Welcome to the East of England

Norfolk and Suffolk. Each of the region's counties has its very own unique character, and all of them have a wealth of places to explore, treasures to discover and places to eat and shop. From historic houses, museums and gardens, to animal collections, country parks and beaches - you'll find all these plus lots more in the East of England.

Whether you are on a short break or holiday, visiting friends or family or a local resident planning to explore your neighbourhood, this guide gives you all the information you need to discover this beautiful region.

Contents

How to use this Guide . . . . 4 - 5

Money-Off Vouchers . . . . 7 - 10

Tourist Information Centres 11

Useful Web Sites . . . . 12 - 14

Diary of Events 2004 . . . . 15 - 25

Lights, Camera, Action . . . . 26 - 38

Aviation Heritage . . . . 39 - 40

SPECIAL FEATURE St. Edmundsbury Cathedral . . 41 - 42

SPECIAL FEATURE Glenn Miller's Anniversary . . . . 43 - 44

County Sections (includes Places to Visit):

Bedfordshire & Hertfordshire 45

Cambridgeshire 91

Essex 127

Norfolk 189

Suffolk 251

Index 304

This picture: Ely, Cambridgeshire

eastofengland

How to use this Guide

This guide contains all the information you need to plan Great Days Out in the East of England. Each section has its own colour coding. The first section includes general information such as Tourist Information Centres, Useful Web Sites, Diary of Events, Lights, Camera, Action (film and TV locations) and Aviation Heritage. There are also Money-off Vouchers, and special features focusing on the completion of England's last unfinished Anglican Cathedral in 2004 (Bury St. Edmunds, Suffolk), and the 100th anniversary of famous big band leader Glenn Miller's birth.

We've then spilt the rest of the guide into useful county sections, which contain the following information:

- Map of County
- County Information (including facts and figures)
- Cities, Towns & Villages (for that county)
- Good Beach Guide (Essex, Norfolk and Suffolk sections only)
- Tourist Information (Centres & Points for that county)
- Guided Tours

- Places to Visit (listed alphabetically by location name), under the following categories:

History & Heritage (Historic Houses, Ancient Monuments, Museums & Galleries, Machinery & Transport, Mills).
Bloomin' Beautiful (Gardens, Nurseries & Garden Centres).
Family Fun (Animal & Bird Collections, Amusement/Theme Centres & Parks, Children's Indoor Play Centres, Leisure Pools).
Countryside (Special Areas, Country Parks & Nature Reserves, Picnic Sites).
Activities (Activity Centres, Boat Trips, Golf Courses, Cycling, Walking, Specialist Holidays and Tours).
Food & Drink (Regional Produce, Breweries & Vineyards, Restaurants, Afternoon Teas).
Stop & Shop (Craft Centres & Speciality Shopping).

- Discovery Tours (at the end of each county section these tours give you a few suggestions on what to see and how to fit it all in).

Entries within this guide include contact details for each attraction, along with a short description, details of opening times, fees and facilities available.

Biggleswade
Shuttleworth Collection Map ref. F6 ❶
Old Warden Aerodrome
Tel: (01767) 627288 Web: www.shuttleworth.org
A unique historical collection of aircraft, from a 1909 Bleriot to a 1942 Spitfire in flying condition, and cars dating from an 1898 Panhard in running order.
Times: Open Apr-Oct, daily, 1000-1700. ❷
Fee: £6.00/£3.00/£1.50/£12.00. ❸
Facilities: ❹
SAMPLE ENTRY

❶ **MAP REFERENCE**
Map references are given for each attraction. You should refer to the relevant map at the beginning of each county section, which will indicate its approximate position.

❷ **OPENING TIMES**
Opening times are correct at the time of going to press, but we strongly recommend you contact the attraction prior to your visit.

❸ **FEE**
All prices for attractions appear in the order of Adult/Child/Concessions/Family - in some cases prices were not available at the time of going to press. If no price is quoted you should check with the attraction concerned before you visit. Some places to visit are free or may suggest a voluntary donation. Remember that prices can go up and those provided to us by the attractions are provisional for 2004.

❹ **FACILITIES**
In order to give you as much information as possible in the space available, we have used the following symbols in this guide:

Indicates that the attraction is in the Commercial Membership Scheme of the East of England Tourist Board.

Q These places to visit participate in the Visitor Attraction Quality Assurance Service. They have all been independently assessed and offer an assured level of quality for the visitor.

G Green Tourism Business Award Winner

P Parking (on site)

Indicates a public bus service stops within 1/4 mile of the attraction.

- Indicates a train station within 1 mile of the attraction.
- T(1 hr) Indicates the time that should be allowed for a visit to this attraction.
- Guided Tours (for individuals) available
- Restaurant/Café
- Picnic Site
- Dogs Permitted
- Indicates that all/most of the attraction is accessible to the wheelchair visitor. But we strongly recommend you telephone in advance of your visit to check the exact details, particularly regarding access to toilets and refreshment facilities.
- **EH** English Heritage
- **NT** National Trust

Please note that all of the places to visit in this guide have signed the National Code of Practice for Visitor Attractions.

PLEASE NOTE

All information contained in this guide is given in good faith, based on the information supplied by the individual establishments listed. Whilst every care has been taken to ensure the accuracy of the information published herein, the East of England Tourist Board cannot accept responsibility in respect of any error or omission which may have occurred.

Compiled and published by:
East of England Tourist Board
Toppesfield Hall, Hadleigh, Suffolk IP7 5DN
Tel: 0870 225 4800 Fax: 0870 225 4890
Email: information@eetb.org.uk
Web: www.visiteastofengland.com

Editor and Production Manager: Stephen Rampley
Production Assistant: Lyn Mowat
Graphic Design: PRS Advertising Ltd, Ipswich, Suffolk
Maps: ©Maps in Minutes™2003. ©Crown Copyright, Ordnance Survey 2003
Printed: in the UK by Warners Midlands PLC
ISBN: 1 873246 692

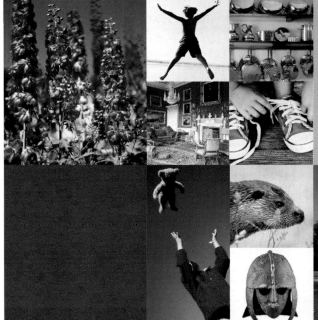

Hatfield House

(Gardens only)

Hatfield, Hertfordshire

Offer: Two adults for the price of one (full paying adult).
This offer does not apply to groups or entry during major events or on Fridays. Valid from 10/4/04.

Closing Date: 30 September 2004

(See entry in Hertfordshire - Historic Houses section)

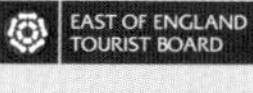

Ingatestone Garden Centre

Roman Road, Ingatestone, Essex

Offers: (1) Reward Card for quarterly voucher.
(2) As displayed on visit - frequently changed.

Closing Date: 30 December 2004

(See entry in Essex - Nurseries & Garden Centres section)

REWARD

EAST OF ENGLAND TOURIST BOARD

TruckFest

East of England Showground

Offer: One child goes free per two full paying adults.

Monday 3 May 2004 only

(See advert in Events section)

ONE CHILD FREE

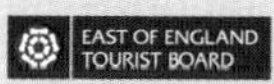

Mole Hall Wildlife Park & Butterfly Pavilion

Saffron Walden, Essex

Offer: One child goes free per two full paying adults.

Closing Date: 30 November 2004

(See entry in Essex - Family Fun section)

ONE CHILD FREE

Colchester Castle Museum

Colchester, Essex

Offer: One free entry with one full paying adult.

Closing Date: 30 November 2004

(See entry in Essex - Museums & Galleries section)

ONE FREE ENTRY

The Original Great Maze

Blake House Craft Centre, Blake End, Braintree, Essex

Offer: One child goes free with two full paying adults.

Closing Date: 11 September 2004

(See entry in Essex - Family Fun section)

ONE CHILD FREE

Electric Palace Cinema, Harwich

Harwich, Essex

Offer: 10% off full adult price - One ticket only.
Cannot be added to any other concessions.

Closing Date: 31 December 2004

(See advert in Events section)

10% OFF

Banham Zoo

Banham, Norfolk

Offer: One child goes free with every two full paying adults.
Does not apply to Bank Holidays, event weekends or in conjunction with any other offer.

Closing Date: 21 November 2004

(See entry in Norfolk - Family Fun section)

ONE CHILD FREE

Hylands House

Writtle, near Chelmsford, Essex

Offer: One free cream tea with paid admission to Hylands House.
Voucher only redeemable by one paying visitor per party.

Closing Date: 31 December 2004

(See entry in Essex - Historic Houses section)

FREE CREAM TEA

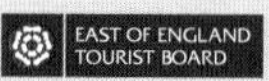

Bure Valley Railway

Aylsham, Norfolk

Offer: 50p off standard adult return ticket.
Cannot be used in conjunction with boat/train tickets or on Day Out with Thomas or Santa Special events.

Closing Date: October 2004

(See entry in Norfolk - Machinery & Transport section)

Ingatestone Garden Centre

Roman Road, Ingatestone, Essex
Offers: (1) Reward Card for quarterly voucher.
(2) As displayed on visit - frequently changed.
Closing Date: 30 December 2004
(See entry in Essex - Nurseries & Garden Centres section)

REWARD

Mole Hall Wildlife Park & Butterfly Pavilion

Saffron Walden, Essex
Offer: One child goes free per two full paying adults.
Closing Date: 30 November 2004
(See entry in Essex - Family Fun section)

ONE CHILD FREE

The Original Great Maze

Blake House Craft Centre, Blake End, Braintree, Essex
Offer: One child goes free with two full paying adults.
Closing Date: 11 September 2004
(See entry in Essex - Family Fun section)

ONE CHILD FREE

Banham Zoo

Banham, Norfolk
Offer: One child goes free with every two full paying adults.
Does not apply to Bank Holidays, event weekends or in conjunction with any other offer.
Closing Date: 21 November 2004
(See entry in Norfolk - Family Fun section)

ONE CHILD FREE

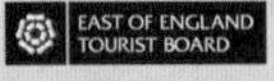

Bure Valley Railway

Aylsham, Norfolk
Offer: 50p off standard adult return ticket.
Cannot be used in conjunction with boat/train tickets or on Day Out with Thomas or Santa Special events.
Closing Date: October 2004
(See entry in Norfolk - Machinery & Transport section)

50p OFF

Hatfield House
(Gardens only)

Hatfield, Hertfordshire
Offer: Two adults for the price of one (full paying adult
This offer does not apply to groups or entry during maj
events or on Fridays. Valid from 10/4/04.
Closing Date: 30 September 2004
(See entry in Hertfordshire - Historic Houses section)

TWO FOR ONE

EAST OF ENGLAND
TOURIST BOARD

TruckFest

East of England Showground
Offer: One child goes free per two full paying adults.
Monday 3 May 2004 only
(See advert in Events section)

ONE CHILD FREE

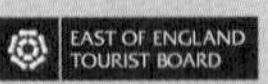

Colchester Castle Museum

Colchester, Essex
Offer: One free entry with one full paying adult.
Closing Date: 30 November 2004
(See entry in Essex - Museums & Galleries section)

ONE FREE ENTRY

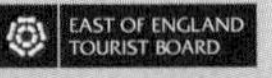

Electric Palace Cinema, Harwic

Harwich, Essex
Offer: 10% off full adult price - One ticket only.
Cannot be added to any other concessions.
Closing Date: 31 December 2004
(See advert in Events section)

10% OFF

Hylands House

Writtle, near Chelmsford, Essex
Offer: One free cream tea with paid admission to Hylands House.
Voucher only redeemable by one paying visitor per par
Closing Date: 31 December 2004
(See entry in Essex - Historic Houses section)

FREE CREAM TEA

Fairhaven Woodland & Water Garden

School Road, South Walsham, Norfolk
Offer: Two for the price of one.
Closing Date: 30 December 2004
(See entry in Norfolk - Gardens section)

Somerleyton Hall and Gardens

Lowestoft, Suffolk
Offer: Save up to £3.00. 50p off normal admission price for up to six people
(not to be used in conjunction with any other offer).
Closing Date: October 2004
(See entry in Suffolk - Historic Houses section)

The Muckleburgh Collection

Holt, Norfolk
Offer: Two for the price of one.
Closing Date: 31 October 2004
(See entry in Norfolk - Machinery & Transport section)

Suffolk Wildlife Park

Kessingland, Suffolk
Offer: One child goes free with every two full paying adults. Does not apply to Bank Holidays, event weekends or in conjunction with any other offer.
Closing Date: 21 November 2004
(See entry in Suffolk - Family Fun section)

Kids Klub

Gt. Finborough, Suffolk
Offer: 10% discount (Total £243).
Closing Date: December 2004
(See advert in Suffolk - Activities section)

East of England Cycling Discovery Map

Please select which map you would like from the list at the bottom of this page. Please note this offer does not include the Suffolk Coastal Cycle Route or The Fens Cycle Way packs. Return this voucher to our address shown on page 5.

Name of map...

Closing Date: 31 December 2004

Cycling Discovery Maps

For more information on these routes, please visit the Activities section for each county within this guide. The location name listed in brackets is the starting point of the route.

Beds

The Great Ouse - 25 miles (Bedford)
The Thatcher's Way - 24 miles (Bedford)

Cambs

Apples and Ale - 13 miles (Wisbech)
Katherine's Wheels - 15 miles (Grafham Water, nr. Huntingdon)
The Peterborough Green Wheel (North) - 29 miles (Peterborough)

Essex

Two Rivers' Way - 25 miles (Burnham-on-Crouch)
The Witchfinder's Way - 27 miles (Harwich)

Herts

Literary Landscapes - 25 miles (Welwyn)
Roisia's Path - 28 miles (Therfield, nr. Royston)
Romans and Royalty - 16 miles (Hatfield)

Norfolk

The Bishop's Chapel - 23 miles (Dereham)
The Brecks - 20 miles (Swaffham)
Lords of the Manor - 29 miles (Aylsham)
The Lost Villages of Breckland - 23 miles (Gressenhall, nr. Dereham)
Nelson's Norfolk - 29 miles (Fakenham)

Suffolk

Churches, Copses and Country Lanes - 24 miles (Carlton Colville, nr. Lowestoft)
The Jockey's Trail - 28 miles (Newmarket)
The Miller's Trail - 23 miles (Ixworth, nr. Bury St. Edmunds)

Somerleyton Hall and Gardens

Lowestoft, Suffolk
Offer: Save up to £3.00. 50p off normal admission price for up to six people
(not to be used in conjunction with any other offer).
Closing Date: October 2004
(See entry in Suffolk - Historic Houses section)

REDUCED ADMISSION

Fairhaven Woodland & Water Garden

School Road, South Walsham, Norfolk
Offer: Two for the price of one.
Closing Date: 30 December 2004
(See entry in Norfolk - Gardens section)

EAST OF ENGLAND TOURIST BOARD

Suffolk Wildlife Park

Kessingland, Suffolk
Offer: One child goes free with every two full paying adults. Does not apply to Bank Holidays, event weekends or in conjunction with any other offer.
Closing Date: 21 November 2004
(See entry in Suffolk - Family Fun section)

ONE CHILD FREE

The Muckleburgh Collection

Holt, Norfolk
Offer: Two for the price of one.
Closing Date: 31 October 2004
(See entry in Norfolk - Machinery & Transport section)

TWO FOR ONE

East of England Cycling Discovery Map

Please select which map you would like from the list at the bottom of this page. Please note this offer does not include the Suffolk Coastal Cycle Route or The Fens Cycle Way packs. Return this voucher to our address shown on page 5.
Name of map...
Closing Date: 31 December 2004

FREE FREE FREE FREE

Kids Klub

Gt. Finborough, Suffolk
Offer: 10% discount (Total £243).
Closing Date: December 2004
(See advert in Suffolk - Activities section)

10% DISCOUNT

Cycling Discovery Maps

For more information on these routes, please visit the Activities section for each county within this guide. The location name listed in brackets is the starting point of the route.

Beds

The Great Ouse - 25 miles (Bedford)
The Thatcher's Way - 24 miles (Bedford)

Cambs

Apples and Ale - 13 miles (Wisbech)
Katherine's Wheels - 15 miles (Grafham Water, nr. Huntingdon)
The Peterborough Green Wheel (North) - 29 miles (Peterborough)

Essex

Two Rivers' Way - 25 miles (Burnham-on-Crouch)
The Witchfinder's Way - 27 miles (Harwich)

Herts

Literary Landscapes - 25 miles (Welwyn)
Roisia's Path - 28 miles (Therfield, nr. Royston)
Romans and Royalty - 16 miles (Hatfield)

Norfolk

The Bishop's Chapel - 23 miles (Dereham)
The Brecks - 20 miles (Swaffham)
Lords of the Manor - 29 miles (Aylsham)
The Lost Villages of Breckland - 23 miles (Gressenhall, nr. Dereham)
Nelson's Norfolk - 29 miles (Fakenham)

Suffolk

Churches, Copses and Country Lanes - 24 miles (Carlton Colville, nr. Lowestoft)
The Jockey's Trail - 28 miles (Newmarket)
The Miller's Trail - 23 miles (Ixworth, nr. Bury St. Edmunds)

Tourist Information Centres

* Not open all year

Bedfordshire

Bedford, St. Paul's Square. Tel: (01234) 215226

Dunstable, The Library, Vernon Place. Tel: (01582) 471012

Luton, Central Library, St. George's Square. Tel: (01582) 401579

Mid Bedfordshire, 5 Shannon Court, High Street, Sandy. Tel: (01767) 682728

Cambridgeshire

Cambridge, The Old Library, Wheeler Street. Tel: 0906 586 2526

Ely, Oliver Cromwell's House, 29 St. Mary's Street. Tel: (01353) 662062

Huntingdon, The Library, Princes Street. Tel: (01480) 388588

Peterborough, 3-5 Minster Precincts. Tel: (01733) 452336

St. Neots, The Old Court, 8 New Street. Tel: (01480) 388788

Wisbech and the Fens, 2-3 Bridge Street. Tel: (01945) 583263

Essex

Braintree, Town Hall Centre, Market Square. Tel: (01376) 550066

Brentwood, Pepperell House, 44 High Street. Tel: (01277) 200300

Clacton-on-Sea, Town Hall, Station Road. Tel: (01255) 423400

Colchester, 1 Queen Street. Tel: (01206) 282920

Maldon, Coach Lane. Tel: (01621) 856503

Saffron Walden, 1 Market Place, Market Square. Tel: (01799) 510444

Southend-on-Sea, 19 High Street. Tel: (01702) 215120

Thurrock, Moto Services, M25, Grays. Tel: (01708) 863733

Waltham Abbey, 2-4 Highbridge Street. Tel: (01992) 652295

Hertfordshire

Birchanger Green, Welcome Break Services, Junction 8, M11 Motorway. Tel: (01279) 508656

Bishop's Stortford, The Old Monastery, Windhill. Tel: (01279) 655831

Hemel Hempstead, Marlowes. Tel: (01442) 234222

Hertford, 10 Market Place. Tel: (01992) 584322

Letchworth Garden City, 33-35 Station Road. Tel: (01462) 487868

St. Albans, Town Hall, Market Place. Tel: (01727) 864511

Norfolk

Aylsham, Bure Valley Railway Station, Norwich Road. Tel: (01263) 733903

Burnham Deepdale, Deepdale Farm. Tel: (01485) 210256

Cromer, Prince of Wales Road. Tel: (01263) 512497

Diss, Mere's Mouth, Mere Street. Tel: (01379) 650523

Downham Market *, The Priory Centre, 78 Priory Road. Tel: (01366) 387440

Great Yarmouth *, Marine Parade. Tel: (01493) 842195

Holt *, 3 Pound House, Market Place. Tel: (01263) 713100

Hoveton *, Station Road. Tel: (01603) 782281

Hunstanton, Town Hall, The Green. Tel: (01485) 532610

King's Lynn, The Custom House, Purfleet Quay. Tel: (01553) 763044

Mundesley *, 2A Station Road. Tel: (01263) 721070

Norwich, The Forum, Millennium Plain. Tel: (01603) 727927

Sheringham *, Station Approach. Tel: (01263) 824329

Swaffham *, Market Place. Tel: (01760) 722255

Wells-next-the-Sea *, Staithe Street. Tel: (01328)710885

Wymondham *, Market Cross, Market Place. Tel: (01953) 604721

Suffolk

Aldeburgh, 152 High Street. Tel: (01728) 453637

Beccles *, The Quay, Fen Lane. Tel: (01502) 713196

Bury St. Edmunds, 6 Angel Hill. Tel: (01284) 764667

Felixstowe, 91 Undercliff Road West. Tel: (01394) 276770

Flatford *, Flatford Lane. Tel: (01206) 299460

Ipswich, St. Stephens Church, St. Stephens Lane. Tel: (01473) 258070

Lavenham *, Lady Street. Tel: (01787) 248207

Lowestoft, East Point Pavilion, Royal Plain. Tel: (01502) 533600

Mid Suffolk, Wilkes Way, Stowmarket. Tel: (01449) 676800

Newmarket, Palace House, Palace Street. Tel: (01638) 667200

Southwold, 69 High Street. Tel: (01502) 724729

Sudbury, Town Hall, Market Hill. Tel: (01787) 881320

Woodbridge, Station Buildings. Tel: (01394) 382240

See each county section for further TIC details.

Useful Web Sites

Surf the web to discover the East of England on-line. Over the next three pages we have brought together a selection of both informative and fun web sites, giving you lots of useful information about the region.

Regional Information

East of England Tourist Board
www.visiteastofengland.com

Arts Council England (East)
www.artscouncil.org.uk
East Anglian Brewers
www.eastanglianbrewers.com
East of England Development Agency (EEDA)
www.eeda.org.uk
Eastern Cathedrals Association
www.easterncathedrals.org.uk
Screen East (regional film and television)
www.screeneast.co.uk
Tastes of Anglia (regional food and drink)
www.tastesofanglia.com

Bedfordshire

Bedfordshire County Council
www.bedfordshire.gov.uk
Bedfordshire, Hertfordshire and Luton
www.bedshertsluton.com
Bedford Borough Council
www.bedford.gov.uk
Luton Borough Council
www.luton.gov.uk
Mid Bedfordshire District Council
(Ampthill, Biggleswade, Sandy and Woburn)
www.midbeds.gov.uk
South Bedfordshire District Council
(Dunstable and Leighton Buzzard)
www.southbeds.gov.uk
Bedfordshire Museums
www.museums.bedfordshire.gov.uk
The Chilterns
www.chilternsaonb.org
Forest of Marston Vale
www.marstonvale.org
The Greensand Trust
www.greensand-trust.org.uk
The Wildlife Trust for Bedfordshire, Cambridgeshire and Peterborough
www.wildlifetrust.org.uk/bcnp

Cambridgeshire

Cambridgeshire County Council
www.camcnty.gov.uk
Cambridge City Council
www.cmsc.co.uk
Cambridge Tourist Information Centre
www.tourismcambridge.com
East Cambridgeshire District Council (Ely)
www.eastcambs.gov.uk
Fenland District Council (March, Whittlesey and Wisbech)
www.fenland.gov.uk
The Fens Tourism Group (The Fens)
www.fenswaterways.com
Huntingdonshire District Council
(Huntingdon, St. Ives and St. Neots)
www.huntsdc.gov.uk www.huntsleisure.org
Peterborough City Council
www.peterborough.gov.uk
South Cambridgeshire District Council
www.scambs.gov.uk
University of Cambridge
www.cam.ac.uk
The Wildlife Trust for Bedfordshire, Cambridgeshire and Peterborough
www.wildlifetrust.org.uk/bcnp

Essex

Essex County Council
www.essexcc.gov.uk www.realessex.co.uk
Basildon District Council
www.basildon.gov.uk
Braintree District Council
(Braintree, Coggeshall and Halstead)
www.braintree.gov.uk www.enjoybraintree.co.uk
Brentwood Borough Council
www.brentwood-council.gov.uk
Castle Point Borough Council
www.castlepoint.gov.uk
Chelmsford Borough Council
www.chelmsfordbc.gov.uk www.enjoychelmsford.co.uk
Colchester Borough Council (Dedham)
www.colchesterwhatson.co.uk www.colchester.gov.uk
Epping Forest District Council
(Epping and Waltham Abbey)
www.eppingforestdc.gov.uk
Harlow Council
www.harlow.gov.uk

Maldon District Council (Burnham-on-Crouch)
www.maldon.gov.uk
Rochford District Council (Rayleigh)
www.rochford.gov.uk
Southend-on-Sea Borough Council
www.southend.gov.uk
Tendring District Council (Brightlingsea, Clacton, Frinton, Harwich, Manningtree and Walton)
www.tendringdc.gov.uk
www.essex-sunshine-coast.org.uk
Thurrock Council
www.thurrock.gov.uk
Uttlesford District Council
(Great Dunmow, Saffron Walden and Thaxted)
www.uttlesford.gov.uk www.saffire.org.uk
Essex Tourism Association
www.hidden-treasures.co.uk
Essex Wildlife Trust
www.essexwt.org.uk

Hertfordshire

Hertfordshire County Council
www.hertsdirect.org
Bedfordshire, Hertfordshire and Luton
www.bedshertsluton.com
Broxbourne Borough Council
(Cheshunt, Hoddesdon and Waltham Cross)
www.broxbourne.gov.uk
Dacorum Borough Council
(Berkhamsted, Hemel Hempstead and Tring)
www.dacorum.gov.uk
East Hertfordshire District Council
(Bishop's Stortford, Hertford and Ware)
www.eastherts.gov.uk
Hertsmere Borough Council
(Borehamwood, Bushey, Elstree and Potters Bar)
www.hertsmere.gov.uk
Letchworth Garden City Heritage Foundation
www.letchworth.com
North Hertfordshire District Council
(Baldock, Hitchin, Letchworth Garden City and Royston)
www.north-herts.gov.uk
Stevenage Borough Council
www.stevenage.gov.uk
St. Albans District Council
www.stalbans.gov.uk
Three Rivers District Council (Rickmansworth)
www.3rivers.gov.uk
Watford Borough Council
www.watford.gov.uk www.watfordtourism.co.uk
Welwyn/Hatfield Council (Welwyn Garden City)
www.welhat.gov.uk
The Chilterns
www.chilternsaonb.org
Hertfordshire Museums
www.hertsmuseums.org.uk
Hertfordshire Wildlife Trust
www.wildlifetrust.org.uk/herts

Norfolk

Norfolk County Council
www.norfolk.gov.uk www.visitnorfolk.co.uk
Breckland Council
(Attleborough, Dereham, Thetford, Swaffham and Watton)
www.breckland.gov.uk
Broadland District Council
(Aylsham and Wroxham/Hoveton)
www.broadland.gov.uk
Broads Authority (The Broads)
www.broads-authority.gov.uk
Great Yarmouth Borough Council
www.great-yarmouth.gov.uk
Greater Yarmouth Tourist Authority
www.great-yarmouth.co.uk
North Norfolk District Council (Cromer, Fakenham, Holt, Little Walsingham, Mundesley, North Walsham, Sheringham and Wells)
www.northnorfolk.org
www.northnorfolk.roomcheck.co.uk
Norwich Area Tourism Agency
www.visitnorwich.co.uk
Norwich City Council
www.norwich.gov.uk
South Norfolk Council
(Diss, Harleston, Loddon and Wymondham)
www.south-norfolk.gov.uk
West Norfolk Borough Council
(Downham Market, King's Lynn and Hunstanton)
www.west-norfolk.gov.uk
The Brecks Countryside Project
www.brecks.org.uk
Independent Traveller's Norfolk
www.itnorfolk.co.uk
The Norfolk Coast Partnership
www.norfolkcoastaonb.org.uk
Norfolk Countryside Access Team
www.countrysideaccess.norfolk.gov.uk
Norfolk Museums and Archaeology Service
www.norfolk.gov.uk/leisure/museums
Norfolk Tourist Attractions Association
www.norfolktouristattractions.co.uk
Norfolk Wildlife Trust
www.wildlifetrust.org.uk/norfolk
The Peddar's Way and Norfolk Coast Path
www.nationaltrail.co.uk/peddarsway
The Southern Broads
www.southernbroads.com
Where to Go in North Norfolk Group
www.northnorfolkattractions.co.uk

Suffolk

Suffolk County Council
www.suffolkcc.gov.uk www.visit-suffolk.org.uk

Babergh District Council ('Constable Country', Hadleigh, Lavenham, Long Melford and Sudbury)
www.babergh-south-suffolk.gov.uk

Forest Heath District Council (Brandon, Mildenhall and Newmarket)
www.forest-heath.gov.uk

Ipswich Borough Council
www.ipswich.gov.uk

Mid Suffolk District Council (Eye, Needham Market and Stowmarket)
www.mid-suffolk-dc.gov.uk
www.midsuffolkleisure.co.uk

St. Edmundsbury Borough Council (Bury St. Edmunds, Clare and Haverhill)
www.stedmundsbury.gov.uk

Suffolk Coastal District Council (Aldeburgh, Felixstowe, Framlingham, Orford and Woodbridge)
www.suffolkcoastal.gov.uk

Waveney District Council (Beccles, Bungay, Halesworth, Lowestoft, Oulton Broad and Southwold)
www.waveney.gov.uk www.visit-lowestoft.co.uk

The Dedham Vale and Stour Valley Countryside Project
www.dedhamvalestourvalley.org

Heart of Suffolk Tourism Association
www.heart-of-suffolk.co.uk

Invitation to View (privately-owned historic houses offering tours)
www.suffolkhistorichouses.org.uk

The Stour and Orwell Estuaries Management Group
www.stourandorwell.org

Suffolk Coast and Heaths Unit
www.suffolkcoastandheaths.org.uk

Suffolk Museums
www.suffolkmuseums.org

Suffolk's Top Attractions
www.suffolktopattractions.com

Suffolk Wildlife Trust
www.wildlifetrust.org.uk/suffolk

Travelling around

The British Horse Society (horse-riding)
www.bhseast.org.uk

British Waterways
www.british-waterways.org
www.waterscape.com

Cyclists' Touring Club (CTC)
www.ctc.org.uk

National Express (travel by coach)
www.nationalexpress.com

National Rail Enquiries (timetables)
www.nationalrail.co.uk

North Sea Cycle Route
www.northsea-cycle.com

The Ramblers' Association
www.ramblers.org.uk

Sustrans (cycling charity - National Cycle Network)
www.sustrans.org.uk

Traveline (public transport information)
www.traveline.org.uk

Miscellaneous

British Farming
www.cobritishfarming.org.uk

Campaign for Real Ale (CAMRA)
www.camra.org.uk

The Churches Conservation Trust
www.visitchurches.org.uk

The Countryside Agency
www.countryside.gov.uk

English Heritage
www.english-heritage.org.uk

English Nature
www.english-nature.org.uk

English Wine Producers
www.englishwineproducers.com

Forestry Commission
www.forestry.gov.uk

The Good Beach Guide
www.goodbeachguide.co.uk

The Guild of Registered Tourist Guides
www.blue-badge.org.uk

Holiday Care Service (information on disabled holidays)
www.holidaycare.org.uk

The National Gardens Scheme (NGS)
www.ngs.org.uk

The National Trust
www.nationaltrust.org.uk

The Royal Horticultural Society
www.rhs.org.uk

Royal Society for the Protection of Birds (RSPB)
www.rspb.org.uk

Seaside Awards
www.seasideawards.org.uk

Sport England
www.sportengland.org

Visit Britain
www.visitbritain.com

WI (Women's Institute) Country Markets
www.wimarkets.co.uk

Events 2004

The East of England offers a range of exciting and varied events to suit all tastes, from air shows to arts festivals, from historical re-enactments and cheese rolling contests to craft fairs and agricultural shows. Or for the more unusual, try the World Snail Racing and Pea Shooting Championships, all held in the region throughout the year. On the following pages we have brought together a selection of events taking place during the year. For more information on the events listed or other events taking place during 2004, please contact the East of England Tourist Board on 0870 225 4800.

* - Provisional

January

1-3 Jan	Chelmsford Winter Beer Festival, Anglia Polytechnic University, Bishop Hall Lane, Chelmsford, Essex
2 Jan-28 Feb	Floodlit Swan Evenings, Wildfowl and Wetlands Trust, Welney, Cambs
7-11 Jan	Whittlesey Straw Bear Festival, Whittlesey, Cambs
16-18 Jan	Chilford Hall's Home Design and Interiors Exhibition, Balsham Road, nr. Linton, Cambs
23-25 Jan	Woburn Abbey Home Design and Interiors Exhibition, Woburn, Beds

February

1-28 Feb	Walsingham Abbey Snowdrop Walks, Little Walsingham, Norfolk
8-29 Feb	Snowdrop Sundays, Hatfield House, Hatfield, Herts
14/15 Feb	Lee Valley Birdwatching Fair, Lee Valley Park Farms, Stubbins Hall Lane, Crooked Mile, nr. Waltham Abbey, Essex
14-22 Feb	Primrose/Spring Plant Festival, By-pass Nurseries, Capel St. Mary, Suffolk
14-28 Feb	King's Lynn Mart, Tuesday Market Place, King's Lynn, Norfolk
24 Feb	Lowestoft Pancake Races, High Street, Lowestoft, Suffolk
24 Feb	Pancake Races, Town Centre, Hitchin, Herts
24 Feb	Pancake Races, Town Centre, Huntingdon, Cambs
28 Feb-6 Mar	Bedfordshire Festival of Music, Speech and Drama, Corn Exchange, Bedford, Beds
29 Feb	The Centenary Celebration of the Birth of Glenn Miller, Twinwood Airfield, nr. Bedford, Beds
29 Feb-4 Apr	Lambing Sundays and Spring Bulb Days, Kentwell Hall, Long Melford, Suffolk

March

6/7 Mar	Bedfordshire Spring Craft Show at Woburn Safari Park, Woburn, Beds
8-13 Mar	Celebration of Schools Music, Snape Maltings, Snape, Suffolk
12-14 Mar	Fiction Festival, Town Hall, Saturday Market Place, King's Lynn, Norfolk
13 Mar-30 Apr	Early Spring Flowers, Fairhaven Woodland and Water Garden, School Road, South Walsham, Norfolk
14 Mar	St. Patrick's Day Festival, various venues, Luton, Beds
20/21 Mar	The Shire Horse Society Spring Show, East of England Showground, Peterborough, Cambs
20 Mar-4 Apr	Lambing Weekends, Wimpole Hall and Home Farm, Arrington, nr. Royston, Cambs
27/28 Mar	Thriplow Daffodil Weekend, Thriplow, Cambs

April

Apr-Oct	A Good Bet - the History of Betting Exhibition, National Horseracing Museum, High Street, Newmarket, Suffolk
Apr-Oct	Red Rum and the 70s Exhibition, National Horseracing Museum, High Street, Newmarket, Suffolk
4 Apr	Haverhill Country Music Festival, Leisure Centre, Ehringshausen Way, Haverhill, Suffolk
9-11 Apr	Suffolk Spring Garden Show, Suffolk Showground, Ipswich, Suffolk

9-12 Apr	Aldeburgh Easter Music Festival, various venues, Aldeburgh, Suffolk
9-12 Apr	Easter Craft Show, Blickling Hall, Blickling, nr. Aylsham, Norfolk
9-12 Apr	Great Easter Egg Hunt, Quiz and Re-creation of Tudor Life, Kentwell Hall, Long Melford, Suffolk

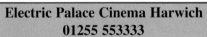

10-12 Apr	Easter Thunderball (National Drag Racing Championships), Santa Pod Raceway, Podington, Beds
11/12 Apr	Easter Fun Days, Barleylands Farm Centre, Barleylands Road, Billericay, Essex
11/12 Apr	Gamekeeper and Countryman's Fair, Hertfordshire County Showground, Redbourn, Herts
11/12 Apr *	Medieval Jousting, Knebworth House, nr. Stevenage, Herts
19-24 Apr	Hertford Theatre Week, Castle Hall, Hertford, Herts
21 Apr	Easter Family Fun Day, Roots of Norfolk, Gressenhall, nr. Dereham, Norfolk
21-24 Apr	The East Anglian Beer Festival, The Corn Exchange, Cornhill, Bury St. Edmunds, Suffolk
23 25 Apr	The National Motorhome Show, East of England Showground, Peterborough, Cambs
24/25 Apr	Minsmere Bird Fair, RSPB Minsmere Nature Reserve, Westleton, nr. Saxmundham, Suffolk
30 Apr-9 May	The Harleston and Waveney Festival 2004, various venues, Harleston, Norfolk

May

May-Oct	The Shuttleworth Collection Flying Displays, Old Warden, nr. Biggleswade, Beds
1 May	King's Lynn May Garland Procession, Town Centre, King's Lynn, Norfolk
1 May	King Street Festival, Norwich, Norfolk
1/2 May	Sagitta Guineas Festival, Rowley Mile Racecourse, Newmarket, Suffolk
1-3 May	Southend Garden Show, Garons Park, Southend-on-Sea, Essex
1-3 May	Tudor May Day Celebrations, Kentwell Hall, Long Melford, Suffolk
1-31 May	Hertford Music Festival, various venues, Hertford, Herts
2 May	33rd Ipswich to Felixstowe Historic Vehicle Run, Ipswich/Felixstowe, Suffolk
2 May	Heritage Coast Run or Walk, Thorpeness Sports Ground, nr. Aldeburgh, Suffolk
2/3 May *	Knebworth Country Show, Knebworth House, nr. Stevenage, Herts
2/3 May	Mendlesham Street Fayre and Art Exhibition, Mendlesham, Suffolk
2/3 May	Suffolk Game and Country Fair, Glemham Hall, Little Glemham, Suffolk
2/3 May	Truckfest 2004, East of England Showground, Peterborough, Cambs

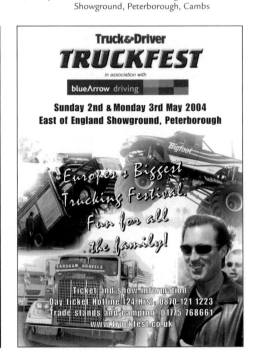

3 May	Dunstable Carnival, Bennett Memorial Recreation Ground, Dunstable, Beds
3 May	Ickwell May Festival, Ickwell Green, nr. Biggleswade, Beds
3 May	Stilton Cheese Rolling, Stilton, nr. Peterborough, Cambs
3 May	Woodbridge Horse Show, Suffolk Showground, Ipswich, Suffolk
3 May	Breckland Family Show, Watton Airfield, Watton, Norfolk
3 May	Reach Fair, Village Green, Reach, Cambs
5-15 May	Norfolk and Norwich Festival, various venues, Norwich, Norfolk
6-9 May	Living Crafts Exhibition, Hatfield House, Hatfield, Herts
7-9 May	East of England Garden Show, East of England Showground, Peterborough, Cambs
7-9 May	St. Neots Folk Festival, The Priory Centre, St. Neots, Cambs
8-15 May	Chelmsford Cathedral Festival, Chelmsford, Essex
8-15 May	Rickmansworth Week 2004, various venues, Rickmansworth, Herts
8-31 May	Candelabra Primula Weeks, Fairhaven Woodland and Water Garden, School Road, South Walsham, Norfolk
9 May	Peterborough Dragon Boat Festival, The Embankment (opposite Key Theatre), Peterborough, Cambs
9 May	South Suffolk Show, Ampton Racecourse, Ampton, nr. Bury St. Edmunds, Suffolk
14-16 May	Norfolk Garden Show, Norfolk Showground, Norwich, Norfolk
14-30 May	Bury St. Edmunds Festival, various venues, Bury St. Edmunds, Suffolk
15 May	Hadleigh Farmer's Agricultural Association May Show, Holbecks Park, Hadleigh, Suffolk
15/16 May *	Kite Festival, Rougham Airfield, nr. Bury St. Edmunds, Suffolk
15-30 May	Norfolk Open Studios, various venues, Norfolk
21-23 May	Essex Garden Show, Brentwood Centre, Doddinghurst Road, Brentwood, Essex
22 May	A Journey through Time, Norwich Cathedral, Norfolk
22-23 May	BMF Bike Show, East of England Showground, Peterborough, Cambs
22-23 May *	Hertfordshire Garden Show, Knebworth House, nr. Stevenage, Herts
22-23 May	Rickmansworth Canal Festival, Grand Union Canal, Rickmansworth, Herts
23 May *	Tour de Tendring (Cycle Race), various venues, Tendring district, Essex

23/24 May Framlingham Gala, Town Centre, Framlingham, Suffolk

29/30 May Hertfordshire County Show, Hertfordshire County Showground, Redbourn, Herts

29/30 May Tring Canal Festival, Grand Union Canal, Tring, Herts

29-31 May The Main Event (FIA European Drag Racing Championships), Santa Pod Raceway, Podington, Beds

29-31 May Aldenham Country Park Craft Fair, Elstree, Herts

29-31 May Felbrigg Coast and Country Show, Felbrigg Hall, Felbrigg, Norfolk

29 May-5 Jun Felixstowe Drama Festival, Spa Pavillion Theatre, Seafront, Felixstowe, Suffolk

30 May * Bury in Bloom Spring Flower Market, The Buttermarket, Bury St. Edmunds, Suffolk

30/31 May * Norfolk Game and Country Fair, Constructional Industry Training Board, Bircham Newton, Norfolk

30/31 May Southend Air Show, Seafront, Southend-on-Sea, Essex

30 May-6 Jun Downham Market Festival, various venues, Downham Market, Norfolk

31 May * Luton International Carnival, Town Centre and Wardown Park, Luton, Beds

31 May Woolpit Street Fair, Woolpit, nr. Bury St. Edmunds, Suffolk

31 May Redoubt Fort Fete, off Main Road, Harwich, Essex

31 May Norfolk History Fair, Roots of Norfolk, Gressenhall, nr. Dereham, Norfolk

June

2-3 Jun Suffolk Show, Suffolk Showground, Ipswich, Suffolk

4-6 Jun Cambridgeshire Garden Show, Wood Green Animal Shelters, London Road, Godmanchester, Cambs

5 Jun Newmarket Carnival, Town Centre, Newmarket, Suffolk

5/6 Jun Thaxted Morris Ring Meeting, various venues in Thaxted and surrounding villages, Essex

5/6 Jun Woolpit Steam Rally, Warren Farm, Wetherden, nr. Stowmarket, Suffolk

5-9 Jun Walpole St. Peter Church Annual Flower Festival, Walpole St. Peter, Norfolk

6 Jun D-Day Anniversary Show, Imperial War Museum, Duxford, Cambs

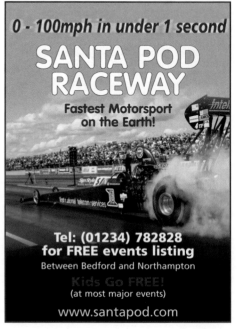

6 Jun Cambridgeshire County Show, Wimpole Hall and Home Farm, Arrington, nr. Royston, Cambs

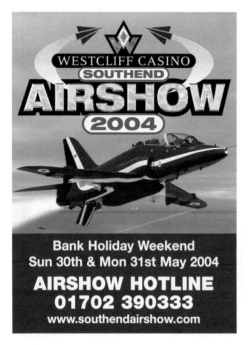

6 Jun	Fayre in the Square, Town Centre, Beccles, Suffolk
10-20 Jun	Woolpit Festival, various venues, Woolpit, Suffolk
11-13 Jun	A1 Festival of Music and Dance, Sacrewell Farm and Country Centre, Thornhaugh, nr. Peterborough, Cambs
11-13 Jun	Festival of Gardening, Hatfield House, Hatfield, Herts
11-27 Jun	Aldeburgh Festival of Music and the Arts (57th), Snape Maltings, Snape, Suffolk
12 Jun	Deepdale Jazz Festival, Marsh Barn, Burnham Deepdale, Norfolk
12 Jun	Strawberry Fair, Shenfield Common, Ingrave Road, Brentwood, Essex
12 Jun	Braintree and Bocking Carnival, various venues, Braintree, Essex
12/13 Jun	Scarecrow Festival, Barton Mills, nr. Mildenhall, Suffolk
12/13 Jun	Magna Carta Celebrations, Town Centre, Bury St. Edmunds, Suffolk
12/13 Jun	Whitwell Steam and Country Fair, St. Pauls Walden, nr. Whitwell, Herts
12/13 Jun *	Bedford International Kite Festival, Russell Park, Bedford, Beds
12/13 Jun	Cressing Temple Craft Festival, Cressing Temple Barns, Cressing, nr. Braintree, Essex
12/13 Jun	Long Melford Garden Show, Melford Hall Park, Long Melford, Suffolk
12/13 Jun	Woburn Garden Show, Woburn Abbey, Woburn, Beds
12 Jun-4 Jul *	East Coast Regatta, various venues, Lowestoft, Suffolk
13 Jun	14th Euston Park Rural Pastimes Show, Euston Hall, Euston, nr. Thetford, Suffolk
13 Jun	Lavenham's Hidden Gardens, Lavenham, Suffolk
13 Jun	Peterborough Kite Festival, Ferry Meadows Country Park, Peterborough, Cambs
13 Jun	Aldham Gardens Open Day, Aldham, nr. Colchester, Essex
18-20 Jun	The East of England Country Show, East of England Showground, Peterborough, Cambs
18-20 Jun	South East Essex Garden Show, Barleylands Farm Centre, Billericay, Essex
18 Jun-11 Jul	Thaxted Festival, Parish Church and various venues, Thaxted, Essex
19 Jun	Lowestoft Fish Fayre, The Docks, Lowestoft, Suffolk
19 Jun	Brightlingsea Carnival, various venues, Brightlingsea, Essex
19 Jun	Woburn Open Gardens Day, Woburn, Bedfordshire
19 Jun-3 Jul	Haverhill Festival, Arts Centre, Haverhill, Suffolk
20 Jun	The Hidden Gardens of Bury St. Edmunds, Bury St. Edmunds, Suffolk
20 Jun	Nowton Park Country Fair, Nowton Road, Bury St. Edmunds, Suffolk
20 Jun	Green Environmental Festival, Fairhaven Woodland and Water Garden, School Road, South Walsham, Norfolk
20 Jun-11 Jul	Great Annual Re-creation of Tudor Life, Kentwell Hall, Long Melford, Suffolk
23-27 Jun	17th Ampthill Music Festival, various venues, Ampthill, Beds
25-27 Jun	Leigh Folk Festival, various venues, Leigh-on-Sea, Essex
25-27 Jun	South Weald Festival, various venues, South Weald, Essex
25 Jun-4 Jul	Harwich Festival of the Arts, various venues, Harwich, Essex
26 Jun	Pin Mill Barge Match, River Orwell, Pin Mill, Suffolk
26/27 Jun	Eye Open Gardens, Eye, Suffolk
26/27 Jun	Sandringham Country Show and Horse Driving Trials, Sandringham Estate, Norfolk
26/27 Jun	Wings and Wheels Model Spectacular, North Weald Airfield, Epping, Essex
26/27 Jun	Summer Nationals (National Drag Racing Championships), Santa Pod Raceway, Podington, Beds
26/27 Jun *	Wings, Wheels and Steam, Rougham Airfield, nr. Bury St. Edmunds, Suffolk
26 Jun-11 Jul	Hitchin Festival, various venues, Hitchin, Herts
26 Jun-11 Jul	Peterborough Festival, various venues, Peterborough, Cambs
27 Jun	Chelsworth Open Gardens Day, Chelsworth, nr. Hadleigh, Suffolk
27 Jun	Old Buckenham Airfield Flying Display, Old Buckenham, Norfolk
27 Jun	Castle Point Borough Show, Waterside Farm Showground, Canvey Island, Essex

27 Jun	Vintage Vehicle Rally, Leighton Buzzard Railway, Page's Park Station, Leighton Buzzard, Beds
27 Jun-4 Jul	Hunstanton and District Festival of Arts, various venues, Hunstanton, Norfolk
28 Jun-11 Jul	IP-Art, various venues, Ipswich, Suffolk
30 Jun-1 Jul	Royal Norfolk Show, Norfolk Showground, Norwich, Norfolk
30 Jun-4 Jul	Southwold Festival of the Sea, Blackshore, The Harbour, Southwold, Suffolk
30 Jun-4 Jul	Wisbech Rose Fair, St. Peter's Parish Church, Wisbech, Cambs

July

Jul/Aug	Theatre in the Parks, various venues, Norwich, Norfolk
2 Jul *	Dame Nora Major's Annual Cricket Match, Recreation Field, Alconbury, Cambs
3 Jul	Clare World Music Festival, Clare Castle Country Park, Clare, Suffolk
3 Jul	Ware Carnival Day, various venues, Ware, Herts
3 Jul *	Firework Concert, Knebworth House, nr. Stevenage, Herts
3 Jul	North Watford Show, Billeverett Community Centre, Watford, Herts
3 Jul	Families Day in Meadow Park, Borehamwood, Herts
3/4 Jul	Silsoe Jazz Festival, Village Hall, Silsoe, Beds
3/4 Jul	Haverhill Show, Recreation Ground, Haverhill, Suffolk
3/4 Jul	The Sheringham Potty Festival, Town Centre, Sheringham, Norfolk
3/4 Jul	Bedford River Festival, The Embankment, Bedford, Beds
3-11 Jul	Wymondham Music Week, various venues, Wymondham, Norfolk
3-11 Jul	Swaffham Carnival, various venues, Swaffham, Norfolk
3-18 Jul	Bungay Festival, various venues, Bungay, Suffolk
3-24 Jul	Bury St. Edmunds Art Society Annual Exhibition, Bury St. Edmunds, Suffolk
4 Jul	Aquafest, Riverside (Willow Walk/Maltings area), Ely, Cambs
4 Jul	Hunstanton Rotary Carnival, The Green, Hunstanton, Norfolk
4 Jul	Ipswich Music Day, Christchurch Park, Ipswich, Suffolk
4 Jul	Model Railway Mania, Leighton Buzzard Railway, Page's Park Station, Leighton Buzzard, Beds

4 Jul Walton Classic Vehicle Show, Bathhouse Meadow, Walton-on-the-Naze, Essex

4/5 Jul * National Stud Fair 2004, The National Stud, Newmarket, Suffolk

4-10 Jul Bloor Homes East of England Tennis Championships, Felixstowe Lawn Tennis Club, Felixstowe, Suffolk

8-11 Jul Bures Music Festival, various venues, Bures, Suffolk

8-18 Jul Cambridge Film Festival, Arts Picture House, Cambridge, Cambs

9-11 Jul Ely Folk Weekend, beside A10, Ely, Cambs

9-11 Jul Lord Mayor's Celebrations, City Centre, Norwich, Norfolk

9-11 Jul Summer in the City 2004, Midsummer Common, Cambridge, Cambs

10 Jul Tendring Hundred Show, Lawford House Park, Lawford, nr. Manningtree, Essex

10 Jul World Pea Shooting Championships, Village Green, Witcham, Cambs

10 Jul Ipswich Community Carnival, Town Centre, Ipswich, Suffolk

10 Jul Hoddesdon Vintage and Classic Car Display, Town Centre, Hoddesdon, Herts

10 Jul Dunmow Flitch Trials, Great Dunmow, Essex

10/11 Jul Bedfordshire Country Show, Old Warden Park, nr. Biggleswade, Beds

10/11 Jul Home and Garden Show, Blickling Hall, Blickling, nr. Aylsham, Norfolk

10/11 Jul Flying Legends Air Show, Imperial War Museum, Duxford, Cambs

10-24 Jul Festival Too, various venues, King's Lynn, Norfolk

10 Jul-1 Aug 26th East Anglian International Summer Music Festival, The Old School, Bridge Street, Hadleigh, Suffolk

11 Jul Watford Rainbow Festival, Cassiobury Park, Watford, Herts

15-18 Jul 37th Snape Antiques and Fine Art Fair, Snape Maltings, nr. Aldeburgh, Suffolk

16-18 Jul Hacheston Rose Festival, various venues, Hacheston, Suffolk

16-18 Jul Weeting Steam Engine Rally, Fengate Farm, Weeting, nr. Brandon, Suffolk

16 Jul-14 Aug 25th Cambridge Summer Music Festival, various venues, Cambridge, Cambs

17 Jul Framlingham Horse Show, Castle Meadow, Framlingham, Suffolk

17 Jul World Snail Racing Championships, The Cricket Field, Grimston, nr. King's Lynn, Norfolk

17/18 Jul Basildon Festival, Wat Tyler Country Park, Pitsea, nr. Basildon, Essex

17/18 Jul * Large Models and Top Gun Show, Rougham Airfield, nr. Bury St. Edmunds, Suffolk

17 Jul-28 Aug Great Yarmouth Summer Festival, Seafront, Great Yarmouth, Norfolk

18 Jul Summer Festival 2004, Needham Lake and Nature Reserve, Needham Market, Suffolk

20-22 Jul East of England July Show, East of England Showground, Peterborough, Cambs

21-25 Jul Southend Cricket Festival, Southchurch Park, Southend-on-Sea, Essex

22-24 Jul * Bedford by the Sea, Harpur Square, Bedford, Beds

22-31 Jul * King's Lynn Festival, various venues, King's Lynn, Norfolk

23-25 Jul Bug Jam VW Beetle Festival, Santa Pod Raceway, Podington, Beds

24 Jul Duxford Flying Proms, Imperial War Museum, Duxford, Cambs

24 Jul Littleport Show, High Field, Ely Road, Littleport, Cambs

24 Jul Blackwater Barge Race, River Blackwater, Maldon, Essex

24/25 Jul West Bergholt Historic Vehicle Rally, Nayland Road, West Bergholt, Essex

24-26 Jul Beccles Carnival, The Quay, Beccles, Suffolk

25 Jul London to Southend Classic Car Run, Western Esplanade, Southend-on-Sea, Essex

28 Jul Sandringham Flower Show, Sandringham Park, Sandringham, Norfolk

29/30 Jul Lowestoft Seafront Air Festival 2004, Seafront, Lowestoft, Suffolk

29 Jul-1 Aug 40th Cambridge Folk Festival, Cherry Hinton Hall Grounds, Cherry Hinton, nr. Cambridge, Cambs

29 Jul-3 Aug Southend's 2nd International Jazz Festival, various venues, Southend-on-Sea, Essex

30 Jul-1 Aug Worstead Village Festival, various venues, Worstead, Norfolk

August

1 Aug	Royston Kite Festival, Therfield Heath, nr. Royston, Herts
1 Aug *	National Amber Hunt, Southwold Beach, Suffolk
1 Aug	Helmingham Festival of Classics, Helmingham Hall, Helmingham, Suffolk
1-7 Aug	The Mundlesey Festival, Coronation Hall, Mundlesey, Norfolk
1-8 Aug *	Wells Carnival, various venues, Wells-next-the-Sea, Norfolk
4 Aug	Sheringham Carnival, various venues, Sheringham, Norfolk
5/6 Aug	Minsmere Family Event, RSPB Minsmere Nature Reserve, Westleton, nr. Saxmundham, Suffolk
6 8 Aug	Art in Clay - National Pottery and Ceramics Festival, Hatfield House, Hatfield, Herts
6-8 Aug	Felixstowe Carnival, various venues, Felixstowe, Suffolk
6-8 Aug *	NSRA Hot Rod Supernationals, Knebworth House, nr. Stevenage, Herts
7 Aug	100th Maldon Carnival, various venues, Maldon, Essex
7/8 Aug	WWII: The Home Front, Kentwell Hall, Long Melford, Suffolk
7/8 Aug	11th Annual Rhythm and Booze Festival, The Angel Inn, Larling, Norfolk
7/8 Aug	Fenmuse 2004, various venues, Wisbech, Cambs
7/8 Aug	Thurlow and Haverhill Steam and Country Show, The Showground, Haverhill, Suffolk
8 Aug *	Annual British Open Crabbing Championship, Ferry Car Park, Walberswick, Suffolk
8 Aug	Frettenham Festival, various venues, Frettenham, Norfolk
8 Aug	Wayland Show, The Meadows, Brandon Road, Watton, Norfolk
8 Aug	Duxford Military Vehicle Show, Imperial War Museum, Duxford, Cambs
8 Aug	Hemsby Lifeboat Day, Hemsby Beach, Norfolk
8 Aug *	Lifeboat Day, The Promenade, Cromer, Norfolk
8 Aug	Sunrise Carnival Procession, various venues, Lowestoft, Suffolk
14 Aug	Westleton Barrel Fair, Westleton, Suffolk
15 Aug	Hunstanton Rotary Kite Festival, Smithdon School Playing Field, Hunstanton, Norfolk
15 Aug	Woburn Commercial Rally and Road Run, Woburn Abbey, Woburn, Beds
15-22 Aug	Clacton Carnival Week, Town Centre, Clacton-on-Sea, Essex
16 Aug	Aldeburgh Olde Marine Regatta and Carnival, High Street and Seafront, Aldeburgh, Suffolk
16-21 Aug	Ponies Association (UK) 2004 Summer Championship Show, East of England Showground, Peterborough, Cambs
18 Aug	Cromer Carnival, various venues, Cromer, Norfolk
19/20 Aug	Thorpeness Regatta and Fireworks, Thorpeness, nr. Aldeburgh, Suffolk
20-22 Aug	Great Yarmouth Carnival, various venues, Great Yarmouth, Norfolk
21 Aug *	Illuminated Carnival Procession and Firework Spectacular, Seafront, Southend-on-Sea, Essex
21 Aug	Walton Carnival, various venues, Walton-on-the-Naze, Essex
21/22 Aug *	Rougham Air Show (Sun) and Fly-in, Rougham Airfield, nr. Bury St. Edmunds, Suffolk
21/22 Aug *	Hertfordshire Craft Show, Knebworth House, nr. Stevenage, Herts
21/22 Aug	V Festival, Hylands Park, Chelmsford, Essex
21/22 Aug *	De Havilland Moth Club Fly-In, Woburn Abbey, Woburn, Beds
22 Aug-10 Sept	Festival of Bowls, Seafront, Great Yarmouth, Norfolk
24-29 Aug	Peterborough Beer Festival, The Embankment, Bishop's Road, Peterborough, Cambs
25-28 Aug	St. Ives Music and Arts Festival, various venues, St. Ives, Cambs

26/27 Aug	Clacton Air Show, Marine Parade, Clacton-on-Sea, Essex
27-30 Aug	High Summer Re-creation of Tudor Life, Kentwell Hall, Long Melford, Suffolk
27-30 Aug	Lavenham Carnival, various venues, Lavenham, Suffolk
27-30 Aug	Suffolk Villages Festival, Boxford/Hadleigh/Stoke-by-Nayland Churches, Suffolk
28 Aug	Kempston Fun Day, Addison Howard Park, Kempston, Beds
28 Aug	RNLI Street Fayre, Aldeburgh, Suffolk
28/29 Aug	Ely Horticultural Society Show, Paradise Sports Centre, Ely, Cambs
28-30 Aug *	Mildenhall Cycling Rally, Riverside Middle School, Mildenhall, Suffolk
28-30 Aug	The International Glenn Miller Festival, Twinwood Airfield, nr. Bedford, Beds
28-30 Aug *	Clacton Jazz Festival, various venues, Clacton-on-Sea, Essex
28-30 Aug *	Chelmsford Spectacular, Hylands Park, Chelmsford, Essex
28 Aug-4 Sept	Burnham Week, various venues, Burnham-on-Crouch, Essex
29/30 Aug	The Countess of Warwick's Country Show, Little Easton, nr. Dunmow, Essex

29/30 Aug	Eye Show, Eye Showground, Dragon Hill, Eye, Suffolk
29/30 Aug	Walsham Le Willows Open Gardens Day, various venues, Walsham Le Willows, Suffolk
29/30 Aug	Fenland Country Fair, Quy Park, Stow Cum Quy, Cambs
29/30 Aug *	Knebworth 2004 - Classic Motor Show, Knebworth House, nr. Stevenage, Herts
30 Aug	Aylsham Agricultural Show, Blickling Park, Blickling, nr. Aylsham, Norfolk
30 Aug *	St. Albans Carnival, various venues, St. Albans, Hertfordshire
30 Aug *	Lowestoft Lions Charity Gala Day, Nicholas Everitt Park, Oulton Broad, Suffolk
30 Aug	Village at War, Roots of Norfolk, Gressenhall, nr. Dereham, Norfolk

September

3-5 Sept	Country Home, Garden and Rare Breeds Show, Hatfield House, Hatfield, Herts
3-5 Sept	Woburn Oyster Festival, Market Place, Woburn, Beds
3-5 Sept	Reedham Ferry Folk Festival, Reedham Ferry Inn, Reedham, Norfolk
3-5 Sept	Suffolk Autumn Garden Show, Suffolk Showground, Ipswich, Suffolk
4/5 Sept	Duxford 2004 Air Show, Imperial War Museum, Duxford, Cambs
4/5 Sept	English Wine Festival and Country Craft Fair, New Hall Vineyards, Purleigh, Essex
4-12 Sept	Bedford Heritage Week, various venues, Bedford, Beds
5 Sept *	Medieval Jousting, Knebworth House, nr. Stevenage, Herts
5 Sept	Burston Strike School Annual Rally, Burston, nr. Diss, Norfolk
5 Sept	Herring Day, Hemsby Beach, nr. Great Yarmouth, Norfolk
7-11 Sept	18th Chappel Beer Festival, East Anglian Railway Museum, Wakes Colne, nr. Colchester, Essex
9-12 Sept	The European Finals (FIA European Drag Racing Championships), Santa Pod Raceway, Podington, Beds
10-12 Sept	Walton Folk Festival, various venues, Walton-on-the-Naze, Essex
11 Sept	Norfolk Churches Trust - Sponsored Cycle Ride, various locations, Norfolk
11/12 Sept	Steam-Up Weekend, Leighton Buzzard Railway, Page's Park Station, Leighton Buzzard, Beds
11/12 Sept	Essex Steam and Country Show, Barleylands Farm Centre, Billericay, Essex
11/12 Sept	Great Yarmouth Maritime Festival, South Quay, Great Yarmouth, Norfolk
11/12 Sept	Haddenham Steam Rally, Haddenham, nr. Ely, Cambs
11/12 Sept	Old Leigh Regatta, Old Leigh Town, nr. Southend-on-Sea, Essex
18 Sept *	Maldon Regatta, various venues, Maldon, Essex

18/19 Sept * Lowestoft Folk Festival, Royal Green, Lowestoft, Suffolk

18/19 Sept Bedfordshire Steam and Country Fayre, Shuttleworth Park, Old Warden, nr. Biggleswade, Bedfordshire

18/19 Sept Grand Henham Steam Rally, Benacre Hall, Wrentham, Suffolk

18-25 Sept Swaffham Arts Week, various venues, Swaffham, Norfolk

21-25 Sept Ipswich Beer Festival, Corn Exchange, Ipswich, Suffolk

24-26 Sept King's Lynn Poetry Festival, Thoresby College, College Lane, King's Lynn, Norfolk

25 Sept Burnham Carnival, various venues, Burnham-on-Crouch, Essex

25 Sept Soham Pumpkin Fayre, Recreation Ground, Soham, Cambs

25/26 Sept Cressing Temple Craft Festival, Cressing Temple Barns, Cressing, nr. Braintree, Essex

25/26 Sept Power of the Past, Wantisden Valley, nr. Woodbridge, Suffolk

25-28 Sept Re-creation of Tudor Life at Michaelmas, Kentwell Hall, Long Melford, Suffolk

26 Sept The Mascot Grand National 2004, Huntingdon Racecourse, Brampton, nr. Huntingdon, Cambs

October

2 Oct Steam Glow, Leighton Buzzard Railway, Page's Park Station, Leighton Buzzard, Beds

2/3 Oct National Finals (National Drag Racing Championships), Santa Pod Raceway, Podington, Beds

2/3 Oct * Aeronauts and Aviators, Rougham Airfield, nr. Bury St. Edmunds, Suffolk

2-9 Oct 'Words in Motion' Bedford's Film and Book Festival, various venues, Bedford, Beds

6-9 Oct * Bedford Beer Festival, Corn Exchange, Bedford, Beds

10 Oct Autumn Air Show, Imperial War Museum, Duxford, Cambs

10 Oct World Conker Championships 2004, The Village Green, Ashton, Cambs

10 Oct East of England Autumn Show, East of England Showground, Peterborough, Cambs

23/24 Oct WWII: The House Requisitioned, Kentwell Hall, Long Melford, Suffolk

24 Oct Apple Day, Roots of Norfolk, Gressenhall, nr. Dereham, Norfolk

25-30 Oct Norwich Beer Festival, St. Andrews and Blackfriars Hall, Norwich, Norfolk

29-31 Oct Crafts for Christmas at Chilford Hall Vineyard, Balsham Road, nr. Linton, Cambs

30/31 Oct Colchester Gift Show, Leisure World, Cowdray Road, Colchester, Essex

31 Oct * Firework Fiesta, Ferry Meadows Country Park, Peterborough, Cambs

November

5 Nov 36th Big Night Out, Melford Hall Park, Long Melford, Sudbury, Suffolk

5 Nov * Grafton Fireworks 2004, Midsummer Common, Cambridge, Cambs

5-7 Nov Aldeburgh Poetry Festival, Jubilee Hall, Aldeburgh, Suffolk

6 Nov Harwich Guy Carnival, Main Road, Harwich, Essex

6 Nov * Guy Fawkes Night Bonfire and Fireworks, Promenade Park, Maldon, Essex

6 Nov Flame and Thunder (Drag Racing and Firework Spectacular), Santa Pod Raceway, Podington, Beds

6 Nov Annual Firework Display, Christchurch Park, Ipswich, Suffolk

6 Nov Gala Fireworks Celebration at St. Albans, Verulamium Park, St. Albans, Herts

6 Nov * Luton Fireworks Spectacular, Popes Meadow, Old Bedford Road, Luton, Beds

6 Nov Sparks in the Park, Earlham Park, Norwich, Norfolk

6-7 Nov Christmas Craft Show, Woburn Safari Park, Woburn, Beds

11-15 Nov Southwold Literary Festival, St. Edmunds Hall, Southwold, Suffolk

13 Nov-23 Dec The Thursford Collection Christmas Spectacular, Thursford, nr. Fakenham, Norfolk

20 Nov Dunstable Tudor Festival, Town Centre, Dunstable, Beds

20/21 Nov Cambridge Gift Show, Wood Green Animal Shelters, London Road, Godmanchester, Cambs

20/21 Nov	Festival of Swans, Wildfowl and Wetlands Trust, Welney, Cambs
27/28 Nov	Norfolk Christmas Gift Show, Norfolk Showground, Norwich, Norfolk
28-30 Nov	Great Yarmouth Christmas Fayre, Market Place, Great Yarmouth, Norfolk

December

2 and 9 Dec	Maldon Victorian Evenings, High Street, Maldon, Essex
3-5 Dec	Magic of Christmas, Blickling Hall, Blickling, nr. Aylsham, Norfolk
3-5 Dec *	Victorian Christmas Fair, Town Centre, Bedford, Beds
4/5 Dec *	Christmas Craft Fair, Knebworth House, nr. Stevenage, Herts
5 Dec	Brentwood Christmas Craft and Gift Show, Brentwood Centre, Doddinghurst Road, Brentwood, Essex
10 Dec	Family Christmas Night and Fireworks, Town Centre, Haverhill, Suffolk
12 Dec	The Celebration of the Life and Music of Glenn Miller, Twinwood Airfield, nr. Bedford, Beds
12 Dec	Hitchin Winter Gala Day, Town Centre, Hitchin, Herts
26 Dec *	Maldon Mud Race, Riverside, Maldon, Essex

Horseracing (contact relevant racecourse for fixture list)

Fakenham, Norfolk - (01328) 862388
www.fakenhamracecourse.co.uk

Great Yarmouth, Norfolk - (01493) 842527
www.greatyarmouth-racecourse.co.uk

Huntingdon, Cambridgeshire - (01480) 453373
www.huntingdon-racecourse.co.uk

Newmarket, Suffolk - (01638) 675500
www.newmarketracecourses.co.uk

Motor Sports (contact relevant venue for fixture list)

Oulton Broad Powerboat Racing, nr. Lowestoft, Suffolk (regular race meetings) - www.lobmbc.co.uk

Santa Pod Raceway, Podington, Bedfordshire (drag-racing and other events) - (01234) 782828
www.santapod.com

Snetterton Circuit, nr. Attleborough, Norfolk (various car and bike events) - (01953) 887303
www.snetterton.co.uk

Stock car/banger racing:
Arena Essex, Purfleet, Essex - (01708) 867728
www.arenaessex.co.uk

Also stadiums at Bovingdon, Hertfordshire; Great Yarmouth, Norfolk; Swaffham, Norfolk; and Ipswich, Suffolk. More information on these on (01420) 588020
www.spedeworth.co.uk

Open Gardens

British Red Cross (on-line listing of gardens open) - (0207) 235 5454 www.redcross.org.uk

County offices (for printable programmes):
Bedfordshire (01234) 349166
Cambridgeshire (01223) 868686
Essex (01245) 291014
Hertfordshire (01992) 586609
Norfolk (01603) 426361
Suffolk (01284) 767215

The National Gardens Scheme - (01483) 211535
www.ngs.org.uk

St. John's Ambulance - Essex (01245) 265678, Norfolk (01603) 621649

Miscellaneous

The following organisations have a wide and varied range of events at their properties in the East of England.

English Heritage - (01223) 582700
www.english-heritage.org.uk

Forestry Commission (Enterprise) - (01842) 810271
www.forestry.gov.uk

The National Trust - 0870 609 5388
www.nationaltrust.org.uk

RSPB (Royal Society for the Protection of Birds) - (01603) 661662 www.rspb.org.uk

The Wildlife Trusts - www.wildlifetrusts.org

County offices:
Bedfordshire and Cambridgeshire (01223) 712400
Essex (01621) 862960
Hertfordshire (01727) 858901
Norfolk (01603) 625540
Suffolk (01473) 890089

Lights, Camera, Action

Discover the scenes and locations of your favourite films and television programmes in the East of England. From Chariots of Fire, Lovejoy, Dad's Army and Vanity Fair to James Bond, EastEnders and Star Wars, you'll find them all here, plus lots more.

Screen East - is the regional screen agency for the East of England dedicated to developing, supporting and promoting every aspect of film, television and the moving image - from production and locations, film company development and training to education and heritage. Screen East Locations, based at Leavesden Studios in Hertfordshire, provides support and advice across all aspects of shooting in the region. They are proud to have assisted a number of prestigious productions, and endeavours to bring the East of England to cinema and television screens around the world. Visit www.screeneast.co.uk for more information.

The Tourist Board would like to thank Screen East for their help with this feature.

A special information sheet 'Lights, Camera, Action' has been produced by the East of England Tourist Board, and provides more comprehensive information about the films and television programmes mentioned here. For your free copy, please contact us on 0870 225 4800.

Scene from GoldenEye (James Bond), Nene Valley Railway, Peterborough, Cambridgeshire

BEDFORDSHIRE & HERTFORDSHIRE

Film

Ali G in da House (2002) - comedy starring Sacha Baron Cohen as 'hip-hop journalist' Ali G. Scenes filmed at Mentmore Towers (nr. Leighton Buzzard) in Beds.

Batman (1989) - superhero fantasy directed by Tim Burton, and starring Jack Nicholson and Michael Keaton. The exterior of Knebworth House (nr. Stevenage) in Herts was used for 'Wayne Manor'.

Birthday Girl (2001) - comedy thriller starring Nicole Kidman. Scenes were filmed at North Church Common on the Ashridge Estate (nr. Berkhamsted) in Herts.

Boston Kickout (1995) - gritty youth drama shot on location in Stevenage, Herts. Barclays School was one location.

Chaand Kaa Tukdaa (1994) - 'Bollywood' romance with scenes filmed at London Luton Airport in Beds.

Chitty Chitty Bang Bang (1968) - classic family film starring Dick van Dyke. Scenes were filmed at Cardington in Beds.

28 Days Later (2002) - virus/zombie based horror, directed by Danny Boyle. Scenes filmed at Luton Hoo in Beds.

The Dirty Dozen (1967) - classic wartime adventure starring Lee Marvin. Scenes filmed at the village of Aldbury, and the Ashridge Business School (nr. Berkhamsted) in Herts.

Dulhan Banoo Mein Teri (2000) - 'Bollywood' romance with scenes filmed at the Bhaktivedanta Manor at Aldenham (nr. Watford) in Herts.

Empire of the Sun (1987) - war drama, directed by Steven Spielberg. Scenes shot at Luton Hoo in Beds.

Enigma (2001) - World War II thriller starring Kate Winslett and Dougray Scott. Scenes filmed at several locations in Herts, including a farm, cottage and church. Luton Hoo in Beds was also used.

Eyes Wide Shut (1999) - erotic drama, directed by Stanley Kubrick, starring Tom Cruise and Nicole Kidman. Partly filmed at Woburn Abbey in Beds.

First Knight (1995) - romantic King Arthur adventure with Sean Connery and Richard Gere. Scenes were filmed at the Ashridge Estate (nr. Berkhamsted) in Herts (where a complete hill village was built), and the Cathedral and Abbey Church in St. Albans, Herts.

Four Weddings and a Funeral (1994) - romantic comedy. Scenes shot at Luton Hoo in Beds. Starred Hugh Grant.

From Hell (2001) - Jack the Ripper story starring Johnny Depp and Heather Graham. Scenes filmed at the Goldings stately home, nr. Hertford in Herts.

Gosford Park (2001) - drama/murder mystery set around the British class system. Starring Jude Law. Scenes were filmed at Wrotham Park (nr. Potters Bar) in Herts.

The Great Escape (1963) - classic wartime drama. Scenes were filmed at Luton Hoo in Beds.

Harry Potter and the Chamber of Secrets (2002) - the second film in the adventures of a boy wizard. The Weasley family home (The Burrow) was built on land in Gypsy Lane, Hunton Bridge (nr. Watford) in Herts.

Haunted Honeymoon (1986) - comedy with Gene Wilder. Filmed at Knebworth House (nr. Stevenage) in Herts.

The Hours (2002) - Oscar-winning Virginia Woolf biopic starring Nicole Kidman and Meryl Streep. Scenes filmed at two private houses in Herts (which represented Woolf's Richmond and Sussex based homes).

The Importance of Being Earnest (2002) - Oscar Wilde adaptation starring Colin Firth, Rupert Everett and Judi Dench. Scenes filmed at Hatfield House in Herts.

Johnny English (2003) - James Bond spoof starred Rowan Atkinson. Scenes shot in Herts at Bovingdon Airfield, MEPC Leavesden Park (which doubled as Canary Wharf), and the Cathedral and Abbey Church in St. Albans (which doubled as Westminster Abbey).

The Lair of the White Worm (1988) - Ken Russell horror film shot at Knebworth House (nr. Stevenage) in Herts. Starred Hugh Grant.

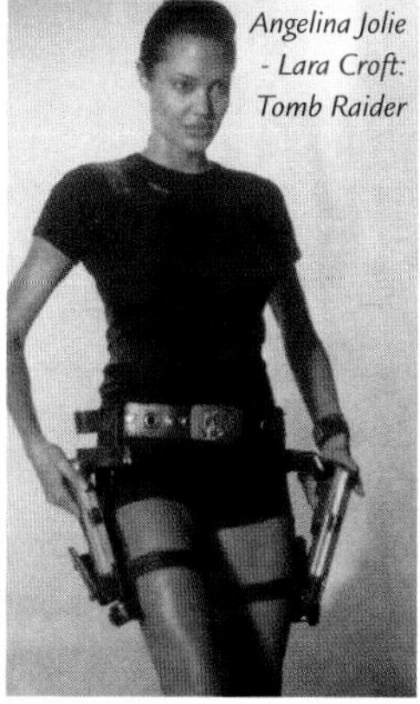
Angelina Jolie - Lara Croft: Tomb Raider

Lara Croft: Tomb Raider (2001) - action/adventure based on the popular computer game, starring Angelina Jolie. Exterior shots for Lara's home were filmed at Hatfield House in Herts.

Lara Croft Tomb Raider: The Cradle of Life (2003) - second of the films based on the popular computer game. Again exterior scenes for Lara's home were filmed at Hatfield House in Herts. This time around though there are also scenes filmed inside the house, including a stick-fight along the stately library.

Lucky Break (2001) - comedy starring James Nesbitt and Olivia Williams. An empty psychiatric hospital near St. Albans in Herts doubles as a prison.

The Martins (2001) - comedy drama starring Lee Evans and Kathy Burke. The Martins' family home is at Hatfield in Herts.

Mean Machine (2001) - prison comedy drama starring Vinnie Jones. Filmed at the Napsbury Hospital in St. Albans, Herts.

Mike Bassett: England Manager (2001) - football comedy starring Ricky Tomlinson. Scenes filmed in St. Albans city centre in Herts.

The Monster Club (1980) - horror comedy featuring three different stories. Starred Vincent Price. Scenes shot at Knebworth House (nr. Stevenage) in Herts.

The Mummy Returns (2001) - action/adventure starring Brendan Fraser. An exterior set used for filming was constructed at Bovingdon Airfield in Herts.

My Brother Tom (2001) - drama about two teenagers escaping suburban childhood. Shot around Watford, St. Albans and Hatfield in Herts.

Never Say Never Again (1983) - James Bond film with scenes shot at Luton Hoo in Beds. Starred Sean Connery.

Nicholas Nickleby (2002) - film version of the Charles Dickens classic starring Jim Broadbent, Christopher Plummer and Jamie Bell. Scenes filmed at Berkhamsted Park and the Bushey Campus both in Herts.

Peter's Friends (1992) - drama directed by Kenneth Brannagh, and filmed at Wrotham Park (nr. Potters Bar) in Herts.

Princess Caraboo (1994) - comedy with scenes shot at both Luton Hoo in Beds and Wrotham Park (nr. Potters Bar) in Herts. Starred Jim Broadbent.

Quills (2000) - drama about the Marquis de Sade. Starred Geoffrey Rush. Scenes were filmed at Luton Hoo in Beds.

Revelation (2001) - supernatural thriller which was filmed at two locations in the west of Herts. Starred Terence Stamp and Derek Jacobi.

Hertfordshire - Britain's very own Hollywood

The southeast of Hertfordshire has developed as a focal point for film and television production, particularly the town of Borehamwood, better known as Elstree. The first studio opened in 1914, and six more followed. Elstree became known as the 'British Hollywood', as it had the greatest number of production facilities outside Hollywood itself. Elstree gave us the first talkie to be made in Britain, the first British musical colour film, the first British colour talking film, and the first film to use Dolby sound. During the 1980s Borehamwood could boast six out of the top ten box office hits of all time. Today only two of the original studios remain open:-

BBC Elstree Centre - opened in 1914, as the historic Neptune Studio. Over the years it has played host to many different owners. In the 1960s it became part of ATV Television, home of big entertainment specials with Shirley Bassey and Tom Jones. Then in the 1980s it became part of the BBC, with the sets of EastEnders, Grange Hill and Holby City based here.
Elstree Film Studios - opened in 1926, and is home to over 500 feature films, including the Star Wars and Indiana Jones trilogies, The Shining, Get Carter, Murder on the Orient Express, The Dambusters, Moby Dick and Who Framed Roger Rabbit? Hammer Films (noted for their horrors) were also based here between 1959-1975. Recent productions include Enigma (2001) and Shanghai Knights (2003). Famous directors to have passed through the doors include Steven Spielberg, Stanley Kubrick and Alfred Hitchcock. George Lucas filmed part of Episode II of Star Wars (Attack of the Clones) here, and in recognition 'Stage One' has been named after him. Popular television shows past and present have also been made here, including The Saint, The Avengers, The Muppet Show, The Tweenies and Who Wants to be a Millionaire? The house from series 3 and 4 of the reality show 'Big Brother' is also sited at the studios. Today Elstree Film Studios (www.elstreefilmtv.com) are owned by Hertsmere Borough Council.

You can discover Borehamwood/Elstree's film heritage, by following a special walk. This includes 'Shenley Road' with its plaques commemorating many famous stars, and the site of the MGM British Studios (demolished 1970) where Ivanhoe, The Dirty Dozen and 2001: A Space Odyssey were made.

Just to the north, (beside the M25) at Abbots Langley, is Leavesden Studios, Britain's most exciting film making complex. Here a former wartime plane factory, once owned by Rolls Royce, has been transformed into over one million square feet of studio space and hundreds of acres of back lot. It has been used for GoldenEye (James Bond), Mortal Kombat Annihilation, The Beach, Sleepy Hollow, Star Wars 'The Phantom Menace' and the Harry Potter films (Philosopher's Stone, Chamber of Secrets, and the yet to be released Prisoner of Azkaban). Visit www.leavesdenpark.com for further information.

Harry Potter and the Philosophers's Stone

Saving Private Ryan (1998) - directed by Steven Spielberg, this wartime epic was shot on vast sets constructed on the former British Aerospace facility at Hatfield in Herts. Starred Tom Hanks.

The Shooting Party (1984) - drama starring James Mason and Edward Fox. Scenes shot at Knebworth House (nr. Stevenage) in Herts.

Spygame (2002) - spy thriller starring Robert Redford and Brad Pitt. The exteriors of the GlaxoSmithKline research centre at Stevenage in Herts doubled as the entrance to the CIA headquarters in Washington, USA.

Those Magnificent Men in their Flying Machines (1965) - classic film which used many of the planes now displayed at The Shuttleworth Collection, Old Warden in Beds. A scene from the film was shot on the former railway line between Cardington and Old Warden. This is where a plane lands on top of a moving train.

Thunderpants (2002) - children's comedy starring Rupert Grint, Simon Gallow and Stephen Fry. Scenes filmed at Cumberland House National Grid in St. Albans, Herts.

To Kill a King (2003) - historical drama starring Rupert Everett, Dougary Scott and Olivia Williams. Scenes filmed at Hatfield House in Herts.

Topsy-Turvy (1999) - Mike Leigh drama/musical based on the story of Gilbert and Sullivan. Scenes shot at the former Langleybury School, nr. Watford, Herts (just off junction 19 of M25).

The Wings of the Dove (1997) - drama by Henry James. Scenes filmed at Luton Hoo in Beds.

Yaadein (2001) - 'Bollywood' romance. Scenes were filmed in the town of Rickmansworth in Herts.

Scene from Lady Audley's Secret, Ingatestone Hall, Essex

Television

2,000 Acres of Sky (BBC) - a medical centre and cottage in Herts double for locations in Scotland in this drama starring Michelle Collins.

The Alchemist (Channel 5) - four part thriller filmed at Leavesden Studios (Abbots Langley), and throughout Herts.

As Time Goes By (BBC) - romantic comedy starring Judi Dench and Geoffrey Palmer. One episode featured scenes shot at Aldenham and Letchmore Heath in Herts.

Auf Wiedersehen Pet (BBC) - comedy drama featuring an intrepid band of British brick layers trying their luck aboard. Scenes filmed at a manor house in Radlett in Herts. Starred Jimmy Nail and Timothy Spall.

The Avengers (ITV) - cult 1960s adventure series with Patrick Macnee. Many scenes shot in Herts, including Aldbury, Ashridge Business School (nr. Berkhamsted), Borehamwood/Elstree, Bovington Airfield, Brocket Hall (nr. Welwyn), Knebworth House (nr. Stevenage), St. Albans and Watford.

Band of Brothers (UStv/BBC) - major wartime mini-series. A number of spectacular sets were built on the former British Aerospace facility at Hatfield, Herts. The area around the village of Wilstone, nr. Tring (Herts) replicated Brecourt Manor in Normandy, whilst the Ayot Estate, nr. Welwyn Garden City (Herts) saw a major tank battle. A large area within the pine woodland of Hatfield House (Herts) was cleared to build the concentration camp at Landsberg.

Bugs (BBC) - hi-tech adventure series which filmed at locations throughout Herts.

The Canterville Ghost (ITV) - two versions of this classic tale have been filmed at Knebworth House (nr. Stevenage) in Herts. The most recent (1997) starred comedian Rik Mayall.

Celeb (BBC) - comedy series about Gary Bloke, an aging rock star who is determined to carry on behaving like a teenager. Starring Harry Enfield. Scenes shot at Knebworth House (nr. Stevenage) in Herts.

The Champions (ITV) - 1960s action/adventure series featuring three secret agents. Many scenes shot in Herts, including Aldbury, Knebworth House (nr. Stevenage) and Moor Park Golf Club (Batchworth).

The Comic Strip Presents: Four Men in a Car (Channel 4) - zany comedy with Rik Mayall. Scenes were filmed on closed section's of the A1 and A41 in Herts.

Daddy's Girl (ITV) - psychological thriller starring Martin Kemp. Scenes filmed at various locations in Herts, including North Watford Cemetary, Bushey police station, Phasell's Wood in Hemel Hempstead, the Ashridge Estate (nr. Berkhamsted) and the village of Aldbury.

Danger Man (ITV) - 1960s intrigue/espionage thriller, with Patrick McGoohan. Scenes shot at the Dunstable Downs in Beds, and Knebworth House (nr. Stevenage) and Elstree Aerodrome in Herts.

Daniel Deronda (BBC) - adaptation of George Eliot's novel, with scenes filmed at Wrotham Park (nr. Potters Bar) in Herts. Starred Hugh Dancy and Edward Fox.

Danielle Cable Eye Witness (ITV) - dramatisation of events surrounding the M25 road rage killing of Stephen Cameron in 1996. Scenes filmed at the Edgwarebury Hotel, Elstree in Herts.

Dead Ringers (BBC) - impressions show starring Jon Culshaw and Jan Ravens. Sketches filmed at Gorhambury House, and amongst the ruins of Verulamium (both in St. Albans) in Herts.

Dinotopia (UStv) - series based on the best-selling children's books. Scenes were filmed on the Ashridge Estate (nr. Berkhamsted) in Herts.

Double Take (BBC) - satirical series with lookalikes of famous people caught in compromising or amusing situations. Gaddesden Place in Hemel Hempstead (Herts) doubled as interiors of Buckingham Palace.

EastEnders (BBC) - soap opera, filmed at the BBC Elstree Studios in Borehamwood, Herts. Storylines are sometimes filmed at outside locations, such as Shenley, Herts (Michelle and Lofty's marriage) and Watford, Herts (where Arthur Fowler is buried). Hatfield Courthouse, Herts was used for the court appearance of Grant Mitchell. Aberford and Meadow Parks in Borehamwood (Herts) are also popular locations.

French and Saunders Christmas Special (BBC) - scenes filmed in Abbots Langley and Sarrat village, both in Herts. Starred Dawn French and Jennifer Saunders.

The Gentlemen Thief (BBC) - 'Raffles' drama, starring Michael French and Nigel Havers. Scenes shot at the former Langleybury School, nr. Watford, Herts (just off junction 19 of M25).

The Inspector Lynley Mysteries (BBC) - detective drama starring Nathaniel Parker. The interiors of a large Elizabethan house in Hatfield (Herts) doubled for the main location in Yorkshire.

Hope and Glory (BBC) - school drama starring Lenny Henry. Filmed at the former Langleybury School, nr. Watford, Herts (just off junction 19 of M25).

In Deep (BBC) - police drama with scenes shot around St. Albans and Watford, Herts.

Inspector Morse (ITV) - hugely popular detective series, starring John Thaw and Kevin Whatley. Scenes filmed at Luton Hoo in Beds, and throughout Herts, including Aldbury, Brocket Hall (nr. Welwyn), Hertford (McMullen Brewery), St. Albans (Fighting Cocks pub and cathedral) and Wrotham Park (nr. Potters Bar).

Jack and the Beanstalk: The Real Story (UStv) - new version of the fairy story, which takes the tale beyond its traditional end. Scenes were shot in Leighton Buzzard, Beds.

Jane Eyre (ITV) - the recent adaptation of this Charlotte Bronte novel, filmed scenes at Knebworth House (nr. Stevenage) in Herts.

Lavenham, Suffolk - Lovejoy Country

Kavanagh QC (ITV) - courtroom drama starring John Thaw. Scenes were shot at Hatfield Courthouse in Herts.

Lady Chatterley (BBC) - recent version of D.H. Lawrence novel, shot at Wrotham Park (nr. Potters Bar) in Herts.

Lorna Doone (BBC) - adaptation of classic novel set in 17th C. England. Scenes filmed on the Ashridge Estate (nr. Berkhamsted) in Herts.

Love in a Cold Climate (BBC) - drama following the fortunes of three girls. Scenes filmed at Wrotham Park (nr. Potters Bar) in Herts.

Lovejoy (BBC) - based on the books by Essex writer Jonathan Gash, this comedy drama was set around the adventures of antiques rogue 'Lovejoy' played by Ian McShane. Scenes filmed at Bishop's Stortford, Hertford, Aldbury, Knebworth House (nr. Stevenage), Wrotham Park (nr. Potters Bar) and The Pelham villages in Herts.

Madame Bovary (BBC) - romantic drama starring Keith Barron. Scenes filmed on the Ashridge Estate (nr. Berkhamsted) in Herts.

The Magical Legend of the Leprechauns (UStv) - mini-series starring Whoopi Goldberg. Scenes filmed on the Ashridge Estate (nr. Berkhamsted) in Herts.

The Man (BBC) - story of a singing travel agent, starring Lenny Henry. Two shops in Chorleywood High Street (Herts) were used for filming.

Merlin (UStv) - Camelot adventure set in AD800, and partially shot at the Ashridge Estate (nr. Berkhamsted) in Herts.

Midsummer Murders (ITV) - the latest series of these murder mysteries (with a humorous twist), and set in the fictional idyllic English county of Midsomer, filmed scenes at Rickmansworth Police Station and Sparrow Herne mansion (Bushey), both in Herts.

Scene from Shakespeare in Love, Holkham Beach, Norfolk

Murder in Mind (BBC) - drama series of psychological thrillers. Several locations have been used, including the former Langleybury School, nr. Watford, Herts (just off junction 19 of M25).

Murder Most Horrid (BBC) - comedy murder mysteries starring Dawn French. One episode featured Luton Hoo in Beds.

Murder Rooms (BBC) - series of dramas looking at Sherlock Holmes' creator Sir Arthur Conan Doyle, and the people/places which inspired his stories. A large Georgian house in Elstree, Herts was used for filming.

The Persuaders (ITV) - 1970s series with Roger Moore and Tony Curtis as millionaire playboys. Scenes shot throughout Herts, including Bovington, Knebworth House (nr. Stevenage) and Watford.

Pie in the Sky (BBC) - comedy drama with Richard Griffiths. The restaurant exterior used can be found at Hemel Hempstead Old Town in Herts.

Playing the Field (BBC) - drama about a woman's football team, filmed in the Herts area.

Porridge (BBC) - classic 70s comedy set in Slade Prison, and starring Ronnie Barker. The opening shot features the gatehouse of the old prison in Victoria Road, St. Albans in Herts.

The Prisoner (ITV) - cult series from 1967/8, featuring Patrick McGoohan as 'No. 6'. Scenes shot at the Dunstable Downs in Beds, and Borehamwood, Shenley and South Mimms in Herts.

The Professionals (ITV) - cult 1970/80s crime/action drama with Lewis Collins and Martin Shaw. Brocket Hall (nr. Welwyn) in Herts, and London Luton Airport in Beds featured in episodes.

Randall and Hopkirk Deceased (ITV) - original 1960/70s series, featuring detectives Jeff Randall and Marty Hopkirk. Scenes filmed at Woburn Abbey in Beds, and St. Albans, Shenley and Watford in Herts.

Randall and Hopkirk Deceased (BBC) - comedy drama starring Vic Reeves and Bob Mortimer. Several episodes have been filmed at locations in the area, including Luton Hoo (Beds), Wrotham Park, nr. Potters Bar (Herts), the McMullen Brewery in Hertford (Herts) and Bushey Grange, nr. Watford (Herts).

The Saint (ITV) - cult 1960s series starring Roger Moore as Simon Templar. Scenes shot at London Luton Airport in Beds, and Aldbury, Elstree, St. Albans, Shenley and Watford in Herts.

The Scold's Bridle (BBC) - dark mystery story starring Miranda Richardson. Scenes filmed at the Benington Lordship Garden, nr. Stevenage, Herts.

The Shillingbury Tales (ITV) - comedy drama set around a typical English village. Starred Robin Nedwell and Diane Keen. Many scenes filmed at Aldbury in Herts.

Smack the Pony (Channel 4) - off-beat comedy series filmed at various locations in Herts, including French Row in St. Albans, Stockers Farm in Rickmansworth, Elstree Aerodrome and West Herts College in Watford.

Some Mothers do have em' (BBC) - classic 70s comedy, with scenes filmed at Short Street in Bedford, Beds. Starred Michael Crawford.

Spooks (BBC) - drama series about the security service MI5. Starring Matthew Macfadyen. One episode filmed scenes at the Hillside School, Borehamwood in Herts.

Station Jim (BBC) - a mansion house in Herts, became a Victorian railway station for this television film starring George Cole.

Trial and Retribution II (ITV) - Lynda La Plante drama filmed in South Herts.

Vanity Fair (BBC) - classic 19th C. story starring Natasha Little. A house in the southwest of Herts was used for filming.

The Vice (ITV) - hard-hitting drama series which filmed at locations around the Watford, Herts area.

Behind the Scenes, Vanity Fair

CAMBRIDGESHIRE

Film

Chariots of Fire (1981) - Oscar-winning film based on the true story of the Olympic runners Harold Abrahams and Eric Liddell, and the 1924 games. Street scenes were filmed in Cambridge. The famous race around the college precinct was based on the actual event at Trinity College, but filmed at Eton College in Berkshire.

Dad Savage (1998) - kidnap and revenge film starring Patrick Stewart (Star Trek). Scenes shot in the Fens.

GoldenEye (1995) and Octopussy (1983) - two James Bond adventure's with scenes filmed at the Nene Valley Railway at Peterborough.

Peter's Friends (1992) - drama directed by Kenneth Brannagh. Scenes filmed at the Nene Valley Railway at Peterborough.

Sylvia (2003) - true story of the 20th C. poets, Ted Hughes and Sylvia Plath, as they meet as students at Cambridge University. Scenes filmed in Cambridge at King's and Trinity Colleges.

Waterland (1992) - intense and intriguing drama starring Jeremy Irons. Filmed in the Fens.

Television

An Unsuitable Job for a Lady (ITV) - detective drama with an episode filmed in Cambridge. Starred Helen Baxendale.

Bliss (ITV) - set in Cambridge, Simon Shepherd takes the lead as a scientific investigator.

Casualty (BBC) - popular medical drama which filmed its dramatic train crash episodes at the Nene Valley Railway at Peterborough.

Cold Enough for Snow (BBC) - drama with Maureen Lipman. Scenes filmed in Cambridge.

David Copperfield (BBC) - adaptation of Dickens novel starring Bob Hoskins and Nicholas Lyndhurst. Areas of Wisbech (The Crescent, Castle and Peckover House) were used in the filming.

Doctor Who (BBC) - cult sci-fi series with Tom Baker playing the Time Lord. The story 'Shada' was filmed in Cambridge (including Emmanuel College, King's Parade and the River Cam).

Honey for Tea (BBC) - Clare College in Cambridge provided scenes for this comedy series.

The Inspector Lynley Mysteries (BBC) - detective drama starring Nathaniel Parker. Scenes were filmed in Cambridge.

London's Burning (ITV) - fire fighting drama series. Scenes filmed at the Nene Valley Railway at Peterborough.

Lovejoy (BBC) - based on the books by Essex writer Jonathan Gash, this comedy drama was set around the adventures of antiques rogue 'Lovejoy' played by Ian McShane. Scenes filmed in Cambridge at Queens' College, the University Arms Hotel and the American Military Cemetery at nearby Madingley.

Martin Chuzzlewit (BBC) - adaptation of classic Dickens novel starring Keith Allen. Scenes were filmed in Wisbech, including Peckover House.

Micawber (ITV) - drama series based on Dickens character from 'David Copperfield'. Filmed in Wisbech (including Peckover House), which depicted London in the 1820s. Starred David Jason.

Murder in Mind (BBC) - drama series of psychological thrillers. One episode ('Tracks') filmed at the Nene Valley Railway at Peterborough.

A Sense of Guilt (BBC) - controversial drama with Trevor Eve, featuring scenes of Cambridge.

Silent Witness (BBC) - drama formally set in Cambridge, with Amanda Burton as pathologist Sam Ryan.

The Student Prince (BBC) - drama with Robson Green. Filmed at Queens' College, Cambridge.

The Winds of War (UStv) - 80s mini series set against the backdrop of the Second World War. Starred Robert Mitchum. Scenes were filmed at the American Military Cemetery at Madingley (nr. Cambridge).

Jonathan Creek - Caroline Quentin and Alan Davies

ESSEX

Film

The Battle of Britain (1969) - wartime epic starring Michael Caine and Trevor Howard. Scenes were filmed at North Weald Airfield.

Bridget Jones' Diary (2001) - romantic comedy about a 30-something singleton searching for true love. Starring Rene Zellweger. Scenes were filmed at Stansted Airport.

Brothers in Arms (1996) - immigration drama. Scenes filmed at Clacton-on-Sea railway station, and Mistley Quay.

Clockwork Mice (1995) - poignant drama starring Art Malik and Ian Hart. Shot at Chipping Ongar.

Essex Boys (2000) - gangland thriller starring Sean Bean and Alex Kingston. Filming took place at Brightlingsea, Jaywick, Clacton and Southend.

The Fourth Protocol (1987) - spy thriller starring Michael Caine and Pierce Brosnan. Shot at Colchester (railway station) and Chelmsford (where there is a memorable car chase scene).

Four Weddings and a Funeral (1994) - romantic comedy starring Hugh Grant. Scenes shot at St. Clement's Church, West Thurrock.

GoldenEye (1995) - James Bond adventure, with scenes shot at Stansted Airport.

Killing Dad (1989) - drama starring Richard E. Grant. Filmed at the Pier and Palace Hotels in Southend.

The Reckoning (2001) - the story of a 14th C. disgraced priest who joins a travelling band of actors as cover. Starring Willem Dafoe. Scenes were filmed at Hedingham Castle in Castle Hedingham.

Television

Band of Brothers (UStv/BBC) - major wartime mini-series. Scenes showing aircraft taking off for the D-Day sequences were filmed at North Weald Airfield.

EastEnders (BBC) - soap opera, which has featured both Southend-on-Sea and Clacton-on-Sea in past episodes.

Hi-de-Hi (BBC) - comedy series centred around Maplin's Holiday Camp. Scenes for the show were filmed at a former holiday camp in Dovercourt.

Holby City (BBC) - popular medical drama series. Scenes were filmed at Stansted Airport.

Ivanhoe (BBC) - classic adventure tale, filmed at Hedingham Castle, Castle Hedingham.

Jonathan Creek (BBC) - comedy drama. One episode featured Stansted Airport.

Lady Audley's Secret (ITV) - scandalous Victorian tale of a man's obsession with a woman. Ingatestone Hall became Audley House, which is where the novel was actually written.

London's Burning (ITV) - fire fighting drama series. Scenes were filmed at Southend-on-Sea, where the team rescued a beached whale.

Lovejoy (BBC) - based on the books by Essex writer Jonathan Gash, this comedy drama was set around the adventures of antiques rogue 'Lovejoy' played by Ian McShane. Scenes filmed at Belchamp St. Paul (pub), Braintree, Chelmsford, Coggeshall, Colchester (Town Hall), Felsham Hall (home of Lady Jane) can be found in the village of Belchamp Walter. Next door is the workshop where Lovejoy was based. Finchingfield (the Green and Fox pub), Gosfield (hall and Green Man pub), Great Bardfield, Great Dunmow, Halstead (Townsford Mill), Harlow, Harwich (Stena ferry to Hook of Holland), Hedingham Castle, Ingatestone Hall, Kelvedon, Layer Marney Tower, Little London, Maldon (quayside, onboard Thames barge in Blackwater estuary), Moyns Park, Saffron Walden (Town Hall, Barclays Bank, Market Square and Tourist Information Centre), Stansted Mountfitchet, Thaxted (Town Street), Tollesbury and Wakes Colne.

Man and Boy (BBC) - adaptation of best-selling novel. Starring Ioan Gruffudd. Scenes filmed at Stansted Airport.

Plotlands (BBC) - 1920s drama about a new community. Filmed at Wivenhoe. Starred Saskia Reeves.

Randall and Hopkirk Deceased (BBC) - comedy drama starring Vic Reeves and Bob Mortimer. Scenes were filmed in the county at ruined Copped Hall and Home Farm, nr. Epping.

Sharpe's Regiment (ITV) - military adventure starring Sean Bean. Scenes filmed at Tilbury Fort.

Spooks (BBC) - drama series about the security service MI5. Starring Matthew Macfadyen. One episode filmed scenes at Bradwell Power Station, nr. Maldon.

NORFOLK

Film

The Beach (1999) - although the film was not shot in the county, it is worth noting that the video for the related No.1 single by the girl group 'All Saints' was filmed on Holkham Beach.

The Care of Time (1990) - murder mystery with Christopher Lee. Hemsby became Miami Beach USA.

Pierce Brosnan - Die Another Day

Conflict of Wings (1953) - comedy about a small Norfolk village up in arms over a proposed RAF airfield. Scenes were filmed in the county.

Dad Savage (1998) - kidnap and revenge film starring Patrick Stewart (Star Trek). Scenes shot in Hunstanton and Wells-next-the-Sea.

The Dambusters (1955) - classic war film which used Langham Airfield (nr. Holt) for some scenes.

Die Another Day (2002) - James Bond adventure. Scenes filmed at RAF Marham, and on the North Norfolk Coast at Deepdale Farm, Burnham Deepdale (where a Korean paddy field was recreated). Starred Pierce Brosnan.

The Eagle has Landed (1976) - classic war-based adventure with Michael Caine. Scenes were filmed in the county.

The Go Between (1971) - drama with Alan Bates. Scenes filmed at Melton Constable Hall, Heydon Hall and village and Norwich (Maids Head Hotel, Cathedral area, Tombland and railway station).

The Grotesque (1995) - comedy starring Sting and Alan Bates. Filmed at Heydon Hall.

Julia (1977) - drama filmed at Winterton-on-Sea, which doubled as a 1930s Cape Cod, USA. Starred Jane Fonda.

Out of Africa (1985) - Oscar-winning film, starring Robert Redford and Meryl Streep. The opening shots which seem to show Denmark, were actually filmed at Castle Rising.

Revolution (1985) - King's Lynn became 18th C. New York for this film starring Al Pacino, and set against the background of the American War of Independence.

Shakespeare in Love (1998) - romantic comedy starring Gwyneth Paltrow. Scenes based around a dramatic shipwreck were filmed at Holkham Beach. The nearby lake at Holkham Hall was also used.

Tarka the Otter (1979) - classic family film, which follows the life of a real otter, and its adventures in the wild. Scenes were filmed at Bintree Mill (nr. Dereham).

Television

A Fatal Inversion (BBC) and Gallowglass (BBC) - two chilling tales from East Anglian writer, Ruth Rendall. Both were filmed at locations in the county.

The Adventures of Sherlock Holmes (ITV) - drama series based on the Baker Street detective. Part of 'The Sign of Four' story was filmed at Burgh Castle (nr. Great Yarmouth).

Allo Allo (BBC) - comedy series set in France during the Second World War. Scenes were filmed in Thetford Forest, and at 19th C. Lynford Hall, nr. Mundford. A cobbled courtyard at the back of the hall was used as the Nouvion town square, complete with the 'Café Rene' in the corner.

All the King's Men (BBC) - First World War drama starring David Jason and Maggie Smith. Filmed on the royal estate at Sandringham and other locations in the area (Cromer, West Newton, Sheringham and Burnham Deepdale). The Great Saloon at Holkham Hall was used for a dinner scene, and the east front/parterre at Blickling Hall (Aylsham) was used to represent Sandringham House.

The Avengers (ITV) - cult 1960s adventure series with Patrick Macnee. One episode featured the National Construction College at Bircham Newton, Wighton and Gun Hill (nr. Wells-next-the-Sea).

Campion (BBC) - 1930s based detective drama starring Peter Davidson. Scenes for a two-part story were filmed at Bintree Mill (nr. Dereham).

Scene from The Mill on the Floss , Bintree Mill (nr. Dereham), Norfolk

The Chief (ITV) - drama set around the head of the regional police force and filmed throughout the county.

Dad's Army (BBC) - comedy classic, focusing on a World War II Home Guard platoon in an English coastal town, Walmington-on-Sea. Eighty episodes were filmed over nine years during the 1960/70s. Nearly all the episodes featured scenes of Norfolk, some of these on the restricted MOD land to the north of Thetford. This includes Frog Hill where the famous closing titles were shot. Other locations included Bardwell (Six Bells pub), Brandon (railway station), Great Yarmouth (Britannia Pier), High Lodge in Thetford Forest, Honington, Lynford Hall (Mundford), North Norfolk Railway (Sheringham), Oxburgh Hall (Oxborough), Thetford (Anchor Hotel, Church of St. Mary the Less and Nether Row) and Winterton beach. The Bressingham Steam Experience and Gardens, nr. Diss is home to the Dad's Army Museum, featuring vehicles used in the show including Corporal Jones' butchers van, a Leyland fire engine, "Birtha" the tractor engine and a threshing machine. There is also a reconstructed street scene of Walmington-on-Sea.

Dangerfield (BBC) - medical/police drama, which for two episodes was filmed on the North Norfolk coast. Starred Nigel Le Valliant.

David Copperfield (BBC) - adaptation of Dickens novel starring Bob Hoskins and Nicholas Lyndhurst. Areas of King's Lynn (King Street) were used in the filming.

Death in Holy Orders (BBC) - murder, greed and corruption in this tale from P.D. James. Starring Martin Shaw as Adam Dalgleish. Scenes were filmed in the county.

EastEnders (BBC) - soap opera which featured episodes filmed in the Norfolk Broads (including the Ferry Boat Inn at Horning).

Great Expectations (BBC) - adaptation of Dickens novel starring Ioan Gruffudd. The area around Thornham (nr. Hunstanton) was used to recreate the Essex marshes where Pip first meets Abel Magwitch. Whilst a derelict coal barn on the harbour was used as the Gargery house and forge where Pip grew up.

I'm Still Alan Partridge (BBC) - comedy series starring the Norwich DJ and failed television star, Alan Partridge. Starring Steve Coogan. Scenes filmed in Norwich.

Kavanagh QC (ITV) - courtroom drama starring John Thaw. Scenes shot at Norwich.

Keeping up Appearances (BBC) - comedy series which in 1995 filmed scenes in Great Yarmouth (Pleasure Beach). Starred Patricia Routledge.

Love on a Branch Line (BBC) - nostalgic drama, filmed at Oxburgh Hall at Oxborough and on the North Norfolk Railway at Sheringham. Starred Leslie Phillips.

Lovejoy (BBC) - based on the books by Essex writer Jonathan Gash, this comedy drama was set around the adventures of antiques rogue 'Lovejoy' played by Ian McShane. Scenes were filmed in Norwich (Elm Hill, Market Place and Cathedral) and at Blakeney on the North Norfolk Coast.

Martin Chuzzlewit (BBC) - adaptation of classic Dickens novel starring Pete Postlewaite. Scenes were filmed in King's Lynn, which was designed to represent London at the time.

The Mill on the Floss (BBC) - adaptation of George Eliot novel. Filmed at Bintree Mill (nr. Dereham), and Heydon Hall and village (which became St. Ogg's).

The Moonstone (BBC) - costume detective drama, filmed at Heydon Hall and village. Starred Greg Wise.

Murder Rooms (BBC) - series of dramas looking at Sherlock Holmes' creator Sir Arthur Conan Doyle, and the people/places which inspired his stories. Filming took place at Cromer, including the beach, pier and North Lodge council offices. Scenes were also shot at the North Norfolk Railway in Sheringham and Holt Country Park.

A scene from Murder Rooms

P.D. James Mysteries (ITV) - drama series based on the novels written by East Anglian writer P.D. James, and featuring detective Adam Dalgleish. Filmed throughout the county including the coastline, Norfolk Broads and Norwich.

The Prisoner (ITV) - cult series from 1967/8, featuring Patrick McGoohan as 'No. 6'. The opening titles feature McGoohan driving his car at the Lotus factory test track at Hethel (nr. Norwich).

The Rainbow (BBC) - adaptation of D.H. Lawrence novel. Scenes filmed in the walled garden at Felbrigg Hall, nr. Cromer.

Sansaar (India Zee TV) - India soap opera which filmed scenes in Cromer (pier and Runton Road) and Norwich.

September Song (ITV) - comedy drama starring Russ Abbot. Filmed at Cromer.

The Uninvited (ITV) - sci-fi drama starring Leslie Grantham, and filmed throughout the county.

Up Rising (ITV) - saucy comedy starring Michelle Collins and Anton Rogers. Heydon was transformed to become the village of 'Up Rising' for the series.

Vanity Fair (BBC) - adaptation of William Thackeray's tale. Filmed at Rainthorpe Hall, nr. Flordon; Barningham Hall, nr. Holt and Thelveton Hall, nr. Diss. These three appear on screen as one property, the grand Elizabethan Queens Crawley.

SUFFOLK

Film

Barry Lyndon (1975) - Stanley Kubrick film starring Ryan O'Neal. Scenes filmed in the village of Lavenham, where The Guildhall became an 18th C. inn.

The Bridge (1991) - drama with scenes filmed at Walberswick and Yoxford. Starred Saskia Reeves and Geraldine James.

David Copperfield (1970) - adaptation of Dickens novel, starring Laurence Olivier. The isolated beaches between Lowestoft and Southwold was the location for Peggotty's boat. Filming was also done in Southwold itself.

Defence of the Realm (1985) - drama starring Denholm Elliot. Scenes filmed at RAF Lakenheath.

Drowning by Numbers (1988) - drama starring Bernard Hill and Joan Plowright. Scenes filmed at Thorpeness and Southwold.

Eyes Wide Shut (1999) - erotic drama, directed by Stanley Kubrick, starring Tom Cruise and Nicole Kidman. Scenes were filmed at Elveden Hall, nr. Thetford.

The Fourth Protocol (1987) - spy thriller with Michael Caine. Scenes shot in Ipswich (wet dock) and along the River Orwell (Orwell Bridge).

The Golden Bowl (2000) - Merchant/Ivory costume drama starring Uma Thurman and Anjelica Huston. Scenes shot at Helmingham Hall.

Dame Judi Dench - Iris

Iris (2002) - bio-pic of the novelist/philosopher Iris Murdoch. Starring Dame Judi Dench and Kate Winslet. Scenes were filmed on Southwold beach, Walberswick and at St. Lawrence's Church in South Cove.

Lara Croft: Tomb Raider (2001) - action/adventure based on the popular computer game, starring Angelina Jolie. Some of the scenes were shot at Elveden Hall, nr. Thetford.

The Lost Son (1999) - detective drama starring Natassja Kinski. Scenes were shot at Landguard Point, Felixstowe.

Princess Caraboo (1994) - comedy with scenes shot at Elveden Hall, nr. Thetford. Starred Jim Broadbent.

Requiem Apache (1994) - drama with Julie Walters. Scenes were filmed in the village of Stoke-by-Nayland, and in Ipswich (nightclub and car park).

Tomorrow Never Dies (1997) - James Bond adventure with Pierce Bronsan. Scenes were shot at RAF Mildenhall, which doubled as the US airbase at Okinawa in Japan, complete with fake palm trees. RAF Lakenheath was transformed into an Afghan arms dump.

The Wind in the Willows (1997) - Kentwell Hall at Long Melford became Toad Hall for the latest film adaptation of Kenneth Cranham's animal adventures.

The Witchfinder General (1968) - story of Matthew Hopkins, starring Vincent Price. Filmed throughout Suffolk, mainly in the fields/country lanes around Debenham and Eye. The village of Lavenham was also used.

Yangste Incident (1957) - wartime drama starring Richard Todd. Scenes filmed on the River Orwell (which doubled for China).

Yesterday's Hero (1979) - football drama starring Ian McShane. Scenes filmed at the Ipswich Town Football Club.

Television

A Fatal Inversion (BBC) and Gallowglass (BBC) - two chilling tales from East Anglian writer, Ruth Rendall. Both were filmed at locations in the county.

Between the Lines (BBC) - police series, mainly based in London. One storyline had scenes filmed in the town of Felixstowe and at the riverside hamlet of Pin Mill.

Canterbury Tales (BBC) - adaptation of Geoffrey Chaucer's poem. Scenes were filmed in Lavenham, which represented a London street of the time.

The Chief (ITV) - drama set around the head of the regional police force and filmed throughout the county.

The Children of Green Knowe (BBC) - classic children's story. Scenes were filmed at Wingfield College (nr. Diss).

Dark Ages (ITV) - comedy starring Phil Jupitus and Alistair McGowan. The programme used the West Stow Anglo-Saxon Village (nr. Bury St Edmunds) for its location shots.

David Copperfield (BBC) - adaptation of Dickens novel starring Bob Hoskins and Nicholas Lyndhurst. Areas of Southwold were used in the filming.

Death in Holy Orders (BBC) - murder, greed and corruption in this tale from P.D.James. Starring Martin Shaw as Adam Dalgleish. Scenes were filmed in the county.

Deceit (BBC) - thriller based on Clare Francis novel. Various locations were used around the Rivers Deben and Orwell (including Pin Mill).

Great Expectations (BBC) - Ramsholt Church (nr. Woodbridge) featured in the adaptation of this Dickens novel. Starred Ioan Gruffudd.

Gullivers Travels (UStv) - mini series based on the classic tale. Starred Ted Danson. Scenes were filmed at Elveden Hall, nr. Thetford.

A Line in the Sand (ITV) - thriller starring Ross Kemp. Scenes were filmed at Walberswick.

Jonathan Creek (BBC) - one of the episodes from the first series of this comedy drama was filmed at The Bell pub in Middleton, and at locations in Wangford and Wrentham.

Lovejoy (BBC) - based on the books by Essex writer Jonathan Gash, this comedy drama was set around the adventures of antiques rogue 'Lovejoy' played by Ian McShane. Scenes filmed at Boxford, Bungay, Bury St. Edmunds (Angel Hill, Borough Offices, One Bull pub), Cavendish, Clare (Market Hill), Dunwich, Elmswell, Flatford Mill, Hadleigh (churchyard, cricket pitch, Corn Exchange and Market Place), Helmingham Hall, Hintlesham Hall, Ickworth House, Ipswich (wet dock), Kersey (used for very first shot in the series), Lavenham (Angel Hotel, Great House Restaurant, Shilling Street, Swan Hotel), Leiston, Lindsey (Red Rose pub), Long Melford (Bull Hotel, Kentwell Hall, High Street), Lowestoft, Newmarket, Orford, Pin Mill (Butt and Oyster pub), Preston St. Mary (Priory Farm used as Charlotte Cavendish's auction rooms), Somerleyton Hall, Sudbury (North Street) and Wingfield College.

Miss Marple (BBC) - Agatha Christie's elderly female sleuth, starring Joan Hickson. Scenes filmed at Wingfield College (nr. Diss).

The Moonstone (BBC) - costume detective drama, filmed at Elveden Hall, nr. Thetford. Starred Greg Wise.

Murder in Mind (BBC) - drama series of psychological thrillers. One episode ('Rage') filmed at Walberswick beach and church, Ipswich, Westleton and Woodbridge.

Only Fools and Horses (BBC) - classic comedy with David Jason as Del Boy. Scenes filmed at Helmingham Hall.

P.D. James Mysteries (ITV) - drama series based on the novels written by East Anglian writer P.D. James, and featuring detective Adam Dalgleish. Filmed throughout the county, including Ipswich, Felixstowe Ferry, Bawdsey and Sizewell Power Station.

Spooks (BBC) - drama series about the security service MI5. Starring Matthew Macfadyen. One episode filmed scenes at the Dunwich Heath Coastal Centre and Beach, nr. Saxmundham.

The Witchfinder General (Channel 4) - history docu-drama highlighting the infamous witch-hunts of East Anglia in the mid 17th C. Scenes were filmed in the Market Place at Lavenham.

Aviation Heritage in the East of England

On December 17th 1903, the Wright Brothers lifted their aircraft into the skies - and the birth of aviation was forced upon an unbelieving world. Since then the progress of aviation has developed as a result of our challenge to conquer the skies and space. In the East of England, you can discover Britain's great aviation heritage, from the very beginnings of flight with balloons and airships, to the former and present day airfields of the Royal Air Force (RAF) and United States Air Force (USAF). Discover exciting museums, spectacular air shows and poignant memorials.

Balloons and Airships

In September 1784, Britain's first hot air balloon flight was undertaken by Vincenzo Lunardi. He ascended from London, then touched down first at Welham Green (Herts), then twelve miles later in the hamlet of Standon Green End (Herts), where a boulder now marks the spot. The East of England has two major airship connections - an airship factory was constructed at Cardington (Beds) from 1916, later becoming one of the world's best facilities, home of the R101 and R100. They were housed in two gigantic sheds which remain today. To the east of the region, Pulham St. Mary (Norfolk), was another world famous airship station from 1915-1935. The R33 airship is shown on the village sign here.

de Havilland

During the 1920s, one of the greatest names in aircraft design/construction was born 'The de Havilland Aircraft Company'. Their greatest creations are the Moth and Mosquito - the latter designed in secret at Salisbury Hall, nr. St. Albans (Herts) in 1940. A huge factory complex was also built at Hatfield (Herts). In 1977, de Havilland became part of British Aerospace, who developed the Comet and Trident at Hatfield.

RAF and United States Army Air Force (USAAF)

With its flat landscape and proximity to Europe, the East of England was ideal for the construction of airfields. From the mid 1930s, with war looming, the RAF began a massive programme of expansion. In 1942, the Americans arrived, and many RAF airfields were made available to the USAAF, so by 1943 there were over 100,000 US airmen based in Britain. The largest concentration was in the East of England, where most of the 8th Air Force and some of the 9th were located on almost a hundred bases. The 8th Air Force was the largest air striking force ever committed to battle, the first units arriving in May 1942.

With the end of the war, many of the wartime airfields were closed down, whilst others were developed for peacetime duties. Today the East of England is home to some of Britain's most important airbases:-

RAF Coltishall (Norfolk) - opened 1940. During the Second World War many fighter squadrons (and famous pilots) were based here. Later it became the first RAF Station to operate the English Electric Lightning all-weather fighter. Home today to entire RAF Jaguar force.

RAF Lakenheath (Suffolk) - assumed full station status in 1943, with RAF Bomber Command. In 1948, the USAF arrive. Home of the 48th Tactical Fighter Wing (since 1960), flying F-15 Eagles.

RAF Marham (Norfolk) - developed in 1930s as bomber/fighter station. Became RAF's major reconnaissance base in 1993. Home today to Tornado and Canberra squadrons.

RAF Mildenhall (Suffolk) - opened 1934, and used for the start of the world's greatest air race to Australia. Began life with RAF Bomber Command. The USAF arrive in 1950, and in 1959, the airfield becomes the 'Gateway to the UK' for US forces, and later the HQ of the Third Air Force. Aerial refuelling, special operations, reconnaissance and intelligence are some of the key roles today.

RAF Wittering (Cambs) - started life as a training airfield from 1916. Once home to Central Flying School. Became fighter station from 1935. Today known as 'the home of the Harrier'.

Other RAF sites include: Neatishead (Norfolk) - the control and reporting centre responsible for the southern UK air defence region; Honington (Suffolk) - home of the RAF Regiment Depot; Wattisham (Suffolk) - with its search and rescue helicopter unit; and RAF Brampton Wyton Henlow (Bedfordshire and Cambridgeshire) - which has three separate sites under Personnel and Training Command.

Old Airfields

Alongside these present day bases, visitors can discover many of the old airfields, which have found new uses or have been returned to agricultural land. Some are identified by special signs, memorials to past squadrons, or original control towers lovingly restored.

Monuments and Memorials

Throughout the region there are poignant reminders of the men and women who served their country during the two World Wars, including special memorials and monuments. One of the most famous is at Madingley, nr. Cambridge. Here you will find the only Second World War American military cemetery and memorial in Britain.

Museums

There are lots of aviation museums and collections in the area, such as the impressive Imperial War Museum at Duxford (Cambs). For a full listing, please refer to the 'Machinery & Transport' sections (for each county) within this guide.

Famous People

There are lots of famous names connected to the history of aviation in the East of England, such as Thomas Scott and Charles Black, who took part in the famous air race (1934) from Mildenhall to Melbourne, 'Mary the Flying Duchess' of Woburn Abbey who flew her de Havilland Moth on a record-breaking flight to Cape Town in 1937, and the two Hollywood celebrities Clark Gable and James Stewart, who served in the East of England during the Second World War. The famous US bandleader Glenn Miller and his band were based in Bedford during the Second World War (as part of a special radio station set up by the BBC to entertain the troops). They played at venues in the town, and at air bases around the region.

American Air Museum, Imperial War Museum, Duxford, Cambridgeshire

Air Shows

The region holds an impressive range of air shows during the year. Please refer to the 'Diary of Events' for full details (pages 15-25).

USAAF Airfields Official Map

Highlighting the American airforce (USAAF) links with the East of England, the Tourist Board has produced a unique full colour fold-out map (scale 1:425,000) which will help you navigate around the places of aviation interest in the region. All the former USAAF airfields (8th and 9th Air Forces) are marked, and a detailed gazetteer describes their current use. There is also a complete list of memorials and where to find them. A must for any visitor with an interest in aviation history. The map can be ordered directly from the East of England Tourist Board, priced £4.95 (excl. postage & packing) - please call 0870 225 4852 for further information.

If you are interested in finding out more about aviation heritage in the East of England, why not visit our website: **www.visiteastofengland.com** The aviation section includes a car tour 'Fortresses and Fighters', plus lots more information on aviation-related places to visit and events.

St. Edmundsbury Cathedral

Come and see the completion of England's last unfinished Anglican Cathedral in 2004.

The skyline in Bury St. Edmunds, Suffolk is being dramatically changed with the magnificent 150ft Gothic lantern tower over the central crossing of St. James Cathedral (Angel Hill) reaching completion. Five years in the building, the Millennium Tower brings to a close development work over nearly half a century on a project which is probably unique in England.

The tower and the other most recent works - the North Transept, Chapel of the Apostles and East Cloisters - have been built employing medieval materials and methods. Lime mortar was used virtually throughout and required the masons and bricklayers to learn fresh skills. The tower, which has similarities to the Bell Harry Tower at Canterbury, is unique in that it is built externally mainly with Barnack stone. This was the best English limestone in the Middle Ages, but was largely worked out over five hundred years ago. Unexpectedly six years ago, a sufficient amount became available for the building of the tower. Some Clipsham stone is also used on the tower, and elsewhere, Doulting. Safety regulations prevent public access to the top of the tower, but interactive computerised displays of the view are available at ground level.

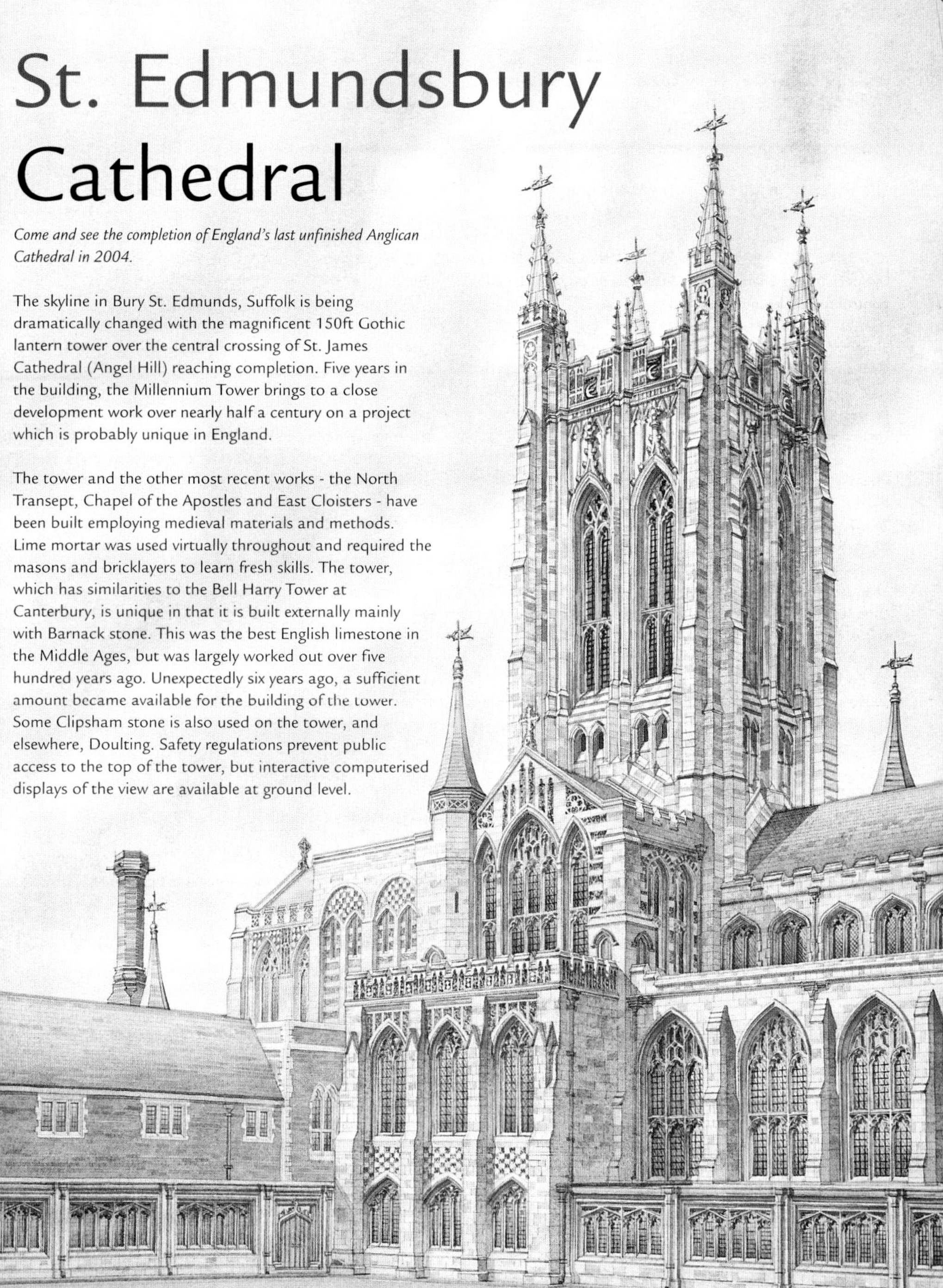

 SPECIAL FEATURE

The lantern tower allows light to fall on the Nave altar below. Whilst the Cathedral's bells are hung in the adjacent Norman Tower - built over eight hundred years ago, also in Barnack stone. The new tower will weather to a similar appearance over the next few centuries. The Millennium Tower derives its strength from the 600,000 bricks, which form the core between outer and inner stone courses. Over twenty miles of scaffolding was raised to support the work.

The North Transept was the first of the recent works to be finished. Below it is a vaulted cloister, one bay of which houses a lift to enable wheelchair users to access the Nave from street level. Above is a tiered gallery with seating overlooking the Nave altar. Next to the St. Edmund Chapel (1967), a new Chapel of the Apostles holds the Reserved Sacrament. There is also a Crypt chapel intended for private prayer. Another door opens onto stairs leading to a small chamber with a fine Oriel window. The final part of the newest work is the East side cloister which offers covered access from the North Door to the Cathedral Centre. This houses the Vestries, the Song School, the Refectory and other hospitality facilities. The completion of St. Edmundsbury Cathedral since the late 1950s has been the inspiration of Stephen Dykes Bower (1903-94), who was architect here between 1943-1988.

Trained by F. C. Eden, he sought to blend seamlessly early 16th C. work with modern gothic design in a relatively plain style, but supported with richly decorated ironwork, joinery and furnishings.

Within stone and lime-washed plaster walls, ceilings are vibrantly coloured panels of striking motifs, the Nave Roof decorations, all done with stencils, having been completed only in the 1980s. This effect is carried down by the handsome Font cover, a memorial of the First World War, to the Victorian tiled floor, laid in 1865. In contrast, the floors at the East end are in randomly coloured Suffolk paving. The stained glass windows are mostly Victorian, and in the Nave, relate to the Old Testament (North side) and to the New Testament (South side). Those at the West end are full of detail, not least of wildlife, for the sharp-eyed. Glazing in the tower and the other recent work is clear - known as white glass - having only random coloured tints in some panes.

Elegantly carved timber furnishings are a feature of the Cathedral. The initial impression will be dominated by the Victorian pews and pulpit in the Nave. New work is in limed oak, notably the stalls in the Quire, but replicated by those in the North Transept Gallery which were made only two years ago. Perhaps the most important sculpture work in the Cathedral is the Elisabeth Frink 'Crucifixion' at the head of the Treasury stairs. Suffolk born, Miss Frink also sculpted the statue of St. Edmund in the Great Churchyard, a memorial to the old West Suffolk County Council dissolved in 1973. Other modern works include the Madonna and Child in the Lady Chapel, which contrast with much older memorials and carved panels elsewhere.

The individual kneelers in the Nave and Quire were created in the 1960s. The designs, based on the blue woollen cloth of the Middle Ages, from which the wealth of Suffolk was then derived, represent every parish and many other organisations in the Diocese - all are different. Communion Rail kneelers, cushions and other soft furnishings are all part of the same original concept. Displayed over the Treasury Stairs arch, a tapestry worked in France only five years ago depicts Christ in Majesty as drawn by Master Hugo in the Bury Bible, created in the 12th C. in the great Benedictine Abbey of which St James's was a daughter church.

The Treasury was built with financial help from the USA in 1990. It displays a selection of the marvellous Communion vessels and other plate from the Cathedral and other parish churches in Suffolk. Rarely on show otherwise, these are complemented by paintings, tapestries and vestments.

The Cathedral caters for visitors with a licensed Refectory in the Cathedral Centre. The Cathedral Shop is next to the main entrance to the Cathedral, and offers a selection of gifts, books and CDs. Adjacent to the shop, the Tower Room interprets the recent building works. A DVD illustrates the various stages of building work and the craftsmen on site. Computer operated consoles bring down the view from the top of the tower and offer the facility to zoom in on more distant buildings. The Cathedral is open all year, daily, 0800-1800 (1900 from 1 May-31 Aug), and there are regular guided tours. Special themed tours, especially about the most recent works, can be booked with the Visitor's Officer on (01284) 754933. More information at www.stedscathedral.co.uk

Glenn Miller's 100th Anniversary (1904-2004)

2004 marks the 100th anniversary of the birth of Glenn Miller. It was in Jun 1944 that Miller and his band arrived in England - primarily here to entertain the huge numbers of American Servicemen in the European Theatre of Operations, they also became extremely popular with millions of Britons tuning into their radio broadcasts. Major Glenn Miller's loss on the 15 Dec 1944 came as a complete and devastating surprise to the world - but he will always be remembered, and it is a tribute to him that his music is as popular today as it was then.

Biography

Miller was born on the 1 Mar 1904 in Clarinda, Iowa, USA. Aged 17, he got his first full time job in Boyd Senter's Band. Two years later he enrolled at the University of Colorado - but left after just three terms to pursue his musical career. In 1937, Miller formed his first full time band, having worked with other key bandleaders such as the Dorsey Brothers and Ray Noble. On the 4 Apr 1939 "Moonlight Serenade" is recorded for the first time, and a year later in Feb, the band is voted America's No. 1 in a dance band poll. In 1942, Miller is presented with the world's first Gold Disc for "Chattanooga Choo Choo".

Miller clearly loved his country, and although being over the call up age he decided on the 15 Feb 1942 (at the age of 38) to join the armed forces. He became a captain and was assigned to the Army Air Core - becoming leader of the US Army Air Force Band.

In 1944, the long awaited allied invasion of Europe was in an advanced stage of preparation. General Eisenhower was acutely aware of the need to sustain the morale of the thousands of American servicemen gathering in Southern England. To that end, Supreme Headquarters Allied Expeditionary Forces agreed with the BBC to set up a new radio service "The Allied Expeditionary Forces Programme" - and a cornerstone of this was to be the AAF Band. On the 28 Jun 1944, Miller and his band arrived in Scotland aboard the "Queen Elizabeth", and after a brief period in London, was moved to the town of Bedford in Jul. By 1944, the BBC had a number of studios in various church halls in the town, as well as the Corn Exchange and Co-Partners Hall. On Sun 9 Jul, the band made their first 'live' broadcast from the Corn Exchange for the AEF Programme. In between the huge broadcasting schedule, the band undertook live performances at many of the US Air Bases throughout the South of England, playing to troop audiences totalling 1 1/2 million.

The band were due to leave Bedford for Paris on Sat 16 Dec to play a series of concerts. Miller decided that he would go on ahead of the band. But bad weather from the 13 Dec until the Fri, meant that Miller's departure was frustrated. In the Officers' Club at Milton Ernest Hall (HQ of the 8th Air Force Service Command) Miller discovered that a certain Col. Baessell was going to Paris at lunchtime on Fri 15 in a single engine Norseman Aircraft. Baessell offered Miller a lift, and shortly after lunch the two officers climbed aboard the aircraft at Twinwood Farm Airfield (nr. Milton Ernest). Neither Miller, Baessell nor their pilot were ever seen again. On Wed 20 Dec, the 8th Air Force HQ at Milton Ernest issued an official notification that Major Alton Glenn Miller and his two companions were "missing in flight, presumed to be lost". But in England and Europe, the unique Miller sound continued to please audiences until Sat 28 Jul 1945 when the band gave their last concert at La Havre.

SPECIAL FEATURE

Glenn Miller Trail

Start your tour in the town of *Bedford*, which during World War II became a mecca for music making - home of the BBC Music Department and the BBC Symphony Orchestra, which were moved here from Bristol. In Jul 1944, this was further enhanced by the start of the AEF radio station, and the music of Glenn Miller. The Corn Exchange was 'Studio 1', the major broadcast and concert venue, and you will find a bust of Miller outside the building.

Head north now along the A6 to Clapham, and the former *RAF Twinwoods Farm* (www.twinwoodevents.com). This was not an American bomber base, but was used by the AEF Band as a departure and arrival base. From here the band flew to give concerts throughout the country. The original control tower has been restored, and houses an exhibition dedicated to Glenn Miller.

Continue along the A6 to *Milton Ernest*, where the hall was the HQ of the 8th Air Force Service Command. Miller's band played here on several occasions. *Thurleigh Airfield* (to the north east) was the wartime home of the 306th Bombardment Group, and a museum houses displays, artefacts and uniforms. The AEF Band played a hanger concert here in 1944, with an audience of 3,000 men.

From here, it is only a short journey east to the University city of *Cambridge*, where you can visit the only Second World War Military cemetery and memorial in Britain. Here on the "Wall of the Missing" you will find MILLER, ALTON G. .... AEF BAND. End your tour at the *Imperial War Museum, Duxford* (just to the south of the city, beside the M11), home of the American Air Museum, with its outstanding collection of aircraft including a B-17 Flying Fortress.

Special Events

A number of special events are being held to mark the 100th anniversary, including:

Sun 29 Feb
Centenary Celebration of the birth of Glenn Miller - Twinwood Airfield

Sat 3 and Sun 4 Jul
Bedford River Festival (with an American Independence Day)

Sat 28-Mon 30 Aug
The International Glenn Miller Festival - Twinwood Airfield

Sat 4-Sun 12 Sept
Bedford History and Heritage Week - talks, film shows and exhibitions

Sun 12 Dec
The Celebration of the Life and Music of Glenn Miller - Twinwood Airfield

Bedfordshire & Hertfordshire

Map of County 46

County Information 47

Cities, Towns & Villages 49

Tourist Information (Centres & Points) . . . 56

Guided Tours 58

History & Heritage
Historic Houses 59
Ancient Monuments 62
Museums & Galleries 64
Machinery & Transport 69
Mills 70

Bloomin' Beautiful
Gardens 71
Nurseries & Garden Centres 73

Family Fun
Animal & Bird Collections 76
Children's Indoor Play Centres 78
Leisure Pools 79

Countryside
Special Areas 80
Country Parks & Nature Reserves 81
Picnic Sites 83

Activities
Activity Centres 85
Boat Trips 85
Cycling 85
Walking 86

Food & Drink
Regional Produce 87
Restaurants 87
Afternoon Teas 87

Discovery Tours 88

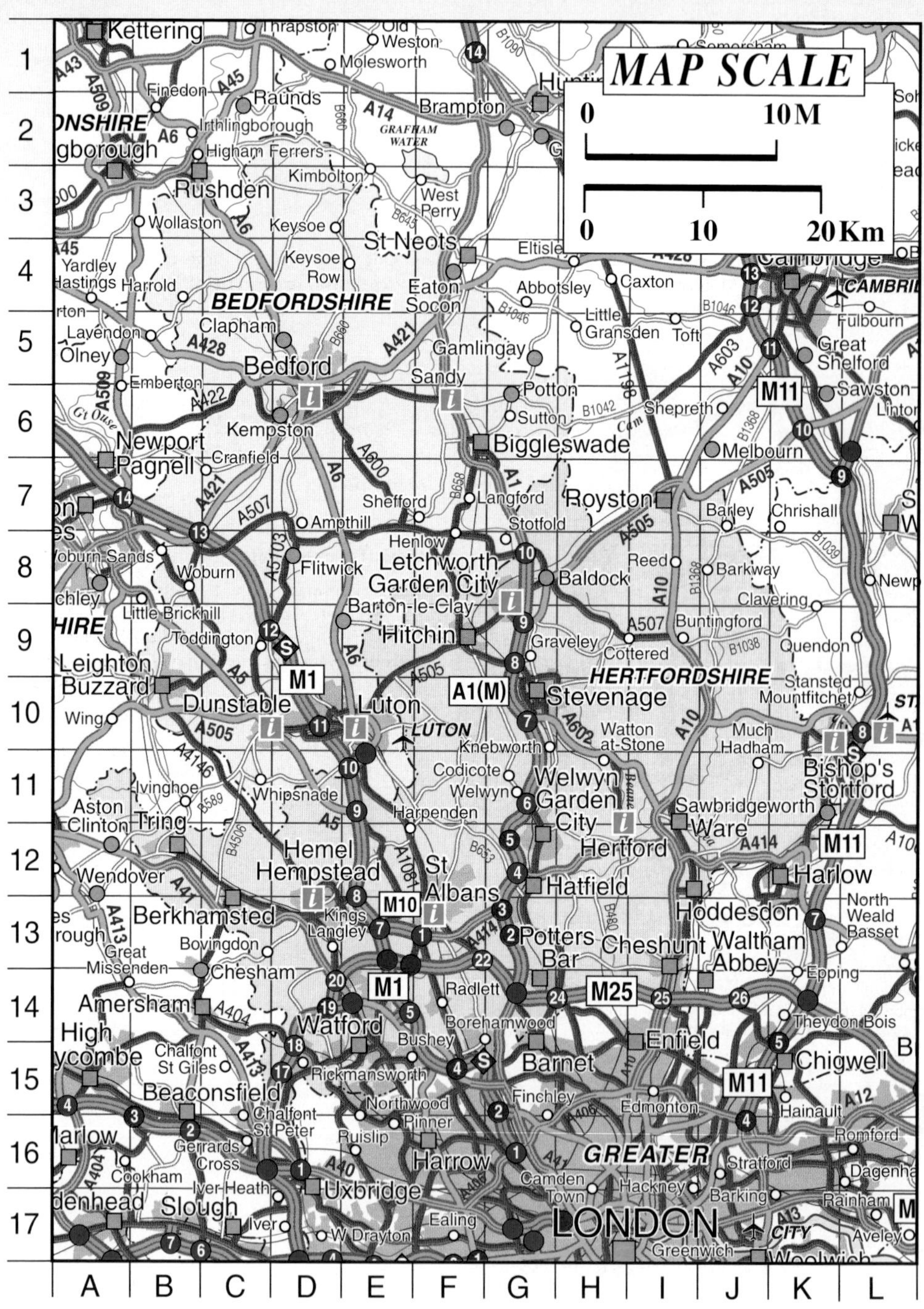
MAP SCALE
0
10M
0
10
20Km
Kettering
Thrapston
Weston
Molesworth
Raunds
Finedon
Irthlingborough
Higham Ferrers
Brampton
GRAFHAM WATER
Kimbolton
West Perry
Rushden
Wollaston
Keysoe
St Neots
Keysoe Row
Eaton Socon
Yardley Hastings
Harrold
BEDFORDSHIRE
Eltisley
Caxton
Abbotsley
Little Gransden
Toft
Cambridge
CAMBRIDGE
Fulbourn
Great Shelford
Sawston
Lavendon
Olney
Clapham
Bedford
Gamlingay
Sandy
Potton
Sutton
Emberton
Kempston
Biggleswade
Shepreth
Melbourn
Newport Pagnell
Cranfield
Langford
Royston
Shefford
Ampthill
Stotfold
Henlow
Barley
Chrishall
Woburn Sands
Woburn
Flitwick
Letchworth Garden City
Baldock
Reed
Barkway
Little Brickhill
Barton-le-Clay
Clavering
Toddington
Hitchin
Buntingford
Cottered
Graveley
Quendon
Leighton Buzzard
HERTFORDSHIRE
Stansted Mountfitchet
Dunstable
Luton
Stevenage
Wing
LUTON
Watton at-Stone
Much Hadham
Knebworth
Bishop's Stortford
Codicote
Welwyn
Welwyn Garden City
Ivinghoe
Whipsnade
Aston Clinton
Tring
Harpenden
Sawbridgeworth
Hertford
Ware
Hemel Hempstead
St Albans
Wendover
Hatfield
Harlow
Berkhamsted
Kings Langley
Hoddesdon
North Weald Basset
Bovingdon
Potters Bar
Cheshunt
Waltham Abbey
Great Missenden
Chesham
Epping
Radlett
Amersham
Watford
Borehamwood
Theydon Bois
High Wycombe
Chalfont St Giles
Bushey
Barnet
Enfield
Chigwell
Rickmansworth
Beaconsfield
Northwood
Finchley
Edmonton
Hainault
Chalfont St Peter
Pinner
Marlow
Gerrards Cross
Ruislip
Harrow
GREATER
Stratford
Romford
Cookham
Iver Heath
Uxbridge
Camden Town
Hackney
Barking
Dagenham
Slough
Iver
Ealing
LONDON
Rainham
W Drayton
CITY
Greenwich
Aveley
Woolwich
M1
M10
M11
M25
A1(M)
1 2 3 4 5 6 7 8 9 10 11 12 13 14 15 16 17
A B C D E F G H I J K L

Bedfordshire

County Town: Bedford.
Population: 566,400 approx. (including Luton).
Highest Point: Dunstable Downs 244m (801 feet).
Rivers: Beane, Flit, Grand Union Canal, Hiz, Ivel, Lea, Ouse, Ouzel.
Landmarks: A1 (Great North Road), Cardington airship hangers, Dunstable Downs (chalk lion), The Greensand Ridge, London Luton Airport, M1 Motorway (Britain's first motorway), The Icknield Way (ancient road), Woburn Abbey.

Welcome to Bedfordshire:

Explore the ancient town of Bedford, with its riverside gardens and connections to John Bunyan and Glenn Miller. To the north west are pretty limestone villages, and to the east, the giant airship hangers at Cardington and the unique Swiss Garden at Old Warden. Lovers of antiques should head to the Georgian towns of Ampthill or Woburn, which is also home to the magnificent abbey - seat of the Dukes of Bedford. Get back to nature in Luton's landscaped parkland, amongst the chalk-life flora and fauna of the magnificent Dunstable Downs or on the Grand Union Canal at Leighton Buzzard.

Industry Past & Present:

Luton has long been recognised as the centre of British *hat making*. The industry that thrives today has its roots deep in the 17th C. when local straw was plaited, then sewn together to form hats. Soon special plait schools were developed, and in 1919 production began on felt hats. Visit the 'Plaiter's Lea' conservation area, home of today's hat manufacturers. To the north of the county, Bedford and the villages of the Ouse Valley, saw a thriving *pillow-lace* industry from the late 16-19th C. Made with bobbins, the cotton was woven to create intricate lace designs of beauty. This was reputedly started by Katherine of Aragon (Henry VIII's first wife), whilst held at Ampthill Castle. Today *arable farming (cereal production)* has taken over much of the county, but *market gardening* flourishes around Biggleswade and Sandy. To the west, *clay, sand* and *chalk* have been quarried in vast quantities around Leighton Buzzard and Marston Moretaine. Up until the 1960s around 3,000 tons of sand were carried away each week at Leighton Buzzard. *Aeronautical* and *agricultural research* figures prominently at Cranfield (with its own airfield) and Silsoe (biology). Whilst London Luton Airport is the headquarters to several well-known airline companies including Britannia, Easyjet and Monarch. In 1916, an airship factory was constructed at Cardington, later becoming one of the world's best facilities, home of the R101 and R100 airships. They were housed in two gigantic sheds which remain today. Recently airship construction has returned to Cardington, with airships designed for police surveillance, advertising and TV work. Millbrook (nr. Ampthill) is Europe's leading *commercial test/validation centre* for the automotive and transport industries. Famous names of the county include - Jordans (breakfast cereals/crunchy bars), Charles Wells (brewing), Gossard (lingerie) and Vauxhall (head office/parts).

Famous People:

Katherine of Aragon *(Henry VIII's first wife)*, Lady Margaret Beaufort *(mother of Henry VII)*, Mary the 'flying' Duchess of Bedford (*Woburn Abbey*), Dukes of Bedford *(Woburn Abbey)*, Robert Bloomfield *(poet)*, John Bunyan *(author/preacher)*, Henry VIII, John Howard *(prison reformer)*, Glenn Miller *(US bandleader)*, Mary Norton *(author)*, Dorothy Osborne *(17th C. letter writer)*, Sir Joseph Paxton *(English gardener)*, Richard Shuttleworth (*aviator*), Thomas Tompion *(watch and clock maker)*, Samuel Whitbread *(brewer)*.

Cardington, Bedfordshire

Hertfordshire

County Town: Hertford.
Population: 1,033,977 approx.
Highest Point: Hastoe 245m (803 feet).
Rivers: Colne, Grand Union Canal, Ivel, Lea, Mimram, Rib, Stort, Ver.
Landmarks: A1 (Great North Road), Ashridge Estate, The Chiltern Hills, Grand Union Canal, Hatfield House, Lee Valley Park, Letchworth Garden City, M1 & M25 Motorways, St. Albans Cathedral, Verulamium.

Welcome to Hertfordshire:

Discover St. Albans, a city shaped by over 2,000 years of history, including Roman remains and a magnificent cathedral. South from here is Borehamwood, famed for its film/television studios. Watford is great for shopping, or why not visit the world's first Garden City at Letchworth? There are also interesting market towns, such as Berkhamsted, Bishop's Stortford, Hertford, Hitchin and Tring. To the west of the county is the 4,000 acre 'Ashridge Estate' with its commons and woodland, and to the east, the waterways and green open spaces of the Lee Valley Park.

Industry Past & Present:

Hertfordshire has always been an *agricultural* county, long famous for its *market gardening, watercress* and *roses*. The Gade Valley (nr. Hemel Hempstead) was once a major *paper-making* centre. In 1809, John Dickinson bought Apsley Mill (and later two other mills), so by 1838, they had a combined output of 41 tons of paper per week. During the 20th C. the company became the market leader. The river valleys of the Lea and the Stort have been described as the cradle of the *malting* industry in England. From the 1700s the industry grew rapidly, and from then until the early 1900s, huge amounts of malt were exported to brewers in London. The Lea Valley also became one of the largest areas in the country for *market gardening*. By the 1930s almost half the glasshouses in England were here, growing a variety of fruit, vegetables and flowers. Although greatly diminished, there are still many glasshouses mainly growing plants and shrubs for the garden centres around London. The extraction of good quality *gravel* also became a major activity between Waltham Cross and Ware. The south of the county is noted as a focal point for *film* and *television* production, particularly the town of Borehamwood (Elstree), Britain's very own Hollywood since 1914. To the north, the former Rolls Royce factory at Leavesden is now a major film studio, whilst St. Albans saw early experiments in film. The county also has a place in the history of *aviation*, Britain's first hot air balloon flight landed at Standon, the Mosquito Bomber was manufactured at London Colney and British Aerospace were based at Hatfield. St. Albans was once home to Ryder Seeds, remembered in golf's 'Ryder Cup', whilst Letchworth Garden City is noted for its former 'Spirella' corset factory. Famous names of the county include - GlaxoSmithKline (pharmaceuticals), Kodak (photographic), McMullen and Sons (brewing) and Tesco (head office).

Famous People:

Saint Alban *(first martyr for the Christian faith to die in Britain)*, Francis Bacon *(essayist/statesman)*, Nicholas Breakspear *(only English pope)*, Edward Bulwer-Lytton *(author)*, Dame Barbara Cartland *(author)*, William Cowper *(poet)*, Charles Dickens *(author)*, Elizabeth I, Captain William Earl Jones *(author)*, Lady Katherine 'the wicked lady' Ferrers *(highwaywoman)*, EM Forster *(author)*, Graham Greene *(author)*, Charles Lamb *(essayist)*, Henry Moore *(sculptor)*, George Orwell *(author)*, Beatrix Potter *(author)*, Cecil Rhodes *(British Empire builder)*, George Bernard Shaw *(author)*, Anthony Trollope *(author)*, HG Wells *(author)*.

Tring, Hertfordshire

Cities, Towns & Villages

MD: Market Day
FM: Farmers' Market
EC: Early Closing
Tourist Information Centre (see page 56)
Guided Tours (see page 58)

Bedfordshire

Ampthill Map ref. D7
Ancient market town, under the brow of the Greensand Ridge. Picturesque narrow streets are lined with fine Georgian buildings and quaint antique shops. Ampthill Park was once home to a 15th C. castle, where Henry VIII stayed, and his wife Katherine of Aragon was kept during their divorce proceedings. A stone cross now marks the spot. **MD**: Thurs. **FM**: last Sat in month.

Bedford Map ref. D5/6
Ancient county town, dating back to before Saxon times. Fine buildings and mound of Norman castle. The Embankment is one of the country's finest river settings, with tree-lined walkways, gardens, bandstand and elegant suspension bridge. Connections to John Bunyan, preacher/author ('The Pilgrim's Progress'); Glenn Miller, the World War II bandleader; and the former Bedfordshire lace industry. **MD**: Wed and Sat. **FM**: 2nd Thurs in month.

Biggleswade Map ref. F6
Set on the River Ivel, this busy town is in the heart of market gardening country. During the 18th C. it was an important coaching centre on the Great North Road, and many old inns remain today. Dan Albone (1860-1906), racing cyclist and inventor of the tandem bicycle, established the Ivel Cycle Works in the town. **MD**: Sat.

Dunstable Map ref. C/D10
Set at the junction of the 4,000 year old Icknield Way and 'Roman' Watling Street, this ancient market town was started in the 12th C. by Henry I. The Augustinian priory, founded in 1131, was chosen by Henry VIII for the divorce proceedings of his first wife Katherine of Aragon. Later the town became a major coaching centre, and was noted for its straw plait and hat making industries. **MD**: Wed and Sat, plus small market on Fri.

Flitwick Map ref. D8
The older part of this large village sits around the church of St. Peter with its large lychgate. Several timber-framed/brick cottages and 17/18th C. manor house. Flitwick Moor is a wetland area consisting of old peat workings. **MD**: Fri.

Houghton Regis Map ref. D10
Once a royal manor at the time of Edward the Confessor, Houghton Regis is noted for its fine 18th C. mansion which stands beside a green where cricket is still played. The church has a chequer-work exterior of flint and local stone.

Leighton Buzzard Map ref. B10
Situated on the Grand Union Canal, the town has always been famous for its sand. Fine Georgian buildings line the wide High Street, alongside a medieval market cross, 19th C. town hall and charming mews. The 13th C. parish church is noted for its 191 feet high spire. Adjoining Linslade is popular with boaters, anglers and walkers. **MD**: Tues and Sat. **FM**: 3rd Sat in month. **EC**: Thurs.

 CITIES, TOWNS & VILLAGES

Luton Map ref. E10
Situated on the edge of the Chiltern Hills, Luton is a thriving town with a long history. From the 17th C. it was noted for its straw plait and hat making industries. There is also a long association with the car industry. St. Mary's Church has one of the finest double arch stone screens in Europe. The famous Luton Shopping Centre, excellent entertainment/leisure facilities and several landscaped parks are other key attractions. **MD**: Mon to Sat.

Potton Map ref. G6
Ancient market town, centred on an enclosed medieval square. Red-brick 18th C. houses and Neo-Georgian clock house. Narrow streets radiate out from the square, lined with Georgian and ironstone buildings. The 13/14th C. church has gravestones adorned with angels and skulls.

Sandy Map ref. F6
Set against a backdrop of greensand hills, with their parklands, woodlands and heath, Sandy is one of the earliest places in the county where market gardening was recorded. Excavations show the town dates back to Roman times. An Elizabethan-style mansion (The Lodge) is now the headquarters of the RSPB. **MD**: Fri.

Shefford Map ref. F7
Small market town, which in the 19th C. enjoyed a brief status of an inland port - when the Ivel Navigation was built to transport coal and other goods by boat. The famous 19th C. poet Robert Bloomfield lived here from 1812-1823. **MD**: Fri.

Woburn Map ref. B8
Surrounded by wooded countryside and parkland, this beautifully preserved Georgian town is acknowledged as one of the most historically important in Britain. 18/19th C. houses and period shop-fronts line the High Street. Today it has become an excellent centre for antiques and collectables. The old church is now a Heritage Centre.

Pavenham, Bedfordshire

Pick of the villages

1 **Aspley Guise** - former 19th C. health resort, set amid sandy pine woods. Map ref. B8
2 **Biddenham** - lies in a loop of the river. Stone and colour-washed houses. Map ref. D5
3 **Billington** - hilltop village with thatched cottages and 13th C. church. Map ref. B10
4 **Bletsoe** - castle remains, once home of Lady Margaret Beaufort, mother of Henry VII. Map ref. D4
5 **Bromham** - 13th C. medieval bridge and restored water mill (17th C.). Map ref. C5
6 **Cardington** - well-kept green, with 200 year old cottages. Huge airship sheds. Map ref. E6
7 **Clophill** - 17/18th C. buildings, former lockup/pound and ruined hilltop church. Map ref. E7
8 **Elstow** - 16th C. timber-framed Moot Hall. John Bunyan was born nearby in 1628. Map ref. D6
9 **Felmersham** - hilltop village, with finest early English church in county. Map ref. C4
10 **Harlington** - connections to John Bunyan. 17th C. manor house and half-timbered cottages. Map ref. D9
11 **Harrold** - tree-lined green with 18th C. butter cross and circular lock-up. Map ref. B4
12 **Heath and Reach** - old cottages set beside a green, with pump and clock tower. Map ref. B9
13 **Ickwell** - classic English village with cricket pitch and permanent maypole. Map ref. F6
14 **Milton Bryan** - timber framed houses. Birthplace of Sir Joseph Paxton, designer of the Crystal Palace. Map ref. C9
15 **Northill** - 18th C. thatched cottages and the church sit beside a little pond. Map ref. F6
16 **Old Warden** - picturesque village recreated in Swiss-style by the 3rd Lord Ongley. Map ref. F6
17 **Pavenham** - limestone houses and splendid church. Former rush-matting industry. Map ref. C4
18 **Shelton** - tiny hamlet with pretty cottages and a Georgian rectory. Map ref. D2
19 **Silsoe** - small village with over 130 listed buildings. Close by is Wrest Park. Map ref. D/E8
20 **Southill** - estate village, with Southill Park, home of the Whitbread Family since 1795. Map ref. F7
21 **Stevington** - 14th C. medieval market cross where John Bunyan once preached. Map ref. C5
22 **Studham** - one of the highest villages in Beds. Once noted for its hat-making. Map ref. D11
23 **Sutton** - 14th C. packhorse bridge and ford. Church has 19th C. barrel organ. Map ref. G6
24 **Swineshead** - pretty main street, including limestone spire of 14th C. church. Map ref. D3
25 **Thurleigh** - remains of Norman castle. Timber-framed and thatched buildings. Map ref. D4
26 **Toddington** - hilltop village with elegant houses/cottages. Large green with pump. Map ref. C9
27 **Totternhoe** - set below a chalkland spur, and once noted for its building stone. Map ref. C10
28 **Turvey** - 19th C. estate village, set beside the River Great Ouse. 13th C. bridge. Map ref. B5
29 **Whipsnade** - set on famous downs, surrounded by common land. Unusual tree cathedral. Map ref. C11
30 **Willington** - 16th C. stables and stone dovecote (once housing 1,500 nesting birds). Map ref. E5

 CITIES, TOWNS & VILLAGES

Hertfordshire

Abbots Langley Map ref. E14
This large village was granted to the abbot of St. Albans at the time of Edward the Confessor. To the north is the hamlet of Bedmond where the only English Pope, Nicholas Breakspear was born (1100). Former Ovaltine factory and dairy farm.

Baldock Map ref. G8
An important Iron Age/Roman settlement, whose borough was founded in 1250 by the Knights Templar. The town gained importance in the coaching era when it was the first main stop on the Great North Road out of London. It has retained much of its old-world charm, with handsome 16-18th C. buildings. The town's greatest feature is St. Mary's Church tower. **MD**: Wed. **FM**: at nearby Sandon, 3rd Sat in month. **EC**: Thurs.

Berkhamsted Map ref. C12/13
This thriving town is steeped in history, with a large section of the elegant High Street designated a conservation centre. Close by are the romantic ruins of the former 11th C. castle. The town has strong literary links, including Graham Greene, William Cowper and J.M. Barrie. Just to the north is the 4,000 acres of The National Trust's 'Ashridge Estate'. **MD**: Sat. **EC**: Wed.

Bishop's Stortford Map ref. K10/11
Set on the River Stort, this ancient market town is the birthplace (1853) of Cecil Rhodes, who went to South Africa and found his fortune in the diamond mines.
A former coaching centre, the town prospered from the malting and brewing industry. There are many fine 16/17th C. buildings, alongside the remains of a Norman castle. **MD**: Thurs and Sat. **FM**: at nearby Little Hadham, last Sat in month. **EC**: Wed.

Borehamwood and Elstree Map ref. F/G14/15
Borehamwood is largely a modern town with much postwar housing. It is historically associated with the film industry, although today only two studios remain. The BBC Elstree Centre is home to the set of 'EastEnders'. The much older settlement of Elstree, sits on the 'Roman' Watling Street with old houses and inns of timber-framed and brick construction. **MD**: Tues and Sat.

Brookmans Park Map ref. G13
Attractive residential area, built in the grounds of two former 16th C. estates - Brookmans and Gobions. Both are long demolished, with 'Gobions' belonging to Sir Thomas More. All that remains is the Folly Arch (circa 1750).
EC: Wed.

Buntingford Map ref. I9
Once an important coaching town in the 18/19th C. Buntingford lies on the 'Roman' Ermine Street. Many fine listed buildings can be found in the High Street, including St. Peter's Church, the first brick built church in England, and the rare 16th C. turret clock. The River Rib, well known for kingfishers, runs through the town. **MD**: Mon. **FM**: at nearby Great Hormead, 1st Sat in month. **EC**: Wed.

Bushey Map ref. E/F15
Small town, retaining its village atmosphere. Links with the Monro Circle of early English watercolourists, and the Victorian artist, Sir Hubert von Herkomer, who founded an art/film studio here (a rose garden now stands on the site). Attractive green, pond and 13th C. church with hammerbeam roof. **EC**: Wed

Cheshunt and Waltham Cross Map ref. I13/14
These adjoining towns are set on the edge of the Lee Valley Park. Cheshunt is a popular shopping centre, with a pond and fountain at its centre. Waltham Cross (to the south) is noted for its beautiful 'Eleanor Cross', a Grade I listed monument, erected by King Edward I in 1290 in memory of his beloved queen. **MD**: Wed and Fri (Waltham Cross).

Harpenden Map ref. E/F11/12
From agricultural origins, Harpenden has developed into an attractive small town. Designated a conservation area, the tree-lined High Street has many listed 17/18th C. buildings, interesting shops and a variety of pubs and restaurants. The town boasts many fine open spaces, such as Rothamsted Park and the Common with its ponds and nature trail.

Aldbury, Hertfordshire

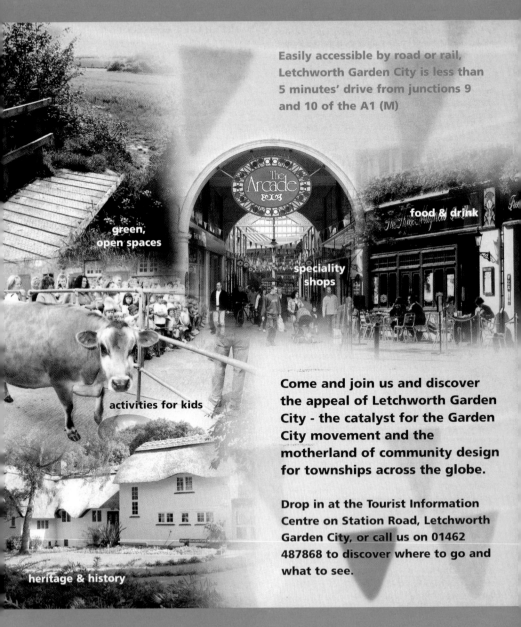

CITIES, TOWNS & VILLAGES

Hertford, Hertfordshire

Hatfield Map ref. G12
The old town dates back to Saxon times, with Georgian houses and former coaching inns. Charles Dickens visited The Eight Bells, and later featured it in 'Oliver Twist'. During the 1930s, Hatfield's growth was linked to the aviation industry, with both the Mosquito and Trident built here. In 1948, the 'new town' of Hatfield was established. **MD**: Wed and Sat. **FM**: 1st Sat in month. **EC**: Thurs.

Hemel Hempstead Map ref. D12/13
Unlike most New Towns, Hemel Hempstead developed around a charming old settlement, centred on St. Mary's Church (which dates from c.1150). The preserved High Street has 17/18th C. houses, specialist shops and a lively arts centre. The New Town is a vibrant centre with an undercover shopping mall, parkland and water gardens. **MD**: Thurs to Sat (antiques market on Wed). i

Hertford Map ref. H/I12
Historic county town, at the meeting place of four rivers, and a royal borough for more than 1,000 years. The former castle with its Norman mound, massive walls and 15th C. gatehouse stand in attractive gardens. Impressive 18th C. Shire Hall, and the oldest 'Quaker' Friend's Meeting House (c.1670) in the world. The town has also become famed as an antiques centre, especially along St. Andrew Street. **MD**: Sat. **EC**: Thurs. i

Hitchin Map ref. F9
Ancient market town dating back to Saxon times. A former Royal Manor, Hitchin prospered from the wool trade, and retains its medieval plan with narrow streets and lanes. The large market square is surrounded by Tudor and Georgian buildings, and overlooked by the largest parish church in the county. Close by is Hitchin Priory, an 18th C. mansion. **MD**: Tues, Fri and Sat. **FM**: Tues. **EC**: Wed.

Hoddesdon Map ref. I12
Set on the edge of the Lee Valley Park, this bustling market town has several fine listed buildings, including the Swan Inn and the Salisbury Arms, both of which date from the 17th C. The town centre has been designated a conservation area, and the Clock Tower (built in 1835) is an historic focal point. There has been a market here since the 13th C. **MD**: Wed and Fri. **EC**: Thurs.

Kings Langley Map ref. D13
Large and thriving village set beside the Grand Union Canal. A former royal palace was the birthplace (1341) of Edmund de Langley, first Duke of York and fifth son of Edward III. His tomb can be seen in the church.

Letchworth Garden City Map ref. G8
The world's first Garden City, founded in 1903 - its unique design based on the ideas of Ebenezer Howard. His dream was to combine "the health of the country with the comfort of the town", with carefully planned and well designed housing and industries. Wide tree-lined avenues, parks and gardens add to its unique appeal. Famous black squirrels. **MD**: (indoor market) Mon to Sat (except Wed). **EC**: Wed. i

Berkhamsted, Hertfordshire

CITIES, TOWNS & VILLAGES

London Colney Map ref. F13
This small town has a long main street with old inns and a restored bridge. To the south, flooded gravel pits have been transformed into a nature reserve. The nearby All Saints Pastoral Centre is noted for its ruined medieval chapel.

Much Hadham Map ref. J11
This is one of Hertfordshire's showpiece villages, and for 800 years the country seat of the Bishops of London. The long High Street has well-preserved timber/brick houses, and grand 18/19th C. residences. The former home of sculptor Henry Moore is at nearby Perry Green.

Potters Bar Map ref. G14
The name of this town is thought to derive from a Roman pottery which once operated in the area. Its later growth is connected to the arrival of the railway in 1850, which made it an attractive commuter town. **EC**: Thurs.

Redbourn Map ref. E12
Named after the River Red, this small town sits on the 'Roman' Watling Street. During the 17/18th C. it was a popular coaching stop. Ancient pubs and restored water mill. The Common was the site of the first recorded cricket match in Hertfordshire in 1666. **EC**: Wed.

Rickmansworth Map ref. D15
A former market town with a charter dating from 1542. The town boasts a fine conservation area, including St. Mary's Church with its 17th C. tower. Basing House has associations with William Penn, famous Quaker statesmen and founder of the state of Pennsylvania, USA. To the south east of the town is Rickmansworth Aquadrome, offering water-based activities.

St. Albans, Hertfordshire

Royston Map ref. I7
Busy market town, which grew up around a cross erected by Lady Roisia (around 1066). This marked the intersection of the ancient Icknield Way and 'Roman' Ermine Street. In the 17th C. Royston became a hunting base for James I. Several historic buildings, award-winning gardens and an unusual man-made cave, with medieval carvings. **MD**: Wed and Sat. **EC**: Thurs.

St. Albans Map ref. F13
An historic city shaped by 2,000 years of history. Named after St. Alban, Britain's first Christian martyr, the city is built beside the site of Verulamium, the third largest Roman town in Britain. Today's settlement developed in Saxon times, around the precincts of the 10th C. monastery. Discover Roman remains, the magnificent 11th C. Cathedral/Abbey Church, historic buildings/inns, attractive parkland and bustling shopping areas. **MD**: Wed and Sat. **FM**: 2nd Sun in month.

Sawbridgeworth Map ref. K11
Described as 'one of the best small towns in the county', Sawbridgeworth prospered from the malting industry, and is dominated by the 13th C. church spire. The riverside maltings have been converted into an antiques centre. The town centre is a conservation area with picturesque streets and Georgian/Victorian buildings. **EC**: Thurs.

Stevenage Map ref. G10
Sitting amongst open farmland, Stevenage was a small market town until 1946, when it was designated Britain's first New Town. Divided into neighbourhoods, Stevenage is noted for its parks, leisure facilities and Britain's first pedestrianised shopping centre. The quaint 'old town' offers pubs, restaurants and shops. **MD**: Wed and Sat (outdoor); and Wed to Sat (indoor). **FM**: at nearby Dane End, 2nd Sat in month.

Tring Map ref. B12
Lying amidst the wooded Chiltern Hills, on the Grand Union Canal, this small attractive market town has been important since the 17th C. The wealthy Rothschild family had a strong influence on the town, their mansion (now a private school) is set in 300 acres of landscaped parkland. Famous zoological museum, beautiful memorial garden and brick maze. **MD**: Fri. **FM**: Sat bi-monthly. **EC**: Wed.

Ware Map ref. I11/12
Once a major centre for brewing, this delightful town is set on the navigable section of the River Lea. The town has many historic buildings, including old coaching inns, 18th C. riverside gazebos and the unique flint and shell decorated Scott's Grotto. Lady Jane Grey was proclaimed Queen in the town in 1553, but only reigned for nine days. **MD**: Tues. **EC**: Thurs.

 CITIES, TOWNS & VILLAGES

Watford Map ref. E14/15
Hertfordshire's largest town is a busy and prosperous regional centre for shopping and entertainment. Impressive 'Harlequin Shopping Centre', elegant Edwardian theatre and popular football club, supported by Sir Elton John. To the south is Cassiobury Park with open space, woodland and boat trips on the Grand Union Canal. **MD**: Tues, Fri and Sat.

Welwyn Map ref. G11
Set on the River Mimram, this historic town has Georgian houses and former coaching inns. The sister of artist Vincent Van Gogh taught at a former school. Just outside the town are the remains of a 3rd C. Roman bathing suite, discovered in 1960.

Welwyn Garden City Map ref. G12
The town was developed from 1920, as England's second Garden City (after Letchworth). Based on the ideas of Ebenezer Howard, its design saw separate residential and industrial areas laid out amongst landscaped parkland and tree-lined boulevards. The neo-Georgian town centre has shopping areas set around a fountain and lawns.

Little Hadham, Hertfordshire

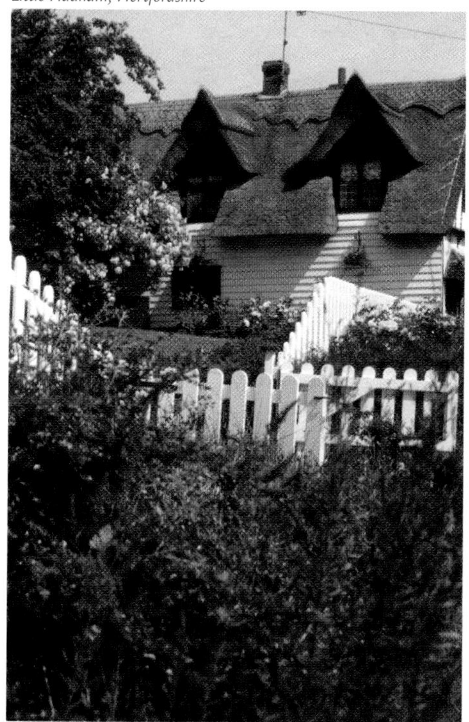

Pick of the villages

1 **Aldbury** - classic English village. Green with duck pond, stocks and whipping post. Map ref. C12
2 **Aldenham** - mentioned in Domesday book. Reservoir and country park. Map ref. F14
3 **Ardeley** - green with horseshoe of thatched cottages, well and church. Map ref. H9
4 **Ashwell** - fine houses, 19th C. lock up and elegant church tower. Source of River Cam. Map ref. G7
5 **Ayot St. Lawrence** - secluded woodland village. Former home of George Bernard Shaw. Map ref. F11
6 **Ayot St. Peter** - set amongst narrow lanes and fine trees. Red-brick church spire. Map ref. G11
7 **Barkway** - former coaching centre, with elegant High Street and 18th C. milestone. Map ref. J8
8 **Barley** - noted for its early Tudor town house, lock-up and rare 'gallows' pub sign. Map ref. J7
9 **Benington** - timbered cottages and church set around green/duck pond. Map ref. H10
10 **Braughing** - once important Roman centre. 17th C. cottages, ford and green. Map ref. J9/10
11 **Brent Pelham** - hilltop village. Stocks/whipping post and tomb of dragon slayer. Map ref. J9
12 **Chipperfield** - wooded common with cricket pitch and Apostles Pond. Map ref. D14
13 **Great Amwell** - source of 17th C. (artificial) 'New River'. Pretty islands with monuments. Map ref. I12
14 **Great Gaddesden** - set beside River Gade. Restored church and 18th C. mansion. Map ref. D12
15 **Hunsdon** - weather-boarded/timbered cottages set around green. Map ref. J11/12
16 **Kings Walden** - hamlet of cottages and farms in parkland. Neo-Georgian mansion. Map ref. F10
17 **Little Berkhamsted** - wooded village, overlooking Lea Valley. 18th C. Stratton's Folly. Map ref. H13
18 **Little Gaddesden** - set amongst woods/common, on edge of Ashridge estate. Map ref. C12
19 **Little Hadham** - fine timber-framed cottages, Elizabethan hall and windmill. Map ref. K10
20 **Markyate** - set on 'Roman' Watling Street. Many listed buildings. Map ref. D11
21 **Reed** - Hertfordshire's highest village. Winding lanes with traces of medieval moats. Map ref. I8
22 **St. Pauls Walden** - well-wooded parish. Childhood home of The Queen Mother. Map ref. F10
23 **Shenley** - quiet village. Former hospital now developed as park. 18th C. lock-up cage and pond. Map ref. F14
24 **Standon** - former market town. Detached church tower and puddingstone. Map ref. J10
25 **Stanstead Abbotts** - thriving village, once a brewing centre. Listed buildings and marina. Map ref. J12
26 **Therfield** - pretty houses, 12th C. castle mound and extensive chalk/grass heathland. Map ref. I8
27 **Walkern** - 17/18th C. houses, dovecote, water mill and Hertfordshire's oldest church. Map ref. H9/10
28 **Westmill** - neat village with triangular green, tile-roofed pump and thatched cottages. Map ref. I9
29 **Wheathampstead** - dates back to pre-Roman times. Devil's Dyke earthwork. Map ref. F12
30 **Wilstone** - pretty village set between the Grand Union Canal and Wilstone reservoir. Witchcraft stories. Map ref. A11

Tourist Information

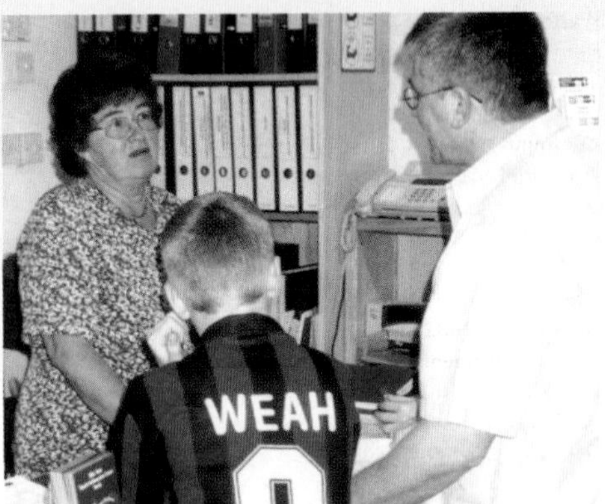

Mid Bedfordshire Tourist Information Centre

Tourist Information Centres

With so much to see and do in this area, it's impossible for us to mention all of the places you can visit. You will find Tourist Information Centres (TICs) throughout Bedfordshire and Hertfordshire, with plenty of information on all the things that you can do and places you can visit.

TICs can book accommodation for you, in their own area, or further afield using the 'Book A Bed Ahead' Scheme. They can also be the ideal place to purchase locally made crafts or gifts, as well as books covering a wide range of local interests.

Bedfordshire

Bedford, St. Paul's Square.
Tel: (01234) 215226
Email: bedford@eetb.info Web: www.bedford.gov.uk

Dunstable, The Library, Vernon Place.
Tel: (01582) 471012
Email: dunstable@eetb.info

Luton, Central Library, St. George's Square.
Tel: (01582) 401579
Email: luton@eetb.info Web: www.luton.gov.uk

Mid Bedfordshire, 5 Shannon Court, High Street, Sandy.
Tel: (01767) 682728
Email: sandy@eetb.info Web: www.midbeds.gov.uk

Hertfordshire

Birchanger Green, Welcome Break Services, Junction 8, M11 Motorway.
Tel: (01279) 508656

Bishop's Stortford, The Old Monastery, Windhill.
Tel: (01279) 655831
Email: bishopsstortford@eetb.info
Web: www.bishopsstortford.org

Hemel Hempstead, Marlowes.
Tel: (01442) 234222
Email: hemelhempstead@eetb.info
Web: www.dacorum.gov.uk

Hertford, 10 Market Place.
Tel: (01992) 584322
Email: hertford@eetb.info Web: www.hertford.net

Letchworth Garden City, 33-35 Station Road.
Tel: (01462) 487868
Email: letchworth@eetb.info Web: www.letchworth.com

St. Albans, Town Hall, Market Place.
Tel: (01727) 864511
Email: stalbans@eetb.info Web: www.stalbans.gov.uk

Tourist Information Points

Limited information is also available from the following information points.

* Not open all year.

Bedfordshire

Ampthill, Mid Beds District Council, The Limes, Dunstable Street. Tel: (01525) 402051

Woburn Heritage Centre *, Old St. Mary's Church, Bedford Street. Tel: (01525) 290631

Hertfordshire

Baldock, Baldock Library, Simpson Drive.
Tel: (01438) 737333

Berkhamsted, Berkhamsted Library, Kings Road.
Tel: (01438) 737333

Borehamwood, Central Reception, Civic Offices, Elstree Way.
Tel: (0208) 207 7496
Email: customer.services@hertsmere.gov.uk

Buntingford, The Manor House, High Street.
Tel: (01763) 272222
Email: btc.manorhouse@btclick.com

Cheshunt, One Stop Shop (personal callers only),
Windmill Lane.

Goffs Oak, (personal callers only) The Library, Goffs Lane.

Harpenden, Town Hall, Leyton Road.
Tel: (01582) 768278
Email: harpenden.town.council@hertscc.gov.uk

Hitchin, 27 Churchyard.
Tel: (01462) 453335 Email: htci@hitchin.net

Hoddesdon, One Stop Shop (personal callers only),
42 Tower Centre.

Rickmansworth, Three Rivers House, Northway.
Tel: (01923) 776611
Email: enquiries@threerivers.co.uk

Stevenage, Central Library, Southgate.
Tel: (01438) 737333

Tring, 99 Akeman Street.
Tel: (01442) 823347 Email: info@tring.gov.uk

Waltham Cross, One Stop Shop (personal callers only),
123 High Street.

Bishop's Stortford Tourist Information Centre

Guided Tours

Why not enjoy a guided tour exploring one of the area's towns and cities? Some of these tours (indicated with a *) are conducted by Registered Blue Badge Guides, who have attended a training course sponsored by the East of England Tourist Board. Many of these guides also have a further qualification to take individuals around the region for half day, full day or longer tours if required. For more information on the guided tours listed, please telephone the relevant contact.

Bedfordshire

Bedford

- **Regular town tours:** summer programme of Sun morning guided walks which take place at 1100, departing from the Tourist Information Centre. Walks last approximately 90 mins and pre-booking is essential.
- **Group tours:** available throughout the year by prior arrangement. A choice of six titles on offer, plus ghost walks which are available throughout the winter months.
- For further information contact the Tourist Information Centre on (01234) 215226.

Hertfordshire

St. Albans *

- **Regular city walks:** depart from the Tourist Information Centre. Easter-end Oct, Wed and Sat at 1500. Sun at 1115 and 1500.
- **Ghost walk:** departs from the Tourist Information Centre. 8pm on Weds (twice monthly in summer; once monthly in winter).
- **Verulamium walk:** departs from the Verulamium Museum. Easter-end Oct, Sun at 1500. Guides also on duty at Roman Theatre from Easter-end Oct, on Sat and Sun at various times.
- **Themed coach tours:** in Bedfordshire and Hertfordshire in your own coach.
- For further information contact the Tourist Information Centre on (01727) 864511.

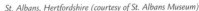

St. Albans, Hertfordshire (courtesy of St. Albans Museum)

Historic Houses

Bedfordshire

Bedford
Cecil Higgins Art Gallery Map ref. D5/6
See entry in Museums & Galleries section.

Elstow (nr. Bedford)
Elstow Moot Hall Map ref. D6
Elstow Green, Church End
Tel: (01234) 266889 Web: www.bedfordshire.gov.uk
A medieval market hall containing exhibits of 17th C. life, including beautiful period furniture. Publications and antique maps for sale.
Times: Open 1 Apr-30 Sept, Tues-Thurs, Sun and Bank Hols, 1300-1600.
Fee: £1.00/50p/50p.
Facilities: T(40 mins)

Moggerhanger (nr. Bedford)
Moggerhanger Park Map ref. E6
Park Road
Tel: (01767) 641007
Web: www.the-park.net/moggerhangerpark
Georgian Grade I listed building designed by Sir John Soane, with grounds landscaped by Humphry Repton. Undergoing restoration. Historic rooms, tea rooms, exhibition and visitor centre.
Times: Park, visitor centre and tea rooms open all year. Historic rooms open Jul-Sept. Please contact for further details.
Fee: £4.00/free.
Facilities: T(1 hr) (park only)

Shefford
Chicksands Priory Map ref. E7
Tel: (01525) 860497
12th C. priory of the Gilbertine Order - only one cloister remains. After the dissolution, it became the ancestral seat of the Osborn Family until 1936. Medieval roof timbers and 13th C. vaulting.
Times: By appointment only - 1st and 3rd Sun of each month from Apr-Oct at 1400.
Fee: Donations welcome (suggested £5, includes refreshments).
Facilities: T(1 hr)

Woburn
Woburn Abbey Map ref. C8
Tel: (01525) 290666 Web: www.woburnabbey.co.uk
An 18th C. Palladian mansion, altered by Henry Holland, the Prince Regent's architect, containing a collection of English silver, French and English furniture and art.
Times: Open 3 Jan-7 Mar, Sat, 1100-1600; Sun, 1100-1700. 13 Mar-31 Oct, Mon-Sat, 1100-1600; Sun, 1100-1700.
Fee: £9.00/£4.50/£8.00.
Facilities: T(2 hrs) (park only)

Hertfordshire

Ayot St. Lawrence (nr. Welwyn Garden City)
Shaw's Corner Map ref. F11
Tel: (01438) 820307 Web: www.nationaltrust.org.uk
The home of George Bernard Shaw from 1906 until his death in 1950, with literary and personal effects on display. 3 1/2 acre garden.
Times: Open 20 Mar-31 Oct, Wed-Sun and Bank Hol Mon, garden 1200-1730, house 1300-1700. Last admission to house and garden at 1630.
Fee: £3.80/£1.90/£9.50 (family).
Facilities: T(1 1/2 hrs) NT

Gorhambury (nr. St. Albans)
Gorhambury Map ref. E13
Tel: (01727) 854051
A classical-style mansion, built from 1777-1784 by Sir Robert Taylor. 16th C. enamelled glass, 17th C. carpet and historic portraits of the Bacon and Grimston families.
Times: Open 6 May-30 Sept, Thurs, 1400-1700.
Fee: £6.00/£3.00/£4.00.
Facilities: T(1 1/2 hrs)

Elstow Moot Hall, Bedfordshire

Hatfield

Hatfield House, Park and Gardens Map ref. G12/13
Tel: (01707) 287010 Web: www.hatfield-house.co.uk
Magnificent Jacobean house, home of the Marquess of Salisbury. Exquisite gardens, model soldiers and park trails. Childhood home of Queen Elizabeth I.
Times: Open 10 Apr-30 Sept, daily, house 1200-1600, park and gardens 1100-1730.
Fee: House, park and gardens £7.50/£4.00/£21.00 (family). Park only £2.00/£1.00. Park and gardens £4.50/£3.50.
Facilities: Q P T(2½ hrs) (park only)

Hoddesdon

Rye House Gatehouse Map ref. J12
Rye House Quay, Rye Road
Tel: (01992) 702200 Web: www.leevalleypark.com
A 15th C. moated building, the scene of the 'Rye House Plot' to assassinate King Charles II in 1683. Features include an exhibition and a shop.
Times: Open Easter-26 Sept, Sat, Sun and Bank Hol Mon, 1100-1700.
Fee: £1.30/80p/80p.
Facilities: P T(30 mins)

DID YOU KNOW

St. Andrew's Church at Ampthill in Bedfordshire contains the tomb of Colonel Richard Nicolls (first Governor of New York) who died at the Battle of Sole Bay in 1672. The cannonball which killed him is set in the pediment above the monument.

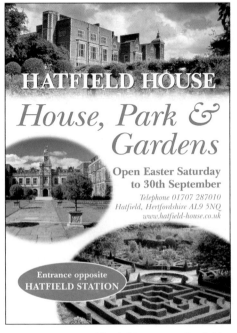

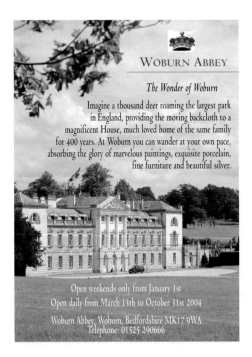

Knebworth (nr. Stevenage)

Knebworth House, Gardens and Park Map ref. G10/11
Tel: (01438) 812661 Web: www.knebworthhouse.com
Tudor manor house, re-fashioned in the 19th C., housing a collection of manuscripts, portraits and Jacobean banquet hall. Formal gardens and adventure playground.
Times: Open 27, 28 Mar, Sat and Sun; 3-18 Apr, daily; 24 Apr-23 May, Sat, Sun and Bank Hols; 29 May-6 Jun, daily; 12-27 Jun, Sat and Sun; 3 Jul-31 Aug, daily; 4-26 Sept, Sat and Sun. House open 1200-1700 (last admission at 1615). Park open 1100-1730.
Fee: House, park and gardens £8.50/£8.00/£8.00/£29.00. Park and gardens £6.50/£6.50/£6.50/£22.00.
Facilities: T(2½ hrs) (on leads)

Ware

Ware Priory Map ref. I11/12
High Street
Tel: (01920) 460316 Web: www.warepriory.co.uk
Grade I Listed, the Priory stands in 7 acres of picturesque riverside grounds. Founded as a Franciscan Friary in 1338.
Times: Open all year, Mon-Fri, 0900-1700. Weekends by arrangement.
Fee: Free.
Facilities: T(1-2 hrs)

Shaw's Corner, Ayot St. Lawrence, Hertfordshire

DID YOU KNOW

The only chalk lion in Britain can be seen on the Dunstable Downs in Bedfordshire. It was dug from 1932-35, and measures 160 yards from nose to tail.

Ancient Monuments

Bedfordshire

Ampthill

Houghton House Map ref. D7
Tel: (01234) 228337 Web: www.english-heritage.org.uk
The ruins of a 17th C. country house, built in the heights near Ampthill, and believed to be the House Beautiful in Bunyan's The Pilgrim's Progress.
Times: Open at any reasonable time.
Fee: Free.
Facilities: T(45 mins) EH

Colmworth (nr. Bedford)

Bushmead Priory Map ref. E4
Tel: (01234) 376614 Web: www.english-heritage.org.uk
A small Augustinian priory founded in about 1195, with a magnificent 13th C. timber roof of crown-post construction. Medieval wall paintings and stained glass.
Times: Please contact for details of opening times.
Fee: Please contact for details of admission prices.
Facilities: T(45 mins) EH

Dunstable

Priory Church of St. Peter Map ref. C/D10
Church Street
Tel: (01582) 477422
Web: www.dunstableparish.freeserve.co.uk
A Grade I Listed building which is an active parish church. It is the surviving part of an Augustinian priory founded in 1131. Scene of the annulment of Henry VIII's marriage to Katherine of Aragon.
Times: Open all year, daily, 0930-1600. Closed 26 Dec.
Fee: Free.
Facilities: T(45 mins)

Flitton

De Grey Mausoleum Map ref. D8
Tel: (01525) 860094 Web: www.english-heritage.org.uk
A large mortuary chapel of the de Greys of Wrest Park, containing fine sculptured tombs of monuments from 16th-19th C. and some brass and alabaster.
Times: Open all year, Sat and Sun. Please contact Mrs Stimson (key keeper) on (01525) 860094.
Fee: Free.
Facilities: T(1 hr) EH

Willington (nr. Bedford)

Willington Dovecote and Stables Map ref. E6
Church End
Tel: (01480) 301494 Web: www.nationaltrust.org.uk
A distinctive 16th C. stable and stone dovecote, lined internally with nesting boxes for 1,500 pigeons. They are the remains of an historical manorial complex.
Times: Open Bank Hol Mons, 1300-1700. At other times by appointment.
Fee: £1.00/£1.00/£1.00.
Facilities: T(1 hr) (on leads) NT

Hertfordshire

Berkhamsted

Berkhamsted Castle Map ref. C12
Tel: (01536) 402840 Web: www.english-heritage.org.uk
The extensive remains of an 11th C. motte-and-bailey castle which was the work of Robert of Mortain, half brother of William of Normandy, who learnt he was king here.
Times: Please contact for details of opening times.
Fee: Free.
Facilities: T(30 mins) EH

Bishop's Stortford

Castle Mound Map ref. K10/11
The Castle Gardens
Tel: (01279) 655261 Web: www.bishopsstortford.org
Remaining mound of a castle built by William I, set in the gardens just minutes from the town. Key to gate available from Bishop's Stortford Tourist Information Centre.
Times: Open all year, Mon-Fri, 0930-1600. Closed Bank Hols. Key needs to be collected from Bishop's Stortford Tourist Information Centre.
Fee: Free.
Facilities: T(30 mins)

Gorhambury (nr. St. Albans)

Roman Theatre of Verulamium Map ref. E13
Tel: (01727) 835035
The only completely exposed Roman theatre in Britain, with the remains of a townhouse and underground shrine.
Times: Open 1 Jan-29 Feb, daily, 1000-1600. 1 Mar-31 Oct, daily, 1000-1700. 1 Nov-31 Dec, daily, 1000-1600. Closed 25 and 26 Dec.
Fee: £1.50/£1.50/£1.00.
Facilities: T(20 mins) (on leads)

DID YOU KNOW

The church at Brent Pelham (nr. Buntingford in Hertfordshire) contains the 11th C. tomb of dragon slayer - Piers Shonks. It depicts a cross (driven like a spear) through the dragon's jaws.

Hertford

Hertford Castle Map ref. H/I12
The Castle
Tel: (01992) 552885
A 15th C. Edward IV gatehouse, Mayor's parlour and robing room with 15th C. stone, brick and timber screens. The town's insignia is also on display on special open days.
Times: Castle grounds open all year, except Bank Hols. Open by arrangement within the castle gatehouse.
Fee: Free.
Facilities: P T(1½ hrs) (on leads)

Royston

Royston Cave Map ref. I7
Melbourn Street
Tel: (01763) 245484 Web: www.roystoncave.com
A man-made cave with medieval carvings made by the Knights Templar dated from around the beginning of the 14th C. Possibly a secret meeting place for initiations.
Times: Open 10 Apr-26 Sept, Sat, Sun and Bank Hol Mon, 1430-1700.
Fee: £2.00/free/£1.00.
Facilities: T(45 mins)

St. Albans

Cathedral and Abbey Church of St. Alban Map ref. F13
Tel: (01727) 860780 Web: www.stalbanscathedral.org.uk
A Norman abbey church on the site of the martyrdom of St. Alban, Britain's first Christian martyr. The 13th C. shrine has been restored and is a centre of ecumenical worship.
Times: Open all year, daily, 0900-1745.
Fee: Free. Donations requested
Facilities: Q T(1½ hrs)

St. Albans

Clock Tower Map ref. F13
Market Street
Tel: (01727) 866380
A curfew tower, built in approximately 1405, with small exhibitions on aspects of local history. The belfry and 1866 clock mechanism can be viewed. Fine views from the roof.
Times: Open 9 Apr-19 Sept, Sat, Sun and Bank Hols, 1030-1700.
Fee: 30p/15p.
Facilities: T(30 mins)

Waltham Cross

Eleanor Cross Map ref. I14
High Street
Tel: (01992) 785537 Web: www.broxbourne.gov.uk
One of 12 crosses erected between 1291 and 1294 to mark the overnight stops of Eleanor of Castile's funeral cortege (wife of King Edward I), on its way to Westminster Abbey.
Times: Open all year, daily - can be viewed at any reasonable time.
Fee: Free.
Facilities: T(15 mins)

Ware

Scott's Grotto Map ref. I11/12
Scotts Road
Tel: (01920) 464131 Web: www.scotts-grotto.org
Grotto extending 67ft into the hillside, including passages and six chambers decorated with fossils, shells, pebbles and flints. Unlit so torches are necessary. Garden and Summerhouse
Times: Open 3 Apr-25 Sept, Sat and Bank Hol Mons, 1400-1630.
Fee: Free.
Facilities: T(30 mins)

Welwyn

Welwyn Roman Baths Map ref. G11
Welwyn Bypass
Tel: (01707) 271362 Web: www.welhat.gov.uk
The baths are a small part of a villa which was built at the beginning of the 3rd C. and occupied for over 150 years. The villa had at least four buildings.
Times: Open 1 Jan-28 Nov, Sat, Sun and Bank Hols, 1400-1700 (or dusk if earlier). Also Hertfordshire school holidays.
Fee: £1.00/free.
Facilities: P T(45 mins)

Museums & Galleries

Bedfordshire

Bedford
BCA Gallery Map ref. D5/6
33 Castle Lane
Tel: (01234) 273580 Web: www.bedfordcreativearts.org
Contemporary art gallery offering a changing programme of lens based work by local, national and international living artists. Shows include photography, film and new media work.
Times: Open all year, Tues-Sat, 1100-1700. Please contact for Christmas openings.
Fee: Free.
Facilities: P T(15 mins)

Bedford
Bedford Museum Map ref. D5/6
Castle Lane
Tel: (01234) 353323 Web: www.bedfordmuseum.org
Housed in the former Higgins and Sons Brewery, Bedford Museum is situated within the gardens of bygone Bedford Castle. Changing programme of temporary exhibitions.
Times: Open all year, Tues-Sat, 1100-1700; Sun and Bank Hol Mon, 1400-1700. Closed 9 Apr. Telephone for Christmas opening times.
Fee: £2.20/free.
Facilities: Q P T(1 hr)

Bedford
Cecil Higgins Art Gallery Map ref. D5/6
Castle Lane
Tel: (01234) 211222
Web: www.cecilhigginsartgallery.org
A Victorian mansion, furnished in late 19th C. style. A large collection of watercolours, prints, drawings, glass, ceramics, porcelain and lace in modern galleries.
Times: Open all year, Tues-Sat, 1100-1700; Sun and Bank Hol Mon, 1400-1700. Closed 9 Apr, 23-28 Dec and 1 Jan.
Fee: £2.20/free.
Facilities: T(1½ hrs)

DID YOU KNOW
The foundations of England's earliest known windmill (14th C.) was found in the village of Sandon (nr. Baldock) in Hertfordshire.

Bedford
John Bunyan Museum and Bunyan Meeting Free Church
Map ref. D5/6
Mill Street
Tel: (01234) 213722
Museum housing the personal effects of John Bunyan (1628-1688) and copies of The Pilgrim's Progress in over 170 languages, together with other works by Bunyan.
Times: Open 2 Mar-30 Oct, Tues-Sat, 1100-1600. Closed 9 Apr.
Fee: Free. Donations appreciated.
Facilities: T(1 hr)

Clapham (nr. Bedford)
Twinwood Arena and The Glenn Miller Museum
Map ref. D5
Twinwood Road
Tel: (01234) 350413 Web: www.twinwoodevents.com
Restored airfield control tower housing an audio and visual exhibition dedicated to the famous band leader Glenn Miller. RAF room, aviation art gallery and collection of military vehicles. Landscaped showground arena.
Times: Open all year, Sat, Sun and Bank Hols, 1030-1630. Closed 24-26 Dec and 1 Jan.
Fee: £3.00/free/£3.00.
Facilities: P T(2½ hrs)

Elstow (nr. Bedford)

Elstow Moot Hall Map ref. D6
See entry in Historic Houses section.

Luton

Luton Museum and Gallery Map ref. E10
Wardown Park
Tel: (01582) 546722
Web: www.luton.gov.uk/enjoying/museums
Housed in a Victorian mansion, displays present the development of Luton from prehistory to the present day. Free parking and admission. Gift shop.
Times: Open all year, Tues-Sat, 1000-1700; Sun, 1300-1700. Closed Mon (except Bank Hol Mon), 25, 26 Dec and 1 Jan.
Fee: Free.
Facilities: T(1½ hrs)

Luton

Stockwood Craft Museum and Gardens Map ref. E10
Farley Hill
Tel: (01582) 738714
Web: www.luton.gov.uk/enjoying/museums
The craft museum illustrates the crafts and trades of pre-industrial Bedfordshire; period gardens; the Mossman Collection of carriages, sculpture gardens and tea room.
Times: Open 3 Jan-27 Mar, Sat and Sun, 1000-1600. 28 Mar-30 Oct, Tues-Sun, 1000-1700. 31 Oct-19 Dec, Sat and Sun, 1000-1600.
Fee: Free.
Facilities: T(3 hrs)

Sandy

Roman Sandy Story Map ref. F6
Council Offices, 10 Cambridge Road
Tel: (01767) 681491 Web: www.roman-sandy.com
Permanent exhibition (mini museum) telling the story of Roman Sandy, using many of the artefacts of a five year programme of archaeology. Artists impressions and finds.
Times: Open all year, Mon-Fri, 0900-1600. Closed Bank Hols.
Fee: Free.
Facilities: T(1 hr)

Thurleigh (nr. Bedford)

306th Bombardment Group Museum Map ref. D4
Bedford Autodrome, Thurleigh Airfield Business Park
Tel: (01234) 708715
Museum commemorating the 306th Bombardment Group, and the social impact of the 'Friendly Invasion' on the surrounding area during the war years. Large collection of artefacts, uniforms and photographs.
Times: Open 6 Mar-31 Oct, Sat, Sun and Bank Hols, 1030-1600. At other times by arrangement.
Fee: £3.00/free.
Facilities: T(1½ hrs)

Woburn

Woburn Heritage Centre Map ref. B8
Old St. Mary's Church, Bedford Street
Tel: (01525) 290631
Small registered museum covering the local history of Woburn. Housed in the redundant Old St. Mary's Church. Tourist Information Point.
Times: Open 9 Apr-30 Sept, Mon-Fri, 1400-1630; Sat, Sun and Bank Hols, 1000-1700. 1-31 Oct, Sat and Sun, 1000-1700.
Fee: Free.
Facilities: T(45 mins)

Hertfordshire

Ashwell (nr. Baldock)

Ashwell Village Museum Map ref. G7
Swan Street
Tel: (01462) 742956
A collection of village bygones and agricultural implements set in a small but interesting timber building.
Times: Open all year, Sun and Bank Hol Mon, 1430-1700. Please phone for Christmas openings.
Fee: £1.00/25p.
Facilities: T(30 mins)

Baldock

Baldock Museum Map ref. G8
Town Hall, Hitchin Street
Tel: (01462) 892640
Permanent display on the history of Baldock. Plus series of changing displays focusing on particular aspects of the town's history.
Times: Open 4 Jan-19 Dec, Wed, 1000-1500 and Sun, 1400-1600.
Fee: 25p/free/25p.
Facilities: T(1 hr)

Cecil Higgins Art Gallery, Bedford, Bedfordshire

Bushey

Bushey Museum and Art Gallery Map ref. E/F15
Rudolph Road
Tel: (0208) 950 3233 Web: www.busheymuseum.org
Community museum telling the story of Bushey. Archaeology, social history, local trades and industries. Art galleries show changing exhibitions.
Times: Open all year, 2 Jan-19 Dec, Thurs-Sun, 1100-1600.
Fee: Free.
Facilities: T(1½ hrs)

Hatfield

Mill Green Museum and Mill Map ref. G12
Mill Green
Tel: (01707) 271362 Web: www.welhat.gov.uk
An 18th C. watermill, restored to working order, with a museum in the adjoining miller's house displaying local and social history and archaeology. Riverside gardens
Times: Open all year, Tues-Fri, 1000-1700; Sat, Sun and Bank Hols, 1400-1700. Closed 24-26 Dec.
Fee: Free.
Facilities: T(1 hr)

Hertford

Hertford Museum Map ref. H/I12
18 Bull Plain
Tel: (01992) 582686 Web: www.hertford.net/museum
A 17th C. building with main exhibits on the archaeology, natural and local history of Hertfordshire, with a collection of Hertfordshire Regiment regalia and changing exhibitions.
Times: Open all year, Tues-Sat, 1000-1700.
Closed 24-28 Dec.
Fee: Free.
Facilities: T(1 hr)

Hitchin

The Hitchin British Schools Map ref. F9
41/42 Queen Street
Tel: (01462) 420144
Web: www.hitchinbritishschools.org.uk
Rare elementary school buildings including 1837 monitorial school room for 330 boys and 1853 galleried classroom demonstrating period lessons. Family trail activities.
Times: Open 3 Feb-30 Nov, Tues, 1000-1600. Also Sun, 4 Apr-31 Oct, 1430-1700.
Fee: £2.00/£1.00.
Facilities: T(2 hrs)

DID YOU KNOW

The founder of inland navigation in Britain is the third Duke of Bridgewater or the 'canal duke' as he was known. His monument on the Ashridge Estate in Hertfordshire was erected in 1832.

Hitchin

Hitchin Museum and Art Gallery Map ref. F9
Paynes Park
Tel: (01462) 434476 Web: www.north-herts.gov.uk
A converted 19th C. house on two floors with displays of costume, local history, a Victorian chemist's shop and a physic garden. Changing temporary exhibitions and active events programme.
Times: Open all year, Mon-Sat, except Wed, 1000-1700. Closed on Bank Hols.
Fee: Free.
Facilities: T(40mins)

Hoddesdon

Lowewood Museum Map ref. I12
High Street
Tel: (01992) 445596 Web: www.lowewood.com
A listed Georgian building housing a museum of artefacts and photographs concerning the Borough of Broxbourne, along with temporary exhibitions.
Times: Open all year, Wed-Sat, 1000-1600. Closed 9 Apr, 25, 26 and 31 Dec.
Fee: Free.
Facilities: T(1 hr)

Ivinghoe (nr. Tring)

Pitstone Green Museum Map ref. B11
Vicarage Road (off B489)
Web: http://website.lineone.net/~pitstonemus
Rural life museum, with displays and exhibits relating to farming, country life, trades and professions. Also model railway, stationary engines and WWII military aviation room.
Times: Open Easter Mon (Apr 12); May Bank Hols (3rd and 31st); Suns 13 Jun, 11 Jul, 8 Aug, 12 Sept; Bank Hol Mon 30 Aug, 1100-1700.
Fee: £3.00/£1.50/£3.00.
Facilities: T(3-4 hrs)

Letchworth Garden City

First Garden City Heritage Museum Map ref. G8
296 Norton Way South
Tel: (01462) 482710 Web: www.letchworth.com
A museum housing displays relating to the Garden City movement and the social history of Letchworth including a collection of Parker and Unwin architectural drawings.
Times: Open all year, Mon-Sat, 1000-1700. Closed 25, 26 Dec and 1 Jan.
Fee: Non-residents £1.00/free. Residents 50p/free.
Facilities: T(1 hr)

Letchworth Garden City

Letchworth Museum Map ref. G8
Broadway
Tel: (01462) 685647 Web: www.north-herts.gov.uk
A museum which features local wildlife, archaeological displays and a programme of temporary exhibitions.
Times: Open all year, Mon, Tues and Thurs-Sat, 1000-1700. Please phone for Easter and Christmas opening.
Fee: Free.
Facilities: T(45 mins)

Letchworth Garden City

Standalone Farm Map ref. G8
See entry in Family Fun section.

Much Hadham

The Forge Museum and Victorian Cottage Garden
Map ref. J11
High Street
Tel: (01279) 843301 Web: www.hertsmuseums.org.uk
Grade II Listed building. Houses displays on blacksmithing, beekeeping, the parish of Much Hadham and the Page family who were blacksmiths for over 150 years.
Times: Open 26 Mar-19 Dec, Fri-Sun and Bank Hol Mon, 1100-1700.
Fee: £1.00/50p/50p/£2.00.
Facilities: T(1 hr)

Much Hadham

The Henry Moore Foundation Map ref. J11
Dane Tree House, Perry Green
Tel: (01279) 843333 Web: www.henry-moore-fdn.co.uk
A sculpture garden and studios with a permanent exhibition of monumental sculptures by Henry Moore.
Times: Open Apr-Sept, by appointment only. Closed Bank Hols (9, 12 Apr; 3, 31 May and 30 Aug).
Fee: £7.00/free/£3.00.
Facilities: P T(2½ hrs)

Potters Bar

Potters Bar Museum Map ref. G14
Wyllyotts Centre, Darkes Lane
Tel: (01707) 645005
Local history museum tracing the development of Potters Bar from pre-history, through Roman, medieval and recent history, up to the present day. Also temporary exhibitions throughout year.
Times: Open all year, Tues and Wed, 1430-1630; Sat, 1100-1300. Museum is open on Sun when the antiques fair is open, please phone for details. Please also phone for Easter and Christmas openings.
Fee: Free.
Facilities: P T(1 hr)

Redbourn

Redbourn Village Museum Map ref. E12
Silk Mill House, The Common
Tel: (01582) 793397 Web: www.redbourn.org.uk
History of Redbourn and surrounding area from Iron Age to present day. Housed in a Grade II listed building standing in its own grounds.
Times: Open 3 Jan-19 Dec, Sat, 1400-1700; Sun, 1200-1700. Please contact for Bank Hol Mon opening times.
Fee: £1.00/50p.
Facilities: P T(1 hr)

Rickmansworth

Batchworth Lock Canal Centre Map ref. D15
99 Church Street
Tel: (01923) 778382
Batchworth Lock provides information to boaters and walkers using the Rickmansworth area. Canal history, narrowboat 'Roger' and shop. Boat trips in summer.
Times: Open 28 Mar-28 Sept, Mon, 0900-1700; Tues, 0900-1300; Sat, 1200-1700; Sun, 0900-1700.
Fee: Free.
Facilities: T(30 mins)

Batchworth Lock Canal Centre, Rickmansworth, Hertfordshire

St. Albans
Museum of St. Albans Map ref. F13
Hatfield Road
Tel: (01727) 819340 Web: www.stalbansmuseums.org.uk
Displays include craft tools and local/natural history, telling the St. Albans story from Roman times to the present day. Wildlife garden.
Times: Open all year, Mon-Sat, 1000-1700; Sun, 1400-1700. Closed 24-26 Dec and 1 Jan.
Fee: Free.
Facilities: Q P T(1½ hrs)

St. Albans
Saint Albans Organ Museum Map ref. F13
320 Camp Road
Tel: (01727) 768652
Web: www.saintalbansorganmuseum.org.uk
A collection of mechanical organs by Mortier, DeCap, Bursens; Weber and Steinway duo-art reproducing pianos; Mills violano-virtuoso; music boxes and Wurlitzer and Rutt theatre pipe organs.
Times: Open all year, Sun, 1400-1630. Closed 26 Dec.
Fee: £3.50/£1.00/£2.50/£8.00.
Facilities: P T(1½ hrs)

St. Albans
Verulamium Museum Map ref. F13
St. Michaels
Tel: (01727) 781810 Web: www.stalbansmuseums.org.uk
The museum of everyday life in Roman Britain. Award-winning displays of re-created Roman rooms, 'hands-on' areas and videos of Roman Verulamium.
Times: Open all year, Mon-Sat, 1000-1730; Sun, 1400-1730. Closed 24-26 Dec and 1 Jan.
Fee: £3.30/£2.00/£2.00/£8.00.
Facilities: Q P T(2 hrs)

Stevenage
The Boxfield Gallery Map ref. G10
Stevenage Arts and Leisure Centre, Lytton Way
Tel: (01438) 242642 Web: www.stevenage-leisure.co.uk
Contemporary art gallery exhibiting a variety of work by both local and national artists. Approximately twelve exhibitions a year, ranging from paintings and textiles to sculptures and installations.
Times: Open all year, daily, 1000-1800. Closed 11 Apr, 25 Dec and 1 Jan.
Fee: Free.
Facilities: P T(1 hr)

Stevenage
Stevenage Museum Map ref. G10
St. George's Way
Tel: (01438) 218881 Web: www.stevenage.gov.uk/museum
Award-winning museum which tells the story of Stevenage from the Stone Age to the present. Displays include a 1950s living room and a programme of exhibitions.
Times: Open all year, Mon-Sat, 1000-1700; Sun, 1400-1700. Closed 9, 11, 12 Apr, 24-26 Dec and 1 Jan.
Fee: Free.
Facilities: T(1½ hrs)

Tring
College Lake Wildlife Centre Map ref. B12
See entry in Countryside section.

Tring
The Walter Rothschild Zoological Museum Map ref. B12
Akeman Street
Tel: (0207) 942 6171 Web: www.nhm.ac.uk/museum/tring
The former private zoological collection of Lionel Walter, 2nd Baron Rothschild. More than 4,000 mounted animal and bird specimens on display in a unique Victorian setting.
Times: Open all year, Mon-Sat, 1000-1700; Sun, 1400-1700. Closed 24-26 Dec.
Fee: Free.
Facilities: P T(2 hrs)

Ware
Ware Museum Map ref. I11/12
The Priory Lodge, High Street
Tel: (01920) 487848 Web: www.waremuseum.org.uk
An independent museum featuring the story of Ware from the Roman town through to the malting industry. Also a World War II command bunker and changing exhibitions.
Times: Open summer - Tues, Thurs and Sat, 1100-1700; Sun, 1400-1700. Winter - Tues, Thurs and Sat, 1100-1600; Sun, 1400-1600. Please phone for Easter and Christmas openings.
Fee: Free. Donations welcome.
Facilities: T(30 mins)

Watford
Watford Museum Map ref. E14/15
194 High Street
Tel: (01923) 232297 Web: www.hertsmuseums.org.uk
A museum building, built in 1775, with displays of local history, brewing, printing and archaeology.
Times: Open all year, Thurs-Sat, 1000-1700. Closed 9 Apr, 25 Dec and 1 Jan.
Fee: Free.
Facilities: P T(1½ hrs)

Machinery &Transport

Bedfordshire

Biggleswade

Shuttleworth Collection Map ref. F6

Old Warden Aerodrome

Tel: (01767) 627288 Web: www.shuttleworth.org

A unique historical collection of aircraft from a 1909 Bleriot to a 1942 Spitfire in flying condition, and cars dating from an 1898 Panhard in running order.

Times: Open 2 Jan-31 Mar, daily, 1000-1600. 1 Apr-31 Oct, daily, 1000-1700. 1 Nov-24 Dec, daily, 1000-1600.

Fee: Non-event days - £7.50/free (up to 16yrs and accompanied by an adult)/£6.00. Seperate fees for air displays/events.

Facilities: P T(2½ hrs)

Clapham (nr. Bedford)

Twinwood Arena and The Glenn Miller Museum

Map ref. D5

See entry in Museums & Galleries section.

Ivinghoe (nr. Tring)

Pitstone Green Museum Map ref. B11

See entry in Museums & Galleries section.

Stondon Museum, Lower Stondon, Bedfordshire

Leighton Buzzard

Leighton Buzzard Railway Map ref. B10

Page's Park Station, Billington Road

Tel: (01525) 373888 Web: www.buzzrail.co.uk

An authentic narrow-gauge light railway, built in 1919, offering a 70-minute return journey into the Bedfordshire countryside. Most trains hauled by historic steam locos.

Times: Open every Sun from 14 Mar-31 Oct. Bank Hol weekends. Weds from Jun-Aug. Tues, Thurs and Sat in Aug. Please contact for train times.

Fee: £5.50/£2.50/£4.50.

Facilities: P T(2 hrs)

Lower Stondon

Stondon Museum Map ref. F8

Station Road

Tel: (01462) 850339 Web: www.transportmuseum.co.uk

The largest private transport museum in the country, with over 400 exhibits covering 100 years of motoring, mostly undercover. Full size replica of Captain Cook's ship 'The Endeavour'.

Times: Open all year, daily, 1000-1700. Closed 22-31 Dec.

Fee: £6.00/£3.00/£5.00/£16.00.

Facilities: P T(2½ hrs)

Luton

Mossman Collection Map ref. E10

Stockwood Craft Museum and Gardens, Farley Hill

Tel: (01582) 738714

Web: www.luton.gov.uk/enjoying/museums

The Mossman Collection is Britain's largest collection of horse-drawn carriages, illustrating the history of road transport from Roman times to the 1930s.

Times: Open 3 Jan-27 Mar, Sat and Sun, 1000-1600. 28 Mar-30 Oct, Tues-Sun, 1000-1700. 31 Oct-19 Dec, Sat and Sun, 1000-1600.

Fee: Free.

Facilities: P T(3 hrs)

Hertfordshire

London Colney

de Havilland Aircraft Heritage Centre Map ref. G14

Salisbury Hall

Tel: (01727) 822051 Web: www.dehavillandmuseum.co.uk

Museum showing the restoration and preservation of a range of de Havilland aircraft, including the prototype Mosquito. Also engines, propellers, missiles, memorabilia and a de Havilland story board.

Times: Open 7 Mar-31 Oct, Tues, Thurs and Sat, 1430-1730; Sun and Bank Hols, 1030-1730.

Fee: £5.00/£3.00/£3.00/£13.00.

Facilities: P T(2½ hrs)

Mills

Bedfordshire

Bromham (nr. Bedford)

Bromham Mill Map ref. C5
Bridge End
Tel: (01234) 824330 Web: www.bedfordshire.gov.uk
Restored watermill in working condition. Wholemeal stoneground flour for sale. Refreshments overlooking River Great Ouse. Art gallery, craft sales and picnic site.
Times: Open 4 Apr-31 Oct, Sun and Bank Hol Mon, 1300-1700.
Fee: Donations requested.
Facilities: T(1½ hrs)

Stevington (nr. Bedford)

Stevington Windmill Map ref. C5
Tel: (01234) 228330 Web: www.bedfordshire.gov.uk
A fully-restored 18th C. postmill. Entry is via keys which are available from the pubs in the village for a small returnable deposit.
Times: Open all year, daily, 1000-1900 (or dusk in winter). Collect keys from the pubs in the village.
Fee: Free.
Facilities: T(1 hr)

Stevington Windmill, Bedfordshire

Hertfordshire

Cromer (nr. Buntingford)

Cromer Windmill Map ref. H9
Tel: (01279) 843301 Web: www.hertsmuseums.org.uk
Hertfordshire's sole-surviving postmill. Video and audio display. Exhibitions on Hertfordshire's windmills, the history of Cromer Mill and the restoration of the mill.
Times: Open 8 May-12 Sept, Sun, Bank Hol Mon, 2nd and 4th Sat in month, 1430-1700.
Fee: £1.50/25p.
Facilities: T(1 hr)

Hatfield

Mill Green Museum and Mill Map ref. G12
See entry in Museums & Galleries section.

Ivinghoe (nr. Tring)

Ford End Watermill Map ref. B11
Station Road (B488)
Tel: (01582) 600391 Web: www.fordendwatermill.co.uk
Grade II listed watermill built about 1700 on site of an earlier mill. Now restored to working order as it was in late 1800s. Stoneground wholemeal flour for sale when milling.
Times: Open *12 Apr; 3*, 9*, 23, 31* May; 13, 27 Jun; 11, 25 Jul; 8, 22, 30* Aug; 12, 26 Sept. 1430-1730.
* - indicates milling demonstrations on these dates between 1500-1700.
Fee: £1.20/40p.
Facilities: T(1 hr)

St. Albans

Kingsbury Watermill Map ref. F13
St. Michael's Street
Tel: (01727) 853502
A 16th C. watermill with working machinery, a collection of farm implements, an art gallery and gift shop. There is also the Waffle House tearoom and restaurant.
Times: Open all year. Summer - Mon-Sat, 1000-1800; Sun, 1100-1800. Winter - Mon-Sat, 1000-1700; Sun, 1000-1700. Closed 25 and 26 Dec.
Fee: £1.10/60p/75p.
Facilities: T(30 mins)

St. Albans

Redbournbury Watermill Map ref. E12
Redbournbury Lane
Tel: (01582) 792874 Web: www.redbournmill.co.uk
An 18th C. working watermill with riverside walks. Organic flours and bread for sale.
Times: Open 4 Apr-26 Sept, Sun, 1430-1700.
Fee: £1.50/80p/80p/£4.00.
Facilities: T(1½ hrs)

Gardens

Bedfordshire

Luton

Stockwood Craft Museum and Gardens Map ref. E10
See entry in Museums & Galleries section.

Old Warden (nr. Biggleswade)

The Swiss Garden Map ref. F6
Old Warden Park
Tel: (01767) 627666 Web: www.bedfordshire.gov.uk
19th C. landscape garden created in the picturesque/Swiss manner. A garden of continued vistas leading the eye to several significant architectural features. Tiny folly buildings and ornamental ponds and bridges.
Times: Open 1 Mar-31 Oct, daily, 1000-1700.
Fee: £3.00/£2.00/£2.00/£8.00.
Facilities: T(1½ hrs)

Shefford

Hoo Hill Maze Map ref. E7
Hitchin Road
Tel: (01462) 813475
Hedge maze, 2m high and approx 30m by 30m square. Set in a small apple, pear and plum orchard of about 3 acres. Picnic areas and marquee/summer house for shelter.
Times: Open all year, daily, 0900-1800.
Fee: £3.00/£3.00 (under 5's £2.00).
Facilities: T(1-2 hrs)

Silsoe

Wrest Park Gardens Map ref. E8
Tel: (01525) 860152 Web: www.english-heritage.org.uk
One hundred and fifty years of English gardens laid out in the early 18th C. including painted pavilion, Chinese bridge, lakes, classical temple and Louis XV-style French mansion.
Times: Please contact for details of opening times.
Fee: Please contact for details of admission prices.
Facilities: Q T(1 hr) (audio tours) (on leads) **EH**

Woburn

Woburn Abbey Map ref. C8
See entry in Historic Houses section.

Hertfordshire

Ayot St. Lawrence (nr. Welwyn Garden City)

Shaw's Corner Map ref. F11
See entry in Historic Houses section.

Benington (nr. Stevenage)

Benington Lordship Gardens Map ref. H10
Tel: (01438) 869228 Web: www.beningtonlordship.co.uk
Edwardian garden and historic site. Ornamental, vegetable, rose/water garden. Herbaceous borders, lakes and contemporary sculptures.
Times: Open all year, Sun, 1400-1700; Bank Hol Mon, 1200-1700.
Fee: £3.50/free.
Facilities: T(1 hr)

Enfield

Capel Manor Gardens Map ref. I14
Bullsmoor Lane
Tel: (0208) 366 4442 Web: www.capel.ac.uk
Thirty acres of richly planted themed gardens including Italianate maze, historical gardens and Japanese garden. Gardening Which? Magazine demonstration/theme gardens. National Gardening Centre with specially designed gardens.
Times: Open all year, daily, 1000-1800. Last admission at 1630.
Fee: £5.00/£2.00/£4.00/£12.00.
Facilities: T(2-3 hrs)

Biggleswade in Bedfordshire was the home of Daniel Albone, a famous racing cyclist, who in the 1880s established the Ivel Cycle Works in Shortmead Street. He invented the tandem and ladies bicycle.

 BLOOMIN' BEAUTIFUL

Harrold, Bedfordshire

Enfield
Myddelton House Gardens Map ref. I14
Bulls Cross
Tel: (01992) 702200 Web: www.leevalleypark.com
A garden for all seasons, created by famous plantsman, expert botanist and author E.A. Bowles. Unusual varieties and rarities of plants. Home to the National Collection of award-winning Bearded Iris.
Times: Open Apr-Sept, Mon-Fri, 1000-1630. Oct-Mar, Mon-Fri, 1000-1500. Suns and Bank Hol Mons from Apr-Oct, 1200-1600.
Fee: £2.10/£1.50/£1.50.
Facilities: T(1½ hrs)

Gorhambury (nr. St. Albans)
Gorhambury Map ref. E13
See entry in Historic Houses section.

Hatfield
Hatfield House, Park and Gardens Map ref. G12/13
See entry in Historic Houses section.

Hitchin
Hitchin Museum and Art Gallery Map ref. F9
See entry in Museums & Galleries section.

Hitchin
St. Pauls Walden Bury Garden Map ref. F10
St. Pauls Walden Bury
Tel: (01438) 871218
Formal woodland garden laid out in about 1730, and covering 60 acres with temples, statues, lake, ponds and flower gardens. The childhood home of the late Queen Mother.
Times: Open 18 Apr and 16 May, Sun, 1400-1900. Also 4 Jul, 1400-1800 (followed by concert).
Fee: Open days £3.00/50p/£3.00. Open by arrangement days £5.00.
Facilities: T(1-2 hrs)

Knebworth (nr. Stevenage)
Knebworth House, Gardens and Park Map ref. G10/11
See entry in Historic Houses section.

Much Hadham
The Forge Museum and Victorian Cottage Garden
Map ref. J11
See entry in Museums & Galleries section.

Much Hadham
The Henry Moore Foundation Map ref. J11
See entry in Museums & Galleries section.

St. Albans
The Gardens of the Rose Map ref. E13
Chiswell Green
Tel: (01727) 850461 Web: www.rnrs.org
The Royal National Rose Society's Garden, including the international trials of new roses. The garden may be undergoing a major re-development in 2004, so please contact for full details.
Times: Please contact for details of opening times.
Fee: Please contact for details of admission prices.
Facilities: T(1-3 hrs)

Sandy
RSPB Lodge Nature Reserve Map ref. F6
See entry in Countryside section.

Waltham Cross
Cedars Park Map ref. I13/14
See entry in Countryside section.

Ware
Ware Priory Map ref. I11/12
See entry in Historic Houses section.

Wrest Park Gardens, Silsoe, Bedfordshire

Nurseries & Garden Centres

Hertfordshire

Bragbury End (nr. Stevenage)

The Van Hage Garden Company Map ref. H10
Bragbury Lane, Bragbury End, nr. Stevenage SG2 8TJ
Tel: (01438) 811777 Fax: (01438) 815485
Café: (01438) 813172 Web: www.vanhage.co.uk
Junction 7, off A1(M) at Stevenage South, follow signs A602 to Ware. A series of listed farm buildings linked together, each retaining many original features and individuality. The emphasis is on top-quality plants and inspirational displays in the award winning Plant Nursery and Houseplant Department. The courtyard Café serves a fine selection of homemade food. Other attractions include a children's play area, Aquatics Centre and Christmas Grotto. Information, Free Parking, Coaches (limited at weekends), WC, Disabled facilities, Wheelchairs, Baby Changing. P T(3 hrs)

St. Albans in Hertfordshire is the birthplace of the famous golf tournament 'The Ryder Cup'. On Holywell Hill is the old seed packing company started/run by Samuel Ryder. He enjoyed a round of golf, and donated the Ryder Cup to the game.

Chenies (nr. Rickmansworth)

The Van Hage Garden Company Map ref. C14
Chenies, nr. Rickmansworth WD3 6EN
Tel: (01494) 764545 Fax: (01494) 762216
Web: www.vanhage.co.uk
Junction 18, M25 on A404 towards Amersham. Established over 23 years ago this delightful garden centre, nestling in the Hertfordshire/Buckinghamshire countryside, offers customers a fantastic selection of both indoor and outdoor plants. Staff are always on hand to offer comprehensive information, and the centre is full of inspirational ideas for the garden. Coffee Shop, Aquatics, BBQ's, Garden Buildings, Garden Furniture, Hard Landscape, Statues, Christmas Grotto.
P T(3 hrs)

Baldock, Hertfordshire

Great Amwell (nr. Ware)

The Van Hage Garden Company Map ref. I12
Great Amwell, nr. Ware SG12 9RP
Tel: (01920) 870811 Fax: (01920) 871861
Web: www.vanhage.co.uk
On A1170 (Junction 25 off M25). One of Europe's top gardening retailers offering an outstanding selection of products and inspirational displays to meet all gardening requirements. Van Hage is a leisure destination for the whole family, with landscaped animal gardens, seasonal events and attractions, and a 200 seater air-conditioned restaurant with a courtyard setting - you can spend the whole day here. Don't miss our Christmas Wonderland which includes a free Santa's Grotto, the ultimate festive shopping experience. Entrance to Garden Centre FREE. Disabled, Information, Parking (Ample - FREE), Coaches, WC, Shops, Catering - Hot Meals, Snacks, Beverages, Self-service, Groups welcome.

St. Albans

Aylett Nurseries Limited Map ref. F13
North Orbital Road, St. Albans AL2 1DH
Tel: (01727) 822255 Web: www.aylettnurseries.co.uk
Undoubtedly one of the best Garden Centres in the southeast. Famous for our Dahlias having been awarded Gold medals by the Royal Horticultural Society for 36 consecutive years. In spring our greenhouses are well worth a visit to see our geraniums, fuchsias, hanging baskets and other summer bedding plants. Our plant area is a gardener's paradise, with all year round displays. Houseplants are another speciality. Light lunches and snacks are available at our Coffee House. Visit our Gift Shop before you leave. Christmas Wonderland opens mid-Oct. Open daily including Sun except Easter Sun, Christmas and Boxing Day. P T(1-2 hrs)

Bushey, Hertfordshire

St. Albans

Notcutts Garden Centres Map ref. F13
Hatfield Road, Smallford, nr. St. Albans AL4 0HN
Tel: (01727) 853224 Web: www.notcutts.co.uk
Discover a world of ideas and inspiration around every corner for you, your home and your garden. From fabulous plants to gifts and treats galore, there's so much to see. Gift ideas from around the world, houseplants, books, fresh cut and silk flowers, 3,000 varieties of hardy plants (with a 2 year replacement guarantee), pet centre, restaurant, expert friendly advice about seasonal and bedding plants, garden furniture and barbecues. Keep an eye open for regular offers on key garden products. Notcutts open 7 days a week, free car-parking.

Braughing, Hertfordshire

DID YOU KNOW

The de Havilland Aircraft Heritage Centre is the oldest aircraft museum in Britain. Based at the historic 17th C. Salisbury Hall, nr. London Colney in Hertfordshire, the famous de Havilland 'Mosquito Bomber' was designed here in secret in 1940.

Ware, Hertfordshire

Family Fun

Animal & Bird Collections

Bedfordshire

Aspley Guise

HULA Animal Rescue: South Midlands Animal Sanctuary
Map ref. B7
Glebe Farm, Salford Road
Tel: (01908) 584000 Web: www.hularescue.org
A 17-acre registered agricultural holding, headquarters of the registered charity founded in 1972. Visitors can see round the animal houses, and feed the resident ponies, pigs, goats and cows.
Times: Open all year, Sat, Sun and Bank Hols, 1300-1500. Closed 20 Dec-4 Jan.
Fee: £1.00/50p.
Facilities: T(2 hrs)

Biggleswade

The English School of Falconry - Bird of Prey and Conservation Centre Map ref. F6
Old Warden Park, Old Warden
Tel: (01767) 627527 Web: www.birdsofpreycentre.co.uk
One of the country's largest collections of birds of prey (over 300), including rare species. Walk-through barn owl aviary and daily displays featuring different birds of prey.
Times: Open 1 Feb-end Oct, daily, 1000-1600 (1700 in summer months).
Fee: £6.00/£4.00/£5.00/£16.00.
Facilities: T(5 hrs)

Dunstable

Whipsnade Wild Animal Park Map ref. C11
Tel: (01582) 872171 Web: www.whipsnade.co.uk
Whipsnade Wild Animal Park has over 2,500 animals set in 600 acres of beautiful parkland. Fun-filled and informative daily events run throughout the day.
Times: Open 1 Jan-31 Mar, daily, 1000-1600. 1 Apr-31 Oct, daily, 1000-1800. 1 Nov-31 Dec, daily, 1000-1600. Closed 25 Dec.
Fee: £13.50/£10.10/£11.50/£42.50.
Facilities: T(5 hrs)

Leighton Buzzard

Mead Open Farm Map ref. B10
Stanbridge Road, Billington
Tel: (01525) 852954 Web: www.meadopenfarm.co.uk
Wide range of farm animals, including pets corner. Indoor and outdoor play areas, daily hands on activities and tractor/trailer rides. Voted "Farm Attraction of the Year 2003".
Times: Open Feb-Oct, daily, 1000-1700. Nov-Jan, daily, 1000-1600. Contact for Christmas and New Year openings.
Fee: £4.75/£3.75/£4.25/£17.00.
Facilities: Q P T(4 hrs)

Slip End (nr. Luton)

Woodside Animal Farm Map ref. D11
Woodside Road
Tel: (01582) 841044 Web: www.woodsidefarm.co.uk
100's of farm and exotic animals to see and feed. Indoor and outdoor play areas, tractor rides, animal encounters, trampolines and crazy golf. Farm shop, pet store and coffee shop.
Times: Open all year, daily, summer 0800-1800, winter 0800-1700. Closed 25, 26 Dec and 1 Jan.
Fee: £4.95/£3.95/£3.95.
Facilities: P T(3 hrs)

Thurleigh (nr. Bedford)

Thurleigh Farm Centre Map ref. D4
Cross End
Tel: (01234) 771597 Web: www.thurleighfarmcentre.co.uk
Working farm with indoor and outdoor play facilities. Trampoline centre. Meet and feed the animals both large and small. Nature trail. Tearoom and special seasonal attractions.
Times: Open all year - please contact for days and times.
Fee: Various, depending upon activity - please contact for details.
Facilities: P T(4 hrs)

Wilden (nr. Bedford)

Bedford Butterfly Park Map ref. E5
Renhold Road
Tel: (01234) 772770 Web: www.bedford-butterflies.co.uk
Set in landscaped hay meadows, the park features a tropical glasshouse where visitors walk through lush foliage with butterflies flying. Tearoom, gift shop, trails and playground.
Times: Open 14 Feb-31 Oct, daily, 1000-1700 (last entry 1600).
Fee: £4.50/£2.75/£3.50.
Facilities: Q G P T(2½ hrs)

Woburn

Woburn Safari Park Map ref. C8
Woburn Park
Tel: (01525) 290407 Web: www.woburnsafari.co.uk
Drive through the safari park with 30 species of animals in natural groups just a windscreen's width away, plus the action-packed Wild World Leisure Area with shows for all.
Times: Open all year. Winter - weekends only, 1100-1500 (or dusk). 13 Mar-31 Oct, daily, 1000-1700.
Fee: Please contact for details of admission prices.
Facilities: Q P T(6 hrs)

Hertfordshire

Broxbourne

Paradise Wildlife Park Map ref. I13
White Stubbs Lane
Tel: (01992) 470490 Web: www.pwpark.com
A marvellous day out for the family with many daily activities, children's rides, catering outlets, picnic areas, paddling pool and an excellent range of animals.
Times: Open 1 Jan-29 Feb, daily, 1000-1700 (or dusk if earlier). 1 Mar-31 Oct, daily, 0930-1800. 1 Nov-31 Dec, daily, 1000-1700 (or dusk if earlier). Contact for Easter and Christmas openings.
Fee: 1 Mar-31 Oct, £10.00/£7.00/£7.00/£32.00. 1 Nov-28 Feb, £9.00/£6.00/£6.00.
Facilities: G P T(5 hrs)

Bushey

Activity World and Farmyard Funworld Map ref. E/F15
See entry in Children's Indoor Play Centres.

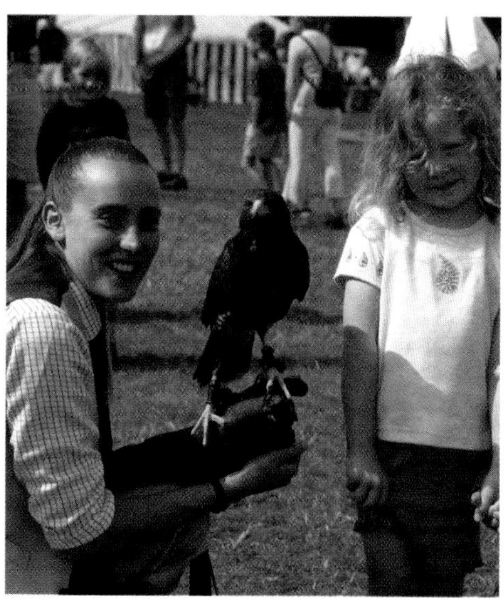

Elstree

Aldenham Country Park Map ref. F15
See entry in Countryside section.

Letchworth Garden City

Standalone Farm Map ref. G8
Wilbury Road
Tel: (01462) 686775
An open farm with cattle, sheep, pigs, poultry, shire horses a wildfowl area, natural history museum, farm walk and daily milking demonstration.
Times: Open 1 Mar-30 Sept, daily, and Oct half term week (Hertfordshire), 1100-1700.
Fee: £3.95/£2.95/£2.95/£14.95.
Facilities: T(2 hrs)

London Colney

Willows Farm Village Map ref. F13
Coursers Road
Tel: (01727) 822444 Web: www.willowsfarmvillage.com
At the unique Willows Farm Village families discover their true animal instincts, roaming free in the countryside and running wild with the adventure activities. Daft Duck Trials, Bird-o-matic falconry displays and country fun fair.
Times: Open 27 Mar-31 Oct, daily, 1000-1730.
Fee: £8.50/£7.50.
Facilities: Q T(4 hrs)

Whitwell

Waterhall Farm and Craft Centre Map ref. F10
Tel: (01438) 871256
An open farm featuring rare breeds, and offering a 'hands-on' experience for visitors. Craft centre and tea-room.
Times: Open all year, Sat, Sun and daily during school holidays. Summer 1000-1700. Winter 1000-1600. Closed 25 and 26 Dec.
Fee: £2.75/£1.75/£1.75.
Facilities: T(3 hrs)

Children's Indoor Play Centres

Bedfordshire

Dunstable

Toddler World Map ref. C/D10
Dunstable Leisure Centre, Court Drive
Tel: (01582) 604307 Web: www.activityworld.co.uk
Indoor adventure play area for children under the height limit of 1.2m.
Times: Open all year, daily, 0930-1700. Closed 25, 26 Dec and 1 Jan.
Fee: Child £2.95.
Facilities: T(1 hr)

Hertfordshire

Bishop's Stortford

Little Legs Playhouse Map ref. K10
Unit 3, Birchanger Industrial Estate, Stansted Road
Tel: (01279) 656646 Web: www.littlelegsplayhouse.co.uk
Children's indoor soft play centre with cafeteria and private party rooms. Under 4's area with non-walker section. Larger over 4's apparatus with many features.
Times: Open all year, Mon, 1200-1730; Tues-Sun, 1000-1730. During school holidays, daily, 1000-1730. Closed 24-26, 31 Dec and 1 Jan.
Fee: Various, please contact for further details.
Facilities: T(2-3 hrs)

Bushey

Activity World and Farmyard Funworld Map ref. E/F15
The Lincolnsfield Children's Centre, Bushey Hall Drive
Tel: (01923) 219902 Web: www.lincolnsfields.co.uk
The best of both worlds for children. Activity World is a giant indoor adventure playground. Farmyard Funworld has lots of animals to see and feed in our outdoor farmyard and play area.
Times: Open all year, daily, 1000-1800. Last admission one hour before closing time. Farmyard Funworld closes at dusk during the winter months. Closed 25, 26 Dec and 1 Jan.
Fee: Child (under 2) £1.50/Child (under 5) £4.00/Child (over 5) £5.00/Adult £1.00. Special discounts on term time weekdays.
Facilities: T(4 hrs)

Hatfield

Activity World Map ref. G12
Longmead, Birchwood
Tel: (01707) 270789 Web: www.activityworld.co.uk
A large children's indoor adventure play centre with 6,000 sq ft of giant slides, ball pools and mazes. Birthday parties are catered for and special schemes for playgroups.
Times: Open all year, daily, 0930-1830. Closed 25, 26 Dec and 1 Jan.
Fee: Child £2.95. Weekends and school holidays £3.95.
Facilities: T(1½ hrs)

Hatfield

Toddler World Map ref. G12
The Galleria, Comet Way
Tel: (01707) 257480 Web: www.activityworld.co.uk
Indoor adventure play area for children under the height limit of 1.2m.
Times: Open all year, Mon-Sat, 1000-1800; Sun, 1100-1700. Closed 25, 26 Dec and 1 Jan.
Fee: Child £2.95.
Facilities: T(1 hr)

Hemel Hempstead

Toddler World Map ref. D12/13
Leisureworld, Jarman Park
Tel: (01442) 212901 Web: www.activityworld.co.uk
Indoor adventure playground for children under the height limit of 1.2m.
Times: Open all year, daily, 1000-1700. Closed 25, 26 Dec and 1 Jan.
Fee: Child £2.95.
Facilities: T(1 hr)

Sawbridgeworth

Adventure Island Playbarn Map ref. K11
Parsonage Lane
Tel: (01279) 600907
A £200,000 high-quality barn conversion into an indoor children's play centre incorporating a toddler area for the under 3's, soft play, slides and much more.
Times: Open all year, daily, 1000-1800. Closed 24-26 Dec and 1 Jan.
Fee: Child from £1.30-£3.80.
Facilities: T(1½ hrs)

Hemel Hempstead

Aquasplash Map ref. D12/13
Leisureworld, Jarman Park
Tel: (01442) 292203
Indoor tropical water park with space bowl, super flume, tyre ride, drag race, multi slide, falling rapids and lazy river.
Times: Open all year. Please contact for details.
Fee: £4.90/£4.10/£3.50/£15.80.
Facilities: T(2-3 hrs)

Letchworth Garden City

North Herts Leisure Centre Map ref. G8
Baldock Road
Tel: (01462) 679311 Web: www.leisure-centre.com
Tropical leisure pool with wave machine, giant flume, swan slide and inflatable. Health and fitness studio, sports hall and squash courts.
Times: Open all year, Mon-Fri, 0700-2200; Sat, 0800-2200; Sun, 0700-2200; Bank Hols, 1000-1800.
Fee: Prices vary depending upon activity.
Facilities: T(2-3 hrs)

Leisure Pools

Bedfordshire

Bedford

Bedford Oasis Beach Pool Map ref. D5/6
Cardington Road
Tel: (01234) 272100 Web: www.bedford.gov.uk
Fun pool with two giant waterslides, spa baths, bubble burst area, lazy river ride, outside water lagoon, water cannon, wave machine and water mushroom.
Times: Open all year. Weekdays in term times, 1200-1930; weekdays in holidays, 1100-1930; weekends, 0945-1830. Other sessions available.
Fee: £2.60-£4.60/£2.10-£3.60/£2.10-£2.60/£5.75-£11.50.
Facilities: T(2-3 hrs)

Hertfordshire

Broxbourne

Lee Valley Leisure Pool Map ref. I13
New Nazeing Road
Tel: (01992) 467899 Web: www.leevalleypark.com
Large indoor pool with beach area, fountain and wave machine. Toddlers' soft play area and fitness suite.
Times: Open all year, Mon-Fri, 0600-2200; Sat, 0800-1800; Sun, 0800-1900.
Fee: Prices vary depending upon activity.
Facilities: T(2-3 hrs)

Ampthill, Bedfordshire

Countryside

The countryside of Bedfordshire rises and falls in gentle hills and valleys, from a rather, flat clay plain in the north (with the pretty river valleys of the Ouse and Ivel), through to the high ridge of chalk downs (The Chiltern Hills) in the south. In between is the Greensand Ridge, with its wooded sandy slopes and abundant wildlife. The county is dominated by intensive arable farming, although horticultural production and market gardening is also present. Mineral extraction has created several new natural habitats.

The countryside of Hertfordshire is bounded by the rivers Lea and Stort on the east of the county, and on the north and north-west by the curve of The Chilterns - magnificent chalk hills (rising to just over 900 feet) with downland and extensive beech woodland. Most of the county is a rolling landscape spilt by a series of broad valleys, containing the major rivers and areas of broadleaved woodlands. Crop production is the dominant land use, alongside a multi-million pound market gardening industry.

Special Areas

Bedfordshire

The Dunstable Downs - are the highest point in the East of England at 244m (801 feet), providing superb views over Bedfordshire and the Vale of Aylesbury. Part of The Chiltern Hills, they were formed by chalk deposited on the seabed when the area was still underwater about 70 million years ago. This is a great place for a picnic, and for flying kites - you can buy them from the countryside centre, which also has a downs exhibition. There are miles of footpaths, ancient remains (burial mounds), and an abundance of plants and wildlife - or you could take a flight in a glider. More information at www.nationaltrust.org.uk and www.chilternsaonb.org

The Greensand Ridge - a narrow ridge of sandstone running for about 40 miles from Leighton Buzzard to Gamlingay. Iron deposits give the stone a distinctive rust-brown colour, and in some areas 'glauconite' (an iron-bearing mineral) colours the stone an amazing green - the origin of the name 'Greensand'. Today you can see it used in local villages, churches, walls and bridges. The ridge is well-wooded because the sandy soils derived from the greensand are low in nutrients, and so make poor agricultural land. Another key feature of the area is the number of historic estates, such as Woburn. More information at www.greensand-trust.org.uk

Hertfordshire

The Ashridge Estate - runs along the main ridge of The Chiltern Hills, on the borders of Hertfordshire and Buckinghamshire. There are around 4,000 acres of ancient woodland, commons and chalk downland, supporting a rich variety of wildlife. Explore on the extensive network of paths, or head to the visitor centre to pick up self-guided walking leaflets. Next to the centre is the 105ft high monument (erected 1832) to the third Duke of Bridgewater, Francis Thomas Egerton (1736-1803), "the father of British inland waterways". More information at www.nationaltrust.org.uk and www.chilternsaonb.org

The Chilterns - covering around 517 sq. miles, this 'Area of Outstanding Natural Beauty', offers a landscape of rolling chalk hills, farmland, quiet valleys, charming brick and flint villages, and magnificent beechwoods (planted in the 18th C. to provide valuable timber to the local furniture-making industry). Rich in flora and fauna - the woodlands are carpeted with bluebells in spring, whilst in the autumn, the trees are turned to magnificent golden colours. Look out also for the kite, a bird of prey re-introduced here in the early 1990s. The area is excellent for cycling, horse-riding and walking. More information at www.chilternsaonb.org

Grand Union Canal - opened in 1806, this is the most famous and prosperous of all the British canals, built to provide a direct link between London and Birmingham. Running for 137 miles, with 160 locks, the canal passes through a section of Bedfordshire and Hertfordshire, and offers great opportunities for boating, walking, fishing and cycling. Along the way you can discover the Batchworth Lock Canal Centre (Rickmansworth), Cassiobury Park (Watford), the locks at Wilstone and Marsworth, and the Tring Reservoirs (built to supply the canal with water lost through the operation of locks). More information at www.waterscape.com

The Lee Valley Park - a unique mosaic of landscapes and habitats, with lakes and watercourses, nature reserves, meadows, open spaces, farm and woodland, inlaid with centres for leisure, sports, heritage and entertainment. It covers some 10,000 acres, and stretches 23 miles on both sides of the river Lea, from the more rural areas of Hertfordshire and Essex, down into the heart of London's East End. This was once a great industrial area - the river powering many mills producing flour, gunpowder and paper. Whilst barges transported goods along the important navigation to London. More information at www.leevalleypark.org.uk

Country Parks & Nature Reserves

Bedfordshire

Bedford

Priory Country Park Map ref. D6
Tel: (01234) 211182
Over 300 acres of open space with two lakes and riverside. Fishing facilities, water sports, bird-watching hides, guided walks and talks.
Times: Open at any reasonable time. Visitor centre open all year, daily, except Sat, opening times may vary.
Fee: Free.
Facilities: P T(1½ hrs)

Dunstable

Dunstable Downs Countryside Centre Map ref. C11
Whipsnade Road
Tel: (01582) 608489 Web: www.nationaltrust.org.uk
Scenic views over the vale of Aylesbury. Countryside Centre where kites, souvenirs and publications can be purchased. Site of Specific Scientific Interest.
Times: Countryside Centre open 3 Jan-31 Mar, Sat, Sun and Bank Hols, 1000-1600. 1 Apr-31 Oct, Mon-Sat, 1000-1700; Sun and Bank Hols, 1000-1800. 1 Nov-31 Dec, Sat, Sun and Bank Hols, 1000-1600. Closed 25 Dec.
Fee: Free.
Facilities: P T(2 hrs) NT

Harrold

Harrold-Odell Country Park Map ref. B4
Carlton Road
Tel: (01234) 720016 Web: www.ivelandouse.co.uk
A 150-acre country park with three lakes and riverside. Posted walks in meadow, lakeside and by river. Visitors centre with tearoom and facilities.
Times: Open all year, daily, at any reasonable time.
Fee: Free.
Facilities: P T(2½ hrs)

Luton

John Dony Field Centre Map ref. E10
Hancock Drive, Bushmead
Tel: (01582) 486983
Web: www.luton.gov.uk/enjoying/museums
Natural history site with displays featuring local/natural history, conservation and archaeology.
Times: Open 2 Jan-16 Apr, Mon-Fri, 0930-1645. 22 Apr-20 Aug, Mon-Fri, 0930-1645. 26 Aug-24 Dec, Mon-Fri, 0930-1645.
Fee: Free.
Facilities: P T(1 hr)

Luton

Sundon Hills Country Park Map ref. D9
Sundon
Tel: (01582) 608489 Web: www.nationaltrust.org.uk
Chalk downland within the Chilterns Area of Outstanding Natural Beauty, a Site of Specific Scientific Interest, and adjoining the Icknield Way long distance footpath. Outstanding landscape views.
Times: Open at any reasonable time.
Fee: Free.
Facilities: P T(2 hrs) NT

Marston Moretaine

The Marston Vale Millennium Country Park Map ref. C7
Tel: (01234) 767037 Web: www.marstonvale.org
Country park with visitor centre. Bike hire, exhibition, café and bar, bistro, art gallery and shop. Rare wetland habitat.
Times: Open all year. Spring/summer, daily, 1000-1800. Autumn/winter, daily, 1000-1600. Closed 25, 26 Dec and 1 Jan.
Fee: Free. Small charge for exhibition/wetlands reserve.
Facilities: P T(2 hrs)

Dunstable Downs, Bedfordshire

Leighton Buzzard, Bedfordshire

Moggerhanger (nr. Bedford)

Moggerhanger Park Map ref. E6
See entry in Historic Houses section.

Sandy

RSPB Lodge Nature Reserve Map ref. F6
Tel: (01767) 680551 Web: www.rspb.org.uk
A reserve with mixed woodland and heathland supporting a wide variety of birds and wildlife. Also formal gardens which are run by organic methods open to the public.
Times: Nature Reserve open daily, dawn-dusk. Visitor Centre open all year, Mon-Fri, 0900-1700; Sat and Sun, 1000-1700. Closed 25 and 26 Dec.
Fee: £3.00/£1.00/£1.50/£6.00.
Facilities: T(2 hrs)

DID YOU KNOW

Bedmond (nr. Hemel Hempstead) in Hertfordshire is the birthplace (around 1100) of Nicholas Breakspear, England's first and only pope (1154-59).

Hertfordshire

Berkhamsted

Ashridge Estate Map ref. C12
Ringshall
Tel: (01442) 851227 Web: www.nationaltrust.org.uk
Six square miles of woodlands, commons, chalk downland and farmland, with the focal point of the Bridgewater Monument. Visitor centre.
Times: Open end Mar-2nd week in Dec, Mon-Fri, 1300-1700; Sat and Sun, 1200-1700.
Fee: Monument £1.20/60p.
Facilities: T(2 hrs) NT

Elstree

Aldenham Country Park Map ref. F15
Aldenham Road
Tel: (0208) 953 9602 Web: www.hertsdirect.org/aldenham
Meadow and woodland consisting of 175 acres with Rare Breeds Farm, playgrounds, angling, nature trail and toilets. Refreshments. Site of 'Winnie the Pooh's' 100 Aker Wood.
Times: Open 1 Jan-29 Feb, daily, 0900-1600. 1 Mar-30 Apr, daily, 0900-1700. 1 May-31 Aug, daily, 0900-1800. 1 Sept-31 Oct, daily, 0900-1700. 1 Nov-31 Dec, daily, 0900-1600. Closed 25 Dec.
Fee: Car park £3.00.
Facilities: T(4 hrs)

Hatfield

Hatfield House, Park and Gardens Map ref. G12/13
See entry in Historic Houses section.

Knebworth (nr. Stevenage)

Knebworth House, Gardens and Park Map ref. G10/11
See entry in Historic Houses section.

Fairlands Valley Park, Stevenage, Hertfordshire

Rickmansworth

Rickmansworth Aquadrome Map ref. D15
Frogmoor Lane, off Harefield Road
Tel: (01923) 727031
100 acres of water, woodland and semi-landscaped parkland with walks (including scenic Alder trail), picnic and BBQ areas, children's playground, day fishing tickets and water sports.
Times: Open all year, daily, from 0800. Closing times vary.
Fee: Free.
Facilities: T(1 hr)

Stanstead Abbots

RSPB Rye Meads Nature Reserve Map ref. J12
Rye Meads Visitor Centre, Rye Road
Tel: (01992) 708383 Web: www.rspb.org.uk
Rye Meads has a wide range of wetland habitats and is particularly suited to family visits. The reed bed, open water and meadows attract many different birds.
Times: Open all year, daily, 1000-1700 (or dusk if earlier). Closed 25 and 26 Dec.
Fee: Free.
Facilities: T(2 hrs)

Stevenage

Fairlands Valley Park Map ref. G10
Tel: (01438) 353241
Web: www.stevenage-leisure.co.uk/fairlands
120 acres of parkland, including watersports, dinghy, windsurfing and powerboat courses. Private tuition and angling. Play area, cafe and disabled toilets on site.
Times: Open all year, daily, at any reasonable time. Closed 25 Dec, afternoon of 26 Dec and 1 Jan.
Fee: Free.
Facilities: T(2 hrs)

Tring

College Lake Wildlife Centre Map ref. B12
Bulbourne (off B488)
Tel: (01865) 775476 Web: www.bbowt.org.uk
Created from a worked-out chalk quarry, College Lake has been transformed into an outstanding centre for wildlife. Visitor centre, farming/wildlife museum, bird hides and two mile walk.
Times: Visitor permit required from Warden's office on request. Open all year, daily (except Mon), 1000-1700.
Fee: Free.
Facilities: T(3-4 hrs)

Waltham Abbey

River Lee Country Park Map ref. I/J13/14
See entry in Countryside section (Essex).

Waltham Cross

Cedars Park Map ref. I13/14
Theobalds Lane
Tel: (01992) 785537 Web: www.broxbourne.gov.uk
Steeped in history - this magnificent park hosts the remains of Theobalds Palace, first visited by Elizabeth I in 1564. Ornamental gardens, lake, pets' corner, rose walk and arboretum.
Times: Open all year, daily, 1000-dusk.
Fee: Free.
Facilities: T(1 hr)

Welwyn Garden City

Stanborough Park Map ref. G12
Stanborough Road
Tel: (01707) 327655 Web: www.welhat.gov.uk
Stanborough Park is a high quality public open space providing a focus of activity for many varied user groups. Watersports centre, nature trail, picnic areas and fishing.
Times: Open all year, daily, at any reasonable time.
Fee: Car park charge - weekends, £2.50. Car park charge - school hols, £1.50
Facilities: T(2 hrs)

Picnic Sites

Bedfordshire

Brogborough Hill - beside A421, 7 miles south west of Bedford. Map ref. C7
Bromham Mill - beside river bridge, just off A428, 1 1/2 miles west of Bedford. Map ref. C5
Daisy Bank - beside minor road between Carlton and Felmersham, 6 miles north west of Bedford. Map ref. C4
Deadman's Hill - beside A6, 1 mile north west of Clophill. Map ref. D7
Dunstable Downs - beside B4541, 1 mile south of Dunstable. Map ref. C11
Maulden Wood (Forestry Enterprise) - access from Deadman's Hill, beside A6, 1 mile north west of Clophill. Map ref. D7
Rowney Warren Wood (Forestry Enterprise) - beside Sandy Lane, just off A600, 2 miles north west of Shefford. Map ref. E7
Totternhoe Knolls - access from unclassified road at Totternhoe (off B489), 2 miles west of Dunstable. Map ref. C10
Whipsnade Heath - beside B4541/B4540, 2 1/2 miles south of Dunstable. Map ref. C11

Hertfordshire

Ashridge Estate - beside minor road, off B4506, 4 miles north west of Berkhamsted. Map ref. C12
Baas Hill Common - beside A10 at Broxbourne, access from A1170 along Bell Lane. Map ref. I13
Broxbourne Woods - beside minor road, 2 miles west of A10 at Broxbourne. Access from A1170 along Bell Lane. Map ref. I13
Cole Green Way - beside minor road between Cole Green and Letty Green. Access off A414 roundabout, 1 mile east of Welwyn Garden City. Map ref. H12
Lee Valley Park picnic sites - Broxbourne: Old Mill and Meadows; Rusheymead. Cheshunt: Cadmore Lane; Cheshunt Lock; Pindar/Turner Hill Marsh and Turnford Brook. Hoddesdon: Rye House. Wormley: Wharf Road. Map ref. I12/13 and J12
Mardley Heath - 1 3/4 miles north east of Welwyn, along unclassified road off B197. Map ref. G11
Northaw Great Wood - beside B157, 1 mile north west of Cuffley. Map ref. H13
Stocker's Lake - 1/4 mile south of Rickmansworth (off the A404), on minor road towards Woodcock Hill. Map ref. D15
Symondshyde Great Wood - 1/2 mile north of minor road between St. Albans and Stanborough. Map ref. F12
Tring Reservoirs - 3/4 mile north of Tring, off B489. Map ref. B12
Whippendell Wood - 3/4 mile west of Watford. Access via minor roads off A411 or A412. Map ref. D14
Wilbury Hill - beside minor road, 1 mile north from the roundabout on the A505 at Hitchin (eastern outskirts). Map ref. G8

Countryside Organisations - Bedfordshire and Hertfordshire

English Nature (Bedfordshire)
Ham Lane House, Ham Lane, Nene Park, Orton Waterville, nr. Peterborough, Cambs PE2 5UR
Tel: (01733) 405850 Web: www.english-nature.gov.uk

English Nature (Hertfordshire)
Harbour House, Hythe Quay, Colchester, Essex CO2 8JF
Tel: (01206) 796666 Web: www.english-nature.gov.uk

Forest Enterprise - East Anglia Forest District
Santon Downham, nr. Brandon, Suffolk IP27 0TJ
Tel: (01842) 810271 Web: www.forestry.gov.uk

The National Trust - Regional Office for East Anglia
Angel Corner, 8 Angel Hill, Bury St. Edmunds, Suffolk IP33 1UZ
Tel: 0870 609 5388 Web: www.nationaltrust.org.uk

The Royal Society for the Protection of Birds (RSPB) - Regional Office for East Anglia
Stalham House, 65 Thorpe Road, Norwich, Norfolk NR1 1UD
Tel: (01603) 661662 Web: www.rspb.org.uk

The Wildlife Trust (Bedfordshire)
3B Langford Arch, London Road, Sawston, nr. Cambridge, Cambridgeshire CB2 4EE
Tel: (01223) 712400 Web: www.wildlifetrust.org.uk/bcnp

The Wildlife Trust (Hertfordshire)
Grebe House, St. Michaels Street, St. Albans, Hertfordshire AL3 4SN
Tel: (01727) 858901 Web: www.wildlifetrust.org.uk/herts

Bedford, Bedfordshire

Activities

Activity Centres

Bedfordshire

Thurleigh (nr. Bedford)
Monster Events Centre Map ref. D4
Milton Road
Tel: (01234) 771904 Web: www.monster-events.co.uk
Off-road activity centre for all ages. Activities include quad bikes, 4x4, monster truck and radio control trucks. All activities must be pre-booked in advance.
Times: By appointment only.
Fee: Prices vary depending upon activity.
Facilities: T(1-3 hrs)

Boat Trips

Bedfordshire

Leighton Buzzard
Leighton Lady Cruises Map ref. B10
Brantoms Wharf, Canal Side
Tel: (01525) 384563
Web: www.leightonlady.freeuk.com
70 foot narrow boat. Heated passenger saloon with cushioned seats, seating up to 54. Cream teas and buffet available on request.
Times: Please contact for public trips list.
Fee: Please contact for details of admission prices.
Facilities: T(1 hr)

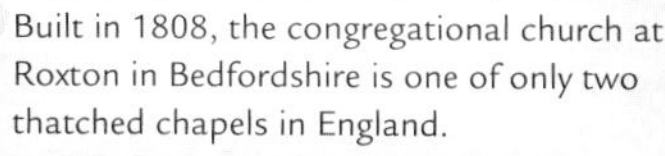

Built in 1808, the congregational church at Roxton in Bedfordshire is one of only two thatched chapels in England.

Hertfordshire

Broxbourne
The Lady of Lee Valley Map ref. I13
Lee Valley Boat Centre Limited, Old Nazeing Road
Tel: (01992) 462085
Web: www.riverleecruises.co.uk www.leevalleyboats.co.uk
Regular river cruises - public trips and private hire (some with meals/refreshments), aboard 'The Lady of Lee Valley'. Also day boats and hourly electric/rowing boats available.
Times: Open 29 Mar-31 Oct, daily, 1000-1800. Please contact for times of cruises.
Fee: Various - please contact for details.
Facilities: T(1-5 hrs)

Cycling

Bedfordshire

The Great Ouse is a 25 mile circular route starting in Bedford, and exploring the Ouse Valley with its ancient limestone villages and medieval bridges.
The Thatcher's Way is a 24 mile circular route starting in Bedford - discover picturesque thatched villages, a magnificent collection of flying machines and the unique Swiss Garden. Saleable maps for these two routes from the East of England Tourist Board on 0870 225 4852.
The Marston Vale Millennium Country Park is the starting point for a 6 mile family ride, or a 4 mile route around Stewartby Lake - there is cycle hire too. More information on (01234) 767037. Enjoy twelve different 'easy' cycle rides (for all ages) around the town of Bedford, with the help of a saleable guide available from the Tourist Information Centre on (01234) 215226. Or head to Mid Bedfordshire, to try The Greenwood Trail (23 mile circular route around the Marston Vale); The Jubilee Way (21 mile circular route starting from the town of Shefford); or The Shannon Trail (21 mile route starting from the town of Potton) - saleable leaflets from the Mid Bedfordshire Tourist Information Centre on (01767) 682728.

Ayot Green, Hertfordshire

Hertfordshire

The best place to visit for cycling information is the Hertfordshire County Council web site at www.hertsdirect.org They have a special section on cycling, including details on a series of routes throughout the county (many downloadable). You can also pick up leaflets for some of these routes at local Tourist Information Centres or libraries. The East of England Tourist Board has also produced a range of routes - try Roisia's Path, a 28 mile circular route starting from Therfield (nr. Royston), and offering panoramic views and pretty timber-framed villages. Three separate maps link together to create the Great North Way through the county (with two currently available). Romans and Royalty (16 miles) is a circular route taking in St. Albans and Hatfield, including The Alban Way. Literary Landscapes (25 miles) starts in Welwyn, and includes a visit to George Bernard Shaw's country retreat. Saleable maps for all these routes from the East of England Tourist Board on 0870 225 4852. For more great cycling try The Chilterns (to the west of the county), where there are miles of country roads, quiet lanes, byways, tracks and bridleways to explore. Contact The Chilterns Conservation Board for their cycling leaflet on (01844) 271300.

Walking

Long Distance Walks

The Greensand Ridge Walk (40 miles) - runs from Leighton Buzzard to Gamlingay. Leaflet (send self-addressed envelope) from The Greensand Trust, The Forest Office, Haynes West End, Bedfordshire MK45 3QT. Tel: (01234) 743666.

The Hertfordshire Way (166 miles) - circular route around the county. Saleable guide available from The Friends of the Hertfordshire Way, 53 Green Drift, Royston, Hertfordshire SG8 5BX. Tel: (01763) 244509.

The Icknield Way Path (105 miles) - runs from Ivinghoe Beacon (Buckinghamshire) to Knettishall Heath Country Park (Suffolk), passing through parts of Bedfordshire and Hertfordshire. Saleable guide available from the Icknield Way Association, 19 Boundary Road, Bishop's Stortford, Hertfordshire CM23 5LE. Tel: (01279) 504602.

The Lea Valley Walk (50 miles) - runs from Luton, via Hertfordshire to London's East End. Saleable guide available from the Lee Valley Park Information Centre, Stubbins Hall Lane, Crooked Mile, Waltham Abbey, Essex EN9 2EG. Tel: (01992) 892781.

Bedfordshire

Shorter Walks

The Dunstable Downs offers three circular walks - two of 2 miles and one of 4 miles. A map is available from the Countryside Centre on (01582) 608489. Discover the Ivel and Ouse with a range of walking options: The Kingfisher Way is a 21 mile long linear walk along the banks of the River Ivel, or try The Navigator's Way, a 7 mile circular walk linking Shefford and Stanford. Also available - The Potton-Sutton Circular Walk (5 miles), The Sandy-Blunham Circular Walk (7 miles) and the Biggleswade Common Circular Walks (1-6 miles). More information on all these walks on (01767) 626326. Mid Bedfordshire District Council has a range of circular walks, such as around Ampthill, Old Warden and Woburn. More information on (01767) 682728. On the west side of the county, The Marston Vale Millennium Country Park has both short and long walks around its wetlands and lakes, and is also the starting point for the 13 mile circular Timberland Trail. More information on (01234) 767037. For woodland trails try Maulden Wood (nr. Clophill) or Rowney Warren Wood (nr. Shefford). Of course don't forget the area's country parks, with their various walks and nature trails - see the 'Countryside' section for further information.

Hertfordshire

Shorter Walks

Your first port of call should be the Countryside Management Service at Hertfordshire County Council www.hertsdirect.org/cms They have downloadable routes available, alongside a programme of guided walks throughout the year. You can also pick up leaflets for some of these routes at local Tourist Information Centres or libraries. Walk the railway lines of the past on the 6 mile linear Alban Way from St. Albans to Hatfield - leaflet from St. Albans Tourist Information Centre (01727) 864511, or the 9 mile linear Nicky Line from Hemel Hempstead to Harpenden - leaflet from Hemel Hempstead Tourist Information Centre (01442) 234222. For a woodland walk, try Broxbourne Wood or The Great Wood at Northaw. Watery views can be had on the 14 mile Beane Valley Walk between Hertford and Walkern - leaflet on (01279) 843067; the Ebury Way which crosses the Colne, Chess and Gade rivers - leaflet on (01923) 776611, and the Ver Valley Walk from Redbourn to St. Albans - leaflet on (01727) 848168. From St. Albans you can jump on the train to Watford, and enjoy the 'Alban Flyer' walks at each station along the route, or head to the west of the county to discover one of the 'Chilterns Country' walks - leaflets on these last two walks on (01727) 848168. Of course don't forget the area's country parks, with their various walks and nature trails - see the 'Countryside' section for further information.

Food & Drink

Regional Produce

Bedfordshire - try a clanger, a local delicacy of baked suet crust with savoury meat at one end, and something sweet at the other - a complete meal in one handy parcel. Originally it was made by the women for their men folk labouring in the fields. Pick one up from Gunns Bakery in Sandy. The family firm of Jordan's have been milling since 1855, and are renowned today for their crunchy breakfast cereals and bars. Visit their mill shop at Holme Mills (nr. Biggleswade). Wash it all down with a pint of Bombardier Bitter from the famous brewer Charles Wells, which was established in Bedford in 1876. Teetotallers can head to Woburn Abbey, where the tradition of afternoon tea was started by Anna Maria, the 7th Duchess of Bedford. At certain times of the year you can also purchase delicious venison from Woburn's naturally reared deer.

Hertfordshire - at one time the county was known as the 'cradle of the malting industry', its rich barley harvest used to make the essential ingredient of beer. Malting took place throughout the area, and by 1855, there were 44 breweries in Hertfordshire. Today this tradition continues with McMullen and Sons, who have been brewing beer in Hertford for over 170 years. Teetotallers will appreciate Hertfordshire's very own natural spring water - Hadham Water. It is reputedly one of the purest available, drawn from 500 feet below the chalk layers of the Ash Valley. Another local speciality is watercress, and you might spot some growing on farms in the Whitwell area. The county is also noted for its mills - at the Mill Green Museum and Mill in Hatfield you can buy freshly milled flour, whilst at Kingsbury Watermill in St. Albans, delicious waffles are the speciality.

Woburn, Bedfordshire

Restaurants

Hertfordshire

St. Albans

Waffle House Map ref. F13
Kingsbury Watermill Museum Limited,
St. Michael's Street, St. Albans AL3 4SJ
Tel: (01727) 853502 Fax: (01727) 730459
Freshly baked, Belgian-style waffles are the star attraction in this delightfully informal venue on the outskirts of town. The menu ranges from best-seller ham and mushroom to pecan with butterscotch sauce. The kitchen cares about quality, making use of organically farmed beef, stoneground flour and free-range eggs. Situated next to a historic watermill, museum and gift shop. Eat in the rustic dining room (once the Miller's Parlour), or outside in the shade of huge parasols. Open: Mon-Sat, 1000-1800. Sun and Bank Hols, 1100-1800 (1700 winter). Waffles from £2.10 to £7.00. £12.00 per head for three courses, without drinks (unlicensed).

Afternoon Teas

Hertfordshire

Hare Street Village (nr. Buntingford)

The Old Swan Teashop Map ref. J9
Hare Street Village (on the B1368),
nr. Buntingford SG9 ODZ
Tel: (01763) 289265
A picturesque hall house dating back to 1475. Set in two acres of beautiful east Hertfordshire countryside, the teashop specialises in traditional home baking, licenced, serving breakfast, lunch, afternoon tea and early evening meals. Sunday roasts but please book. Open 1000-1800 Thurs-Sun, and all Bank Hols except Christmas.

Discovery Tours

Bloomin' Beautiful

Enjoy the spectacular colours and delicate fragrances of some of England's finest gardens.

Tour 1

Starting point: St. Albans, Herts Map ref. F13
Mileage: 10m/16km
Morning - enjoy a stroll amongst the parkland and lakes of Verulamium, the site of Britain's third largest Roman town. Then take the B4630 to Chiswell Green, and the sweet-smelling *Gardens of the Rose*.
Afternoon - return to St. Albans, and take the A1057 to Hatfield. Visit the 17th C. gardens of *Hatfield House*.

Tour 2

Starting point: Luton, Beds Map ref. E10
Mileage: 21m/34km
Morning - explore nine centuries of gardening history at the *Stockwood Craft Museum and Gardens*.
Afternoon - take the A6 north for 10 miles, to visit the unusual follies at *Wrest Park Gardens* (Silsoe). Then return to the A6, and at the roundabout with the A507, turn right. 4 miles later, turn left onto the A600, then at the next roundabout, turn right onto the B658. After 4 miles, turn left to Old Warden and the eccentric *Swiss Garden*.

Ashridge Estate, Hertfordshire

Wings and Wheels

Transport yourself to the world of planes, trains and automobiles.

Tour 1

Starting point: Bedford, Beds Map ref. D5/6
Mileage: 18m/29km
Morning - follow the A603 to the roundabout with the A421. Join the road to *Cardington*, and its giant airship hangers. At the T-junction in the village, turn right to Old Warden, and the vintage planes of *The Shuttleworth Collection*.
Afternoon - turn right from the exit gate, then at the roundabout with the B658 turn right again. After 4 miles, turn left at the first roundabout on the A600, then left again at the second one. 1 1/2 miles later (at the third roundabout), turn right remaining onto the A600. 1 1/2 miles later, turn right to Lower Stondon, and visit the private transport collection of the *Stondon Museum*.

Tour 2

Starting point: Luton, Beds Map ref. E10
Mileage: 15m/24km
Morning - start at *The Mossman Collection*, Britain's largest collection of horse-drawn carriages. Then take the A505 to Dunstable. Follow the B489 onto the *Dunstable Downs*, to enjoy the gliders soaring overhead.
Afternoon - leave the Downs on the B489 towards Tring. At the roundabout with the A4146, turn right to Leighton Buzzard. Enjoy a ride on the *Leighton Buzzard Railway*, then end the day with a cruise along the Grand Union Canal, aboard *Leighton Lady Cruises*.

Hollywood Hertfordshire

Lights, Camera, Action! Discover the locations of your favourite films and television programmes.

Starting point: Borehamwood, Herts Map ref. F/G14/15
Mileage: 17m/27km
Morning - explore the *Borehamwood* Film Walk, home to historic and present-day film/television studios. Watch out, you might spot a famous face or two!
Afternoon - take the A1 north to junction 7, passing the former airfield at *Hatfield*, used for the vast sets of the wartime epic 'Saving Private Ryan' (1998). End the day at *Knebworth House*, used as Wayne Manor in 'Batman' (1989).

DID YOU KNOW

St. Albans in Hertfordshire is named after Britain's first Christian martyr. 'Alban' was a Roman soldier living in Verulamium (Britain's third largest Roman city), beheaded for his religious beliefs in AD209.

Walk on the Wildside

Enjoy a wild adventure, on our animal safari into deepest Beds and Herts.

Starting point: Tring, Herts Map ref. B12
Mileage: Walter Rothschild Zoological Museum and Whipsnade Wild Animal Park 8m/13km
Walter Rothschild Zoological Museum and Woburn Safari Park 20m/32km
Morning - visit the unique *Walter Rothschild Zoological Museum*, with its 4,000 species of animals and birds.
Afternoon - take the B488/B489 to the roundabout with the A4146. Two choices, either go straight ahead, remaining on the B489, then at the next roundabout, turn right onto the B4540 to *Whipsnade Wild Animal Park*. Or turn left onto the A4146 to Leighton Buzzard, then take the A4012 to *Woburn*, and its famous *Safari Park*.

Antiques, Auctions, Bids and Bargains

Explore priceless antique towns and stately homes filled with heirlooms.

Tour 1
Starting point: Bishop's Stortford, Herts Map ref. K10/11
Mileage: 32m/51km
Morning - take the A1184 south to *Sawbridgeworth*, and lose yourself in the large antique centres. Continue on the A1184 to Harlow, where you join the A414 west to historic *Hertford*, noted for its antique shops.
Afternoon - remain on the A414/A1057 to *St. Albans*. Explore the narrow streets and lanes of this historic city, including the interesting antique and curio shops of George Street.

Tour 2
Starting point: Hitchin, Herts Map ref. F9
Mileage: 22m/35km
Morning - begin in *Hitchin*, with its speciality shopping and regular antiques fairs. Then take the B655 to Barton-le-Clay, where you join the A6 north to Clophill. Turn left at the roundabout on the A507. After a short distance, visit *Ampthill*, with its quaint antique shops.
Afternoon - rejoin the A507/A4012 to *Woburn* with its antique shops. Visit the famous *Woburn Abbey*, home to a large antiques centre.

DID YOU KNOW

All Saints Church in Leighton Buzzard, Bedfordshire contains an eagle lectern which is believed to be the oldest wooden lectern in England, dating from the 13th C.

The Pilgrim Trail

In the pursuit of heavenly inspiration, follow our trail of the area's spiritual heritage.

Starting point: Bedford, Beds Map ref. D5/6
Mileage: 30m/48km
Morning - discover Bedford's connections to the preacher/author John Bunyan (1628-88). Visit the *John Bunyan Museum*, then head to nearby *Elstow* (where he grew up), and the timber-framed Moot Hall.
Afternoon - take the B530 south to Ampthill, then the A5120 to *Dunstable*. Visit the 12th C. Augustinian Priory, where Henry VIII got his divorce. End the day by taking the A5/A5183 to *St. Albans*, and the Cathedral and Abbey Church, built on the execution site of St. Alban, Britain's first Christian martyr.

Birds and Bees

Wander amongst the rich countryside and wildlife of Bedfordshire.

Starting point: Sandy, Beds Map ref. F6
Mileage: 18m/29km
Morning - start the day amongst the birds at the *Lodge Nature Reserve* (RSPB headquarters). Then take the A603 towards Bedford. In the village of Willington, turn right to Great Barford. Then at the traffic lights, turn left (over the bridge) to reach the crossroads with the A421. Go straight ahead to Wilden, and the tropical *Bedford Butterfly Park*.
Afternoon - head to the B660, and take this south to Bedford. Then take the A428 to the village of Bromham. Explore the working 17th C. *Bromham Mill*, set in meadows rich in bird and plant life.

RSPB Lodge Nature Reserve, Sandy, Bedfordshire

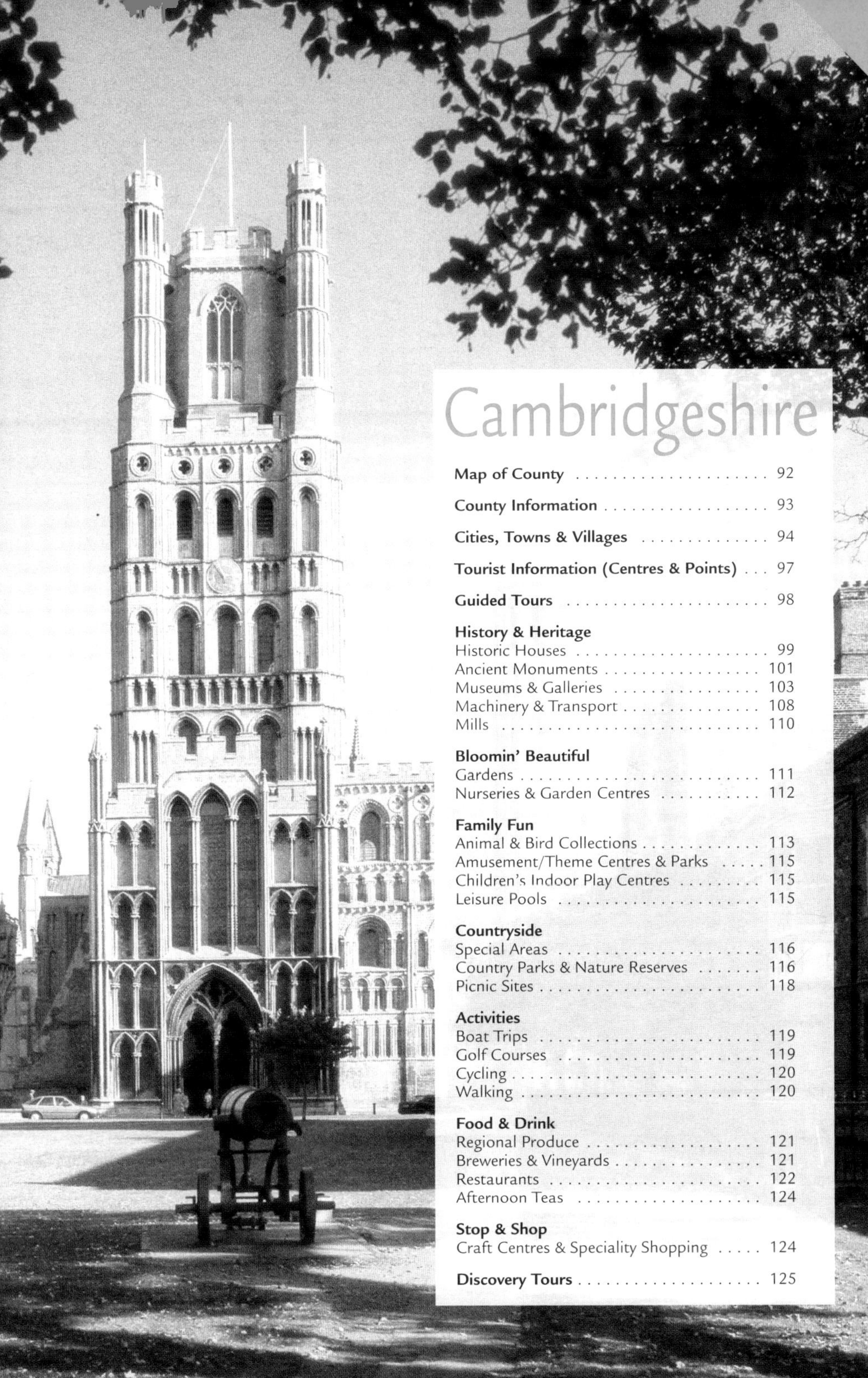

Cambridgeshire

Map of County 92

County Information 93

Cities, Towns & Villages 94

Tourist Information (Centres & Points) ... 97

Guided Tours 98

History & Heritage
Historic Houses 99
Ancient Monuments 101
Museums & Galleries 103
Machinery & Transport 108
Mills 110

Bloomin' Beautiful
Gardens 111
Nurseries & Garden Centres 112

Family Fun
Animal & Bird Collections 113
Amusement/Theme Centres & Parks 115
Children's Indoor Play Centres 115
Leisure Pools 115

Countryside
Special Areas 116
Country Parks & Nature Reserves 116
Picnic Sites 118

Activities
Boat Trips 119
Golf Courses 119
Cycling 120
Walking 120

Food & Drink
Regional Produce 121
Breweries & Vineyards 121
Restaurants 122
Afternoon Teas 124

Stop & Shop
Craft Centres & Speciality Shopping 124

Discovery Tours 125

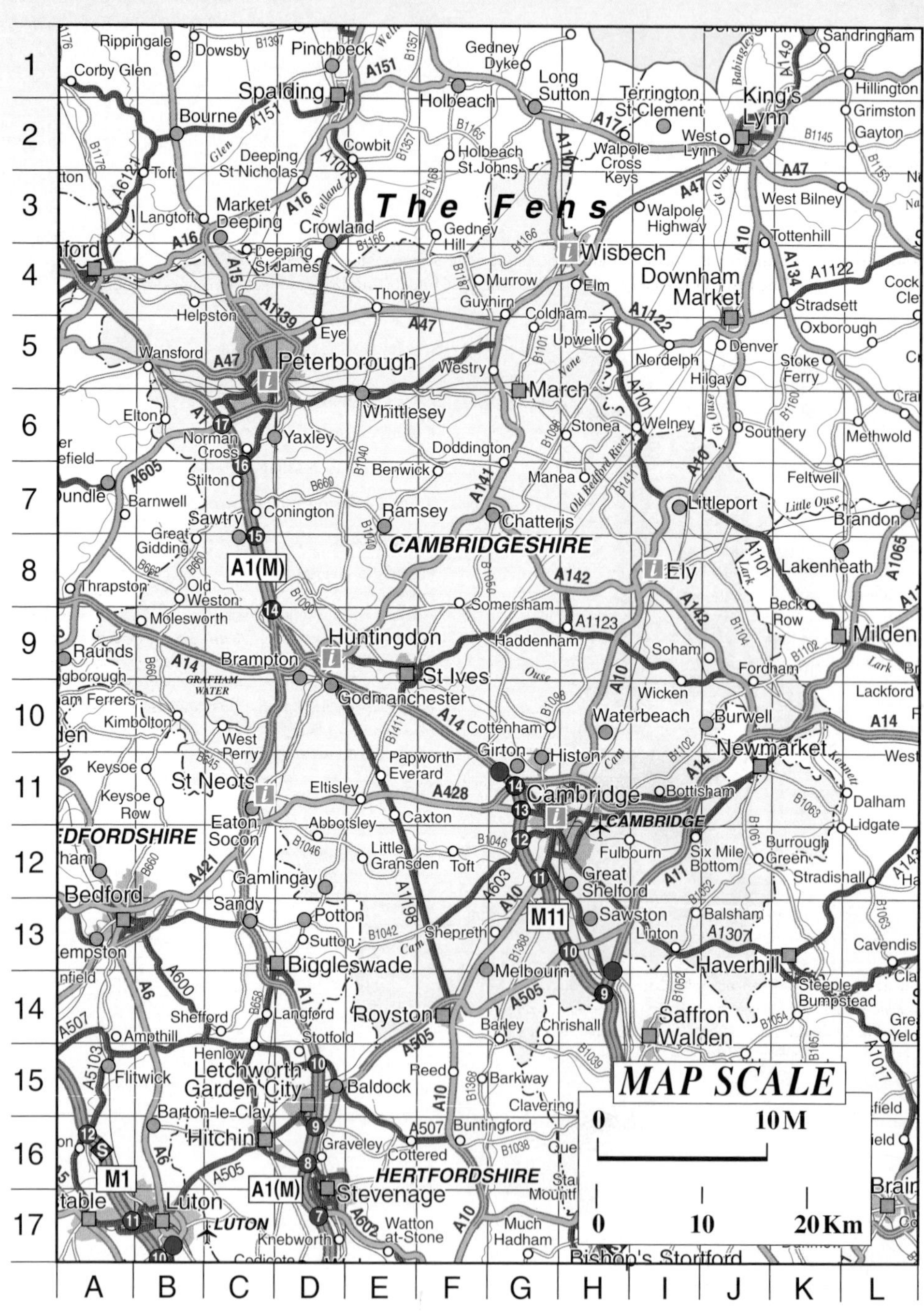

The Fens
CAMBRIDGESHIRE
BEDFORDSHIRE
HERTFORDSHIRE
Rippingale
Dowsby
Pinchbeck
Gedney Dyke
Sandringham
Corby Glen
Spalding
Holbeach
Long Sutton
Terrington St Clement
King's Lynn
Hillington
Grimston
Gayton
Bourne
Deeping St Nicholas
Cowbit
Holbeach St Johns
Walpole Cross Keys
West Lynn
Toft
West Bilney
Market Deeping
Langtoft
Crowland
Gedney Hill
Walpole Highway
Tottenhill
Deeping St James
Wisbech
Downham Market
Murrow
Elm
Stradsett
Thorney
Guyhirn
Coldham
Helpston
Eye
Upwell
Oxborough
Denver
Wansford
Peterborough
Westry
Nordelph
Stoke Ferry
Hilgay
Whittlesey
March
Elton
Norman Cross
Yaxley
Stonea
Welney
Southery
Methwold
Doddington
Stilton
Benwick
Manea
Feltwell
Barnwell
Littleport
Brandon
Sawtry
Conington
Ramsey
Chatteris
Great Gidding
Lakenheath
Thrapston
Old Weston
Ely
Somersham
Beck Row
Molesworth
Haddenham
Mildenhall
Huntingdon
Raunds
Soham
Brampton
St Ives
Fordham
Grafham Water
Godmanchester
Wicken
Lackford
Kimbolton
Cottenham
Waterbeach
Burwell
West Perry
Girton
Histon
Newmarket
Keysoe
Papworth Everard
St Neots
Keysoe Row
Eltisley
Cambridge
Bottisham
Dalham
Caxton
Lidgate
Eaton Socon
Abbotsley
Fulbourn
Six Mile Bottom
Burrough Green
Little Gransden
Toft
Stradishall
Gamlingay
Great Shelford
Bedford
Sandy
Potton
Sawston
Balsham
Sutton
Shepreth
Linton
Kempston
Biggleswade
Melbourn
Haverhill
Cavendish
Steeple Bumpstead
Shefford
Langford
Royston
Saffron Walden
Ampthill
Barley
Chrishall
Stotfold
Henlow
Letchworth Garden City
Reed
Barkway
Flitwick
Baldock
Clavering
Barton-le-Clay
Hitchin
Buntingford
Graveley
Cottered
Stevenage
Luton
LUTON
CAMBRIDGE
Watton at-Stone
Much Hadham
Knebworth
Bishop's Stortford
A1(M)
M11
M1
A1
A10
A14
A47
A16
A15
A605
A142
A141
A428
A505
A507
A6
A600
A421
A603
A1198
A1307
A11
A1101
A1122
A1123
A134
A149
A17
A151
A1139
MAP SCALE
0
10M
0
10
20Km
1
2
3
4
5
6
7
8
9
10
11
12
13
14
15
16
17
A
B
C
D
E
F
G
H
I
J
K
L

Cambridgeshire

County Town: Cambridge.
Population: 708,719 approx. (including Peterborough).
Highest Point: Great Chishill 146m (480 feet).
Rivers: Cam, Granta, Nene, New Bedford, Old Bedford, Ouse.
Landmarks: Cambridge American Cemetery, Cambridge Science Park, Ely Cathedral, The Fens, Gog Magog Hills, King's College Chapel (Cambridge), Peterborough Cathedral.

Welcome to Cambridgeshire:

Visit the University city of Cambridge, with its historic colleges and punting along the river. To the north is the distinctive Fens, an area drained by man to create some of the most fertile land in Britain. Discover towering church spires, important nature reserves and market towns such as Georgian Wisbech, and Ely dominated by its cathedral. Peterborough also has a superb cathedral, while Huntingdon is the birthplace of Oliver Cromwell. Pretty villages can be found along the attractive Nene and Ouse Valley's.

Industry Past & Present:

Before technology, the county flourished with the *wool* trade, and through the production of its *worsted cloth*. In the 18th C. *pillow lace, straw plaiting* and *lime-burning* were also common. One of the oldest industries was *coprolite-digging* - the extraction of phosphatised clay nodules for fertiliser. It occurred in a belt running from Soham to Barrington, but was exhausted between 1850 and 1890. To the north of the county, the village of Barnack became famous for its *stone*, worked from Roman times until the 18th C. *Agriculture* remains the key industry, dominated by large-scale *cereal* production. The 17th C. Fen drainage gave the county some of the richest soil in Britain, where *cereals, root crops, fruit* and *flowers* are grown. Associated businesses include *food processing, packaging* and *haulage*. Wisbech is the main *rose-growing* area of the country, with hundreds of thousands of rose bushes distributed nationwide each year, mainly by mail order. The town is also surrounded by numerous fruit orchards, notably growing Bramley apples. Other traditional Fen industries include *wildfowling, peat-cutting, willow basket-making* and *reed-cutting* (for thatch). Cambridge also started life as an agricultural market town, but later, *academic studies* (the University), *tourism* and *scientific/hi-tech research* (Cambridge Science Park) have become the key industries. To the north, March was once home to Britain's largest *railway marshalling* yard. Whilst Peterborough was once noted for its manufacture of *bricks* - on such a large scale, that London builders were supplied. Today Peterborough is the headquarters for many well-known companies, such as Thomas Cook/Travelex (travel), AMP Pearl (insurance), EMAP (media), Perkins (engineering) and Freemans (shopping). Other famous names of the county include - Anglian Water (head office), Elgood and Sons (brewing), Huntingdon Life Sciences (research), and Marshall of Cambridge (aviation/motoring).

Famous People:

Sixty-two Nobel prize-winners, thirteen British prime ministers and nine archbishops of Canterbury are linked with Cambridge and its University. Those who attended/taught at colleges include - Rupert Brooke *(poet)*, Lord Byron *(poet)*, Prince Charles, Charles Darwin, Professor Stephen Hawking, AA Milne *(author)*, Sir Issac Newton and Samuel Pepys. Other famous names of the county include - Katherine of Aragon *(Henry VIII's first wife)*, Capability Brown *(landscape gardener)*, Thomas Clarkson *(slavery abolisher)*, Oliver Cromwell *(statesman)*, St. Etheldreda *(founder of Ely)*, Octavia Hill *(National Trust founder)*, Thomas Hobson *(carrier of 'Hobson's Choice' fame)*, John Major *(former prime minister)*, Hereward the Wake *(Saxon rebel)*.

Wisbech

CITIES, TOWNS & VILLAGES

Cities, Towns & Villages

MD: Market Day
FM: Farmers' Market
EC: Early Closing
Tourist Information Centre (see page 97)
Guided Tours (see page 98)

Cambridge

Buckden Map ref. D10
Former coaching centre set beside the Great North Road - once the haunt of highwayman Dick Turpin. The High Street has old inns and brick houses. Former palace of the Bishops of Lincoln (where Katherine of Aragon was held in 1533), now a Christian retreat.

Burwell Map ref. J10
Large Fen-edge village, which in the 17th C. was a busy inland port. Earthworks of 12th C. castle built by King Stephen. The 15th C. church is noted for its 'Flaming Heart' gravestone, marking the burial site of 78 people who perished in a barn fire in 1727.

Cambridge Map ref. G/H11/12
Famous university city, noted for its historic colleges (the first founded in 1284), complete with their courtyards and bridges across the River Cam. The crowning glory is King's College Chapel, noted for its fan-vaulted ceiling. Enjoy a walking tour of the city, or take a river trip through the watermeadows and gardens of 'The Backs', aboard the famous punts. Explore medieval churches, parks, bookshops and specialist museums.
MD: Mon to Sat. **FM**: Sun.

Chatteris Map ref. G7
This small town has a long main street lined with Georgian/Victorian buildings. The 14th C. church tower overlooks a square of lawns and trees. A fire in the 14th C. destroyed most of the abbey founded in 980AD. Chatteris is thought to have been the last refuge of Queen Boudicca.
MD: Fri. **EC**: Wed.

Ely Map ref. I8
One of England's most beautiful cities, dominated by its spectacular cathedral. Ely was once an island surrounded by marshes. Narrow streets and lanes are lined with historic buildings, such as the former home of Oliver Cromwell, now a visitor centre. Sweeping parkland leads to the attractive riverside area with its marina and antique shops. **MD**: Thurs and Sat. **FM**: 2nd and 4th Sat in month. **EC**: Tues.

Godmanchester Map ref. D9/10
Delightful little town, separated from Huntingdon by attractive water meadows and a 13th C. bridge. Originally an important Roman settlement, it became one of England's first boroughs in 1212. Elegant 17/18th C. town houses and timber-framed cottages. The charming Island Hall and Chinese Bridge were originally built in 1827 by the architect Gallier.

Huntingdon Map ref. D9
Historic market town, the birthplace (1599) of Oliver Cromwell. The town grew up around an important crossing of the River Great Ouse, then from the 16-18th C. prospered as a coaching stop on the Great North Road. The old stone river bridge is one of England's finest medieval bridges. Close by is the Hinchingbrooke Country Park and the National Hunt Racecourse. **MD**: Wed and Sat. **FM**: alternate Fri.

 CITIES, TOWNS & VILLAGES

Kimbolton Map ref. B10
This attractive village was once an important medieval town, with both a market and fair. Interesting alleyways and lanes. Handsome 17/18th C. buildings, displaying pan-tiled roofs and Georgian facades. The 13th C. church has a 'Tiffany' window and painted medieval screen.

Linton Map ref. I13
A large village with a long, narrow High Street. Adjacent lanes contain thatched cottages and timber-framed buildings. 13/14th C. church, and early half-timbered Guildhall (16th C.). From the Middle Ages until the 1860's, this was a thriving market town. A Saxon burial ground has been found nearby. **FM**: at nearby Chilford Hall Vineyard, 1st Sat in month.

Littleport Map ref. I7
Before the Fens drainage, this ancient small town was an island, joined to Ely by a causeway. It has been both a coaching centre, and a busy port for barges. In 1816, the Littleport riots saw local men violently demonstrating their anger at their low wages, and the high price of bread. **MD**: Tues. **EC**: Wed.

March Map ref. G5/6
Busy market town, which originally prospered as a minor port, trading and religious centre. The 'West End' riverside area, has been likened to a Thames-style village in miniature, with its old cottages and attractive gardens. St. Wendreda's Church is noted for its outstanding timber roof, a double hammer-beam with 120 carved angels. **MD**: Wed and Sat. **EC**: Thurs.

Peterborough Map ref. C/D5/6
Steeped in history, Peterborough was originally founded around a Saxon monastery. It has developed into a modern city, that tastefully combines the old with the new. The historic centre is dominated by the magnificent Norman cathedral, and the excellent undercover Queensgate Shopping Centre. To the west of the city centre is the Nene Park, with its landscaped parkland and lakes, nature reserves, sporting activities and steam train rides. **MD**: Tues to Sat.

Ramsey Map ref. E7
This quiet market town grew up around its 10th C. abbey, founded on the edge of the Fens. In the 12/13th C. it became one of the most important in England. Ramsey later prospered from the rich agricultural land created after the Fen drainage. Remnant of 15th C. Abbey Gatehouse, and 12th C. church containing oak lectern. **MD**: Sat.

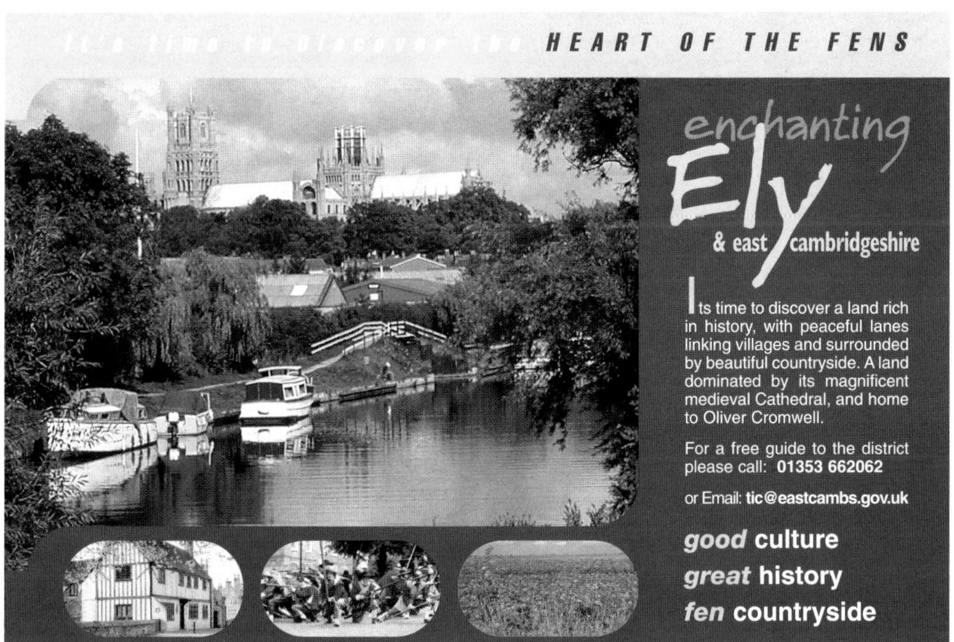

 CITIES, TOWNS & VILLAGES

St. Ives Map ref. E/F9
Attractive, riverside market town. The Chapel of St. Leger is one of only four surviving bridge chapels in the country, set midstream on the 15th C. stone bridge spanning the river. On the Market Hill is the statue of Oliver Cromwell, who lived here from 1631-1636. In between here and the Riverside are 'The Lanes' a maze of little alleys. **MD**: Mon (main) and Fri.

St. Neots Map ref. C/D11
Set beside the River Great Ouse, this is the largest town in the county. It grew up around a priory founded in 974AD, and takes its name from the Cornish saint whose remains were interred here. The large market square is overlooked by the 15th C. church - the 'Cathedral of Huntingdonshire'. Riverside Park offers boat trips and band concerts. **MD**: Thurs. **FM**: 2nd Sat in month.

Soham Map ref. J9
Small Fenland town, which grew up in the 7th C. beside the former 'Soham Mere'. The 12th C. church has a splendid beamed roof and tower. The Fountain Inn is noted for its 17th C. steelyard, once used for weighing wagons. 18th C. restored windmill and annual Pumpkin Fair. **MD**: Fri. **EC**: Wed.

Whittlesey Map ref. E5/6
Small Fenland town, with fine examples of 17/18th C. houses and a butter cross. St. Mary's Church is noted for its beautiful mid 15th C. spire. The local hero, Sir Harry Smith, one of Wellington's generals, is commemorated by the South Chapel in the church. The town is famous for its annual 'Straw Bear Festival' (held each January). **MD**: Fri. **FM**: alternate Fri, swaps with Wisbech. **EC**: Thurs.

Wisbech Map ref. H3/4
Prosperous market town, which grew up around its port, trading from medieval times. After the Fen drainage, it became a busy agricultural centre, evident today in some of the finest Georgian street architecture in Britain (such as North Brink, The Crescent and Museum Square). The town remains at the heart of a fruit and flower growing area. **MD**: Thurs and Sat. **FM**: alternate Fri, swaps with Whittlesey. **EC**: Wed.

Godmanchester

Pick of the villages

1 **Alwalton** - conservation village with fine Norman church and pretty cottages. Map ref. C6
2 **Ashley** - thatched and colour-washed houses set around a green and duck pond. Map ref. K11
3 **Barnack** - once noted for its limestone quarries. Stone-built houses and 18th C. windmill. Map ref. B4
4 **Barrington** - attractive village set beside one of the largest greens in England. Map ref. G13
5 **Chippenham** - attractive estate village, set beside Lord Orford's 17th C. park. Map ref. K10
6 **Elm** - tree-canopied street, with 17/18th C. houses and pastel-washed cottages. Map ref. H4
7 **Eltisley** - beautifully kept green (cricket pitch) bordered by attractive houses. Map ref. E11
8 **Elton** - fine 17th C. houses, set beside parkland of hall. River Nene with old mill. Map ref. B6
9 **Emneth** - surrounded by fruit orchards. Connections to Thomas the Tank Engine. Map ref. H4
10 **Fenstanton** - 17th C. lock up/clock tower. Tomb of landscape gardener 'Capability' Brown. Map ref. F10
11 **Gamlingay** - former market town, with many fine buildings, including 17th C. almshouses. Map ref. D12
12 **Grantchester** - idyllic setting beside River Cam. Former home of poet Rupert Brooke. Map ref. G12
13 **Haddenham** - one of the highest Fen villages. Pleasant High Street and restored 13/14th C. church. Map ref. H9
14 **Helpston** - grey-stone village with 12th C. butter-cross. Memorial to 18th C. poet John Clare. Map ref. B4
15 **Hemingford Abbots** - brick, timber and thatched houses cluster around a 12th C. church. Map ref. E9
16 **Hemingford Grey** - beautiful riverside setting. Old cottages and 12th C. manor house. Map ref. E9
17 **Houghton** - riverside village. Thatched/white-washed cottages and water mill. Map ref. E9
18 **Leverington** - outstanding church, 17/18th C. houses and Elizabethan hall. Map ref. G3
19 **Little Downham** - remains of former 15th C. country palace of the Bishops of Ely. Map ref. I7/8
20 **Madingley** - Elizabethan mansion, post-mill and American Military Cemetery. Map ref. G11
21 **Marholm** - cream-coloured and thatched houses set around a green. Map ref. C5
22 **Meldreth** - 18th C. whipping post and stocks. Base of medieval cross. Map ref. F13
23 **Northborough** - many fine stone and thatched cottages. 14th C. manor house. Map ref. C4
24 **Prickwillow** - typical Fens village, with houses overlooked by steep river banks. Map ref. J8
25 **Reach** - once the medieval port for Cambridge. Pretty green, a venue for annual fairs. Map ref. I10
26 **Stilton** - named after the cheese, which was once distributed from the 17th C. Bell Inn. Map ref. C7
27 **Swaffham Prior** - noted for its two churches in the same churchyard. Map ref. I10/11
28 **Thorney** - remains of Norman abbey (now part of church). 19th C. houses by Duke of Bedford. Map ref. E4
29 **Thriplow** - ancient settlement, with an old smithy. Annual daffodil festival. Map ref. G13
30 **Wicken** - thatched houses, pond and four separate greens. Britain's oldest nature reserve. Map ref. I9

Tourist Information

Tourist Information Centres

With so much to see and do in this area, it's impossible for us to mention all of the places you can visit. You will find Tourist Information Centres (TICs) throughout Cambridgeshire, with plenty of information on all the things that you can do and places you can visit.

TICs can book accommodation for you, in their own area, or further afield using the 'Book A Bed Ahead' Scheme. They can also be the ideal place to purchase locally made crafts or gifts, as well as books covering a wide range of local interests.

Cambridge, The Old Library, Wheeler Street.
Tel: 0906 586 2526 (charged at 60p per min)
Email: cambridge@eetb.info
Web: www.tourismcambridge.com

Ely, Oliver Cromwell's House, 29 St. Mary's Street.
Tel: (01353) 662062
Email: ely@eetb.info Web: www.eastcambs.gov.uk

Huntingdon, The Library, Princes Street.
Tel: (01480) 388588
Email: huntingdon@eetb.info Web: www.huntsleisure.org

Peterborough, 3-5 Minster Precincts.
Tel: (01733) 452336
Email: peterborough@eetb.info
Web: www.peterborough.gov.uk

St. Neots, The Old Court, 8 New Street.
Tel: (01480) 388788
Email: stneots@eetb.info Web: www.huntsleisure.org

Wisbech and the Fens, 2-3 Bridge Street.
Tel: (01945) 583263
Email: wisbech@eetb.info Web: www.fenland.gov.uk

Peterborough Tourist Information Centre

Guided Tours

Why not enjoy a guided tour exploring one of the area's towns and cities? Some of these tours (indicated with a *) are conducted by Registered Blue Badge Guides, who have attended a training course sponsored by the East of England Tourist Board. Many of these guides also have a further qualification to take individuals around the region for half day, full day or longer tours if required. For more information on the guided tours listed, please telephone the relevant contact.

Cambridge *

- **Daily walking tours:** of the city and colleges depart from the Tourist Information Centre up to four times a day in summer. Ticket price includes entrance to either King's or St. John's College, other colleges included as available. For further information contact the Tourist Information Centre on (01223) 457574.
- **Group tours:** tours for groups can be arranged in ten different languages, and can include city and colleges, walking/punting, science tours, Royal Cambridge, ghost tours and other themed tours. Coach tours of Cambridge and East Anglia can also be arranged. For bookings and enquiries, Tel: (01223) 457574. Fax: (01223) 457588. Email: tours@cambridge.gov.uk Web: www.tourismcambridge.gov.uk

Cambridge

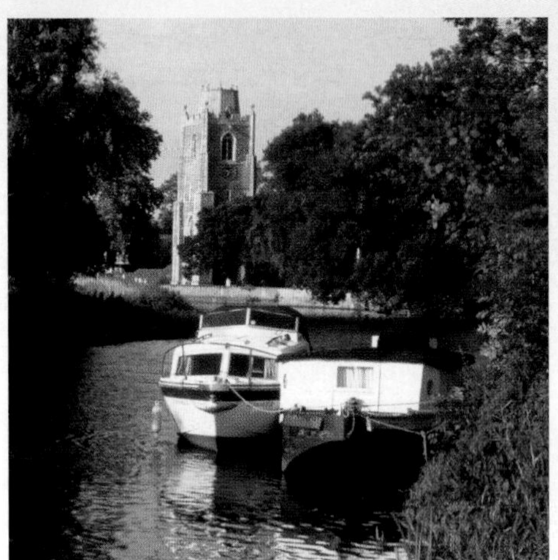

Hemingford Grey

- **Important information:** all parties of ten or more who intend to tour the colleges should be accompanied by a Cambridge Registered Blue Badge Guide. Colleges which charge for admission are only included on request (cost added to tour price). Most colleges are closed to the public during University examination time, mid Apr-end Jun.

Ely *

- **Cathedral and city tours, and city only tours:** guides available for pre-booked groups by appointment. Tours can include the cathedral and city, or Oliver Cromwell's House. For cathedral tours, please contact The Chapter Office on (01353) 667735.
- **Oliver Cromwell's House, tours and visits:** available for pre-booked groups. Evening tours can be arranged. Special rate for school parties and costumed guides are popular.
- **Ghost tours and alternative Ely tours:** with costumed guides, can be arranged direct with the guides.
- For further information contact the Tourist Information Centre on (01353) 662062.

Peterborough *

- **Group tours:** guides are available for city and cathedral tours at any time for private groups, each tour lasts approximately 1 1/2 hours. For further information contact the Tourist Information Centre on (01733) 452336.

Wisbech

- **Regular town tours:** themed guided walks on Wed evenings from May-Jul, lasting 1 1/2 hours.
- **Group tours:** town tour and themed walks can be arranged for groups.
- For further information contact the Tourist Information Centre on (01945) 583263.

Historic Houses

Arrington (nr. Royston)

Wimpole Hall and Home Farm Map ref. F12
Tel: (01223) 207257 Web: www.wimpole.org
An 18th C. house in a landscaped park with a folly and Chinese bridge. Plunge bath and yellow drawing room in the house, the work of John Soane. Home Farm with rare breeds centre.
Times: Hall - open 20 Mar-31 Oct: Tues-Thurs, Sat, Sun, Bank Hol Mons and 9 Apr (Good Fri). Aug: Tues-Sun and Bank Hol Mon. Nov: Sun, 7, 14, 21 and 28. 1300-1700 (Bank Hol Mons 1100-1700, closes 1600 after 31 Oct). Home Farm and Gardens - open 20 Mar-31 Oct: Tues-Thurs, Sat, Sun, Bank Hol Mons and 9 Apr (Good Fri). Jul and Aug: Tues-Sun. 6 Nov-Mar 2005: Sat and Sun (also open everyday Easter Hols, Spring, Oct and Feb half term). 1030-1700 (20 Mar-31 Oct), 1100-1600 (Nov-Mar). Restaurant, shop and gallery - open all year, Tues-Thurs, Sat, Sun, plus Fri in Aug, 1100-1700 (gallery 1300-1700). Park - open all year, dawn to dusk.
Fee: Hall only £6.60/£3.20. Farm only £5.10/£3.20. Hall and farm £9.80/£5.20/£25.00 (family).
Facilities: T(4 hrs) NT

Elton (nr. Peterborough)

Elton Hall Map ref. B6
Tel: (01832) 280468
An historic house and gardens open to the public with a fine collection of paintings, furniture, books and Henry VIII's prayer book. There is also a restored rose garden.
Times: Open 31 May; Wed in Jun; Wed, Thurs and Sun in Jul and Aug, plus Bank Hol Mon (30) Aug. 1400-1700.
Fee: House and garden £6.00. Garden only £3.00.
Facilities: T(1 hr)

Peckover House, Wisbech

Ely

Oliver Cromwell's House Map ref. I8
29 St. Mary's Street
Tel: (01353) 662062 Web: www.eastcambs.gov.uk
The family home of Oliver Cromwell with a 17th C. kitchen, parlour, a haunted bedroom, a Tourist Information Centre, souvenirs and a craft shop.
Times: Open 2 Jan-31 Mar, Mon-Fri, 1100-1600; Sat, 1100-1700; Sun, 1115-1600. 1 Apr-31 Oct, daily, 1000-1730. 1 Nov-31 Dec, Mon-Fri, 1100-1600; Sat, 1100-1700; Sun, 1115-1600. Closed 25 Dec and 1 Jan
Fee: £3.75/£2.50/£3.25/£10.00.
Facilities: Q T(45 mins)

Godmanchester

Island Hall Map ref. D9/10
Tel: (01480) 459676
A mid-18th C. mansion of architectural importance on the Great Ouse river. A family home with interesting ancestral possessions.
Times: Open by appointment for groups only, May-Sept. Closed Aug.
Fee: £4.00/£2.00.
Facilities: T(1 hr)

Hemingford Grey (nr. St. Ives)

The Manor Map ref. E9
Tel: (01480) 463134 Web: www.greenknowe.co.uk
The 'Green Knowe' children's books were based on this ancient house. Also see the Lucy Boston patchworks. Garden is 4 1/2 acres with topiary.
Times: Garden open all year, daily, 1100-1700 (dusk in winter). House tours are available by appointment only.
Fee: House £4.00/£1.50/£3.50. Garden £2.00.
Facilities: T(1 1/2 hrs)

DID YOU KNOW

Revd. Wilbert Awdry, author of the famous Thomas the Tank Engine books, was vicar of Emneth Church, nr. Wisbech. In 1947, he re-named engine number 1800 at the Nene Valley Railway at Peterborough as 'Thomas'.

Kimbolton

Kimbolton Castle Map ref. B10
Tel: (01480) 860505 Web: www.kimbolton.cambs.sch.uk
A Tudor house, remodelled by Vanbrugh with Pellegrini mural paintings, an Adam gatehouse and fine parklands. The castle is now occupied by an independent school.
Times: Open 7 Mar and 7 Nov, Sun, 1300-1600.
Fee: Please contact for details of admission prices.
Facilities: P T(1½ hrs)

Lode (nr. Cambridge)

Anglesey Abbey, Gardens and Lode Mill Map ref. I11
Quy Road
Tel: (01223) 810080 Web: www.nationaltrust.org.uk
A 13th C. abbey with a later Tudor house and the famous Fairhaven collection of paintings and furniture. There is also an outstanding 100-acre garden and arboretum. Watermill.
Times: 1 Jan-21 Mar (winter walk, shop, plant centre and restaurant only), Wed-Sun, 1030-1630. Also mill open on Sat and Sun, 1100-1500. 24 Mar-7 Nov, Wed-Sun and Bank Hols - house and mill, 1300-1700; garden, shop, plant centre and restaurant, 1030-1730. Not open Good Fri. 5 Jul-29 Aug, daily, 1030-1730 (Thurs until 2000). 10 Nov-23 Dec (winter walk, shop, plant centre and restaurant only), Wed-Sun, 1030-1630. Also mill open on Sat and Sun, 1100-1500.
Fee: Abbey, gardens and mill £6.60/£3.30. Gardens and mill only £4.10/£2.05. Winter walk £3.40/£1.70.
Facilities: Q P T(4 hrs) NT

Nassington (nr. Peterborough)

The Prebendal Manor Medieval Centre Map ref. B6
Church Street
Tel: (01780) 782575 Web: www.prebendal-manor.co.uk
Discover life during the Middle Ages at this 13th C. Grade I listed building, once King Cnut's Royal Manor. Europe's largest recreated medieval garden, rare breed animals and tithe barn exhibition.
Times: Open Easter-Sept, Wed and Sun, 1300-1730; Bank Hol Mons, 1300-1730.
Fee: £4.50/£2.00/£4.50. Gardens only £4.00/£1.50/£4.00
Facilities: P T(2-3 hrs) (audio tours)

DID YOU KNOW

Cambridge was the home of Thomas Hobson, who ran a carrier business. He gave his name to the phrase 'Hobson's Choice', because he would only lend out its horses in strict rotation, the customer taking the horse nearest the stable door, whatever its quality (hence no choice at all).

Stamford

Burghley House Map ref. A4
Tel: (01780) 752451 Web: www.burghley.co.uk
Immense Elizabethan stately home. Built by William Cecil in 1587, and occupied by his descendants ever since. 18 state rooms including art collections, woodcarvings and magnificent ceilings.
Times: Open 27 Mar-31 Oct, daily, 1100-1700 (last admission 1630). Mon-Sat - guided tours only; Sun - free flow in house. Closed 4 Sept.
Fee: £7.80/£3.50/£6.90/£19.50.
Facilities: P T(3-4 hrs)

Wisbech

Peckover House and Gardens Map ref. H4
North Brink
Tel: (01945) 583463 Web: www.nationaltrust.org.uk
A merchant's house on the North Brink of the River Nene, built in 1722, with a plaster and wood rococo interior and a notable 2 acre Victorian garden with unusual trees.
Times: Garden open 21 Mar-31 Oct, daily (except Fri), 1230-1700. House open 21 Mar-28 Apr, Wed, Sat and Sun, 1330-1630; 1 May-29 Aug, Wed, Thurs, Sat and Sun, 1330-1630; 1 Sept-31 Oct, Wed, Sat and Sun, 1330-1630. Shop open same dates and days as above, but 1230-1700.
Fee: House and gardens £4.25/£2.00. Garden only £2.75/£1.50.
Facilities: T(3 hrs) NT

Wimpole Hall and Home Farm, Arrington

Ancient Monuments

Cambridge

King's College Chapel Map ref. H11
Tel: (01223) 331212 Web: www.kings.cam.ac.uk
The chapel, founded by Henry VI, includes the breathtaking fan-vault ceiling, stained glass windows, a carved oak screen and Ruben's masterpiece 'The Adoration of the Magi'.
Times: Open all year, during term - Mon-Fri, 0930-1530; Sat, 0930-1515; Sun, 1315-1430 and during BST, 1700-1730. Out of term - Mon-Sat, 0930-1630; Sun 1000-1700.
Fee: £4.00/£3.00/£3.00.
Facilities: T(1 hr)

Coton (nr. Cambridge)

Cambridge American Cemetery Map ref. G11
Tel: (01954) 210350
A cemetery with a visitor reception for information, the graves area and a memorial chapel. Operated and maintained by the American Battle Monuments Commission.
Times: Open all year, daily, 0900-1700. Closed 25 Dec-1 Jan.
Fee: Free.
Facilities: P T(30 mins)

Ely

Ely Cathedral Map ref. I8
Tel: (01353) 667735 Web: www.cathedral.ely.anglican.org
One of England's finest cathedrals with guided tours and tours of the Octagon and West Tower. Monastic precincts, brass rubbing centre and Stained Glass Museum.
Times: Open 1 Jan-27 Mar, Mon-Sat, 0730-1800; Sun, 0730-1700. 29 Mar-30 Oct, daily, 0700-1900. 31 Oct-31 Dec, Mon-Sat, 0730-1800; Sun, 0730-1700.
Fee: £4.80/free/£4.20.
Facilities: T(1½ hrs)

Isleham

Isleham Priory Church Map ref. J9
Tel: (01223) 582700 Web: www.english-heritage.org.uk
Rare example of early Norman church with herringbone masonry. Little altered despite later conversion to a barn.
Times: Open at any reasonable time.
Fee: Free.
Facilities: T(30 mins) EH

Longthorpe (nr. Peterborough)

Longthorpe Tower Map ref. C5
Thorpe Road
Tel: (01733) 268482 Web: www.english-heritage.org.uk
The 14th C. tower of a fortified manor house, with wall paintings which form the most complete set of domestic paintings of the period in northern Europe.
Times: Please contact for details of opening times.
Fee: Please contact for details of admission prices.
Facilities: T(1 hr) EH

March

Saint Wendreda's Church Map ref. G6
Church Street
Tel: (01354) 654783
This church is noted for its exceptional double hammerbeam timber roof which contains 120 carved angels. Probably the finest of all such East Anglian timber roofs.
Times: Open all year, daily, 1000-1600. When church is locked, the availability of the key nearby is advertised.
Fee: Free.
Facilities: P T(30 mins)

Peterborough

Flag Fen Bronze Age Centre Map ref. D5
The Droveway, Northey Road
Tel: (01733) 313414 Web: www.flagfen.com
Visitor Centre with landscaped park, summer archaeological excavation, rare breed animals, roundhouses and museum of the Bronze Age.
Times: Open all year, daily, 1000-1700 (last admission 1600). Closed 24 Dec-2 Jan.
Fee: £4.00/£3.00/£3.50/£11.00.
Facilities: P T(2½ hrs)

Peterborough

Peterborough Cathedral Map ref. D5
Tel: (01733) 343342
Web: www.peterborough-cathedral.org.uk
Norman cathedral with an Early English west front, a 13th C. painted nave ceiling and the tomb of Katherine of Aragon. It was also the former burial place of Mary Queen of Scots.
Times: Open all year, Mon-Sat, 0900-1700; Sun, 1200-1700. Closed 25 and 26 Dec.
Fee: Donations requested.
Facilities: T(1 hr)

Ramsey

Ramsey Abbey Gatehouse Map ref. E7
Tel: 0870 609 5388 Web: www.nationaltrust.org.uk
The ruins of a 15th C. gatehouse.
Times: Open 1 Apr-31 Oct, daily, 1000-1700.
Fee: Free. Donations appreciated.
Facilities: T(1 hr) NT

St. Ives

Saint Ives Bridge Chapel Map ref. E/F9
Bridge Street
Tel: (01480) 497314
A 15th C. chapel built onto the bridge in midstream. One of only four in England, with a balcony over the river.
Times: Open 5 Jan-30 Apr, Mon-Sat, 1000-1700. 1 May-30 Sept, Mon-Sat, 1000-1700; Sun, 1400-1700. 1 Oct-31 Dec, Mon-Sat, 1000-1700. Closed 3 Jan, 9 Apr and 25-28 Dec.
Fee: Free.
Facilities: T(20 mins)

DID YOU KNOW

The Fens are the legendary haunt of Jack O' Lanterns, a highly dangerous fairy whose flickering lights would weave an hypnotic spell, enticing unwary travellers off the paths to their doom in the boggy marshes.

Thorney

Thorney Abbey Church Map ref. E4
Tel: (01733) 270388
Abbey church with a Norman nave (c.1100), a fine church organ originally built in 1787-1790 and a stained glass east window depicting the miracles of St. Thomas Becket.
Times: Open all year, daily, 1000-dusk.
Fee: Free.
Facilities: T(45 mins)

Waterbeach

The Farmland Museum and Denny Abbey Map ref. H10
See entry in Museums & Galleries section.

Whittlesford

Duxford Chapel Map ref. H13
Tel: (01223) 443180 Web: www.english-heritage.org.uk
A 14th C. chapel which was once part of the Hospital of St. John.
Times: Open at any reasonable time.
Fee: Free.
Facilities: T(1 hr) EH

Museums & Galleries

Bassingbourn (nr. Royston)
Bassingbourn Tower Museum Map ref. F14
Bassingbourn Barracks
Tel: (01763) 243500
Web: http://members.aol.com/an6530/museum.htm
Museum housed in original airfield control tower. Exhibits, photographs and documents covering the history of this important military establishment, including the RAF, USAAF 91st BG (H) and British Army.
Times: Open by appointment only - 7 Apr-31 Oct, Wed, 1000-1600 and Sun, 1000-1300. Please phone for Easter openings.
Fee: Free. Donations appreciated.
Facilities: P T(3 hrs)

Bourn (nr. Cambridge)
Wysing Arts Map ref. F12
Fox Road
Tel: (01954) 718881 Web: www.wysingarts.org
Art centre and gallery exhibiting contemporary art. Continuous programme of courses for adults and children. Eleven acre site open all year round.
Times: Open all year, daily, 0900-1800.
Fee: Free.
Facilities: P T(1½ hrs)

Burwell Museum

Cromwell Museum, Huntingdon

Burwell
Burwell Museum Map ref. J10
Mill Close
Tel: (01638) 605544
Web: http://mysite.freeserve.com/burwell_museum
A rural village museum housed in a re-erected 18th C. timber-framed barn. Also war memorabilia, forge, wagons and carts. Displays of village shop and old school room. Roman potter's display.
Times: Open 11 Apr-31 Oct, Thurs, Sun and Bank Hol Mon, 1400-1700.
Fee: £2.00/50p.
Facilities: T(2 hrs)

Cambridge
Cambridge and County Folk Museum Map ref. G11
2-3 Castle Street
Tel: (01223) 355159 Web: www.folkmuseum.org.uk
A part timber-framed 17th C. inn, retaining many original fittings. Established as a museum of Cambridgeshire life in 1936. Strong collections. Extra display room from Jun 2004.
Times: Closed for redevelopment until Jun 2004. Exact date of reopening to be confirmed, please contact for details.
Fee: £2.50/75p/£1.50.
Facilities: T(1 hr) (from Jun 2004)

Cambridge
Cambridge Contemporary Art Map ref. H11
6 Trinity Street
Tel: (01223) 324222 Web: www.cambridgegallery.co.uk
Changing exhibitions highlight paintings, sculpture, hand-made prints and crafts. With work by acknowledged masters and established artists.
Times: Open all year, Mon-Sat, 0900-1730. Closed 9 Apr, 25, 26 Dec and 1 Jan.
Fee: Free.
Facilities: T(1 hr)

Cambridge

Fitzwilliam Museum Map ref. H11
Trumpington Street
Tel: (01223) 332900 Web: www.fitzmuseum.cam.ac.uk
A large, internationally-renowned collection of antiquities, applied and fine arts. The original buildings are mid-19th C. with later additions.
Times: Closed until 1 Jun 2004 for completion of courtyard development. From Jun, open Tues-Sat and Bank Hol Mon, 1000-1700; Sun, 1200-1700. Closed 24-26, 31 Dec and 1 Jan.
Fee: Free.
Facilities: T(2 hrs)

Cambridge

Kettle's Yard Map ref. G11
Castle Street
Tel: (01223) 352124 Web: www.kettlesyard.co.uk
A major collection of 20th C. paintings and sculpture, exhibited in a house of unique character. Also changing contemporary art exhibitions in the gallery.
Times: Open all year. Gallery - Tues-Sun, 1130-1700. House - Tues-Sun, 1400-1600 (extended in summer).
Fee: Free.
Facilities: T(1½ hrs)

Cambridge

Rupert Brooke Museum Map ref. G12
The Orchard, 45-47 Mill Way, Grantchester
Tel: (01223) 845788 Web: www.rupertbrooke.com
Small, privately owned museum depicting the life in words and photographs of the poet Rupert Brooke (1887-1915), who lived at Orchard House whilst at University.
Times: Open all year, daily, 1100-1800.
Fee: Free.
Facilities: T(15 mins)

Cambridge

Sedgwick Museum Map ref. H11
Department of Earth Sciences, Downing Street
Tel: (01223) 333456 Web: www.sedgwickmuseum.org
A large collection of fossils from all over the world, both invertebrate and vertebrate with some mounted skeletons of dinosaurs, reptiles and mammals. Mineral gallery.
Times: Open all year, Mon-Fri, 0900-1300 and 1400-1700; Sat, 1000-1300. Closed 9-12 Apr and 25 Dec-3 Jan.
Fee: Free.
Facilities: T(1 hr)

Cambridge

University Museum of Archaeology and Anthropology
Map ref. H11
Downing Street
Tel: (01223) 333516
Web: http://museum-server.archanth.cam.ac.uk
Displays relating to world prehistory and local archaeology, with anthropology displays, opened in July 1990.
Times: Open all year, Tues-Sat, 1400-1630. Extended opening hours from Jun-Sept.
Fee: Free.
Facilities: T(2 hrs)

Cambridge

University Museum of Zoology Map ref. H11
Downing Street
Tel: (01223) 336650 Web: www.zoo.cam.ac.uk/museum
Spectacular displays of internationally important specimens, including fossils, mammal skeletons, birds, dinosaurs, beautiful shells and a huge whale. Temporary exhibitions throughout the year.
Times: Open all year, Mon-Fri, 1000-1645. Closed 9-12 Apr and 24 Dec-1 Jan.
Fee: Free.
Facilities: T(45 mins)

Fitzwilliam Museum, Cambridge

Cambridge
Whipple Museum of the History of Science
Map ref. H11
Free School Lane
Tel: (01223) 330906 Web: www.hps.cam.ac.uk/whipple
The Whipple Museum houses a designated collection of scientific instruments and models, dating from the Middle Ages to the present.
Times: Open all year, Mon-Fri, 1330-1630. Closed Bank Hols.
Fee: Free.
Facilities: T(1 hr)

Chatteris
Chatteris Museum Map ref. G7
14 Church Lane
Tel: (01354) 696319
A small museum with artefacts, ephemera and photographs relating to the history of the town of Chatteris, its people and its environs.
Times: Open 8 Jan-1 Apr, Thurs, 1400-1600; Sat, 1000-1200. 3 Apr-21 Oct, Thurs, 1400-1630; Sat, 1000-1300. 23 Oct-18 Dec, Thurs, 1400-1600; Sat, 1000-1200.
Fee: Free.
Facilities: T(1 hr)

Ely
Babylon Gallery Map ref. I8
Waterside
Tel: (01353) 669022 Web: www.babylongallery.co.uk
The Babylon Gallery offers a mixture of national touring exhibitions, and high quality curated exhibitions of work by local and regional artists.
Times: Open all year, Tues-Sat, 1000-1600; Sun and Bank Hol Mon, 1100-1700. Closed 25, 26 Dec and 1 Jan.
Fee: Free.
Facilities: T(1 hr)

Ely
Ely Museum Map ref. I8
The Old Gaol, Market Street
Tel: (01353) 666655 Web: www.ely.org.uk
Tells the story of Ely from prehistory to the present day. Collections include archaeology and social history, as well as displays of the condemned gaol cells. Events throughout the year.
Times: Open 3 Jan-28 Mar, Mon and Wed-Sat, 1030-1600; Sun, 1300-1600. 29 Mar-31 Oct, Mon-Sat, 1030-1700; Sun, 1300-1700 (last admission 1630). 1 Nov-19 Dec, Mon and Wed-Sat, 1030-1600; Sun, 1300-1600.
Fee: £3.00/free (up to 16yrs and accompanied by an adult)/£2.00.
Facilities: T(1 hr)

Ely
Oliver Cromwell's House Map ref. I8
See entry in Historic Houses section.

Ely
Stained Glass Museum Map ref. I8
Ely Cathedral
Tel: (01353) 660347 Web: www.sgm.abelgratis.com
A museum housing examples of stained glass from the 13th C. to the present day in specially lighted display boxes, with models of a modern workshop.
Times: Open 1 Jan-31 Mar, Mon-Fri, 1030-1630; Sat, 1030-1700; Sun, 1200-1630. 1 Apr-31 Oct, Mon-Fri, 1030-1700; Sat, 1030-1730; Sun, 1200-1800. 1 Nov-31 Dec, Mon-Fri, 1030-1630; Sat, 1030-1700; Sun, 1200-1630. Last admission half an hour before closing. Closed 9 Apr and 25, 26 Dec.
Fee: £3.50/£2.50/£2.50/£7.00.
Facilities: T(40 mins)

Eynesbury (nr. St. Neots)
St. Neots Picture Gallery Map ref. D11
23 St. Mary's Street
Tel: (01480) 215291
Watercolours, pastels and photographs of St. Neots and surrounding area. Comprehensive range of artists materials.
Times: Open all year, Tues-Fri, 0900-1730; Sat, 0900-1700. Closed 9-12 Apr and 25 Dec-3 Jan.
Fee: Free.
Facilities: T(30 mins)

Great Staughton (nr. St. Neots)
Taggart Tile Museum Map ref. C10
Robin Hood Cottage
Tel: (01480) 860314 Web: www.taggartgallery.co.uk
15th C. cottage (next to the church), housing a permanent and extensive exhibition of tiles covering the period of 1650-2000.
Times: Open all year, Wed-Sat, 0930-1700; Sun (Oct-May), 1100-1500. Closed 24 Dec-3 Jan.
Fee: Free.
Facilities: T(30 mins)

Huntingdon
Blacked-Out Britain War Museum Map ref. D9
1 St. Marys Street
Tel: (01480) 450998
Everyday items of life from 1939-45. From evacuation to rationing, bus tickets to bombs.
Times: Open all year, Mon-Sat, 0900-1700; Sun, 1000-1400. Closed 11 Apr and 25, 26 Dec.
Fee: Free.
Facilities: T(30 mins)

Huntingdon

Cromwell Museum Map ref. D9
Grammar School Walk
Tel: (01480) 375830 Web: www.cromwell.argonet.co.uk
A museum with portraits, signed documents and other articles belonging to Cromwell and his family.
Times: Open 1 Apr-31 Oct, Tues-Fri, 1100-1300 and 1400-1700; Sat and Sun, 1100-1300 and 1400-1600. 1 Nov-31 Mar 2005, Tues-Fri, 1300-1600; Sat, 1100-1300 and 1400-1600; Sun, 1400-1600.
Fee: Free.
Facilities: T(1 hr)

March

March and District Museum Map ref. G5/6
High Street
Tel: (01354) 655300
A general collection of artefacts relating to social history, agricultural tools, many local photographs and records. A restored blacksmith's forge and Victorian cottage parlour.
Times: Open all year, Wed and Sat, 1030-1530. Suns - 6 Jun; 4 Jul; 1 Aug and 5 Sept, 1400-1630.
Fee: Free.
Facilities: P T(1 hr)

Parson Drove (nr. Wisbech)

The Cage Map ref. F4
The Village Green, Station Road
Tel: (01945) 700501
Built in 1829 by John Peck as a lock-up. The clock tower was added in 1897. Houses displays covering the history of the building and local land drainage.
Times: Open 18 Apr-26 Sept, Wed and Sun, 1400-1700.
Fee: Free.
Facilities: P T(45 mins)

Peterborough

Flag Fen Bronze Age Centre Map ref. D5
See entry in Ancient Monuments section.

Peterborough

Peterborough Museum and Art Gallery Map ref. D5
Priestgate
Tel: (01733) 343329
Web: www.peterboroughheritage.org.uk
Museum of local history, geology, archaeology, natural and social history. World-famous collection of Napoleonic POW work. Varied programme of temporary exhibitions and weekend events. Local ghost walk.
Times: Open all year, school term time, Tues-Fri, 1200-1700. School hols, Tues-Sat, 1000-1700; Sun and Bank Hol Mon, 1200-1600. Closed 1 Jan, 9-12 Apr and 24-26 Dec.
Fee: Free.
Facilities: T(1½ hrs)

Flag Fen Bronze Age Centre, Peterborough

Ramsey

Ramsey Rural Museum Map ref. E7
Wood Lane
Tel: (01487) 815715/814304 Web: www.ramseytown.com
17th C. farm buildings with collection covering the history of Fenland life. Well restored agricultural machinery, Victorian chemists, cobblers, blacksmiths and schoolroom. Local and family history archive.
Times: Open 1 Apr-30 Sept, Thurs, 1000-1700; Sun and Bank Hols, 1400-1700.
Fee: £2.00/£1.00/£1.00.
Facilities: P T(1-3 hrs)

St. Ives

Norris Museum Map ref. E/F9
The Broadway
Tel: (01480) 497314
Museum displaying the history of Huntingdon from earliest times to the present day with fossils, archaeology, history, an art gallery and library.
Times: Open 2 Jan-30 Apr, Mon-Fri, 1000-1300 and 1400-1600; Sat 1000-1200. 1 May-30 Sept, Mon-Fri, 1000-1300 and 1400-1700; Sat, 1000-1200 and 1400-1700; Sun, 1400-1700. 1 Oct-31 Dec, Mon-Fri, 1000-1300 and 1400-1600; Sat, 1000-1200. Closed 9 Apr, 25-28 Dec and 1 Jan.
Fee: Free.
Facilities: T(1 hr)

St. Neots

Saint Neots Museum Map ref. C/D11
The Old Court, 8 New Street
Tel: (01480) 214163
A former police station and Magistrates' Court, now housing the local history museum.
Times: Open 4 Feb-18 Dec, Wed-Sat, 1030-1630. Closed 25 and 26 Dec.
Fee: £2.00/£1.00.
Facilities: T(45 mins)

Thorney

Thorney Heritage Museum Map ref. E4
Station Road
Tel: (01733) 270780
Showing the development from monastic days, Walloon and Flemish influence after Vermuydens drainage; also 19th C. model housing by the Duke of Bedford.
Times: Open 10 Apr-26 Sept, Sat and Sun, 1400-1700.
Fee: Free.
Facilities: T(45 mins)

Thornhaugh (nr. Peterborough)

Sacrewell Farm and Country Centre Map ref. B5
Sacrewell
Tel: (01780) 782254 Web: www.sacrewell.org.uk
A 500-acre farm with a working watermill, farmhouse gardens, shrubberies, farm/nature/general interest trails, 18th C. buildings, displays of the farm, bygones and animals.
Times: Open all year, daily, 0930-1700. Closed 24 Dec-2 Jan.
Fee: £3.50/£2.00/£2.50/£9.00.
Facilities: T(3 hrs)

Waterbeach (nr. Cambridge)

The Farmland Museum and Denny Abbey Map ref. H10
Ely Road
Tel: (01223) 860988/860489
Web: www.dennyfarmlandmuseum.org.uk
An agricultural estate since medieval times, with an abbey and an interactive museum. Remains of 12th C. Benedictine abbey, and a 14th C. hall of a religious house.
Times: Please contact for details of opening times.
Fee: Please contact for details of admission prices.
Facilities: T(1½ hrs) EH

Wendy (nr. Royston)

British Museum of Miniatures Map ref. F13
Maple Street
Tel: (01223) 207025 Web: www.maplestreet.co.uk
Dolls house and miniatures museum, including the largest dolls house in the world. Dolls house and miniatures shop. New crafts and toy department.
Times: Open all year, Mon-Sat, 1000-1700; Sun, 1200-1600. Please ring for Bank Hol opening times. Closed 25, 26 Dec and 1 Jan.
Fee: £2.50/£1.50.
Facilities: T(2 hrs)

Whittlesey

Whittlesey Museum Map ref. E5/6
Town Hall, Market Street
Tel: (01733) 840986
Museum of archaeology, agriculture, hand tools, brickmaking, local photographs, a Sir Harry Smith exhibition, costume display and temporary exhibitions.
Times: Open all year, Fri and Sun, 1430-1630; Sat, 1000-1200. Closed 26 Dec.
Fee: 50p/20p.
Facilities: T(1 hr)

Wisbech

Octavia Hill Birthplace Museum Map ref. H4
1 South Brink Place
Tel: (01945) 476358 Web: www.octaviahillmuseum.org
Grade II* Georgian house in which Octavia Hill, social reformer and co-founder of the National Trust was born. Museum commemorates her life, work and legacy.
Times: Open 17 Mar-31 Oct, Wed, Sat, Sun and Bank Hol Mon, 1400-1730 (last admission 1700). Closed 25 and 26 Dec.
Fee: £2.00/free.
Facilities: T(1 hr)

Wisbech

Skylark Studios Map ref. G2/3
Hannath Road, Tydd Gote
Tel: (01945) 420403 Web: www.skylarkstudios.co.uk
An art gallery showing monthly exhibitions by local and national artists, along with a permanent display of art and crafts.
Times: Open all year, Tues-Sat, 1000-1700. Closed 11, 12 Apr and 25 Dec-6 Jan.
Fee: Free.
Facilities: T(45 mins)

Wisbech

Wisbech and Fenland Museum Map ref. H4
Museum Square
Tel: (01945) 583817
One of the oldest purpose-built museums in the country, situated next to Wisbech's fine Georgian crescent. Displays on Fen landscape, local history, geology and archaeology.
Times: Open Jan-Mar, Tues-Sat, 1000-1600. Apr-Sept, Tues-Sat, 1000-1700. Oct-Dec, Tues-Sat, 1000-1600.
Fee: Free.
Facilities: T(45 mins)

Machinery & Transport

Burwell

Burwell Museum Map ref. J10

See entry in Museums & Galleries section.

Cambridge

Museum of Technology Map ref. H11

The Old Pumping Station, Cheddars Lane

Tel: (01223) 368650

Web: www.museumoftechnology.com

A Victorian pumping station housing unique Hathorn Davey steam pumping engines, electrical equipment and a working letterpress print shop. Hands-on pumps.

Times: Steaming days - 11, 12 Apr; 30, 31 May; 29, 30 Aug; 30, 31 Oct, 1100-1700. Non-steaming days - every Sun from Easter-Oct, plus 1st Sun in month from Jan-Easter and Nov/Dec, 1400-1700.

Fee: Steaming days - £4.00/£2.00/£2.00/£10.00. Non-steaming days - £2.00/£1.00/£1.00/£5.00.

Facilities: T(1 hr)

Duxford (nr. Cambridge)

Imperial War Museum Map ref. H13

Tel: (01223) 835000 Web: www.iwm.org.uk

One of the world's most spectacular aviation heritage complexes, with almost 200 aircraft on display. Collection of military vehicles, tanks and guns. Special exhibitions and air shows throughout the year.

Times: Open 1 Jan-12 Mar, daily, 1000-1600. 13 Mar-30 Oct, daily, 1000-1800. 31 Oct-31 Dec, daily, 1000-1600. Closed 24-26 Dec.

Fee: Please contact for details of admission prices.

Facilities: Q T(4 hrs)

Peterborough

Railworld Map ref. C5

Oundle Road

Tel: (01733) 344240 Web: www.railworld.net

Railworld highlights modern trains and the environment. Superb model railway, films and hands-on displays for children. 'Steam age' displays, large locomotives and hovertrains. Visitors have all day free parking

Times: Open 1 Jan-27 Feb, Mon-Fri, 1100-1600. 1 Mar-31 Oct, daily, 1100-1600. 1 Nov-31 Dec, Mon-Fri, 1100-1600. Closed 9 Apr.

Fee: £4.00/£2.00/£3.00/£10.00.

Facilities: T(1 hr)

Prickwillow

Prickwillow Drainage Engine Museum Map ref. J8
Main Street
Tel: (01353) 688360
A museum housing a Mirrlees Bickerton and Day diesel engine, a 5-cylinder, blast injection, 250 bhp working unit and a Vicker-Petter, 2-cylinder, 2-stroke diesel and others.
Times: Open 6 Mar-25 Apr, Sat, Sun and Bank Hols, 1100-1600. 1 May-28 Sept, Sun-Tues, Fri and Sat, 1100-1630. 2-31 Oct, Sat and Sun, 1100-1600. Special run days, please contact for details.
Fee: £2.00/£1.00/£1.50/£5.00. Run days £3.00/£1.50/£2.00/£7.00.
Facilities: T(1 hr)

Stibbington (nr. Peterborough)

Nene Valley Railway Map ref. B5
Wansford Station
Tel: (01780) 784444 Web: www.nvr.org.uk
A 7½ mile track between Wansford and Peterborough via Yarwell Jct and Nene Park, with over 28 steam and diesel locomotives. Regular steam trains operate over the line.
Times: Open all year, daily, 0930-1630. Closed 25 Dec. Please contact for details of train services.
Fee: Rover Ticket £10.00/£5.00/£7.50/£25.00. Other adult and child single/return tickets available.
Facilities: T(1-2 hrs)

Imperial War Museum, Duxford

Wimpole Hall and Home Farm. Arrington

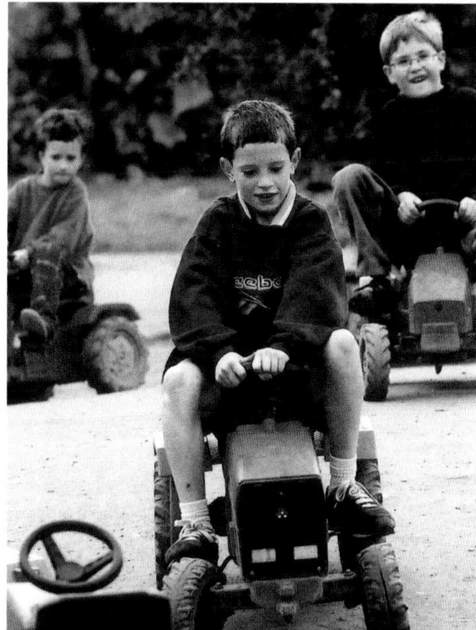

Mills

Houghton (nr. Huntingdon)

Houghton Mill Map ref. E9

Tel: (01480) 301494 Web: www.nationaltrust.org.uk

A large, timber-built watermill on an island in the River Ouse, with much of the 19th C. mill machinery intact and some restored to working order.

Times: Open 3 Apr-30 May, Sat and Sun, 1300-1700. 31 May-29 Sept, Sat-Wed, 1300-1700. 2-31 Oct, Sat and Sun, 1300-1700.

Fee: £3.20/£1.50/£7.00 (family).

Facilities: T(1 hr) NT

Lode (nr. Cambridge)

Anglesey Abbey, Gardens and Lode Mill Map ref. I11

See entry in Historic Houses section.

Swaffham Prior

The Windmill Map ref. I10/11

Tel: (01638) 741009 Web: www.fostersmill.co.uk

Four sailed working windmill, built in 1857, and worked commercially until 1946. Restored by the present owner, and producing stoneground flours. Visitors can climb the mill. Photographic display.

Times: Open 11 Jan; 8 Feb; 14 Mar; 4 Apr; 9 May; 13 Jun; 11 Jul; 8 Aug; 12 Sept; 10 Oct; 14 Nov; 12 Dec, Sun, 1300-1700.

Fee: Free. Donations appreciated.

Facilities: T(30 mins)

Thornhaugh (nr. Peterborough)

Sacrewell Farm and Country Centre Map ref. B5

See entry in Museums & Galleries section.

Wicken (nr. Soham)

Wicken Corn Windmill Map ref. I9

23 High Street

Tel: (01664) 822751 Web: www.geocities.com/wickenmill

One of the country's finest windmills, built in the 19th C. Probably the world's only working 12-sided smock windmill. The mill grinds wholemeal flour on open days.

Times: Open all year. Jan and Feb, 1st Sat in month, 1000-1730. Mar-Nov, 1st Sat and Sun in month, 1000-1730. Dec, 1st Sat in month, 1000-1730.

Fee: Free. Donations appreciated.

Facilities: T(1 hr)

Wicken (nr. Soham)

Wicken Fen National Nature Reserve Map ref. I10

See entry in Countryside section.

DID YOU KNOW

The village of Warboys (nr. Huntingdon) became renowned for one of the most notorious trials in English witch-hunting, when in the 16th C. a 10 year old girl of a prosperous local family fell ill, and a neighbour Alice Samuel was accused of witchcraft.

Wicken Fen National Nature Reserve

Gardens

Arrington (nr. Royston)
Wimpole Hall and Home Farm Map ref. F12
See entry in Historic Houses section.

Cambridge
Cambridge University Botanic Garden Map ref. H12
Bateman Street
Tel: (01223) 336265 Web: www.botanic.cam.ac.uk
Forty-acre oasis of beautiful gardens and glasshouses, with some 10,000 plant species. Rock, winter and dry gardens, tropical rainforest and lake. Unique systematic beds and several important plant collections.
Times: Open all year. Feb and Oct, daily, 1000-1700. Mar-Sept, daily, 1000-1800 (glasshouses close at 1630). Jan, Nov and Dec, daily, 1000-1600 (glasshouses close at 1545). Closed 25 Dec-1 Jan.
Fee: £2.50/£2.00/£2.00.
Facilities: T(3½ hrs) (daily in summer, weekends only in winter)

Elton (nr. Peterborough)
Elton Hall Map ref. B6
See entry in Historic Houses section.

Hemingford Grey (nr. St. Ives)
The Manor Map ref. E9
See entry in Historic Houses section.

Lode (nr. Cambridge)
Anglesey Abbey, Gardens and Lode Mill Map ref. I11
See entry in Historic Houses section.

Nassington (nr. Peterborough)
The Prebendal Manor Medieval Centre Map ref. B6
See entry in Historic Houses section.

Shepreth
Crossing House Map ref. G13
78 Meldreth Road
Tel: (01763) 261071
The crossing keeper's cottage and a small plantsman's garden with a very wide variety of plants.
Times: Open all year, daily, dawn-dusk.
Fee: Free.
Facilities: T(1 hr)

Elton Hall

Shepreth
Docwra's Manor Garden Map ref. G13
2 Meldreth Road
Tel: (01763) 261473
Walled gardens around an 18th C. red-brick house, approached by 18th C. wrought iron gates. There are barns, a 20th C. folly and unusual plants.
Times: Open all year, Wed and Fri, 1000-1600. 7 Mar; 4 Apr; 2, 9 May; 6 Jun; 4 Jul; 1 Aug; 5 Sept; 3 Oct, Sun 1400-1600. Closed Easter and Christmas.
Fee: £3.00/free/£3.00.
Facilities: P T(1½ hrs)

Walpole St. Peter (nr. Wisbech)
Walpole Water Gardens Map ref. H3
Chalk Road
Tel: 07718 745935
Dominated by water and rocks, with a sub-tropical atmosphere, 3/4 acres. Eucalyptus, rockeries and palms. Koi carp, black swans, ducks and peacocks.
Times: Open all year, daily, summer 1000-2100; winter 1000-1900.
Fee: Free.
Facilities: P T(30 mins)

Wilburton (nr. Ely)
Herb Garden Map ref. H9
Nigel House, 67 High Street
Tel: (01353) 740824
A herb garden laid out in collections: culinary, aromatic, medical, biblical, Shakespearean, dye bed and astrological.
Times: Open 1 May-30 Sept, daily. Please phone to confirm times.
Fee: Free.
Facilities: P T(1 hr)

Wisbech
Elgood's Brewery and Garden Map ref. H4
See entry in Food & Drink section.

Wisbech
Peckover House and Gardens Map ref. H4
See entry in Historic Houses section.

Nurseries & Garden Centres

Cambridge

Notcutts (Ansells) Garden Centres Map ref. H11
High Street, Horningsea, Cambridge CB5 9JG
Tel: (01223) 860320 Web: www.notcutts.co.uk
Discover a world of ideas and inspiration around every corner for you, your home and your garden. From fabulous plants to gifts and treats galore, there's so much to see. Gift ideas from around the world, houseplants, books, fresh cut and silk flowers, 3,000 varieties of hardy plants (with a 2 year replacement guarantee), pet centre, restaurant, expert friendly advice about seasonal and bedding plants, garden furniture and barbecues. Keep an eye open for regular offers on key garden products. Notcutts open 7 days a week, free car-parking plus children's play area.

Peterborough

Notcutts Garden Centres Map ref. D5
Oundle Road, Orton Waterville, nr. Peterborough PE2 5UU
Tel: (01733) 234600 Web: www.notcutts.co.uk
Discover a world of ideas and inspiration around every corner for you, your home and your garden. From fabulous plants to gifts and treats galore, there's so much to see. Gift ideas from around the world, houseplants, books, fresh cut and silk flowers, 3,000 varieties of hardy plants (with a 2 year replacement guarantee), pet centre, restaurant, expert friendly advice about seasonal and bedding plants, garden furniture and barbecues. Keep an eye open for regular offers on key garden products. Notcutts open 7 days a week, free car-parking plus children's play area.

DID YOU KNOW

Peterborough Cathedral contains a memorial to Robert Scarlett, a Tudor gravedigger who buried both Katherine of Aragon and Mary Queen of Scots. He is also claimed to have buried two members of each Peterborough household during his life.

Benwick

Family Fun

Animal & Bird Collections

Arrington (nr. Royston)

Wimpole Hall and Home Farm Map ref. F12
See entry in Historic Houses section.

Godmanchester

Wood Green Animal Shelters Map ref. E10
King's Bush Farm, London Road
Tel: (01480) 830014 Web: www.woodgreen.org.uk
Europe's busiest animal rescue and rehoming site with lots to see, including farm animals, cats, dogs and small animals. Some permanent residents, others awaiting caring new homes.
Times: Open all year, daily, 1000-1600. Closed 25 Dec.
Fee: Free.
Facilities: P T(1½ hrs)

Linton

Linton Zoo Map ref. I13
Hadstock Road
Tel: (01223) 891308
The zoo has big cats, lynx, wallabies, lemurs, toucans, parrots and reptiles, a wonderful combination of beautiful gardens and wildlife.
Times: Open all year, daily, please contact for times. Closed 25 and 26 Dec.
Fee: £6.00/£4.50 (up to 13 yrs)/£5.50.
Facilities: P T(6 hrs)

St. Ives

Sawtry

Hamerton Zoo Park Map ref. C8
Tel: (01832) 293362 Web: www.hamertonzoopark.com
A wildlife park with tigers, lemurs, marmosets, meerkats, wallabies, and a unique bird collection with rare and exotic species from around the world.
Times: Open all year, daily, from 1030. Closed 25 Dec.
Fee: Please contact for details of admission prices.
Facilities: P T(3 hrs)

Shepreth (nr. Royston)

Shepreth Wildlife Park (Willersmill) Map ref. G13
Station Road
Tel: (01763) 262226 Web: www.sheprethwildlifepark.co.uk
A great day out for the whole family. See tigers, puma, lynx, wolves, reptiles and many more, at one of East Anglia's major attractions. See our full page advert on page 114.
Times: Open all year, daily, summer, 1000-1800; winter, 1000-dusk. Closed 25 Dec.
Fee: £5.50/£3.95/£4.50.
Facilities: Q P T(4 hrs)

DID YOU KNOW

The Wandlebury Country Park (nr. Cambridge) is the burial site of the famous breeding stallion, The Godolphin Arabian. It is said to be the racehorse that all others are descended from.

Thornhaugh (nr. Peterborough)
Sacrewell Farm and Country Centre Map ref. B5
See entry in Museums & Galleries section.

Woodhurst (nr. Huntingdon)
The Raptor Foundation Map ref. E9
The Heath, St. Ives Road
Tel: (01487) 741140 Web: www.raptorfoundation.org.uk
A collection of injured birds of prey and wild birds. Hand-reared owls used for fund raising for the hospital. Tearoom, gift shop, craft village and falconry flying area.
Times: Open all year, daily, 1030-1700. Closed 25 Dec and 1 Jan.
Fee: £3.50/£2.00/£2.50.
Facilities: Q T(3 hrs)

Amusement/Theme Centres & Parks

Milton (nr. Cambridge)
The Milton Maize Maze Map ref. H11
Rectory Farm Shop, A10 Milton Bypass
Tel: (01223) 860374
Web: www.rectoryfarmshop.co.uk/maizemaze
A giant walk through puzzle to challenge any age! A field full of family fun. Farm shop. New for 2004 - pets' paddock and small coffee shop.
Times: Maze open 17 Jul-5 Sept, daily, 1000-1700 (last entry at 1615).
Fee: £3.00/£2.00/£10.00 (family).
Facilities: T(2 hrs)

Children's Indoor Play Centres

Peterborough
Activity World Map ref. D5
Padholme Road East
Tel: (01733) 314446 Web: www.activityworld.co.uk
An indoor and outdoor adventure playground, plus the Laser Maze arena.
Times: Open all year, daily, 0930-1830. Closed 25, 26 Dec and 1 Jan.
Fee: Activity World £1.00/£3.95. Laser Maze £3.00/£3.00.
Facilities: T(1½ hrs)

Peterborough
Big Sky Adventure Play Map ref. C6
24 Wainman Road, Shrewsbury Avenue, Woodston
Tel: (01733) 390810
An indoor children's soft play activities centre, with electric mini go-karts and a monorail rocket ship ride. Trampoline arena, plus six metre climbing wall.
Times: Open all year, daily, 1030-1830. Closed 25, 26 Dec and 1 Jan.
Fee: Main play area £4.50. Pre-school play area £3.50. Extra charge for go-karts, monorail and climbing wall.
Facilities: T(2 hrs)

Leisure Pools

Cambridge
Parkside Pools Map ref. H11
Gonville Place
Tel: (01223) 446100
Web: www.cambridge.gov.uk/leisure/parkside.htm
Eight lane 25 metre pool, diving pool, two giant flume rides, children's water area and health suite.
Times: Open all year. Mon-Fri, 0700-2130; Sat and Sun, 0800-1730; Bank Hol Mon, 0800-1730. Closed 0900-1000 on Mon. Closes at 1600 on Tues, and 1700 on Thurs.
Fee: Prices vary depending upon activity.
Facilities: T(2-3 hrs)

Linton Zoo

DID YOU KNOW

Grafham Water (nr. Huntingdon) is the third largest man-made reservoir in Britain. Constructed in the 1960's, it covers 2½ square miles, and holds 59,000 million litres of water.

Countryside

The countryside of Cambridgeshire is one of contrasts, from the distinctive flat plains of The Fens in the north of the county, to the chalk downland of the Gog Magog Hills (named after the legendary giants) in the south. Around Peterborough you will find the Nene Valley with its quaint old cottages, or follow the river south from Huntingdon along the pretty Ouse Valley. The county has a higher proportion of quality land than any other county in England, with large-scale cereal crops, vegetables, fruit and flowers.

Special Areas

The Fens - stretching out from the Wash, the Fen landscape of today is the result of man's desire to tame and control this former wet wilderness, and in turn, create some of the most fertile land in Britain. The Romans were the first to try their hand at drainage, but it was not until the 17th C. that a major scheme was undertaken, with expert engineers such as Cornelius Vermuyden. Today you can discover a unique panorama, criss-crossed by waterways, and offering stunning skyscapes and unforgettable sunsets. This is also one of the country's most important wildlife areas, home to an array of birdlife. More information at www.visitthefens.co.uk

Country Parks & Nature Reserves

Arrington (nr. Royston)
Wimpole Hall and Home Farm Map ref. F12
See entry in Historic Houses section.

Babraham (nr. Cambridge)
Wandlebury Country Park Map ref. H12
Wandlebury Ring, Gog Magog Hills
Tel: (01223) 243830 Web: www.cpswandlebury.org
Countryside park and nature reserve, the site of an Iron Age ring ditch. Woodlands, circular walks, wildlife and public footpaths leading to a Roman road.
Times: Open all year, daily, dawn-dusk.
Fee: £2.00 car park charge.
Facilities: P T(2 hrs)

Brampton (nr. Huntingdon)
Brampton Wood Map ref. C10
Tel: (01223) 712400 Web: www.wildlifetrust.org.uk/bcnp
Consists primarily of ash and field maple with hazel coppice. Supports wide variety of plants and animals, and is particularly well known for butterflies. CWT.
Times: Open all year, daily, any reasonable time.
Fee: Free.
Facilities: P T(4 hrs)

Fowlmere (nr. Royston)
RSPB Fowlmere Nature Reserve Map ref. G13
Tel: (01763) 208978 Web: www.rspb.org.uk
An 100-acre nature reserve incorporating a nature trail and three bird-watching hides. Attractions include unspoilt wetland scenery and birdlife including the kingfisher.
Times: Open at any reasonable time.
Fee: Admission free to RSPB members, donations requested from non-members.
Facilities: P T(3 hrs)

Gamlingay (nr. Sandy)
Gamlingay Wood Map ref. D12
Tel: (01223) 712400 Web: www.wildlifetrust.org.uk/bcnp
Ancient ash and maple wood, which grows on a mixture of soils and contains an unusual variety of woodland types. Special habitat for mosses, fungi and insects. New woodland creation project. CWT.
Times: Open all year, daily, any reasonable time.
Fee: Free.
Facilities: P T(2 hrs)

Grafham (nr. Huntingdon)
Grafham Water Map ref. C10
Tel: (01480) 812154 Web: www.anglianwater.co.uk
Water park with extensive views, sailing, trout fishing, nature reserve, trails and walks, picnic areas, play areas, refreshments and gift shop.
Times: Open 3 Jan-28 Mar, daily, 1100-1600. 29 Mar-31 Oct, Mon-Fri, 1100-1600; Sat, Sun and Bank Hols, 1100-1700. 1 Nov-19 Dec, daily, 1100-1600.
Fee: Car park charge £2.00 (1 Apr-30 Sept); £1.00 (Oct-Mar).
Facilities: P T(3 hrs) (on leads)

DID YOU KNOW

The village of Stilton (nr. Peterborough) is where the famous cheese was first distributed from (not made). This is celebrated each May Bank Holiday, by rolling wooden 'cheeses' down the High Street.

Huntingdon

Hinchingbrooke Country Park Map ref. D9
Brampton Road
Tel: (01480) 451568
Web: www.huntsleisure.org/countryside/hinchingbrooke
Open grasslands, meadows, woodlands and lakes covering 180 acres with a wealth of wildlife. Ideal for family outings and picnics. Visitor centre.
Times: Open all year, daily, any reasonable time.
Fee: Free.
Facilities: T(2 hrs)

Longstowe (nr. St. Neots)

Hayley Wood Map ref. E12
Tel: (01223) 712400 Web: www.wildlifetrust.org.uk/bcnp
Mostly ancient woodland of oak, ash and maple - resplendent with bluebells and oxlips in spring. Whilst in summer the rides and glades are filled with wildflowers and butterflies. CWT.
Times: Open at any reasonable time.
Fee: Free.
Facilities: T(2 hrs)

March

RSPB Ouse Washes Map ref. H7
Welches Dam
Tel: (01354) 680212 Web: www.rspb.org.uk
Nature reserve in the heart of the Fens, with ten bird-watching hides, visitor centre and a programme of events.
Times: Open at any reasonable time.
Fee: Free
Facilities: T(2 hrs)

Milton (nr. Cambridge)

Milton Country Park Map ref. H11
Cambridge Road
Tel: (01223) 420060 Web: www.scambs.gov.uk
Milton Country Park comprises 95 acres of woodland, grass and water areas with many sites for picnics, and a play area for children.
Times: Open all year, daily, from 0800. Closing times vary throughout the year. Closed 25 Dec.
Fee: Free.
Facilities: T(2 hrs)

St. Neots

Paxton Pits Nature Reserve Map ref. D11
High Street, Little Paxton
Tel: (01480) 406795 Web: www.paxton-pits.org.uk
Restored gravel pits, made up of lakes, meadows, grassland, scrub and woodland. Famous for its nightingales in summer and wildfowl in winter. Visitor centre, trails and bird-watching hides.
Times: Open all year, daily, dawn-dusk.
Fee: Free.
Facilities: T(3 hrs)

Waresley

Waresley and Gransden Woods Map ref. E12
Tel: (01223) 712400 Web: www.wildlifetrust.org.uk/bcnp
Both woods are fine examples of the ancient woodland which once covered much of the boulder clay uplands in this area. Both woods are ash and oak. New Woodland creation project. CWT.
Times: Open at any reasonable time.
Fee: Free.
Facilities: T(2 hrs)

Wansford

Welney

Wildfowl and Wetlands Trust Map ref. I6
Hundred Foot Bank
Tel: (01353) 860711 Web: www.wwt.org.uk
A wetland nature reserve of 1,000 acres attracting large numbers of ducks and swans in winter, waders in spring and summer, plus a range of wild plants and butterflies.
Times: Open all year, daily, 1000-1700. Closed 25 Dec.
Fee: £3.65/£2.00/£2.90/£9.25.
Facilities: Q T(2 hrs)

Wicken (nr. Soham)

Wicken Fen National Nature Reserve Map ref. I10
Tel: (01353) 720274 Web: www.wicken.org.uk
The last remaining undrained portion of the great Fen levels of East Anglia, rich in plant and invertebrate life, and good for birds. Also a working windpump and restored Fen cottage.
Times: Open all year, daily except Mon (unless Bank Hol Mon), 1000-1700. Closed 25 Dec.
Fee: £3.90/£1.25/£3.90.
Facilities: T(2½ hrs) NT

Picnic Sites

Brandon Creek picnic site - beside A10, 3½ miles north of Littleport. Map ref. J6
Bryon's Pool (Grantchester) - on Grantchester Road, 2 miles south of Cambridge (off A1309 at Trumpington). Map ref. G12
High Lode - on the Great Whyte Road (B1040) at Ramsey. Map ref. E7
Holywell Front - 7 miles east from Huntingdon, off the A1123 at Needingworth, then south to Holywell. Map ref. F9
Magog Down picnic site - beside minor road off A1307, 1¾ miles south east of Cambridge. Map ref. H12
Riverside Park - on minor road between Shepreth and Barrington, 7 miles south west of Cambridge (off A10). Map ref. G13
St. Neots Riverside Park - off the B1428 in the centre of the town, just off Market Square. Map ref. C/D11
Southery Wood (Forest Enterprise) - off minor road between Upton and Ufford, 5 miles north west of Peterborough. Map ref. B5

DID YOU KNOW

The Old Cavendish Laboratory on Free School Lane in Cambridge is where the atom was spilt for the first time in 1932. Then in the 1950's, DNA was discovered here.

Countryside Organisations - Cambridgeshire

English Nature (Cambridgeshire)
Ham Lane House, Ham Lane, Nene Park, Orton Waterville, nr. Peterborough, Cambs PE2 5UR
Tel: (01733) 405850 Web: www.english-nature.gov.uk

Forest Enterprise - East Anglia Forest District
Santon Downham, nr. Brandon, Suffolk IP27 0TJ
Tel: (01842) 810271 Web: www.forestry.gov.uk

The National Trust - Regional Office for East Anglia
Angel Corner, 8 Angel Hill, Bury St. Edmunds, Suffolk IP33 1UZ
Tel: 0870 609 5388 Web: www.nationaltrust.org.uk

The Royal Society for the Protection of Birds (RSPB) - Regional Office for East Anglia
Stalham House, 65 Thorpe Road, Norwich, Norfolk NR1 1UD
Tel: (01603) 661662 Web: www.rspb.org.uk

The Wildlife Trust (Cambridgeshire) (CWT)
3B Langford Arch, London Road, Sawston, nr. Cambridge, Cambridgeshire CB2 4EE
Tel: (01223) 712400 Web: www.wildlifetrust.org.uk/bcnp

Houghton Mill

Activities

Boat Trips

Cambridge
Riverboat Georgina Map ref. H11
Jubilee Gardens, Jesus Lock, Chesterton Road
Tel: (01223) 307694 Web: www.georgina.co.uk
River cruises with a 1st class service in the magnificent surroundings of the River Cam. Private charter available.
Times: Please contact for details of opening times.
Fee: Various rates, including 2hr river cruise £10.00/£7.00/£10.00.
Facilities: T(2 hrs)

Peterborough
Key Ferry Cruises Map ref. C5
The Embankment
Tel: (01933) 680743
30 min river trips from Ferry Meadows Country Park, with full commentary. Private charter trips from Peterborough.
Times: Please contact for details of opening times.
Fee: £2.20/£1.20/£2.20 (Ferry Meadows trips).
Facilities: T(1 hr)

Golf Courses

Peterborough
Orton Meadows Golf Course Map ref. C6
Ham Lane, Orton Waterville PE2 5UU
Tel: (01733) 237478
Email: Enquiries@ortonmeadowsgolfcourse.co.uk
Web: www.ortonmeadowsgolfcourse.co.uk
18 holes, 5613 yards Par 67. Top Pay As You Play Course with lakes and streams in picturesque setting surrounded by trees. Booking necessary. Club/Trolley hire available.
Web: www.experiencedgolfclubs.co.uk
Orton Meadows hosts Eastern England's only Golf Factory Clearance Shop providing excellent value and top quality refurbished second hand clubs. P

Peterborough
Orton Meadows Pitch & Putt Course Map ref. C6
Ham Lane, Orton Waterville PE2 5UU
Tel: (01733) 237478
This 12 hole Pitch & Putt Course is very popular with players of all ages and all levels, and provides fun for all the family. An introduction to the game for those who would like to take up golf, or opportunity for players to improve their short game. Clubs and Balls provided.

Peterborough
Thorpe Wood Golf Course Map ref. C5
Thorpe Wood PE3 6SE
Tel: (01733) 267701
Email: Enquiries@thorpewoodgolfcourse.co.uk
Web: www.thorpewoodgolfcourse.co.uk
18 holes, 7086 yards, Par 73. Top UK Pay As you Play Course designed by Peter Alliss and Dave Thomas (designers of The Belfry), set in undulating parkland maintained in superb condition and always open whatever the weather. Popular with golfers of all ages/abilities. Booking necessary. Club/Trolley hire available. P

Ramsey
Old Nene Golf and Country Club Ltd Map ref. E7
Muchwood Lane, Bodsey
Tel: (01487) 815622
Quality Golf Course, 9 holes, 18 tees, floodlit driving range, fishing and fully licensed bar. (Eastern Area Environmental Winner 1996). Excellent drainage and well constructed greens mean play is possible throughout the year. Measuring (5.675) yards par 68 the fairways are separated by numerous trees and wildlife.

Cambridge

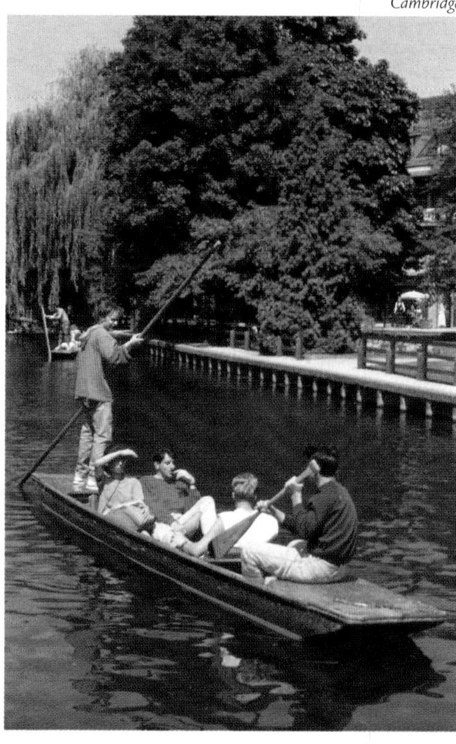

Cycling

Katherine's Wheels is a 15 mile circular route starting at Grafham Water (nr. Huntingdon), and travelling via the final two residences of Queen Katherine of Aragon (includes the mainly off-road circuit of 10 miles around the reservoir). The Peterborough Green Wheel (North) takes you on a 29 mile journey to the north of the city, including cream-coloured villages and prehistoric remains. Or head to Wisbech to try the Apples and Ale route (13 miles), combining acres of fruit orchards with a chance to try a pint of real ale at a Georgian brewery. Saleable maps for these three routes from the East of England Tourist Board on 0870 225 4852. For more information on cycling in the county contact the Countryside Services Team at Cambridgeshire County Council on (01223) 717445, or visit www.camcnty.gov.uk/sub/cntryside They have a range of leaflets and information available (small charge), including Spokes & Saddles (six routes near Ely), Cycling in the Fens - with routes around March and Wisbech, and Cycling in the Ouse Valley - pretty waterside and countryside based routes in the Huntingdon, St. Ives and St. Neots area.

The Fens Cycle Way - discover the unique panorama of the Fens, criss-crossed by waterways, and offering stunning skyscapes and unforgettable sunsets. This cycle pack contains two separate loops, one starting at Wisbech (40 miles) and the other at Ely (34 miles). They are shown on two fold-out maps, together with an information guide containing places to stay and cycle hire information. This saleable pack is available from the East of England Tourist Board on 0870 225 4852.

Walking

Long Distance Walks

Black Fen Trail (65 miles) - way-marked circular route linking Ely, March and Downham Market. Information on walk (including other Fenland trails) from Fens Tourism, Ayscoughfee Hall, Churchgate, Spalding, Lincolnshire PE11 2RA. Tel: (01775) 722773.
The Fen Rivers Way (50 miles) - runs from Cambridge to The Wash in Norfolk. Saleable guide to route available from Bernard Hawes, 52 Maid's Causeway, Cambridge, Cambridgeshire CB5 8DD. Tel: (01223) 560033.
The Hereward Way (110 miles) - runs from Oakham (nr. Stamford), via Peterborough, March, Ely and Brandon to East Harling in Norfolk. A leaflet covering the Cambridgeshire section is available from the Countryside Services Team (Cambridgeshire County Council) on (01223) 717445.
The Icknield Way Path (105 miles) - runs from Ivinghoe Beacon (Buckinghamshire) to Knettishall Heath Country Park (Suffolk), passing through parts of Cambridgeshire. Saleable guide available from the Icknield Way Association, 19 Boundary Road, Bishop's Stortford, Hertfordshire CM23 5LE. Tel: (01279) 504602.
The Ouse Valley Way (26 miles) - runs from Bluntisham to Eaton Socon, following the River Great Ouse. It can be shortened into six circular routes. Saleable guide to route available from Huntingdon Tourist Information Centre on (01480) 388588.

Shorter Walks

Your first port of call should be the Countryside Services Team at Cambridgeshire County Council on (01223) 717445. Visit their web site www.camcnty.gov.uk/sub/cntryside for lots of information on walks around the county, plus a range of saleable guides and leaflets. This includes a pack of 10 Cambridgeshire based walks and 'Footloose & Car Free' routes. For a walk beside the water, try The Nene Way, a 10 mile waymarked trail along the River Nene, nr. Peterborough - leaflet on (01223) 717445; or the 10 mile circuit around the shores of Grafham Water, Britain's third largest reservoir - more information on (01480) 812154. Discover the unique Fenland landscape on The Bishops Way, a circular 9 mile route from Ely; The Woodmans Way, a circular route of 6 miles from March, or on one of the circular walks around the Fen villages of Haddenham, Manea, Mepal, Stretham and Wicken - leaflets for all these walks on (01223) 717445. Take a walk through history on the 7th C. defensive earthwork of the Devil's Dyke, with walks of 1-9 miles in length - leaflet on (01223) 717445; go in search of the 5th C. Iron Age hill fort at Wandlebury Country Park - more information on (01223) 243830; or walk to 18th C. Wimpole Hall from Cambridge on the 13 mile Wimpole Way - leaflet on (01223) 717445. Of course don't forget the area's country parks, with their various walks and nature trails - see the 'Countryside' section for further information.

Peterborough

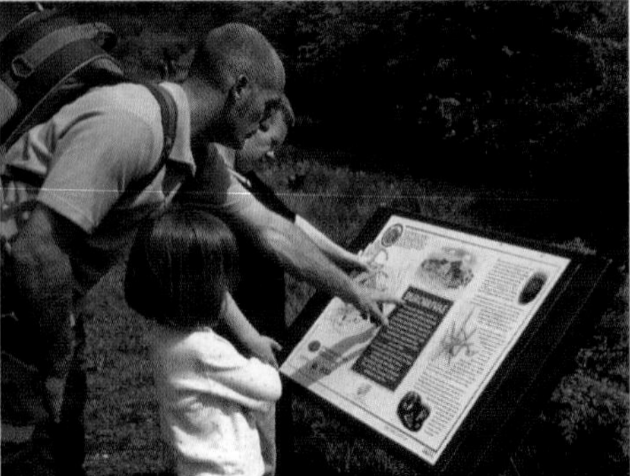

Food & Drink

Regional Produce

Cambridgeshire is home of The Fens 'the food basket of Britain', noted for some of the most fertile soil in the country - the rich dark peat used to grow cereals, flowers, fruit and vegetables. Pick up some of this delicious produce from the many markets, farm shops and road side stalls. Surrounding Wisbech you will find apple orchards and soft fruits, whilst carrots and celery thrive around Ely. A local Fen delicacy is eel, a common fish in the waterways here, alongside bream, roach, rudd, pike and zander. The village of Stilton is named after the famous English cheese. Although not made here, the cheese was distributed from the village, and every May this is celebrated by rolling wooden cheeses down the High Street. Wash all this down with a tasting of fine English wine at Chilford Hall Vineyard (nr. Linton), or a pint of real ale at Elgood's Georgian brewery in Wisbech.

Grafham Water, nr. Huntingdon

Breweries & Vineyards

Linton

Chilford Hall Vineyard Map ref. I13
Chilford Hundred Limited, Balsham Road, Linton, nr. Cambridge CB1 6LE
Tel: (01223) 895625 Web: www.chilfordhall.co.uk
Taste and buy award winning wines from the largest vineyard in Cambridgeshire. See the grapes growing in the eighteen acre vineyard, learn how English wine is made and appreciate the subtle difference between each of the Chilford quality wines. Also on sale, a range of local specialities - browse and buy! Take the A11/A1307 then just follow - 'Chilford Hall Vineyard' signs.
Times: Open 1 Mar-31 Oct, daily, 1100-1730. Group visits by arrangement throughout the year.
Fee: Vineyard tours £4.50 per person or £3.75 for groups of over 15. Free tastings. Telephone for group bookings.
Facilities: P T(2 hrs)

Wisbech

Elgood's Brewery and Garden Map ref. H4
North Brink Brewery
Tel: (01945) 583160 Web: www.elgoods-brewery.co.uk
Independent family brewery established in 1795. Visitors can watch traditional methods of brewing and sample a range of real ales. 4-acre garden contains many features and maze.
Times: Open 27 Apr-30 Sept, Tues-Thurs, 1130-1630.
Fee: Brewery, garden and tasting £6.00. Garden only £2.50.
Facilities: P T(2 hrs) (garden and visitor centre)

Restaurants

Cambridge

Arundel House Hotel Map ref. G11
Chesterton Road, Cambridge CB4 3AN
Tel: (01223) 367701 Fax: (01223) 367721
Email: info@arundelhousehotels.co.uk
Web: www.arundelhousehotels.co.uk

Elegant, privately owned, 103 bedroom, 19th C. Victorian terrace hotel set in a beautiful location overlooking the River Cam and open parkland. Only a few minutes walk from the historic city centre and famous University colleges. The hotel is well known for its friendly relaxed atmosphere and has a reputation for providing some of the best food in the area, at very modest prices, in its award winning restaurant. The hotel's magnificent Victorian style conservatory, which overlooks an attractive walled garden adjacent to the bar, offers an alternative menu throughout the day, including cream teas with additional seating outside. The hotel facilities also include a large car park.

Ely

Cambridge

Midsummer House Restaurant Map ref. H11
Midsummer Common, Cambridge CB4 1HA
Tel: (01223) 369299 Fax: (01223) 302672
Email: reservations@midsummerhouse.co.uk
Web: www.midsummerhouse.co.uk

Midsummer House is set in an idyllic location on the banks of the River Cam. This Victorian house, with enchanting conservatory boasts the finest dining in Cambridge. Outstanding French Mediterranean Cuisine produced by Chef/Patron Daniel Clifford incorporates the freshest, finest local produce, wherever possible. This, accompanied by arguably the Best Wine List outside London, adds to an unforgettable meal in 'picture-postcard' surrounds. Open for lunch/dinner. Closed Sun and Mon. Prices from 2-course lunch @ £20.00 to 3-course A La Carte Meal @ £45.00.

Hemingford Abbots

Cambridge

Panos Map ref. H12
154-156 Hills Road, Cambridge CB2 2PB
Tel: (01223) 212958
Elegant professional standards, close to Botanic Gardens, with easy access to the railway station and historic centre. The cuisine has its own special interest and originality, offering a variety of Greek and French dishes - even a traditional 'Mezze' as a first course. Desserts, all home-made, include Crêpe Suzette and Baklava. Turkish coffee and Cappuccino are offered. The expertly chosen range of wines is very reasonably priced. Daily "special" always available. Restaurant open Mon-Sat dinner and Mon-Fri lunch. Sun closed. 3 course dinner £14.95. 2 course lunch £11.50.

Duxford (nr. Cambridge)

Duxford Lodge Hotel Map ref. H13
Ickleton Road, Duxford CB2 4RT
Tel: (01223) 836444 Fax: (01223) 832271
Email: admin@duxfordlodgehotel.co.uk
Web: www.duxfordlodgehotel.co.uk
Beautiful gardens, village setting just south of Cambridge, and close to Duxford Air Museum, the pretty villages of Essex and Suffolk and Newmarket Races. The attractive hotel has much going for it. Beautifully maintained public rooms and delightful bedrooms provide a relaxed informal atmosphere. Modern French cooking is the theme for 'Le Paradis' Restaurant, one of only a few 2 Rosette Restaurants in the Cambridgeshire area. Tourist Board Gold award for Quality. Cheerful enthusiastic service and an excellent wine list. Lunch from £9.99 (2 courses), Dinner from £25.00 (3 courses), Sun lunch £17.95, children under 10 half price. Private dining our speciality.

Ely

The Old Fire Engine House Map ref. I8
25 Saint Mary's Street, Ely CB7 4ER
Tel: (01353) 662582 Fax: (01353) 668364
The Old Fire Engine House is a restaurant and gallery, which has been owned and run by the same family since 1968. An 18th C. brick building close to Ely Cathedral, it has a large walled garden, friendly staff and an informal atmosphere. The cooking is based on local ingredients and classic English dishes form the mainstay of the menus. There is an extensive wine list and afternoon teas are also served. Art Gallery features monthly exhibitions of work by local and national artists. Open for coffee, lunch, tea and dinner - telephone for details.

Huntingdon

The Old Bridge Hotel Map ref. D9
1 High Street, Huntingdon PE29 3TQ
Tel: (01480) 424300 Web: www.huntsbridge.co.uk
The ultimate 'country hotel in a town'. The lounges extend into a really splendid conservatory with attractive and comfortable cane chairs and tables. Here one can enjoy exceptional brasserie style food. There is also a top-class, panelled restaurant with a wine list regularly named as one of the finest in the UK, including a selection of 20 wines served by the glass. Enjoy tea, coffee and drinks (including a fine selection of real ales) any time of day in the comfortable lounge and bar or outside on the patio. Open: daily. Average prices: 3 course restaurant meal £24.00. Brasserie meals from £4.50.

Kimbolton

The New Sun Inn Map ref. B10
20-22 High Street, Kimbolton PE28 0HA
Tel: (01480) 860052
16th C. beamed Inn and Restaurant. Real Ales and home made food using local produce. Bar meals £2.25-£7.25. Three-course à la carte meal at an average of £18.75. Traditional Sun lunch £6.75. Open 365 days of the year. House Specials include Home-made Steak and Kidney Pudding, Chocolate Fudge and Walnut Pudding.

Afternoon Teas

Ely

Steeplegate Map ref. I8
16-18 High Street, Ely CB7 4JU
Tel: (01353) 664731
Proprietor: Mr J S Ambrose. Seats: 40. Home-made cakes, scones and fresh cream teas, served in an historic building backing onto the cathedral. Medieval vault on view. Craft goods also sold. Small groups welcome. Open: Daily except Sun.

Stop & Shop

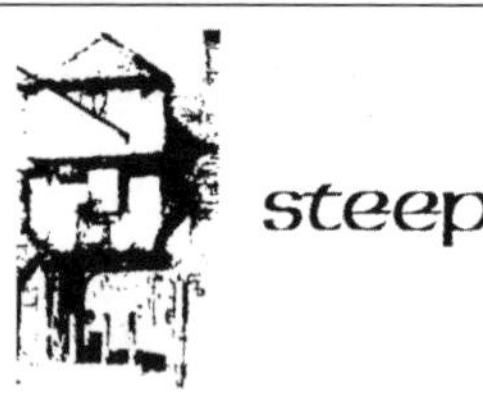

Ely

Steeplegate Map ref. I8
16-18 High Street, Ely CB7 4JU
Tel: (01353) 664731
Unusual gifts of good taste in Craft Gallery beside the cathedral. Tearoom. We sell woodwork, books, ceramics, jewellery, lace and toys. Open all year, daily except Sunday, 0900-1730.

Discovery Tours

Cromwell Country

Follow in the footsteps of Oliver Cromwell (1599-1658), the great Lord Protector.

Starting point: Huntingdon, Cambs Map ref. D9
Mileage: 21m/34km
Morning - Cromwell was born in *Huntington*. Start at the *Cromwell Museum* with its artefacts and portraits, then take the A1123 to *St. Ives* with its unusual Bridge Chapel and statue of Cromwell.
Afternoon - remain on the A1123 to Stretham (about 12 miles), where at the roundabout you turn left onto the A10 to *Ely*. Visit the magnificent *Cathedral* and *Oliver Cromwell's House* - but watch out for his ghost!

Time Travel East

Jump aboard our time machine, for a journey through the centuries.

Starting point: Peterborough, Cambs Map ref. C/D5/6
Mileage: 7m/11km
Morning - start the day in the Bronze Age with the prehistoric excavations at *Flag Fen*, then it's into Norman times at the beautiful *Peterborough Cathedral*, where the tomb of Katherine of Aragon can be seen.
Afternoon - enjoy a Victorian-style steam train ride aboard the *Nene Valley Railway*, then take the A605 to *Elton Hall*, a romantic 18th C. house.

Anglesey Abbey, Gardens and Lode Mill

The Friendly Invasion

Discover the special bond developed between the UK and US during the Second World War.

Starting point: Cambridge, Cambs Map ref. G/H11/12
Mileage: 11m/18km
Morning - enjoy a walking tour of the city, then have a pint in the *Eagle pub*, noted for its Air Force bar.
Afternoon - follow the A1303 to Madingley, and the *Cambridge American Cemetery*. Then retrace your steps to the M11, and follow this south to junction 10. End the day at Europe's top aviation attraction, the *Imperial War Museum* at Duxford, with its impressive American Air Museum.

Birds and Bees

Wander amongst the rich countryside and wildlife of the Fens.

Starting point: Wisbech, Cambs Map ref. H3/4
Mileage: 30m/48km
Morning - take the A1101 to the *Wildfowl and Wetlands Trust* at Welney, home to ducks and swans. Then retrace your steps to *Wisbech* for a wander around the pretty Georgian streets and squares.
Afternoon - visit *Peckover House* with its Victorian garden, complete with an orangery and fernery. Then end the day with a tour of the *Elgood's Brewery*, and enjoy a pint in the adjacent garden with its rare trees.

Oliver Cromwell's House, Ely

Bloomin' Beautiful

Enjoy the spectacular colours and delicate fragrances of some of England's finest gardens.

Starting point: Cambridge, Cambs Map ref. G/H11/12
Mileage: Cambridge and Anglesey Abbey 5m/8km
Cambridge and Wimpole Hall 9m/14km
Morning - visit the famous *Cambridge University Botanic Garden*. Then try your hand at punting through 'The Backs'.
Afternoon - two choices: either leave the city on the A1303 towards Newmarket. Then at the roundabout with the A14, take the B1102 to Lode and visit 17th C. *Anglesey Abbey*, renowned for its outstanding 100 acre garden. Alternatively take the A603 to visit *Wimpole Hall*, with its parterre and vegetable gardens.

Tales of the Fenland

Discover the story of the Fens, its history, drainage and people.

Starting point: Ely, Cambs Map ref. I8
Mileage: 25m/40km
Morning - start at *Oliver Cromwell's House*, and watch the 'drainage of the Fens' video. Then take the B1382 to *Prickwillow*, and visit the *Drainage Engine Museum*.
Afternoon - return to Ely, and take the A10 south to Stretham. At the roundabout, turn left onto the A1123 to *Wicken*. Visit the last remaining undrained Fen, and a 1930's 'Fen' cottage. End the day by returning to the A10, and heading south to *The Farmland Museum and Denny Abbey* (Waterbeach).

Writers and Wine

Hunt out great English writers and wine on this vintage tour.

Starting point: Cambridge, Cambs Map ref. G/H11/12
Mileage: 29m/47km
Morning - enjoy a literary tour of the city (including Grantchester), and learn of A.A. Milne, Rupert Brooke and Lord Byron. Then take the A603 to 18th C. *Wimpole Hall*, the former home of Rudyard Kipling's daughter.
Afternoon - retrace your steps to Cambridge, and take the A1307 south east to Linton. Turn left here onto the B1052 towards Balsham. End the day with a tour and tasting at *Chilford Hall Vineyard*.

Katherine's Haunt

Visit the last homes of Katherine of Aragon, the first queen of Henry VIII. But watch out for her ghost!

Starting point: St. Neots, Cambs Map ref. C/D11
Mileage: 12m/19km
Morning - start in the riverside town of St. Neots. Then take the A1 north to the pretty village of *Buckden*, where Katherine was held (by Henry VIII) in 1533, at the former palace of the Bishops of Lincoln.
Afternoon - take the B661 to *Grafham Water*, where you can enjoy a stroll around Britain's third largest reservoir. Remain on the B661 to Great Staughton, where you turn right onto the B660 to *Kimbolton*. Visit the castle where Katherine spent her last years, dying as a prisoner in 1536.

Wildfowl and Wetlands Trust, Welney

Essex

Map of County 128

County Information 129

Cities, Towns & Villages 130

Good Beach Guide 138

Tourist Information (Centres & Points) . . 139

Guided Tours 140

History & Heritage
Historic Houses 141
Ancient Monuments 143
Museums & Galleries 147
Machinery & Transport 157
Mills 159

Bloomin' Beautiful
Gardens 160
Nurseries & Garden Centres 165

Family Fun
Animal & Bird Collections 166
Amusement/Theme Centres & Parks 168
Children's Indoor Play Centres 170
Leisure Pools 171

Countryside
Special Areas 172
Country Parks & Nature Reserves 173
Picnic Sites 176

Activities
Boat Trips 177
Cycling 177
Walking 178

Food & Drink
Regional Produce 179
Breweries & Vineyards 179
Restaurants 180
Afternoon Teas 184

Stop & Shop
Craft Centres & Speciality Shopping 185

Discovery Tours 186

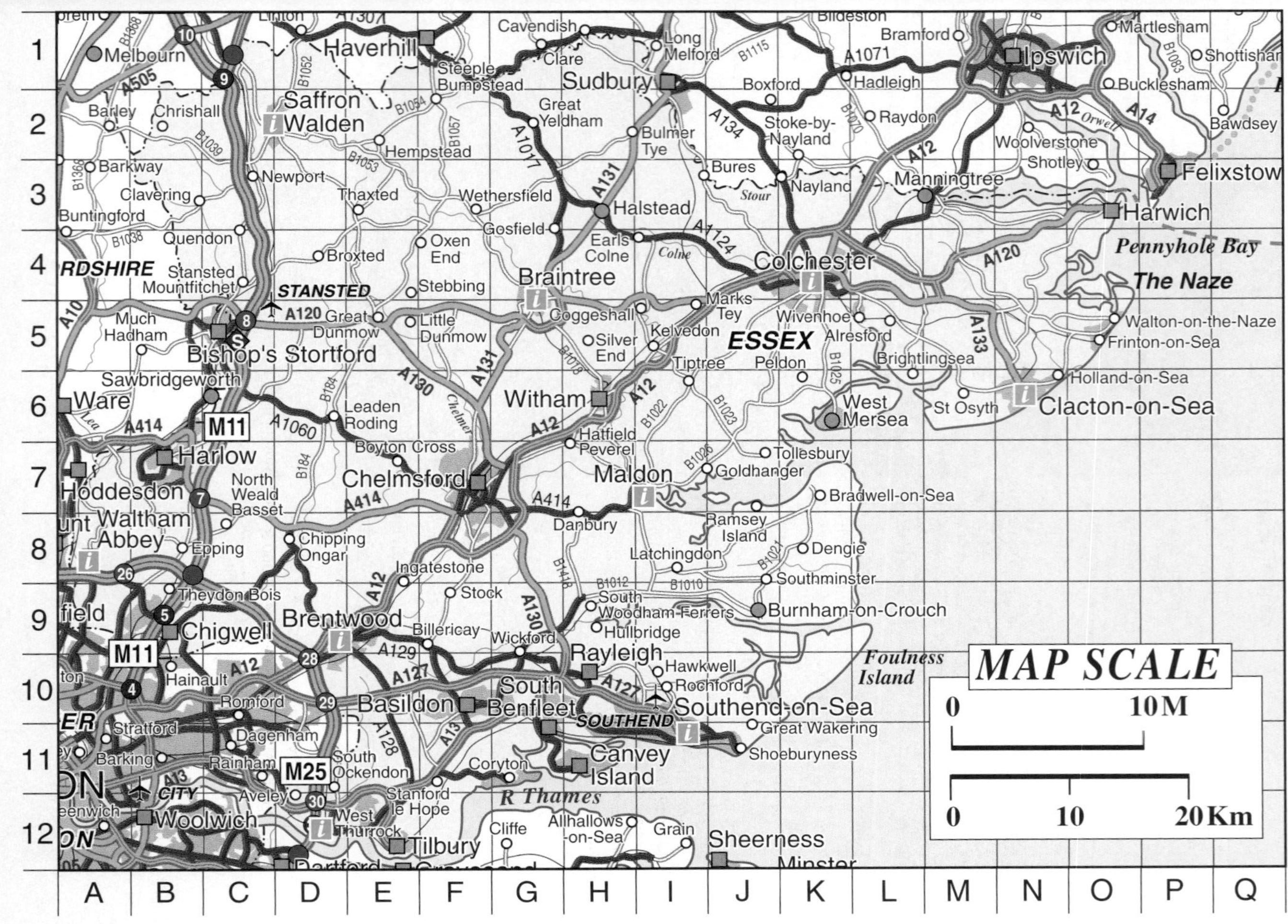
MAP SCALE
0
10M
0
10
20Km
ESSEX
Melbourn
Haverhill
Cavendish
Clare
Long Melford
Bildeston
Bramford
Ipswich
Martlesham
Shottishar
Bucklesham
Bawdsey
Steeple Bumpstead
Sudbury
Hadleigh
Boxford
Barley
Chrishall
Saffron Walden
Great Yeldham
Raydon
Hempstead
Bulmer Tye
Stoke-by-Nayland
Woolverstone
Shotley
Felixstow
Barkway
Newport
Bures
Nayland
Manningtree
Clavering
Thaxted
Wethersfield
Stour
Harwich
Buntingford
Halstead
Gosfield
Quendon
Oxen End
Earls Colne
Colne
Pennyhole Bay
Broxted
Colchester
RDSHIRE
Stansted Mountfitchet
STANSTED
Braintree
The Naze
Stebbing
Much Hadham
Great Dunmow
Little Dunmow
Coggeshall
Marks Tey
Wivenhoe
Walton-on-the-Naze
Bishop's Stortford
Silver End
Kelvedon
Alresford
Frinton-on-Sea
Tiptree
Peldon
Brightlingsea
Sawbridgeworth
Holland-on-Sea
Ware
Leaden Roding
Witham
West Mersea
St Osyth
Clacton-on-Sea
Harlow
Boyton Cross
Hatfield Peverel
Tollesbury
Hoddesdon
North Weald Basset
Chelmsford
Maldon
Goldhanger
Bradwell-on-Sea
Waltham Abbey
Epping
Chipping Ongar
Danbury
Ramsey Island
Dengie
Latchingdon
Ingatestone
Southminster
Theydon Bois
Stock
South Woodham Ferrers
Burnham-on-Crouch
Chigwell
Brentwood
Billericay
Wickford
Hullbridge
Rayleigh
Foulness Island
Hainault
Hawkwell
Rochford
Romford
Basildon
South Benfleet
Southend-on-Sea
Stratford
Dagenham
SOUTHEND
Great Wakering
Barking
Rainham
South Ockendon
Coryton
Canvey Island
Shoeburyness
CITY
Aveley
Stanford le Hope
R Thames
Woolwich
West Thurrock
Allhallows-on-Sea
Grain
Cliffe
Tilbury
Sheerness
Minster
M11
M25
A10
A12
A13
A14
A120
A127
A128
A129
A130
A131
A133
A134
A414
A505
A1017
A1060
A1071
A1124
B184
B1008
B1018
B1022
B1023
B1025
B1026
B1053
B1054
B1057
B1070
B1083
B1115
B1368
A B C D E F G H I J K L M N O P Q
1 2 3 4 5 6 7 8 9 10 11 12

Essex

County Town: Chelmsford.
Population: 1,614,220 approx. (including Southend/Thurrock).
Highest Point: High Wood, nr. Langley 146m (480 feet).
Rivers: Brook, Blackwater, Brain, Can, Chelmer, Colne, Crouch, Lea, Roach, Roding, Rom, Stour, Ter, Wid.
Landmarks: Colchester Castle, 'Constable Country', Dartford Tunnel and Queen Elizabeth II Bridge, Epping Forest (over 6,000 acres), Harwich International Port, M25 Motorway, The Naze, Southend Pier (longest in the world), Stansted Airport, Tilbury Port.

Welcome to Essex:

A county of gently rolling countryside and pockets of ancient woodland. Numerous picturesque villages can be explored such as Finchingfield, Castle Hedingham and Dedham. Most of the coastline is unspoilt with saltmarshes, mudflats and tiny creeks, once the haunt of smugglers. Discover historic maritime centres, such as Harwich and Maldon, or the seaside fun of Clacton and Southend. Inland, visit Colchester, Britain's oldest recorded town, the antiques centres of Coggeshall and Halstead, and Saffron Walden with its pargetted buildings and mazes.

Industry Past & Present:

Essex has always been an *agricultural* county, with superb *corn-growing* countryside - the subsequent grain giving rise to associated *milling, malting* and *brewing* industries. The rich soil was also used to grow the much-needed *gardener's seeds*, remembered in such names as the 'Kelvedon Wonder' pea. Essex is also the *jam (soft fruit)* capital of Britain, with both 'Wilkin and Sons' (started 1885) and 'Elsenham' producing their preserves here. Saffron Walden gets part of its name from the 'Saffron Crocus' which was once grown in the area (15-18th C.). It's bright orange stigma used for dyeing, medicine and flavouring. The coastline has also brought great wealth, with important *trading, fishing* and *shipbuilding* centres. Many goods were carried on the famous Thames Sailing Barges. Today you can try *sea salt* from Maldon, *oysters* from Colchester and *cockles* at Leigh-on-Sea. To the south of the county there were *cement works* and *brick-making* at Grays, and *gravel extraction* in the Lea Valley. In the Middle Ages, Colchester owed its prosperity to the *cloth* trade which had declined by the 1550's. It was revitalised by Flemish refugees who settled in the town in the late 16th C. (now the Dutch Quarter). The exiled French Huguenots first bought *silk weaving* to this country, and the trade arrived in Braintree early in the 19th C. After the collapse of the wool industry, Pound Mill in the town was bought by Warners, who went on to become the best known silk weavers in Britain. Nearby Coggeshall was one of the principal centres of *cloth making* in the region in the 15/16th C. then later for *Tambour Lace*. Whilst Halstead manufactured the first artificial silk *Rayon*. Today Essex is home to Tilbury Docks, the Port of Harwich and Bradwell Power Station. Famous names of the county include - Britvic (beverages), Ford Motor Company (head office), Marconi (communications and information technology) and Ridley's (brewing).

Famous People:

Margery Allingham *(author)*, Thomas Audley *(Lord Chancellor)*, Anne Boleyn *(Henry VIII's second wife)*, Queen Boudicca, John Constable *(artist)*, Daniel Defoe *(author)*, Queen Elizabeth I, Dr William Gilberd *(pioneer of the study of magnetism)*, King Harold, William Harvey *(discovered circulation of blood)*, Gustav Holst *(composer)*, Matthew Hopkins *(Witchfinder General)*, Christopher Jones *(Master of the Mayflower)*, Lionel Lukin *(inventor of lifeboat)*, Guglielmo Marconi *(father of wireless)*, Frances Evelyn Maynard *('Darling Daisy')*, Alfred Munnings *(artist)*, Captain Oates *(explorer)*, Samuel Pepys, John Ray *(botany)*, Dorothy L. Sayers *(author)*, Alfred Lord Tennyson *(poet)*, Dick Turpin *(highwayman)*, Lawrence Washington *(great, great grandfather of George Washington)*.

Bradwell-on-Sea

Cities, Towns & Villages

MD: Market Day
FM: Farmers' Market
EC: Early Closing
Tourist Information Centre (see page 139)
Guided Tours (see page 140)

Basildon Map ref. F10
Until the railway arrived in the 19th C. Basildon was a small rural village, whose cottages clustered around the 14th C. Holy Cross Church. In 1949 it became a New Town, and now has a population of around 160,000. The Eastgate Centre is one of the county's major shopping centres. **MD**: Mon (second-hand), Tues, Thurs, Fri and Sat.

Billericay Map ref. F9
Small town, set in well-wooded countryside. Numerous Georgian and period houses. The impressive church tower was built around 1500. Chantry House was the 17th C. home of Christopher Martin, treasurer to the Pilgrim Fathers. Nearby is Norsey Wood Nature Reserve, where 500 men were massacred by King Richard's soldiers in the Peasant's Revolt of 1381. **FM**: at nearby Barleylands Farm Centre, 2nd and last Sat in month.

Braintree Map ref. G4/5
Bustling market town standing on the old Roman road. King John gave Braintree its market charter in 1199. The textile industry has brought prosperity here for more than 400 years, firstly with wool, then from the 19th C. silk-weaving. Bradford Street has fine houses once occupied by those in the industry. Close by is the Freeport Designer Outlet village. **MD**: Wed and Sat.

Brentwood Map ref. D/E9
The town grew up in the late 12th C. (around a forest clearing), as a convenient stopping place for pilgrims travelling from East Anglia and the Midlands to Canterbury. It later developed as an 18th C. coaching centre with some good inns. Surrounding the town are rural areas of countryside and parkland, offering an excellent centre for walking.

Brightlingsea Map ref. L6
A maritime heritage town, Brightlingsea is the only cinque port outside Kent and Sussex. Sitting at the mouth of the River Colne, it is a major yachting centre with one of the best stretches of sailing on the East Coast. The town is also home to one of England's oldest timber-framed buildings, the 13th C. Jacobes Hall. Superb walks alongside the creek and river. **EC**: Thurs.

Burnham-on-Crouch Map ref. J9
Quiet, unspoilt riverside town, one of England's leading yachting centres. Known as the 'Cowes of the East Coast', the attractive quayside is lined with colour-washed houses, boat-building yards and sailing clubs. The famous clock tower dates from 1877. The town is also noted for its annual regatta, oysters, smuggling tales and long walks along the sea walls. **EC**: Wed.

Canvey Island Map ref. H11
This silt island was created by the currents of the Thames estuary. In the 17th C. the land was reclaimed by a group of Dutchmen, under the guidance of Cornelius Vermuyden. From an agricultural area, with a few villages, the island has developed into a large residential area. 16th C. inn, old Dutch cottages and watersports.

Brightlingsea

Chelmsford Cathedral

Castle Hedingham Map ref. H2/3
A former market town, granted a charter by King John in the 13th C. Today the winding lanes of this medieval village are lined with timber-framed buildings and elegant Georgian houses. Dominating the village is the magnificent 12th C. castle keep of the de Vere family, Earls of Oxford.

Chelmsford Map ref. F7
Founded in 1199, Chelmsford has been the county town of Essex for more than 700 years. Imposing 18th C. Shire Hall, and 15th C. parish church, designated a cathedral in 1914. Pedestrianised shopping areas and excellent entertainment/leisure facilities, including the Essex County Cricket Ground. In 1899, the world's first radio factory was opened here by Guglielmo Marconi. **MD**: Tues, Wed, Fri and Sat (second hand/collectable market on Thurs).

Chipping Ongar Map ref. D8
Surrounded by open farmland, this pleasant little country town owes its existence to the Normans. In 1162, Richard de Lucy, Chief Justice of England, built a great castle here. It was demolished in the 16th C. and today only the impressive mound remains. The wide High Street has houses dating from 1642, and within its parish church are Roman bricks. **MD**: Wed. **EC**: Wed.

Clacton-on-Sea Map ref. N6
The capital of the 'Essex Sunshine Coast', Clacton is a popular seaside town with tree-lined streets, long sandy beaches and beautiful seafront gardens. The 19th C. pier offers a range of entertainment and attractions. Water sports, two theatres and good shopping area. Close by is the Clacton Factory Shopping Village. **MD**: Tues and Sat (covered market Mon to Sat).

Coggeshall Map ref. I5
Once an important place in the trade of wool and lace-making, Coggeshall is now a major antiques centre. There are many fine timber-framed buildings, including 16th C. Paycockes, once home to a wealthy wool merchant. Grange Barn, erected by Cisterican monks in 1140, is all that remains of the former abbey. The clock tower was built in 1887. **MD**: Thurs. **FM**: at nearby Marks Hall Garden and Arboretum, last Sat in month. **EC**: Wed.

Colchester Map ref. K4
Britain's oldest recorded town, with over 2,000 years of history to explore. Discover the largest Norman castle keep in Europe (now an award-winning museum), and Britain's best preserved Roman gateway. Close by are the quaint narrow streets of the Dutch Quarter, where the cloth industry once flourished. Excellent shopping and leisure facilities. Lovely parkland and gardens. **MD**: Fri and Sat. **FM**: 1st Fri in month.

Danbury Map ref. H7/8
Hilltop town, built on the site of an Iron Age fort. There are views of the Blackwater Estuary with its barges and yachts. The church is 600 years old and contains notable wooden effigies of knights. Set within a country park is the 19th C. Danbury Palace, a former bishop's residence.

Colchester

CITIES, TOWNS & VILLAGES

Dedham Map ref. L3
Set by the River Stour, Dedham is in the heart of Constable Country. It was here that the 18th C. landscape artist went to school. The attractive main street is lined with Georgian-fronted houses, old inns and a large arts/crafts centre. The magnificent 15th C. church is noted for its heraldic symbols. East of the village is the former home of the artist Sir Alfred Munnings. **EC**: Wed.

Epping Map ref. B8
Founded in the 13th C. by the canons of Waltham Abbey, Epping is set on the old coaching route from London. Its long, wide High Street is full of attractive buildings and old inns. To the north is the famous Epping Forest, covering some 6,000 acres. This former royal hunting ground was the haunt of legendary highwayman Dick Turpin. **MD**: Mon. **EC**: Wed.

Frinton-on-Sea Map ref. O5
With a reputation as an exclusive resort, Frinton retains an atmosphere of the 1920s and 30s. Tree-lined residential avenues sweep down to the elegant Esplanade and cliff-top greensward. The long stretch of sandy beach is quiet and secluded. The main shopping street (Connaught Avenue) has been dubbed the "Bond Street" of East Anglia.
EC: Wed.

Grays/Thurrock Map ref. D/E12
The manor of Thurrock was granted to Henry de Grai by Richard the Lionheart in 1195. In those early days, fishing was the local industry, but later Grays became renowned as a cement and brick-making centre. To the west is the popular Lakeside Shopping Centre, and Europe's longest cabled-stayed bridge. **MD**: Fri and Sat. **EC**: Wed. i

Great Dunmow Map ref. E5
Historic market town, which prospered from the medieval wool trade. It is home of the Flitch Trials, which date from 1104. This custom takes place every four years, and awards a flitch of bacon to a newly married couple who can prove that they have lived in harmony for a year and a day. The Doctor's Pond is the scene of the first lifeboat experiments in 1784. **MD**: Tues. **FM**: at nearby Barnston, 4th Sat in month. Also at nearby Takeley, 1st Sat in month. **EC**: Wed.

Halstead Map ref. H3
Lively and picturesque town with a 600 year old church and interesting country-style shops. With the decline of the wool industry, Halstead turned to silk manufacture, started by the Courtauld family in the 1800s. Their weather-boarded mill, which straddles the River Colne, is now a large antiques centre. **MD**: Fri and Sat.

Maldon

Harlow Map ref. B7
Designed to relieve the congestion of London in 1947, this New Town has set residential and industrial areas. Its long history still survives though, in the rural parishes that surround 'The High', its modern centre. 'The Lawn' is the first tower block built in Britain in 1951, now listed for preservation. Wide range of sculpture. **MD**: Mon, Tues, and Thurs to Sat (bric-a-brac on Mon).

Harwich and Dovercourt Map ref. O3
Harwich is famous for its sea-faring history and heritage. It was once the headquarters of the King's Navy, and home of Christopher Jones 'Master of the Mayflower'. Narrow streets, historic buildings and museums, including the Redoubt Fort. Adjacent is the Edwardian style resort of Dovercourt with its sandy beaches, boating lake and park. **MD**: Fri. **EC**: Wed.

Ingatestone Map ref. E8/9
Lying beside the busy A12, this little country town has Georgian brick houses and a 16th C. inn. The church is noted for its 15th C. red-brick tower. Inside is a chapel housing the tombs of the Petre family. Sir William Petre moved here in 1539, building Ingatestone Hall.

Dovercourt

CITIES, TOWNS & VILLAGES

Dedham

Maldon Map ref. I7
Ancient hilltop town, port and sailing centre, at the head of the Blackwater estuary. Famed for its unique crystal salt and majestic Thames Sailing Barges. Attractive lanes and 'chases', with many historic buildings, including the 15th C. Moot Hall and 17th C. Dr Plume's Library. All Saints' Church has a unique triangular shaped tower. Edwardian Promenade Park. **MD**: Thurs and Sat. **FM**: 1st Tues in month. **EC**: Wed.

Manningtree and Mistley Map ref. M3
At the head of the Stour Estuary, these two small towns are joined by a waterfront area, noted for its swans. Manningtree is a sailing town with fine Georgian buildings, while Mistley with its swan fountain, was all set to become a spa town in the 18th C. Both places are connected with Matthew Hopkins, the infamous 17th C. 'Witchfinder General'. **MD**: Wed and Sat. **EC**: Wed.

Mersea Island Map ref. K/L6
Britain's most easterly inhabited island, accessed by 'The Strood' - which at high tide floods, making the island separate from the mainland. Noted for its sailing, fishing and oyster farming. West Mersea is a quiet resort with old fishing cottages and a shingly beach.

North Weald Bassett Map ref. C8
Large residential village. 18th C. half-timbered inn, and 13th C. church with fine Tudor tower. North Weald Airfield was first established in 1917, and used as an RAF station from 1928 - playing a major role in the Battle of Britain.

Rayleigh and Rochford Map ref. H/I10
Rayleigh is noted for its handsome 14th C. church, and the mound of its former royal castle built by the Saxons. Adjacent Rochford has a square surrounded by attractive buildings, the oldest dating from 1270. The red-brick tower of the church was once used by smugglers. Nearby is 15th C. Rochford Hall, reputed birthplace of Anne Boleyn. **MD**: Wed (Rayleigh), Tues (Rochford). **FM**: 1st Sat in month (Rochford). **EC**: Wed (Rayleigh), Tues (Rochford).

 CITIES, TOWNS & VILLAGES

Saffron Walden Map ref. C/D2
This ancient town takes its name from the Saffron Crocus, which grew here in the 16th C. Once a centre for wool production, the wealth generated has left many lovely timber framed buildings, some decorated with pargetting. The parish church, with its elegant spire, is one of the largest in Essex. Also remains of Norman castle and rare turf maze. **MD**: Tues and Sat. **FM**: at nearby Great Chesterford, 2nd Sat in month.

South Woodham Ferrers Map ref. H9
'New Town' located on the edge of the Dengie Peninsula. Housing is represented in different styles, whilst the major shops are gathered around a brick-paved and traffic-free area. Attractive 'nautical themed' gardens, riverside walks and country park.

Southend-on-Sea Map ref. I11
Traditional family seaside resort with seven miles of seafront, award-winning beaches, and magnificent parks and gardens. The famous 100 year old pier is the longest in the world - take a ride to the end aboard the little trains. Also excellent shopping centre, Kursaal entertainment complex, Adventure Island theme park, bandstand concerts, theatre and full calendar of special events. **MD**: Thurs. **FM**: 3rd Wed in month. Also at nearby Leigh-on-Sea, last Fri in month. **EC**: Thurs.

Stansted Mountfitchet Map ref. C4
Best known for its airport, this small town owes its earlier importance to a castle built here by the Mountfitchet family. The extensive earthworks are now home to the world's only reconstructed motte and bailey castle. The main part of the town is grouped along a hill. 18th C. windmill. **FM**: at nearby Ugley, 3rd Sat in month.

Thaxted Map ref. E3
Developed from a Saxon settlement, Thaxted prospered from the cutlery industry in the 14th C. Quaint streets are lined with fine medieval buildings, including the 15th C. Guildhall and thatched almshouses. Beautiful church with 181 feet high tower, and John Webb's 19th C. windmill. Home of the British composer, Gustav Holst and highwayman Dick Turpin. **MD**: Fri.

Tilbury Map ref. E12
Modern town, now one of Europe's largest container ports. Henry VIII built riverside block houses at East and West Tilbury, these later becoming Coalhouse and Tilbury Forts. In 1588, Queen Elizabeth I gave her morale boosting speech at Tilbury Fort, as her troops prepared to meet the Spanish Armada. **MD**: Fri.

Tiptree Map ref. I6
Best-known for its production of jam, this little town is surrounded by orchards. Fruit farming began here in 1864, and today the family firm of Wilkin and Sons is world-famous for their jams and preserves. The brick windmill was reputed used to hide contraband smuggled up the River Blackwater. **EC**: Wed.

Waltham Abbey Map ref. A8
Well preserved town, home to one of the county's most outstanding Norman buildings, 'Waltham Abbey'. It was endowed by King Harold, who was reputedly buried here. Beside the abbey is a lovely area of parkland and gardens. Sitting on the Meridian Line, the town has former coaching inns, and a fine 'Art Nouveau' Town Hall. **MD**: Tues and Sat. **FM**: 3rd Thurs in month. **EC**: Thurs.

Finchingfield

Walton-on-the-Naze Map ref. O5
Family seaside resort with clean sandy beaches, seafront gardens and quaint narrow streets. The pier is the second longest in Britain. The Naze is a headland jutting into the sea, where the heathland nature reserve is a haven for birdwatchers. Behind the town are 'The Backwaters', a series of saltings and little creeks leading into Harwich harbour. **MD**: Mon (Jun-Sept) and Thurs.

Witham Map ref. H6
Standing on the River Brain, the manor of Witham was given to the Knights Templar in 1148. It has been a cloth-making centre, spa and coaching town. Newland Street has many fine Georgian buildings, including the council offices with its period garden. Statue of crime-writer Dorothy L. Sayers who lived in the town for 27 years from 1929. **MD**: Sat. **FM**: 2nd and 4th Tues in month. **EC**: Wed.

Wivenhoe Map ref. L5
Set on the wooded slopes of the River Colne, Wivenhoe has attractive old inns and a pretty quayside. The earliest record of boat-building was in 1575, then in the 18th C. it developed as a port and shipyard. An earthquake in 1884 damaged the church. On the outskirts of the town is Wivenhoe Park, home of the University of Essex.

Clacton-on-Sea

CITIES, TOWNS & VILLAGES

Pick of the villages

1 **Arkesden** - pretty hamlet set around a green. Buildings of wood, plaster and thatch. Map ref. C3
2 **Battlesbridge** - attractive riverside village, famed today as a major antiques centre. Map ref. H9
3 **Bradwell-on-Sea** - unusual lock-up, marina and England's oldest Saxon church. Map ref. K7
4 **Canewdon** - tales of witchcraft. Massive church tower, village cage and stocks. Map ref. J9
5 **Clavering** - remains of former castle, 14th C. church and thatched 'Dolls House'. Map ref. B/C3
6 **Felsted** - delightful village with a well-known public school. Victorian brewery. Map ref. F5
7 **Finchingfield** - picture postcard village clustered around its green and duck pond. Map ref. F3
8 **Goldhanger** - farming/fishing hamlet. Village pump, oyster beds and sea-wall walks. Map ref. J7
9 **Great Bardfield** - former market town with pargetted cottages and 19th C. lock-up. Map ref. F3
10 **Great Bentley** - reputedly the largest village green in England at 42 acres. Map ref. M5
11 **Great Waltham** - restored Guildhall with Tudor chimneys. Large flint/stone church. Map ref. F6
12 **Greensted** - home to the oldest wooden church in the world, dating from 945AD. Map ref. D8
13 **Hempstead** - quiet village. Birthplace of highwayman Dick Turpin in 1705. Map ref. E2
14 **Kelvedon** - attractive village set beside the A12, now an antiques centre. Map ref. I5
15 **Leigh-on-Sea** - quaint 'cockle' fishing centre. Cobbled street and weather-boarded cottages. Map ref. H/I11
16 **Little Easton** - pargetted cottages, Tudor chimneys and superb 12th C. church. Map ref. E4
17 **Matching** - idyllic setting with church, pond, moated hall and 15th C. 'Wedding Feast House'. Map ref. C6
18 **Manuden** - plastered and white-washed houses, some with pargetting. Map ref. C4
19 **Newport** - former market town, its main street lined with handsome houses. 15th C. barn. Map ref. C3
20 **Paglesham** - hamlet between the rivers Roach and Crouch. Noted for its oysters. Map ref. J9/10
21 **Pleshey** - impressive remains of 12th C. castle, including huge mound and 15th C. bridge. Map ref. E6
22 **Purleigh** - the great-great grandfather of George Washington was rector here in the 17th C. Map ref. H/I8
23 **The Rodings** - eight pretty villages/hamlets set along the valley of the River Roding. Map ref. D6/7
24 **St. Osyth** - ancient village, with a 12th C. priory, complete with magnificent gatehouse. Map ref. M6
25 **Stock** - pretty village with weather-boarded houses. 19th C. windmill. Map ref. F9
26 **Terling** - estate village, with pretty cottages, 15th C. manor house and church. Map ref. G6
27 **Tillingham** - property of St. Paul's Cathedral since c.610AD. Weather-boarded cottages. Map ref. K8
28 **Tollesbury** - former fishing centre. 19th C. sail lofts. Little square with lock-up. Map ref. J7
29 **Wendens Ambo** - colour-washed cottages, thatched and tiled. Large timber-framed barn. Map ref. C3
30 **Writtle** - village green and pond, with period buildings. Famous agricultural college. Map ref. F7

Good Beach Guide

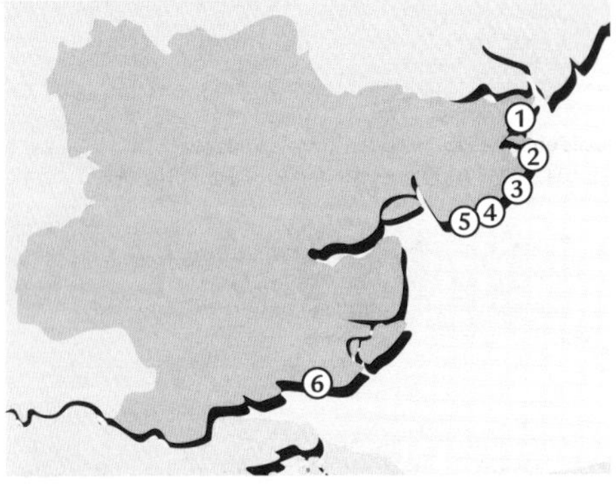

Key

TIC: Tourist Information Centre (see page 139)

TIP: Tourist Information Point (see page 139)

Dog ban: 1 May-30 September, dogs banned from the main beach areas. Further details from the nearest TIC.

Good Beach Guide 2004
The Good Beach Guide is the ultimate independent guide to UK beaches. By checking the water quality grade and the level of sewage treatment - you can choose a safe beach to visit this summer. The guide is available from the Marine Conservation Society from May 2004.
Tel: (01989) 566017 or visit www.goodbeachguide.co.uk

1 Dovercourt Bay
Holder of the Blue Flag award. Cliffs, superb beaches and excellent amenities. Café. Tennis, sports and fitness centre, skateboard park and boating lake nearby.

2 Walton-on-Naze
Gently shelving sandy beach. The Naze has groynes, dunes and a grassy area on high sandy cliffs giving excellent views of the busy shipping lanes around Harwich and Felixstowe. Pier. Deck-chairs. Putting and tennis. Refreshment kiosks at regular intervals along the seafront. Car parking. Toilets. TIP.

3 Frinton-on-Sea
Wide expanse of greensward on top of low cliffs above a gently shelving sandy beach. A first-class golf course plus excellent cricket, tennis and squash facilities. Deck-chairs. Toilets. Car parking. Dog ban.

4 Holland-on-Sea
Good sandy beaches which are usually quieter and less crowded than nearby Clacton. Groynes. Deck-chairs. Adjoining is the Holland Haven Country Park and Nature Reserve. Picnic facility. Car parking. Toilets. Dog ban.

5 Clacton-on-Sea
Gently sloping, long sandy beach. Amusements and entertainments. Pier featuring rides, roller skating rink and Seaquarium. Deck-chairs. Car parking. Toilets. Dog ban. TIC.

6 Southend-on-Sea
Seven miles of sea and foreshore with award-winning sand and shingle beaches. Expanse of seaside provides walks, traditional seaside entertainment, special events, boat trips, watersports, restaurants, kiosks, archway cafes, deckchairs, car parking, toilets (including disabled). Dog ban. TIC. Longest pleasure pier in the world, with pier trains to transport passengers the 1.33 miles. Sea Life Adventure, Adventure Island, ten-pin bowling at the historic Kursaal and seafront illuminations. Shoebury East Beach - small, sandy with grassy headland. Car parking, café, recreation area, shower and toilets. Zoned for watersports. Three Shells Beach - small family beach valeted every day. Shower and children's climbing frame. Shoebury Common Beach - long pebble/sand beach. Controlled slipway for personal watercraft and dinghies. Café and car parking. Jubilee Beach - stretches from Southend Pier to Thorpe Bay. Marine Parade section has cafes, restaurants, beach goods shops, amusements and car parking close by. Kite surfing area managed by Southend Kite Surfing Club. Chalkwell - long, narrow sandy beach. Refreshments and car parking. Bell Wharf Beach (Leigh Old Town) - very small, sandy beach. Close to historical, working fishing village. Shops, cafes and car parking nearby.

Southend-on-Sea

Tourist Information

Tourist Information Centres

With so much to see and do in this area, it's impossible for us to mention all of the places you can visit. You will find Tourist Information Centres (TICs) throughout Essex, with plenty of information on all the things that you can do and places you can visit.

TICs can book accommodation for you, in their own area, or further afield using the 'Book A Bed Ahead' Scheme. They can also be the ideal place to purchase locally made crafts or gifts, as well as books covering a wide range of local interests.

Braintree, Town Hall Centre, Market Square.
Tel: (01376) 550066
Email: braintree@eetb.info Web: www.enjoybraintree.co.uk

Brentwood, Pepperell House, 44 High Street.
Tel: (01277) 200300
Email: brentwood@eetb.info
Web: www.brentwood-council.gov.uk

Clacton-on-Sea, Town Hall, Station Road.
Tel: (01255) 423400 Email: clactononsea@eetb.info
Web: www.essex-sunshine-coast.org.uk

Colchester, 1 Queen Street.
Tel: (01206) 282920
Email: colchester@eetb.info Web: www.colchester.gov.uk

Maldon, Coach Lane.
Tel: (01621) 856503
Email: maldon@eetb.info Web: www.maldon.gov.uk

Saffron Walden, 1 Market Place, Market Square.
Tel: (01799) 510444
Email: saffronwalden@eetb.info
Web: www.uttlesford.gov.uk

Southend-on-Sea, 19 High Street.
Tel: (01702) 215120 Email: southendonsea@eetb.info
Web: www.southend.gov.uk

Thurrock, Moto Services, M25, Grays.
Tel: (01708) 863733
Email: thurrock@eetb.info Web: www.thurrock.gov.uk

Waltham Abbey, 2-4 Highbridge Street.
Tel: (01992) 652295 Email: walthamabbey@eetb.info
Web: www.walthamabbey.org.uk

Tourist Information Points

Limited information is also available from the following information points.

* Not open all year.

Basildon, The Library, St. Martin's Square.
Tel: (01268) 526097 Email: bas-cip@care4free.net

Burnham-on-Crouch, The Old Customs House, The Quay.
Tel: (01621) 784962

Freeport Braintree, Charter Way, Chapel Hill.
Tel: (01376) 348168

Halstead, The Mill House, The Causeway.
Tel: (01787) 476480 Email: halsteadtown@btconnect.com

South Woodham Ferrers, 34 Baron Road.
Tel: (01245) 327200

Walton-on-the-Naze *, Princes Esplanade.
Tel: (01255) 675542

Witham, Town Hall, Newland Street.
Tel: (01376) 502674 Email: witham-tourism@yahoo.co.uk

Maldon Tourist Information Centre

Guided Tours

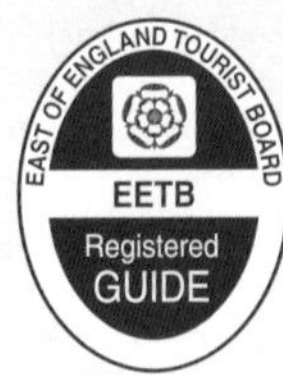

Why not enjoy a guided tour exploring one of the area's towns and cities? Some of these tours (indicated with a *) are conducted by Registered Blue Badge Guides, who have attended a training course sponsored by the East of England Tourist Board. Many of these guides also have a further qualification to take individuals around the region for half day, full day or longer tours if required. For more information on the guided tours listed, please telephone the relevant contact.

Colchester *

- **Regular town tours:** depart from the Visitor Information Centre. Duration of 1 3/4 hours. For further information (including times and costs) contact the Visitor Information Centre on (01206) 282920, or visit www.colchesterwhatson.co.uk
- **Group tours:** may be booked at any time of year.

Harwich

- **Regular town tours:** meet at the Ha'penny Pier Visitor Centre on Wed and Sat at 1400, between the 1 May-mid Sept. Free guided walks in Harwich.
- **Group tours:** for pre-booked groups. Guided tour of Harwich, visit to museums, including Harwich Redoubt Fort. Charges include museum entrance and small charge for guide.
- For further information contact Lyn Kingsbury on (01255) 502668.

Saffron Walden and surrounding areas *

- **Group tours:** guides available at any time to conduct tours for private groups. Variety of walking tours in Saffron Walden, Great and Little Dunmow, Thaxted and Newport - some tours themed (eg Saffron Walden Quakers). Can design tours to meet specific needs of groups. Tours last for about 2 hours - but can be scaled down to fit into existing itinerary. Prices on application.
- **Day or half day coach tours:** Uttlesford and Essex guides available to guide tours in a large area of North West Essex, and well into Hertfordshire and Suffolk. Wide range of standard tours (visits to churches a speciality). Can also assist with the design of special and themed tours for particular interests and occasions.
- For further information contact the Tours Organiser on (01799) 526109.

Colchester

Historic Houses

Chingford

Queen Elizabeth's Hunting Lodge Map ref. A9
Rangers Road
Tel: (0208) 529 6681
Web: www.cityoflondon.gov.uk/openspaces
Timber-framed hunting lodge built for King Henry VIII in 1543. Surrounded by the ancient forest of Epping.
Times: Open all year, Wed-Sun, 1300-1600.
Fee: Free.
Facilities: P ≹ T(45 mins)

Coggeshall

Paycockes Map ref. I5
West Street
Tel: (01376) 561305 Web: www.nationaltrust.org.uk
A half-timbered merchant's house, built in the 16th C. with a richly-carved interior and a small display of Coggeshall lace. Very attractive garden.
Times: Open 4 Apr-10 Oct, Tues, Thurs, Sun and Bank Hol Mon, 1400-1730. Last admission 1700.
Fee: £2.30/£1.15. Joint ticket with Grange Barn £3.40.
Facilities: T(30 mins) NT

Gosfield (nr. Halstead)

Gosfield Hall Map ref. G4
Tel: (01787) 472914 Web: www.cha.org.uk
A Tudor house built around a courtyard with later alterations, an old well and pump house with a 100ft Elizabethan gallery with oak panelling.
Times: Open 5 May-30 Sept, Wed and Thurs, 1400-1700.
Fee: £3.50/£1.50.
Facilities: P T(1 hr)

Layer Marney Tower

Ingatestone Hall

Hartford End (nr. Braintree)

Leez Priory Map ref. F5
Tel: (01245) 362555 Web: www.brideshead.co.uk
13th C. priory ruins and 16th C. redbrick Tudor mansion and tower. 40 acres of parkland, lakes, walled gardens, Tudor tunnels and oak-panelled Great Hall.
Times: Open all year, by appointment only.
Fee: Free.
Facilities: P T(3 hrs)

Ingatestone

Ingatestone Hall Map ref. E9
Hall Lane
Tel: (01277) 353010
Tudor house and gardens, the home of the Petre family since 1540. Family portrait collection, furniture and other heirlooms on display.
Times: Open 10 Apr-18 Jul, Sat, Sun and Bank Hol Mons, 1300-1800. 21 Jul-3 Sept, Sat, Sun, Bank Hol Mons and Wed-Fri, 1300-1800. 4-26 Sept, Sat, Sun and Bank Hol Mons, 1300-1800.
Fee: £4.00/£2.00/£3.50.
Facilities: P ≹ T(2 hrs)

DID YOU KNOW

The railway station platform at Colchester is the longest in England, whilst the platform at nearby Manningtree is the second longest!

Layer Marney (nr. Colchester)

Layer Marney Tower Map ref. J5
Tel: (01206) 330784 Web: www.layermarneytower.co.uk
A 1520 Tudor-brick gatehouse, 8 storeys high with Italianate terracotta cresting and windows. Gardens, park, rare breed farm animals and also the nearby church.
Times: Open 1 Apr-3 Oct, Sun-Fri, 1200-1700. Bank Hols, 1100-1800. Aug daily, 1100-1700.
Fee: £3.50/£2.00/£10.00 (family).
Facilities: T(2 hrs)

Rayleigh

Dutch Cottage Map ref. H10
Crown Hill
Tel: (01702) 318150 Web: www.rochford.gov.uk
This tiny octagonal cottage, based on the design of the 17th C. Dutch settlers, must be one of the smallest, and certainly most unusual 'council houses' in Britain.
Times: Open all year (by appointment), Wed, 1330-1630.
Fee: Free.
Facilities: T(40 mins)

Rochford

The Old House Map ref. I10
South Street
Tel: (01702) 318144 Web: www.rochford.gov.uk
History is revealed in the rooms of this elegant house, originally built in 1270, lovingly restored and now housing the District Council offices.
Times: Open all year (by appointment), Wed, 1400-1630.
Fee: Free.
Facilities: T(40 mins)

Hylands House, Widford

Saffron Walden

Audley End House and Park Map ref. C2
Audley End
Tel: (01799) 522399 Web: www.english-heritage.org.uk
A palatial Jacobean house remodelled in the 18th-19th C. Magnificent Great Hall with 17th C. plaster ceilings. Rooms and furniture by Robert Adam, and park by 'Capability' Brown. Parterre and organic kitchen garden.
Times: Please contact for details of opening times.
Fee: Please contact for details of admission prices.
Facilities: T(3 hrs) (on leads) **EH**

Southend-on-Sea

Southchurch Hall Museum Map ref. I11
See entry in Museums & Galleries section.

Widford (nr. Chelmsford)

Hylands House Map ref. F8
Hylands Park, London Road
Tel: (01245) 496800 Web: www.hylandshouse.org.uk
Originally built in 1730. Currently six restored rooms are available to view. Exhibitions on the history of the house, as well as monthly art exhibitions are on display.
Times: Open 4 Jan-29 Mar, Sun, 1100-1800; Mon, 1100-1630. 4 Apr-27 Sept, Sun and Mon, 1100-1800. 3 Oct-27 Dec, Sun, 1100-1800; Mon, 1100-1500. Closed 25 Dec and 1 Jan.
Fee: £3.30/free/£2.30.
Facilities: T(1½ hrs)

DID YOU KNOW

Great Dunmow is famous for its Flitch Trials, which sees the award of a side of bacon or flitch, to a couple who having been married for at least a year, can prove in front of a judge and jury, that they have not regretted their marriage nor quarrelled.

Ancient Monuments

Billericay

St. Mary Magdalene Church Map ref. F10
Church Street, Great Burstead
Tel: (01277) 652701
Web: www.greatburstead.freewire.co.uk
Saxon church with 14th C. medieval wall paintings. Christopher Martin, the church warden, led the Pilgrim Fathers' journey to Billericay (nr. Boston) in the USA.
Times: Open all year, daily, dawn to dusk.
Fee: Free.
Facilities: P T(30 mins)

Bradwell-on-Sea

Saint Peters-on-the-Wall Map ref. L7
East End Road
Tel: (01621) 776203
Built by St. Cedd of Lindisfarne in AD654, this is England's oldest Saxon church. Small exhibition about its history. Bookstall. Evening services every Sun at 1800 during Jul and Aug.
Times: Open at any reasonable time.
Fee: Free.
Facilities: P T(30 mins)

Brentwood

Cathedral Church of St. Mary and St. Helen
Map ref. D/E9
Ingrave Road
Tel: (01277) 210107
Web: www.brentwood-cathedral.co.uk
Roman Catholic cathedral designed by Mr Quinlan Terry in the Classical style. Dedicated in May 1991.
Times: Open all year, Mon-Sat, 1000-1800; Sun, 1400-1700. Please contact for Christmas and Easter openings.
Fee: Free.
Facilities: P T(1 hr)

St. Andrew's (Minster) Church, Ashingdon

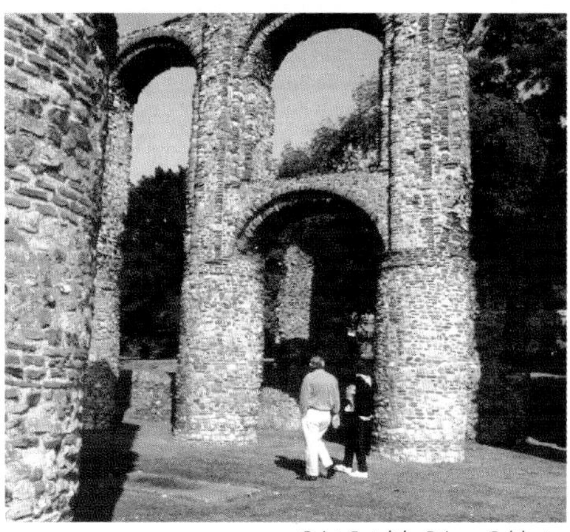

Saint Botolphs Priory, Colchester

Castle Hedingham

Hedingham Castle Map ref. H2
Tel: (01787) 460261 Web: www.hedinghamcastle.co.uk
The finest Norman keep in England, built in 1140 by the de Veres, Earls of Oxford. Visited by Kings Henry VII and VIII and Queen Elizabeth I, and besieged by King John. Lake walks and woodland.
Times: Open Apr-Oct, Thurs, Fri and Sun, 1100-1600. School holiday special opening - 4-16 Apr; 30 May-3 Jun; 26 Jul-26 Aug and 24-29 Oct, 1000-1700.
Fee: £4.00/£3.00/£3.50.
Facilities: P T(1½ hrs)

Chelmsford

Chelmsford Cathedral Map ref. F7
Tel: (01245) 294480
Web: www.cathedral.chelmsford.anglican.org
A late-medieval church, reordered in 1983 and blending old with new. Became a cathedral in 1914, when the Diocese of Chelmsford was created. Modern sculpture and tapestry.
Times: Open all year, daily, 0815-1800.
Fee: Donations requested.
Facilities: T(1 hr) (by arrangement)

Coggeshall

Grange Barn Map ref. I5
Grange Hill
Tel: (01376) 562226 Web: www.nationaltrust.org.uk
One of the oldest surviving timber framed barns in Europe, dating from around 1240, and originally part of a Cistercian Abbey. Restored in the 1980s.
Times: Open 4 Apr-10 Oct, Tues, Thurs, Sun and Bank Hol Mon, 1400-1700.
Fee: £1.70/85p. Joint ticket with Paycockes £3.40.
Facilities: P T(30 mins) NT

Colchester
Colchester Castle Museum Map ref. K4
See entry in Museums & Galleries section.

Colchester
Saint Botolphs Priory Map ref. K4
Tel: (01206) 282920 Web: www.english-heritage.org.uk
The remains of a 12th C. priory near the town centre, with a nave which has an impressive arcaded west end. One of the first Augustinian priories in England.
Times: Open at any reasonable time.
Fee: Free.
Facilities: Q T(45 mins) EH

Colchester
Saint Michael and All Angels Church Map ref. J5
Church Road, Copford Green
Tel: (01621) 815434
A 12th C. church in Romanesque style, with an apse that is decorated with medieval wall paintings.
Times: Open all year, daily, 0915-1730 (or dusk). Sun service, 1100-1200.
Fee: Free.
Facilities: P T(40 mins)

Cressing (nr. Braintree)
Cressing Temple Barns Map ref. H5
Witham Road
Tel: (01376) 584903 Web: www.essexcc.gov.uk
The site of a Knights Templar settlement dating from 1137. Two magnificent 13th C. timber-framed barns and Tudor walled garden.
Times: Open Mar-Oct, Sun, 1030-1700. May-Sept, Wed-Fri, 1030-1630.
Fee: £3.50/£2.50/£2.50/£9.00.
Facilities: P T(2½ hrs)

East Tilbury
Coalhouse Fort Map ref. F12
Princess Margaret Road
Tel: (01375) 844203
Web: www.coalhousefort.freeserve.co.uk
Best example of a Victorian armoured casemate fortress in the south east. Built as a frontline defence for the Thames. Guided tours and displays, including Thameside Aviation Museum.
Times: Open 28 Mar; 12, 25 Apr; 3, 30, 31 May; 27 Jun; 11, 25 Jul; 29, 30 Aug; 11, 12, 26 Sept; 29, 30 Oct; 1100-1600.
Fee: £2.50/free/£2.00.
Facilities: P T(2 hrs)

Waltham Abbey Church

Great Dunmow

Great Dunmow Maltings Map ref. E5
Mill Lane
Tel: (01371) 878979
Dating from 1560, the Maltings retain much of the original malting infrastructure used to produce malt by hand. They are superb examples of 16th C. and 18th C. architecture. Houses town museum.
Times: Open all year. 3 Jan-12 Apr, Sat, Sun and Bank Hols, 1100-1600. 13 Apr-26 Oct, Sat, Sun, Tues and Bank Hols, 1100-1600. 30 Oct-12 Dec, Sat, Sun and Bank Hols, 1100-1600.
Fee: £1.00/50p/50p.
Facilities: T(1½ hrs)

Greensted (nr. Chipping Ongar)

St. Andrews Church Map ref. C8
Church Lane, Greensted Road
Tel: (01277) 364694
The oldest wooden church in the world, and the oldest wooden (stave built) building in Europe.
Times: Open daily, 1 Jan-31 Mar, 0900-1700. 1 Apr-30 Sept, 0900-1800. 1 Oct-31 Dec, 0900-1700.
Fee: Free.
Facilities: P T(1 hr)

Mistley Towers

Hadleigh

Hadleigh Castle Map ref. H11
Tel: (01760) 755161 Web: www.english-heritage.org.uk
Familiar from Constable's painting, the castle stands on a bluff overlooking the Leigh Marshes with a single, large 50ft tower and 13th C. and 14th C. remains.
Times: Open at any reasonable time.
Fee: Free.
Facilities: T(45 mins) EH

Harwich

Harwich Redoubt Fort Map ref. O3
Behind 29 Main Road
Tel: (01255) 503429 Web: www.harwich-society.com
An anti-Napoleonic circular fort commanding the harbour. Eleven guns on battlements.
Times: Open 4 Jan-25 Apr, Sun and Bank Hols 1000-1600. 1 May-31 Aug, daily, from 1000 (last admission 1630). 5 Sept-Dec, Sun, 1000-1600. Closed Christmas.
Fee: £1.00/free/50p.
Facilities: T(1½ hrs)

Little Tey (nr. Coggeshall)

St. James the Less Church Map ref. I4
Church Lane
Tel: (01206) 211652
A 12th C. church with 13/14th C. wall paintings, which have been uncovered and conserved without any restoration. They are virtually untouched since their original painting.
Times: Open all year, Thurs-Sun, 1000-dusk. Key available on request.
Fee: Free. Donations appreciated.
Facilities: P T(30 mins)

Mistley

Mistley Towers Map ref. M3
Tel: (01206) 393884 Web: www.english-heritage.org.uk
Two towers designed by Robert Adam in 1776, as part of the parish church. A rare example of Robert Adam's ecclesiastical work. Key from Mistley Quay Workshops.
Times: Open at any reasonable time.
Fee: Free.
Facilities: T(45 mins) EH

Rayleigh

Rayleigh Mount Map ref. H10
Tel: 0870 609 5388 Web: www.nationaltrust.org.uk
Former site of the Domesday castle built by Sweyn of Essex.
Times: Open summer, daily, 0700-1800; winter, daily, 0700-1700.
Fee: Free.
Facilities: T(1 hr) NT

Rivenhall (nr. Witham)
Saint Mary and All Saints Church Map ref. H5
Church Road
Tel: (01376) 511161 Web: www.rivenhall.org.uk
A Saxon church on the earthworks of a Roman villa, restored by early Victorians with 12th C. glass and interesting monuments.
Times: Open 2 May-3 Oct, Sun, 1430-1630; Wed, 0900-1130.
Fee: Free. Donations appreciated.
Facilities: T(30 mins)

Southend-on-Sea
St. Andrew's (Minster) Church Map ref. I9
Church Road, Ashingdon
Tel: (01702) 203358
Built by Canute in 1020, this small hilltop church offers panoramic views. Very peaceful, and with many features of great historic interest.
Times: Open 12 Apr-30 Sept, daily (except Sun), 1400-1600.
Fee: Free.
Facilities: T(45 mins)

Southminster
Rural Discovery Church Map ref. J8
Saint Lawrence
Tel: (01621) 779319
An active church, sited on a hill overlooking the River Blackwater. Exhibitions of local interest.
Times: Open 29 May-26 Sept, Sat, Sun and Bank Hols, 1430-1630.
Fee: Free.
Facilities: T(1 hr)

Stansted Mountfitchet
Mountfitchet Castle Map ref. C4
Tel: (01279) 813237 Web: www.mountfitchetcastle.com
A re-constructed Norman motte-and-bailey castle, and village of the Domesday period. Grand Hall, church, prison and siege tower. Domestic animals roam the site.
Times: Open 14 Mar-14 Nov, daily, 1000-1700.
Fee: £6.00/£5.00/£5.00. 10% discount on admission to castle and toy museum (see page 155) next door, if visiting both places on the same day.
Facilities: T(2 hrs)

Thaxted
Thaxted Guildhall Map ref. E3
See entry in Museums & Galleries section.

Tilbury
Tilbury Fort Map ref. F12
Tel: (01375) 858489 Web: www.english-heritage.org.uk
One of Henry VIII's coastal forts, re-modelled and extended in the 17th C. in continental style. The best and largest example of 17th C. military engineering in England.
Times: Please contact for details of opening times.
Fee: Please contact for details of admission prices.
Facilities: T(2 hrs) (audio tours) (on leads) EH

Waltham Abbey
Waltham Abbey Church Map ref. A8
Highbridge Street
Tel: (01992) 767897
Web: www.walthamabbeychurch.co.uk
A Norman church, the reputed site of King Harold's tomb. The Lady Chapel and crypt (now a visitors' centre and shop) date from the 14th C.
Times: Open 1 Jan-27 Mar, Mon, Tues and Thurs-Sat, 1000-1600; Wed, 1100-1600; Sun, 1200-1600. 28 Mar-30 Oct, Mon, Tues and Thurs-Sun, 1000-1800; Wed, 1100-1800; Sun, 1200-1800. 31 Oct-31 Dec, Mon, Tues and Thurs-Sat, 1000-1600; Wed, 1100-1800; Sun, 1200-1800. Closed 9 Apr and 25 Dec.
Fee: Donations welcome.
Facilities: T(1 hr)

Widdington
Priors Hall Barn Map ref. D3
Tel: (01223) 582700 Web: www.english-heritage.org.uk
One of the finest surviving medieval barns in south east England, representative of the type of aisled barn in North West Essex, 124 x 30 x 33 ft high.
Times: Please contact for details of opening times.
Fee: Please contact for details of admission prices.
Facilities: T(30 mins) EH

Willingale (nr. Chipping Ongar)
Willingale Churches Map ref. D7
Tel: (01277) 896353
Two ancient churches in one churchyard, side by side. On this site since Norman times. A village setting on The Essex Way.
Times: Open all year, daily, dawn-dusk.
Fee: Free.
Facilities: T(1½ hrs)

DID YOU KNOW

The famous Victorian water tower at Colchester (built in 1882) is known as 'Jumbo' after a 6½ ton African elephant which once lived at London Zoo. It stands 30 metres high and held 230,000 gallons of water.

Museums & Galleries

Basildon

Langdon Visitor Centre and Nature Reserve Map ref. F10
See entry in Countryside section.

Battlesbridge

Battlesbridge Motorcycle Museum and Antiques Centre
Map ref. H9
The Old Granary, Hawk Hill
Tel: (01268) 575000 Web: www.battlesbridge.com
Five interesting old buildings housing over 70 dealers of antiques, reproductions and crafts. Motorcycle Museum.
Times: Open all year, daily, 1000-1730. Museum open Sun, 1100-1600 (or by appointment). Closed 25 and 26 Dec.
Fee: Antiques Centre free. Motorcycle museum £1.00.
Facilities: P T(2 hrs)

Billericay

Barleylands Farm Centre Map ref. F10
See entry in Family Fun section

Billericay

Cater Museum Map ref. F9
74 High Street
Tel: (01277) 622023
A folk museum of bygones with a Victorian sitting room, bedroom and kitchen, as well as a World War II exhibition.
Times: Open all year, Mon-Sat, 1400-1700. Closed Easter, 24-26 Dec and 1 Jan.
Fee: Free.
Facilities: T(1 hr)

Braintree

Braintree District Museum Map ref. G4/5
Manor Street
Tel: (01376) 325266 Web: www.braintree.gov.uk
Threads of Time is a permanent exhibition housed in a converted Victorian school, telling the story of Braintree district and its important place in our history.
Times: Open all year, Mon-Sat, 1000-1700. Sun and Bank Hols (Oct-Dec) 1300-1600. Closed 25 and 26 Dec.
Fee: £2.00/£1.00/£1.00.
Facilities: P T(2 hrs)

Braintree

Freya's Ponyland Rescue Centre and Farm Museum
Map ref. H4
See entry in Family Fun section.

Tymperleys Clock Museum, Colchester

Braintree

Great Notley Country Park and Discovery Centre
Map ref. F/G5
See entry in Countryside section.

Braintree

The Town Hall Centre Map ref. G4/5
Market Square
Tel: (01376) 557776 Web: www.braintree.gov.uk
Art gallery in Grade II* listed building with Tourist Information Centre on site. Situated in historic market square dating back to 1199.
Times: Open all year, Mon-Fri, 0900-1700; Sat, 1000-1600. Please contact for details of Christmas and Easter opening times.
Fee: Free.
Facilities: P T(1 hr)

Brentwood

Brentwood Museum Map ref. D/E9
Cemetery Lodge, Lorne Road
Tel: (01277) 223326/210333
A small cottage museum covering social and domestic history with special reference to Brentwood. It includes a 1930s kitchen, toys and exhibits from two World Wars.
Times: Open 4 Apr, 2 May, 6 Jun, 4 Jul, 1 Aug, 5 Sept, 3 Oct, Sun, 1430-1630.
Fee: Free.
Facilities: P T(40 mins)

Brentwood

Kelvedon Hatch Nuclear Bunker Map ref. D8
Kelvedon Hall Lane, Kelvedon Hatch
Tel: (01277) 364883 Web: www.secretnuclearbunker.co.uk
A large, 3-storey, ex-government regional headquarters buried some 100ft below ground, complete with canteen, BBC studio, dormitories, plant room and plotting floor.
Times: Open 1 Jan-29 Feb, Thurs-Sun, 1000-1600. 1 Mar-31 Oct, Mon-Fri, 1000-1600; Sat and Sun, 1000-1700. 1 Nov-31 Dec, Thurs-Sun, 1000-1600. Closed 25 Dec.
Fee: £5.00/£3.00/£12.00 (family).
Facilities: Q P T(2 hrs)

Brightlingsea

Brightlingsea Museum Map ref. L6
1 Duke Street
Tel: (01206) 303286
The maritime and social history museum of Brightlingsea (a limb of the Cinque Port of Sandwich) showing collections relating to the town's Cinque Port connections.
Times: Open 3 Apr-26 Sept, Sun and Mon, 1400-1700; Sat, 1000-1600.
Fee: 50p/25p/25p.
Facilities: T(1 hr)

Burnham-on-Crouch

Burnham-on-Crouch and District Museum Map ref. J9
Tucker Brown Boathouse, Coronation Road
Tel: (01621) 783444
A small museum devoted to local history with maritime and agricultural features of the Dengie Hundred.
Times: Open Apr-end Nov, Sat, Sun, Wed and daily in school hols, 1400-1700.
Fee: £1.00/20p.
Facilities: T(30 mins)

Canvey Island

Dutch Cottage Museum Map ref. H11
Canvey Road
Tel: (01268) 794005
An early 17th C. cottage of one of Vermuyden's Dutch workmen who was responsible for drainage schemes in East Anglia.
Times: Open 31 May, then every Sun from 6 Jun-5 Sept, plus Wed in Jul and Aug, 1430-1700.
Fee: Free.
Facilities: T(45 mins)

Canvey Island

Heritage Centre Map ref. H11
Canvey Village, Canvey Road
Tel: (01268) 694317
The Heritage Centre is housed in the now redundant parish church of St. Katherine, built in 1876. It contains an art and craft centre and a folk museum.
Times: Open 3 Jan-19 Dec, Sat and Sun, 1100-1600. Please telephone for Easter openings.
Fee: Free.
Facilities: T(30 mins)

The Sir Alfred Munnings Art Museum, Dedham

Chelmsford

Chelmsford Museum Map ref. F7
Oaklands Park, Moulsham Street
Tel: (01245) 615100
Web: www.chelmsfordmuseums.co.uk
Local and social history, from prehistory to present day. Essex Regiment history, fine and decorative arts (ceramics, costume, glass), coins, natural history, events and talks.
Times: Open all year, Mon-Sat, 1000-1700. 28 Mar-24 Oct, Sun, 1400-1700. 4 Jan-21 Mar and 31 Oct-19 Dec, Sun, 1300-1600. Closed 9 Apr and 25, 26 Dec.
Fee: Free.
Facilities: T(1½ hrs)

Chelmsford

Essex Police Museum Map ref. F7
Essex Police Headquarters, Springfield
Tel: (01245) 457150 Web: www.essex.police.uk/museum
Covers the history of policing in Essex, from its Victorian origins to the present day, including Moat Farm murder and the death of PC Gutteridge. Hands-on police equipment.
Times: Open by appointment only. All year, Mon-Fri, 0900-1700. Evenings by arrangement.
Fee: Free.
Facilities: T(1½ hrs)

DID YOU KNOW

The Sun Inn at Saffron Walden is famed for its pargeting. One scene shows local folk hero Thomas Hickathrift, who beat a nasty giant of the area, armed with just a sword made from the axle of his wagon, and a cartwheel for a shield.

Coggeshall

Coggeshall Heritage Centre Map ref. I5
St. Peter's Hall, Stoneham Street
Tel: (01376) 563003
Web: www.btinternet.com/~coggeshall
Ever-changing historical depiction of this medieval wool and market town. Large exhibition of Coggeshall lace, working wool loom and old photographs.
Times: Open 4 Apr-31 Oct, Sun, Bank Hol Sat and Mon, 1415-1645.
Fee: Free.
Facilities: T(45 mins)

Colchester

Colchester Castle Museum Map ref. K4
Tel: (01206) 282939
Web: www.colchestermuseums.org.uk
A Norman keep on the foundations of a Roman temple. The archaeological material includes much on Roman Colchester (Camulodunum). Exciting hands-on displays.
Times: Open all year, Mon-Sat, 1000-1700; Sun, 1100-1700. Closed 25, 26 Dec and 1 Jan.
Fee: £4.00/£2.70/£2.70.
Facilities: Q T(2½ hrs)

Colchester

firstsite @ The Minories Art Gallery Map ref. K4
74 High Street
Tel: (01206) 577067 Web: www.firstsite.uk.net
firstsite presents a diverse programme of innovative contemporary art exhibitions and events at the Minories Art Gallery - an inpressive Georgian townhouse with a shop, cafe and beautiful walled garden.
Times: Open 1 Jan-30 Jun, Mon-Sat, 1000-1700. 1 Jul-31 Aug, Mon-Sat, 1000-1700; Sun, 1100-1700. 1 Sept-31 Dec, Mon-Sat, 1000-1700. Closed all Bank Hols.
Fee: Free.
Facilities: Q T(45 mins)

Colchester

Hollytrees Museum Map ref. K4
High Street
Tel: (01206) 282940
Web: www.colchestermuseums.org.uk
A collection of toys, costumes and decorative arts from the 18th-20th C., displayed in an elegant Georgian town house, built in 1718.
Times: Open all year, Mon-Sat, 1000-1700; Sun, 1100-1700. Closed 25, 26 Dec and 1 Jan.
Fee: Free.
Facilities: Q T(1 hr)

Barleylands Farm Centre, Billericay

Colchester
Natural History Museum Map ref. K4
All Saints Church, High Street
Tel: (01206) 282932
Web: www.colchestermuseums.org.uk
Hands-on displays and events giving the whole family an interesting perspective on the local natural history of Essex.
Times: Open all year, Mon-Sat, 1000-1700; Sun, 1100-1700. Closed 25, 26 Dec and 1 Jan.
Fee: Free.
Facilities: T(40 mins)

Colchester
Pam Schomberg Gallery Map ref. K4
12 St. Johns Street
Tel: (01206) 769458
Gallery situated in centre of town with changing exhibition programme. Featuring a wide range of ceramics, glass, jewellery, wood textiles, prints and paintings.
Times: Open all year, Mon-Sat, 1000-1700. Closed 25 Dec-2 Jan.
Fee: Free.
Facilities: T(1 hr)

Colchester
Tymperleys Clock Museum Map ref. K4
Trinity Street
Tel: (01206) 282931
Web: www.colchestermuseums.org.uk
A fine collection of Colchester-made clocks from the Mason collection, displayed in a 15th C. timber-framed house which Bernard Mason restored and presented to the town.
Times: Open 1 Apr-31 Oct, Tues-Sat, 1000-1300 and 1400-1700.
Fee: Free.
Facilities: T(45 mins)

Dedham
Dedham Centre Toy Museum Map ref. L3
High Street
Tel: (01206) 322666
Collection of dolls, teddies, toys, games, play houses and pictures displayed in a beautifully converted church. Touch and try corner, doll and teddy hospital.
Times: Open all year - please contact to confirm exact opening days and times.
Fee: Free. Donations requested.
Facilities: T(1 hr)

Dedham
The Sir Alfred Munnings Art Museum Map ref. L3
Castle House, Castle Hill
Tel: (01206) 322127 Web: www.siralfredmunnings.co.uk
The home, studios and grounds where Sir Alfred Munnings, KCVO, lived and painted for 40 years. A large collection, also includes pictures on loan from private collections.
Times: Open 11 Apr-3 Oct, Sun, Wed and Bank Hol Mon, 1400-1700. Also Thurs and Sat in Aug, 1400-1700
Fee: £4.00/£1.00/£3.00.
Facilities: T(1½ hrs)

Finchingfield
Finchingfield Guildhall and Heritage Centre Map ref. F3
Church Hill
Tel: (01371) 810456
The Guildhall is open for exhibitions, lectures and meetings. Heritage Centre is open for details of the Guildhall, church and other ancient properties in the village.
Times: Open 10 Apr-26 Sept, Sat and Sun, 1400-1800.
Fee: Free.
Facilities: T(1½ hrs)

Goldhanger (nr. Maldon)
Maldon and District Agricultural and Domestic Museum
Map ref. J7
47 Church Street
Tel: (01621) 788647
An extensive collection of farm machinery, domestic items of every kind, products of Maldon Ironworks, printing machines from 1910, photographs and stuffed birds.
Times: Please contact for details of opening times.
Fee: Please contact for details of admission prices.
Facilities: T(1 hr)

DID YOU KNOW

Lionel Lukin demonstrated the world's first unsinkable lifeboat on the Doctors Pond at Great Dunmow in 1784.

Grays

Thurrock Museum Map ref. E12
Thameside Complex, Orsett Road
Tel: (01375) 382555
Over 1,500 artefacts interpreting 250,000 years of Thurrock's Heritage. From prehistory through to our recent industrial developments.
Times: Open all year, Mon-Sat, 0900-1700. Closed Bank Hols.
Fee: Free.
Facilities: P T(1 hr)

Great Bardfield

Bardfield Cage Map ref. F3
Bridge Street
Tel: (01371) 810516
Great Bardfield Cage is a 19th C. village lock-up. There is a figure of a man in the cage and an audio tape player.
Times: Open 3 Apr-26 Sept, Sat, Sun and Bank Hol Mon, 1400-1700.
Fee: Free. Donations appreciated.
Facilities: P T(20 mins)

Great Bardfield

Cottage Museum Map ref. F3
Dunmow Road
Tel: (01371) 810516
A 16th C. charity cottage with a collection of 19th C. and 20th C. domestic and agricultural artefacts and some rural crafts. Mainly straw plaiting and corn dollies.
Times: Open 3 Apr-26 Sept, Sat, Sun and Bank Hol Mon, 1400-1700.
Fee: Free. Donations appreciated.
Facilities: P T(1 hr)

Museum of Power, Langford

Great Dunmow

Great Dunmow Maltings Map ref. E5
See entry in Ancient Monuments section.

Great Warley (nr. Brentwood)

Hazle Ceramics Workshop Map ref. D10
Stallion's Yard, Codham Hall
Tel: (01277) 220892 Web: www.hazle.com
Discover the background to our award-winning designs, especially 'A Nation of Shopkeepers'. Learn how to cast clay into moulds, and watch demonstrations of the whole ceramic process. Hobby painting.
Times: Open all year, Fri, Sat and Bank Hols, 1100-1700. Closed 24-31 Dec.
Fee: Free.
Facilities: P T(1 hr)

Harlow

The Museum of Harlow Map ref. B7
Muskham Road, Off First Avenue
Tel: (01279) 454959 Web: www.tmoh.com
Museum showing the history of Harlow from earliest times to the present day. Also includes a bicycle collection, local history library and three walled gardens.
Times: Open all year, Tues-Fri, 1000-1700; Sat, 1000-1230 and 1330-1700. Closed 9, 11, 12 Apr; 25, 26 Dec and 1 Jan.
Fee: Free.
Facilities: P T(1½ hrs)

Harwich

Ha'penny Pier Visitor Centre Map ref. O3
The Quay
Tel: (01255) 503429 Web: www.harwich-society.com
Visitor information centre for everything in Harwich. Includes a small Harwich and the New World exhibition.
Times: Open 1 May-31 Aug, daily, from 1000. Last admission 1630.
Fee: Free.
Facilities: P T(20 mins)

Harwich

Harwich Lifeboat Museum Map ref. O3
Timberfields, off Wellington Road
Tel: (01255) 503429 Web: www.harwich-society.com
The Harwich Lifeboat Museum contains the last Clacton off-shore 37ft lifeboat, the Oakley class, and a fully-illustrated history of the lifeboat service in Harwich.
Times: Open 1 May-31 Aug, daily, from 1000. Last admission 1630.
Fee: 50p/25p.
Facilities: P T(30 mins)

Harwich
Harwich Maritime Museum Map ref. O3
Low Lighthouse, Harbour Crescent
Tel: (01255) 503429 Web: www.harwich-society.com
A museum with special displays related to the Royal Navy and commercial shipping, with fine views over the unending shipping movements in the harbour.
Times: Open 1 May-31 Aug, daily, from 1000. Last admission 1630.
Fee: 50p/25p.
Facilities: T(30 mins)

Kelvedon (nr. Coggeshall)
Feering and Kelvedon Local History Museum Map ref. I5
Aylett's School, Maldon Road
Tel: (01376) 571206
Artefacts from the Roman settlement of Canonium, manorial history, agricultural tools and bygones.
Times: Open 3 Jan-28 Feb, Sat, 0930-1230. 1 Mar-30 Oct, Mon, 1400-1700; Sat, 0930-1230. 6 Nov-18 Dec, Sat, 0930-1230. Closed Bank Hols.
Fee: Free.
Facilities: T(1 hr)

Lindsell (nr. Great Dunmow)
Lindsell Art Gallery Map ref. E4
Tel: (01371) 870777
Art gallery specialising in paintings, prints, sculptures and greeting cards by local artists. Pictures of local interest.
Times: Open all year, daily (except Wed), 0930-1730. Closed 25-31 Dec.
Fee: Free.
Facilities: T(30 mins)

Southchurch Hall Museum, Southend-on-Sea

Linford (nr. Tilbury)
Walton Hall Museum Map ref. F12
Walton Hall Road
Tel: (01375) 671874 Web: www.waltonhallmuseum.com
The main collection is housed in a 17th C. English barn and other farm buildings. Bygones, tools, wagons, militaria, domestic and motoring displays. Old-time dairy, blacksmith and printshop displays.
Times: Open 3 Apr-18 Dec, Thurs-Sun and Bank Hol Mon, 1000-1700. Please contact for school holiday openings.
Fee: £3.00/£1.50/£1.50.
Facilities: T(4 hrs)

Maldon
Maeldune Heritage Centre Map ref. I7
Plume Building
Tel: (01621) 851628
The Maeldune Centre houses the celebrated Maldon embroidery and exhibitions of paintings and local history. Large archive of old Maldon photographs.
Times: Open 2 Jan-27 Mar, Thurs-Sat, 1300-1600. 1 Apr-31 Oct, Mon-Sat, 1300-1600. 4 Nov-24 Dec, Thurs-Sat, 1300-1600. Closed 25, 26 Dec and 1 Jan.
Fee: Free.
Facilities: T(1 hr)

Maldon
Maldon District Museum Map ref. I7
47 Mill Road
Tel: (01621) 842688
Web: www.maldonmuseum.fsnet.co.uk
A small museum devoted to Maldon town with many articles of a general and domestic nature.
Times: Open 2 Apr-31 Oct, Wed-Fri, 1400-1600; Sat, Sun and Bank Hol Mon, 1400-1700.
Fee: £1.00/25p.
Facilities: T(1 hr)

Manningtree
Manningtree and District Local History Museum Map ref. M3
Manningtree Library, High Street
Tel: (01206) 392747
Displays of old photographs, artefacts, books and local maps. Some permanent displays, with two exhibitions yearly.
Times: Open 3 Jan-24 Dec, Wed, 1000-1200; Fri, 1400-1600; Sat, 1000-1200. Closed 9, 10 Apr and 25-31 Dec.
Fee: Free. Donations welcome.
Facilities: T(1 hr)

Navestock (nr. Romford)
Norpar Flowers Map ref. D9
See entry in Gardens section.

 HISTORY & HERITAGE

Colchester Castle Museum

Ongar
Blake Hall Gardens and Museum Map ref. D7
See entry in Gardens section.

Purfleet
Purfleet Heritage and Military Centre Map ref. D12
Royal Gunpowder Magazine, Centurion Way
Tel: (01708) 866764/523409
The Royal Gunpowder Magazine dates from 1760. The heritage centre displays local history, photographs, artefacts and memorabilia.
Times: Open Nov-Mar, Thurs and Sun, 1000-1500. Apr-Oct, Thurs, Sun and Bank Hols, 1000-1630.
Fee: £2.00/75p/£5.00 (family).
Facilities: P T(4 hrs)

Rayleigh
Rayleigh Windmill and Museum Map ref. H10
See entry in Mills section.

DID YOU KNOW

The Electric Palace Cinema in Harwich, is the oldest unaltered, purpose-built cinema in Britain, dating from 1911

Ridgewell
Ridgewell Airfield Commemorative Museum Map ref. G2
Tel: (01787) 277310 Web: www.381st.com
Small private collection of military/civilian memorabilia, dedicated to the USAAF 381st Bomb Group and 90 Squadron, RAF who flew from Ridgewell. Housed in US base hospital building.
Times: Open 11 Apr, 9 May, 13 Jun, 11 Jul, 8 Aug, 12 Sept, Sun, 1100-1700. Other times by appointment.
Fee: Free.
Facilities: P T(1½ hrs)

Saffron Walden
Fry Public Art Gallery Map ref. C/D2
Bridge End Gardens, Castle Street
Tel: (01799) 513779 Web: www.fryartgallery.org
Permanent exhibition of 20th C. British artists who have lived and worked in North West Essex. Additionally two or three changing exhibitions are on show in parallel.
Times: Open 11 Apr-31 Oct, Tues, Sat, Sun and Bank Hols, 1400-1700.
Fee: Free.
Facilities: T(45 mins)

 HISTORY & HERITAGE

Saffron Walden

Saffron Walden Museum Map ref. C/D2
Museum Street
Tel: (01799) 510333
A friendly, family-sized museum of local history, decorative arts, ethnography, archaeology and natural history. Museum of the Year Award: Best Museum of Social History.
Times: Open 1 Jan-29 Feb, Mon-Sat, 1000-1630; Sun and Bank Hols, 1400-1630. 1 Mar-31 Oct, Mon-Sat, 1000-1700; Sun and Bank Hols, 1400-1700. 1 Nov-31 Dec, Mon-Sat, 1000-1630; Sun and Bank Hols, 1400-1630. Closed 24 and 25 Dec.
Fee: £1.00/free/50p.
Facilities: T(1 hr)

Southend-on-Sea

Central Museum and Planetarium Map ref. I11
Victoria Avenue
Tel: (01702) 434449 Web: www.southendmuseums.co.uk
An Edwardian building housing displays of archaeology, natural history, social and local history. Hands-on Discovery Centre. Planetarium.
Times: Open all year, Tues-Sat, 1000-1700. Closed 9 Apr, 25, 26 Dec and 1 Jan.
Fee: Museum free. Charge for Planetarium £2.40/£1.70.
Facilities: T(1 hr)

Southend-on-Sea

Focal Point Gallery Map ref. I11
Southend Central Library, Victoria Avenue
Tel: (01702) 612621 Web: www.focalpoint.org.uk
A regularly changing exhibition programme of the best of contemporary photography, digital and video art. Artists' talks and workshops accompany most shows.
Times: Open all year, Mon-Fri, 0900-1900; Sat, 0900-1700. Closed Bank Hols, 25, 26 Dec and 1 Jan. Closed between exhibitions, please contact for details.
Fee: Free.
Facilities: T(1 hr)

Southend-on-Sea

Prittlewell Priory Map ref. I11
Priory Park, Victoria Avenue
Tel: (01702) 342878 Web: www.southendmuseums.co.uk
The remains of a 12th C. priory with later additions housing displays of medieval religious life, radios, gramophones and televisions.
Times: Open all year, Tues-Sat, 1000-1300 and 1400-1700 (or dusk). Closed 9 Apr, 25, 26 Dec and 1 Jan.
Fee: Free.
Facilities: T(30 mins)

Southend-on-Sea

Southchurch Hall Museum Map ref. I11
Southchurch Hall Gardens, Southchurch Hall Close
Tel: (01702) 467671 Web: www.southendmuseums.co.uk
A moated, timber-framed 14th C. manor-house with Tudor extensions set in attractive gardens. Rooms in period settings.
Times: Open all year, Tues-Sat, 1000-1300 and 1400-1700 (or dusk). Mornings reserved for schools during term time. Closed 9 Apr, 25, 26 Dec and 1 Jan.
Fee: Free.
Facilities: T(1 hr)

Southend-on-Sea

Southend Pier Museum Map ref. I11
Southend Pier, Marine Parade
Tel: (01702) 611214/614553
Situated in redundant pier workshops underneath the pier station (Shore End). Depicts the history of the longest pier in the world from 1830. Pictures and antique slot machines.
Times: Open 1 May-31 Oct, Tues, Wed, Sat, Sun and Bank Hols, 1100-1700 (1730 on school hols). Open 26 Dec and 1 Jan.
Fee: 60p.
Facilities: T(1 hr) (by arrangement)

Southend-on-Sea

Southend Planetarium Map ref. I11
Central Museum, Victoria Avenue
Tel: (01702) 434449 Web: www.southendmuseums.co.uk
Projector provides a clear illusion of the night sky with stars and the Milky Way which lasts 40 minutes. No children under 5 admitted.
Times: Open all year, Wed-Sat, shows at 1100, 1400 and 1600. Closed 9 Apr, 25, 26 Dec and 1 Jan.
Fee: £2.40/£1.70.
Facilities: T(45 mins)

Stansted Mountfitchet

House on the Hill Toy Museums Adventure Map ref. C4
Tel: (01279) 813237 Web: www.mountfitchetcastle.com
An exciting, animated toy museum covering 7,000 sq ft and featuring a huge collection of toys from Victorian times to the 1970s. Offers a nostalgic trip back to childhood.
Times: Open all year, daily, 1000-1700. Closed Mons in Jan. Please contact for Christmas openings.
Fee: £4.00/£3.20/£3.50. 10% discount on admission to toy museum and castle (see page 146) next door, if visiting both places on the same day.
Facilities: T(2 hrs)

Thaxted
Thaxted Guildhall Map ref. E3
Town Street
Tel: (01371) 830226 Web: www.thaxted.co.uk
A 15th C. building housing a permanent display of old photographs and relics, mainly relating to the history of Thaxted. Exhibitions on some weekends and small museum.
Times: Open 9 Apr-26 Sept, Sun and Bank Hol weekends, 1400-1730.
Fee: 50p/10p.
Facilities: T(30 mins)

Tiptree
Tiptree Tearoom, Museum and Shop Map ref. I6
Wilkin and Sons Ltd
Tel: (01621) 814524 Web: www.tiptree.com
Tearoom and shop with a museum displaying how life was and how the art of jam-making has advanced over the years at Tiptree.
Times: Open 5 Jan-30 Apr, Mon-Sat, 1000-1700. 1 May-31 Aug, Mon-Sat, 1000-1700; Sun, 1200-1700. 1 Sept-24 Dec, Mon-Sat, 1000-1700. Closed 25 Dec-1 Jan.
Fee: Free.
Facilities: Q T(1½ hrs)

Waltham Abbey
Epping Forest District Museum Map ref. A8
39-41 Sun Street
Tel: (01992) 716882
Web: www.eppingforestdistrictmuseum.org.uk
Tudor and Georgian timber-framed buildings with a herb garden, a Tudor-panelled room, temporary exhibitions, the social history of Epping Forest and many special events.
Times: Open 2 Jan-30 Apr, Mon, 1400-1700; Tues, 1200-1700; Fri, 1400-1700; Sat, 1000-1700. 1 May-28 Sept, Mon, 1400-1700; Tues, 1200-1700; Fri, 1400-1700; Sat, 1000-1700; Sun, 1400-1700. 1 Oct-Dec, Mon, 1400-1700; Tues, 1200-1700; Fri, 1400-1700; Sat, 1000-1700. Closed 25 and 26 Dec.
Fee: Free.
Facilities: T(1 hr)

Waltham Abbey
Royal Gunpowder Mills Map ref. A8
Beaulieu Drive
Tel: (01992) 707370 Web: www.royalgunpowdermills.com
Combining fascinating history, exciting science and 175 acres of natural parkland, the Royal Gunpowder Mills offers a truly unique day out for the family. Exhibitions and displays.
Times: Open 24 Apr-26 Sept, Sat, Sun and Bank Hols, 1100-1700 (last entry at 1530).
Fee: £5.50/£2.50/£4.50/£16.00.
Facilities: Q T(3½ hrs)

Walton-on-the-Naze
Walton Maritime Museum Map ref. O5
East Terrace
Tel: (01255) 678259
A 100-year-old former lifeboat house, carefully restored with exhibitions of local interest, particularly maritime, urban, geological seaside and development.
Times: Open 9-12 Apr; 1-3 May; 29-31 May, 1400-1600. 3 Jul-26 Sept, daily, 1400-1600.
Fee: 50p/free.
Facilities: T(30 mins)

Westcliff-on-Sea
Beecroft Art Gallery Map ref. I11
Station Road
Tel: (01702) 347418 Web: www.beecroft-art-gallery.co.uk
An Edwardian building housing a permanent collection of works of art. Varied programme of temporary exhibitions. Panoramic estuary views.
Times: Open all year, Tues-Sat, 1000-1300 and 1400-1700. Closed 9 Apr, 25, 26 Dec and 1 Jan.
Fee: Free.
Facilities: T(1½ hrs)

West Mersea
Mersea Island Museum Map ref. K6
High Street
Tel: (01206) 385191
Museum of local, social and natural history with displays of methods and equipment used in fishing and wildfowling. Fossils and a mineral display. Also special exhibitions.
Times: Open 1 May-26 Sept, Wed-Sun and Bank Hol Mon, 1400-1700.
Fee: 50p/25p/25p.
Facilities: T(1 hr)

Witham
Dorothy L. Sayers Centre Map ref. H6
Witham Library, 18 Newland Street
Tel: (01376) 519625
A reference collection of books by/about Dorothy L. Sayers. The centre is only 100m from the house where Sayers lived, and a statue of her stands just across the road.
Times: Open all year, Thurs, 1400-1700. Closed 25 Dec and 1 Jan.
Fee: Free.
Facilities: T(30 mins)

Machinery & Transport

Audley End (nr. Saffron Walden)

Audley End Miniature Railway Map ref. C2
Tel: (01799) 541354 Web: www.audley-end-railway.co.uk
Steam and diesel locomotives in 10.25 gauge, running through attractive woodland for 1 1/2 miles. The railway crosses the River Cam twice.
Times: Open 20 Mar-31 Oct, Sat and Sun, 1400-1700. Daily in school hols, 1400-1700. Bank Hols, 1100-1700.
Fee: All day ticket £5.00/£3.00.
Facilities: T(1 hr)

Burnham-on-Crouch

Mangapps Railway Museum Map ref. J9
Tel: (01621) 784898 Web: www.mangapps.co.uk
A large collection of railway relics, two restored stations, locomotives, coaches and wagons with a working railway line of 1 mile.
Times: Open all year, every weekend and Bank Hol Mon (except Jan and 17/18 Jul). Daily in Easter and summer school hols, 1130-1700.
Fee: Prices vary, please contact for details.
Facilities: T(2 hrs)

Canvey Island

Canvey Railway and Model Engineering Club Map ref. H11
Waterside Farm Leisure Centre
Tel: (01268) 413235 Web: www.cramec.org
Two miniature railways, both live steam and/or diesel. Approx. 1 mile of track.
Times: Open 4 Apr-10 Oct, Sun, 1000-1730.
Fee: Free entry. Train rides 70p/70p. Multi ride tickets £7.00 for 12 rides.
Facilities: T(1 hr)

Canvey Island

Castle Point Transport Museum Map ref. H11
105 Point Road
Tel: (01268) 684272
A 1935 museum housing a collection of buses, coaches and commercial vehicles in restored and unrestored condition. Some examples of these vehicles are unique.
Times: Open 4 Apr-10 Oct, Sun, 1000-1630.
Fee: Free.
Facilities: T(1 hr)

Castle Hedingham

Colne Valley Railway Map ref. G2/3
Yeldham Road
Tel: (01787) 461174 Web: www.colnevalleyrailway.co.uk
An award-winning station. Ride in the most pleasant part of the Colne Valley. A large, interesting collection of operational heritage railway rolling stock.
Times: Open 28 Mar-31 Oct, Sun, 1030-1700. Also Wed and Thurs in school hols, and daily in Aug.
Fee: Operational steam days (includes rides) £6.00/£3.00/£5.00/£18.00.
Facilities: T(2 hrs)

Colchester

East Anglian Railway Museum Map ref. I4
Chappel Station, Wakes Colne
Tel: (01206) 242524 Web: www.earm.co.uk
A large and varied collection of working and static railway exhibits from the age of steam, set in original surroundings of a once important Victorian country junction station.
Times: Open all year, daily, 1000-1700. Closed 25 Dec.
Fee: £6.00/£3.00/£4.50/£15.00 (event days). £3.00/£1.50/£2.50/£8.00 (non-event days).
Facilities: Q T(3 hrs)

East Tilbury

Coalhouse Fort (Thameside Aviation Museum)
Map ref. F12
See entry in Ancient Monuments section.

Goldhanger (nr. Maldon)

Maldon and District Agricultural and Domestic Museum
Map ref. J7
See entry in Museums & Galleries section.

East Anglian Railway Museum, Colchester

Langford (nr. Maldon)

Museum of Power Map ref. H7

Steam Pumping Station, Hatfield Road

Tel: (01621) 843183 Web: www.museumofpower.org.uk

Housed in an impressive 1920s building. A large triple-expansion steam engine is the main exhibit with many other sources of power on show.

Times: Open 1 Jan, 1000-1600. 2-31 Jan, by arrangement only. 1 Feb-1 Apr, Fri-Sun, 1000-1600. 2 Apr-31 Oct, Wed-Sun, 1000-1700. 1 Nov-Christmas, Fri-Sun, 1000-1600. Open all Bank Hol Mons.

Fee: Free. Charges for special events

Facilities: T(1½ hrs)

Linford (nr. Tilbury)

Walton Hall Museum Map ref. F12

See entry in Museums & Galleries section.

North Weald

North Weald Airfield Museum Map ref. C8

Astra House, Hurricane Way

Tel: (01992) 523010 Web: www.fly.to/northweald

A fine old house at the former main gate of North Weald Airfield, standing adjacent to an impressive memorial. Artifacts, photographs and models telling story of airfield.

Times: Open 28 Mar-31 Oct, Sun and Bank Hols, 1200-1700.

Fee: £1.50/£1.00/£1.00.

Facilities: T(2½ hrs)

Pitsea (nr. Basildon)

The Motorboat Museum Map ref. G11

Wat Tyler Country Park

Tel: (01268) 550077

A museum devoted to the history and evolution of the motorboat in the sports and leisure field.

Times: Open all year, Mon and Thurs-Sun, 1000-1630. Daily during school hols, 1000-1630. Closed 24 Dec-3 Jan.

Fee: Free.

Facilities: T(3½ hrs)

St. Osyth (nr. Clacton-on-Sea)

East Essex Aviation Society and Museum Map ref. M6

Martello Tower, Point Clear

An exhibition of aircraft parts from local recoveries. There are also displays from World War I up to the late 1940s. Housed in a 19th C. Martello tower.

Times: Open all year, Mon, 1900-2130; 1 Feb-31 Oct, Sun, 1000-1400. 2 Jun-29 Sept, Wed, 1000-1400. Open additional hours on Bank Hols.

Fee: Free.

Facilities: T(1½ hrs)

Thaxted

Glendale Forge Map ref. E3

Monk Street

Tel: (01371) 830466

Forge with a comprehensive range of wrought ironwork, gates, lanterns, fireguards, blacksmith work and a small collection of unusual half-size vehicles.

Times: Open all year, Mon-Sat, 0900-1700; Sun, 1000-1200. Train shed open, Wed, 1400-1700; Sun, 1000-1200. Please phone for Christmas openings.

Fee: Free. Donations appreciated.

Facilities: T(1½ hrs)

DID YOU KNOW

Guglielmo Marconi established the world's first radio factory here in 1899. In the same year he established the first radio link between Britain and France. Then in 1901 the first radio link with America. It was also the birthplace of radio broadcasting, as the location for Dame Nellie Melba's pioneering radio recital in 1920. The BBC's first long-wave radio station was "Chelmsford 5XX".

Southend-on-Sea

Mills

Aythorpe Roding

Aythorpe Roding Postmill Map ref. D6
Tel: (01245) 437663
An 18th C. postmill (the largest remaining in Essex) restored to working order. It is winded by a fantail arrangement, which runs along a stone track around the mill.
Times: Open 25 Apr; 9, 30 May; 27 Jun; 25 Jul; 29 Aug; 26 Sept, Sun, 1400-1700.
Fee: Free.
Facilities: T(2 hrs)

Bocking (nr. Braintree)

Bocking Windmill Map ref. G4
Church Street
Tel: (01376) 341339
Postmill built in 1721. Small collection of historic agricultural items.
Times: Open 3, 9 May, 1000-1700. 31 May, 27 Jun, 25 Jul, 30 Aug, 1400-1700.
Fee: Free. Donations appreciated.
Facilities: P T(1 hr)

Colchester

Bourne Mill Map ref. K4
Bourne Road
Tel: (01206) 572422 Web: www.nationaltrust.org.uk
The mill was originally built as a fishing lodge in 1591, and features stepped Dutch Gables. There is a mill pond, and some of the machinery, including the waterwheel is working.
Times: Open 1 Jun-31 Aug, Tues and Sun, 1400-1700.
Fee: £2.00/£1.00.
Facilities: P T(2 hrs) NT

Finchingfield

Finchingfield (Duck End) Postmill Map ref. F3
Tel: (01245) 437663
A small, simple, mid-18th C. feudal or estate-type postmill with a wooden wind shaft and one pair of stones.
Times: Open 18 Apr; 9, 16 May; 20 Jun; 18 Jul; 15 Aug; 19 Sept, Sun, 1300-1700.
Fee: Free.
Facilities: T(2 hrs)

DID YOU KNOW

The descendants of the first US president came from Purleigh. Lawrence Washington was rector of the 14th C. All Saints Church from 1633-1643.

Mountnessing (nr. Ingatestone)

Mountnessing Windmill Map ref. E9
Roman Road
Tel: (01245) 437663
An early 19th C. postmill restored to working order. Visitors may climb the windmill and see the wooden machinery.
Times: Open 9, 16 May; 20 Jun; 18 Jul; 15 Aug; 19 Sept; 17 Oct, Sun, 1300-1700.
Fee: Free.
Facilities: P T(1¾ hrs)

Rayleigh

Rayleigh Windmill and Museum Map ref. H10
Mill Hall Car Park, Bellingham Lane
Tel: (01268) 771072
A windmill with sails but no mechanism. On the ground floor, the museum has bygones and local artefacts.
Times: Open 3 Apr-25 Sept, Sat, 1030-1300.
Fee: 20p/10p/20p.
Facilities: P T(30 mins)

Stansted Mountfitchet

Stansted Mountfitchet Windmill Map ref. C4
Millside
Tel: (01279) 647213
Brick tower windmill built in 1787. Not working, but contains most of original machinery. Scheduled ancient monument.
Times: Open 11, 12 Apr; 2, 9, 30, 31 May; 6 Jun; 4 Jul; 1, 29, 30 Aug; 5 Sept; 3 Oct, Sun and Bank Hols, 1400-1800.
Fee: 50p/25p.
Facilities: T(45 mins)

Stock (nr. Ingatestone)

Stock Towermill Map ref. F9
Mill Lane
Tel: (01245) 437663
A 19th C. towermill, recently restored to working order and typical of the latest in millwrights techniques just before windmills became obsolete.
Times: Open 11 Apr; 9 May; 13 Jun; 11 Jul; 8 Aug; 12 Sept; 10 Oct, Sun 1300-1700.
Fee: Free.
Facilities: P T(2 hrs)

Thorrington (nr. Wivenhoe)

Thorrington Tidemill Map ref. L5
Brightlingsea Road
Tel: (01245) 437663
An early 19th C. tidal watermill, restored by Essex County Council. Visitors may climb to the top of the mill.
Times: Open 25 Apr; 9, 30 May; 27 Jun; 25 Jul; 29 Aug; 26 Sept, Sun, 1400-1700.
Fee: Free.
Facilities: P T(1¾ hrs)

Gardens

Abridge (nr. Romford)
BBC Essex Garden Map ref. B/C9
Ongar Road
Tel: (01708) 688581 Web: www.gardeningwithken.com
Garden with lawn, borders and small vegetable area. Linked to Ken's programme 'Down to Earth' on Sats. Also farmyard pets, teashop, superb plants and clematis on sale.
Times: Open all year, daily, 0900-1700. Closed 23 Dec-2 Jan
Fee: Free.
Facilities: P T(1 hr)

Ardleigh (nr. Colchester)
Green Island Garden Map ref. L4
Green Island, Park Road
Tel: (01206) 230455
Beautiful gardens situated in 19 acres of woodland, with a huge variety of unusual plants. Lots of interest all year. New sculpture trail.
Times: Open 7 Apr-14 Oct, Wed, Thurs and Bank Hol Mons, 1300-1700. Also Suns, 11, 25 Apr; 9, 16, 30 May; 6, 20, 27 Jun; 11, 25 Jul; 15 Aug; 12, 26 Sept.
Fee: £2.50/50p.
Facilities: P T(1½ hrs)

Bocking
Roundwood Garden Centre Map ref. G4
Bocking Church Street
Tel: (01376) 551728
Drought and Millennium gardens, nature trail with ponds and wildflower meadow. Aviary.
Times: Open all year, Mon-Fri, 0915-1700. Closed 9, 12 Apr and 23 Dec-2 Jan.
Fee: Free.
Facilities: P T(1 hr)

Cressing Temple Barns, Cressing

Coggeshall
Marks Hall Garden and Arboretum Map ref. H/I4
Tel: (01376) 563796 Web: www.markshall.org.uk
Newly re-opened walled garden, designed for summer. Winter walks and snowdrops. Wildlife walks through woodland. Visitor centre with teashop and gift shop.
Times: Open 1 Jan-26 Mar, Fri-Sun, 1030-dusk. 27 Mar-31 Oct, Tues-Sun and Bank Hol Mon, 1030-1700. 1 Nov-31 Dec, Sat and Sun, 1030-dusk.
Fee: £3.50 per car.
Facilities: P T(2½ hrs)

Coggeshall
Paycockes Map ref. I5
See entry in Historic Houses section.

Colchester
firstsite @ The Minories Art Gallery Map ref. K4
See entry in Museums & Galleries section.

Cressing (nr. Braintree)
Cressing Temple Barns Map ref. H5
See entry in Ancient Monuments section.

Dedham
Gnome Magic Map ref. L3
New Dawn, Old Ipswich Road (off A12)
Tel: (01206) 231390 Web: www.gnomemagic.co.uk
An unusual treat, with a delightful garden and an amazing wood (5 acres) where gnomes and their friends live. Come and meet them.
Times: Open 1 Apr-Oct, daily, 1000-1730 (last entry at 1630).
Fee: £3.50/£2.00/£3.00.
Facilities: P T(2 hrs)

Dedham

The Sir Alfred Munnings Art Museum Map ref. L3

See entry in Museums & Galleries section.

Elmstead Market

The Beth Chatto Gardens Map ref. L4

Tel: (01206) 822007 Web: www.bethchatto.co.uk

Drought tolerant plants furnish the gravel garden throughout the year, the dappled wood garden is filled with shade lovers, while the water garden fills the spring fed hollow.

Times: Open 3 Jan-29 Feb, Mon-Fri, 0900-1600. 1 Mar-31 Oct, Mon-Sat, 0900-1700. 1 Nov-23 Dec, Mon-Fri, 0900-1600. Closed 11 Apr and 24 Dec-2 Jan.

Fee: £3.50/free.

Facilities: Q P T(3 hrs)

Feering (nr. Coggeshall)

Feeringbury Manor Map ref. I5

Tel: (01376) 561946

Six acre plantsman's garden with constant running water over a Victorian water-wheel. Ebullient planting within an interesting design. Many plants grown from seed. Wildflowers and pots a special feature.

Times: Open 1 Apr-30 Jul and 2 Sept-1 Oct, Thurs and Fri, 0800-1600.

Fee: £2.00/free.

Facilities: P T(1 hr)

Gosfield (nr. Halstead)

Gosfield Hall Map ref. G4

See entry in Historic Houses section.

Harlow

The Gibberd Garden Map ref. B7

Marsh Lane, Gilden Way

Tel: (01279) 442112 Web: www.thegibberdgarden.co.uk

Important 20th C. garden designed by Sir Frederick Gibberd, master planner for Harlow New Town, with some fifty sculptures. Shop.

Times: Open 3 Apr-29 Sept, Wed, Sat, Sun and Bank Hol Mon, 1400-1800. Last admission 1700.

Fee: £4.00/free/£2.50.

Facilities: P T(1½ hrs) (on leads)

Visit COLCHESTER Castle *park*

COLCHESTER'S CASTLE PARK is an oasis of horticultural splendour in the town centre. This award winning classic Victorian park is a delight for the senses all the year round. But it's not just the gardens that makes the park such a delight to visit. Castle Park's 23 gently sloping acres (9.3ha) provide the perfect venue for fairs, festivals, open-air concerts and displays.

Variety is the essence of Castle Park. There are formal flower beds and gardens, a Sensory Garden, a children's playground, the newly planted herb beds and rhododendron borders, the new Hollytrees museum where you can discover life in Colchester over the last 300 years, and a summertime Pitch & Putt. A magnificent weeping willow provides an impressive backdrop to the boating lake and you can take picturesque walks along the river. Stroll through the park to the oldest Roman wall in Britain, for a treat in the café near the Victorian bandstand or bring your own picnic.

No trip to Castle Park is complete without a visit to the award-winning Castle Museum, popular for its hands-on displays and holiday events. Visit the Castle Museum and its Roman foundations and discover the major historical events which took place in and around the Castle almost 2000 years ago.

EAST OF ENGLAND TOURIST BOARD
QUALITY ASSURED VISITOR ATTRACTION

COLCHESTER

*f*OR FURTHER INFORMATION ABOUT COLCHESTER AND EVENTS IN CASTLE PARK
☞ PLEASE CALL THE COLCHESTER VISITOR INFORMATION CENTRE
1 QUEEN STREET · COLCHESTER · ESSEX · CO1 2PG ☎ 01206 282920
OR CLICK ONTO **www.colchesterwhatson.co.uk**

Harlow

The Museum of Harlow Map ref. B7
See entry in Museums & Galleries section.

Hartford End (nr. Braintree)

Leez Priory Map ref. F5
See entry in Historic Houses section.

Ingatestone

Ingatestone Hall Map ref. E9
See entry in Historic Houses section.

Layer Marney (nr. Colchester)

Layer Marney Tower Map ref. J5
See entry in Historic Houses section.

Little Easton (nr. Great Dunmow)

The Gardens of Easton Lodge Map ref. D/E4
Warwick House, Easton Lodge
Tel: (01371) 876979 Web: www.eastonlodge.co.uk
23 acres of beautiful historic gardens, famous for their peaceful atmosphere. Featuring the splendid formal gardens created by leading Edwardian designer Harold Peto. Former home of the Countess of Warwick.
Times: Open 9 Apr-31 Oct, Fri-Sun and Bank Hols, 1200-1800. Please contact to confirm snowdrops opening times.
Fee: £3.80/£1.50/£3.50.
Facilities: T(2 hrs) (on leads)

Little Easton (nr. Great Dunmow)

Little Easton Manor and Barn Theatre Map ref. D/E4
Park Road
Tel: (01371) 872857
Little Easton Manor has gardens, lakes and fountains. Also The Barn Theatre, angling, a caravan and rally site and refreshments.
Times: Open 3 Jun-30 Sept, Thurs, 1300-1700.
Fee: £2.50/free/£2.00.
Facilities: T(2 hrs)

Messing (nr. Tiptree)

Red House Visitor Centre Map ref. I5
School Road
Tel: (01621) 815219
Sensory and artists gardens, pond, children's play area and junior farm. Coffee shop, plant and craft sales.
Times: Open all year, Mon-Thurs, 0930-1700; Fri 0930-1600. Weekends from Easter-Aug Bank Hol, 1000-1530.
Fee: Free.
Facilities: T(2 hrs) (on leads)

RHS Garden: Hyde Hall, Rettendon

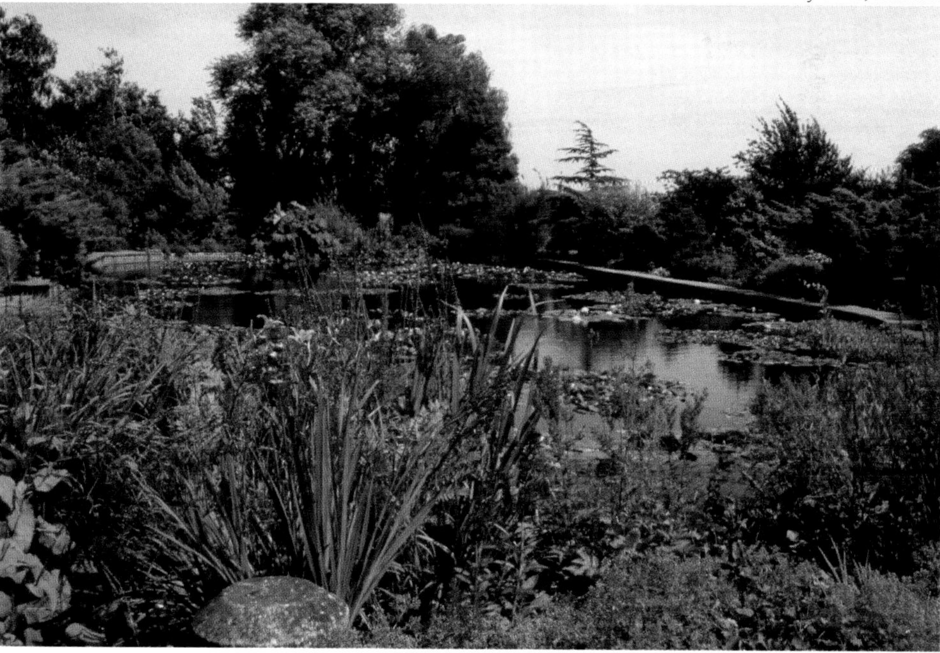

Navestock (nr. Romford)
Norpar Flowers Map ref. D9
Navestock Hall
Tel: (01277) 374968 Web: www.norpar.co.uk
Dried flowers grown and dried on the premises. Demonstrations, country walk, 10th C. church and antique farm implement museum.
Times: Open all year, Mon-Fri, 0900-1700; Sat, 1000-1700; Sun, 1100-1700.
Fee: Free.
Facilities: P T(2 hrs)

Ongar
Blake Hall Gardens and Museum Map ref. D7
Bobbingworth
Tel: (01277) 362502 Web: www.blakehall.co.uk
Twenty five acres of beautiful gardens, with many species of trees, peat and herbaceous borders, old ice house, rose garden and tropical house. Also World War II museum.
Times: Open 9 Apr-29 Sept, Good Fri and Sat-Wed, 1100-1700.
Fee: £3.00/£1.50/£3.00/£8.00.
Facilities: P T(1½ hrs)

2003 REGIONAL EXCELLENCE IN ENGLAND WINNER SMALL ATTRACTION

Rettendon (nr. Chelmsford)
RHS Garden: Hyde Hall Map ref. G9
Buckhatch Lane
Tel: (01245) 400256 Web: www.rhs.org.uk
20 acre garden with all year round interest, including dry garden, roses, flowering shrubs, perennial borders and alpines. National Collection of Viburnum. New garden for wildlife.
Times: Open Jan-Mar, daily, 1000-dusk. Apr-Sept, daily, 1000-1800. Oct-Dec, daily, 1000-dusk. Closed 25 Dec.
Fee: £4.50/£1.00
Facilities: P T(3 hrs)

Saffron Walden
Audley End House and Park Map ref. C2
See entry in Historic Houses section.

DID YOU KNOW

Coggeshall is said to be the most unluckiest place in Britain. It is said that ley lines cross here creating friction. It could be the cause of the unusually high number of disturbing things that have happened.

Saffron Walden
Bridge End Gardens Map ref. C/D2
Tel: (01799) 510445
Victorian garden featuring fine trees, garden ornaments, a rose garden, Dutch garden, pavilions and a hedge maze.
Times: Open all year, daily, 0800-dusk. Contact Tourist Information Centre for opening times of maze.
Fee: Free.
Facilities: T(1½ hrs)

Thaxted
The Thaxted Garden for Butterflies Map ref. E3
Aldboro Lodge, Park Street
Tel: (01371) 830780
A 1-acre retirement garden especially planted and developed to be attractive to butterflies and moths. Exhibition of photographs of the butterflies that have visited the garden.
Times: Open 1 May-30 Sept, daily, 1000-1700.
Fee: Free.
Facilities: P T(30 mins)

Widford (nr. Chelmsford)
Hylands House Map ref. F8
See entry in Historic Houses section.

Seafront Gardens, Clacton-on-Sea

Nurseries & Garden Centres

Ardleigh (nr. Colchester)

Notcutts Garden Centres Map ref. L4
Station Road, Ardleigh CO7 7RT
Tel: (01206) 230271 Web: www.notcutts.co.uk

Discover a world of ideas and inspiration around every corner for you, your home and your garden. From fabulous plants to gifts and treats galore, there's so much to see. Gift ideas from around the world, houseplants, books, 3,000 varieties of hardy plants (with a 2 year replacement guarantee), expert friendly advice about seasonal and bedding plants, garden furniture and barbecues. Keep an eye open for regular offers on key garden products. Notcutts open 7 days a week, free car-parking plus children's play area.

Southend-on-Sea

Coggeshall

The Dutch Nursery Garden Centre Map ref. I5
West Street, Coggeshall CO6 1NT
Tel: (01376) 561287

In picturesque Coggeshall, The Dutch Nursery is well worth a visit. The large shop has an interesting range of houseplants, silk flowers, gift items, pots, garden furniture and seasonal bulbs direct from Holland. The Plant Area has a varied range of trees, shrubs, climbing plants, roses and seasonal bedding. A large selection of terracotta and glazed pots and containers offer excellent value. Relax in our Coffee Shop or outdoor sun terrace with a delicious home-made cake or snack. Coach parties welcome by appointment. Finally, visit the water gardens and other shops adjacent to the large car park.

Morning coffee, teas, delicious home made cakes and lunches, served in our Café du Jardin next to our pleasant relaxing gardens. Play area for children. Gift shop and extensive ranges of home and garden items, plants, stoneware, cane and wooden furniture.

Open 7 days a week. In fine weather enjoy your meal in our gardens. Parties welcome, by appointment.

Roman Road *(on A12 slip road)*
Ingatestone, Essex.
Tel: (01277) 353268

Family Fun

Animal & Bird Collections

Billericay
Barleylands Farm Centre Map ref. F10
Barleylands Road
Tel: (01268) 290229 Web: www.barleylands.co.uk
Unique family attraction. Feed our friendly farm animals, cuddle a rabbit in the bunny barn, feed the ducks on the pond, have fun in the adventure play area. Museum, tearoom and miniature steam train (Sun only).
Times: Open 1 Mar-31 Oct, daily, 1000-1700.
Fee: £2.50/£2.50/£2.50.
Facilities: T(2 hrs)

Braintree
Freya's Ponyland Rescue Centre and Farm Museum
Map ref. H4
Gowers Farm, Tumblers Green
Tel: (01376) 325155
Pony rescue centre (mainly Shetlands) - which you can pet and groom. Also open farm with rare breeds, and museum offering an insight into farming over the last 150 years.
Times: Open all year, Fri-Sun, 1000-1600.
Fee: £3.50/£2.00/£2.00.
Facilities: T(2 hrs)

Chigwell
Hainault Forest Country Park Map ref. C10
See entry in Countryside section.

Marsh Farm Country Park, South Woodham Ferrers

Clacton-on-Sea
Clacton Pier (Seaquarium) Map ref. N6
See entry in Amusement/Theme Centres & Parks.

2003 REGIONAL EXCELLENCE IN ENGLAND WINNER LARGE ATTRACTION

Colchester
Colchester Zoo Map ref. J5
Maldon Road, Stanway
Tel: (01206) 331292 Web: www.colchester-zoo.co.uk
One of Europe's finest zoos, with over 200 species in 60 acres of gardens. New Playa Patagonia Sealion experience with 24 metre tunnel under the water. Don't miss the African Zone.
Times: Open all year, daily, from 0930. Closed 25 Dec.
Fee: £10.99/£6.99/£6.99.
Facilities: T(5 hrs)

Layer Marney (nr. Colchester)
Layer Marney Tower Map ref. J5
See entry in Historic Houses section.

Messing (nr. Tiptree)
Red House Visitor Centre Map ref. I5
See entry in Gardens section.

Mistley
Mistley Place Park Animal Rescue Centre Map ref. M3
New Road
Tel: (01206) 396483
Twenty five acres of woodlands and lakeside walks with goats, horses, sheep, rabbits, ducks, gift shop and a nature trail.
Times: Open all year, Tues-Sun and Bank Hol Mon, 1000-1800 (or dusk if earlier). Open daily in school hols. Please contact to check winter opening times.
Fee: £3.00/£2.00/£2.50.
Facilities: T(2 hrs)

Nazeing (nr. Harlow)

Ada Cole Rescue Stables Map ref. B7
Broadlands, Broadley Common
Tel: (01992) 892133 Web: www.adacole.co.uk
A horse rescue charity with 47 acres of paddocks and stables. Gift shop, information room, and pet's corner.
Times: Open all year, daily, 1400-1700. Closed 25, 26 Dec and 1 Jan.
Fee: £1.50/free.
Facilities: T(1½ hrs)

South Weald (nr. Brentwood)

Old MacDonalds Educational Farm Park Map ref. D9
Weald Road
Tel: (01277) 375177 Web: www.oldmacdonaldsfarm.org.uk
We tell the whole story of British livestock farming, keeping rare breeds, cattle, pigs, sheep, shire horses and poultry, red squirrels, owls, otters and lots more.
Times: Open 2 Jan-31 Mar, daily, 1000-dusk. 1 Apr-30 Sept, daily, 1000-1700. 1 Oct-31 Dec, daily, 1000-dusk. Closed 25, 26 Dec and 1 Jan.
Fee: £3.25/£2.00/£2.75.
Facilities: Q T(2 hrs)

South Woodham Ferrers

Marsh Farm Country Park Map ref. H9
Marsh Farm Road
Tel: (01245) 321552
Web: www.marshfarmcountrypark.co.uk
A farm centre with sheep, a pig unit, free-range chickens, milking demonstrations, an indoor and outdoor adventure play area, nature reserve, walks, picnic area and pet's barn.
Times: Open 14 Feb-29 Oct, daily, from 1000. Closing times vary. Contact for openings in Nov and Dec.
Fee: £5.60/£3.00/£4.00/£16.50.
Facilities: T(2½ hrs)

South Woodham Ferrers

Tropical Wings Butterfly and Bird Gardens Map ref. H9
Wickford Road
Tel: (01245) 425394 Web: www.tropicalwings.co.uk
Over 6,000 sq ft of tropical house, home to free-flying exotic butterflies, birds and tropical plants. Outdoor bird gardens. Children's play area.
Times: Open all year, daily, summer, 0930-1730; winter, 1030-1630.
Fee: £4.25/£2.75/£3.50/£12.00.
Facilities: T(3 hrs)

Great Bentley (nr. Clacton-on-Sea) is home of the largest village green in England.

Southend-on-Sea

Southend Sea Life Adventure Map ref. I11
Eastern Esplanade
Tel: (01702) 601834 Web: www.sealifeadventure.co.uk
The very latest in marine technology brings the secrets of the mysterious underwater world closer than ever before. An amazing underwater tunnel allows an all-round view. Daily talks and presentations.
Times: Open all year, daily, from 1000 (last admission 1700). Closed 25 Dec.
Fee: Please contact for details of admission prices.
Facilities: Q T(1½ hrs)

Waltham Abbey

Lee Valley Park Farms Map ref. A8
Stubbins Hall Lane, Crooked Mile
Tel: (01992) 892781 Web: www.leevalleypark.com
Two farms in one. Hayes Hill, a traditional-style farm with visitor facilities, including tearooms and play area. Holyfield Hall, a modern arable farm. Also information centre on the whole of the Lee Valley Regional Park.
Times: Open all year, Mon-Fri, 1000-1630; Sat, Sun and Bank Hols, 1000-1730 (or dusk if earlier). Closed 25, 26 Dec and 1 Jan.
Fee: £3.50/£2.00/£3.00/£14.00.
Facilities: T(3½ hrs)

Clacton Pier

Amusement/Theme Centres & Parks

Braintree

The Original Great Maze Map ref. F5
Blake House Craft Centre
Tel: (01376) 553146 Web: www.maze.info
This challenging maize maze is known as one of the biggest mind benders in the world. It has more than five miles of pathways laid out in over 10 acres of the idyllic north Essex countryside.
Times: Open 10 Jul-12 Sept, daily, 1000-1700.
Fee: £4.00/£2.50/£2.50.
Facilities: T(2-5 hrs)

Wethersfield (nr. Braintree)

Boydells Dairy Farm Map ref. F3
Tel: (01371) 850481 Web: www.boydellsdairy.co.uk
A small dairy farm where you can watch the milking of cows, sheep and goats. Also pigs, poultry and bees. Goat and donkey cart rides. Farm shop.
Times: Open 3 Apr-26 Sept, Fri-Sun and Bank Hols, 1400-1700. Also 3-18 Apr; 1-6 Jun; 22 Jul-31 Aug, daily, 1400-1700. Closed 9 Apr.
Fee: £3.50/£2.50.
Facilities: T(2 hrs)

Widdington (nr. Saffron Walden)

Mole Hall Wildlife Park Map ref. D3
Tel: (01799) 540400 Web: www.molehall.co.uk
Park with otters, chimps, guanaco, lemurs, wallabies, deer, a butterfly pavilion, attractive gardens, picnic/play areas and pet's corner.
Times: Open 1 Jan-31 Mar, daily, 1030-dusk (cafe, gift shop and butterfly pavilion closed). 1 Apr-31 Oct, daily, 1030-1800. 1 Nov-31 Dec, daily, 1030-dusk (cafe, gift shop and butterfly pavilion closed). Closed 25 Dec.
Fee: Please contact for details of admission prices.
Facilities: T(2½ hrs)

Clacton-on-Sea
Clacton Pier Map ref. N6
Tel: (01255) 421115 Web: www.clactonpier.co.uk
Fun pier with fairground rides, arcades, shops, cafes, restaurants, side shows, children's play area and seaquarium.
Times: Open all year, daily, from 1000. Rides open 1 Mar-end Oct. Closed 25 Dec.
Fee: Free. Individual charges for rides/attractions.
Facilities: T(3 hrs)

Colchester
PC Arena Map ref. K4
14 Queen Street
Tel: (01206) 542905
Web: www.pcarenas.com/colchester2.htm
East Anglia's only themed multiplayer PC gaming arena. Play all the latest games against your friends, or others. Lighting and an excellent sound system add to the atmosphere.
Times: Please contact for details of opening times.
Fee: Please contact for details of admission prices.
Facilities: T(1 hr)

Colchester
Quasar at Rollerworld Map ref. K4
Eastgates
Tel: (01206) 868868 Web: www.rollerworld.co.uk
East Anglia's largest quasar (laser game) arena. Futuristic briefing room, space age vesting room and industrial wasteland arena, complimented by fully interactive lights, UV effects, smoke generators and sub bass sound system.
Times: Open all year, please contact for further details.
Fee: Please contact for details of admission prices.
Facilities: T(2 hrs)

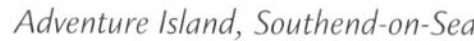
Adventure Island, Southend-on-Sea

Colchester
Rollerworld Map ref. K4
Eastgates
Tel: (01206) 868868 Web: www.rollerworld.co.uk
Great Britain's largest roller-skating rink, 25m x 50m maple floor. RollerHire, RollerCafe and RollerBar - stunning sound and light show.
Times: Open all year, please contact for further details.
Fee: Please contact for details of admission prices.
Facilities: T(2-3 hrs)

Dedham
Gnome Magic Map ref. L3
See entry in Gardens section.

Rayleigh
Megazone Laser Arena Map ref. H10
The Warehouse Centre, 7 Brook Road
Tel: (01268) 779100 Web: www.rayleighmegazone.co.uk
A game of stealth, strategy and skill, played in the laser arena in Essex with the most advanced laser system.
Times: Open all year, Mon-Fri, 1500-2200; Sat and Sun, 1000-2200; school hols, 1000-2300. Closed 9 Apr, 25, 26 Dec and 1 Jan.
Fee: Non-member £3.95, member £3.45.
Facilities: T(1½ hrs)

Southend-on-Sea
Adventure Island Map ref. I11
Sunken Gardens West, Western Esplanade
Tel: (01702) 443400 Web: www.adventureisland.co.uk
One of the best value 'theme parks' in the South East, with over 40 great rides and attractions, for all ages. No admission charge, you only 'pay if you play'!
Times: Open Jan-2 Apr, Sat and Sun, from 1100. Also daily in Feb school half term week. 3 Apr-5 Sept, daily, 1100-late. 6 Sept-Dec, Sat and Sun, and school half term weeks and holidays from 1100.
Fee: Free. Individual charges for rides/attractions.
Facilities: T(3-4 hrs)

Southend-on-Sea
Kursaal Map ref. I11
Eastern Esplanade
Tel: (01702) 322322 Web: www.kursaal.co.uk
The Kursaal has something for everyone. Among the features are ten pin bowling, a sports bar with big screen entertainment, amusement machines, rides, McDonalds, and the Rendezvous Casino.
Times: Open all year, daily, 1000-late. Closed 25 Dec.
Fee: Free. There are charges for bowling etc - prices vary, so please contact for details.
Facilities: T(2½ hrs)

Southend-on-Sea
Mr B's Space Chase Quasar Map ref. I11
5/8 Marine Parade
Tel: (01702) 467720
A quasar arena situated within a family entertainment centre with prize bingo and video games.
Times: Open all year, daily and summer school half terms, 1000-2200. Closed 25 Dec.
Fee: £2.00/£2.00.
Facilities: T(20 mins)

Southend-on-Sea
Southend-on-Sea Pier Map ref. I11
Western Esplanade
Tel: (01702) 215620 Web: www.southendpier.co.uk
The world's longest pleasure pier. Train ride along the pier. Pier Museum at North Station, amusements, novelty shop, restaurant and licensed public house. Guided tours at Lifeboat House.
Times: Open Spring, Mon-Fri, 0800-1800; Sat and Sun 0800-2000. Summer, Mon-Fri, 0800-2100; Sat and Sun 0800-2200. Autumn, Mon-Fri, 0800-1800; Sat and Sun 0800-2000. Winter, Mon-Fri, 0800-1600; Sat and Sun 0800-1800. Closed 25 Dec.
Fee: Free. Train £2.50/£1.25/£6.00 (family). Walk and ride £1.80/£1.00/£4.00 (family).
Facilities: T(2 hrs)

Stansted Mountfitchet
House on the Hill Toy Museums Adventure Map ref. C4
See entry in Museums & Galleries section.

DID YOU KNOW

Manningtree is England's smallest town. It is 22 acres (9 hectares) at low tide, but only 17 acres (7 hectares) at high tide. It is so small that one end of the High Street is in Lawford, the other in Mistley.

Walton-on-the-Naze
Walton Pier Map ref. O5
Pier Approach
Tel: (01255) 682400 Web: www.waltonpier.co.uk
Adult and junior rides (one price to pay - ride all day wristbands). Family amusement area, tenpin bowling, Pirate Pete's soft play area, Seaspray Diner, Mermaid Bar and fishing.
Times: Open all year. Weekends only in low/winter season. Daily during school holidays and Jun. Please contact for details of exact opening times.
Fee: Free. Individual charges for rides/attractions.
Facilities: T(2 hrs)

Children's Indoor Play Centres

Clacton-on-Sea
Play Rascals Map ref. N6
Rascals House, Telford Rd, Gorse Lane Ind Estate
Tel: (01255) 475755 Web: www.playrascals.co.uk
Giant children's indoor play centre, with seperate toddler section. Restaurant.
Times: Open all year, Mon, 1200-1830; Tues-Sun, 1000-1830. Closed 24-26 Dec and 1 Jan.
Fee: 0-12 mths free/12 mths-5yrs £3.50/over 5yrs £4.50.
Facilities: T(2 hrs)

Colchester
Childsplay Adventureland Map ref. K4
Clarendon Way
Tel: (01206) 366566
Web: www.childsplayadventureland.com
Indoor play facility for under 9's. ROSPA safety inspected. Ball pools, slides and special area for babies/toddlers.
Times: Open all year, daily, 0930-1830. Closed 25 Dec.
Fee: Child (under 5) £3.20. Child (over 5) £3.75.
Facilities: Q T(2 hrs)

Colchester
Go Bananas Map ref. K4
9-10 Mason Road, Cowdray Centre
Tel: (01206) 761762 Web: www.go-bananas.co.uk
Children's indoor adventure playground. 3-storey adventure frame for 5-12 year-olds, an under 5's play village, climbing wall, spaceball ride and cafeteria.
Times: Open all year, daily, 0930-1830. Closed 25, 26 Dec and 1 Jan.
Fee: Child (under 5) £3.40. Child (5-12yrs) £3.95.
Facilities: Q T(2 hrs)

Halstead

Tumblewood Map ref. H3
Whitehouse Business Park, Whiteash Green
Tel: (01787) 474760 Web: www.tumblewood.co.uk
Children's indoor adventure playground with facilities for parties. Separate play areas and baby/toddler area.
Times: Open all year, daily, 1000-1800. Closed 25, 26 Dec and 1 Jan.
Fee: Child (under 5) £2.95. Child (over 5) £3.45.
Facilities: T(2 hrs)

Southend-on-Sea

Kids Kingdom Map ref. I11
Garon Park, Eastern Avenue
Tel: (01702) 462747
Exciting range of indoor adventure play activities for children up to 12 years of age. Slides, inflatables, ball ponds, swing bridges, and special under 5 section.
Times: Open all year, daily, 1000-1800. Closed 25, 26 Dec and 1 Jan.
Fee: Child (under 5) £3.50. Child (over 5) £4.50.
Facilities: T(1½ hrs)

Colchester

Colchester Leisure World Map ref. K4
Cowdray Avenue
Tel: (01206) 282000
Web: www.colchesterleisureworld.co.uk
Leisure pool with flumes, wave machine and rapids ride. Separate fitness pool, sports hall, squash courts and 'Aqua Springs' sauna/spa experience.
Times: Open all year. Please contact for further details.
Fee: Prices vary depending upon activity.
Facilities: T(2-3 hrs)

Maldon

Blackwater Leisure Centre Map ref. I7
Park Drive
Tel: (01621) 851898 Web: www.blackwaterleisure.co.uk
Leisure pool with jungle river, flume ride and jacuzzi bubble ledge. Toddler pool. Gym, sauna and multi-purpose sports hall.
Times: Open all year. Please contact for further details.
Fee: Prices vary depending upon activity.
Facilities: T(2-3 hrs)

Leisure Pools

Chelmsford

Riverside Ice and Leisure Centre Map ref. F7
Victoria Road
Tel: (01245) 615050 Web: www.riversideiceandleisure.com
National sized ice arena, and three swimming pools including flume ride and triple-diving platform. Fitness centre, sports hall, squash and children's indoor adventure playground.
Times: Open all year. Please contact for further details.
Fee: Prices vary depending upon activity.
Facilities: T(2-3 hrs)

DID YOU KNOW

The railway viaduct at Chappel (nr. Colchester) has a total of 32 arches and is made up of approx. 6,000,000 bricks. This makes it the second largest amount of bricks used in any construction in Britain.

Mountfitchet Castle, Stansted Mountfitchet

Countryside

The countryside of Essex is a rich, fertile landscape - fairly flat in the south, but with gently rolling hills to the north. Here you can discover traditional market towns, picturesque villages and tiny hamlets linked by quiet country lanes. Whilst pockets of ancient woodland, and the great forests of Epping, Hatfield and Hainault (once part of the Royal Hunting Forest) can be explored. Much of the agricultural land is of the highest grade, with large scale cereal production, horticulture (fruit-farming) and market gardening.

Special Areas

Essex Coastline - stretching for 310 miles, it is not widely known that most of the coastline has been designated an Environmentally Sensitive Area (ESA). This status will help preserve the flat salt-marshes, backwaters, creeks and mudflats that are a paradise for bird-watchers and yachtsmen. Mini tour - start at the steep, well-wooded banks of the River Stour, one of the most important areas in Britain for breeding birds. Heading south are the Walton Backwaters, a solitary wilderness of tidal saltings, mud/sand flats and reed-fringed islands. Whilst the Naze is a headland of grass and gorse jutting out into the sea - it's 70 feet high cliffs (rich in fossils) are being severely eroded away by the sea. Between Brightlingsea and Burnham-on-Crouch is a series of pretty river estuaries and creeks, once the haunt of smugglers. Pay a visit to Britain's most easterly island at Mersea, reached by its causeway. The Blackwater estuary is recognised as a 'Site of Special Scientific Interest', its open water and mudflats important for wintering birds. Two islands sit in the estuary, the private Osea, and Northey - the site of the Battle of Maldon in 991. Look out for the Thames sailing barges in this area. Between the Rivers Blackwater and Crouch is the Dengie Peninsula, where much of the countryside was once waterlogged, then reclaimed in the 17th C. by Dutch engineers to create rich farming land. Further south is the remote Foulness Island, the fourth largest off the coast of England, and the inter-tidal flats/marshes of Maplin Sands, a haven for wildfowl.

The Dedham Vale - an 'Area of Outstanding Natural Beauty', sitting on the borders of Essex and Suffolk, and famous worldwide through the paintings of John Constable (1776-1837). Many of the scenes which brought him inspiration can still be seen today. The area is characterised by some of the finest lowland landscape in England, dissected by the winding course of the attractive River Stour. Grazing meadows, ancient woodlands and hedgerows provide habitats for many species of flora and fauna. Leave your car at home, and discover this beautiful area on foot or by bicycle. More information at www.dedhamvalestourvalley.org

Epping Forest - covering some 6,000 acres, this is the largest public open space in the vicinity of London, although it is only a tenth of its original size. Dating from ancient times, it once formed part of the great royal hunting forest of Essex, whose function was to supply deer for the monarch. In 1878, the 'Epping Forest Act' was passed, and the management of the forest was given to the Corporation of London. Today the forest stretches for about 12 miles, and is noted for its fine woodlands (hornbeams, beech and oak), heath, reed fringed ponds and grassland. More information at www.cityoflondon.gov.uk/living_environment/open_spaces

The Lee Valley Park - see the Countryside section in Bedfordshire and Hertfordshire for further information.

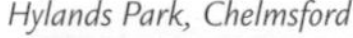

Hylands Park, Chelmsford

Country Parks & Nature Reserves

Basildon

Langdon Visitor Centre and Nature Reserve Map ref. F10
Third Avenue, Lower Dunton Road
Tel: (01268) 419103 Web: www.essexwt.org.uk
460 acres of meadow, woodland and plotland gardens. Eighteen miles of footpaths and bridleways. A former plotland home, The Haven, has been restored to 1930s style, and is open as a museum. EWT.
Times: Open all year, Tues-Sun, 0900-1700; Bank Hol Mon, 1000-1700. Closed 25 and 26 Dec.
Fee: Free.
Facilities: P T(2 hrs)

Billericay

Hanningfield Reservoir Visitor Centre Map ref. G9
Hawkswood Road
Tel: (01268) 711001 Web: www.essexwt.gov.uk
The visitor centre has refreshments, toilets, gift shop and full disabled access. It will help you discover the 100-acre nature reserve on the shores of Hanningfield Reservoir. Bird hides and walks. EWT.
Times: Open all year, Tues-Sun and Bank Hol Mon, 0900-1700. Closed 25 and 26 Dec.
Fee: Free. Donations appreciated.
Facilities: P T(2 hrs)

Braintree

Great Notley Country Park and Discovery Centre
Map ref. F/G5
Tel: (01376) 347134
Ecologically built discovery centre with permanent exhibition of ecological principals. Wind turbine. Set within a 100 acre country park, providing beautiful walks around lakes, meadows and woods.
Times: Open all year. Discovery Centre - Mon-Fri, 1000-1630; Sun, 1000-1600.
Fee: Free.
Facilities: P T(1-2 hrs)

Brentwood

Thorndon Country Park Map ref. E10
The Avenue
Tel: (01277) 211250 Web: www.essexcc.gov.uk
Public open space of 540 acres. Woodlands, meadows, picnic and barbeque areas. Fishing lake and two visitor centres. Horse, cycle and walking routes.
Times: Open all year, daily, 0800-dusk.
Fee: Free.
Facilities: P T(2 hrs)

Castle Hedingham

Hedingham Castle Map ref. H2
See entry in Ancient Monuments section.

Chelmsford

Chelmer and Blackwater Navigation Map ref. G/H/I7
See entry in Activities section.

Chigwell

Hainault Forest Country Park Map ref. C10
Romford Road
Tel: (0208) 500 7353 Web: www.hainaultforest.co.uk
600 acres of ancient woodland, a lake and rare breeds farm. Managed by the London Borough of Redbridge and the Woodland Trust for Essex County Council. Visitor and interpretation centre.
Times: Open all year, daily, 0700-dusk.
Fee: Free.
Facilities: P T(2 hrs)

Clacton-on-Sea

Holland Haven Country Park Map ref. O5
Tel: (01255) 253235
Unspoilt coastal grazing marshes with footpaths through meadows. Cliff-top walks to Frinton-on-Sea. Bird-watching hides. Access to beaches.
Times: Open at any reasonable time.
Fee: Free.
Facilities: P T(2 hrs)

Coggeshall

Marks Hall Garden and Arboretum Map ref. H/I4
See entry in Gardens section.

Colchester

High Woods Country Park Map ref. K4
Visitors Centre, Turner Road
Tel: (01206) 853588
A 330 acre country park situated to the north of central Colchester, with a variety of landscape and wildlife. Visitor centre, toilets, bookshop and small shop.
Times: Visitor Centre open, 1 Jan-31 Mar, Sat and Sun, 1000-1600. 1 Apr-30 Sept, Mon-Sat, 1000-1630; Sun, 1100-1730. 1 Oct-19 Dec, Sat and Sun, 1000-1600. Car park open at any reasonable time.
Fee: Free.
Facilities: Q P T(2 hrs)

Corringham (nr. Stanford-le-Hope)

Langdon Hills Country Park Map ref. F11
One Tree Hill
Tel: (01268) 542066 Web: www.essexcc.gov.uk
Country park consisting of Westley Heights and One Tree Hill. Picnic areas, wildflower meadows and ancient woodlands overlooking the Thames estuary.
Times: Open all year, daily, 0800-dusk.
Fee: Free.
Facilities: P T(5 hrs)

Lee Valley Park

Danbury (nr. Chelmsford)
Danbury and Lingwood Commons Map ref. H7/8
Tel: 0870 609 5388 Web: www.nationaltrust.org.uk
Danbury Common is composed of a mixture of woodland, shrub, grassland and heath. Napoleonic defences are evidence of Danbury's military past.
Times: Open at any reasonable time.
Fee: Free. Donations for parking.
Facilities: T(2 hrs) NT

Danbury (nr. Chelmsford)
Danbury Country Park Map ref. H8
Woodhill Road
Tel: (01245) 222350 Web: www.essexcc.gov.uk
Country park set in the gardens and old deer park of Danbury Palace. Walled garden, lakes and woodland. The site offers a place for quiet recreation.
Times: Open all year, daily, 0800-dusk. Closing times are displayed at the entrance to the site car parks.
Fee: Free. Car parking charges (upto 1 hr) £1.00, all day £2.00.
Facilities: T(1½ hrs)

East Mersea
Cudmore Grove Country Park Map ref. L6
Bromans Lane
Tel: (01206) 383868 Web: www.essexcc.gov.uk
Situated next to the entrance of the Colne estuary, the park consists of grassland and a sandy beach, ideally suited to walking, picnics, informal games and wildlife watching.
Times: Open all year, daily, 0800-dusk.
Fee: Car park charge - £1.00 per hour, £2.00 all day.
Facilities: Q T(1½ hrs)

Fingringhoe (nr. Colchester)
Fingringhoe Wick Nature Reserve Map ref. L5
South Green Road
Tel: (01206) 729678 Web: www.essexwt.org.uk
125 acres of woodland, lakes and saltmarsh on the Colne estuary, with nature trails and eight hides. Observation room, tower and gift shop. EWT.
Times: Open all year, Tues-Sun and Bank Hol Mon, 0900-1700. Closed 25 and 26 Dec.
Fee: £1.00/50p.
Facilities: Q T(4 hrs)

Gosfield (nr. Halstead)
Gosfield Lake Resort Map ref. G4
Church Road
Tel: (01787) 475043 Web: www.gosfieldlake.co.uk
A leisure park with something for everyone. Lake with fishing, water-sking and children's playground.
Times: Open 1 Apr-30 Sept, daily, 0930-dusk.
Fee: £1.00/50p/50p. Extra charges for activities.
Facilities: T(2 hrs)

Hadleigh
Hadleigh Castle Country Park Map ref. H11
Chapel Lane
Tel: (01702) 551072 Web: www.essexcc.gov.uk
Large area of unspoilt countryside (fields and woodland), with superb views over the Thames estuary. Remains of castle close by, picnic areas, horse rides, bird hides and way-marked trails.
Times: Open all year, daily, 0800-dusk.
Fee: Free (car park charge).
Facilities: T(2 hrs)

Harwich
RSPB Stour Estuary Nature Reserve Map ref. O3
Tel: (01255) 886043 Web: www.rspb.org.uk
The Stour Estuary is one of the most important estuaries in Britain for breeding birds, with internationally important numbers of grey plovers, knots, redshanks and dunlin.
Times: Open any reasonable time. Closed 25 Dec.
Fee: Free. Donations appreciated.
Facilities: T(3 hrs)

Layer de la Haye (nr. Colchester)
Abberton Reservoir Visitor Centre Map ref. K5
Church Road
Tel: (01206) 738172 Web: www.essexwt.org.uk
Nature reserve providing superb bird-watching over the 1,200 acre expanse of Abberton Reservoir. Shop with toilets and displays. Adult and children's activities. EWT.
Times: Open all year, Tues-Sun, 0900-1700. Closed 25 and 26 Dec.
Fee: Free. Donations appreciated.
Facilities: Q T(3 hrs)

Leigh-on-Sea

Belfairs Park Map ref. I11
Eastwood Road North
Tel: (01702) 520202 Web: www.southend.gov.uk
Woodland gardens and walks. Golf course, pitch and putt and 92-acre nature reserve.
Times: Open all year, daily, 0730-dusk.
Fee: Free.
Facilities: T(2½ hrs)

Little Wigborough (nr. Colchester)

Copt Hall Marshes Map ref. K5
Tel: 0870 609 5388 Web: www.nationaltrust.org.uk
Site of Specific Scientific Interest. The salt marshes are rich in overwintering wildfowl and wading birds. Grass headland paths give access to the sea wall.
Times: Open at any reasonable time.
Fee: Free.
Facilities: T(2 hrs) NT

Pitsea (nr. Basildon)

Wat Tyler Country Park Map ref. G11
Pitsea Hall Lane
Tel: (01268) 550088 Web: www.basildon.gov.uk
125 acres of thorn woodland, meadows, coastal grassland, saltings and ponds. Motorboat museum, adventure play area, craft units, boat pond and miniature railway.
Times: Open all year, daily, 0900-dusk.
Fee: Free.
Facilities: T(3 hrs)

The Naze

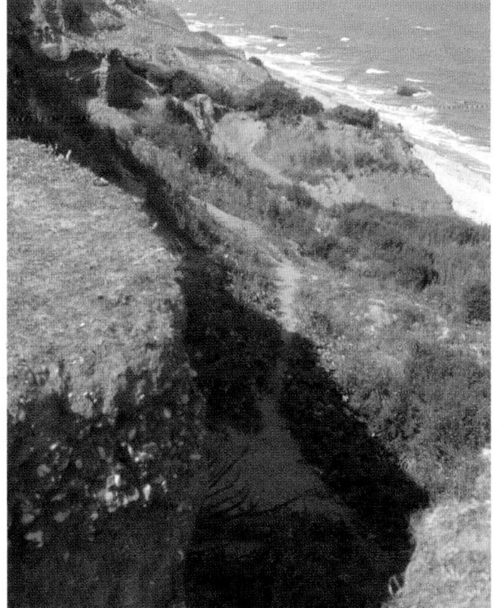

Rayleigh

Hockley Woods Map ref. H10
Main Road, Hockley
Tel: (01702) 203078
Ancient semi natural woodland, 300 acres - freedom to roam. Picnic area, play area and two self guided trails. Horse routes. Rare animals, birds and insects. Local nature reserve.
Times: Open at any reasonable time.
Fee: Free.
Facilities: T(3½ hrs)

Rayne (nr. Braintree)

Flitch Way Country Park Map ref. C/D/E/F/G5
Rayne Station Centre, Station Road
Tel: (01376) 340262 Web: www.essexcc.gov.uk
15 miles of linear country park along the old Bishop's Stortford to Braintree railway. Rayne Station Centre has been renovated, and now has an exhibition of local heritage.
Times: Open all year, daily, dawn-dusk. Rayne Station Centre open all year, daily, 0900-1700. Exhibition Room open all year, Sun, 1300-1600.
Fee: Free.
Facilities: T(2 hrs)

Romford

Bedfords Park Visitor Centre Map ref. C9/10
Broxhill Road
Tel: (01708) 748646 Web: www.essexwt.org.uk
Set in the grounds of Bedfords Park, an historic parkland site, the Visitor Centre is built on the site of the former mansion. Exotic trees and superb views over area. EWT.
Times: Open all year, Tues-Sun, 0900-1700. Closed 25 and 26 Dec.
Fee: Free.
Facilities: T(2 hrs)

South Ockendon

Belhus Woods Country Park Map ref. D11
Romford Road, Aveley
Tel: (01708) 865628 Web: www.essexcc.gov.uk
A mixed landscape of ancient woodlands, grasslands and lakes created from gravel extraction. Offering quiet recreation, including fishing, walking and bird watching. Visitor Centre.
Times: Open all year, daily, 0800-dusk.
Fee: Free (car park charge).
Facilities: T(3 hrs)

South Weald (nr. Brentwood)
Weald Country Park Map ref. D9
Weald Road
Tel: (01277) 216297/261343 Web: www.essexcc.gov.uk
Visitor Centre with interactive exhibition. Gift shop, light refreshments, deer paddock, country walks, fishing, lakes and own horse-riding.
Times: Open all year, daily, 0800-dusk.
Fee: Free. Car park charge - 1 hour £1.00, over 1 hour £2.00.
Facilities: T(5 hrs)

South Woodham Ferrers
Marsh Farm Country Park Map ref. H9
See entry in Family Fun section.

Takeley (nr. Bishop's Stortford)
Hatfield Forest Map ref. D5
Tel: (01279) 870678 Web: www.nationaltrust.org.uk
Over 400 hectares of ancient coppice woodland, grassland, magnificent pollarded trees, two ornamental lakes, 18th C. Shell house and stream.
Times: Open all year, at any reasonable time. Vehicle access to forest, 1 Apr-31 Oct, daily, 1000-1700.
Fee: 1 Apr-31 Oct, £3.20 per car. Outside this period, £1.00 per car.
Facilities: T(3-4 hrs) NT

Waltham Abbey
River Lee Country Park Map ref. A8
Situated on either side of the River Lea, between Waltham Abbey and Broxbourne
Tel: (01992) 702200 Web: www.leevalleypark.com
Unique patchwork of lakes, waterways, green open spaces and countryside areas, covering 1,000 acres. A haven for wildlife - great for cycling, walking, angling and bird-watching. Dragon-fly sanctuary.
Times: Open all year, daily, 0830-1630.
Fee: Free.
Facilities: T(2 hrs)

Waltham Abbey
Royal Gunpowder Mills Map ref. A8
See entry in Museums & Galleries section.

Widford (nr. Chelmsford)
Hylands House Map ref. F8
See entry in Historic Houses section.

DID YOU KNOW

The Plume Library in Maldon is the second oldest public library in England, dating from 1704. It contains over 5,000 rare gems, including 16/17th C. books.

Picnic Sites

Epping Forest - several areas around forest, including High Beach, reached along minor road off A104 roundabout. Map ref. A9
Great Dunmow - beside minor road leading east from the town centre to the A120. Map ref. E5
Lee Valley Park picnic sites - Waltham Abbey: Abbey Gardens and Fishers Green. Also barbeque area at Showground car park, Station Road, Waltham Abbey. Map ref. A8
The Naze - 1/4 mile north east of the town centre at Walton-on-the-Naze. Map ref. O4/5
Norsey Wood picnic site - beside minor road running to the east of Billericay, between the A129 and B1007. Map ref. F9

Countryside Organisations - Essex

English Nature
Harbour House, Hythe Quay, Colchester, Essex CO2 8JF
Tel: (01206) 796666 Web: www.english-nature.gov.uk

Essex Wildlife Trust (EWT)
Abbotts Hall Farm, Great Wigborough, nr. Colchester, Essex CO5 7RZ
Tel: (01621) 862960 Web: www.essexwt.org.uk

The National Trust - Regional Office for East Anglia
Angel Corner, 8 Angel Hill, Bury St. Edmunds, Suffolk IP33 1UZ
Tel: 0870 609 5388 Web: www.nationaltrust.org.uk

The Royal Society for the Protection of Birds (RSPB) - Regional Office for East Anglia
Stalham House, 65 Thorpe Road, Norwich, Norfolk NR1 1UD
Tel: (01603) 661662 Web: www.rspb.org.uk

Activities

Maldon

Boat Trips

Chelmsford

Chelmer and Blackwater Navigation Map ref. G/H/17
Paper Mill Lock, North Hill, Little Baddow
Tel: (01245) 225520 Web: www.cbn.co.uk
Historic canal with 14 miles of towpath - excellent for walkers, boaters and anglers. Canal centre at Paper Mill Lock offers a teashop, boat hire and river trips aboard the barge 'Victoria'.
Times: Canal centre open all year, daily, 1000-1800. River trips between Apr-Oct.
Fee: Canal centre free. Charge for boat hire and river trips.
Facilities: T(2 hrs)

Cycling

The Witchfinder's Way is a 27 mile circular route starting at the historic sea-faring town of Harwich, and visiting the haunts of Matthew Hopkins - 'The Witchfinder General'. Whilst the Two Rivers' Way takes you on a 25 mile journey from Burnham-on-Crouch, via weather-boarded villages, sailing hamlets and England's oldest Saxon chapel. Saleable maps for these two routes from the East of England Tourist Board on 0870 225 4852. For more information on cycling in the county contact Essex County Council on (01245) 437118, or visit www.essexcc.gov.uk They have a range of leaflets and information available (some with a small charge), including Get on your bike and cycle around Chelmsford, Bike it! Cycle Routes in Harlow, and Leisure Cycle Routes - Colchester. Many of the country parks in Essex offer cycling opportunities, such as The Flitch Way, which runs for 15 miles along the length of the old Bishop's Stortford to Braintree railway. Or why not try the Colne Valley Cycle Trails, offering four different routes - leaflets are available from Braintree Tourist Information Centre on (01376) 550066.

The Essex Cycle Route - offers 250 miles of cycling (between Epping and Harwich) through some of the county's most beautiful countryside and charming villages and towns. You can dip into small sections, or try some of the loops and links around it. The route conveniently links with the National Cycle Network Route 1 (Hull to Harwich). A map/guide to the cycle route (priced £2.50) is available from Essex County Council on (01245) 437118.

DID YOU KNOW

The Balkerne Gate in Colchester is the largest surviving Roman gateway in Britain.

Walking

Long Distance Walks

The Essex Way (81 miles) - linear walk stretching right across the county from Epping to Harwich. Saleable guide to route available from PROW Team, Essex County Council, County Hall, Chelmsford, Essex CM1 1QH. Tel: (01245) 437274.
The Roach Valley Way (23 miles) - circular walk around south-east Essex. Saleable guide to route available from PROW Team, Essex County Council, County Hall, Chelmsford, Essex CM1 1QH. Tel: (01245) 437274.
The Three Forests Way (60 miles) - circular walk linking the ancient forests of Epping, Hainault and Hatfield. Saleable guide to route available from PROW Team, Essex County Council, County Hall, Chelmsford, Essex CM1 1QH. Tel: (01245) 437274.
The St. Peter's Way (45 miles) - linear walk from Chipping Ongar to Bradwell-on-Sea. Saleable guide to route available from PROW Team, Essex County Council, County Hall, Chelmsford, Essex CM1 1QH. Tel: (01245) 437274.

Shorter Walks
Your first port of call should be the Public Rights of Way Team at Essex County Council on (01245) 437274, or visit www.essexcc.gov.uk (downloadable order form). They have a range of saleable guides and leaflets, including two Wildside Walks packs, featuring country parks and wildlife sites. Also available is The John Ray Walk, a linear trail linking Braintree and Witham, and Danbury Walks - six scenic walks around the town. To the south of the county, explore the countryside around Brentwood with the help of eight different leaflets, available from the Borough Council on (01277) 261111. Or why not visit the Norsey Wood Local Nature Reserve at Billericay, download the trail leaflet at www.basildon.gov.uk Epping Forest has a 1 1/4 mile tree trail, starting at High Beach, or try the circular 6 mile long Jubliee Walk - leaflets from the Epping Forest Information Centre on (0208) 508 0028. For a walk with a sea view, follow the North Blackwater Trail from Maldon, leaflet from the Tourist Information Centre on (01621) 856503. The historic town of Saffron Walden can be explored with the help of Discover Walden, available from the Tourist Information Centre on (01799) 510444. Or walk the landscapes that inspired John Constable with the help of the Constable Country: Keep it Special visitor's guide. Contact the Flatford Tourist Information Centre for a copy on (01206) 299460. Of course don't forget the area's country parks, with their various walks and nature trails - see the 'Countryside' section for further information.

Dedham

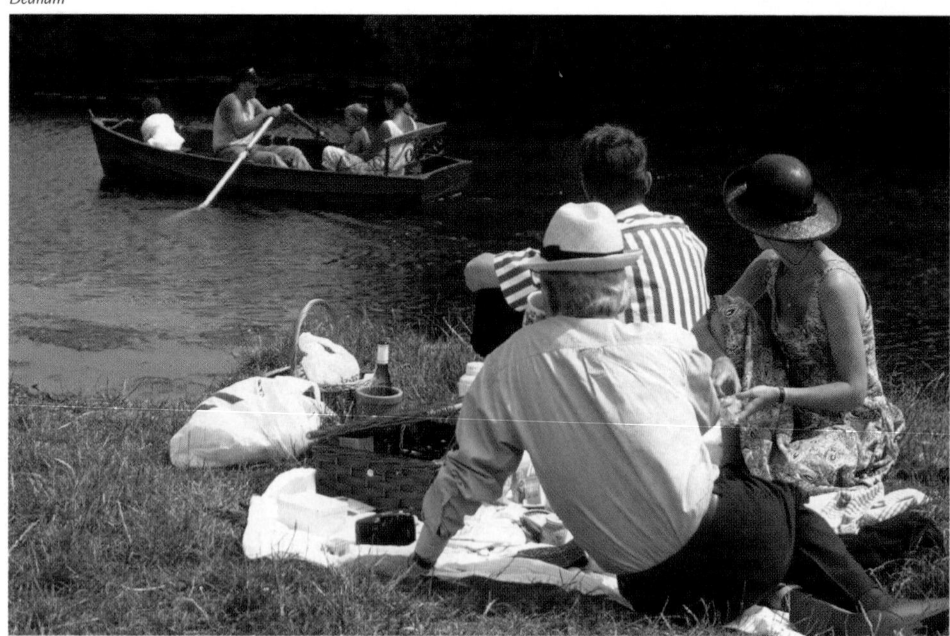

Food & Drink

Regional Produce

Essex is a great place for trying seafood. Start in Colchester, whose oysters have been farmed since Roman times. Known as 'English Natives' - Mersea Island is the centre of the industry. Each October, the town holds a private oyster festival attended by the Mayor. South from here samphire, 'the asparagus of the sea', grows alongside the coast, whilst Maldon is the only place in the country where sea water is used to make crystalline salt (recommended by Delia Smith). Further south is the fishing village of Leigh-on-Sea, where you can try cockles and jellied eels. The county is also noted for its fruit-growing used to make delicious jams. Visit the museum and tearoom (see page) at Wilkin and Sons in Tiptree, where the first jams were made in 1885. Wash it all down at Hartford End (nr. Chelmsford), home of Ridley's Brewery, a family-run brewer producing cask ales and bottled beers.

Breweries & Vineyards

Boxted (nr. Colchester)

Carter's Vineyards Map ref. K3
Green Lane
Tel: (01206) 271136 Web: www.cartersvineyards.co.uk
Vineyards and a winery with an alternative energy project and a conservation area. Fishing facilities (day licence) are available.
Times: Open 12 Apr-end Oct, daily, 1100-1700.
Fee: £3.50.
Facilities: T(2 hrs)

East Mersea

Mersea Vineyard Map ref. L6
Rewsalls Lane
Tel: (01206) 385900 Web: www.merseawine.com
10 acre site (established 1985) overlooking the Blackwater and Colne estuaries. Tasting and vineyard walk. Conducted tours of winery and vineyard by appointment only.
Times: Open Apr-end Jun, Sat and Sun, 1200-1600. Jul and Aug, Wed-Sun, 1200-1600. At other times by appointment.
Fee: Free.
Facilities: T(1 hr)

Felsted (nr. Great Dunmow)

Felsted Vineyard Map ref. F5
The Vineyards, Crix Green
Tel: (01245) 361504
Set on a 12 acre site. Working vineyard and brewery - see how wine is made and how to brew. Children welcome to view animals.
Times: Open all year, Sat and Sun, 1000-dusk. Closed 24 Dec-1 Jan. Other times by appointment.
Fee: Free.
Facilities: T(1½ hrs)

Great Bardfield

Bardfield Vineyard Map ref. F3
Great Lodge
Tel: (01371) 810776
Web: www.thegreatlodgeexperience.com
The vineyard was planted in 1990, on a south facing slope behind a Grade I listed brick and tile barn built by Anne of Cleves. The aromatic grape varieties are hand-picked.
Times: Open 9 Apr-29 Sept, Wed-Sat, 1100-1600.
Fee: £3.50.
Facilities: T(1½ hrs)

Purleigh (nr. Maldon)

New Hall Vineyards Map ref. H8
Chelmsford Road
Tel: (01621) 828343 Web: www.newhallwines.co.uk
Guided tours of the vineyards, with a trail through the vines and the cellars where wine can be tasted. Also visit the press house with slide shows. See fermentation/bottling.
Times: Open all year, Mon-Fri, 1000-1700; Sat and Sun, 1000-1330.
Fee: Free.
Facilities: T(2-3 hrs)

Carter's Vineyards, Boxted

Restaurants

Earls Colne (nr. Colchester)
Carved Angel Map ref. I4
Upper Holt Street, Earls Colne, nr. Colchester CO6 2PG
Tel: (01787) 222330 Web: www.carvedangel.com
AA and Les Routiers commendations highlight a twenty-first century vision of the country pub in this 15th C. building. Award-winning food, extensive range of wines, real ales, international and bottled beers suit all occasions. A la carte seven days a week, with optional fixed-priced menu and light snacks at lunch.

Earls Colne (nr. Colchester)
de Vere Arms Map ref. I4
High Street, Earls Colne, nr. Colchester CO6 2PB
Tel: (01787) 223353 Web: www.deverearms.com
Refurbished during 2001-2002, this stylish yet extremely comfortable restaurant and hotel quickly drew praise from professionals, critics and public alike. The AA (3 stars and two rosettes), the RAC (3 stars and a grade three dining award) and Johansens were all impressed by the elegance and quality evident throughout. Nine bedrooms (one for disabled guests) are individually furnished and decorated, and the 65-seat restaurant is a shrine to fine dining. The kitchen staff offer a sophisticated take on traditional and modern dishes, supported by impressive technical skill and creative energy. 'A very special dining experience' was one restaurant critic's verdict.

DID YOU KNOW

St. Lawrence's Church at Bradfield (nr. Mistley) has a memorial to Edwin Harris Dunning of the Royal Flying Corps. He was the first officer to land an aircraft successfully on the deck of a moving ship in August 1917.

Felsted (nr. Great Dunmow)
Reeves Restaurant Map ref. F5
Rumbles Cottage, Braintree Road, Felsted,
nr. Great Dunmow CM6 3DJ
Tel: (01371) 820996 Web: www.reeves-restaurant.co.uk
In the centre of the picturesque and historic village of Felsted, an enchanting Grade II Listed building provides an idyllic setting for Reeves Restaurant. Relax and enjoy superb food freshly prepared by our two highly experienced chefs. Menus to entice with a contemporary twist on traditional fine dining. Open Tues-Sat from 1200-1400 for a fixed price or a la carte lunch. Dinner from 1900 when the a la carte menu is served. We are also open Sun for traditional lunch from 1200-1600.

Felsted (nr. Great Dunmow)
The Swan at Felsted
Station Road, Felsted, nr. Great Dunmow CM6 3DG
Tel: (01371) 820245 Fax: (01371) 821393
Email: info@theswanatfelsted.co.uk
Web: www.theswanatfelsted.co.uk
The Swan at Felsted is located in the heart of the pretty village of Felsted, only 15 minutes from Chelmsford, just off the A120. Freshly prepared dishes from light snacks at lunchtime to an extensive evening menu that changes every month. Specials at the weekend and traditional roasts on Sun. A great selection of wines and well kept real ales. All served in clean and pleasant surroundings by happy, polite staff. A refreshing change! Open Mon-Sat from 1100-1500 and 1700 onwards and we are open all day on Sun.

Great Tey (nr. Colchester)

The Barn Brasserie Map ref. I4
Great Tey, nr. Colchester CO6 1JE
Tel: (01206) 212345 Fax: (01206) 211522
Web: www.barnbrasserie.co.uk
The Barn Brasserie, Great Tey, can be found just a five minute journey along the A120 from the main A12 near Colchester. Set in the heart of beautiful countryside, this award-winning conversion of a Grade Two Listed 16th C. barn is one of the most popular and successful restaurants in the region. Offering fantastic dining with a range of set menus as well as a superb a la Carte menu, and a choice of 100 fine wines, the Barn Brasserie has a reputation for excellent service, excellent food and excellent value for money. Open all day every day with plenty of car parking.

Great Yeldham (nr. Halstead)

The White Hart Map ref. G2
Poole Street (A1017), Great Yeldham,
nr. Halstead CO9 4HJ
Tel: (01787) 237250 Web: www.whitehartyeldham.co.uk
An imposing 16th C. building with full a la carte menu available in restaurant, and in bar, where lighter meals and snacks are also served. 100 wines on list, several served by the glass. Bar offers ever-changing range of quality real ales and bottled beers, an impressive range of cognacs and malt whiskies. Patio overlooking riverside garden. Ideal venue for weddings and special occasions, equally popular for those wanting just a relaxing drink. John Dicken is one of the country's most accomplished chefs. Open all day, seven days a week; telephone booking essential for restaurant at weekends, but bar always available.

Messing (nr. Colchester)

Crispin's Map ref. I5
The Street, Messing, nr. Colchester CO5 9TR
Tel: (01621) 815868
Crispin's, built around 1475, is an oak-beamed, candlelit restaurant with en-suite rooms, with four-poster beds. B&B for two is £57.50. It's international cuisine is outstanding, and the restaurant is open from 1930 Wed-Sat and for lunch on Sun. We are just a few miles from the A12 south of Colchester.

Walton-on-the-Naze

Harbour Lights (Walton-on-the-Naze) Ltd Map ref. O5
Titchmarsh Marina, Coles Lane,
Walton-on-the-Naze CO14 8SL
(off B1034-Lower Kirby Road)
Tel: (01255) 851887
Where better to enjoy our Waterside location with:
Welcoming and friendly surroundings,
Unique dishes made with the freshest ingredients,
Ideal for any occasion,
Open all year.

Pleshey

Afternoon Teas

Aldham (nr. Colchester)

Mill Race Nursery Coffee Shop Map ref. J4
New Road, Aldham, nr. Colchester CO6 3QT
Just off the A1124, formerly A604 at Ford Street.
Tel: (01206) 242521 Web: www.millracenursery.co.uk
Enjoy home-made and speciality cakes, cream teas or light lunches in our conservatory style coffee lounge or courtyard garden. Riverside garden and boat hire, large plant centre, silk and dried flower shop and giftware. Open daily including Sun 0930-1700.

DID YOU KNOW

The longest pleasure pier in the world, opened in 1899 at Southend-on-Sea. It stretches 1.33 miles into the Thames estuary. The largest pleasure pier in the world at Clacton-on-Sea was built in 1871. It was widened in the 1930s to over 300 feet wide.

Wivenhoe

Ingatestone

Café du Jardin Map ref. E9
Ingatestone Garden Centre, Roman Road,
Ingatestone CM4 9AU
Tel: (01277) 353268
Web: www.ingatestone-gardencentre.co.uk
Café du Jardin has established a good reputation for home cooked lunch and home baked cakes. It is in attractive gardens where you can sit in warm weather to enjoy the food and gardens. Come once and you'll come again! Open 7 days a week. T(2 hrs)

Hatfield Forest

Stop & Shop

Billericay

Barleylands Craft Village Map ref. F9
Barleylands Farm, Barleylands Road, Billericay CM11 2UD
Tel: (01268) 290219 Email: info@barleylands.co.uk
Web: www.barleylands.co.uk
Probably the largest collection of working crafts in East Anglia. Stroll around Barleylands Craft Village, and visit over 23 impressive individual specialist workshops demonstrating their crafts including blacksmiths and glassblowing. Relax and enjoy a cream tea in our new tea-room. Free parking and free entry all year round (closed Mons). Q P T(2 hrs)

Braintree

Blake House Craft Centre Map ref. F5
Blake End, nr. Braintree CM7 8SH
Tel: (01376) 552553
Web: www.blakehousecraftcentre.co.uk
The courtyard of listed farm buildings, which have been converted into craft shops and units as specialised businesses. Open all year, 7 days a week and Bank Hols 1000-1700. Closed 25 Dec-3 Jan. P

Brentwood

Hazle Ceramics Workshop Map ref. D10
Stallion's Yard, Codham Hall, Great Warley, nr. Brentwood CM13 3JT
Tel: (01277) 220892 Web: www.hazle.com
See where the award-winning collectable ceramic wall plaques, "A Nation of Shopkeepers" are made. Hobby ceramic painting sessions on Fri/Sat and school hols - phone for details/book. Open all year, Fri-Sat and Bank Hols, 1100-1700. Shop open Tues-Sat. Closed 24 Dec-4 Jan. P T(1 hr)

Chelmsford

Moulsham Mill Map ref. F7
Parkway, Chelmsford CM2 7PX
Tel: (01245) 608200 Web: www.moulshammill.co.uk
A mill on the site of an ancient watermill, dating back to Domesday. The watermill is not working, and has been restored to a retail craft and business centre. Refreshments available. Open all year, Mon-Sat, 0900-1700. Closed on all Bank Hols.

Colchester

Greyfriars Books: the Colchester Bookshop Map ref. K4
92 East Hill, Colchester CO1 2QN
Tel: (01206) 563138
Web: www.colchesterbooks.co.uk
Browse through five rooms of fascinating books on literature, art, philosophy, history, science and local interest, less than 5 minutes walk from Colchester Castle, just beyond Hollytrees Museum and the Minories Art Gallery, at the top of East Hill. Good books also bought. Open Mon-Sat, 1000-1730. P T(1 hr)

Saffron Walden

Debden Antiques Map ref. D3
Elder Street, Debden, nr. Saffron Walden CB11 3JY
Tel: (01799) 543007 Web: www.debden-antiques.co.uk
A large collection of fine antiques for the home and garden, displayed in a magnificent 17th C. Essex barn. Outside is a lovely courtyard and a large private car park. Open all year, Mon-Sat 1000-1730; Sun and Bank Hols, 1100-1600. P T(1 hr)

Colchester

Discovery Tours

Bloomin' Beautiful

Enjoy the spectacular colours and delicate fragrances of some of England's finest gardens.

Tour 1
Starting point: Chelmsford, Essex Map ref. F7
Mileage: Hylands House, Cressing Temple Barns and Marks Hall Garden and Arboretum 23m/37km
Hylands House, Cressing Temple Barns and The Gardens of Easton Lodge 30m/48km
Morning - enjoy a stroll in the parkland of *Hylands House*, then take the A12 to Witham. Follow the B1018 to *Cressing Temple Barns* and its Tudor walled garden.
Afternoon - remain on the B1018 to Braintree. Two choices, either take the A120 east for 6 miles, then the B1024 to the landscaped parkland of the *Marks Hall Garden and Arboretum*. Or take the A120 west for 10 miles to Great Dunmow. Follow the B184 for 2 miles, then turn left to Little Easton and *The Gardens of Easton Lodge*.

Tour 2
Starting point: Southend-on-Sea, Essex Map ref. I11
Mileage: 12m/19km
Morning - enjoy the award-winning parks and gardens of *Southend-on-Sea*.
Afternoon - leave on the A127 towards Basildon. After 7 miles, turn right onto the A130. 5 miles later in the village of Rettendon, follow signs to the *RHS Garden: Hyde Hall* with its roses and waterlilies.

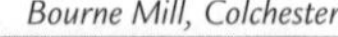

Bourne Mill, Colchester

Coggeshall

Raptors, Romans and Roundabouts

A fun-packed family tour, based around Britain's oldest recorded town.

Starting point: Colchester, Essex Map ref. K4
Mileage: 22m/35km
Morning - leave the town on the B1022 to visit the excellent *Colchester Zoo*, one of Europe's finest.
Afternoon - return to Colchester, and discover the *Castle Museum*, where mum can try on a Roman toga! End the day by taking the A133 to *Clacton-on-Sea*, and its fun-packed pier. Smash into dad on the dodgems and scare your little sister in the haunted house.

Antiques, Auctions, Bids and Bargains

Explore priceless antique towns and stately homes filled with heirlooms.

Starting point: Halstead, Essex Map ref. H3
Mileage: 29m/47km
Morning - explore *Halstead's* speciality shops and weather-boarded antiques centre. Then take the A1124 to Earls Colne, where you turn right onto the B1024 to historic *Coggeshall*, a mecca for antiques lovers.
Afternoon - remain on the B1024 south to *Kelvedon* (with more shops to enjoy), then join the A12 south towards London. After 12 miles, take the A130 to the antiques village of *Battlesbridge*.

A Taste of Essex

If you are in search of culinary adventure, then this tour is full of tasty surprises.

Starting point: Southend-on-Sea, Essex Map ref. I11
Mileage: 30m/48km
Morning - start the day with a cockle or two in the fishing village of *Leigh-on-Sea*. Then enjoy a stroll along the world's longest pier at *Southend*, with some delicious fish and chips.
Afternoon - follow the A127 for 7 miles, before turning right onto the A130. 3 miles later (at the roundabout), turn right onto the A132. At South Woodham Ferrers, turn left onto the B1418. Then 5 miles later (at the roundabout) join the A414 to the hilltop town of *Maldon*, noted for its sea salt production. End the day by taking the B1022 to *Tiptree*, and enjoy afternoon tea at the jam factory.

Country Classics

Discover the historic houses and castles of the rich and famous.

Starting point: Saffron Walden, Essex Map ref. C/D2
Mileage: 19m/31km
Morning - explore charming *Saffron Walden*, then follow signs to the Jacobean *Audley End House and Park*.
Afternoon - take the B1053 via *Finchingfield* (a picture postcard village) to Wethersfield, where you turn left onto the unclassified road to Sible Hedingham. At the T-junction with the A1017, turn left to reach *Castle Hedingham*, and its magnificent castle keep.

The Witchfinder's Way

Watch out for black cats and broomsticks in Witch Country!

Starting point: Harwich, Essex Map ref. O3
Mileage: 18m/29km
Morning - explore the medieval seafaring town of *Harwich*. Then take the B1352 (with its spectacular river views) to *Mistley* and *Manningtree*, the former haunt of Matthew Hopkins, The Witchfinder General.
Afternoon - take the A137 south to *Colchester*. If you dare, visit the dungeons of the Castle Museum, where the screams of the witches can still be heard!

DID YOU KNOW

Maldon was the home of Edward Bright. He died in 1750, reputedly the biggest man in England at 44 stones. He is buried in All Saints Church.

Leez Priory, Hartford End

Stand and Deliver!

Visit the haunts and hideaways of Britain's most famous highwayman Dick Turpin (1705-39).

Starting point: Saffron Walden, Essex Map ref. C/D2
Mileage: 42m/68km
Morning - follow the B1053/B1054 to *Hempstead*, birthplace of Turpin. Then take the B1053/B1051 to the medieval town of *Thaxted*, where his house stands in Stoney Street. Now head south along the B184 to '*The Rodings*', a group of attractive villages where Turpin found safe places to hide.
Afternoon - remain on the B184 to Chipping Ongar, then turn right onto the A414. After 3 miles, turn left onto the B181/B1393 to *Epping*. Take a walk in the famous forest, where Turpin held up the passing coaches. Then take the A121 to *Waltham Abbey*, reputedly the burial place of King Harold.

Defence of the Realm

Explore the military defences of the area, built to safeguard against invasion and attack.

Starting point: Waltham Abbey, Essex Map ref. A8
Mileage: 38m/61km
Morning - trace the evolution of gunpowder technology at the *Royal Gunpowder Mills*.
Afternoon - join the M25 to junction 28, then take the A1023/A128 (via Brentwood) to *Kelvedon Hatch*. Go underground to explore the *Nuclear Bunker*. Then head back along the A128 (via Brentwood) and onto the junction with the A13, where you turn right. Just over a mile later, turn left onto the A1089 to 17th C. *Tilbury Fort*.

Norfolk

Map of County 190

County Information 191

Cities, Towns & Villages 192

Good Beach Guide 197

Tourist Information (Centres & Points) . . 199

Guided Tours 201

History & Heritage
Historic Houses 202
Ancient Monuments 205
Museums & Galleries 208
Machinery & Transport 217
Mills 221

Bloomin' Beautiful
Gardens 223
Nurseries & Garden Centres 226

Family Fun
Animal & Bird Collections 230
Amusement/Theme Centres & Parks 232
Children's Indoor Play Centres 234
Leisure Pools 234

Countryside
Special Areas 235
Country Parks & Nature Reserves 236
Picnic Sites 238

Activities
Boat Trips 239
Golf Courses 241
Cycling 241
Walking 241
Specialist Holidays & Tours 242

Food & Drink
Regional Produce 243
Breweries & Vineyards 243
Restaurants 243
Afternoon Teas 244

Stop & Shop
Craft Centres & Speciality Shopping 245

Discovery Tours 249

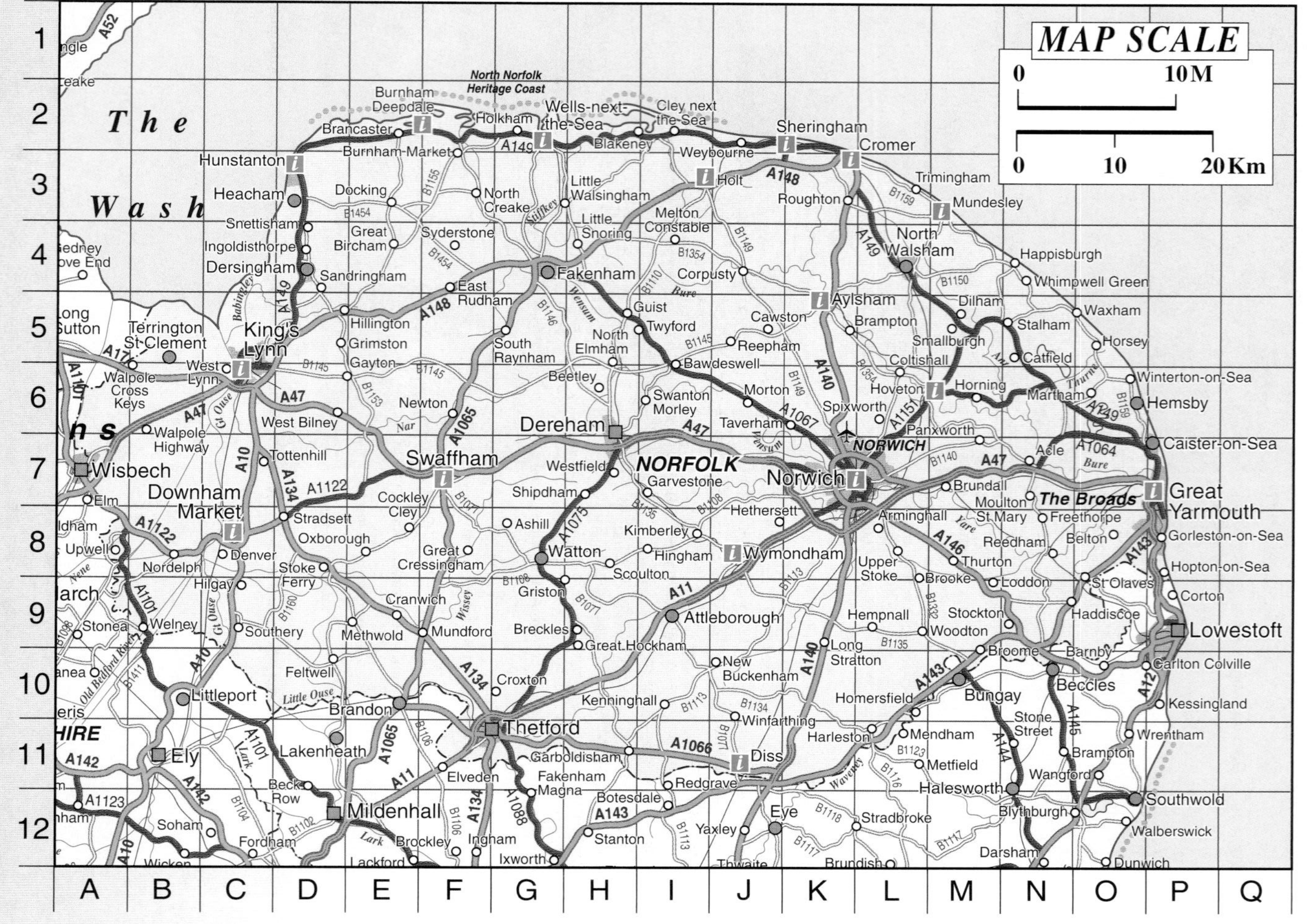
MAP SCALE
0
10M
0
10
20Km
The Wash
North Norfolk Heritage Coast
NORFOLK
The Broads
Hunstanton
Heacham
Snettisham
Ingoldisthorpe
Dersingham
Sandringham
King's Lynn
West Lynn
Brancaster
Burnham Deepdale
Burnham-Market
Docking
Great Bircham
Syderstone
North Creake
Holkham
Wells-next-the-Sea
Little Walsingham
Little Snoring
Blakeney
Cley next the Sea
Weybourne
Sheringham
Cromer
Holt
Melton Constable
Fakenham
East Rudham
South Raynham
Hillington
Grimston
Gayton
West Bilney
Newton
Swaffham
Downham Market
Denver
Stoke Ferry
Oxborough
Methwold
Feltwell
Hilgay
Southery
Wisbech
Walpole Highway
Walpole Cross Keys
Terrington St Clement
Long Sutton
Littleport
Ely
Soham
Fordham
Lakenheath
Mildenhall
Brandon
Thetford
Elveden
Mundford
Croxton
Watton
Ashill
Shipdham
Dereham
Swanton Morley
Bawdeswell
Reepham
Aylsham
Norwich
NORWICH
Wymondham
Attleborough
Hingham
Diss
Eye
Harleston
Bungay
Beccles
Halesworth
Southwold
Lowestoft
Great Yarmouth
Caister-on-Sea
Hemsby
North Walsham
Mundesley
Trimingham
Happisburgh
Whimpwell Green
Horning
Acle
Kessingland
Walberswick
Dunwich
Corton
Gorleston-on-Sea
Hopton-on-Sea
Winterton-on-Sea

Norfolk

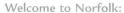

County Town: Norwich.
Population: 797,900 approx.
Highest Point: Roman Camp, Sheringham 102m (336 feet).
Rivers: Ant, Babingley, Burn, Bure, Chet, Glaven, Great Ouse, Little Ouse, Nar, Ouse, Stiffkey, Tas, Thet, Waveney, Wensum, Wissey, Yare.
Landmarks: Blakeney Point, The Brecks, The Fens, Little Walsingham, The Norfolk Broads, Norwich Cathedral, Sandringham, Thetford Forest Park, The Wash.

Welcome to Norfolk:

Start in Norwich, with its beautifully preserved medieval centre, Norman cathedral and castle. Then explore the Norfolk Broads, England's newest National Park with over 125 miles of navigable waterways. While to the west are Royal Sandringham, and the maritime town of King's Lynn. Take a drive along the coastline from the flat tidal marshes of the Wash, via the nature reserves and flint fishing villages of North Norfolk, to the seaside fun of Cromer, Hunstanton and Great Yarmouth. Or explore the unique landscape of the Brecks, home of Britain's largest lowland pine forest.

Industry Past & Present:

Noted for its rich *agricultural* heritage, Norfolk has led the way in farming developments. One of the great reformers was Thomas Coke of Holkham Hall who experimented with farming techniques, such as transforming his land from sheep pastures to productive mixed farms. Today most of the county is given over to *cereal* and *vegetable crops*. In the Middle Ages, pastures supported vast flocks of sheep, and this local wool started the important *weaving* industry. The village of Worstead gives its name to a type of cloth, woven there by Flemish weavers. Later (17th C.) the industry became more centred on Norwich. The wealth generated can be seen in medieval guildhalls, merchants' houses and churches. On the coast, Great Yarmouth (home of North Sea *gas/oil production*) had a huge *herring* industry, which reached its peak at the start of the 20th C. with large numbers of steam drifters. But over-fishing led to the collapse of the industry after the Second World War. Today *shellfish* is more important - with *cockles/shrimps* from the Wash, *mussels/whelks* from North Norfolk, and *crabs/lobsters* at Cromer and Sheringham. *Smoked fish (bloaters/kippers)* have also long been a speciality. One of England's major ports from the 12-18th C. King's Lynn was chosen by the Hanseatic merchants as a base for their warehouses. Today the town is home to the only remnant (a warehouse) of the Hanse left in Britain. Similarly Norwich has traded its goods throughout Europe, noted for its *banking/insurance* (Norwich Union), *brewing, printing* (Jarrolds), *shoe making* and *mustard* (Colman's). To the north, the Norfolk Broads were created, when *peat* (used for fuel) diggings of the 12-14th C. became flooded. Here *reed/sedge* are cut for thatch. While to the south, the vast Thetford Forest provides valuable *timber*. Famous names of the county include - Bernard Matthews (poultry), Cirio Del Monte Foods (fruit drinks), Group Lotus (sports cars) and Jeyes (pharmaceuticals).

Famous People:

Queen Boudicca, Henry Blogg *(Cromer lifeboatman)*, Anne Boleyn *(Henry VIII's second wife)*, George Borrow *(author)*, Thomas Browne *(author)*, Nurse Edith Cavell, The Coke Family *(Holkham)*, John Crome & John Sell Cotman *(Norwich School of Painting)*, William Cowper *(poet)*, Edward VII, Elizabeth Fry *(social reformer)*, Richard Lincoln *(Abraham Lincoln's ancestor)*, Admiral Lord Nelson, Thomas Paine *(political writer)*, Arthur Ransome *(author)*, Humphry Repton *(landscape gardener)*, John Rolfe *(married Red Indian princess Pocahontas)*, Anna Sewell *(author)*, Captain George Vancouver *(seafarer)*, Sir Robert Walpole *(Britain's first Prime Minister)*.

The Norfolk Broads

 CITIES, TOWNS & VILLAGES

Cities, Towns & Villages

MD:	Market Day
FM:	Farmers' Market
EC:	Early Closing
i	Tourist Information Centre (see page 199)
	Guided Tours (see page 201)

Acle Map ref. N7
This small town, situated halfway between Norwich and Great Yarmouth, sits on the edge of the Halvergate Marshes. It originally stood on the coast, until the reclamation of the river estuaries. The large green is surrounded by 17/18th C. buildings, while the church has a detached, round Saxon tower. Acle is noted for its regular auctions. **MD**: Thurs.

Attleborough Map ref. I9
Pleasant market town. It was once famous for its cider works (depicted on the town sign) and for producing turkeys, which used to make the journey to the London markets on foot. The small shopping centre is set around an attractive green, while the parish church was once the centre of a much larger building, whose remains can be seen. **MD**: Thurs. **EC**: Wed.

Attleborough

Aylsham Map ref. K5
For 500 years, this picturesque small town was an important centre for the manufacture of linen, then worsted cloth. The open market place is surrounded by handsome 18th C. buildings. Humphry Repton, the famous 18th C. landscape gardener is buried in the churchyard. The town is noted for its regular antique auctions. **MD**: Mon and Fri. **FM**: 1st Sat in month. **EC**: Wed. i

Blakeney Map ref. H/I2
Attractive village and small port at the mouth of the River Glaven, which in summer is busy with yachts and pleasure craft. Narrow lanes of flint cottages, fine church and medieval guildhall. Boat trips to Blakeney Point, a 3 mile long sand and shingle spit.

Burnham Market Map ref. F3
This is the largest of the seven 'Burnham' villages. Attractive main street and green, with elegant 18th C. houses and pretty flint cottages. Antique, book and craft shops. Bolton House was the home of Lord Nelson's sister, while his daughter was married at St. Mary's Church in 1823. **EC**: Wed. i (at Burnham Deepdale)

Caister-on-Sea Map ref. P7
Popular seaside resort, with a wide sandy beach and famous volunteer lifeboat service. Remains of fortified Roman town/port. Ruins of 15th C. castle, built by Sir John Fastolf, who features in Shakespeare's Henry VI. Several holiday centres, caravan and chalet parks.

Cley-next-the-Sea Map ref. I2
Once an important wool port, Cley is a popular holiday centre, with narrow lanes, brick/flint houses and old-fashioned shops. The famous 18th C. windmill overlooks the surrounding salt-marshes and nature reserve leading to the sea.

Cromer Map ref. K3
Dominated by the tower of its parish church (the tallest in the county), this sedate seaside town stands on a cliff top, with wide sandy beaches running down to the sea. Cromer is famous for its crabs, caught by its little fishing boats which still work from the beach. The fine pier is noted for its end-of-the-pier theatre and lifeboat station. **MD**: Fri. **EC**: Wed. i

Dereham Map ref. H6/7
Lively market town, established as a religious community by St. Withburga in the 7th C. 18th C. buildings surround the market place, while the partly Norman church has a detached bell tower. Bishop Bonner's Cottages are noted for their pargetting. The poet William Cowper lived here from 1796 until his death. **MD**: Tues and Fri. **FM**: 2nd Sat in month. **EC**: Wed.

Diss Map ref. J11
Set in the Waveney Valley, this thriving market town borders a six acre mere, home to a variety of wildfowl. Diss still retains much of its picturesque old world charm, with a maze of streets clustered around St. Mary's Church, its tower dating from 1300. 16th C. timber-framed houses, and later buildings of the 18/19th C. surround the market place. **MD**: Fri (also auction). **FM**: 2nd Sat in month. **EC**: Tues.

Downham Market Map ref. C8
Dating back to Saxon times, this small hillside settlement is one of Norfolk's oldest market towns. Lying on the edge of the Fens, Downham Market is noted for its 19th C. black and white clock tower and local carrstone buildings, some showing a Dutch influence. 15th C. church with unusual spire. **MD**: Fri and Sat. **EC**: Wed.

Fakenham Map ref. G4
Thriving market town set on the River Wensum. The large market place is surrounded by handsome 18/19th C. buildings, interesting courtyards and tiny lanes. The patronage of the partly 15th C. church has rested with Trinity College in Cambridge since 1547. The town boasts one of the finest National Hunt courses in the country. **MD**: Thurs. **FM**: 4th Sat in month. **EC**: Wed.

Gorleston-on-Sea Map ref. P8
Sitting on the other side of the River Yare from its more busy neighbour, Great Yarmouth, Gorleston-on-Sea is ideal for those looking for a quieter holiday. The town has interesting 19th C. villas, and its own theatre, lifeboat station and inshore fishing fleet. The sandy beach is backed by low cliffs to form a bay. **EC**: Wed.

Great Yarmouth Map ref. P7
One of Britain's most popular seaside resorts with wide sandy beaches, colourful gardens and traditional seaside attractions and entertainment. Built on a spit of sand, between the sea and the River Yare, the town's wealth comes from its port, and the former herring industry. The historic quayside has old merchants' houses and 'rows' (narrow medieval alleys). Remains of the town wall and the largest parish church in England. **MD**: Wed, Fri (summer only) and Sat. **EC**: Thurs.

Harleston Map ref. L11
Lying in the Waveney Valley, this old-fashioned market town borders countryside made famous by the local artist, Sir Alfred Munnings. Harleston has fine timber-framed buildings and Georgian town houses. In the Old Market Place are courtyards where weavers and basketmakers once lived. **MD**: Wed. **FM**: 3rd Sat in month. **EC**: Thurs.

Hingham Map ref. I8
Pretty market town, with two splendid greens bordered by Georgian period houses and linked by narrow streets. The large church contains a bust of Abraham Lincoln, a descendant of Samuel Lincoln, a local weaver and Quaker, who sailed to religious freedom in the America's in 1637.

Holt Map ref. I3
One of the most attractive small towns in Norfolk, with a main street lined with elegant Georgian buildings, mostly built after the fire of 1708. The town is best known for Greshams, a public school founded in 1555 by Sir John Gresham, a former Lord Mayor of London. Holt is a mecca for antique and bric-a-brac collectors. **EC**: Thurs.

Norwich

CITIES, TOWNS & VILLAGES

Horning Map ref. M6
Broads holiday village stretching for about a mile alongside the River Bure. Edwardian lodges and thatched cottages mix with shops, restaurants, pubs and boathouses, with gardens and lawns sweeping down to the water. Annual regatta.

Hunstanton Map ref. D3
This is England's only east coast resort which faces west. Hunstanton is a traditional seaside town with a range of attractions, large sandy beaches and gardens. Ornate Victorian and Edwardian houses overlook wide open greens. To the north is Old Hunstanton, a residential village with distinctive red and white striped cliffs. **MD**: Wed and Sun. **EC**: Thurs.

King's Lynn Map ref. C5/6
Historic port and market town, dating back to the 12th C. and steeped in maritime history. Two magnificent market places and two medieval guildhalls; one is the largest in Britain, the other houses the town's regalia. Former merchants' houses, hidden courtyards and attractive waterfront area with 18th C. Custom House. 12th C. church with rare moon/tide dial. **MD**: Tues, Fri and Sat.

Little Walsingham Map ref. G/H3
Picturesque village, a famous pilgrimage centre since 1061, when the Lady of the Manor had a vision of the Virgin Mary. The subsequent shrine became one of the most important in Europe. Timber-framed buildings and Georgian facades line the High Street and Market Place, with its 16th C. pump-house. Also extensive ruins of Augustinian abbey set in attractive parkland.

Loddon Map ref. M9
Broadland market town on the River Chet, with an imposing and beautiful 15th C. church. The town is a popular boating centre, with Georgian and Victorian houses lining the main street. Its small shopping centre has a waterside picnic area. Loddon was once a commercial port, and there are old warehouses and a watermill still remaining. **MD**: Mon.

Long Stratton Map ref. K9
This large village, almost a small town, has a long main street bordered by 16/17th C. half-timbered buildings. St. Mary's Church has a round tower and very rare sexton's wheel. Preserved 19th C. ice house which once served the demolished Manor House. **EC**: Wed.

Mundesley Map ref. M3
Built at the mouth of the tiny river Mund, this is one of Norfolk's best kept secrets. The town prospered at the start of the 20th C. when the railway arrived, and for a time it was something of a health resort with two sanatoriums. Today Mundlesey is a quiet holiday town with a clean beach, and shallow pools left by the turning tide.
EC: Wed.

North Walsham Map ref. L4
This busy market town became a centre for the wool industry in the late medieval period. The wealth generated enabled the local people to build St. Nicholas Church, which dates back to 1330. The 16th C. market cross is the focal point of the town. Lord Nelson spent his schooldays at 'The Paston School'. **MD**: Thurs. **EC**: Wed.

Norwich Map ref. K/L7
East Anglia's capital, and the most complete medieval city in Britain. Surrounded by its old walls are over 1,500 historic buildings, and an intricate network of winding streets and lanes, such as cobbled Elm Hill. Norwich is dominated by its magnificent cathedral, and impressive 12th C. castle keep. Lively cultural scene with museums, galleries, theatres, restaurants and pubs. Excellent shopping centre, including the Castle Mall, famous Mustard Shop and colourful open air market. **MD**: Mon to Sat. **FM**: 2nd Sat in month.

Reepham Map ref. J5
Attractive market town, with narrow winding streets lined with Georgian/half-timbered buildings. Dominating the market place is 'The Dial House', so called because of the sun-dial over the door. Reepham is unique in having three churches in one churchyard (although one is now a ruin). **MD**: Wed. **EC**: Thurs

King's Lynn

 CITIES, TOWNS & VILLAGES

Sheringham Map ref. J/K2
This traditional seaside town grew up around its old fishing village, and a band of little boats still bring in the daily catch. A mixture of Edwardian and Victorian buildings, Sheringham is home of the North Norfolk Railway (The Poppy Line), which operates steam train rides to Holt. At low tide the large sandy beach reveals rock pools.
MD: Sat. **EC**: Wed.

Stalham Map ref. N5
Peaceful little market town on the edge of the Norfolk Broads. Still a centre for boat building, Stalham has pretty Georgian houses, shops, inns and cafes. The large 15th C. church contains a magnificent richly carved font. The staithe, once busy with the wherry trade, is built on an artificial cut (or dyke) leading from the river. **MD**: Tues. **FM**: 1st and 3rd Sat in month. **EC**: Wed.

Swaffham Map ref. F7
Charming old market town, once a fashionable centre for the gentry in the 18th C. The triangular-shaped market place has handsome Georgian buildings (such as the Assembly Rooms) and a butter market. The 15th C. church is one of the finest in the region, with its double hammerbeam angel roof, and memorial to the famous Pedlar of Swaffham. **MD**: Sat.

Thetford Map ref. F/G11
Thriving market town, which a thousand years ago was the capital of East Anglia. Its importance continued during the early Middle Ages, and has left a legacy of historic sites, such as the Iron Age earthworks, a Norman castle mound and the remains of the 12th C. priory. The town centre is a conservation area with fine medieval and Georgian buildings. **MD**: Tues and Sat. **EC**: Wed.

Watton Map ref. G8
Busy rural centre with an unusual clock tower dated 1679. The wide High Street has late 18/19th C. houses offering many family-run shops. Watton has the only church in the country that is wider than it is long. To the south is Wayland Wood, which is connected to the famous story of the 'Babes in the Wood'. This is depicted on the town sign. **MD**: Wed. **FM**: 1st Sat in month. **EC**: Thurs.

Wells-next-the-Sea Map ref. G2
Picturesque small town, a busy port for coasters and the local whelk and shrimp boats. Not quite on the sea, but sitting on an estuary, Wells has narrow streets lined with traditional flint buildings. While on the green (The Buttlands) is a series of Georgian houses. A little railway takes visitors from the port to the nearby sandy beach.
EC: Thurs.

Cley-next-the-Sea

 CITIES, TOWNS & VILLAGES

Blakeney

Wroxham and Hoveton Map ref. L/M6
The adjoining villages of Wroxham and Hoveton are known as the 'capital of the Broads'. Linked together by a hump-backed bridge over the River Bure, Hoveton offers the main shopping and tourist centre with its boatyards, chandleries and 'Roys' (the largest village store in the world). Various boat excursions available.

Wymondham Map ref. J8
Wymondham (pronounced "Win-dum") retains all the character of a historic market town. The town has more listed buildings than any similar sized town in the county, including the 17th C. octagonal market cross. The twin towers of the beautiful abbey dominate the skyline, and are the result of a 14th C. dispute between the townspeople and the monks. **MD**: Fri. **FM**: 3rd Sat in month. **EC**: Wed.

Diss

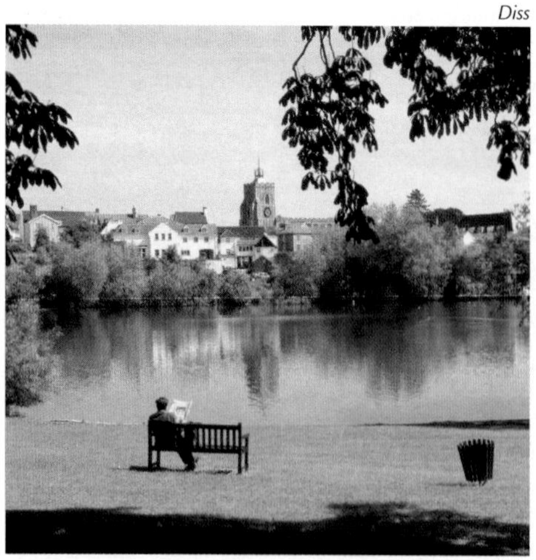

Pick of the villages

1 **Baconsthorpe** - remains of 15th C. partly-moated, semi-fortified house. Map ref. J3
2 **Beachamwell** - ancient village set around its green and thatched church. Map ref. E8
3 **Binham** - flint cottages and elegant houses. 11th C. priory remains. Map ref. H3
4 **Brancaster** - fisherman's cottages, sailing boats and earthworks of Roman fort. Map ref. E2
5 **Burnham Thorpe** - wide open green with brick/flint buildings. Birthplace of Lord Nelson. Map ref. F3
6 **Castle Acre** - flint-built village with castle mound, priory ruins and 13th C. bailey gate. Map ref. F6
7 **Caston** - small and pretty village with thatched church, green and windmill. Map ref. H9
8 **The Creakes (North and South)** - two riverside villages. Flint houses and 13th C. abbey ruins. Map ref. F3
9 **Coltishall** - former wherry port. 18th C. buildings, thatched church and green. Map ref. L6
10 **Denver** - famous sluice controls vast Fenland waterways. 19th C. restored windmill. Map ref. C8
11 **East Lexham** - tiny hamlet. Butter market, round-towered church and 17th C. hall. Map ref. F6
12 **Great Massingham** - huge village green with flint houses and three large ponds. Map ref. E5
13 **Happisburgh** - seaside village with flint houses and red/white striped lighthouse. Map ref. N4
14 **Heydon** - attractive, privately owned village. Used in numerous TV/film productions. Map ref. J5
15 **Letheringsett** - set in wooded Glaven valley. 18th C. hall and water mill. Map ref. I3
16 **Litcham** - handsome village on banks of River Nar. Elegant 18th C. town houses. Map ref. G6
17 **Neatishead** - Broadland village at head of wooded creek. Georgian houses. Map ref. M6
18 **Martham** - wide open green with Georgian houses. Splendid church tower. Map ref. O6
19 **New Buckenham** - planned medieval village. 17th C. market house and castle ramparts. Map ref. J10
20 **North Elmham** - ecclesiastical centre of Saxon Norfolk. Remains of Norman chapel. Map ref. H5/6
21 **Outwell/Upwell** - adjoining Fenland villages. 'Dutch-style' houses, gardens and boats. Map ref. A8
22 **Pulham Market** - green with 16/17th C. colour-washed houses. Airship connections. Map ref. K10
23 **Ranworth** - 'cathedral of the Broads' (views from tower) and floating conservation centre. Map ref. M6
24 **Reedham** - on the banks of the River Yare, noted for the last chain ferry on the Broads built in 1914. Map ref. N8
25 **Stiffkey** - narrow winding street with fishermen's cottages. Famous for its shellfish. Map ref. H2
26 **Surlingham** - thatched cottages beside River Yare. 'Wherry graveyard'. Map ref. M7
27 **Swanton Morley** - the family of US President Abraham Lincoln originated in this village. Map ref. I6
28 **Walpole St. Peter** - 'Marshland' village, noted for one of the finest churches in Britain. Map ref. B6
29 **Woodbastwick** - estate village with thatched cottages and church. Map ref. M6
30 **Worstead** - medieval weaving centre. 15th C. wool church and elegant 17th C. houses. Map ref. M5

Good Beach Guide

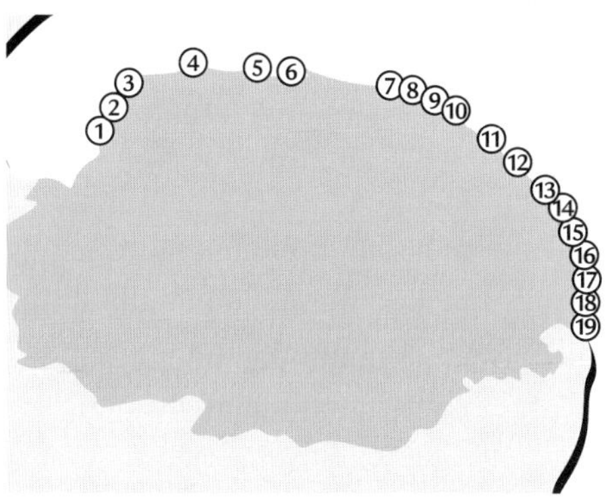

Key

TIC: Tourist Information Centre (see page 199)

TIP: Tourist Information Point (see page 200)

Dog ban: 1 May-30 September, dogs banned from the main beach areas. Further details from the nearest TIC.

Good Beach Guide 2004
The Good Beach Guide is the ultimate independent guide to UK beaches. By checking the water quality grade and the level of sewage treatment - you can choose a safe beach to visit this summer. The guide is available from the Marine Conservation Society from May 2004.
Tel: (01989) 566017 or visit www.goodbeachguide.co.uk

1 Heacham

Winner of the Seaside Award for rural beaches, this beach has safe, gently shelving sands and a limited number of amenities. Car parking and parking for the disabled is available, and there is a ramp to the beach from the disabled parking area. Small cafe and boat launch facilities. Toilets.

2 Hunstanton

Winner of Seaside Awards for the last five years. Sandy beaches make an ideal playground for children, whilst windsurfers find the Wash an excellent location for their sport. The beach is very gently shelving and when the tide goes out it makes a pleasant walk to the sea for a swim. Deck-chairs. Pony rides. Pitch and putt, bowls, adventure golf courses and a fun fair. Specially designed route for wheelchairs along the seafront. Car parking. Toilets. Dog ban. TIC.

3 Old Hunstanton

A quieter and more rural beach than its near neighbour Hunstanton. There are red and white cliffs, sand dunes and beach huts, a small café, shop, toilets and the local lifeboat station. Limited parking.

4 Brancaster

Very quiet broad sandy beach with dunes. Approached by a lane leading north from the village. The tide retreats for more than a mile to the east, but not so far to the west. Car parking. Toilets.

5 Holkham

A huge private sheltered sandy beach with dunes backed by pine trees. A favourite spot for picnics and swimming. The tide goes out for miles. Car parking along Lady Anne's Drive on payment of fee in summer, but free in winter.

6 Wells-next-the-Sea

The wide spacious beach is a mile from the town and is reached by road, or by the narrow gauge railway. Consisting of sand and shingle with pine trees on one side and the harbour channel on the other. Car parking. Toilets. Dog ban. TIC.

Old Hunstanton

7 Sheringham
A beach of sloping pebbles and shingle above sand. Rocks and groynes with shallow pools at low tide. Low cliffs. Fishing boats are hauled up on the beach. Blue Flag and Seaside Award. Amusements and refreshments. Deck-chairs. Car parking. Toilets. Dog ban. TIC.

8 East Runton & West Runton
Gently shelving sand and shingle beaches backed by low crumbling cliffs. Groynes. Rocky at low tide. Car park. Dog ban at West Runton. Toilets.

9 Cromer
Gently shelving sandy beach with shingle and pebbles. Shallow pools at low tide. Cliffs. Blue Flag and Seaside Award. Pier with entertainment. Famous lifeboat. Deck-chairs. Car parking. Toilets. Dog ban. TIC.

10 Overstrand
Gentle shelving sandy beach with pedestrian access. Groynes, pleasant cliff-top walks. Small car park. Toilets. Dog ban.

11 Mundesley
Quiet holiday resort built in a dip in the coast line. Cliff path access to a smooth sandy beach between groynes. Blue Flag and Seaside Awards. Deck-chairs. Car parking. Toilets. Dog ban. TIC.

12 Sea Palling
Wide and long sandy beach backed by low sand dunes. Blue Flag and Seaside Award. Cafés, picnic area, beach pub and sun loungers on the beach. Car parking. Toilets. Dog ban.

13 Winterton-on-Sea
Very wide sandy beach backed by extensive sand dunes. Pools at low tide. Nature reserve. Car parking. Toilets.

14 Hemsby
Wide sandy beach scattered with stones and backed by grassy dunes. Amusements and deck-chairs. Restaurants and refreshment stalls. Car parking. Toilets.

15 Scratby/California
Low cliffs and wide sandy beach. Shallow pools at low tide. Amusements on cliff top at California. Car park at Scratby. Toilets.

16 Caister-on-Sea
Wide sandy beach which shelves steeply in some places. At the north end, towards California, there are low sandy cliffs. Low sea wall with dunes behind. Boat trips. Volunteer Lifeboat Station. Deck-chairs. Car parking on Beach Road (central beach). Toilets. Picnic area.

17 Great Yarmouth
Very long sandy beach lined by the Marine Parade with its colourful gardens and countless attractions and amenities. Two piers with entertainment and amusements. Dunes at North Beach. Boat trips, trampolines and numerous refreshment stalls. Marina Centre. Deck-chairs. Beach huts and tents. Car parking. Toilets. Dog ban. TIC.

18 Gorleston-on-Sea
Wide sandy beach. Dog ban on northern section from ravine to harbour. Pier, forming part of harbour entrance. Amusements, yacht pond and paddling pool. Low cliffs between sea wall and promenade. Beach chalets. Deck-chairs. Car parking. Toilets. Dog ban.

19 Hopton
Flat sandy beach with some shingle beneath low cliffs.

Gorleston-on-Sea

Tourist Information

Tourist Information Centres

With so much to see and do in this area, it's impossible for us to mention all of the places you can visit. You will find Tourist Information Centres (TICs) throughout Norfolk, with plenty of information on all the things that you can do and places you can visit.

TICs can book accommodation for you, in their own area, or further afield using the 'Book A Bed Ahead' Scheme. They can also be the ideal place to purchase locally made crafts or gifts, as well as books covering a wide range of local interests.

* Not open all year.

Aylsham, Bure Valley Railway Station, Norwich Road.
Tel: (01263) 733903
Email: aylsham@eetb.info Web: www.broadland.gov.uk

Burnham Deepdale, Deepdale Farm.
Tel: (01485) 210256 Email: info@deepdalefarm.co.uk
Web: www.deepdalefarm.co.uk

Wymondham Tourist Information Centre

Norwich Tourist Information Centre

Cromer, Prince of Wales Road.
Tel: (01263) 512497
Email: cromer@eetb.info Web: www.northnorfolk.org

Diss, Mere's Mouth, Mere Street.
Tel: (01379) 650523
Email: diss@eetb.info Web: www.south-norfolk.gov.uk

Downham Market *, The Priory Centre, 78 Priory Road.
Tel: (01366) 387440
Email: downhammarket@eetb.info
Web: www.west-norfolk.gov.uk

Great Yarmouth *, Marine Parade.
Tel: (01493) 842195 Email: greatyarmouth@eetb.info
Web: www.great-yarmouth.co.uk

Holt *, 3 Pound House, Market Place.
Tel: (01263) 713100
Email: holt@eetb.info Web: www.northnorfolk.org

Hoveton *, Station Road.
Tel: (01603) 782281 Email: hoveton@eetb.info
Web: www.broads-authority.gov.uk

Hunstanton, Town Hall, The Green.
Tel: (01485) 532610 Email: hunstanton@eetb.info
Web: www.west-norfolk.gov.uk

King's Lynn, The Custom House, Purfleet Quay.
Tel: (01553) 763044
Email: kingslynn@eetb.info Web: www.west-norfolk.gov.uk

Mundesley *, 2A Station Road.
Tel: (01263) 721070
Email: mundesley@eetb.info Web: www.northnorfolk.org

Norwich, The Forum, Millennium Plain.
Tel: (01603) 727927
Email: norwich@eetb.info Web: www.norwich.gov.uk

Sheringham *, Station Approach.
Tel: (01263) 824329
Email: sheringham@eetb.info Web: www.northnorfolk.org

Swaffham *, Market Place.
Tel: (01760) 722255
Email: swaffham@eetb.info Web: www.breckland.gov.uk

Wells-next-the-Sea *, Staithe Street.
Tel: (01328) 710885 Email: wellsnextthesea@eetb.info
Web: www.northnorfolk.org

Wymondham *, Market Cross, Market Place.
Tel: (01953) 604721 Email: wymondham@eetb.info
Web: www.wymondham-norfolk.co.uk

Tourist Information Points

Limited information is also available from the following information points.

* Not open all year.

Dereham *, Church House, Church Street.
Tel: (01362) 698992 Email: derehamtourism@tesco.net

Fakenham *, Fakenham Connect, Oak Street.
Tel: (01328) 850102

Great Yarmouth, Town Hall. Tel: (01493) 846345

Little Walsingham *, Shirehall Museum, Common Place.
Tel: (01328) 820510

Loddon *, The Old Town Hall, Bridge Street.
Tel: (01508) 521028

Ludham *, Toad Hole Cottage Museum, How Hill.
Tel: (01692) 678763
Email: toadholeinfo@broads-authority.gov.uk

North Walsham *, Brentnall House, 32 Vicarage Street.
Tel: (01692) 407509

Potter Heigham *, The Staithe. Tel: (01692) 670779
Email: potterinfo@broads-authority.gov.uk

Ranworth *, The Staithe. Tel: (01263) 270453
Email: ranworthinfo@broads-authority.gov.uk

Stalham *, The Museum of the Broads, The Staithe.
Tel: (01692) 581681

Watton *, The Clock Tower, High Street.
Tel: 07818 670694

Wells-next-the-Sea

Guided Tours

Why not enjoy a guided tour exploring one of the area's towns and cities? Some of these tours (indicated with a *) are conducted by Registered Blue Badge Guides, who have attended a training course sponsored by the East of England Tourist Board. Many of these guides also have a further qualification to take individuals around the region for half day, full day or longer tours if required. For more information on the guided tours listed, please telephone the relevant contact.

Great Yarmouth

- **Regular town tours:** a choice of four heritage walks running on certain dates between May-Oct. Medieval Town Walls; Maritime Connections; Historic Town Centre and Old Yarmouth. All accompanied by an official town guide.
- Private tours may be booked throughout the year.
- For further information contact the Tourist Information Centre on (01493) 842195.

King's Lynn *

- **Regular town tours:** individuals may join the tours which depart from The Tales of the Old Gaolhouse, from May-Oct. For further information of days and times contact the Tourist Information Centre on (01553) 763044.
- **Group tours:** guided tours can be arranged throughout the year for groups by contacting King's Lynn Town Guides on (01553) 765714.

Little Walsingham

Walking guided tours around the historic village of Walsingham. Easter-30 Sept, Wed and Thurs at 1100. Also Sat from Jun-Sept at 1400. Group tours throughout the year by arrangement. For further information contact the Tours Organiser on (01328) 820250.

Norwich *

- **Regular city tours:** 'Norwich - City of Century' walking tours lasting 1 1/2 hours, depart from the Tourist Information Centre in the Forum. Up to three times daily from Apr-Oct, plus Suns from Jun-Sept.
- **Evening tours:** themed tours including 'Tales of the Riverside' and 'When George was King', twice weekly at 1900 from Jun-Sept.
- **Group tours:** a variety of themed walking tours are available for pre-booked groups. A 'Panoramic Norwich' coach tour can be arranged. Itineraries can also be arranged for longer half or full day tours, including the Norfolk Broads or North Norfolk Coast.
- For further information contact the Tourist Information Centre on (01603) 727927. Fax: (01603) 765389. Email: tourism@norwich.gov.uk

King's Lynn

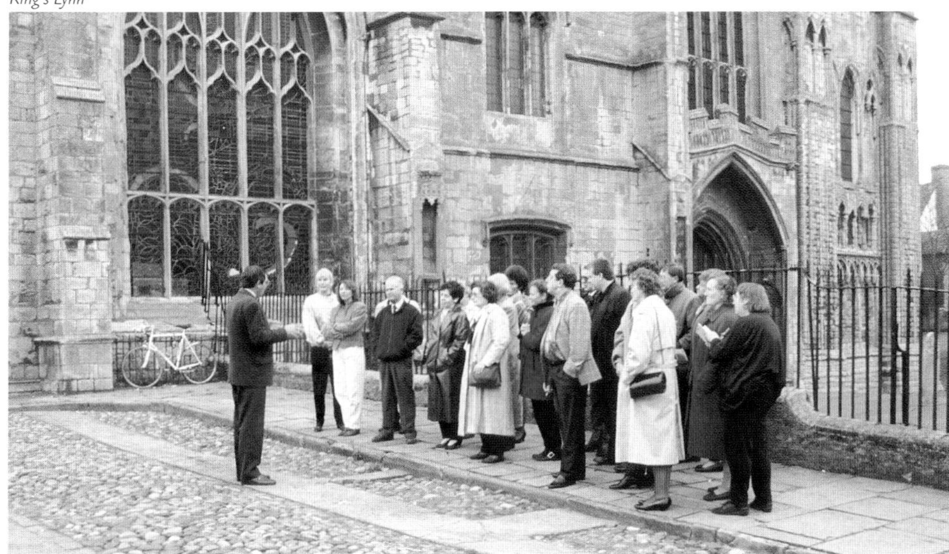

Historic Houses

Blakeney

Blakeney Guildhall Map ref. H/I2

Tel: (01223) 582700 Web: www.english-heritage.org.uk

The remains of the 14th C. basement to a merchant's house which was most likely used for storage.

Times: Open at any reasonable time.

Fee: Free.

Facilities: T(30 mins) EH

Blickling (nr. Aylsham)

Blickling Hall, Garden and Park Map ref. K4

Tel: (01263) 738030 Web: www.nationaltrust.org.uk

A Jacobean redbrick mansion with garden, orangery, parkland and lake. Spectacular long gallery, superb plasterwork ceilings and fine collections of furniture, pictures, books and tapestries. Walks.

Times: House open - 20 Mar-3 Oct, Wed-Sun, 1300-1700. 6-31 Oct, Wed-Sun, 1300-1600. Garden open - 20 Mar-31 Jul, Wed-Sun, 1015-1715. 1 Sept-31 Oct, Wed-Sun, 1015-1715. 4 Nov-19 Dec, Thurs-Sun, 1100-1600. Park open all year, daily, dawn-dusk.

Fee: House and garden £7.00/£3.50. Garden only £4.00/£2.00.

Facilities: P T(2 hrs) NT

Erpingham (nr. Aylsham)

Wolterton Park Map ref. K4

Tel: (01263) 584175 Web: www.manningtongardens.co.uk

A beautiful Georgian house with lake and extensive parkland. Park has a playground, walks and orienteering. House with fascinating history.

Times: Park open all year, daily, 0900-dusk. Hall open 30 Apr-29 Oct, Fri, 1400-1700. Last admission 1600.

Fee: Hall £5.00/£2.50. Park free, but car park charge of £2.00.

Facilities: P T(2 hrs)

Felbrigg (nr. Cromer)

Felbrigg Hall Map ref. K3

Tel: (01263) 837444 Web: www.nationaltrust.org.uk

A 17th C. country house with original 18th C. furniture and pictures. There is also a walled garden, orangery, park and woodland with way-marked walks, shops and catering.

Times: Open 29 Mar-31 Oct, Sat-Wed, house 1300-1700; gardens 1100-1700. 22 Jul-8 Sept, gardens daily, 1100-1700. Estate walks, all year, daily, dawn-dusk.

Fee: Hall and gardens £6.30/£3.00/£15.50 (family). Gardens only £2.60/£1.00.

Facilities: P T(2 hrs) NT

Great Yarmouth

Elizabethan House Museum Map ref. P7

See entry in Museums & Galleries section.

Great Yarmouth

Old Merchant's House, Row III House and Greyfriars Cloisters Map ref. P7

See entry in Museums & Galleries section.

Houghton

Houghton Hall Map ref. E4

Tel: (01485) 528569 Web: www.houghtonhall.com

Splendid Palladian house built by Sir Robert Walpole. Magnificently furnished State Rooms. 5-acre walled garden - full of colour all summer. 20,000 Model Soldier Museum. Tearoom and Shop.

Times: Open 10 Apr-30 Sept, Wed, Thurs, Sun and Bank Hol Mon. Gates, gardens, Soldier Museum, tearoom and shop, 1300-1730. House 1400-1730 (last admission 1700).

Fee: £6.50/£3.00. Excluding house £4.00/£2.00.

Facilities: Q P T(2 hrs)

King's Lynn

Guildhall of St. George Map ref. C5/6

See entry in Museums & Galleries section.

Felbrigg Hall

Norwich

Dragon Hall Map ref. K/L7
115-123 King Street
Tel: (01603) 663922
Medieval merchant's hall with outstanding timber-framed structure. The 15th C. Great Hall has a crown-post roof with an intricately carved and painted dragon.
Times: Open 2 Jan-31 Mar, Mon-Fri, 1000-1600. 1 Apr-30 Oct, Mon-Sat, 1000-1600. 31 Oct-20 Dec, Mon-Fri, 1000-1600. Closed 9, 12 Apr and 20 Dec-1 Jan.
Fee: £2.50/£1.00/£2.00.
Facilities: T(1 hr)

Norwich

Strangers' Hall Museum Map ref. K/L7
See entry in Museums & Galleries section.

Oxborough (nr. Swaffham)

Oxburgh Hall Map ref. E8
Tel: (01366) 328258 Web: www.nationaltrust.org.uk
A 15th C. moated redbrick fortified manor-house with an 80ft gatehouse, Mary Queen of Scot's needlework, a Catholic priest's hole, garden, woodland walks and a Catholic chapel.
Times: House open 20 Mar-7 Nov, Sat-Wed, 1300-1700. Garden open 28 Feb-14 Mar, Sat and Sun, 1100-1600. 20 Mar-28 Jul, Sat-Wed, 1100-1730. 31 Jul-27 Aug, daily, 1100-1730. 28 Aug-7 Nov, Sat-Wed, 1100-1730. 13 Nov-19 Dec, Sat and Sun, 1100-1600. Shop and restaurant (dates as garden) 1100-1700. Closed 9 Apr.
Fee: House and garden £5.75/£2.90/£15.00 (family). Garden and estate £2.90/£1.45.
Facilities: T(3 hrs) NT

Sandringham (nr. King's Lynn)

Sandringham Map ref. D4/5
Tel: (01553) 612908 Web: www.sandringhamestate.co.uk
The country retreat of HM The Queen. A delightful house set in 60 acres of grounds and lakes. Museum of royal vehicles and memorabilia. 600 acre country park. Visitor centre.
Times: Open 10 Apr-23 Jul, daily, house 1100-1645; museum 1100-1700; grounds 1100-1700. 1 Aug-31 Oct, daily, house 1100-1645; museum 1100-1700; grounds 1030-1700.
Fee: House, grounds and museum £6.50/£4.00/£5.00/£17.00. House and grounds £4.50/£2.50/£3.50/£14.00.
Facilities: T(3½ hrs)

Sandringham, (by gracious permission of HM The Queen)

Thetford

Ancient House Museum Map ref. F/G11

See entry in Museums & Galleries section.

Thetford

Thetford Warren Lodge Map ref. F11

Tel: (01223) 582700 Web: www.english-heritage.org.uk

The ruins of a small two storey medieval gamekeeper's lodge which can only be viewed from the outside.

Times: Open at any reasonable time.

Fee: Free.

Facilities: T(20 mins) (on leads) **EH**

DID YOU KNOW

The tale of the Pedlar of Swaffham (depicted on the town's sign) tells of John Chapman - who in a dream was told to go to London Bridge, where he would find his fortune. Here he met a stranger, who told him that a pot of gold lay buried in the garden of a certain Pedlar in Swaffham. Without saying a word, he rushed home and dug in his garden, where he found his riches.

Wells-next-the-Sea

Holkham Hall Map ref. G2

Tel: (01328) 710227 Web: www.holkham.co.uk

A classic 18th C. Palladian-style mansion. Part of a great agricultural estate, and a living treasure house of artistic and architectural history. Bygones Museum with over 4,000 items from cars and crafts to kitchens and steam.

Times: Hall open 3 Jun-27 Sept, daily (except Tues and Wed), 1300-1700 (last admission at 1630). Terraces open Mon, Thurs and Fri (but not weekends on Bank Hol Mons). 6-28 May, audio tour of hall (turn up and join in) at 1500 daily (except Tues and Wed). Hall also open on 10-12 Apr, 1-3 and 29-31 May and 28-30 Aug, 1130-1700 (last admission at 1630). Bygones Museum open 10-12 Apr, then 6 May-27 Sept, daily (except Tues and Wed), 1000-1700 (last admission at 1630).

Fee: Hall £6.50/£3.25. Bygones Museum £5.00/£2.50. Hall and Bygones Museum £10.00/£5.00/£25.00 (family).

Facilities: T(2 hrs) (out of season)

Oxburgh Hall, Oxborough

Ancient Monuments

Baconsthorpe (nr. Holt)
Baconsthorpe Castle Map ref. J3
Tel: (01223) 582700 Web: www.english-heritage.org.uk
A 15th C. part-moated, semi-fortified house. The remains include the inner and outer gatehouse and the curtain wall. Baconsthorpe Post Office sells guide books and postcards.
Times: Open at any reasonable time.
Fee: Free.
Facilities: T(45 mins) (on leads) **EH**

Binham
Binham Priory Map ref. H3
Tel: (01328) 830434 Web: www.english-heritage.org.uk
Extensive remains of an early 12th C. Benedictine priory. The original nave of the church is still used as the parish church.
Times: Open at any reasonable time.
Fee: Free.
Facilities: T(45 mins) **EH**

Burnham Market
Creake Abbey Map ref. F3
Tel: (01223) 582700 Web: www.english-heritage.org.uk
Remains of an abbey church dating from the 13th C., including presbytery and north transept with chapels.
Times: Open at any reasonable time.
Fee: Free.
Facilities: T(45 mins) (on leads) **EH**

Caistor St. Edmund (nr. Norwich)
Caistor Roman Town Map ref. L8
Web: www.norfarchtrust.org.uk
The site of Venta Icenorum, the Roman capital of Norfolk. The Roman fortifications can be seen in several places. Series of interpretation boards on signposted walks.
Times: Open at any reasonable time.
Fee: Free.
Facilities: T(1½ hrs)

Castle Acre (nr. Swaffham)
Castle Acre Castle Map ref. F6
Tel: (01760) 755394 Web: www.english-heritage.org.uk
The remains of a Norman manor-house which became a castle with earthworks, set by the side of a village.
Times: Open at any reasonable time.
Fee: Free.
Facilities: Q T(½ hrs) (on leads) **EH**

Castle Acre (nr. Swaffham)
Castle Acre Priory Map ref. F6
Stocks Green
Tel: (01760) 755394 Web: www.english-heritage.org.uk
Impressive ruins of a Cluniac priory, built by William de Warenne in about 1090. Church and decorated 12th C. west front, 16th C. gatehouse and prior's lodgings.
Times: Please contact for details of opening times.
Fee: Please contact for details of admission prices.
Facilities: Q T(1 hr) (audio tours) (on leads) **EH**

Castle Rising (nr. King's Lynn)
Castle Rising Castle Map ref. D5
Tel: (01553) 631330 Web: www.castlerising.co.uk
Castle Rising Castle is a fine example of a Norman castle. The rectangular keep, one of the largest, was built around 1140 by William D'Albini.
Times: Please contact for details of opening times.
Fee: Please contact for details of admission prices.
Facilities: T(1½ hrs) **EH**

Great Yarmouth
Burgh Castle Map ref. O8
Church Farm, Burgh Castle
Tel: (01223) 582700 Web: www.english-heritage.org.uk
The remains of a 3rd C. Roman fort overlooking the River Waveney. The monument is only approached on foot. There is information and a tearoom available from Easter-Oct.
Times: Open at any reasonable time.
Fee: Free.
Facilities: T(45 mins) (on leads) **EH**

Great Yarmouth
Caister Roman Site Map ref. P7
Caister-on-Sea
Tel: (01223) 582700 Web: www.english-heritage.org.uk
The remains of a Roman commercial port which was possibly a fort. The footings of walls and buildings are seen all along the main street.
Times: Open at any reasonable time.
Fee: Free.
Facilities: T(45 mins) (on leads) **EH**

Little Walsingham
Shirehall Museum and Abbey Gardens Map ref. G/H3
See entry in Museums & Galleries section.

Little Walsingham
Shrine of our Lady of Walsingham Map ref. G/H3
Holt Road
Tel: (01328) 820239 Web: www.walsingham.org.uk
A pilgrimage church containing the Holy House, standing in extensive grounds.
Times: Open all year, daily, dawn-dusk.
Fee: Free.
Facilities: T(1 hr)

Little Walsingham
Slipper Chapel: Roman Catholic National Shrine
Map ref. G3/4
Houghton St Giles
Tel: (01328) 820217 Web: www.walsingham.org.uk
The Roman Catholic National Shrine of Our Lady. A small 14th C. chapel, plus the new Chapel of Reconciliation. Bookshop and tearoom.
Times: Open all year, daily, dawn-dusk.
Fee: Free.
Facilities: T(20 mins)

Loddon
Hales Hall Barn and Gardens Map ref. M9
Tel: (01508) 548507 Web: www.haleshall.com
Fortified manor with fabulous 15th C. brick barn, built by Henry VII's attorney general, Sir James Hobart. Gardens with topiary, fruit, pottager, greenhouses and exotic plants.
Times: Open 6 Jan-23 Dec, Tues-Sat, 1000-1600. Easter-Sept, Sun, 1000-1600.
Fee: £2.00/free/£2.00.
Facilities: T(1 hr)

Ludham
Saint Benets Abbey Map ref. N6
Web: www.norfarchtrust.org.uk
The ruins of a monastery founded in AD1020 by King Canute. A gatehouse with interesting carvings, 18th C. windmill tower, perimeter wall and fishponds.
Times: Open at any reasonable time.
Fee: Free
Facilities: T(1 hr)

DID YOU KNOW

The longest strike in English history took place at Burston (nr. Diss), lasting from 1914 to just before the Second World War. It was sparked by the respect for two schoolteachers who were dismissed from their posts.

Lynford (nr. Thetford)
Grimes Graves Map ref. F10
Tel: (01842) 810656 Web: www.english-heritage.org-uk
Neolithic flint mines. Four thousand years old and first excavated in the 1870s, with over 300 pits and shafts. One open to the public, 30ft deep with radiating gallery.
Times: Please contact for details of opening times.
Fee: Please contact for details of admission prices.
Facilities: T(1½ hrs) (on leads) EH

New Buckenham (nr. Attleborough)
New Buckenham Castle Map ref. J10
Tel: (01953) 860251
A Norman castle and keep, said to be the largest in diameter in England. Remains of later additions.
Times: Open at any reasonable time.
Fee: £1.00.
Facilities: T(30 mins)

North Elmham (nr. Dereham)
North Elmham Chapel Map ref. H5/6
High Street
Tel: (01223) 582700 Web: www.english-heritage.org.uk
The remains of a Norman chapel, later converted into a house and enclosed by earthworks.
Times: Open at any reasonable time.
Fee: Free.
Facilities: T(45 mins) (on leads) EH

Norwich
Norwich Castle Museum and Art Gallery Map ref. K/L7
See entry in Museums & Galleries section.

Norwich
Norwich Cathedral Map ref. K/L7
Tel: (01603) 218321 Web: www.cathedral.org.uk
A Norman cathedral from 1096, with 14th C. roof bosses depicting bible scenes from Adam and Eve to the Day of Judgement. Cloisters, Cathedral Close, shop and restaurant.
Times: Open 1 Jan-14 May, daily, 0700-1800. 15 May-14 Sept, daily, 0700-1900. 15 Sept-31 Dec, daily, 0700-1800.
Fee: Free. Donations requested.
Facilities: T(1½ hrs)

Norwich
Roman Catholic Cathedral of St. John The Baptist
Map ref. K/L7
Unthank Road
Tel: (01603) 624615 Web: www.stjohncathedral.co.uk
A particularly fine example of 19th C. gothic revival by George Gilbert Scott Junior, with fine stained glass, exquisite stonewalk and Frosterley marble.
Times: Open all year, daily, Mon-Fri, 0730-1930; Sat, 0900-1900; Sun, 0800-1930.
Fee: Free.
Facilities: T(1 hr)

Norwich
Saint Peter Mancroft Church Map ref. K/L7
Haymarket
Tel: (01603) 610443
A church with a Norman foundation (1075). The present church was consecrated in 1455, with a 1463 font, a 1573 Flemish tapestry, an east window with medieval glass and the Thomas Browne memorial.
Times: Open all year, Mon-Fri, 1000-1600; Sat, 1000-1230.
Fee: Free.
Facilities: T(30 mins)

Castle Rising Castle

Tasburgh (nr. Norwich)
Tasburgh Hillfort Map ref. K9
Web: www.norfarchtrust.org.uk
Remains of an earthworks fort, probably Iron Age, with the parish church standing within it. The earthwork and northern bank of the fort can be clearly seen. Interpretative panels.
Times: Open at any reasonable time.
Fee: Free.
Facilities: T(1 hr)

Thetford
Thetford Priory Map ref. F/G11
Tel: (01223) 582700 Web: www.english-heritage.co.uk
The 14th C. gatehouse is the best preserved part of this Cluniac priory, built in 1103. The extensive remains include a plan of the cloisters.
Times: Open at any reasonable time.
Fee: Free.
Facilities: T(30 mins) (on leads) **EH**

Walpole St. Peter (nr. Wisbech)
Walpole St. Peter's Church Map ref. B6
Church Road
Tel: (01945) 780206
A masterpiece of 14th C. architecture. Famous annual flower festival.
Times: Open all year, daily, 0930-1700.
Fee: Free.
Facilities: T(1 hr)

Weeting
Weeting Castle Map ref. E10
Tel: (01223) 582700 Web: www.english-heritage.org.uk
The ruins of an early medieval manor-house within a shallow rectangular moat.
Times: Open at any reasonable time.
Fee: Free.
Facilities: T(45 mins) (on leads) **EH**

Wymondham
Wymondham Abbey Map ref. J8
Vicar Street
Tel: (01953) 602269
Web: www.wymondham-norfolk.co.uk/abbey
Magnificent Norman church built in 1107, with ruins of former Benedictine abbey. Splendid interior with 15th C. Lady Chapel, richly carved angel roofs, two 18th C. organs and gold-faced reredos.
Times: Open 1 Jan-31 Mar, Mon-Sat, 1000-1500. 1-30 Apr, Mon-Sat, 1000-1600. 1 May-31 Oct, Mon-Sat, 1000-1700. 1-30 Nov, Mon-Sat, 1000-1600. 1-31 Dec, Mon-Sat, 1000-1500.
Fee: Free.
Facilities: T(45 mins)

Museums & Galleries

Burston (nr. Diss)

Burston Strike School Map ref. J11
Tel: (01379) 741565 Web: www.burstonstrikeschool.org
Scene of the longest strike in British history which lasted 25 years. The building was erected to house a school for scholars of the strike. Artefacts, documents and photographs.
Times: Open all year, daily, during daylight hours. Closed for local and national polling days.
Fee: Free.
Facilities: P T(1 hr)

Cockley Cley (nr. Swaffham)

Iceni Village and Museums Map ref. E8
Tel: (01760) 724588
Iceni tribal village reconstruction, believed to be on the original site. Medieval cottage and forge with museum, Saxon church 630 AD, carriage/vintage engine and farm museum.
Times: Open 1 Apr-31 Oct, daily, 1100-1730. Jul and Aug, 1000-1730.
Fee: £4.00/£2.00/£3.00.
Facilities: P T(2 hrs) (on leads)

Cromer

Cromer Museum Map ref. K3
East Cottages, Tucker Street
Tel: (01263) 513543
Web: www.museums.norfolk.gov.uk
A late-Victorian fisherman's cottage with displays of local history (fishing, bathing resort), geology, natural history and archaeology.
Times: Open all year, Mon-Sat, 1000-1700. Closed 1300-1400 on Mons. Closed 1 Jan, 9 Apr and 23-26 Dec.
Fee: £1.80/90p/£1.40.
Facilities: T(1 hr)

Cromer

Henry Blogg Museum Map ref. K3
The Old Boathouse, The Promenade
Tel: (01263) 511294
World War II Watson Class lifeboat 'H.F Bailey' - Bloggs boat which saved 500 lives between 1935-1945. History of nearly 200 years of Cromer lifeboats.
Times: Open 29 Mar-31 Oct, daily, 1000-1600.
Fee: Free. Donations appreciated.
Facilities: T(1 hr)

Cromer

Little Gems Map ref. K3
2a Mount Street
Tel: (01263) 519519 Web: www.littlegems.info
An Aladdin's cave - fossils, crystals and minerals from around the globe - most for sale, but also many museum pieces, including a 'baby dinosaur' skeleton and 0.25 ton amethyst cave.
Times: Open all year, Mon-Sat, 1000-1700; Sun, 1200-1600. Limited opening hours over Christmas and New Year - please contact for details.
Fee: Free.
Facilities: T(30 mins)

Dereham

Bishop Bonners Cottage Museum Map ref. H6/7
St. Withburga Lane
Tel: (01362) 696764
A timber-framed building, built in 1502 with walls of brick, flint, wattle and daub. It has a thatched roof, coloured pargetting, local artefacts and bygones from local trades.
Times: Open 1 May-30 Sept, Tues and Thurs-Sat, 1400-1630.
Fee: Free.
Facilities: T(1 hr)

Dereham

Hobbies Museum of Fretwork and Craft Centre
Map ref. H6/7
34-36 Swaffham Road
Tel: (01362) 692985 Web: www.hobbies-dereham.co.uk
A museum of fretwork machines dating back to 1880, with magazines and hobbies weeklies from 1895, and samples of old fretwork designs.
Times: Open 1 Apr-30 Aug, Mon-Fri, 1000-1200 and 1400-1600. Closed 9-12 Apr.
Fee: Free.
Facilities: P T(1 hr)

Norwich Castle Museum and Art Gallery

Dickleburgh (nr. Diss)

100th Bomb Group Memorial Museum Map ref. K11
Common Road
Tel: (01379) 740708
A museum housed in an original World War II control tower and other buildings, showing the history of the 100th Bomb Group, plus 8th Air Force exhibits. Visitor Centre.
Times: Open 1 Feb-3 May, Sat, Sun and Bank Hol Mon, 1000-1700. 5 May-29 Sept, Wed, Sat, Sun and Bank Hol Mon, 1000-1700. 2-31 Oct, Sat and Sun, 1000-1700.
Fee: Free.
Facilities: P T(1¾ hrs)

Diss

Diss Museum Map ref. J11
Market Place
Tel: (01379) 650618
Housed in the historic Shambles building, award-winning Diss Museum provides visitors with a variety of changing displays on local history and prehistory.
Times: Open 10 Mar-1 May, Wed and Thurs, 1400-1600; Fri and Sat, 1030-1630. 2 May-31 Aug, Wed and Thurs, 1400-1600; Fri and Sat, 1030-1630; Sun, 1400-1600. 1 Sept-27 Nov, Wed and Thurs, 1400-1600; Fri and Sat 1030-1630. Closed 9 Apr.
Fee: Free.
Facilities: T(45 mins)

Downham Market

The Collectors World of Eric St. John-Foti Map ref. C8
Hermitage Hall, Bridge Farm
Tel: (01366) 383185 Web: www.collectors-world.org
The Collectors World contains unique collections amassed by Eric St. John-Foti - cars, carriages, dolls, farming and household items. Whilst the Magical Dickens Experience takes you back in time.
Times: Open all year, daily, 1100-1700.
Fee: £4.00/£2.50/£3.50/£10.00.
Facilities: P T(2½ hrs)

Fakenham

Fakenham Museum of Gas and Local History
Map ref. G4
Hempton Road
Tel: (01328) 863150
A complete small-town gasworks with a local history section and displays of working gas meters and working exhausters.
Times: Open 6 May-2 Sept, Thurs, 1030-1530. Please contact for openings on other Thurs throughout year. Other days by appointment.
Fee: Free. Donations appreciated.
Facilities: T(2 hrs)

Glandford (nr. Holt)

Glandford Shell Museum Map ref. I3
Tel: (01263) 740081
Sir Alfred Jodrell's unique collection of shells. Various other exhibits including evocative John Craske tapestry showing panorama of the Norfolk coast.
Times: Open 10 Apr-30 Oct, Tues-Sat, 1000-1230 and 1400-1630.
Fee: £1.75/75p/£1.25.
Facilities: P T(30 mins)

Great Yarmouth

Elizabethan House Museum Map ref. P7
4 South Quay
Tel: (01493) 855746
Web: www.museums.norfolk.gov.uk
A 16th C. merchant's house displaying rooms as though still lived in by families in the past. Includes Victorian kitchen/scullery, Tudor bedroom and conspiracy room.
Times: Open 5 Apr-31 Oct, Mon-Fri, 1000-1700; Sat and Sun, 1315-1700.
Fee: £2.70 (£2.20 in a family group)/£1.80 (in a family group)/£2.30.
Facilities: T(1 hr) NT

Great Yarmouth

Great Yarmouth Potteries Map ref. P7
18/19 Trinity Place
Tel: (01493) 850585
Web: www.greatyarmouthpotteries.co.uk
Full working pottery - from liquid clay to finished ware. Herring smoking museum. Video showing fishing era and town wall, 700 years ago. Nautical oil paintings, carvings and sculptures.
Times: Open all year, summer, daily, 0915-1630; winter, daily, 0915-1230 and 1330-1615. Closed 11-25 Jan, 9-12 Apr and 25 Dec.
Fee: £3.50/£1.95/£3.00/£10.00.
Facilities: T(1 hr)

Great Yarmouth

New Great Yarmouth Museum Map ref. P7
Blackfriars Road
Tel: (01493) 745526 Web: www.museums.norfolk.gov.uk
Opening in Great Yarmouth's Tower Curing Works in the summer of 2004, this new museum will tell the story of Great Yarmouth over time, and celebrate the town's maritime and fishing heritage.
Times: Opening summer 2004 - please contact for details of opening days and times.
Fee: Please contact for details of admission prices.
Facilities: T(3 hrs)

Great Yarmouth

Old Merchant's House, Row III House and Greyfriars Cloisters Map ref. P7
South Quay
Tel: (01493) 857900 Web: www.english-heritage.org.uk
Typical 17th C. town houses, one with splendid plaster ceilings containing local original architectural and domestic fittings salvaged from other 'Row' houses. Also remains of Franciscan friary.
Times: Please contact for details of opening times.
Fee: Please contact for details of admission prices.
Facilities: Q T(1 hr) EH

Great Yarmouth

Norfolk Nelson Museum Map ref. P7
26 South Quay
Tel: (01493) 850698 Web: www.nelson-museum.co.uk
Find out about Nelson's amazing career, famous battles and heroic death. Learn about his scandalous personal life and about the times in which he lived. The maritime courtyard is new for 2004.
Times: Open 1 Apr-30 Oct, Mon-Fri, 1000-1700; Sat and Sun, 1400-1700. Last admission at 1630.
Fee: £2.00/£1.00/£1.50/£4.50.
Facilities: P T(1½ hrs)

Great Yarmouth

Tolhouse Museum Map ref. P7
Tolhouse Street
Tel: (01493) 858900
Web: www.museums.norfolk.gov.uk
One of the oldest municipal buildings in England, once the town's courthouse and gaol. Prison cells can still be seen with displays illustrating the long history of the town.
Times: Open 5 Apr-31 Oct, Mon-Fri, 1000-1700; Sat and Sun, 1315-1700.
Fee: £2.70 (£2.20 in a family group)/£1.30/£2.00.
Facilities: T(1 hr)

Gressenhall (nr. Dereham)

Roots of Norfolk Map ref. H6
Norfolk Rural Life Museum
Tel: (01362) 860563
Web: www.museums.norfolk.gov.uk
Georgian workhouse in extensive grounds. Stunning displays on rural life. Rare breed animals on working 1920s farm. Trails, re-enactments, events and activities. Gardens and adventure playground.
Times: Open 15-22 Feb, daily, 1100-1600. 29 Feb-28 Mar, Sun, 1100-1600. 29 Mar-31 Oct, daily, 1000-1700. 7-28 Nov, Sun, 1100-1600.
Fee: £5.45/£4.35/£4.95.
Facilities: Q P T(6 hrs)

Burston Strike School

Hanworth (nr. Cromer)

The Straw Museum Map ref. K3
Conifer Cottage, Buck Bridge
Tel: (01263) 761615
Beautiful and fascinating straw items from around the world. Corn dollies, plain and dyed marquetry, Swiss straw lace, plaits, embroidery, jewellery and quilling. Courses are available.
Times: Open 10 Apr-30 Oct, Wed and Sat, 1100-1600.
Fee: Free.
Facilities: P T(2 hrs)

Harleston

Harleston Museum Map ref. L11
King Georges Hall, Broad Street
Tel: (01379) 853817
A museum housing an exhibition of items of historical interest relating to Harleston and the district.
Times: Open 1 May-2 Oct, Wed, 1000-1200 and 1400-1600; Sat, 1000-1200.
Fee: Free. Donations appreciated.
Facilities: T(30 mins)

Holt

Bircham Contemporary Arts Map ref. I3
14 Market Place
Tel: (01263) 713312 Web: www.birchamgallery.co.uk
Exhibitions of contemporary paintings, prints, ceramics, sculpture and jewellery by the finest artists and craftspeople.
Times: Open all year, Mon-Sat, 0900-1700. Please phone for Bank Hol opening times. Closed 25-28 Dec and 1 Jan.
Fee: Free.
Facilities: T(20 mins)

Holt

Picturecraft of Holt Map ref. I3
North Norfolk's Art Centre, 23 Lees Courtyard, Off Bull Street
Tel: (01263) 711040
Web: www.exploring.co.uk/picturecraft_holt
The newly refurbished gallery is now divided into 32 individual exhibition spaces, and the displays are changed every three weeks. Picture framing specialists and a premier artists' material centre.
Times: Open all year, Mon-Wed, 0900-1700; Thurs, 0900-1300; Fri and Sat, 0900-1700. Closed 24 Dec-3 Jan.
Fee: Free.
Facilities: P T(1 hr)

Houghton

Houghton Hall (Model Soldier Museum) Map ref. E4
See entry in Historic Houses section.

King's Lynn

Caithness Crystal Visitor Centre Map ref. C6
Paxman Road, Hardwick Industrial Estate
Tel: (01553) 765111 Web: www.caithnessglass.co.uk
See glass making at close quarters, watching the skill of our glass makers as they shape and blow the glass in the manner used for centuries. Factory shop.
Times: Open all year, Mon-Sat, 0900-1700; Sun, 1015-1615. Please contact for glassmaking times. Closed 11 Apr, 25, 26 Dec and 1 Jan.
Fee: Free.
Facilities: P T(1½ hrs)

King's Lynn

Custom House - Maritime Exhibition Map ref. C5/6
Tourist Information Centre, Purfleet Quay
Tel: (01553) 763044
The town's most famous landmark. Displays on the merchants, customs men, smugglers and famous mariners (Vancouver and Nelson) of the past. Superb views over the River Great Ouse.
Times: Open all year, daily, 1100-1500. Closed 25, 26 Dec and 1 Jan.
Fee: Free.
Facilities: T(1 hr)

King's Lynn

The Green Quay Environmental Discovery Centre
Map ref. C5/6
See entry in Countryside section.

Cromer Museum

King's Lynn
Guildhall of St. George Map ref. C5/6
27-29 King Street
Tel: (01553) 765565 Web: www.kingslynnarts.co.uk
A regional arts centre, the medieval Guildhall now houses a theatre with a regular programme of daytime and evening events: film, concerts and galleries.
Times: Open all year, Mon-Fri, 1000-1400. Access to view building is dependent on performance schedule.
Fee: Free.
Facilities: T(20 mins) NT

King's Lynn
Lynn Museum Map ref. C5/6
Market Street
Tel: (01553) 775001
Web: www.museums.norfolk.gov.uk
Housed in a Victorian church, Lynn Museum has displays on natural history, archaeology and local history.
Times: Open all year, Tues-Sat, 1000-1700. Closed Bank Hols.
Fee: £1.00/60p/80p.
Facilities: T(40 mins)

King's Lynn
Tales of the Old Gaol House Map ref. C5/6
The Old Gaol House, Saturday Market Place
Tel: (01553) 774297 Web: www.west-norfolk.gov.uk
A personal stereo tour through Lynn's 1930s police station and into the old cells beyond. True stories of infamous smugglers, murderers, highwaymen and even witches. Also Lynn treasury.
Times: Open Jan-1 Apr, Mon, Tues, Fri and Sat, 1000-1600; Sun, 1200-1600. 5 Apr-31 Oct, Mon-Wed, Fri and Sat, 1000-1700; Sun, 1200-1700. 1 Nov-end Dec, Mon. Tues, Fri and Sat, 1000-1600; Sun, 1200-1600. Last admission half an hour before closing.
Fee: Please contact for details of admission prices.
Facilities: Q T(1 hr)

King's Lynn
Town House Museum of Lynn Life Map ref. C5/6
46 Queen Street
Tel: (01553) 773450
Web: www.museums.norfolk.gov.uk
The past comes to life in this friendly museum with historic room displays including costumes, toys, a working Victorian kitchen and a 1950s living room.
Times: Open Jan-Apr, Mon-Sat, 1000-1600. May-Sept, Mon-Sat, 1000-1700; Sun 1400-1700. Oct-Dec, Mon-Sat, 1000-1600. Closed Bank Hols.
Fee: £1.80/90p/£1.40.
Facilities: T(40 mins)

King's Lynn
True's Yard Fishing Heritage Centre Map ref. C5/6
3-5 North Street
Tel: (01553) 770479 Web: www.welcome.to/truesyard
Two fully-restored fisherman's cottages with research facilities for tracing ancestry in King's Lynn. There is a museum, gift shop and tearoom.
Times: Open all year, Mon-Sat, 0930-1545; Suns (Jul-Oct), 0930-1545. Closed 24 Dec-2 Jan.
Fee: £2.25/£1.00/£1.75.
Facilities: T(1 hr)

Langham (nr. Holt)
Langham Glass Map ref. H3
The Long Barn, North Street
Tel: (01328) 830511 Web: www.langhamglass.co.uk
Glassmakers can be seen working with molten glass from the furnace using blowing irons. Also enclosed children's playground, museum/video, walled garden and 6 1/2 acre maize maze.
Times: Open all year, daily. 2 Jan-30 Mar, 1030-1630; 31 Mar-2 Nov, 1000-1700; 3 Nov-31 Dec, 1030-1630. Closed 25, 26 Dec and 1 Jan.
Fee: Langham Glass £3.50/£2.50/£2.50/£10.00. Maize Maze £3.50/£2.50/£2.50/£10.00.
Facilities: Q P T(2 1/2 hrs)

Litcham (nr. Dereham)
Litcham Village Museum Map ref. G6
'Fourways'
Tel: (01328) 701383
A local village museum and underground lime kiln. The museum houses local artifacts from Roman times to date, and a local photograph collection of over 1,000 items.
Times: Open 3 Apr-3 Oct, Sat and Sun, 1400-1700.
Fee: Free.
Facilities: P T(2 1/2 hrs)

Little Walsingham
Shirehall Museum and Abbey Gardens Map ref. G/H3
Common Place
Tel: (01328) 820510 Web: www.walsingham.uk.com
A Georgian country courthouse, local museum and Tourist Information Point. Ruins of the Augustinian abbey, peaceful gardens and woodland walks set in approximately 20 acres.
Times: Open 31 Jan-29 Feb, daily, 1000-1600 (please check before arrival). 1-26 Mar, Sat and Sun, 1000-1600. 27 Mar-31 Oct, daily, 1000-1630. 1 Nov-19 Dec, Sat and Sun, 1000-1600. Closed 20 Dec-3 Jan.
Fee: Combined ticket (grounds and museum) £3.00/£1.50/£1.50/£7.50.
Facilities: T(1 hr)

Ludham

Toad Hole Cottage Museum Map ref. N6
How Hill
Tel: (01692) 678763 Web: www.broads-authority.gov.uk
A small 18th C. cottage with a Broads information area. Museum giving the impression of the home and working life of a family on the marshes.
Times: Open 1 Apr-31 May, Mon-Fri, 1100-1300 and 1330-1700; Sat and Sun, 1100-1700. 1 Jun-30 Sept, daily, 1000-1800. 1-31 Oct, Mon-Fri, 1100-1300 and 1330-1700; Sat and Sun, 1100-1700.
Fee: Free.
Facilities: T(30 mins)

Mundesley

Mundesley Maritime Museum Map ref. M3
Beach Road
Tel: (01263) 720879
Museum housed in former coastguard lookout. Photographs, prints and artefacts illustrating Mundesley's maritime and village history. First floor reinstated as a lookout of the 1930/40 era.
Times: Open 9-12 Apr and 1 May-30 Sept, daily, 1100-1300 and 1400-1600. Please phone for Christmas openings.
Fee: 50p/free.
Facilities: T(30 mins)

North Elmham (nr. Dereham)

Mid Norfolk Railway (County School Station)
Map ref. H5
See entry in Machinery & Transport section.

The Mustard Shop, Norwich

Norwich

Bridewell Museum Map ref. K/L7
Bridewell Alley
Tel: (01603) 629127
Web: www.museums.norfolk.gov.uk
A museum with displays illustrating local industry during the past 200 years, with a re-created 1920s pharmacy and a 1930s pawnbroker's shop. Also temporary exhibits.
Times: Please contact for details of opening times.
Fee: Please contact for details of admission prices.
Facilities: T(1 hr)

Norwich

Inspire Discovery Centre Map ref. K/L7
St. Michael's Church, Coslany Street
Tel: (01603) 612612 Web: www.science-project.org/inspire
Inspire is a hands-on science centre housed in a medieval church. Suitable for all ages, it allows everyone to explore and discover the wonders of science for themselves.
Times: Open all year, daily, 1000-1730 (last admission 1630). Closed 24 Dec-1 Jan.
Fee: £4.20/£3.60/£3.60/£12.00.
Facilities: T(2 hrs)

Norwich

John Jarrold Printing Museum Map ref. K/L7
Whitefriars
Tel: (01603) 660211
John Jarrold was a pioneering figure in British printing, and this museum charts the history of the printing industry over the last 160 years. Impressive collection of printing machines.
Times: Open all year, Wed, 0930-1200.
Fee: Free.
Facilities: T(2 hrs)

Norwich

The Mustard Shop Map ref. K/L7
15 The Royal Arcade
Tel: (01603) 627889 Web: www.mustardshop.com
A decorated 19th C. style shop which houses a museum, with a series of displays illustrating the history of Colman's Mustard.
Times: Open all year, Mon-Sat, 0930-1700. Closed 25, 26 Dec and 1 Jan.
Fee: Free.
Facilities: T(15 mins)

DID YOU KNOW

The church at Stow Bartolph (nr. Downham Market) contains a life-size wax effigy of Sarah Hare, whose in 1744 was punished for working on a Sunday - pricking her finger whilst sewing, she later died.

Norwich

Norwich Castle Museum and Art Gallery Map ref. K/L7
Castle Meadow
Tel: (01603) 493625
Web: www.museums.norfolk.gov.uk
Ancient Norman keep, one of the most important buildings of its kind in Europe. Houses fine regional collections of archaeology, art and natural history. Guided tours of battlements and dungeons.
Times: Core times - Mon-Fri, 1000-1630; Sat, 1000-1700; Sun, 1300-1700. School half-term, Easter and summer holidays, Mon-Sat, 1000-1800; Sun 1300-1700. Closed 23-26 Dec and 1 Jan.
Fee: £4.95/£3.95/£4.50.
Facilities: T(2 hrs)

Norwich

Norwich Gallery Map ref. K/L7
Norwich School of Art and Design, St. George Street
Tel: (01603) 610561 Web: www.norwichgallery.co.uk
Gallery showing temporary exhibitions of contemporary art, design and crafts.
Times: Open all year, Mon-Sat, 1000-1700. Closed all Bank Hols, 13 Apr and 24 Dec-2 Jan
Fee: Free.
Facilities: T(1 hr)

Norwich

Norwich Puppet Theatre Map ref. K/L7
St. James, Whitefriars
Tel: (01603) 629921
Web: www.geocities.com/norwichpuppets
Medieval church converted to a puppet theatre in 1980. Theatre open for viewing, except on performance days. Foyer houses a display of puppets from the last 20 years.
Times: Open all year, Mon-Fri, 0930-1700. Closed Bank Hols, 25 Dec and 1 Jan
Fee: Free. There are charges for performances days.
Facilities: P T(30 mins)

Norwich

Origins Map ref. K/L7
The Forum, Millennium Plain
Tel: (01603) 727922 Web: www.originsnorwich.com
Origins is Norfolk's most original and interactive experience, tracing 2,000 years of Norfolk and Norwich through exhibits and multimedia presentations. Includes England's only 180 degree projected panorama.
Times: Open 1 Jan-31 Mar, Mon-Sat, 1000-1730; Sun, 1030-1630. 1 Apr-31 Oct, Mon-Sat, 1000-1800; Sun, 1030-1630. 1 Nov-31 Dec, Mon-Sat, 1000-1730; Sun, 1030-1630. Closed 25 and 26 Dec.
Fee: £4.95/£3.50/£3.95/£13.50.
Facilities: Q P T(1½ hrs)

Norwich

The Royal Air Force Air Defence Radar Museum
Map ref. M6
RAF Neatishead
Tel: (01692) 633309 Web: www.radarmuseum.co.uk
History of the development and use of radar, in the UK and overseas, from 1935 to date. Housed in an original 1942 building.
Times: Open 10 Jan, 14 Feb, 13 Mar, Sat, 1000-1700. 1 Apr-28 Oct, Tues, Thurs, Bank Hol Mon and 2nd Sat of month, 1000-1700. 13 Nov, 11 Dec, Sat, 1000-1700.
Fee: £4.00/free/£3.50.
Facilities: Q P T(3 hrs)

Norwich

Royal Norfolk Regimental Museum Map ref. K/L7
Market Avenue
Tel: (01603) 493649
Web: www.museums.norfolk.gov.uk
A modern museum with displays about the county regiment from 1685. Includes a reconstructed World War I communication trench.
Times: Open all year, school terms and Christmas holidays, Tues-Fri, 1000-1630; Sat, 1000-1700. School half terms, Easter and Summer holidays, Mon-Sat, 1000-1700.
Fee: £2.00/£1.20/£1.60.
Facilities: T(1½ hrs)

Norwich

Sainsbury Centre for Visual Arts Map ref. K7
University of East Anglia
Tel: (01603) 593199 Web: www.uea.ac.uk/scva
Housing the Sainsbury collection of works by artists such as Picasso, Bacon and Henry Moore, alongside many objects of pottery and art from across cultures and time.
Times: Open all year, Tues-Sun, 1100-1700.
Fee: £2.00/£1.00/£1.00.
Facilities: P T(1 hr)

Norwich

Second Air Division Memorial Library Map ref. K/L7
The Forum, Millennium Plain
Tel: (01603) 774747 Web: www.2ndair.org.uk
An American library, and a war memorial to those who served in the Second Air Division of the 8th Air Force in World War II.
Times: Open all year, Mon-Sat, 0900-1700. Closed Bank Hols.
Fee: Free.
Facilities: T(1 hr)

Norwich

Strangers' Hall Museum Map ref. K/L7
Charing Cross
Tel: (01603) 667229
Web: www.museums.norfolk.gov.uk
Medieval town house with period rooms. Displays from Tudor to Victorian times. Toy collection on display.
Times: Open all year, Sat 1030-1630; Wed - guided tours only at 1030, 1200 and 1400.
Fee: £2.50/£1.50/£2.00.
Facilities: T(1 hr)

Sandringham (nr. King's Lynn)

Sandringham Map ref. D4/5
See entry in Historic Houses section.

Seething (nr. Loddon)

Seething Airfield Control Tower Map ref. M9
Station 146, Seething Airfield
Tel: (01508) 550787
A renovated original wartime control tower holding the 448th Bomb Group honour roll and World War II exhibits. Also pictures/stories from 448th veterans from 1943-1945.
Times: Open 2 May, 6 Jun, 4 Jul, 1 Aug, 5 Sept, 3 Oct, Sun, 1000-1700.
Fee: Free.
Facilities: T(1½ hrs)

Sheringham

The Henry Ramey Upcher Lifeboat Museum Map ref. J/K2
West Cliff
Tel: (01263) 824343
The 'Henry Ramey Upcher' (private) lifeboat is a sailing and pulling boat in service from 1894-1935. Now on display in her original boatshed with original photographs.
Times: Open 9 Apr-30 Sept, daily, 1200-1630.
Fee: Free.
Facilities: T(30 mins)

Sheringham

Sheringham Museum Map ref. J/K2
Station Road
Tel: (01263) 821871
Local social history museum. Displays on lifeboats and fishing heritage, boat-building, the 1½ million year old 'Weybourne Elephant', flint picking, fossils, Roman kiln and art gallery.
Times: Open 6 Apr-31 Oct, Tues-Sat 1000-1600; Sun 1400-1600.
Fee: £1.00/50p/50p.
Facilities: T(1 hr)

Stalham

The Museum of the Broads Map ref. N5
Stalham Staithe
Tel: (01692) 581681
Web: www.norfolkbroads.com/broadsmuseum
Displays of tools from the traditional Broads industries. Many Broads boats, including gunpunts and steam launch.
Times: Open 9 Apr-31 Oct, Mon-Fri, 1100-1700. Daily during school hols.
Fee: £2.00/£1.00/£1.00/£5.00.
Facilities: T(1½ hrs)

Stalham

Stalham Old Firehouse Museum Map ref. N5
High Street (corner of St. Mary's Church ground)
Tel: (01692) 580553
Tiny Grade II building (c.1833) showing 173 years of fire fighting history in the town. Photographs, a 1902 fire engine, brigade log books, uniforms and other artefacts.
Times: Open all year. Jan-May, Tues and Thurs. May-Jul, Tues, Thurs and Fri. Aug, Mon, Tues, Thurs and Fri. Sept-Oct, Tues and Thurs. Nov and Dec, by appointment only. 1000-1200 and 1400-1600.
Fee: Free.
Facilities: T(25 mins)

Ancient House Museum, Thetford

Swaffham

Ecotech Map ref. F7
Turbine Way
Tel: (01760) 726100 Web: www.ecotech.org.uk
Guided tours (pre-book in advance) of the UK's largest wind turbine. Organic garden and cafe.
Times: Open during school hols (except Christmas), Mon-Fri, 1000-1600.
Fee: £3.70/£2.20/£3.20/£11.80.
Facilities: T(1 hr)

Swaffham

Swaffham Museum Map ref. F7
Town Hall, London Street
Tel: (01760) 721230 Web: www.aboutswaffham.co.uk
An 18th C. building, formerly a brewer's home. Small social history museum for Swaffham and the surrounding villages. Annual exhibitions, plus displays from Stone Age to 20th C.
Times: Open 10 Apr-30 Oct, Tues-Sat and Bank Hol Mon, 1000-1600.
Fee: £1.00/free/£1.00.
Facilities: T(1 hr)

Thetford

Ancient House Museum Map ref. F/G11
White Hart Street
Tel: (01842) 752599
Web: www.museums.norfolk.gov.uk
A museum of Thetford and Breckland life in a remarkable early-Tudor house. Displays on local history, flint, archaeology and natural history.
Times: Open 2 Jan-29 May, Mon-Sat, 1000-1230 and 1300-1700. 30 May-29 Aug, Mon-Sat, 1000-1230 and 1300-1700; Sun, 1400-1700. 30 Aug-31 Dec, Mon-Sat, 1000-1230 and 1300-1700. Closed 9 Apr, 24-26 Dec and 1 Jan.
Fee: Free, except Jul and Aug £1.00/60p/80p.
Facilities: Q T(50 mins)

Thetford

Charles Burrell Museum Map ref. F/G11
Minstergate
Tel: (01842) 751166
The Charles Burrell Steam Museum draws together an impressive collection of exhibits to tell the story of Charles Burrell and Son (1770-1932).
Times: Please contact for details of opening times.
Fee: Please contact for details of admission prices.
Facilities: T(1 hr)

Wells-next-the-Sea

Holkham Hall (Bygones Museum) Map ref. G2
See entry in Historic Houses section.

Wymondham

Wymondham Heritage Museum Map ref. J8
10 Bridewell, Norwich Road
Tel: (01953) 600205
Web: www.wymondham-norfolk.co.uk
Museum housed in a prison built in 1785, and telling the story of the Bridewell as a prison, police station and courthouse. Many local history displays. Cell, dungeon and shop.
Times: Open 1 Mar-30 Nov, Mon-Sat, 1000-1600; Sun, 1400-1600.
Fee: £2.00/50p/£1.50.
Facilities: T(45 mins)

DID YOU KNOW

Great Yarmouth is home to the other 'Nelson's Column'. Somewhat shorter than its London counterpart at 43 metres high, the column is surmounted not by Nelson, but by Britannia.

Reedham

Machinery & Transport

North Norfolk Railway, Sheringham

Aylsham

Bure Valley Railway Map ref. K5
Aylsham Station, Norwich Road
Tel: (01263) 733858 Web: www.bvrw.co.uk
A 15-inch narrow-gauge steam railway covering 9 miles of track from Wroxham in the heart of the Norfolk Broads to Aylsham which is a bustling market town.
Times: Open 15-22 Feb, daily, 1000-1730. 4 Apr-26 Sept, daily, 1000-1730. 21-31 Oct, daily, 1000-1730.
Fee: Return train fare: £8.50/£5.00/£8.00. Boat/train fare: £13.50/£9.00/£13.00.
Facilities: T(2 hrs)

DID YOU KNOW

The first pair of spectacles imported to England arrived at the port of King's Lynn.

Bressingham (nr. Diss)

Bressingham Steam Experience and Gardens Map ref. J11
Tel: (01379) 686900 Web: www.bressingham.co.uk
Steam train rides through four miles of woodland. Six acres of island garden beds. Plant centre. Mainline locomotives, the Victorian Gallopers and over 50 steam engines. Dad's Army Collection.
Times: Open 27 Mar-31 Oct, daily, 1030-1730. Closed Mon and Tues in Mar, Apr, Sept and Oct.
Fee: £7.00/£5.00/£6.00. Extra charges for rides.
Facilities: T(4 hrs)

 HISTORY & HERITAGE

Cockley Cley (nr. Swaffham)
Iceni Village and Museums Map ref. E8
See entry in Museums & Galleries section.

Dereham
Mid Norfolk Railway (Dereham to Wymondham Line)
Map ref. H6/7
The Railway Station, Station Road
Tel: (01362) 690633 Web: www.mnr.org.uk
Victorian railway station at Dereham undergoing restoration. Selection of diesel locomotives and heritage railcars. Other vehicles undergoing restoration. Passenger services to Wymondham
Times: Open Mar-Dec, Sat, Sun and Bank Hols, 1030-1630. Additional Wed in summer.
Fee: Please contact for details of admission prices.
Facilities: T(2 hrs)

Downham Market
The Collectors World of Eric St. John-Foti Map ref. C8
See entry in Museums & Galleries section.

Fleggburgh (nr. Great Yarmouth)
The Village Experience Map ref. O6
See entry in Family Fun section.

Forncett St. Mary (nr. Long Stratton)
Forncett Industrial Steam Museum Map ref. K9
Low Road
Tel: (01508) 488277
Web: http://oldenginehouse.users.btopenworld.com
A unique collection of large industrial steam engines including one that used to open Tower Bridge in London. Seven engines can be seen working on steam days.
Times: Open 2 May, 6 Jun, 4 Jul, 1 Aug, 5 Sept, 3 Oct, 7 Nov, Sun, 1100-1800.
Fee: £4.00/free/£3.50.
Facilities: T(2 hrs)

Horsham St. Faith (nr. Norwich)
City of Norwich Aviation Museum Map ref. K6
Old Norwich Road
Tel: (01603) 893080 Web: www.cnam.co.uk
A collection of aircraft and memorabilia showing the aviation history of Norfolk. The collection features many aircraft which have flown from Norfolk.
Times: Open 4 Jan-31 Mar, Wed and Sat, 1000-1600; Sun, 1200-1600. 1 Apr-31 Oct, Tues-Sat, 1000-1700; Sun and Bank Hol Mon, 1200-1700. 1 Nov-22 Dec, Wed and Sat, 1000-1600; Sun, 1200-1600. Open some Mons in Jul and Aug, contact for details.
Fee: Please contact for details of admission prices.
Facilities: T(2½ hrs)

North Elmham (nr. Dereham)
Mid Norfolk Railway (County School Station)
Map ref. H5
Holt Road
Tel: (01362) 668181 Web: www.mnr.org.uk
Built in 1884, County School Station is the northern outpost of the Mid Norfolk Railway. Situated in the heart of the unspoilt Wensum Valley. Small exhibition and walks.
Times: Open Easter-end Sept, Sun, 1030-1630.
Fee: Free.
Facilities: T(30 mins)

North Walsham
Norfolk Motor Cycle Museum Map ref. L4
Railway Yard
Tel: (01692) 406266
A museum displaying a wide collection of motor cycles dating from 1920-1960. Also old bicycles and die cast toys.
Times: Open all year, daily, 1000-1630. Closed Sun from 31 Oct-Easter. Closed 25, 26 Dec and 1 Jan.
Fee: £3.00/free/£2.50.
Facilities: T(1 hr)

Sheringham

North Norfolk Railway Map ref. J/K2
Sheringham Station, Station Approach
Tel: (01263) 820800 Web: www.nnrailway.co.uk
5-mile long steam railway with stations at Sheringham, Weybourne and Holt. Museum of railway memorabilia, static exhibits, station buffet and souvenir shop at Sheringham.
Times: Sheringham Station open all year, daily, from 0900. Please contact for details of train times.
Fee: Rover Ticket (full round trip ticket from any station allowing for unlimited travel on the day of purchase) £8.00/£4.50/£7.00/£23.00.
Facilities: T(1¾ hrs)

Stalham

The Museum of the Broads Map ref. N5
See entry in Museums & Galleries section.

Strumpshaw (nr. Norwich)

Strumpshaw Old Hall Steam Museum and Farm Machinery Collection Map ref. M7/8
Strumpshaw Old Hall, Low Road
Tel: (01603) 714535
Many steam engines, beam engines, mechanical organs, narrow gauge railway and a working toy train for children. There is also a cafe, gift shop, picnic area and free parking.
Times: Open 2 Jul-2 Oct, daily (except Sat), 1100-1600.
Fee: £4.00/£1.00/£2.00.
Facilities: T(1 hr)

Thetford

Charles Burrell Museum Map ref. F/G11
See entry in Museums & Galleries section.

Wells Walsingham Railway, Wells-next-the-Sea

Thursford (nr. Fakenham)

Thursford Collection Map ref. H4
Thursford Green
Tel: (01328) 878477
A live musical show with nine mechanical organs, and a Wurlitzer show starring Robert Wolfe. Also rides on the Venetian Gondola. Traction engines and road rollers.
Times: Open 9 Apr-17 Oct, daily (except Sat), 1200-1700.
Fee: £5.30/£2.80/£5.00.
Facilities: T(2½ hrs)

Wells-next-the-Sea

Wells Harbour Railway Map ref. G2
Beach Road
Tel: (01328) 710964
This 10¼ inch narrow gauge railway, of approximately 1 mile, runs adjacent to Beach Road, carrying passengers to the beach or harbour. Late trains available.
Times: Open 9-18 Apr, daily, 1030-1700. 24 Apr-23 May, Sat and Sun, 1030-1700. 29 May-19 Sept, daily, 1030-1700. 25 Sept-31 Oct, Sat and Sun, 1030-1700. Late train at peak periods.
Fee: Single fare 90p/60p.
Facilities: T(20 mins)

Wells-next-the-Sea

Wells Walsingham Railway Map ref. G2/3
Stiffkey Road
Tel: (01328) 710631
Four miles of railway. The longest 10¼ inch railway in the world, with a new steam locomotive 'Norfolk Hero' now in service (the largest of its kind ever built).
Times: Open 9 Apr-31 Oct, daily, 1000-1800.
Fee: £6.50/£4.50 (return ticket).
Facilities: T(1¼ hrs)

West Runton (nr. Sheringham)

Norfolk Shire Horse Centre Map ref. K3
See entry in Family Fun section.

West Walton (nr. Wisbech)

Fenland and West Norfolk Aviation Museum Map ref. A7
Bambers Garden Centre, Old Lynn Road
Tel: (01945) 584440 Web: www.fawnaps.co.uk
Vampire T11 and Lightning aircraft. Uniforms, aero engines, aircraft components, artefacts, memorabilia, radio equipment, souvenirs, models and a Jumbo Jet cockpit.
Times: Open 6 Mar-31 Oct, Sat, Sun and Bank Hol Mon, 0930-1700.
Fee: £1.50/75p.
Facilities: T(1 1/2 hrs)

Weybourne (nr. Holt)

Muckleburgh Collection Map ref. J2
Weybourne Old Military Camp
Tel: (01263) 588210 Web: www.muckleburgh.co.uk
Collection of over 136 military vehicles and heavy equipment used by the allied armies during and since World War II, including fighting tanks, armoured cars and artillery.
Times: Open 15-22 Feb, daily, 1000-1700. Then Suns until 9 Apr, 1000-1700. Good Fri-31 Oct, daily, 1000-1700.
Fee: £5.50/£3.00/£4.50/£13.50.
Facilities: T(2 1/2 hrs)

Wroxham

Barton House Railway Map ref. M6
Hartwell Road, The Avenue
Tel: (01603) 782470
A 3 1/2 gauge miniature steam passenger railway, and a 7 1/4 gauge steam and battery-electric railway. Full-size M and GN accessories including signals and signal boxes.
Times: Open 12 Apr, Mon, 1430-1730. 18 Apr, 16 May, 20 Jun, 18 Jul, 15 Aug, 19 Sept, 17 Oct, Sun, 1430-1730.
Fee: 50p/25p.
Facilities: ≥ T(2 hrs)

DID YOU KNOW

St. Mary's Church at West Somerton contains the grave of Europe's tallest man of his day - Robert Hales. Born in 1820, he grew to a staggering 7'8" tall, and weighed 452 pounds.

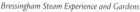

Bressingham Steam Experience and Gardens

Mills

Acle

Stracey Arms Drainage Mill Map ref. N/O7
Tel: (01603) 222705 Web: www.norfolkwindmills.co.uk
An exhibition of photographs, and the history of drainage mills in Broadland. A restored drainage mill with access by two ladders to the cap showing the brakewheel and gears.
Times: Open Easter-end Sept, daily, 0900-2000.
Fee: 70p/30p.
Facilities: P T(30 mins)

Cley-next-the-Sea

Cley Mill Map ref. I2
Tel: (01263) 740209 Web: www.cleymill.co.uk
A towermill used as a flourmill until 1918, and then converted to a guesthouse in 1983. Built in the early 1700s, it is an outstanding example of a preserved mill with sails.
Times: Open 1 Apr-30 Sept, daily, 1400-1700.
Fee: £1.50/75p/75p.
Facilities: P T(15 mins)

Cley Mill

Stracey Arms Drainage Mill, Acle

Denver (nr. Downham Market)

Denver Windmill Map ref. C8
Sluice Road
Tel: (01366) 384009 Web: www.denvermill.co.uk
A fully restored windmill, with all its internal machinery. Unique guided tours to the top of the tower. Visitor's centre, tearoom and bakery.
Times: Open 2 Jan-31 Mar, Mon-Sat, 1000-1600; Sun, 1200-1600. 1 Apr-31 Oct, Mon-Sat, 1000-1700; Sun, 1200-1700. 1 Nov-31 Dec, Mon-Sat, 1000-1600; Sun, 1200-1600. Closed 25, 26 Dec and 1 Jan.
Fee: £3.00/£1.75/£2.75.
Facilities: P T(2 hrs)

Great Bircham (nr. Kings Lynn)

Bircham Mill Map ref. E4
Tel: (01485) 578393 Web: www.birchamwindmill.co.uk
Beautifully restored windmill and on-site working bakery. Tea rooms serve homebaked scones, cakes and light lunches. Gift shop, garden, animals, play-area and cycle hire.
Times: Open 4 Apr-30 Sept, daily, 1000-1700.
Fee: £2.75/£1.50/£2.50.
Facilities: Q P T(2 hrs)

Horsey Windpump

Great Yarmouth

Berney Arms Windmill Map ref. O8

Tel: (01493) 700605 Web: www.english-heritage.org.uk

A most splendid, and the highest remaining Norfolk marshmill with seven floors. Built in the late 19th C. by millwrights Stolworthy, and situated on Halvergate Marsh. Access by boat or train only.

Times: Please contact for details of opening times.

Fee: Please contact for details of admission prices.

Facilities: T(30 mins) EH

Horsey (nr. Great Yarmouth)

Horsey Windpump Map ref. O5

Tel: (01493) 393904 Web: www.nationaltrust.org.uk

Situated on the edge of Horsey Mere, this windmill is four storeys high - the gallery affording splendid views across the marshes.

Times: Open 6-28 Mar, Sat and Sun, 1000-1630. 1 Apr-30 Jun, Wed-Sun, 1000-1630. 1 Jul-31 Aug, daily, 1000-1630. 1 Sept-31 Oct, Wed-Sun, 1000-1630.

Fee: £2.00/£1.00.

Facilities: P T(1½ hrs) NT

DID YOU KNOW

How Hill in The Broads is home to a tree with a sinister past. Once the property of the Boardman family - one member was Christopher, a keen sailor who won a gold medal for Britain at the 1936 Berlin Olympics. He was presented with a oak sapling by Adolf Hitler himself, and today the tree is known as 'Hitler's Oak'.

Letheringsett (nr. Holt)

Letheringsett Watermill Map ref. I3

Riverside Road

Tel: (01263) 713153

Web: www.letheringsettwatermill.co.uk

An historic working watermill with an iron water wheel and main gearing restored with an additional vintage Ruston Hornsby oil engine. Flour, animal and pet feed are for sale.

Times: Open all year, May-Sept, Mon-Fri, 1000-1700; Sat, 0900-1300. Oct-Apr, Mon-Fri, 0900-1600; Sat, 0900-1300.

Fee: Working demonstrations £3.50/£2.00/£3.00. Non-demonstration days £2.50/£1.50.

Facilities: P T(1½ hrs)

Old Buckenham (nr. Attleborough)

Old Buckenham Mill Map ref. I10

Green Lane

Tel: (01603) 222705 Web: www.norfolkwindmills.co.uk

The largest diameter cornmill in the country built in 1818. The mill is static but contains much machinery. It had five sets of stones when operating.

Times: Open 11 Apr, 9 May, 13 Jun, 11 Jul, 8 Aug, 12 Sept, Sun, 1400-1700.

Fee: 70p/30p.

Facilities: P T(45 mins)

Starston (nr. Harleston)

Starston Windpump Map ref. L11

Tel: (01379) 852393

Restored windpump (1832). A hollow postmill built to supply water to Home Farm, Starston. Access by footpath, 150yds from off-road parking.

Times: Open at any reasonable time.

Fee: Free.

Facilities: P T(30 mins)

Gardens

Attleborough

Peter Beales Roses Map ref. I9
London Road
Tel: (01953) 454707 Web: www.classicroses.co.uk
2 1/2 acres of beautiful rose gardens set in rural surroundings. Sweet Briar Bistro and shop.
Times: Open all year, Mon-Fri, 0900-1700; Sat, 0900-1700; Sun and Bank Hols, 1000-1600. Closed 24 Dec-4 Jan.
Fee: Free.
Facilities: T(1-2 hrs) (on leads)

Bayfield (nr. Holt)

Natural Surroundings Map ref. I3
Bayfield Estate
Tel: (01263) 711091 Web: www.hartlana.co.uk/natural
8 acres of demonstration gardens, orchid meadow and woodland walk. Shop, sales area and light refreshments. Red squirrels and family events all summer.
Times: Open 5 Feb-19 Mar, Thurs-Sun, 1000-1600. 23 Mar-30 Sept, Tues-Sun, 1000-1700. 1 Oct-12 Dec, Thurs-Sun, 1000-1600.
Fee: £2.50/£1.50/£1.95/£7.00.
Facilities: T(1½ hrs)

Beeston Regis (nr. Sheringham)

Priory Maze and Gardens Map ref. K2
Cromer Road
Tel: (01263) 822986 Web: www.priorymazegardens.com
Norfolk's only traditional hedge maze set in 10 acres of tranquil and natural woodland, meadow and stream gardens - only 600m from the sea. A must for garden visitor enthausiasts. Plant centre.
Times: Open 1 Apr-31 Oct, daily (except Mon and Wed), 1100-1730. Daily in Aug. Also late night on Thurs from May-Aug, 1100-2100. Open Bank Hol Mons.
Fee: £3.50/£2.00/£3.50/£10.00.
Facilities: T(2 hrs)

Blickling (nr. Aylsham)

Blickling Hall, Garden and Park Map ref. K4
See entry in Historic Houses section.

Bressingham (nr. Diss)

Bressingham Steam Experience and Gardens Map ref. J11
See entry in Machinery & Transport section.

DID YOU KNOW

Breckland is home to Pingos - damp shallow craters left by retreating glaciers during the last Ice Age, about 20,000 years ago. Today filled with water, they are home to a variety of creatures and plants.

Blickling Hall, Garden and Park

East Ruston (nr. Stalham)

East Ruston Old Vicarage Garden Map ref. M4
Tel: (01692) 650432
Web: www.e-ruston-oldvicaragegardens.co.uk
A 20-acre exotic garden separated into sections including the Tropical Borders, Mediterranean Garden, Sunken Garden, Autumn Borders, Kitchen Garden and Wildflower Meadows.
Times: Open 28 Mar-30 Oct, Wed, Fri-Sun and Bank Hols, 1400-1730.
Fee: £4.00/£1.00.
Facilities: T(2 hrs)

Erpingham (nr. Aylsham)

Alby Crafts Gardens Map ref. K4
Cromer Road
Tel: (01263) 761226 Web: www.albycrafts.co.uk
4 1/2 acres of island beds and borders, separated by wide expanses of grass. Specimen trees and wide variety of unusual plants and shrubs. Four ponds and bridge.
Times: Open Mar-Oct, Tues-Sun and Bank Hol Mon, 1000-1700.
Fee: £2.00/free.
Facilities: Q T(1 1/2 hrs)

Felbrigg (nr. Cromer)

Felbrigg Hall Map ref. K3
See entry in Historic Houses section.

Gooderstone (nr. Swaffham)

Gooderstone Water Gardens Map ref. E8
The Street
Tel: (01603) 712913
Created in 1970 from a wet meadow, the gardens cover 6 1/2 acres, with trout stream, four ponds, waterways, mature trees, colourful plants, nature trail and thirteen bridges
Times: Open 4 Jan-11 Apr, Sun, 1300-1600 (or dusk). 13 Apr-29 Sept, Sat, Sun, Tues, Wed and Bank Hols, 1330-1730. 3 Oct-19 Dec, Sun, 1300-1600 (or dusk). Tearoom closed Jan-Apr and Oct-Dec.
Fee: £3.60/£1.00/£3.00.
Facilities: T(1 1/2 hrs)

Grimston (nr. King's Lynn)

Congham Hall Herb Garden Map ref. D5
Lynn Road
Tel: (01485) 600250 Web: www.conghamhallhotel.co.uk
Garden with over 650 varieties of herbs in formal beds, with wild flowers and a potager garden. Over 250 varieties of herbs for sale in pots.
Times: Open 9 Apr-30 Sept, Sun-Fri, 1400-1600.
Fee: Free.
Facilities: T(30 mins)

Heacham (nr. Hunstanton)

Norfolk Lavender Limited Map ref. D3
Caley Mill
Tel: (01485) 570384 Web: www.norfolk-lavender.co.uk
Home of the National Collection of Lavenders. See many varieties of lavender and a large miscellany of herbs. Hear about the harvest, and the ancient process of lavender distillation.
Times: Open 2 Jan-31 Mar, daily, 1000-1600. 1 Apr-31 Oct, daily, 1000-1700. 1 Nov-31 Dec, daily, 1000-1600. Closed 25, 26 Dec and 1 Jan.
Fee: Free.
Facilities: Q T(4 hrs) (on leads)

Houghton

Houghton Hall Map ref. E4
See entry in Historic Houses section.

Little Walsingham

Shirehall Museum and Abbey Gardens Map ref. G/H3
See entry in Museums & Galleries section.

Loddon

Hales Hall Barn and Gardens Map ref. M9
See entry in Ancient Monuments section.

Neatishead (nr. Wroxham)

Willow Farm Flowers Map ref. M5
Cangate
Tel: (01603) 783588 Web: www.willowfarmflowers.co.uk
One of the largest displays of dried, silk and parchment flowers in the region, situated in a magnificent 300-year-old thatched barn in the heart of the Broads.
Times: Open 10 Feb-22 Dec, Tues-Sat, 1000-1600.
Fee: Free.
Facilities: T(30 mins)

Norfolk Lavender, Heacham

Mannington (nr. Saxthorpe Corpusty)
Mannington Gardens and Countryside Map ref. J4
Mannington Hall
Tel: (01263) 584175 Web: www.manningtongardens.co.uk
Gardens with a lake, moat, woodland and an outstanding rose collection. There is also a Saxon church with Victorian follies and countryside walks and trails with guide booklets.
Times: Walks open all year, daily, 0900-dusk. Gardens open 25 Apr-26 Sept, Sun, 1200-1700. 2 Jun-27 Aug, Wed-Fri, 1100-1700.
Fee: £3.00/free/£2.50. Car park £2.00.
Facilities: T(2 hrs)

Norwich
The Plantation Garden Map ref. K/L7
4 Earlham Road
Tel: (01603) 621868 Web: www.plantationgarden.co.uk
A rare surviving example of a private Victorian town garden, created between 1856-1897 in a former medieval chalk quarry and undergoing restoration by volunteers.
Times: Open all year, daily, 0900-1800 (or dusk if earlier).
Fee: £2.00/free.
Facilities: T(2 hrs)

Oxborough (nr. Swaffham)
Oxburgh Hall Map ref. E8
See entry in Historic Houses section.

Pensthorpe (nr. Fakenham)
Pensthorpe Nature Reserve and Gardens Map ref. H4
See entry in Countryside section.

Raveningham (nr. Loddon)
Raveningham Gardens Map ref. N9
The Stables
Tel: (01508) 548152
Extensive gardens surrounding an elegant Georgian house, provide the setting for many rare, variegated and unusual plants and shrubs with sculptures, parkland and a church.
Times: Open 11, 12 Apr; 2, 3, 30, 31 May; 27, 28 Jun; 29, 30 Aug, Sun and Mon, 1400-1700
Fee: £2.50/free/£2.00.
Facilities: T(1½ hrs) (on leads)

Sandringham (nr. King's Lynn)
Sandringham Map ref. D4/5
See entry in Historic Houses section.

Sheringham
Sheringham Park Map ref. J3
See entry in Countryside section.

South Walsham
Fairhaven Woodland and Water Garden Map ref. M6/7
School Road
Tel: (01603) 270449
Web: www.norfolkbroads.com/fairhaven
Delightful natural woodland and water garden, with private broad and a 950 year old oak tree. Spring flowers, candelabra primulas, azaleas and rhododendrons.
Times: Open all year, daily, 1000-1700. 5 May-26 Aug, Wed and Thurs, 1000-2100. Closed 25 Dec.
Fee: £4.00/£1.50/£3.50.
Facilities: T(3 hrs) (on leads)

West Acre (nr. Swaffham)
West Acre Gardens Map ref. E6
Tel: (01760) 755562
D-shaped walled garden. Extensive display beds with year-round interest and beauty. Huge range of unusual plants for sale
Times: Open 2 Feb-30 Nov, Mon-Fri, 1000-1700.
Fee: Free.
Facilities: T(2 hrs)

Wroxham
Hoveton Hall Gardens Map ref. M6
Tel: (01603) 782798
Approximately 15 acres of gardens in a woodland setting, with a large walled herbaceous garden and a Victorian kitchen garden. Woodland and lakeside walks.
Times: Open 11 Apr-mid Sept, Wed, Fri, Sun and Bank Hol Mon. Also Thurs in May. 1100-1700.
Fee: £3.75/£1.00/£2.00.
Facilities: T(2 hrs)

Nurseries & Garden Centres

Attleborough

Peter Beales Roses Map ref. I9
London Road, Attleborough NR17 1AY
Tel: (01953) 454707 Fax: (01953) 456845
Email: Sales@classicroses.co.uk
Web: www.classicroses.co.uk
A large and world famous collection of roses, featuring over 1100 rare, unusual and beautiful varieties of which 250 are unique. The National Collection of Rosa Species is held here. Browse through 2 1/2 acres of gardens. Container roses available in the summer months, or order for winter delivery. Experts are always on hand for advice or help in the selection of new varieties. Open Mon-Fri, 0900-1700; Sat, 0900-1700; Sun and Bank Hols, 1000-1600. Catalogue free on request. New Sweet Briar Shop and Bistro open. P T(1-2 hrs) (on leads)

DID YOU KNOW

Following a newspaper story in the London Evening News in the 1930s, Gimingham became known as the strangest village in England. The report remarked that the village had no butcher, baker, fishmonger, draper, tailor, boot-maker or policeman, and no resident named Smith, Brown, Jones or Robinson. There was no doctor, dentist or chemist. There was a railway but no station, no public house and though next to the sea, no sea view.

Bressingham (nr. Diss)

Blooms of Bressingham Map ref. J11
Bressingham, nr. Diss IP22 2AB
Tel: (01379) 688585
Three miles west of Diss on A1066. Designed to excite and inspire 21st century gardeners, this unique two acre Plant Centre, adjacent to world famous Bressingham Steam Experience and Gardens (featuring the "Dad's Army Exhibition"), gives bigger, better choice for creative gardeners. The famous Blooms range of quality plants, and an increased product range incorporates a new "life-style" approach to gardening. Add the innovative "Into-Food" Café, all set in a striking structure, and it's a must for a great day out. Open: Daily, 0900-1800, Mar-Oct; 0900-1700, Nov-Feb (except Christmas Day/Boxing Day). Plant Centre Sun Trading Hours are:- 1030-1630. See also entry for Bressingham Steam Experience and Gardens under Machinery & Transport on page (217) and Into-Food Café under Afternoon Teas on page (244). P

Fakenham

Fakenham Garden Centre Map ref. G4
Mill Road, Hempton, Fakenham NR21 7LH
Tel: (01328) 863380
Fakenham Garden Centre has so much to offer all under one roof. Our wide selection of indoor and outdoor plants from all over the world will be sure to inspire you. For that special occasion we have a selection of gifts, books and clothing. To entertain the children we have a pet and aquatic centre. Our Coffee Shop offers a tantalising selection of hot and cold food. Our trained staff are always at hand for expert advice. Free car parking, disabled facilities and toilets with baby changing facilities. We are open 7 days a week, Mon-Sat 0900-1730; Sun 1000-1600.

Gressenhall (nr. Dereham)

Norfolk Herbs Map ref. H6
Blackberry Farm, Dillington, nr. Gressenhall, Dereham NR19 2QD
Tel: (01362) 860812
(Approx. 1 mile north of Dereham on the B1110, now signed as the B1146, take the first left to Dillington and we are approx. 1 1/2 miles on right). Norfolk's specialist Herb Farm, in a beautiful wooded valley renowned for its wildlife. Visitors may browse through a vast array of aromatic, culinary and medicinal herb plants, and learn all about growing and using herbs. Open Apr-Jul, daily; Aug, Tue-Sun, 0900-1800; Sept-Mar, Wed-Sat, 0900-1700. Closed Dec 24-Jan 31. For group visits or visiting outside of these hours, please telephone for an appointment.
T(30 mins)

NORFOLK LAVENDER

Heacham (nr. Hunstanton)

Norfolk Lavender Ltd Map ref. D3
Caley Mill, Heacham (on A149) PE31 7JE
Tel: (01485) 570384 Fax: (01485) 571176
Web: www.norfolk-lavender.co.uk
The Fragrant Plant Meadow and Conservatory offer a wide selection of scented plants to add to our lavenders, herb plants and garden collection. Also tours (May-Sept) - learn about the harvest and ancient distillation process. The Gift Shop stocks the full range of Norfolk Lavender's famous fragrant products with a wide choice of other gifts to suit all pockets. Miller's Tearoom - specialising in locally baked cakes, scones, cream teas and lunches. The National Collection of Lavenders. FREE ADMISSION. Open Apr-Oct 1000-1700; Nov-Mar, 1000-1600.
Q T(4 hrs) (on leads)

Fairhaven Woodland and Water Garden, South Walsham

King's Lynn

The African Violet Centre Map ref. B6
Terrington St. Clement, nr. King's Lynn PE34 4PL
Tel: (01553) 828374 Web: www.africanvioletcentre.ltd.uk

The African Violet and Garden Centre offers a wide variety of plants for any enthusiast. Known for our African Violets we boast the best in Britain. A winner of many Chelsea Gold Medals, we place ourselves as the perfect venue, whatever the weather. Our centre enables visitors to share in the secrets and discover the wonderful world of African Violets. Spacious Garden and Gift Shop, Café serving light lunches, children's play area. Ample parking, coach parties welcome. Talks/demonstrations by appointment. Situated by the A17, five miles from King's Lynn. FREE ADMISSION! Open daily: 0900-1700; Sun 1000-1700. Closed Christmas/New Years Day only.

Norwich

Notcutts Garden Centres Map ref. K8
Daniels Road (Ring Road), Norwich NR4 6QP
Tel: (01603) 453155 Web: www.notcutts.co.uk

Discover a world of ideas and inspiration around every corner for you, your home and your garden. From fabulous plants to gifts and treats galore, there's so much to see. Gift ideas from around the world, houseplants, books, fresh cut and silk flowers, 3,000 varieties of hardy plants (with a 2 year replacement guarantee), pet centre, coffee shop, plus expert friendly advice about seasonal and bedding plants, garden furniture and barbecues. Keep an eye open for regular offers on key garden products. Notcutts open 7 days a week, free car-parking plus children's play area.

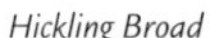

Hickling Broad

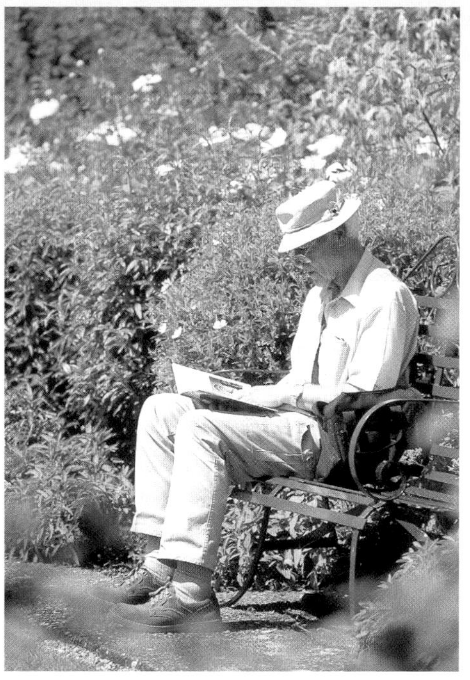

Reymerston (nr. Norwich)

Thorncroft Clematis Nursery Map ref. I8

The Lings, Reymerston, nr. Norwich NR9 4QG

Tel: (01953) 850407 Web: www.thorncroft.co.uk

Come and visit our nursery and garden in the 'heart' of the Norfolk countryside. Our family run nursery stocks many beautiful and unusual clematis cultivars.

Open Tues-Sat, 1000-1600, Closed Sun & Mon. Open Bank Hol Mon. Directions - PLEASE NOTE we are NOT in the village of Reymerston. The nursery is on the B1135, exactly halfway between Wymondham and Dereham.

Family Fun

Animal & Bird Collections

Banham
Banham Zoo Map ref. I10
The Grove
Tel: (01953) 887771 Web: www.banhamzoo.co.uk
Wildlife spectacular, which will take you on a journey to experience some of the world's most exotic, rare and endangered animals, including tigers, leopards and zebra.
Times: Open all year, daily, from 1000. Closing times have seasonal variations. Closed 25 Dec and 1 Jan.
Fee: Please contact for details of admission prices.
Facilities: Q P T(4-6 hrs)

Filby (nr. Great Yarmouth)
Thrigby Hall Wildlife Gardens Map ref. O7
Tel: (01493) 369477 Web: www.thrigbyhall.co.uk
A wide selection of Asian mammals, birds, reptiles, tigers, crocodiles and storks. A 250-year-old landscaped garden with play area and willow pattern gardens.
Times: Open all year, daily, 1000-1700. Winter closing at 1600.
Fee: £6.90/£4.90/£5.90.
Facilities: Q P T(3 hrs)

Frettenham (nr. Norwich)
Hillside Animal Sanctuary Map ref. L6
Hill Top Farm, Hall Lane
Tel: (01603) 736200 Web: www.hillside.org.uk
Visit our rescued farm animals - cows, sheep, goats, horses, ponies and donkeys. Information centre and gift shop.
Times: Open 9-12 Apr, 1300-1700. 18 Apr-27 Jun, Sun, 1300-1700. 4 Jul-30 Aug, Sun and Mon, 1300-1700. 5 Sept-31 Oct, Sun, 1300-1700.
Fee: £3.00/£1.50/£1.50.
Facilities: P T(2 hrs) (on leads)

Fritton (nr. Great Yarmouth)
Fritton Lake Country World Map ref. O8
See entry in Countryside section.

DID YOU KNOW
Norfolk has its very own pyramid - in the grounds of Blickling Hall (nr. Aylsham) it contains the remains of John Hobart, 2nd Earl of Bucks.

Fritton (nr. Great Yarmouth)
Redwings Visitor Centre Map ref. O8
Caldecott Hall
Tel: 0870 040 0033 Web: www.redwings.co.uk
A sanctuary for horses, ponies and donkeys. Stroll along the paddock walks, visit the gift shop and information centre or adopt a rescued horse.
Times: Open 1 Apr-31 Oct, daily during school hols; Sun-Wed, at all other times, 1000-1600. 4/5 Dec, 1000-1500.
Fee: £3.50/£1.50/£2.50.
Facilities: P T(3 hrs) (on leads)

Great Witchingham
Norfolk Wildlife Centre and Country Park Map ref. J6
Fakenham Road
Tel: (01603) 872274 Web: www.norfolkwildlife.co.uk
A large collection of British and European wildlife in 40 acres of parkland with a pet's corner, play areas, model farm and clear-water trout pool. Reptile house. This is not a zoo.
Times: Open Feb half term, then weekends until Easter half term. Easter-end Oct, daily, 1000-1700 (last admission 1600).
Fee: £6.00/£4.50/£5.00/£18.00.
Facilities: P T(3-4 hrs)

Great Yarmouth
Great Yarmouth Sealife Centre Map ref. P7
Marine Parade
Tel: (01493) 330631 Web: www.sealife.co.uk
The centre takes visitors on a fascinating seabed stroll from local waters to tropical depths, including starfish, sharks, stingrays and shrimps. 'Lost City of Atlantis' with underwater tunnel.
Times: Open all year, daily, from 1000. Closed 25 Dec.
Fee: £6.95/£4.95/£5.95.
Facilities: T(2 hrs)

Fritton Lake Country World

Gressenhall (nr. Dereham)
Roots of Norfolk Map ref. H6
See entry in Museums & Galleries section.

Hunstanton
Hunstanton Sea Life Sanctuary Map ref. D3
Southern Promenade
Tel: (01485) 533576 Web: www.sealsanctuary.co.uk
A breath-taking display of British marine life. Over 2,000 fish from 200 different species. Ocean tunnel, rock pools, seal rehabilitation centre, otters and penguins.
Times: Open all year. Jan and Feb, daily, 1000-1500; Mar-Oct, daily, 1000-1600; Nov and Dec, daily, 1000-1500. Closed 25 Dec.
Fee: £6.50/£4.50/£5.50/£21.00.
Facilities: T(1½ hrs)

Long Sutton
Butterfly and Wildlife Park Map ref. A5
Tel: (01406) 363833
Web: www.butterflyandwildlifepark.co.uk
One of Britain's largest walk-through butterfly houses. Insectarium, pet's corner, reptiles and falconry displays (eagles, owls and falcons). New for 2004 'Playfort'.
Times: Open 20 March-31 Oct, daily, from 1000.
Fee: £5.50/£3.80/£4.80/£17.00.
Facilities: P T(5 hrs)

Poringland (nr. Norwich)
The Playbarn Map ref. L8
See entry in Children's Indoor Play Centres.

Reedham
Pettitt's Animal Adventure Park Map ref. N8
Camphill
Tel: (01493) 700094 Web: www.pettittsonline.co.uk
A family park, which includes animals galore including birds of prey, chickens, ducks, miniature Falabella horses, goats, monkeys, parrots, peacocks, rheas and wallabies. Play area.
Times: Open 3 Apr-31 Oct, daily, 1000-1700/1730.
Fee: £7.75/£7.25/£5.85/£29.50.
Facilities: P T(6 hrs)

Scoulton (nr. Watton)
Melsop Farm Park Map ref. H8
Melsop Farm, Ellingham Road
Tel: (01953) 851943
Farm park (rare breeds centre). 17th C. thatched Listed house, set in 11 acres of rural Breckland countryside. Indoor and outdoor play areas.
Times: Open 3 Jan-28 Mar, Sat, Sun and school hols, 1000-1700. 30 Mar-31 Oct, Tues-Sun, 1000-1700. 6 Nov-24 Dec, Sat, Sun and school hols, 1000-1700. Closed 25 Dec-1 Jan.
Fee: £4.00/£3.00/£3.00.
Facilities: P T(3 hrs)

Snetterton (nr. Attleborough)

ILPH Hall Farm Map ref. H10

Tel: (01953) 498898 Web: www.ilph.org

Visit the centre for horses and ponies in beautiful countryside. See the work of the International League for the Protection of Horses. Visit the coffee and gift shops.

Times: Open 7 Jan-22 Dec, Wed, Sat, Sun and Bank Hols, 1100-1600.

Fee: Free.

Facilities: T(2 hrs)

Snettisham (nr. Hunstanton)

Park Farm Snettisham Map ref. D4

Tel: (01485) 542425

Web: www.parkfarms-snettisham.co.uk

Unique red deer safari tours, a visitor centre, adventure play area, crafts centre, art gallery, tearoom and souvenir shop. Indoor and outdoor activities include farm animals and pets.

Times: Open 2 Jan-29 Feb, please ring for information. 1 Mar-31 Oct, daily, 1000-1700. 1 Nov-31 Dec, please ring for information. Closed 25 and 26 Dec.

Fee: Please contact for details of admission prices.

Facilities: Q T(5 hrs)

West Runton (nr. Sheringham)

Norfolk Shire Horse Centre Map ref. K3

West Runton Stables

Tel: (01263) 837339

Web: www.norfolk-shirehorse-centre.co.uk

Shire horses are demonstrated, working twice daily. Native ponies and a bygone collection of horse-drawn machinery. There is also a children's farm.

Times: Open 4 Apr-29 Oct, daily except Sat (unless Bank Hol), 1000-1700. Last admission at 1545.

Fee: £5.50/£4.50/£3.50.

Facilities: T(3 hrs)

Britannia Pier, Great Yarmouth

Wroxham

Junior Farm at Wroxham Barns Map ref. M5

Tunstead Road, Hoveton NR12 8QU

Tel: (01603) 783762 Web: www.wroxham-barns.co.uk

10 acres of converted barns and farmland with something for everyone. Meet, feed and learn about the friendly farmyard animals at Junior Farm. Wroxham Barns Children's Fair with ferris wheel, train, adventure riverboat ride, trampolines, giant slide, jumping jack and kiddies rollercoaster. Resident craftsmen, gift and clothes shops, food and fudge shops and tearoom.

Times: Open all year, daily, 1000-1700. Closed 25, 26 Dec and 1 Jan. Fair (seasonal).

Fee: Free admission and parking. Junior Farm £2.65 per person (under 3s free). Fair rides individually priced. See also our entry under Stop & Shop on page 248.

Facilities: Q T(3 hrs)

Amusement/Theme Centres & Parks

Fleggburgh (nr. Great Yarmouth)

The Village Experience Map ref. O6

Burgh St Margaret

Tel: (01493) 369770 Web: www.thevillage-experience.com

Over 35 acres of rides and entertainment. Traditional fairground rides, adventure play areas and live shows. Crafts and shops. Rides and shows included in price.

Times: Week prior to Easter-end Oct, 1000-1700.

Fee: £6.50/£5.45/£5.75/£20.95.

Facilities: Q T(4 hrs)

Great Yarmouth

Britannia Pier Map ref. P7

Marine Parade

Tel: (01493) 842914 Web: www.britanniapieronline.co.uk

Traditional seaside pier with amusement arcades, children's rides, fun fair, restaurants and bars. Theatre with summer season shows.

Times: Open Apr-end Oct, daily, from 0900.

Fee: Free.

Facilities: T(2-3 hrs)

Great Yarmouth
Joyland Map ref. P7
Marine Parade
Tel: (01493) 844094
Delightful family fun park for young children. Rides include the world famous snails and Tyrolean tub twist. Huge Toytown Mountain with Spook Express kiddie coaster. American family diner.
Times: Open Easter-Oct, daily. Reduced opening hours out of season. Diner open all year (except 25, 26 Dec and 1 Jan).
Fee: Free. Individual charges (tokens) for rides/attractions.
Facilities: Q T(1 hr) (not in diner)

Great Yarmouth
Louis Tussauds House of Wax Map ref. P7
18 Regent Road
A waxworks exhibition with torture chambers, a chamber of horrors, hall of funny mirrors and family amusement arcade.
Times: Open 1 Mar-30 Apr, daily, 1100-1600. 1 May-31 Aug, daily, 1030-1830. 1 Sept-31 Oct, daily, 1100-1600.
Fee: £3.00/£2.00/£9.00 (family).
Facilities: T(1 hr)

Great Yarmouth
Merrivale Model Village Map ref. P7
Marine Parade
Tel: (01493) 842097
A miniature world of town and countryside - now under new ownership. Landscaped gardens with many models, including working fairground and garden railway. New for 2004 - Museum of the old Penny Slot Machine.
Times: Please contact for details of opening times.
Fee: Please contact for details of admission prices.
Facilities: T(1 hr) (on leads)

Great Yarmouth
The Mint Map ref. P7
31 Marine Parade
Tel: (01493) 843968 Web: www.thurston.uk.com
Family entertainment centre, including 'Quasar' the live action laser game.
Times: Open all year, daily, 0900-0100.
Fee: Quasar Centre £2.99/£2.99.
Facilities: T(30 mins)

Wayland Wood at Watton is the setting for the tale of the 'Babes in the Wood', an orphaned brother and sister who starved to death after being left in the woods by their evil uncle so that he could get their inheritance.

Great Yarmouth
Pleasure Beach Map ref. P7
South Beach Parade
Tel: (01493) 844585 Web: www.pleasure-beach.co.uk
9 acre leisure park, with rollercoaster, Terminator, log flume, Twister, monorail, galloping horses, caterpillar, ghost train and fun house. Height restrictions are in force on some rides.
Times: Open Mar-Oct. Please contact for opening days and times.
Fee: Free. Individual charges for rides/attractions.
Facilities: T(2-3 hrs)

Langham (nr. Holt)
Langham Glass (Maize Maze) Map ref. H3
See entry in Museums & Galleries section.

Lenwade (nr. Norwich)
The Dinosaur Adventure Park Map ref. J6
Weston Park
Tel: (01603) 876310 Web: www.dinosaurpark.co.uk
A unique family day out. Attractions include the dinosaur trail, woodland maze, secret animal garden, Climb-a-Saurus, adventure play areas, education centre and lots more.
Times: Open 2 Apr-5 Sept, daily, 1000-1700. 6 Sept-20 Oct, Fri-Sun, 1000-1700. 21-31 Oct, daily, 1000-1700.
Fee: Please contact for details of admission prices.
Facilities: Q P T(4 hrs)

South Creake (nr. Fakenham)
South Creake Maize Maze Map ref. F4
Compton Hall
Tel: (01328) 823224 Web: www.amazingmaizemaze.co.uk
Seven acres of maze to get lost in! Set in 18 acres of unspoilt Norfolk countryside. Crazy golf and panning for gold.
Times: Open 17 Jul-5 Sept, daily, 1000-1800.
Fee: Maze £3.50/£2.50/£2.50/£10.00. Panning for gold £1.50/£1.50/£1.50.
Facilities: P T(3 hrs)

Wroxham
Wroxham Barns Children's Fair Map ref. M5
Tunstead Road
Tel: (01603) 784118 Web: www.wroxham-barns.co.uk
Children's rides including ferris wheel, train, adventure riverboat ride, trampolines, giant slide, jumping jack and kiddies rollercoaster - plus lots more.
Times: Open 20, 21 and 27, 28 Mar; 3-18 and 24, 25 Apr; 1 May-5 Sept, daily; 11, 12, 18, 19, 25, 26 Sept; Oct and Nov, please contact for details. 1000-1700.
Fee: Free. Individual charges (tokens) for rides/attractions.
Facilities: P T(2 hrs)

Children's Indoor Play Centres

Cromer

Funstop Map ref. K3
Exchange House, Louden Road
Tel: (01263) 514976
A children's indoor adventure centre with a giant slide, ball pond, tubes, scrambling nets and a special under-3's area.
Times: Open Jan-Apr, Fri-Sun and daily during school hols, 1000-1800. May-Jun, Thurs-Sun and daily during school hols, 1000-1800. Jul-Sept, daily, 1000-1800. Oct-Dec, Fri-Sun and daily during school hols, 1000-1800. Closed 25-28 Dec and 1 Jan
Fee: Child (under 3) £2.20. Child (over 3) £3.50.
Facilities: P T(2 hrs)

Knapton (nr. Mundesley)

Elephant Playbarn Map ref. M4
Mundesley Road
Tel: (01263) 721080 Web: www.elephantplaybarn.co.uk
A converted Norfolk barn filled with exciting toys for the under 8's. Also a fully enclosed courtyard with pedal toys and an adventure play area.
Times: Open all year, Wed-Sun, 1000-1600. Daily in school hols. Phone for Christmas openings.
Fee: Child £3.50.
Facilities: P T(2 hrs)

Poringland (nr. Norwich)

The Playbarn Map ref. L8
West Green Farm, Shotesham Road
Tel: (01508) 495526 Web: www.theplaybarn.co.uk
Children's indoor and outdoor play centre. Designed for age 7 and under. Large barn and courtyard, beach barn, children's farm, riding school and after school club.
Times: Open all year, Mon-Fri, 0900-1530; Sun, 1000-1700. Closed 25, 26 Dec and 1 Jan.
Fee: £1.00/£4.00.
Facilities: Q P T(2 hrs)

Leisure Pools

Great Yarmouth

Marina Leisure Centre Map ref. P7
Marine Parade
Tel: (01493) 851521
Web: http://marina.leisureconnection.co.uk
Leisure pool with aqua slide and wave machine. Children's indoor soft play area. Piazza with summer entertainment.
Times: Open all year, Mon-Fri, 0630-2200; Sat and Sun, 0900-2200.
Fee: Prices vary depending upon activity. Swimming - £2.90/£2.50/£2.50/£8.80.
Facilities: T(2-3 hrs)

Hunstanton

Oasis Leisure Centre Map ref. D3
Central Promenade
Tel: (01485) 534227 Web: www.west-norfolk.gov.uk
Indoor pool with flume ride. Main sports hall with bowls and multi-sport activities. Squash court, fast tanning sunbeds and fitness suite.
Times: Open all year. Times vary according to season, contact for details.
Fee: Prices vary depending upon activity.
Facilities: P T(2-3 hrs)

Norwich

Aqua Park and Jumping Jacks Map ref. K/7
Norwich Sport Village and Hotel, Hellesdon
Tel: (01603) 788898 Web: www.norwichsportvillage.com
Aqua Park is fun for all the family, with two giant flumes, ride the rapids and laze in the bubble bay. Competition and toddlers pool. Jumping Jacks indoor children's adventure playground.
Times: Open all year, please contact for further details.
Fee: Aqua Park (off peak) £4.35/£3.00/£11.40 (family). Aqua Park (peak) £5.35/£3.50/£13.40 (family). Jumping Jacks £1.50.
Facilities: P T(2 hrs)

Sheringham

The Splash Leisure Pool Map ref. J/K2
Weybourne Road
Tel: (01263) 825675 Web: www.northnorfolk.org
Tropical leisure pool with giant 150ft waterslide and wave machine. Children's paddling area. Sun terrace, saunas, activity hall and health/fitness studios.
Times: Open all year. Times vary according to season, contact for details.
Fee: Prices vary depending upon activity.
Facilities: P T(2-3 hrs)

Thetford

Waterworld Map ref. F/G11
Breckland Leisure Centre, Croxton Road
Tel: (01842) 753110 Web: www.breckland.gov.uk
Fun leisure pool with wave machine, rapids, water cannon, flume and spa pool. Main competition size pool and fitness centre.
Times: Leisure pool open all year. During school term - Mon-Fri, 1530-2030; Sat and Sun, 1000-1800. During school holidays - daily, 1000-1800. Closes at 1730 on Bank Hols.
Fee: Prices vary depending upon activity.
Facilities: P T(2-3 hrs)

Countryside

The countryside of Norfolk offers a variety of landscapes, home to traditional market towns and pretty villages of flint and carrstone. Discover the unspoilt coastline with its saltmarshes and crumbling cliffs, the unique reed-fringed waterways of The Broads, and the sandy heathlands of The Brecks - home of Britain's largest lowland pine forest. This is a county of rich agricultural land, noted for its cereals, oil-seed rape, sugar beet and vegetables, alongside large pig/poultry rearing units and cattle grazing (Broads).

Special Areas

Norfolk Coastline - an 'Area of Outstanding Natural Beauty', with unspoilt beaches, low crumbling cliffs, nature reserves, seaside towns, fishing villages and some of the finest sand dunes and saltmarshes in Britain. Mini tour - start your journey at The Wash, England's largest tidal estuary, and an important winter feeding area for wildfowl. Travelling north, Old Hunstanton is noted for the only red and white striped cliffs in the country, made up of carrstone and red/white chalk. Whilst at Holkham, take a walk on the huge private beach backed by pine trees. Continuing past the little port of Wells-next-the-Sea, the saltmarshes at Stiffkey and Morston are some of the oldest on the coast, and in summer are turned purple by the sea lavender. From here you can take a boat trip to see the seals on the three mile long sand and shingle spit of Blakeney Point. Alternatively enjoy the views over Britain's first designated nature reserve from Cley's windmill - you might spot bitterns, oystercatchers and avocets. At Weybourne, cliffs rich in fossils rise from the marshlands, and you can jump aboard the North Norfolk Railway for a ride along the coast to Sheringham. It is surrounded by attractive heath and woodland, such as Sheringham Park, one of Humphry Repton's most outstanding achievements. Continuing past Cromer, the crumbling cliffs and high-piled sand dunes between Overstrand and Winterton-on-Sea are in a constant battle with the sea, as seen at Happisburgh (noted for its red/white striped lighthouse) where buildings are toppling over the edge.

DID YOU KNOW

West Runton is famous for its elephant skeleton, unearthed from the cliff face in December 1990, having lay buried for between 60-70,000 years. It is said to be the biggest, most complete and best preserved elephant skeleton of its kind ever found.

Burnham Overy Staithe

The Brecks - a unique mix of forest, heath and farmland. Once covering a huge area, the landscape was created by prehistoric farmers, as they cut back the trees to make clearings for crops, and by the constant grazing of sheep and rabbits. 'Breck' is land once cultivated, then a few years later, allowed to return to the wild. Later large areas were planted over with forestry. The pockets of remaining heath-land are fiercely protected today - a rich haven for many rare species of flora and fauna. The area is also dotted with historical sites - burial mounds, deserted villages and Neolithic flint mines. More information at www.brecks.org

The Broads - are man-made, created when peat diggings of the 9-13th C. were later flooded as sea levels rose, making shallow lakes or 'broads'. Today this is Britain's largest protected wetland, with a similar status to a national park. There are around 40 broads, connected by the area's rivers, and making up to 125 miles of lock-free navigable waterways. Whilst the surrounding reed-beds, woodland, meadows and farmland are a haven for some of Britain's rarest flora and fauna. Take a boat trip along the waterways, and visit riverside villages, windmills and important nature reserves. More information at www.broads-authority.gov.uk

The Fens - see the Countryside section in Cambridgeshire for further information.

Thetford Forest Park - Britain's largest lowland pine forest, covering over 50,000 acres. Created in the 1920s, the forest is a patchwork of both Corsican and Scots pines, heath-land and broadleaves, intersected with broad sandy rides and tracks. Rich in animal, bird and plant life - look out for deer, bats and the park's emblem, the red squirrel. Visitors can discover the peace and tranquillity of the forest, or enjoy a great family day out, with numerous way-marked walks, cycle trails and picnic sites. The forest is also rich in archaeological sites, such as Grimes Graves. Regular programme of events. More information at www.forestry.gov.uk

Country Parks & Nature Reserves

Blakeney

Blakeney Point National Nature Reserve Map ref. H/I2
Tel: 0870 609 5388 Web: www.nationaltrust.org.uk
One of Britain's foremost bird sanctuaries, the point is a 31/2 mile long sand and shingle spit noted in particular for its colonies of breeding terns. Seals can also be seen.
Times: Open all year, daily, any reasonable time.
Fee: Car park £2.50.
Facilities: T(3 hrs) NT

Blickling (nr. Aylsham)

Blickling Hall, Garden and Park Map ref. K4
See entry in Historic Houses section.

Cley-next-the-Sea

NWT Cley Marshes Nature Reserve Map ref. I2
Coast Road
Tel: (01263) 740008
Web: www.wildlifetrust.org.uk/norfolk
Coastal nature reserve, with an international reputation. Popular with bird-watchers who come to see migrant and wading birds. Visitor centre overlooks the reserve.
Times: Reserve open all year, daily, dawn-dusk. Closed 25 Dec. Visitor centre open late Mar-early Dec, daily, 1000-1700.
Fee: £3.75/free.
Facilities: T(1-6 hrs)

Erpingham (nr. Aylsham)

Wolterton Park Map ref. K4
See entry in Historic Houses section.

Felbrigg (nr. Cromer)

Felbrigg Hall Map ref. K3
See entry in Historic Houses section.

NWT Broads Wildlife Centre, Ranworth

Foxley (nr. Dereham)

NWT Foxley Wood Map ref. I5
Tel: (01603) 625540
Web: www.wildlifetrust.org.uk/norfolk
The largest ancient woodland in the county (320 acres), with three nature trails existing around the site. The wood is well used by naturalists, the general public and schools.
Times: Open all year, daily (except Thurs), 1000-1700.
Fee: Free.
Facilities: T(2 hrs) (by appointment)

Fritton (nr. Great Yarmouth)

Fritton Lake Country World Map ref. O8
Church Lane
Tel: (01493) 488208 Web: www.frittonlake.co.uk
A 250-acre centre with a children's assault course, putting, adventure playground, golf, fishing, boating, wildfowl, heavy horses, cart rides and falconry flying displays.
Times: Open 28 Mar-3 Oct, daily, 1000-1730. 9 and 10 Oct, Sat and Sun, 1000-1730. 15 Oct-31 Oct, daily, 1000-1700.
Fee: £6.50/£4.50/£5.50.
Facilities: Q T(4 hrs)

Great Yarmouth

RSPB Berney Marshes Nature Reserve (and Breydon Water) Map ref. O7/8
Tel: (01493) 700645 Web: www.rspb.org.uk
Huge expanse of open space, grazing marshes and mudflats. Breydon Water is Britain's most easterly estuary. Home to tens of thousands of wintering and breeding wildfowl and waders.
Times: Open all year, daily, any railonable time.
Fee: Free.
Facilities: T(2 hrs) (on leads)

Hickling

NWT Hickling Broad National Nature Reserve
Map ref. N5/6
Stubb Road
Tel: (01692) 598276
Web: www.wildlifetrust.org.uk/norfolk
Nature reserve beside the largest area of open water in the Broads. Dykes, marshes, fens and woodland, with a visitors centre and water trail. Wintering and resident birds.
Times: Open all year, daily. Visitor's centre open, 1 Apr-30 Sept, 1000-1700.
Fee: £2.75/free. Booking essential for water trail (boat trip).
Facilities: T(1-5 hrs)

Holme-next-the-Sea (nr. Hunstanton)

Holme Bird Observatory Reserve (Norfolk Ornithologist's Association) Map ref. D2
Broadwater Road
Tel: (01485) 525406 Web: www.noa.org.uk
Nature reserve with over 320 species of birds recorded since 1962. One of 18 bird observatories in the UK. Various species of dragonfly. Over 50 species of flora.
Times: Open all year, Tues-Sun and Bank Hol Mons, 1000-1700 (or dusk, if earlier). Closed 25 Dec.
Fee: £2.00.
Facilities: T(2-3 hrs)

Holt

Holt Country Park Map ref. J3
Norwich Road
Tel: (01263) 516001 Web: www.northnorfolk.org
100 acre, mainly coniferous woodland, with children's play area, waymarked trails and a small visitor centre. An observation tower offers attractive views.
Times: Open all year, daily, any reasonable time. Visitor centre only open at peak periods during the summer.
Fee: Free. Car park charge £1.00.
Facilities: T(2 hrs)

King's Lynn

The Green Quay Environmental Discovery Centre
Map ref. C5/6
Marriott's Warehouse, South Quay
Tel: (01553) 818500 Web: www.thegreenquay.co.uk
Set beside the River Great Ouse, the centre promotes the conservation of The Wash estuary and local wildlife. Film shows, bird viewing gallery and hydroponics.
Times: Open all year. 2 Jan-31 Mar, daily, 1000-1600. 1 Apr-30 Sept, daily, 1000-1700. 1 Oct-24 Dec, daily, 1000-1600.
Fee: £1.00/50p/£1.00.
Facilities: T(1 hr)

Mannington (nr. Saxthorpe Corpusty)

Mannington Gardens and Countryside Map ref. J4
See entry in Gardens section.

Mundford

Lynford Arboretum Map ref. F9
Tel: (01842) 810271 Web: www.forestry.gov.uk
A nationally important collection of over 200 species of broad-leaved and coniferous trees. Spring and Autumn are particularly stunning.
Times: Open at any reasonable time.
Fee: Free.
Facilities: T(3 hrs)

Oxborough (nr. Swaffham)

Oxburgh Hall Map ref. E8
See entry in Historic Houses section.

Pensthorpe (nr. Fakenham)

Pensthorpe Nature Reserve and Gardens Map ref. H4
Tel: (01328) 851465 Web: www.pensthorpe.com
Collection of rare and native water birds and migratory visitors. Lakeside, woodland, wildflower meadows, river walks and bird hides. Award-winning Millennium gardens. Cafe, shop and play area.
Times: Open 2 Jan-31 Mar, daily, 1000-1600. 1 Apr-30 Sept, daily, 1000-1700. 1 Oct-31 Dec, daily, 1000-1600. Closed 25, 26 Dec and 1 Jan.
Fee: £5.50/£3.00/£5.00/£15.00.
Facilities: Q T(3-5 hrs)

Ranworth

NWT Broads Wildlife Centre Map ref. M6
Tel: (01603) 270479
Web: www.wildlifetrust.org.uk/norfolk
A nature trail and conservation centre with displays showing history and wildlife. Gallery with telescopes and binoculars over-looking the Ranworth Broad Nature Reserve.
Times: Wildlife centre open 1 Apr-31 Oct, daily, 1000-1700. Boardwalk open all year.
Fee: Free.
Facilities: T(1 hr)

Sandringham (nr. King's Lynn)

Sandringham Map ref. D4/5
See entry in Historic Houses section.

Sheringham

Sheringham Park Map ref. J3
Upper Sheringham
Tel: (01263) 823778 Web: www.nationaltrust.org.uk
One of Humphry Repton's most outstanding achievements, this landscape park contains fine mature woodlands, and a large woodland garden with rhododendrons and azaleas. Stunning views of coast.
Times: Open all year, daily, dawn-dusk.
Fee: Car park £2.80.
Facilities: T(3 hrs) (on leads) **NT**

Snettisham (nr. Hunstanton)

RSPB Snettisham Nature Reserve Map ref. D4
Tel: (01485) 542689 Web: www.rspb.org.uk
At Snettisham you can enjoy one of the country's greatest wildlife spectacles. As the rising tide covers The Wash, waders, ducks and geese move up the beach onto the pools.
Times: Open at any reasonable time.
Fee: Car park £2.00.
Facilities: T(3 hrs)

Strumpshaw (nr. Norwich)
RSPB Strumpshaw Fen Nature Reserve Map ref. M7
Low Road
Tel: (01603) 715191 Web: www.rspb.org.uk
Extensive trails take visitors through unspoilt broadland scenery and habitats - woodland, meadows, fens and reed beds. A great variety of wildlife can be seen. Three bird-watching hides.
Times: Open all year, daily, dawn-dusk. Closed 25 Dec.
Fee: £2.50/50p/£1.50/£5.00.
Facilities: T(3 hrs)

Titchwell (nr. Hunstanton)
RSPB Titchwell Marsh Nature Reserve Map ref. E2
Main Road
Tel: (01485) 210779 Web: www.rspb.org.uk
Nature reserve with three bird-watching hides and two trails. Visitor centre with large shop, food servery, car park and toilets
Times: Open all year, daily, summer 0930-1700; winter 0930-1600. Closed 25 and 26 Dec.
Fee: Car park £3.00.
Facilities: Q T(2 1/2 hrs)

Weeting (nr. Brandon)
NWT Weeting Heath National Nature Reserve
Map ref. E10
Tel: (01842) 827615
Web: www.wildlifetrust.org.uk/norfolk
A nature reserve with grassy heath, pine plantation, meres and associated wildlife. There is also a self-guided nature trail and access to the hide.
Times: Open 1 Apr-31 Aug, daily, dawn-dusk.
Fee: £2.00/free.
Facilities: T(1 hr) (by appointment)

Wells-next-the-Sea
Holkham Hall Map ref. G2
See entry in Historic Houses section.

Picnic Sites

Bacton Wood (Forest Enterprise) - beside minor road, south of B1150, 1 1/2 miles east from North Walsham. Map ref. M4
Bure Park - beside A149 (Caister Road), 1 1/4 miles north of Great Yarmouth. Map ref. P7
Denver Sluice - beside minor road, 2 miles south west of Downham Market. Map ref. C8
Dersingham - beside A149, 1/2 mile south west of village. Map ref. D4
Guy's Head - beside minor road/River Nene, 3 miles north of A17 at Sutton Bridge. Map ref. A5
Pretty Corner - beside A148/A1082, 1 mile south of Sheringham. Map ref. K3
Shouldham Warren (Forest Enterprise) - off A134, on minor road between Shouldham and Marham, 6 miles south east of King's Lynn. Map ref. D7
Wiveton Downs - beside minor road, 1 mile south of Blakeney. Map ref. I3

Forest Enterprise picnic sites in Thetford Forest Park:
Great Hockham - beside A1075, 6 miles north east of Thetford. Map ref. G10
Lynford Stag - beside A134, 1 mile south east of Mundford. Map ref. F10
Rishbeth Wood - beside B1107, 1 mile west of Thetford. Map ref. F11
St. Helens - beside minor road (towards Santon House), 3/4 mile east of Santon Downham. Map ref. F10
Swaffham picnic site - access off A1122, 3 miles west of Swaffham. Map ref. E7
Two Mile Bottom - beside A134, 2 miles north west of Thetford. Map ref. F10

Countryside Organisations - Norfolk

The Broads Authority
18 Colegate, Norwich, Norfolk NR3 1BQ
Tel: (01603) 610734 Web: www.broads-authority.gov.uk

English Nature
60 Bracondale, Norwich, Norfolk NR1 2BE
Tel: (01603) 620558 Web: www.english-nature.gov.uk

Forest Enterprise - East Anglia Forest District
Santon Downham, nr. Brandon, Suffolk IP27 0TJ
Tel: (01842) 810271 Web: www.forestry.gov.uk

The National Trust - Regional Office for East Anglia
Angel Corner, 8 Angel Hill, Bury St. Edmunds, Suffolk IP33 1UZ
Tel: 0870 609 5388 Web: www.nationaltrust.org.uk

Norfolk Wildlife Trust (NWT)
Bewick House, 22 Thorpe Road, Norwich, Norfolk NR1 1RY
Tel: (01603) 625540
Web: www.wildlifetrust.org.uk/norfolk

The Royal Society for the Protection of Birds (RSPB) - Regional Office for East Anglia
Stalham House, 65 Thorpe Road, Norwich, Norfolk NR1 1UD
Tel: (01603) 661662 Web: www.rspb.org.uk

Activities

Boat Trips

Barton Turf

RA Boat Trip Map ref. M5/6
Gay's Staithe, Barton Broad
Tel: (01692) 670779 Web: www.broads-authority.gov.uk
Trips on Barton Broad aboard the solar-powered RA. Enjoy a high tech boating experience and hear about Clear Water 2000 - Europe's leading lake restoration project.
Times: Open Apr, May and Oct weekends, Bank Hols and local half term, departing at 1030, 1200, 1400 and 1530. Jun-Sept, daily, departing at 1030, 1200, 1400 and 1530.
Fee: £4.50/£3.50/£3.50/£9.00.
Facilities: T(1½ hrs)

Blakeney

Bishops Boats Seal Trips Map ref. H/12
Tel: (01263) 740753 Web: www.bishopsboats.co.uk
A boat trip to see the seals and birds on Blakeney Point. See many species of birds, and both grey and common seals in the colony of approximately 500.
Times: Please contact for details, as times vary due to tides.
Fee: £6.00/£4.00.
Facilities: T(2 hrs)

Brundall (nr. Norwich)

Broom Boats Ltd Map ref. M7
Riverside
Tel: (01603) 712334 Fax: (01603) 714803
Email: reservations@broomboats.com
Web: www.broom-boats.co.uk
Brooms operate one of the best fleets of motor cruisers for hire on the Norfolk Broads. Well maintained modern self drive boats for 2 to 7 persons. The Norfolk Broads offer the most attractive area of inland waterways for cruising, with unspoilt countryside, no locks and protected as a national park.

Hickling

NWT Hickling Broad National Nature Reserve (Water Trail) Map ref. N5/6
See entry in Countryside section.

DID YOU KNOW

St. Julian's Church in Norwich has a shrine to Mother Julian, the 14th C. authoress who wrote 'Revelations of Divine Love' - the first known English book written by a woman.

Horning

Mississippi River Boat Map ref. M6
Lower Street
Tel: (01692) 630262 Web: www.southern-comfort.co.uk
Double-decker paddle steamer, which can carry 100 passengers for sightseeing trips and private parties. Three public trips are arranged daily with excellent commentary. Full bar facilities are available plus hot drinks and snacks.
Times: Open Apr-Oct, sailings at 1030, 1300 and 1500.
Fee: £5.00/£4.50/£4.50/£16.00. Booking essential.
Facilities: T(2 hrs)

Horning

Norfolk Broads Yachting Co Ltd Map ref. M6
Southgates Yacht Station, Lower Street NR12 8PF
Tel: (01692) 631330 Fax: (01692) 631133
Email: info@nbyco.com Web: www.nbyco.com
The Norfolk Broads Yachting Company runs the largest fleet of sailing yachts on the Norfolk Broads. The fleet consists of Gaff or Bermudan rigged 2-8 berth yachts. Plus the Wherry yacht "White Moth" 10 berth (skippered). Weekly, short break or daily hire available. Also sailing and rowing dinghies and day boats for hire by the hour, day or week.

Hunstanton

Searles Sea Tours Map ref. D3
South Beach PE36 5BB
Tel: (07831) 321799 or (01485) 534211
Web: www.seatours.co.uk
A choice of 5 guided sea tours providing educational fun for all ages and leaving from Hunstanton's central promenade. Take a trip along the coastline to capture panoramic views of Hunstanton's cliffs and coastline, aboard the 'Wash Monster' (LARC) or DUKW amphibious landing craft. Or take the 'Sandbank Special' and discover the strange creatures of the Wash just at the bottom of the ramp! Take the MV Sealion on the 2-hour, 14-mile sea tour to view the beautiful seals of the Wash, with full commentary given. Please contact for times and fees. Coach parties welcome, but please book to avoid disappointment.

Ludham

Wildlife Water Trail Map ref. N6
How Hill
Tel: (01692) 678763 Web: www.broads-authority.gov.uk
A water trail by electric launch, through the marshes and fens of How Hill Nature Reserve with a guide. Includes short walk to bird hide.
Times: Open 3 Apr-31 May, Sat, Sun, Bank Hols, Easter week and local half term, 1100-1500. 1 Jun-30 Sept, daily, 1000-1700. 2-31 Oct, Sat and Sun, 1100-1500.
Fee: £4.00/£3.00/£3.00/£8.00.
Facilities: T(50 mins)

Morston (nr. Blakeney)

Beans Seal Trips Map ref. H2
Tel: (01263) 740505 Web: www.beansboattrips.co.uk
A family run business for over 50 years, offering daily boat trips to see the seals and birds in their natural habitat on and around Blakeney Point nature reserve.
Times: Open all year. 1 Jan-31 Mar, Sat-Mon and Wed (where possible). 1 Apr-31 Oct, daily, times depend on tides. 1 Nov-31 Dec, Sat-Mon and Wed (where possible). Closed 25 Dec. Please phone for full details.
Fee: £6.00/£4.00/£6.00. Pre-booking recommended.
Facilities: T(2 hrs)

Morston (nr. Blakeney)

Temple Seal Trips Map ref. H2
Tel: (01263) 740791 Web: www.sealtrips.co.uk
Boat trips to see the common and grey seals basking on Blakeney Point, an internationally famous bird sanctuary. Red and white boats depart from Morston Quay.
Times: Open all year, daily, times vary according to tide. Please phone for details.
Fee: £6.00/£4.00/£6.00. Tickets collected from the Anchor pub in Morston.
Facilities: T(2 hrs)

Ranworth

Helen of Ranworth Boat Trip Map ref. M6
The Staithe
Tel: (01603) 270453 Web: www.broads-authority.gov.uk
Trips from Ranworth on Helen (an electric ferry) show what travel was like on a Broads reed lighter - a vessel that traditionally used to carry bundles of reed.
Times: Open Easter-31 Oct, Mon-Sat at 1015. Also ferry service Easter-Oct, every afternoon, at every half-hour from Ranworth Staithe to the Broads Wildlife Centre.
Fee: £5.50/£4.50/£4.50/£11.00. Ferry 80p/40p/40p.
Facilities: T(2 hrs)

Wroxham and Potter Heigham

Broads Tours Ltd Map ref. L/M6 and N6
The Bridge (Wroxham) and The Bridge (Potter Heigham)
Tel: Wroxham (01603) 782207, Potter Heigham (01692) 670711 Web: www.broads.co.uk
Leading passenger boat company on the Norfolk Broads. Enjoy a relaxing and informative trip from either Wroxham (double decker and traditional style passenger boat) or Potter Heigham (traditional style passenger boat).
Times: Open 3 Apr-31 Oct, please contact for further details.
Fee: Varies depending on tour taken, contact for details.
Facilities: T(2½ hrs) (Wroxham only) (Wroxham only)

Golf Courses

Hunstanton

Searles Golf Resort and Country Club Map ref. D3
South Beach PE36 5BB
Tel: (01485) 534211 Fax: (01485) 533815
Web: www.searles.co.uk
9 hole, par-34 resort golf course designed in a links style, with good large greens and enhanced by natural features. Open to the public on a 'pay and play' basis, the course provides a challenge for both experienced and novice golfers alike, with a large 10-bay driving range offering a chance to practice before hitting the course proper. Club hire available. New Country Club overlooking the course is now open and serving refreshments, daytime snacks and evening meals. Changing and shower facilities also provided. Area also incorporates two fishing lakes, bowling green and astro-putting course. Societies welcome.

Cycling

The Brecks is a 20 mile circular route starting at Swaffham, and visiting a unique landscape of heath, pine forests and large open fields. The Lost Villages of Breckland is a 23 mile route, starting from the village of Gressenhall (nr. Dereham), and exploring abandoned medieval hamlets. Whilst The Bishop's Chapel takes you on a 23 mile journey from Dereham, via the ruins of an 11th C. Norman chapel. Nelson's Norfolk (29 miles), starting from Fakenham, takes in Lord Nelson's birthplace and the pilgrimage centre of Little Walsingham. Or why not take a ride past the country estates of the rich and famous on Lords of the Manor (29 miles from Aylsham). Saleable maps for all these routes from the East of England Tourist Board on 0870 225 4852. For some traffic-free rides, try the 9 mile Bure Valley Path between Aylsham and Wroxham, or the numerous trails at the Kelling Heath Holiday Park at Weybourne (nr. Holt), where there is cycle hire too - more details at www.cycle-norfolk.co.uk Alternatively explore the unique landscapes of The Brecks, with their cycling pack of five routes (01842) 765400, or visit www.brecks.org For more information on cycling in the county, contact the Norfolk Countryside Access Team on (01603) 223284, or visit www.countrysideaccess.norfolk.gov.uk

The Norfolk Coast Cycleway - runs for around 103 miles from King's Lynn to Great Yarmouth, using quiet country roads and lanes, situated just inland from the coast. You can dip into small sections, or try some of the loops and links around it. This route connects to the National Cycle Network Route 1 (Hull to Harwich). Maps of the cycleway (small charge) are available from Cromer Tourist Information Centre on (01263) 512497, or for a more detailed guide (with places of interest) visit www.cycle-norfolk.co.uk

Walking

Long Distance Walks

The Angles Way (78 miles) - linear walk running from Great Yarmouth to Knettishall Heath Country Park (Suffolk). Saleable guide to route available from Sheila Smith, Caldcleugh, Old Buckenham, nr. Attleborough, Norfolk NR17 1RU. Tel: (01953) 861094.

The Fen Rivers Way (50 miles) - runs from Cambridge to The Wash, nr. King's Lynn in Norfolk. Saleable guide to route available from Bernard Hawes, 52 Maid's Causeway, Cambridge, Cambridgeshire CB5 8DD. Tel: (01223) 560033.

The Icknield Way Path (105 miles) - runs from Ivinghoe Beacon (Buckinghamshire) to Knettishall Heath Country Park (Suffolk), passing through parts of Norfolk. Saleable guide available from the Icknield Way Association, 19 Boundary Road, Bishop's Stortford, Hertfordshire CM23 5LE. Tel: (01279) 504602.

The Peddar's Way and Norfolk Coast Path (93 miles) - runs from Knettishall Heath Country Park (Suffolk) to Cromer (via Holme-next-the-Sea). Official trail guide by Bruce Robinson, and published by Aurum Press (ISBN: 1-85410-852-2). Basic route and accommodation guide from Sheila Smith, Caldcleugh, Old Buckenham, nr. Attleborough, Norfolk NR17 1RU. Tel: (01953) 861094. www.nationaltrail.co.uk/peddarsway

The Weavers' Way (61 miles) - runs from Cromer to Great Yarmouth. Downloadable maps and information at www.countrysideaccess.norfolk.gov.uk. Accommodation guide available from Sheila Smith, Caldcleugh, Old Buckenham, nr. Attleborough, Norfolk NR17 1RU. Tel: (01953) 861094.

Shorter Walks

Your first port of call should be the Norfolk Countryside Access Team on (01603) 223284, or visit www.countrysideaccess.norfolk.gov.uk where there are on-line walking routes, complete with maps. These include over 70 circular walks (4-6 miles) around villages and towns, plus information on the key long distance walks, such as The Great Eastern Pingo Trail (8 miles of tracks/trails along the eastern edge of The Brecks); The Marriott's Way (21 mile long walk along the former railway line between Norwich and Aylsham); and The Nar Valley Way (34 mile long walk from King's Lynn to Gressenhall, nr. Dereham). For walks with a watery view, try The Peter Scott Walk, a 10 mile trail following the old sea bank alongside the Wash. Leaflet from the King's Lynn Tourist Information Centre on (01553) 763044. Alternatively head to the waterways of The Broads, where there are over 190 miles of footpaths to discover. Contact The Broads Authority for more information on (01603) 610734, or visit www.broads-authority.gov.uk The Thetford Forest Park is Britain's largest lowland pine forest, and offers a wide range of way-marked walks. More information on (01842) 810271, or visit www.forestry.gov.uk Alternatively explore the unique landscapes of The Brecks, with their 'Walking in the Brecks' pack (small charge) - contact (01842) 765400 or visit www.brecks.org for more information. Of course don't forget the area's country parks, with their various walks and nature trails - see the 'Countryside' section for further information.

Specialist Holidays & Tours

Awayadays
Stone Cottage, Front Road, Wood Dalling,
Norwich NR11 6RN
Tel: (01263) 587005 Web: www.awayadays.com
Regular one to seven day tours of the East of England, Norfolk and Norwich for individuals, groups and people with special interests. Open top City sightseeing bus tours of Norwich. Packages can include attractions, accommodation and luxury travel. No car needed. Disabled catered for.

Hilltop Outdoor Centre Map ref. K3
'Old Wood', Sheringham NR26 8TS
Tel/Fax: (01263) 824514
Web: www.hilltopoutdoorcentre.co.uk
Set in 25 acres of wood/fields. Adventure Days, and three to five day Summer Camps offer:- abseiling, giant zip wire, treetop trail, air rifles, trail bikes, archery, assault course, climbing wall, heated outdoor pool, crate stacking, bridges, high ropes and orienteering. Families and parties welcome, B&B available.

Suffolk Cycle Breaks
Bradfield Hall Barn, Alder Carr Farm, PO Box 82,
Needham Market, Suffolk IP6 8BW
Tel: (01449) 721555 Fax: (01449) 721707
Email: enquiry@cyclebreaks.com
Web: www.cyclebreaks.com www.walkingbreaks.com
Gentle cycling and walking holidays in Suffolk and Norfolk. Luggage transfer and accommodation pre-arranged.

Fishing by the River Thet, Thetford

Food & Drink

Regional Produce

During the 18th C. droves of Norfolk turkeys were made to walk to the London markets, their feet coated with tar for protection. Today the county is home to poultry producer Bernard Matthews. The famous mustard maker, Colmans, has been associated with Norwich since 1814, and you can visit The Mustard Shop in the city. Lovers of seafood can try mussels from Stiffkey, lobsters from Sheringham, and Cromer's famous crabs (regarded as some of the best in the country). At Great Yarmouth, once a major fishing port, smoked kippers and bloaters can be sampled, or visit the world's largest seaside rock shop. Head to the windmills at Great Bircham and Denver to try delicious bread and cakes made using the freshly milled flour. Then wash it all down with a trip to Whin Hill Cider at Wells-next-the-Sea, or visit one of the county's breweries - try Iceni at Ickburgh, or Woodforde's at Woodbastwick.

Breweries & Vineyards

Ickburgh (nr. Thetford)
Iceni Brewery Map ref. F9
3 Foulden Road
Tel: (01842) 878922
Tours of the brewery, featuring traditional and new methods of brewing and the history of brewing. Free tasting. Hop Garden and new shop open.
Times: Open all year, Mon-Fri, 0830-1330. Extended opening times from May-Sept, 0830-1630.
Fee: Free.
Facilities: P T(20 mins)

Wells-next-the-Sea
Whin Hill Cider Map ref. G2
Stearmans Yard
Tel: (01328) 711033 Web: www.whinhillcider.co.uk
Cider works in an 18th C. flint barn. Exhibits of cider making equipment, mugs and glasses. Visitors can see bottling, labeling and blending. Opportunity to taste/purchase ciders and apple juice.
Times: Open 3 Apr-25 Jul, Sat and Sun, 1030-1730. 28 Jul-3 Sept, Wed-Sun, 1030-1730. 4-26 Sept, Sat and Sun, 1030-1730.
Fee: Free.
Facilities: T(30 mins)

Woodbastwick (nr. Wroxham/Hoveton)
Woodforde's Brewery Shop and Visitor Centre
Map ref. M6
Broadland Brewery
Tel (01603) 722218 Web: www.woodfordes.co.uk
Woodforde's cask ale brewery shop and visitor centre. Various displays and video of the brewing process. The Fur and Feather Inn is located next door, which is the brewery tap and restaurant.
Times: Open all year, Mon-Fri, 1030-1630. Sat, Sun and Bank Hol Mon, 1130-1630. Closed 25 and 26 Dec.
Fee: Free.
Facilities: P T(30 mins)

Restaurants

Attleborough
Sweet Briar Bistro Map ref. I9
Peter Beales Roses, London Road, Attleborough NR17 1AY
For table reservations and evening dining -
Tel: (01953) 450134 E-mail: mark@classicroses.co.uk
Our licensed Sweet Briar Bistro is set amidst the secluded gardens of Peter Beales Classic Roses, and provides the perfect setting for visitors to relax and enjoy mouth watering food in great surroundings. The 'seasons best' is the motto of our Head Chef, and using only the finest ingredients, offers a variety of new and exciting dishes to tempt you with! A distinctive Table d'hôte menu available for Fri and Sat evening dining - booking essential.
Open 7 days a week, including Bank Hols, Mon-Sat 0930-1700; Sun and Bank Hols 1030-1600; Fri and Sat evening 1900-2100.

Blickling (nr. Aylsham)
The Buckinghamshire Arms Map ref. K4
Blickling, nr. Aylsham NR11 2NF
Tel: (01263) 732133
Probably Norfolk's most attractive inn - standing next to the stunning Blickling Hall. Gorgeous en-suite, four poster accommodation, local produce in delicious dishes, beautiful garden and log fire in the winter. P

Burgh Castle (nr. Great Yarmouth)
Church Farm Public House Map ref. O8
Church Road, Burgh Castle, nr. Great Yarmouth NR31 9QG
Tel: (01493) 780251
Church Farm nestles beside Breydon Water where the rivers Waveney and Yare meet opposite the Berney Arms Windmill, giving the most spectacular views of Norfolk. The towns of Gorleston and Great Yarmouth are 10 minutes drive away with their entertainments, beaches and shops.

Wolterton (North Norfolk)

The Saracen's Head 'With Rooms' Map ref. K4
Wolterton, nr. Aylsham NR11 7LX
Tel: (01263) 768909
Web: www.saracenshead-norfolk.co.uk
Only 20 minutes drive from Norwich, The Saracen's Head is a civilised Inn without piped music or fruit machines. Built in the early 19th C. as a coaching Inn. Impeccably maintained and run by chef/proprietor Robert Dawson-Smith. There are log fires and wicker chairs. It is more a restaurant than a pub. Typical dishes include braised local rabbit, grilled fillets of smoked mackerel, venison, duck and steaks, plus a substantial vegetarian menu. Desserts are traditional favourites such as bread and butter pudding and treacle tart. The wine list is from Australia, South Africa, Spain and France. Open 7 days a week, 1100-1500 and 1800-2300.

Afternoon Teas

Bressingham (nr. Diss)

Into-Food Café Map ref. J11
Blooms of Bressingham, Bressingham, nr. Diss IP22 2AB
Tel: (01379) 688585
Three miles west of Diss on A1066. This impressive building was completed in Spring 2000, and the Tea Rooms renamed. Distinctive daily menus all at a reasonable cost, provide delicious snacks, lunches or tea-time treats in this unique setting, with an outside decking area an added attraction. Open: Daily, 0900-1730, Mar-Oct; 0900-1630, Nov-Feb (except Christmas Day/Boxing Day). See also entry for Blooms of Bressingham under Nurseries & Garden Centres on page 226.

Heacham (nr. Hunstanton)

Norfolk Lavender Ltd Map ref. D3
Caley Mill, Heacham (on A149) PE31 7JE
Tel: (01485) 571965/570384
Web: www.norfolk-lavender.co.uk
Locally baked cakes and scones and cream teas a speciality. Lunches available all year and log fire Oct-Apr. Miller's Tearoom in the middle of lavender/herb gardens and fragrant meadow. Seats: 120 all year, 88 in summer. Free admission. Open Apr-Oct, 1000-1700; Nov-Mar, 1000-1600. Average price: £2.70. Q P T(4 hrs) (on leads)

Thetford

The Mulberry Map ref. F/G11
11 Raymond Street, Thetford IP24 2EA
Tel: (01842) 820099
A new Victorian themed restaurant in the heart of the old town, specialising in homemade, traditional and vegetarian food. Child friendly and non smoking with a delightful courtyard garden for teas and coffee. Full a la carte service, lunch and evenings. Open 1000-1400 and 1800-2100, Mon-Sat; Sun lunch 1230-1400. Average price for 3 courses £19.00.

Thursford (nr. Fakenham)

Thursford Collection Map ref. H4
Thursford, nr. Fakenham NR21 0AS
Tel: (01328) 878477
Proprietor: Mr J Cushing. Afternoon cream teas on the lawn served from our Garden Conservatory. Teas, light refreshments and hot meals also served in our 'Barn'. Seats: 92 inside, 150 outside. Admission: £5.30/£2.80/£5.00. Q P T(2½ hrs)

Walsingham

Sue Ryder Map ref. G/H3
The Martyrs House, High Street, Walsingham NR22 6BZ
Tel: (01328) 820622 Fax: (01328) 820505
Retreat House Accommodation: bed & breakfast and evening meal (non-residents). Groups and individuals welcome. Open all year. Special functions at Easter and Christmas. Coffee Shop: Home-made cakes and light lunches. Seating up to 100. Gift Shop: Extensive range of carefully selected gifts.

DID YOU KNOW

The Hanseatic League were medieval trading links, forged with Northern European countries. These traders came in search of wool, and later some of Europe's finest cloth. King's Lynn was chosen as a base for many of their warehouses, and one of these survives today.

Stop & Shop

VISIT

THE BLACK SHEEP SHOP AND NEW COUNTRYWEAR COLLECTION

Aylsham

Black Sheep Shop - Black Sheep Jerseys Map ref. K5
9 Penfold Street, Aylsham NR11 6ET
Tel: (01263) 733142/732006
Email: Email@blacksheep.ltd.uk
Web: www.blacksheep.ltd.uk
The Black Sheep shop has always been known for the very best in naturally undyed and dyed knitwear, everything from jerseys and cardigans to hats, gloves, scarves and socks. Now we have added an extra dimension with our exclusive countrywear section. Only the best will do and we have introduced sports and hacking jackets, casual coats and jackets as well as boots, belts and tweed caps and a wide range of gift items. If you cannot come and visit us then send for our free colour catalogue. Open Mon-Fri, 0900-1750; Sat, 1000-1700; closed Sun. Free customer parking.

Seething

NORFOLK CHILDREN'S BOOK CENTRE

Between Aylsham and Cromer

Norfolk Children's Book Centre Map ref. K4
Wayside, Alby NR11 7HB
Tel: (01263) 761402 Web: www.ncbc.co.uk
Surrounded by fields, the Centre displays one of the best collections of children's and teachers' books in East Anglia. Here you will find a warm welcome and expert advice. You can browse through the latest and the classics in both fiction and non-fiction. We also sell story cassettes, videos and cards. Find out more about the Centre on www.ncbc.co.uk or telephone (01263) 761402. Open daily, Mon-Sat, 1000-1700, closed Bank Hols. Teachers welcome anytime, please phone. Find us between Aylsham and Cromer just off the A140. Look out for the signposted turn 500 metres north of Alby Craft Centre.

Cley-next-the-Sea

Made in Cley Map ref. I2
High Street, Cley-next-the-Sea, Holt NR25 7RF
Tel: (01263) 740134
Hand-thrown domestic and sculptural Pottery in stoneware, porcelain and raku, contemporary jewellery in silver and gold, prints and sculptures in marble and other stones. Everything is made on the premises and exhibited in a Regency shop which is itself of historical interest. Open daily, closed Wed Oct-Jun.

Cromer

Bond Street Antiques (inc BRIGGS) Map ref. K3
6 Bond Street, Cromer NR27 9DA
Tel: (01263) 513134
Goldsmiths, Silversmiths and Jewellers, incorporating Gem Test Centre. Gems, jewellery, Amber, gifts and objects d'art. Top prices paid for gold, silver and antiques. Valuations for Insurance and Probate. Member of The National Association of Goldsmiths and Fellow of The Gemmological Association of Great Britain.

DID YOU KNOW

Wymondham Abbey is noted for its two towers, the result of a series of disputes between the monks and the townspeople, which led to the building being divided into two in 1249.

Erpingham (nr. Aylsham)

Alby Crafts Map ref. K4
Cromer Road, Erpingham, nr. Norwich NR11 7QE
Tel: (01263) 761590 Web: www.albycrafts.co.uk
Alby Crafts is set amongst superb gardens in beautifully converted farm buildings. Browse in the working studios of some of Norfolk's finest crafts people, including a sculptor, artist, wood turner, silversmith and needleworker. Purchase from them directly or commission your own piece of work. Visit the tearooms, gift and book shop, and the Gallery selling quality British crafts. Or take a relaxing stroll in the beautiful 4 1/2 acre gardens. Open 1000-1700, Tues-Sun (and Bank Hols), from 2nd weekend in Jan-24 Dec.

Great Walsingham (nr. Fakenham)

Great Walsingham Barns Map ref. G/H3
Great Walsingham, nr. Fakenham NR22 6DR
Tel: (01328) 820900 Web: www.walsinghamgallery.co.uk
An attractive range of converted barns comprising: **The Textile Centre Shop & Post Office** - Gifts, casual clothes and books, with an excellent tea room providing light lunches and cream teas. **Great Walsingham Gallery** - Exhibitions of paintings, sculptures, woodcarving, fine-art cards, jewellery and Medici prints. **Oriental Carpets and Rugs.** Open: daily, 0930-1700; weekends and Bank Hols, 1000-1700. T(1 hr)

Great Yarmouth

Candlemaker and Model Centre Map ref. N7
Mill Road, Stokesby, nr. Great Yarmouth NR29 3EY
Tel: (01493) 750242 www.candlemaker-norfolk.co.uk
Situated 9 miles from Great Yarmouth on the banks of the River Bure. Boasts England's largest variety of handcrafted candles, with many that are unique. The candle showroom and workshop is open 1 Apr-31 Oct, 0900-1700, Tues-Sat; closed Sun and Mon. Free admission. Free parking and river moorings. Candle making courses are now available.
T(1 hr)

Heacham (nr. Hunstanton)

Norfolk Lavender Ltd Map ref. D3
Caley Mill, Heacham (on A149) PE31 7JE
Tel: (01485) 570384
Set in the ground floor of Caley Mill, the Gift Shop contains a very wide range of gifts for all the family. There are items to suit every pocket, masses of choice and frequent new ideas. The Old Barn houses the Lavender Shop where you can buy Norfolk Lavender's fragrant products: The English Lavender, Rose, Lily of the Valley and Norfolk Lavender for Men. Open Apr-Oct, 1000-1700; Nov-Mar, 1000-1600. Average price: £2.70. T(4 hrs) (on leads)

Little Ouse River

King's Lynn

Caithness Crystal Visitor Centre Map ref. C6
Paxman Road, Hardwick Industrial Estate,
King's Lynn PE30 4NE Tel: (01553) 765111/765123
Fax: (01553) 767628 Web: www.caithnessglass.co.uk
Glassmaking is a magical craft that can transform sand into exquisite glassware using only the heat of a furnace and the skill of hand and eye. Witness it for yourself at our King's Lynn Visitor Centre and marvel at the demonstration of the skills of glassmaking. Unique factory shopping experience, extensive selection of giftware - stemware paperweights and glass sculptures, also Royal Worcester and Spode. Open: 7 days a week (Factory Shop/Restaurant); glass making Mon-Fri. Free admission. T(1½ hrs)

Langham (nr. Holt)

Langham Glass Map ref. H3
The Long Barn, North Street, Langham, Holt NR25 7DG
Tel: (01328) 830511
Email: langhamglass@talk21.com
Web: www.langhamglass.co.uk
In a large beautiful Norfolk barn complex, teams of glassmakers can be seen working with molten glass using blowing irons and hand tools that have been traditional for hundreds of years. There is an enclosed children's adventure playground, factory gift shops, museum, restaurant, video, rose and clematis walled garden. Many other crafts. Open 7 days a week all year, 1000-1700. Glassmaking, Easter-31 Oct (everyday); 1 Nov-Easter (Mon-Fri). Group visits welcome. Q T(2½ hrs)

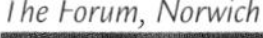

The Forum, Norwich

Sutton (nr. Stalham)

Sutton Pottery Map ref. N5
Church Road, Sutton, Norwich NR12 9SG
Tel: (01692) 580595 Web: www.suttonpottery.com
Follow brown tourist signs from A149 south of Stalham, then traditional finger signs through Sutton. Malcolm Flatman designs and produces a large range of wheel-made microwave and dishwasher-safe stoneware, tableware and decorative items in a choice of glazes. Special "one-off" orders and commissions willingly undertaken. Visitors are welcome in the small workshop to see work in progress and purchase from a wide selection of finished pieces. Price list available by post. Website catalogue and order form. Full postal service. Cards welcome. Usually open Mon-Fri 0900-1800, throughout the year. Please telephone before a special journey, and weekend visits. Free admission. P T(15 mins)

Wroxham

Wroxham Barns Map ref. M5
Tunstead Road, Hoveton NR12 8QU
Tel: (01603) 783762 Web: www.wroxham-barns.co.uk
At the finest rural crafts centre in Norfolk, resident craftsmen bring traditional and contemporary skills to life and produce unique items. From paintings to pine furniture, from apple juice to stained glass, there is something for everyone. A stunning choice of gifts, cards, toys and clothing is available in our shops, together with a selection of tempting foods and homemade fudges. Our tearoom serves delicious cakes and lunches, and children will love Junior Farm and Wroxham Barns Children's Fair. Open daily from 1000-1700 (except Dec 25/26 and Jan 1). Admission is free. Junior Farm £2.65 per person, under 3's free. Fair seasonal - rides priced individually. Guide dogs welcome. Q P T(3 hrs)

Wroxham

Discovery Tours

Family Favourites

Three ideas to keep dad, mum and the children happy in North and West Norfolk.

Tour 1
Starting point: Fakenham, Norfolk Map ref. G4
Mileage: 14m/23km
Morning - take the A1067 to visit *Pensthorpe Nature Reserve and Gardens*, then retrace your steps to Fakenham and follow the A148 towards Cromer. After 4 miles, turn left (following signs) to the musical *Thursford Collection*.
Afternoon - return to the A148 and head to the pretty town of Holt. Jump aboard the *North Norfolk Railway* for a steam train ride to seaside *Sheringham*. Enjoy a walk along the prom with an ice cream!

Tour 2
Starting point: Wells-next-the-Sea, Norfolk Map ref. G2
Mileage: 18m/29km
Morning - explore the quaint fishing town of *Wells*, then take the little steam railway to the pretty pilgrimage centre of *Little Walsingham*.
Afternoon - return to Wells, and take the A149 west to the magnificent *Holkham Hall*. End the day by continuing along the A149 to Hunstanton, and enjoy a watery tour of the *Sea Life Sanctuary*.

Tour 3
Starting point: Cromer, Norfolk Map ref. K3
Mileage: 13m/21km (or 15m/24km with Langham Glass)
Morning - wander the streets of cliff-top *Cromer*, and enjoy a crab tea overlooking the famous pier.
Afternoon - leave Cromer on the A149 to Weybourne, where you can take a ride on the Gama Goat at *The Muckleburgh Collection*. Continue along the A149 to Blakeney, where there are two choices, either take a boat trip to see the seals on *Blakeney Point*. Or head south on the B1156 to the *Langham Glass* workshops.

DID YOU KNOW

Norwich has over 30 medieval churches, more than any other city in Western Europe. Just over 50 years ago, there was said to be a pub for every day of the year, and a church for every Sunday.

Grimes Graves, Lynford

Bloomin' Beautiful

Enjoy the spectacular colours and delicate fragrances of some of England's finest gardens.

Starting point: King's Lynn, Norfolk Map ref. C5/6
Mileage: 23m/37km
Morning - take the A17 to Terrington St. Clement, and visit the *African Violet Centre*. Then retrace your steps to King's Lynn and take the A149 north. After 6 miles, turn right onto the B1439 to *Sandringham*.
Afternoon - enjoy the Queen's favourite blooms. Then take the B1440 to Dersingham. At the T-junction in the village, turn right and follow the road to the A149. Join this north to Heacham, and the home of *Norfolk Lavender*.

Holkham Hall, Wells-next-the-Sea

From Dinosaurs to Dells

Discover the fauna and flora of the world - from the stone age to the present day.

Starting point: Norwich, Norfolk Map ref. K/L7
Mileage: 46m/74km
Morning - follow the A1067 for 8 miles to Morton, then turn left to Weston Longville, and meet T-Rex at *The Dinosaur Adventure Park*. Head south to reach the A47, where you turn left back towards Norwich. After 8 miles, join the A11 towards Thetford. 12 miles later (at Attleborough), turn left onto the B1077 to Cake Street, then turn right along an unclassified road to reach the exotic animals of *Banham Zoo*.
Afternoon - take the unclassified road south via North Lopham to the A1066. Turn left here to reach the world-renowned Dell Garden at the *Bressingham Steam Experience and Gardens*.

Things that go Bump in the Night

Let us send a shiver down your spine with all things spooky and strange!

Starting point: Norwich, Norfolk Map ref. K/L7
Mileage: varied (depending on tour taken)
Morning - wander Norwich's ancient streets and lanes, and visit the eerie dungeons of the *Castle Museum*.
Afternoon - take the A1151 to *Wroxham*, and enjoy a tour of the reed-fringed Norfolk Broads. Scare yourself silly with tales of black devil dogs and ghostly drummer-boys. End the day by leaving Wroxham on the B1354/A140 (via Aylsham) to 17th C. *Blickling Hall*, haunt of Anne Boleyn.

Strange Tales and Curiosities

Discover the flipside of the east, its customs, stories and local characters.

Starting point: Thetford, Norfolk Map ref. F/G11
Mileage: 42m/68km
Morning - head north on the A134. After 5 miles, turn left to explore the bat-infested flint mine at *Grimes Graves*. Continue on the A134/A1065 to *Swaffham*. Visit the church to see the memorial to the famous Pedlar.
Afternoon - take the B1077 to *Watton*, which is connected to the 'Babes in the Wood' story. Then follow the B1108 to *Hingham*, once home of Abraham Lincoln's descendants. Remain on the B1108/B1135 to *Wymondham*, where the abbey's twin towers came from an argument between the monks and townspeople.

The Village Experience, Fleggburgh

Seaside Special

Fun for all the family at one of Britain's most popular seaside resorts.

Starting point: Great Yarmouth, Norfolk Map ref. P7
Mileage: 7m/11km
Morning - start the day with a trip underwater at the *Sealife Centre*, and a ride on the rollercoaster at the *Pleasure Beach*. Before leaving, make a sandcastle on the beach, and enjoy a stroll along the prom.
Afternoon - head north along the A149/A1064 to either the giant crocodiles of *Thrigby Hall Wildlife Gardens* (Filby), or the steam engines and fairground rides at *The Village Experience* (Fleggburgh).

Saints and Sinners

Heavens above! - a tour of 'good versus evil', with naughty monks and devoted saints.

Starting point: King's Lynn, Norfolk Map ref. C5/6
Mileage: 32m/51km
Morning - discover Lynn's infamous murderers, highwaymen and witches at the *Tales of the Old Gaolhouse*. Then take the B1145 east for 16 miles, before turning right onto the A1065, to visit the 12th C. *Castle Acre Priory*. Here relics of godly saints once attracted pilgrims from all over Europe.
Afternoon - remain on the A1065 to Swaffham, then follow the unclassified road (via Cockley Cley) to Oxborough. Visit the 15th C. *Oxburgh Hall*, where you can peer into a Catholic priest's hole.

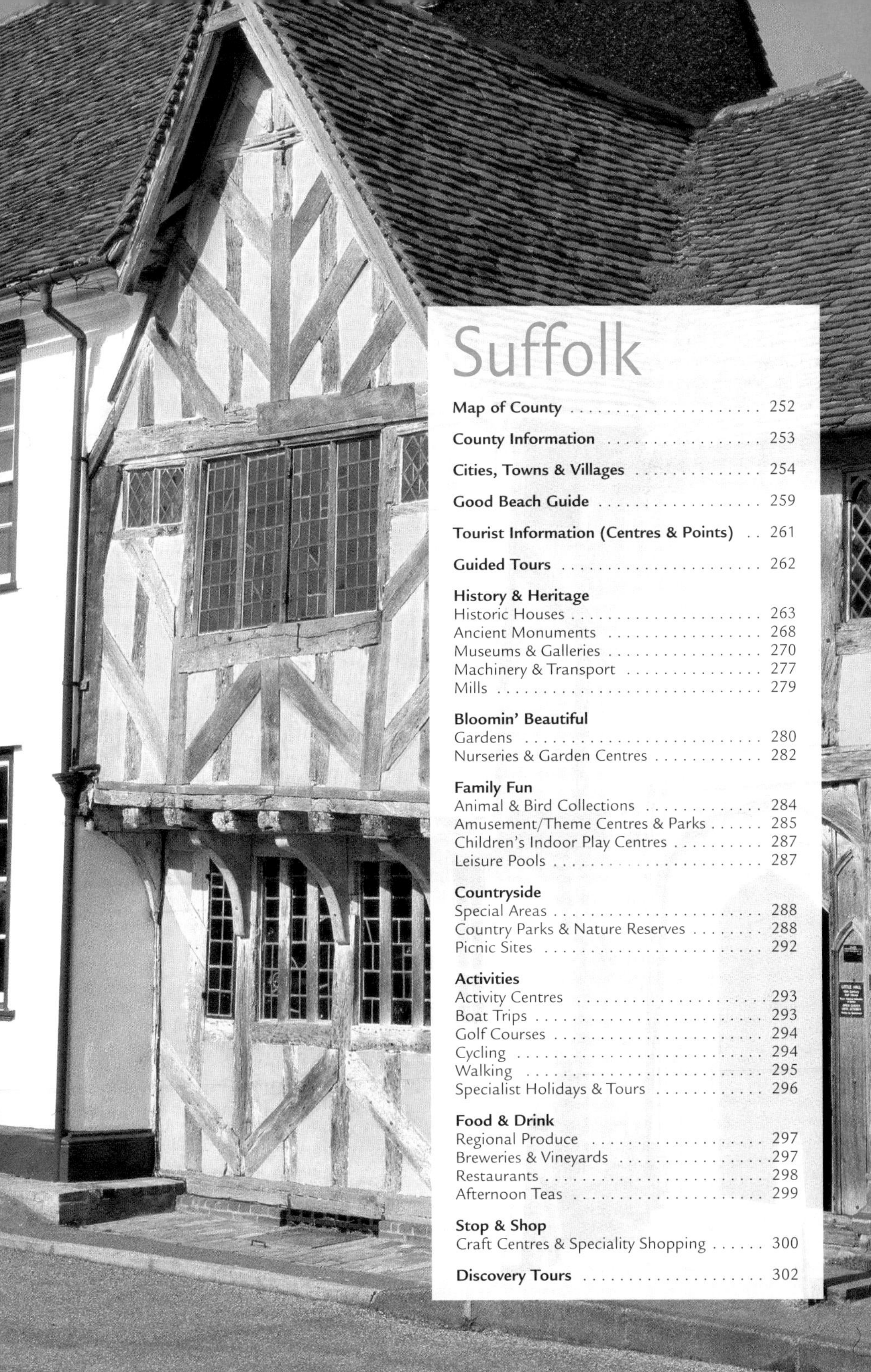

Suffolk

Map of County 252

County Information 253

Cities, Towns & Villages 254

Good Beach Guide 259

Tourist Information (Centres & Points) . . 261

Guided Tours 262

History & Heritage
Historic Houses 263
Ancient Monuments 268
Museums & Galleries 270
Machinery & Transport 277
Mills 279

Bloomin' Beautiful
Gardens 280
Nurseries & Garden Centres 282

Family Fun
Animal & Bird Collections 284
Amusement/Theme Centres & Parks 285
Children's Indoor Play Centres 287
Leisure Pools 287

Countryside
Special Areas 288
Country Parks & Nature Reserves 288
Picnic Sites 292

Activities
Activity Centres 293
Boat Trips 293
Golf Courses 294
Cycling 294
Walking 295
Specialist Holidays & Tours 296

Food & Drink
Regional Produce 297
Breweries & Vineyards 297
Restaurants 298
Afternoon Teas 299

Stop & Shop
Craft Centres & Speciality Shopping 300

Discovery Tours 302

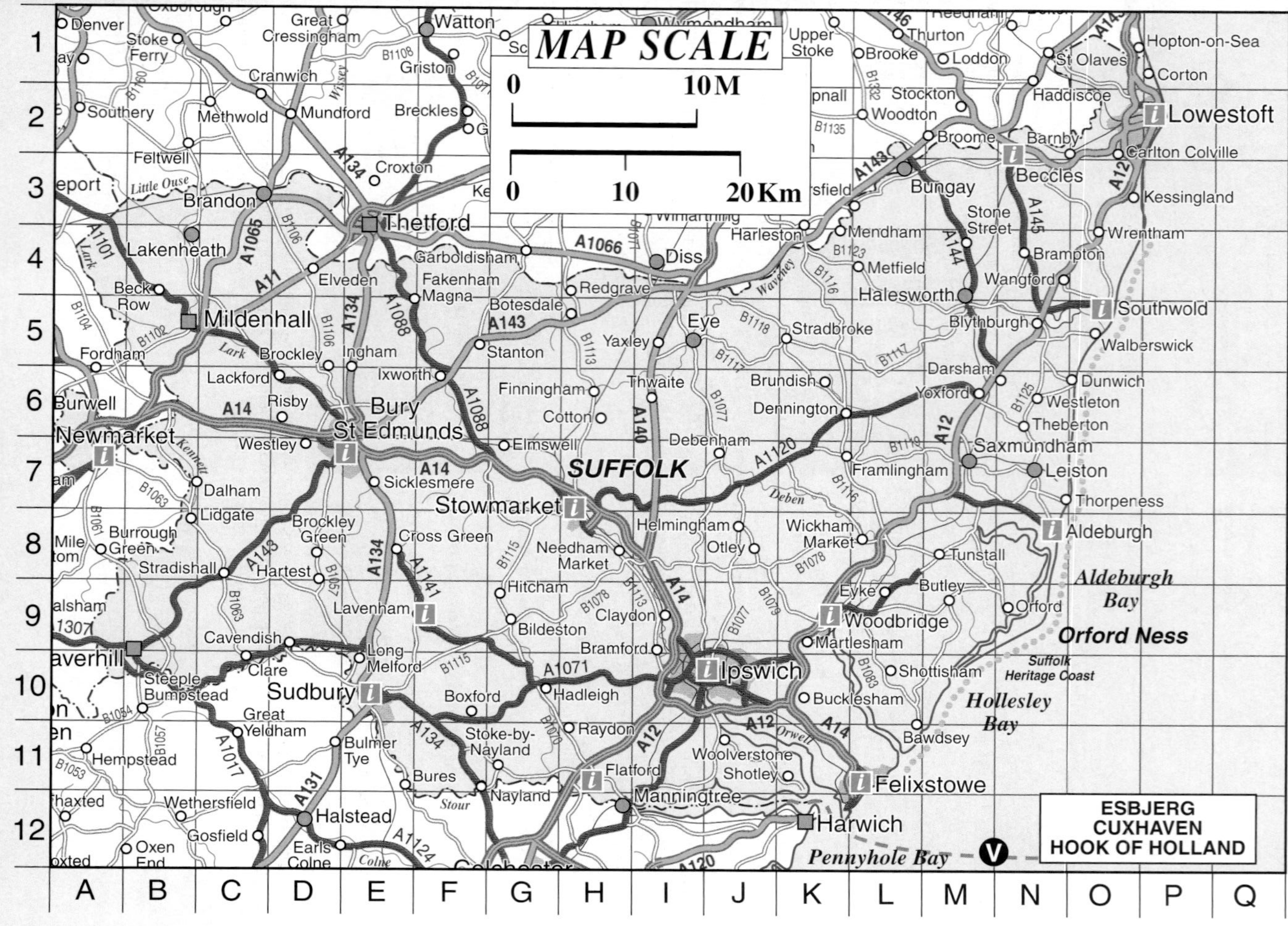
MAP SCALE
0
10M
0
10
20Km
SUFFOLK
Denver
Stoke Ferry
Southery
Feltwell
Methwold
Cranwich
Great Cressingham
Mundford
Watton
Griston
Breckles
Croxton
Brandon
Lakenheath
Thetford
Elveden
Beck Row
Mildenhall
Fordham
Burwell
Newmarket
Garboldisham
Fakenham Magna
Botesdale
Redgrave
Diss
Eye
Yaxley
Stanton
Ixworth
Ingham
Brockley
Lackford
Risby
Bury St Edmunds
Westley
Dalham
Lidgate
Burrough Green
Stradishall
Brockley Green
Hartest
Sicklesmere
Cross Green
Lavenham
Stowmarket
Elmswell
Finningham
Cotton
Thwaite
Debenham
Needham Market
Hitcham
Bildeston
Claydon
Bramford
Ipswich
Haverhill
Steeple Bumpstead
Cavendish
Clare
Long Melford
Sudbury
Great Yeldham
Hempstead
Bulmer Tye
Boxford
Hadleigh
Raydon
Stoke-by-Nayland
Bures
Nayland
Flatford
Manningtree
Halstead
Wethersfield
Gosfield
Oxen End
Earls Colne
Thaxted
Upper Stoke
Brooke
Thurton
Loddon
Stockton
Woodton
Broome
Bungay
Harleston
Mendham
Metfield
Stradbroke
Brundish
Dennington
Framlingham
Helmingham
Otley
Wickham Market
Woodbridge
Martlesham
Eyke
Butley
Tunstall
Orford
Shottisham
Bucklesham
Bawdsey
Woolverstone
Shotley
Felixstowe
Harwich
St Olaves
Haddiscoe
Hopton-on-Sea
Corton
Lowestoft
Barnby
Beccles
Carlton Colville
Kessingland
Wrentham
Stone Street
Brampton
Wangford
Halesworth
Southwold
Blythburgh
Walberswick
Darsham
Dunwich
Yoxford
Westleton
Theberton
Saxmundham
Leiston
Thorpeness
Aldeburgh
Aldeburgh Bay
Orford Ness
Suffolk Heritage Coast
Hollesley Bay
Pennyhole Bay
ESBJERG
CUXHAVEN
HOOK OF HOLLAND
Little Ouse
Lark
Waveney
Deben
Orwell
Stour
Colne
A11
A12
A14
A134
A143
A140
A144
A145
A1065
A1066
A1088
A1101
A1120
A1141
A1071
A1017
A131
A1124
A120
1
2
3
4
5
6
7
8
9
10
11
12
A
B
C
D
E
F
G
H
I
J
K
L
M
N
O
P
Q

Suffolk

County Town: Ipswich.
Population: 669,400 approx.
Highest Point: Rede 128m (420 feet).
Rivers: Alde, Blyth, Brett, Deben, Dove, Gipping, Glem, Lark, Little Ouse, Orwell, Stour, Waveney, Yox.
Landmarks: 'Constable Country', Lowestoft Ness (the most easterly point in England), Newmarket, Orford Ness, Port of Felixstowe, RAF Mildenhall, RSPB Minsmere Nature Reserve, St. Edmundsbury Cathedral (Bury St. Edmunds), Sizewell Power Station, Thetford Forest Park.

Welcome to Suffolk:

The market town of Bury St. Edmunds is noted for its abbey ruins and Britain's smallest pub. To the west is the horseracing capital of the world, Newmarket. To the east 'Constable Country', where the famous artist was inspired. Don't miss the Suffolk Wool Towns, with their timber-framed buildings and magnificent churches, or the many pastel-washed villages of the county. Ipswich dates back to Saxon times, and has a rich maritime heritage. While along the unspoilt coastline discover the seaside town of Lowestoft, or sleepy Southwold and Aldeburgh.

Industry Past & Present:

Suffolk has always been an *agricultural* county, growing rich from its variety of crops and produce. Wind and water mills dot the landscape, once busy with *corn grinding*. The Middle Ages saw the start of the prosperous *cloth/wool* trade, eventually making Suffolk one of the country's most important industrial districts home to skilled weavers and spinners. This reached its height in the late 15th C. when beautiful churches and timber-framed buildings were built. Later came other textile industries - *hemp*, *straw-plaiting* and the *weaving of coconut fibres* and *horsehair*. Then in the 19th C. *silk weaving* factories were opened in South Suffolk, and today there are still companies in Glemsford and Sudbury. *Flint* has also played a major part in the county's past - extracted from mines since neolithic times, and used for tools and building. Brandon was the last British home of the *gun flint* industry. On the coast, the rich pickings of the sea saw busy ports appear at Aldeburgh, Orford and Southwold, but today only a handful of boats remain. Lowestoft, once one of the UK's major *fishing* (herring) centres, is now noted for North Sea *gas/oil production*. Another local industry here in the 18th C. was the making of *porcelain* (which has recently been recreated). To the south is the imposing Sizewell Power Station, and the Port of Felixstowe, the UK's largest container terminal. Ipswich, a port since the 6/7th C. is home to *administration, financial* and *hi-tech companies*, such as the BT research laboratories. This centre has the greatest concentration of IT scientists in Europe and is where Britain's first microchips were made. While to the west of the county is Newmarket, world-famous centre for the *racing, breeding, sale* and *training of horses*. There are also three famous Suffolk brewers, Adnams, Greene King and St. Peter's. Famous names of the county include - Birds Eye Walls, Haywards Pickles, William Clowes (printing) and Wisdom (toothbrushes).

Famous People:

Elizabeth Garrett Anderson *(England's first woman doctor)*, Robert Bloomfield *(poet)*, Benjamin Britten *(composer)*, Lord Byron *(poet)*, Thomas Cavendish *(second Englishman to sail around world)*, John Constable *(artist)*, Edward Fitzgerald *(author)*, George Crabbe *(poet)*, Charles Dickens *(author)*, King Edmund, Thomas Gainsborough *(artist)*, Rider Haggard *(author)*, M.R. James *(author)*, P.D. James *(author)*, Maria Marten and William Corder *(Red Barn Murder)*, Alfred Munnings *(artist)*, George Orwell *(author)*, Beatrix Potter *(author)*, Arthur Ransome *(author)*, Ruth Rendell *(author)*, Thomas Seckford *(benefactor)*, The Taylor Sisters *(authors)*, Robert Watson-Watt *(inventor of radar)*, Cardinal Wolsey *(Chancellor of England)*.

Dunwich

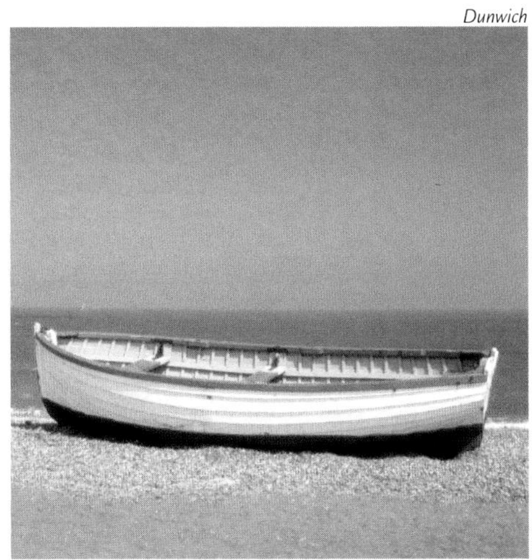

CITIES, TOWNS & VILLAGES

Cities, Towns & Villages

MD: Market Day
FM: Farmers' Market
EC: Early Closing
i Tourist Information Centre (see page 261)
Guided Tours (see page 262)

Aldeburgh Map ref. N8
Charming and sedate seaside town, which grew from an old medieval fishing and shipbuilding centre. The wide High Street has attractive Georgian shop-fronts. Historic buildings include the Moot Hall (c.1520) and the 15th C. church. Fishermen still pull their boats onto the steep shingle beach, and sell their catch each morning. The famous music festival is held in June. **EC**: Wed. i

Beccles Map ref. N2/3
Set on the River Waveney, this fine market town was once a flourishing Saxon seaport. Red-brick Georgian houses and unusual 18th C. octagonal town hall. The magnificent 14th C. church has a detached bell tower. Long gardens run down to the river, now a major boating centre for the Broads. Nearby Roos Hall is one of England's most haunted houses. **MD**: Fri. **FM**: at nearby Barsham, last Sat in month. Also Beccles Heliport, 1st and 3rd Sat in month. **EC**: Wed. i

Bildeston Map ref. G9
Large village, which in 1520 was an important centre for 'blue cloth'. The pleasant square is surrounded by colour-washed buildings and a fine Georgian brick house. At its centre is the Victorian clock tower built in 1864. The Crown Hotel is renowned for its ghosts.

Brandon Map ref. C3
Small town, set beside the Little Ouse River and surrounded by forest and heathland. Brandon stands on flint, is largely built from flint, and was for long the home of England's oldest industry, flint knapping. This provided decorative building materials and also gunflints for firearms. Heritage Centre and country park. **MD**: Thurs and Sat. **FM**: at nearby Elveden, last Sat in month. **EC**: Wed.

Bungay Map ref. L3
Unspoilt market town, set beside a loop of the River Waveney. The Norman castle was rebuilt by the ruthless Bigod Family, but by the 14th C. it was in ruins. After a great fire in 1688, Bungay rebuilt itself as a Georgian town with red-brick facades and Dutch gables. The Butter Cross was built in 1689, while the church tower is noted for its four pinnacles. **MD**: Thurs. **EC**: Wed.

Bury St. Edmunds Map ref. D/E6/7
Named after St. Edmund (the Saxon King of East Anglia), this ancient market town has played an important part in English history. For it was here in 1214, that the barons of England vowed to extract from King John the concessions set out in the 'Magna Carta'. The ruins of the 12th C. abbey (once one of the most powerful in Europe) are overlooked by the cathedral's new gothic tower (opening in 2004). Bury is also noted for its award-winning gardens, Georgian theatre, and the smallest pub in Britain 'The Nutshell'. **MD**: Wed and Sat. i

Clare Map ref. C10
Delightful small town, with colour-washed and timber-framed buildings, many decorated with pargetting. The 13th C. church is linked to the medieval family who founded Clare College in Cambridge. While the country park is dominated by the 100ft high motte of the former Norman castle. Close by is the 13th C. priory, the first Augustinian house in England. **MD**: Mon and Sat. **EC**: Wed.

CITIES, TOWNS & VILLAGES

Debenham Map ref. J7
A former court of East Anglia's Saxon kings, this attractive small town is set near the source of the River Deben. Once a thriving wool centre, many historic buildings (14-17th C.) line the High Street, including old merchants' houses. World-famous teapot pottery.

Eye Map ref. I5
Retaining the peaceful atmosphere and character of a small 18th C. agricultural market town, Eye sits in the heart of the Suffolk countryside. The first definite evidence of a settlement dates from Roman times. The Norman castle mound, which dates back to 1156, affords panoramic views of the town. The west tower of the 15th C. church is one of the best in the county. **EC**: Tues.

Felixstowe Map ref. L11/12
Edwardian resort, retaining much of its original charm, with beautiful south-facing gardens, paved promenade, leisure centre, pier and theatre. Its popularity began with the arrival of the railway in 1887, and a visit in 1891 by the Empress of Germany. The docks, Britain's leading cargo and container port, were developed on marshland in 1886. **MD**: Thurs and Sun. **FM**: 1st Sat in month. **EC**: Wed. i

Framlingham Map ref. K/L7
Ancient market town, which has been a major power in royal fortunes, and once held an important agricultural market. The triangular-shaped market place is bordered by attractive buildings. Framlingham is noted for its well-preserved 12th C. castle, built by the Bigod Family (Earls of Norfolk), and the church with its magnificent tombs and effigies. **MD**: Sat. **EC**: Wed.

Hadleigh Map ref. G10
Once a Viking Royal town, Hadleigh prospered through its wool and cloth trade in the 14th and 15th C. It is the reputed burial place of the Danish King Guthrum. The long High Street is lined with fine timber and plasterwork buildings, some with pargetting. St. Mary's Church with its tall spire is bordered by the 15th C. Guildhall and red-brick Deanery Tower. **MD**: Fri and Sat. **EC**: Wed.

Halesworth Map ref. M4
Nestled in a curve of the River Blyth, Halesworth was a major centre for malting and brewing in the 19th C. There are many fine buildings, including the carved Gothic House, a Tudor Rectory and Elizabethan almshouses. St. Mary's Church has an unusual 18th C. altar, and a memorial to a local father and son who both became directors of Kew Gardens in London. **MD**: Wed. **EC**: Thurs.

Haverhill Map ref. B9/10
Sitting beside an old Roman road, Haverhill's market dates from 1222. Fire destroyed many of the town's older buildings in 1665, although Anne of Cleves' House - reputedly built by Henry VIII in 1540, as his marriage settlement to her - has been restored. Good examples of Victorian architecture. **MD**: Fri and Sat. **EC**: Wed.

Ipswich

Ipswich Map ref. I/J10
Dating back to Saxon times, Ipswich is one of England's oldest towns. Its streets are lined with historic buildings, such as the Ancient House, renowned for its plasterwork. Twelve medieval churches stand testimony to the importance of the town as it developed in the Middle Ages. Close by is 16th C. Christchurch Mansion, which stands in a beautiful landscaped park. Ipswich has a rich maritime heritage, its port founded in the 6/7th C. Visit the redeveloped waterfront with its marina, restaurants and bars. **MD**: Tues, Fri and Sat. **FM**: at nearby Harkstead, 3rd Sat in month.

Lavenham Map ref. E/F9
England's best-preserved medieval town. From the 14-16th C. it was a major wool and cloth-making centre. The wealth generated has left a beautiful legacy of timber-framed houses set along narrow streets and lanes, such as the Guildhall and Swan Hotel. The 13th C. church is noted for its magnificent 141 feet high tower. Numerous gift, craft and tea shops. **EC**: Wed.

Leiston Map ref. N7
Small, mainly modern town, whose prosperity grew in the 19th C. with the success of the Garrett engineering firm. They pioneered steam power in the area, building traction engines and road rollers. The parish church retains its medieval tower, and an unusual 13th C. hexagonal font. Close by are the romantic ruins of 14th C. Leiston Abbey. **MD**: Fri. **EC**: Wed.

Long Melford Map ref. E10
This former wool town is now the 'Antiques Capital of Suffolk'. Its wide, tree-lined High Street is full of antique shops and centres. At one end of the village is the large green, dominated by Melford Hall (c.1550s) and the magnificent 15th C. church, built of carved stone and flint. Just beyond the church is moated Kentwell Hall, renowned for its annual recreations of Tudor life. **FM**: 3rd Sat in month. **EC**: Wed.

Aldeburgh

Bury St. Edmunds

Lowestoft Map ref. P2
Attractive seaside resort at Britain's most easterly point (Lowestoft Ness). It has one of Britain's best sandy beaches, backed by a long promenade. Once a flourishing fishing port, visitors can see the yacht harbour and neighbouring docks, with its small fleet of trawlers. Impressive, glass Edwardian-style pavilion and pedestrianised shopping centre. **MD**: Tues, Fri and Sat. **EC**: Thurs.

Mildenhall Map ref. B5
Busy town, with a timbered 16th C. market cross and pump. The north porch of the 13th C. church is the largest in Suffolk. Mildenhall will be forever associated with a rich treasure of 4th C. Roman silverware which was unearthed in the area in 1942 (it is now in the British Museum). Close by is the large USAF air base (RAF Mildenhall). **MD**: Fri. **EC**: Wed.

Needham Market Map ref. H8
A small town set in the Gipping Valley. The High Street has many historic buildings, including a 17th C. Grammar School, the Friends' Meeting House and numerous Georgian houses. The 15th C. church possesses one of the most superb hammerbeam roofs in England. Nearby Needham Lake offers walks, fishing and picnic sites. **FM**: at nearby Alder Carr Farm, 3rd Sat in month. **EC**: Tues.

Newmarket Map ref. A7
Associated with horses and royalty since Queen Boadicea's day, this is the only place in the world where every aspect of the horseracing industry is in evidence. Over 35 race days a year, two racecourses, The National Horseracing Museum, the heathland "gallops", training yards, studs, a horse hospital and Tattersall's sales rooms. **MD**: Tues and Sat. **EC**: Wed.

CITIES, TOWNS & VILLAGES

Orford Map ref. N9
Steeped in history, this attractive small town is overlooked by its 12th C. castle keep built by Henry VII for coastal defence. From the top, there are panoramic views over the town and marshes. Brick and timber buildings line the streets to the little quayside, where there are boat trips to the mysterious Orfordness (a shingle spit). The town is noted for its oysters.

Oulton Broad Map ref. O2
Forming the southern gateway to The Broads, this is one of the finest stretches of inland water in England. A haven for lovers of watersports, Oulton Broad is perfect for sailing, rowing or taking it easy on a modern cruiser. The Nicholas Everitt Park has bandstand concerts and children's play areas. Regular sailing regattas and motorboat racing events. **EC**: Wed.

Saxmundham Map ref. M7
Small town dating from Saxon times, its market granted in 1272. Later it became a popular coaching stop. The 19th C. town hall displays the arms of the Longs family, who lived at nearby Hurts Hall, a Jacobean mansion. The church has a fine hammerbeam roof. **MD**: Wed. **EC**: Thurs.

Southwold Map ref. O5
This charming town used to be renowned for its herring fishery. St. Edmund's Church is noted for its 15th C. pulpit. Nearby is another landmark, the white lighthouse built in 1890. Nine open greens are surrounded by period houses and fisherman's cottages. Picturesque harbour, colourful beach huts, specialist shops and real ale from the town's own brewery. **MD**: Mon and Thurs. **EC**: Wed. i

Stoke by Nayland Map ref. G11
Sitting on a ridge between the Stour and Box valleys, this village is dominated by its magnificent 15th C. flint/mortar church. The 120 feet high tower is shown in many of John Constable's landscapes. Timber-framed buildings, including 16th C. Guildhall.

Stowmarket Map ref. H7/8
At the centre of Suffolk, this bustling market town is set in the Gipping Valley. Its medieval heart lay around the parish church, and the area leading down to the river. The industrial growth of the town began in 1793 with the opening of the canal to Ipswich. Today Stowmarket is a popular shopping centre and home of the Museum of East Anglian Life. **MD**: Thurs and Sat. **EC**: Tues. i

Sudbury Map ref. E10
Set on the River Stour, this ancient market town is surrounded by water meadows. Mentioned in the Domesday Survey of 1086, Sudbury has thrived on the textile industry, firstly with wool, then silk. The famous artist Thomas Gainsborough was born here in 1727, and his statue stands on the Market Place, overlooked by the 15th C. church. **MD**: Thurs and Sat. **EC**: Wed. i

Thorpeness Map ref. N7
Former holiday village which was created from 1910 by Stuart Oglivie. It was designed to provide self-catering holidays to families -no day-trippers allowed! Disguised water tower (House in the Clouds), post-mill and freshwater boating lake (The Meare).

Lowestoft

Walberswick Map ref. O5
Attractive seaside village at the mouth of the River Blyth. In the early 20th C. it attracted many artists. Tarred wooden huts overlook the river, while pebble, brick and flint houses surround the pretty green. It is best known for its annual crabbing contest.

Wickham Market Map ref. L8
Bypassed by the busy A12, this quiet town has a little square, which was granted a market by Henry VI in about 1440. Georgian and timber-framed buildings. All Saints' Church mainly dates from 1299, but was extensively restored in the 19th C. **FM**: at nearby Easton Farm Park, 4th Sat in month. **EC**: Wed.

Woodbridge Map ref. K9
Set on the River Deben, this attractive market town was once a port, noted for its shipbuilding and sail-making industries. Narrow streets hide many historic buildings, including fine examples of Georgian architecture. On the quayside is the famous Tide Mill, and on the opposite bank of the river, Sutton Hoo, the burial site of Anglo-Saxon kings. **MD**: Thurs. **FM**: 2nd Sat in month. **EC**: Wed.

Thorpeness

Pick of the villages

1 **Blythburgh** - overlooks Blyth estuary. Magnificent 15th C. church with tales of Black Shuck. Map ref. N5
2 **Boxford** - former cloth-making centre, set in the valley of the River Box. Attractive buildings. Map ref. F10
3 **Cavendish** - picture postcard village, with green, almshouses and church. Map ref. D9
4 **Chelsworth** - pretty houses and 18th C. humpbacked bridge. Annual gardens open day. Map ref. G9
5 **Covehithe** - tiny hamlet, severely eroded by the sea. Unusual 'church within a church'. Map ref. O4
6 **Dalham** - set beside River Kennett. Thatched/plastered cottages and little footbridges. Map ref. B7
7 **Dunwich** - former capital of East Anglia, but after centuries of coastal erosion, now just a village. Map ref. O6
8 **East Bergholt** - birthplace of artist John Constable. Unusual wooden bell cage. Map ref. H11
9 **Easton** - estate village, noted for its pretty cottages and crinkle-crankle wall. Map ref. K8
10 **Elveden** - 19th C. hall was former home of the last Maharajah of Punjab, Duleep Singh. Map ref. D4
11 **Euston** - estate village, seat of the Dukes of Grafton. Thatched and flint houses. Map ref. E4
12 **Felixstowe Ferry** - hamlet on River Deben. Weather-boarded houses and fish for sale. Map ref. L11
13 **Haughley** - green and castle remains. The post office is one of the earliest recorded in the UK. Map ref. G7
14 **Hoxne** - bridge where King Edmund met his death at the hands of the Vikings (c.870). Map ref. J5
15 **Ixworth** - attractive main street with ancient buildings and listed petrol pumps. Map ref. F6
16 **Kersey** - one of the prettiest villages in England. Lovely ford with ducks. Map ref. G10
17 **Lakenheath** - large village of flint, brick and chalk. Church has carved 15th C. bench-ends. Map ref. B4
18 **Moulton** - pretty village beside River Kennett, with 15th C. packhorse bridge. Map ref. B7
19 **Nayland** - narrow streets, 16th C. Guildhall and milestone obelisk. Map ref. F11
20 **Pakenham** - last parish in England with working water mill and windmill. Map ref. F6
21 **Peasenhall** - main street with little watercourse and colour-washed houses. Map ref. L6
22 **Pin Mill** - tiny riverside hamlet with quay. Connections to author Arthur Ransome. Map ref. J11
23 **Polstead** - noted for its cherries and notorious Victorian 'Red Barn Murder'. Map ref. G11
24 **Santon Downham** - set in Thetford Forest. Built on shifting sands. Norman church. Map ref. D3
25 **Somerleyton** - Victorian estate village, with cottages grouped around a wide green. Map ref. O1
26 **Thornham Magna** - seat of Lord Henniker. Old houses and parkland with walks. Map ref. I5
27 **Ufford** - set amongst water meadows. Whipping post/stocks. Amazing church font cover. Map ref. L8
28 **Walsham Le Willows** - main street with little stream. Weather-boarded/timbered houses. Map ref. G5
29 **Woolpit** - Georgian brick and Tudor-style houses, covered pump and splendid church. Map ref. F7
30 **Yoxford** - former coaching centre. Variety of architecture styles. Cast-iron signpost. Map ref. M6

Good Beach Guide

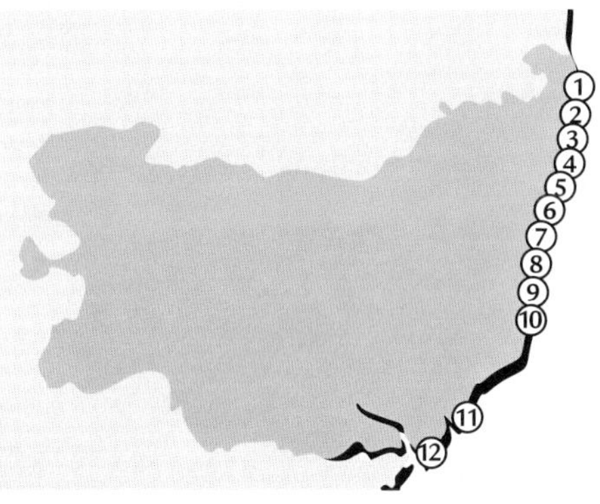

Key

TIC: Tourist Information Centre (see page 261)

TIP: Tourist Information Point (see page 261)

Dog ban: 1 May-30 September, dogs banned from the main beach areas. Further details from the nearest TIC.

Good Beach Guide 2004
The Good Beach Guide is the ultimate independent guide to UK beaches. By checking the water quality grade and the level of sewage treatment - you can choose a safe beach to visit this summer. The guide is available from the Marine Conservation Society from May 2004.
Tel: (01989) 566017 or visit www.goodbeachguide.co.uk

1 Corton
Sand and shingle beach, with southern area available to naturists. Car parking in official car park. Seasonal dog ban.

2 Lowestoft
South of Claremont Pier beach, winner of the Blue Flag Campaign and ENCAMS Seaside Award (Resort Beach Category). Amusements. The East Point Pavilion is an indoor visitor centre with a TIC. North of Claremont Pier beach (sandy), also winner of the Blue Flag Campaign and ENCAMS Seaside Award. Gunton Denes (dunes).

3 Pakefield
Sandy beach scattered with shingle below low grassy cliffs. Car parking. Toilets. Seasonal dog ban.

4 Kessingland
Easy access to pebble and shingle beach with some sand. Low cliffs. Winner of ENCAMS Seaside Award (Rural Beach category). Seasonal dog ban.

5 Southwold
Part sand, part shingle beach depending upon tides, with some dunes for sheltered picnics. Uncommercialised, but pots of tea are available on the beach. Recently refurbished full length pier, with restaurant, bar, amusements and gift shop. Winner of the Pier of the Year 2002. Deck-chairs and beach huts. Parking. Toilets. TIC. Winner of Blue Flag Campaign and ENCAMS Seaside Award (Resort Beach category). Seasonal dog ban.

6 Walberswick
Approached over The Flats, the beach is sand and shingle with sand dunes. It becomes steeper with more shingle to the south and pebbles. Popular with painters and birdwatchers. Stall selling fish on beach. Limited car parking. Toilets.

Felixstowe

7 Dunwich
Short walk to shelving sand and shingle beach. High eroding cliffs should be avoided. Marsh, dunes and more sand to the north. Nature reserve at nearby Dunwich Heath. Car parking. Toilets.

8 Sizewell
Quiet rural beach with long shelving shingle beach. Dunes with a wide variety of flora and fauna, recently re-established. Winner of the ENCAMS Seaside Award (Rural Beach category). Fishing boats hauled onto beach. Toilets. Ample car parking. Tearoom.

9 Thorpeness
Steeply shelving shingle beach with some sand at low tide. Dunes and low cliffs starting to the north. Winner of the ENCAMS Seaside Award (Rural Beach category). Car parking (limited). Toilets.

10 Aldeburgh
Quiet unspoilt resort. Long steeply shelving shingle beach with groynes. Winner of the ENCAMS Seaside Award (Rural Beach category). Lifeboat. Fishing boats hauled up onto the beach, with stalls selling fresh fish daily. Car parking. Toilets. Dog ban. TIC.

11 Shingle Street
As its name suggests, a steep shingle beach particularly good for bracing walks and beachcombing (sometimes you can find amber). Popular for offshore fishing. Very limited roadside parking.

12 Felixstowe
Shelving sand and shingle beach with little tidal movement. Some groynes down to pebbles and sand. Low cliffs to the north. Winner of two ENCAMS Seaside Awards (both Resort and Rural categories for two separate beaches) and also the European Blue Flag for the resort beach. Beach huts for hire. Car parking. Two-mile long promenade with seafront gardens and public seating. Toilets. Dog ban. TIC.

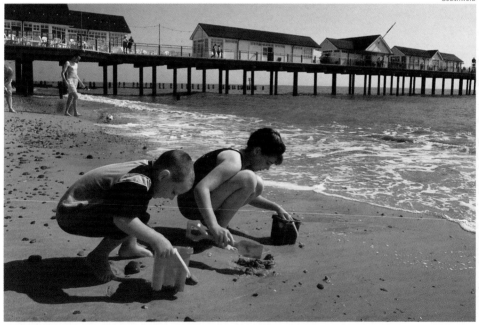

Southwold

 TOURIST INFORMATION

Tourist Information

Tourist Information Centres

With so much to see and do in this area, it's impossible for us to mention all of the places you can visit. You will find Tourist Information Centres (TICs) throughout Suffolk, with plenty of information on all the things that you can do and places you can visit.

TICs can book accommodation for you, in their own area, or further afield using the 'Book A Bed Ahead' Scheme. They can also be the ideal place to purchase locally made crafts or gifts, as well as books covering a wide range of local interests.

* Not open all year.

Aldeburgh, 152 High Street.
Tel: (01728) 453637 Email: aldeburgh@eetb.info
Web: www.suffolkcoastal.gov.uk

Beccles *, The Quay, Fen Lane.
Tel: (01502) 713196 Email: beccles@eetb.info
Web: www.broads-authority.gov.uk

Bury St. Edmunds, 6 Angel Hill.
Tel: (01284) 764667 Email: burystedmunds@eetb.info
Web: www.stedmundsbury.gov.uk

Felixstowe, 91 Undercliff Road West.
Tel: (01394) 276770
Email: felixstowe@eetb.info
Web: www.suffolkcoastal.gov.uk

Flatford *, Flatford Lane.
Tel: (01206) 299460 Email: flatford@eetb.info
Web: www.visit-suffolk.org.uk

Ipswich, St. Stephens Church, St. Stephens Lane.
Tel: (01473) 258070
Email: ipswich@eetb.info Web: www.ipswich.gov.uk

Lavenham *, Lady Street.
Tel: (01787) 248207 Email: lavenham@eetb.info
Web: www.visit-suffolk.org.uk

Lowestoft, East Point Pavilion, Royal Plain.
Tel: (01502) 533600 Email: lowestoft@eetb.info
Web: www.visit-lowestoft.co.uk

Mid Suffolk, Wilkes Way, Stowmarket.
Tel: (01449) 676800 Email: stowmarket@eetb.info
Web: www.visit-suffolk.org.uk

Newmarket, Palace House, Palace Street.
Tel: (01638) 667200 Email: newmarket@eetb.info
Web: www.forest-heath.gov.uk

Southwold, 69 High Street.
Tel: (01502) 724729 Email: southwold@eetb.info
Web: www.visit-lowestoft.co.uk

Sudbury, Town Hall, Market Hill.
Tel: (01787) 881320 Email: sudbury@eetb.info
Web: www.visit-suffolk.org.uk

Woodbridge, Station Buildings.
Tel: (01394) 382240 Email: woodbridge@eetb.info
Web: www.suffolkcoastal.gov.uk

Tourist Information Points

Limited information is also available from the following information points.

* Not open all year.

Brandon, 31 High Street. Tel: (01842) 814955

Hadleigh, The Library, High Street.
Tel: (01473) 823778

Haverhill, The Library, Camps Road.
Tel: (01440) 703971
Email: haverhill.library@libher.suffolkcc.gov.uk

Mildenhall *, Mildenhall Museum, 6 King Street.
Tel: (01638) 715484

Ipswich Tourist Information Centre

Guided Tours

Why not enjoy a guided tour exploring one of the area's towns and cities? Some of these tours (indicated with a *) are conducted by Registered Blue Badge Guides, who have attended a training course sponsored by the East of England Tourist Board. Many of these guides also have a further qualification to take individuals around the region for half day, full day or longer tours if required. For more information on the guided tours listed, please telephone the relevant contact.

Bury St. Edmunds *

- **Regular town tours:** lasting 1 1/2 hours, depart from the Tourist Information Centre. Tickets can be purchased in advance, or on the day. Tours run daily in the summer, including Sat at 1430. Also available are themed walks on summer evenings.
- **Group tours:** guides can be arranged for groups at any time if enough notice is given. Special themes also available.
- For further information (including comprehensive leaflet) contact the Tourist Information Centre on (01284) 764667.

Ipswich *

- **Regular town tours:** individuals may join the tours (lasting approximately 1 1/2 hours) departing from the Tourist Information Centre - May-Sept on Tues and Thurs at 1415.
- **Group tours:** can be arranged for groups anytime all year around.
- For further information contact the Tourist Information Centre on (01473) 258070.

Lavenham *

- **Regular town tours:** weekend walks (with Blue Badge Guides) running from end Mar-end Oct, Sat at 1430 and Sun at 1100 and 1430. Tickets can be purchased in advance or on the day. Tours last approximately 1 1/4 hours, departing from the Tourist Information Centre.
- **Group tours:** can be arranged for groups - contact for details.
- For further information contact the Tourist Information Centre on (01787) 248207.

Lowestoft

- **Regular town tours:** lasting 2 hours, depart from the Town Hall. Tours feature historic tales and ghost stories, and run every Tues and Thurs from Apr-Oct at 1930.
- **Group tours:** can be arranged for groups - contact for details.
- For further information contact the Tourist Information Centre on (01502) 533600.

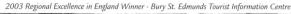

2003 Regional Excellence in England Winner - Bury St. Edmunds Tourist Information Centre

Historic Houses

Bury St. Edmunds
Theatre Royal Map ref. D/E6/7
See entry in Museums & Galleries section.

Flatford (nr. East Bergholt)
Bridge Cottage Map ref. H12
Tel: (01206) 298260 Web: www.nationaltrust.org.uk
A 16th C. thatched cottage, just upstream from Flatford Mill, and housing an exhibition on landscape painter John Constable. Tearoom, shop, information centre and guided walks.
Times: Open Jan and Feb, Sat and Sun, 1100-1530. Mar and Apr, Wed-Sun, 1100-1730. May-Sept, daily, 1000-1730. Oct, daily, 1100-1630. Nov and Dec, Wed-Sun, 1100-1530.
Fee: Free.
Facilities: T(1½ hrs) NT

Hadleigh
Guildhall Map ref. G10
Market Place
Tel: (01473) 823884
Large medieval timber-framed complex, Grade I Listed (with a Victorian addition) dating from the 15th C.
Times: Open 13 Jun-26 Sept, tours on Thurs and Sun, 1400-1700. Cream teas in the garden, Sun-Fri, 1430-1700.
Fee: Free. Donations appreciated.
Facilities: T(45 mins)

DID YOU KNOW

Bawdsey Manor (nr. Felixstowe) is the birthplace of radar. It was developed here in the 1930's by Sir Robert Alexander Watson-Watt.

Haughley (nr. Stowmarket)
Haughley Park Map ref. G7
Tel: (01359) 240701 Web: www.haughleyparkbarn.co.uk
Imposing redbrick Jacobean manor house (1620), set in gardens, park and woodland. Walled kitchen garden, three woodland walks and 17th C. barn.
Times: Gardens and woods open 25 Apr and 2 May for bluebells, Sun, 1400-1730. 4 May-28 Sept, Tues, 1400-1730. House by appointment only.
Fee: Gardens £3.00. House £2.00.
Facilities: T(1½ hrs) (on leads)

Hengrave (nr. Bury St. Edmunds)
Hengrave Hall Map ref. D6
Tel: (01284) 701561 Web: www.hengravehallcentre.org.uk
Hengrave Hall stands in 44 acres, with a lake, varied gardens and parkland. This unique Tudor house is renowned for its Oriel above the gatehouse and stained glass window.
Times: Open by appointment only, please contact for details.
Fee: £5.80/£2.00/£2.00.
Facilities: T(1½ hrs)

Horringer (nr. Bury St. Edmunds)
Ickworth House, Park and Gardens Map ref. D7
Tel: (01284) 735270 Web: www.nationaltrust.org.uk
An extraordinary oval house with flanking wings, begun in 1795. Fine paintings, a beautiful collection of Georgian silver, an Italian garden and stunning parkland. Waymarked woodland walks and vineyard.
Times: Park open all year, daily, 0700-1900. Gardens open 2 Jan-22 Mar, daily, 1000-1600; 23 Mar-31 Oct, daily, 1000-1700; 1 Nov-22 Dec, Mon-Fri, 1000-1600. House open 19 Mar-30 Sept, Fri-Tues, 1300-1700; 1-31 Oct, Fri-Tues, 1300-1630.
Fee: House, park and gardens £6.40/£2.90. Park and gardens £2.95/85p.
Facilities: T(3 hrs) (on leads) NT

Ipswich
Christchurch Mansion Map ref. I/J10
See entry in Museums & Galleries section.

Ipswich

The Ipswich Unitarian Meeting House Map ref. I/J10
Friars Street
Tel: (01473) 218217 Web: www.unitarianipswich.org.uk
A Grade I Listed building, built 1699 (opened in 1700). One of the finest surviving meeting houses, and one of the most important historic structures in Ipswich.
Times: Open 1 May-30 Sept, Tues and Thurs, 1200-1600; Sat, 1000-1600. Closed Easter and Christmas except services.
Fee: Free.
Facilities: T(30 mins)

Ipswich

Pykenham Gatehouse Map ref. I/J10
Northgate Street
Tel: (01473) 255591
15th C. Grade II* timber framed gatehouse to the former residence of Archdeacon Pykenham. Major restoration in 1982/3. Displays on the work of the Ipswich Building Preservation Trust.
Times: Open 1 May, 5 Jun, 3 Jul, 7 Aug, 4 Sept, 2 Oct, Sat, 1030-1230.
Fee: Free.
Facilities: T(30 mins)

Melford Hall, Long Melford

Lavenham

Lavenham Guildhall of Corpus Christi Map ref. E/F9
Market Place
Tel: (01787) 247646 Web: www.nationaltrust.org.uk
Impressive timber-framed building dating from 1530. Originally the hall of the Guild of Corpus Christi, now a local museum with information on the medieval cloth trade. Walled garden.
Times: Open 6-28 Mar, Sat and Sun, 1100-1600. 1-30 Apr, Wed-Sun, 1100-1700. 1 May-31 Oct, daily, 1100-1700. 6-28 Nov, Sat and Sun, 1100-1600. Closed 9 Apr.
Fee: £3.25/free/£3.25.
Facilities: T(1 hr) NT

Lavenham

Little Hall Map ref. E/F9
Market Place
Tel: (01787) 247179 Web: www.suffolksociety.com
A 14th C. hall house with a crown-post roof. Contains the Gayer-Anderson collection of furniture, pictures, sculpture and ceramics. There is also a small walled garden.
Times: Open 9 Apr-31 Oct, Wed, Thurs, Sat and Sun, 1400-1730. Bank Hols, 1000-1730.
Fee: £2.00.
Facilities: T(45 mins)

Long Melford

Kentwell Hall Map ref. E9
Tel: (01787) 310207 Web: www.kentwell.co.uk
Tudor manor house, still a lived-in family home. Winner of the '2001 Heritage Building of the Year' in the Good Britain Guide. Extensive gardens and parkland. Famous Tudor re-creations. Farm with rare breeds.
Times: Open 15-22 Feb, gardens and farm only, daily, 1100-1700. 29 Feb-4 Apr, gardens and farm only (lambing and spring bulb days), Sun, 1100-1700. 5 Apr-19 Jun, house, gardens and farm, Sun, 1200-1700. Also daily, 5-8 Apr, 13-16 Apr and 1-4 Jun. 14 Jul-5 Sept, house, gardens and farm, daily, 1200-1700. 5-24 Sept, house, gardens and farm, Sun, 1200-1700. Oct, house, gardens and farm, Sun, 1200-1700 (also daily 18-22 and 25-29 Oct). Please see the Diary of Events in this guide for details on re-creations.
Fee: House and gardens £6.95/£4.45/£5.95. Gardens only £4.90/£3.20/£4.15.
Facilities: T(5 hrs)

DID YOU KNOW

Holy Trinity Church at Blythburgh is noted for its bench ends depicting the Seven Deadly Sins, whilst the main door is said to show the scorch marks of Black Shuck, the fearsome devil dog.

Lavenham Guildhall of Corpus Christi

Long Melford

Melford Hall Map ref. E9/10

Tel: (01787) 880286 Web: www.nationaltrust.org.uk

Turreted brick Tudor mansion with 18th C. and Regency interiors. Collection of Chinese porcelain, gardens and a walk in the grounds. Memorabilia of Beatrix Potter.

Times: Open 3-30 Apr, Sat, Sun and Bank Hol Mon, 1400-1730. 1 May-30 Sept, Wed-Sun and Bank Hols, 1400-1730. 1-31 Oct, Sat and Sun, 1400-1730. Last admission at 1700. Closed 9 Apr. Contact for Christmas openings.

Fee: £4.50/£2.25/£11.25 (family).

Facilities: T(1 hr) NT

Newbourne (nr. Woodbridge)

Newbourne Hall Map ref. K10

Tel: (01473) 736277

Hall house with timber framing of c.1480, Tudor brick work, pargetting and plaster work of around 1600.

Times: Open all year, by written application only (Newbourne Hall, Newbourne, nr. Woodbridge, Suffolk IP12 4NP).

Fee: £5.00/£10.00.

Facilities: T(1 hr)

Somerleyton (nr. Lowestoft)

Somerleyton Hall and Gardens Map ref. O1

Tel: (01502) 730224 Web: www.somerleyton.co.uk

Early Victorian stately mansion in Anglo-Italian style, with lavish features and fine state rooms. Beautiful 12 acre gardens, with historic Yew hedge maze. Gift shop.

Times: Open 4 Apr-31 Oct, Sun, Thurs and Bank Hol Mon, plus Tues and Wed in Jul and Aug, 1100-1730 (hall 1300-1700).

Fee: £6.20/£3.20/£5.80/£18.00.

Facilities: T(3 hrs)

South Elmham (nr. Harleston)

South Elmham Hall Map ref. L3/4
St. Cross
Tel: (01986) 782526 Web: www.southelmham.co.uk
Grade I Listed medieval bishops palace. Also South Elmham Minster, a ruined Norman chapel in fortified enclosure. Wildlife walks around farm.
Times: Walks to Minster, open at any reasonable time. Tearoom open 9 Apr-30 Sept, Sun, Thurs and Fri, 1000-1700. Hall open 1 May-30 Sept, Thurs and Bank Hol Mon, guided tour at 1400.
Fee: Walks free. Hall £6.00.
Facilities: P T(1 hr)

Sudbury

Gainsborough's House Map ref. E10
See entry in Museums & Galleries section.

Thetford

Euston Hall Map ref. E4
Tel: (01842) 766366 Web: www.eustonhall.co.uk
18th C. hall housing paintings by Van Dyck, Lely and Stubbs, with pleasure grounds designed by John Evelyn and 'Capability Brown'. 17th C. church of St. Genevieve.
Times: Open 17 Jun-16 Sept, Thurs, 1430-1700. Also 27 Jun, 18 Jul and 5 Sept, Sun, 1430-1700.
Fee: £4.00/£2.00/£3.00.
Facilities: P T(2 hrs)

DID YOU KNOW

The High Street at Ixworth (nr. Bury St. Edmunds) contains the only petrol pumps in Britain to be awarded listed status. They date from the 1930s.

Ickworth House, Park and Gardens, Horringer

Ancient Monuments

Bungay

Bungay Castle Map ref. L3
Tel: (01986) 896156
The remains of an original Norman castle with Saxon mounds. Built by the Bigods in 1165. Massive gatehouse towers and curtain walls. Visitor centre with cafe.
Times: Open all year, daily, 1000-1600. Closed Sun in winter (please telephone to confirm).
Fee: £1.00/50p.
Facilities: T(30 mins)

Bury St. Edmunds

Bury St. Edmunds Abbey Map ref. D/E6/7
Tel: (01284) 764667 Web: www.english-heritage.org.uk
The remains of a Benedictine abbey in beautifully kept gardens. The two great gateways (one being 14th C.) are the best preserved buildings.
Times: Open any reasonable time.
Fee: Free.
Facilities: T(1 hr) (on leads) **EH**

Bury St. Edmunds

Saint Edmundsbury Cathedral Map ref. D/E6/7
Tel: (01284) 754933 Web: www.stedscathedral.co.uk
Come and visit in this special year. Millennium tower due for completion in 2004. New stonework and flintwork on view for the first time, as the last unfinished Anglican cathedral is completed. See special feature on pages 41/42.
Times: Open all year, daily, 0730-1800 (1900, 1 May-31 Aug).
Fee: Free.
Facilities: T(1 hr) (summer only)

Leiston Abbey

Clare

Clare Castle Country Park Map ref. C10
See entry in Countryside section.

Eye

Eye Castle Map ref. I5
Castle Street
Tel: (01449) 727150 Web: www.midsuffolkleisure.co.uk
A Norman motte-and-bailey, with medieval walls and a Victorian folly. The castle has always had close associations with royalty since the Norman conquest.
Times: Open 15 Mar-26 Sept, daily, 0900-1900 (or dusk if earlier).
Fee: Free.
Facilities: T(30 mins)

Felixstowe

Landguard Fort Map ref. K/L12
Tel: (01394) 277767 Web: www.landguard.com
An ancient monument, a 1744 fort with 1875 modifications, and additions in 1890, 1901 and 1914.
Times: Open 4-30 Apr, daily, 1000-1700. 1 May-30 Sept, daily, 1000-1800. 1-31 Oct, daily, 1000-1700.
Fee: £3.00/£1.00/£2.50.
Facilities: T(1½ hrs) (on leads) **EH**

Framlingham

Framlingham Castle Map ref. K/L7
Tel: (01728) 724189 Web: www.english-heritage.org.uk
A castle with 12th C. curtain walls, thirteen towers, Tudor-brick chimneys and a wall walk. Built by the Bigod family, the Earls of Norfolk. The home of Mary Tudor in 1553.
Times: Please contact for details of opening times.
Fee: Please contact for details of admission prices.
Facilities: Q T(1½ hrs) (audio tours) (on leads) **EH**

DID YOU KNOW

St. Mary's Church at Blundeston (nr. Lowestoft) has the tallest and narrowest Saxon round tower in England.

HISTORY & HERITAGE

Herringfleet (nr. Lowestoft)

Saint Olave's Priory Map ref. N1
Tel: (01223) 582700 Web: www.english-heritage.org.uk
Remains of an Augustinian priory, with an early 14th C. undercroft and a brick vaulted ceiling.
Times: Open at any reasonable time.
Fee: Free.
Facilities: T(45 mins) (on leads) EH

Leiston

Leiston Abbey Map ref. N7
Tel: (01223) 582700 Web: www.english-heritage.org.uk
The remains of a 14th C. abbey for premonstratensian canons, including the transepts of the church, a range of cloisters and a restored chapel.
Times: Open at any reasonable time.
Fee: Free.
Facilities: T(45 mins) (on leads) EH

Lindsey (nr. Hadleigh)

Saint James's Chapel Map ref. G10
Tel: (01223) 582700 Web: www.english-heritage.org.uk
A small 13th C. medieval chapel, once attached to the nearby castle. Thatched roof and lancet windows.
Times: Open all year, daily, 1000-1600.
Fee: Free.
Facilities: T(30 mins) EH

Orford

Orford Castle Map ref. N9
Tel: (01394) 450472 Web: www.english-heritage.org.uk
A 90ft high keep with views across the River Alde to Orford Ness. Built by Henry II for coastal defence in the 12th C. Local topographical display and sculpture.
Times: Please contact for details of opening times.
Fee: Please contact for details of admission prices.
Facilities: T(1 hr) (audio tours) EH

South Elmham (nr. Harleston)

South Elmham Hall (Minster) Map ref. L3/4
See entry in Historic Houses section.

Bungay Castle

Walpole (nr. Halesworth)

Walpole Old Chapel Map ref. M5
Halesworth Road
Tel: (01986) 798308
17th C. conversion of a hall house into an independent chapel. Many original fittings of late 17th C. - pulpit, chandelier and galleries. Later box pews. Graveyard managed for wildlife.
Times: Open 29 May-11 Sept, Sat, 1400-1630.
Fee: Free. Donations appreciated.
Facilities: T(30 mins)

West Stow (nr. Bury St. Edmunds)

West Stow Anglo-Saxon Village Map ref. D5
Icklingham Road
Tel: (01284) 728718
Web: www.stedmundsbury.gov.uk/weststow.htm
Reconstruction of eight pagan Anglo-Saxon buildings on an original site. Information centre with displays of excavated finds. Costumed events during holiday periods.
Times: Open all year, daily, 1000-1700. Last admission 1600 (1530 in winter). Closed 24-26 Dec.
Fee: £5.00/£4.00/£4.00/£15.00.
Facilities: T(2 hrs)

Woodbridge

Sutton Hoo Burial Site Map ref. K/L9
Tel: (01394) 389700 Web: www.nationaltrust.org.uk
An Anglo-Saxon royal burial site, where the priceless Sutton Hoo treasure was discovered in a huge ship grave. Exhibition tells story including original objects/replicas of treasure. Estate with walks
Times: Open 3 Jan-29 Feb, Sat and Sun, 1000-1600. 20 Mar-30 Sept, daily, 1000-1700. 1-31 Oct, Wed-Sun, 1000-1700. 1 Nov-31 Dec, Fri-Sun, 1000-1600.
Fee: £4.00/£2.00.
Facilities: T(2½ hrs) (on leads) NT

Museums & Galleries

Aldeburgh

The Aldeburgh Museum Map ref. N8
The Moot Hall
Tel: (01728) 454666
A 16th C. Listed ancient building with a museum displaying items of local interest, such as photographs and artefacts depicting life in Aldeburgh (fishing, lifeboat and Anglo-Saxon finds).
Times: Open 3 Apr-30 May, Sat and Sun, 1430-1700. 5-27 Jun, daily, 1430-1700. 3 Jul-29 Aug, daily, 1030-1230 and 1430-1700. 4 Sept-31 Oct, Sat and Sun, 1430-1700.
Fee: £1.00/free.
Facilities: T(45 mins)

Beccles

Beccles and District Museum Map ref. N2/3
Leman House, Ballygate
Tel: (01502) 715722 Web: www.becclesmuseum.org.uk
A Grade I Listed building concerning printing, Waveney, agricultural costumes, cultural and domestic items. Also a model of the town in 1841, and a natural history diorama.
Times: Open 1 Apr-31 Oct, Tues-Sun and Bank Hol Mon, 1430-1700.
Fee: Free.
Facilities: T(1½ hrs)

The Aldeburgh Museum

Beccles

William Clowes Museum of Print Map ref. N2/3
Newgate
Tel: (01502) 712884
One of the largest museums in East Anglia, housing a unique collection of printing memorabilia. Encompasses all aspects including hot metal and litho, early type founding and iron presses.
Times: Open 31 May-3 Sept, Mon-Fri, 1400-1630.
Fee: Free.
Facilities: T(1 hr)

Brandon

Brandon Heritage Centre Map ref. C3
George Street
Tel: (01842) 814955
The centre gives details of the flint, fur and forestry industries in the Brandon area, together with a local interest section housed in the former fire station premises.
Times: Open 10 Apr-31 Oct, Sat and Bank Hol Mon, 1030-1700; Sun, 1400-1700.
Fee: 50p/40p/40p.
Facilities: T(1 hr)

Bungay

Bungay Museum Map ref. L3
Waveney District Council Office, Broad Street
Tel: (01986) 894463
The museum consists of two small upstairs rooms which are inter-connecting. These contain showcases of general items from Norman to Victorian periods.
Times: Open all year, Mon-Fri, 0930-1300 and 1400-1630. Closed 9-12 Apr and 24 Dec-1 Jan.
Fee: 50p/30p/30p.
Facilities: T(30 mins)

Bury St. Edmunds

Bury St. Edmunds Art Gallery Map ref. D/E6/7
The Market Cross, Cornhill
Tel: (01284) 762081
Web: www.burystedmundsartgallery.org
Changing exhibitions of contemporary fine art and craft, plus a programme of talks, events and other educational activities in a magnificent Robert Adam building.
Times: Open all year, Tues-Sat, 1030-1700. Closed 24-28 Dec.
Fee: £1.00/free/50p.
Facilities: T(30 mins)

DID YOU KNOW

In the Abbey Gardens at Bury St. Edmunds is a bench made from the metal framework of a B-17 Flying Fortress plane, commemorating the World War Two US airmen stationed in the area.

Bury St. Edmunds
Greene King Brewery Visitor Centre Map ref. D/E6/7
See entry in Food & Drink section.

Bury St. Edmunds
Manor House Map ref. D/E6/7
5 Honey Hill
Tel: (01284) 757076 Web: www.stedmundsbury.gov.uk
A collection of clocks, watches, costumes and textiles, with fine and decorative arts of national importance in a magnificent 18th C. building.
Times: Open all year, Wed-Sun, 1100-1600. Closed 9 Apr, 25, 26 Dec and 1 Jan.
Fee: £2.50/£2.00/£2.00/£8.00.
Facilities: T(2 hrs)

Bury St. Edmunds
Moyse's Hall Museum Map ref. D/E6/7
Cornhill
Tel: (01284) 706183 Web: www.stedmundsbury.gov.uk
Dating back over 800 years, Moyse's Hall contains local history and archaeology collections, Murder in the Red Barn artifacts and highlights from the Suffolk Regiment.
Times: Open 2 Jan-31 Dec, Mon-Fri, 1030-1730; Sat and Sun, 1100-1600. Closed 9 Apr, 25-27 Dec and 1 Jan.
Fee: £2.50/£2.00/£2.00/£8.00.
Facilities: T(2 hrs)

Bury St. Edmunds
Theatre Royal Map ref. D/E6/7
Westgate Street
Tel: (01284) 769505 Web: www.theatreroyal.org
Built in 1819 by William Wilkins, this is a rare example of a late Georgian playhouse. Presents a full programme of drama to comedy and dance. Theatre tours.
Times: Theatre open for viewing - Jun-Aug, Tues and Thurs, 1100-1300 and 1400-1600; Sat, 1100-1300. Guided tours on Tues and Thurs at 1130 and 1430; Sat at 1130. Subject to theatrical activity.
Fee: Free. Tours £2.50.
Facilities: T(40 mins) NT

Long Shop Museum, Leiston

Cavendish (nr. Sudbury)
Sue Ryder Museum Map ref. D9
High Street
Tel: (01787) 282591
Museum depicting the life and work of Sue Ryder - past present and future.
Times: Open all year, daily, 1000-1700. Closed 24-27 Dec.
Fee: £1.00/50p/50p.
Facilities: T(1 hr)

Clare
Ancient House Museum Map ref. C10
26 High Street
Tel: (01787) 277662
Web: www.clare-ancient-house-museum.co.uk
Set in a 14th C. building, renowned for its pargeting, the museum tells the story of Clare, with graphic displays, computerised records and census returns.
Times: Open 9-12 Apr and 29 Apr-26 Sept, Thurs, Fri and Sun, 1400-1700; Sat and Bank Hols, 1130-1700.
Fee: £1.00/free/£1.00.
Facilities: T(45 mins)

Dunwich
Dunwich Museum Map ref. O6
St James's Street
Tel: (01728) 648796
A museum showing the history of Dunwich from Roman times, chronicling its disappearance into the sea and local wildlife.
Times: Open 1-30 Mar, Sat and Sun, 1400-1630. 1 Apr-30 Sept, daily, 1130-1630. 1-31 Oct, daily 1200-1600.
Fee: Free.
Facilities: T(40 mins)

Felixstowe
Felixstowe Museum Map ref. K/L12
Landguard Point, Viewpoint Road
Tel: (01394) 674355 Web: www.fhms.org.uk
The museum is housed in the Ravelin block adjacent to Landguard Fort. There are exhibits covering local, social and military history of the Felixstowe area.
Times: Open 11 Apr-30 May, Sun and Bank Hol Mon, 1300-1730. 2 Jun-29 Sept, Wed and Sun, 1300-1730. 3-31 Oct, Sun, 1300-1730.
Fee: £1.00/50p.
Facilities: T(1 hr) (on leads)

Flatford (nr. East Bergholt)
Bridge Cottage Map ref. H12
See entry in Historic Houses section.

Framlingham

Lanman Museum Map ref. K/L7
Framlingham Castle
Tel: (01728) 724189
A museum with rural exhibits relating to everyday life in Framlingham and the surrounding area, including paintings and photographs.
Times: Please contact for details of opening times.
Fee: Free.
Facilities: T(30 mins)

Halesworth

Halesworth and District Museum Map ref. M4
The Railway Station, Station Road
Tel: (01986) 873030
Museum housed in the 19th C. railway station building, alongside unique movable platforms. Changing local history displays, railway information and important residents. Also displays of local geology and archaeology.
Times: Open May-Sept, Tues and Wed, 1000-1230 and 1400-1600; Thurs and Sat, 1000-1230; Bank Hols, 1400-1600.
Fee: Free.
Facilities: T(1 hr)

Haverhill

Haverhill and District Local History Centre
Map ref. B9/10
Town Hall Arts Centre, High Street
Tel: (01440) 714962
A collection of over 6,000 items relating to Haverhill and district. There is also a vast collection of photographs.
Times: Open all year, Tues, 1900-2100; Thurs and Fri, 1400-1600; Sat, 1030-1530. Closed 9-12 Apr and 19 Dec-3 Jan.
Fee: Free.
Facilities: T(1 hr)

Ipswich

Christchurch Mansion Map ref. I/J10
Christchurch Park
Tel: (01473) 433554 Web: www.ipswich.gov.uk
Fine Tudor mansion built between 1548-50. Collection of furniture, panelling, ceramics, clocks and paintings from the 16-19th C. Art exhibitions in Wolsey Art Gallery.
Times: Open 1 Jan-31 Mar, Tues-Sat, 1000-1600; Sun, 1430-1600. 1 Apr-31 Oct, Tues-Sat, 1000-1700; Sun, 1430-1630. 1 Nov-31 Dec, Tues-Sat, 1000-1600; Sun, 1430-1600.
Fee: Free.
Facilities: T(2 hrs)

Lowestoft and East Suffolk Maritime Museum

Ipswich

Ipswich Museum Map ref. I/J10
High Street
Tel: (01473) 433550 Web: www.ipswich.gov.uk
Displays of Roman Suffolk, Suffolk wildlife, Suffolk and world geology, the Ogilvie Bird Gallery, 'People of the World' and 'Anglo-Saxons come to Ipswich' displays.
Times: Open all year, Tues-Sat, 1000-1700. Closed 9 Apr, 24, 25 Dec and 1 Jan.
Fee: Free.
Facilities: T(2 hrs)

Ipswich

The John Russell Gallery Map ref. I/J10
4-6 Wherry Lane
Tel: (01473) 212051 Web: www.artone.co.uk
Contemporary art galleries, representing over 160 of the region's painters and sculptors. Demonstrations.
Times: Open all year, Mon-Sat, 0930-1700. Closed 9, 12 Apr and 25 Dec-3 Jan.
Fee: Free.
Facilities: T(30 mins)

Ipswich

Wattisham Airfield Museum Map ref. H9
Wattisham Airfield
Tel: (01449) 728207
Web: www.wattishamairfieldmuseum.fsnet.co.uk
Museum houses an extensive photographic record, models, artefacts and memorabilia depicting the history and squadrons based at the station.
Times: Open 4 Apr-31 Oct, Sun, 1400-1630.
Fee: Free.
Facilities: T(2 hrs)

Kentford (nr. Newmarket)

Animal Health Trust Visitor Centre Map ref. B6
Lanwades Park
Tel: 08700 502424 Web: www.aht.org.uk
The John MacDougall Visitor Centre gives an insight into the veterinary work of the Animal Health Trust charity. Exhibitions and touch screen information. Coffee shop serves light refreshments.
Times: Open all year, Mon-Fri, 0900-1600. Closed 9-12 Apr, 25, 26 Dec and 1 Jan.
Fee: Free.
Facilities: T(1 hr)

Lavenham

Lavenham Guildhall of Corpus Christi Map ref. E/F9
See entry in Historic Houses section.

Laxfield (nr. Framlingham)

Laxfield and District Museum Map ref. L5
The Guildhall, High Street
Tel: (01986) 798026
Museum housed in the early 16th C. Guildhall opposite the church. Displays relate to the domestic and working life of the village in the 19/20th C.
Times: Open 1 May-26 Sept, Sat, Sun and Bank Hol Mon, 1400-1700.
Fee: Free.
Facilities: T(1 hr)

Lowestoft

Heritage Workshop Centre Map ref. P2
Old School House, 80a High Street, Wilde Score
Tel: (01502) 587500
Old school built in 1788, the first to offer free education to sons of fisherfolk. Changing exhibitions and workshops. Archives of local newspapers available to browse.
Times: Open all year, Mon-Fri, 1000-1600.
Fee: Free. Exhibitions - donations appreciated.
Facilities: T(1 hr)

Lowestoft

Lowestoft and East Suffolk Maritime Museum
Map ref. P2
Sparrow's Nest Park, Whapload Road
Tel: (01502) 561963
The museum houses models of fishing and commercial ships, shipwrights' tools, fishing gear, a lifeboat display, an art gallery and a drifter's cabin with models of fishermen.
Times: Open 9-17 Apr, then 1 May-10 Oct, daily, 1000-1630.
Fee: 75p/25p/50p.
Facilities: T(1½ hrs)

Lowestoft

Lowestoft Museum Map ref. O2
Broad House, Nicholas Everitt Park
Tel: (01502) 511457
A museum housing displays on local history, Lowestoft porcelain, fossils, flint implements, medieval artefacts from local sites and domestic history.
Times: Open 29 Mar-3 Oct, Mon-Fri, 1030-1700; Sat and Sun, 1400-1700. 30 May-end Sept, Sat, 1030-1700. Oct half term, Mon-Fri, 1030-1600; Sat and Sun, 1400-1600.
Fee: Free.
Facilities: T(1 hr)

Lowestoft

Lowestoft Porcelain Map ref. P2
Redgrave House, 10 Battery Green Road
Tel: (01502) 572940 Web: www.lowestoftporcelain.com
A little piece of history - the rebirth of an 18th C. English porcelain factory. An opportunity to see fine heritage porcelain and new studio ranges being painted by our artists.
Times: Open all year, Mon-Sat, 0900-1700.
Fee: Free.
Facilities: T(1 hr)

Lowestoft

Lowestoft War Memorial Museum Map ref. P2
Sparrow's Nest Gardens, Whapload Road
Tel: (01502) 587500
Museum and chapel dedicated to all who served in World War II, both service and civillian.
Times: Open 1 May-6 Oct, Sun-Fri, 1200-1630.
Fee: Donations appreciated.
Facilities: T(45 mins)

Lowestoft

Royal Naval Patrol Service Association Museum
Map ref. P2
Sparrow's Nest Gardens, Whapload Road
Tel: (01502) 564344
A museum with photographs and models of World War II officers and crews, minesweepers and anti-submarine vessels.
Times: Open all year, Mon, Wed and Fri, 0900-1200. Other times by appointment.
Fee: Free.
Facilities: T(2 hrs)

DID YOU KNOW

Aldeburgh was the childhood home of Elizabeth Garrett Anderson (1836-1917), the first woman doctor in Britain in 1870. She retired to Aldeburgh, and in 1908 became Britain's first woman's mayor.

Martlesham Heath

Martlesham Heath Control Tower Museum Map ref. K10
Off Parkers Place
Tel: (01473) 435104 Web: www.mhas.org.uk
Original World War II control tower built in 1942. Museum depicts history of this famous airfield 1917-1979. Once important Battle of Britain base and former home to USAAF 356FG.
Times: Open 4 Apr-31 Oct, Sun, 1400-1630.
Fee: Free.
Facilities: T(1 hr)

Mildenhall

Mildenhall and District Museum Map ref. B5
6 King Street
Tel: (01638) 716970 Web: www.mildenhallmuseum.co.uk
A local voluntary museum housed in 19th C. cottages, with modern extensions. Displays include RAF Mildenhall, Fenland and Breckland local archaeology and local history. Complete replica of Mildenhall Treasure.
Times: Open 3 Mar-18 Dec, Wed, Thurs and Sat, 1430-1630; Fri, 1100-1630.
Fee: Free.
Facilities: T(1 hr)

Newmarket

The National Horseracing Museum and Tours
Map ref. A7
99 High Street
Tel: (01638) 667333 Web: www.nhrm.co.uk
Award-winning display of the people and horses involved in racing's amazing history. Minibus tours to gallops, stables and equine pool. Hands-on gallery with horse simulator.
Times: Open 6 Apr-30 Jun, Tues-Sun, 1100-1630. 1 Jul-31 Aug, daily, 1100-1630. 1 Sept-31 Oct, Tues-Sun, 1100-1630. Minibus tours every day when museum open (except Sun), departing at 0920.
Fee: Museum £4.50/£2.50/£3.50/£10.00. Minibus tours £20.00/£18.50/£18.50.
Facilities: T(1½ hrs)

Orford

Dunwich Underwater Exploration Exhibition Map ref. N9
The Orford Craft Shop
Tel: (01394) 450678
Exhibits show progress in the underwater exploration of the former city of Dunwich, and underwater studies off the Suffolk coast. Attraction is not suitable for small children.
Times: Open all year, daily, 1100-1700. Closed 25 and 26 Dec.
Fee: 60p/60p/60p.
Facilities: T(1 hr)

Parham (nr. Framlingham)

Parham Airfield Museum Map ref. L7
Tel: (01728) 621373 (open hours), or (01376) 320848
Museum housed in the original control tower, with aircraft engines, uniforms, photographs and memorabilia. UK Museum of the British Resistance Organisation (Churchill's Secret Army), with many artefacts.
Times: Open 7 Mar-31 Oct, Sun and Bank Hols, 1100-1800. Also Wed from 2 Jun-29 Sept, 1100-1600.
Fee: Free.
Facilities: T(2 hrs)

Shotley Gate (nr. Ipswich)

HMS Ganges Association Museum Map ref. K11
Old Sail Loft, Shotley Marina
Tel: (01473) 684749 Web: www.hmsgangesassoc.org
The history of HMS Ganges, a training establishment for boys aged 15-16 years (closed in 1976). Photographs, artifacts and documentation.
Times: Open 3 Apr-31 Oct, Sat, Sun and Bank Hol Mons, 1100-1700.
Fee: Free.
Facilities: T(1 hr)

Southwold

Alfred Corry Museum Map ref. O5
Ferry Road
Tel: (01502) 722103
The old Cromer lifeboat station transported by sea to Southwold. Restored, and now housing the old Southwold lifeboat. One hundred and ten years old.
Times: Open 3 Jan-28 Mar, Sat and Sun, 1000-1600. 30 Mar-7 Nov, Tues-Fri, 1000-1600; Sat and Sun, 1000-1700. 13 Nov-26 Dec, Sat and Sun, 1000-1600.
Fee: Free.
Facilities: T(40 mins)

Christchurch Mansion, Ipswich

Southwold

The Amber Museum Map ref. O5
15 Market Place
Tel: (01502) 723394 Web: www.ambershop.co.uk
A purpose-built museum telling the story of amber, the precious gem found on the Suffolk shores. Discover how it is formed through historical uses to spectacular modern pieces.
Times: Open all year, Mon-Sat, 0900-1700; Sun, 1100-1600. Closed 25 and 26 Dec.
Fee: Free.
Facilities: T(30 mins)

Southwold

Southwold Lifeboat Museum Map ref. O5
Gun Hill
Tel: (01502) 722422
A museum with RNLI models, photographs of lifeboats and relics from old boats. Housed in former coastguard lookout building.
Times: Open end May-Sept, daily, 1430-1630.
Fee: Free.
Facilities: T(1 hr)

Southwold

Southwold Museum Map ref. O5
9-11 Victoria Street
Tel: (07890) 300532 Web: www.southwoldmuseum.org
Museum housing local history, archaeology, natural history and domestic bygones. Exhibits relating to the Southwold railway and The Battle of Sole Bay.
Times: Open 9 Apr-31 Jul, daily, 1400-1600. 1-31 Aug, daily, 1030-1200 and 1400-1600. 1 Sept-31 Oct, daily, 1400-1600.
Fee: Free.
Facilities: T(1 hr)

Southwold

Southwold Sailors' Reading Room Map ref. O5
East Cliff
A building of character where retired seamen have a social club and reading room. There are maritime exhibits and local history. No unaccompanied children.
Times: Open 1 Jan-9 Apr, daily, 0900-1530. 10 Apr-23 Oct, daily, 0900-1700. 24 Oct-31 Dec, daily, 0900-1530. Closed 25 Dec.
Fee: Free.
Facilities: T(15 mins)

DID YOU KNOW

The unusual crinkle-crankle wall at Easton (nr. Wickham Market) is the longest in the world, built between 1820-1830.

Steeple Bumpstead (nr. Haverhill)

Steeple Bumpstead Pottery and Gallery Map ref. B10
Church Street
Tel: (01440) 730260
Traditional working pottery set in a Victorian village school. Gallery displaying the pots made here.
Times: Open all year, days and times vary - please contact for details.
Fee: Free.
Facilities: T(30 mins)

Stowmarket

Museum of East Anglian Life Map ref. H7/8
Tel: (01449) 612229
Web: www.eastanglianlife.org.uk
East Anglia's open-air museum, set in 70 acres of Suffolk countryside. Displays and special events to interest visitors of all ages. Historic buildings. Suffolk breeds of animals.
Times: Open 28 Mar-31 Oct, Mon-Sat, 1000-1700; Sun, 1100-1700.
Fee: £6.50/£3.50/£5.50/£17.50.
Facilities: T(3 hrs)

Sudbury

Gainsborough's House Map ref. E10
46 Gainsborough Street
Tel: (01787) 372958 Web: www.gainsborough.org
Birthplace of Thomas Gainsborough (1727-88). An elegant Georgian townhouse, which displays more of the artist's work than any other gallery. Walled garden, print workshop and programme of temporary exhibitions.
Times: Open all year, Mon-Sat, 1000-1700; Bank Hol Sun and Mon, 1400-1700. Closed 9 Apr and 24 Dec-1 Jan.
Fee: £3.50/£1.50/£2.80/£8.00.
Facilities: Q T(1 hr)

Walberswick

Walberswick Visitor Centre Map ref. O5
Village Green
Tel: (01394) 384948
Web: www.suffolkcoastandheaths.org.uk
Visitor centre with photographic coverage of the village's history. Fascinating film 'Wild Coasts and Ancient Heaths', containing archive and present day footage on this Area of Outstanding Natural Beauty.
Times: Open 9-12 Apr, Fri-Mon, 1100-1300 and 1400-1700. Apr-Jun, weekends and Bank Hols, 1100-1300 and 1400-1700. Jul and Aug, Mon-Fri, 1400-1700; Sat and Sun, 1100-1300 and 1400-1700. 4, 5, 11 and 12 Sept, Sat and Sun, 1100-1300 and 1400-1700.
Fee: Free.
Facilities: T(30 mins)

Wingfield (nr. Diss)

Wingfield Arts Map ref. J/K4/5
College Yard, Church Road
Tel: (01379) 384505 Web: www.wingfield-arts.co.uk
Award-winning arts centre with art galleries, sculpture garden, shop and tea room. Quality programme of exhibitions, concerts and arts activities for people of all ages in rural settings.
Times: Open 10 Apr-19 Dec, Wed-Fri, 1300-1700; Sat, Sun and Bank Hol Mon, 1400-1700.
Fee: £1.50/£1.00/£1.00.
Facilities: T(1½ hrs)

Woodbridge

Suffolk Horse Museum Map ref. K9
The Market Hill
Tel: (01394) 380643 Web: www.suffolkhorsesociety.org.uk
An indoor exhibition about the Suffolk Punch breed of heavy horse. Paintings, photographs and exhibits.
Times: Open 12 Apr-30 Sept, Tues-Sun and Bank Hol Mon, 1400-1700.
Fee: £2.00/£1.50/£1.50.
Facilities: T(1 hr)

Woodbridge

Woodbridge Museum Map ref. K9
5a Market Hill
Tel: (01394) 380502
The museum tells the story of Woodbridge and its people, from pre-history to the present.
Times: Open 10 Apr-31 Oct, Wed-Sun, 1000-1600. Daily in school holidays.
Fee: £1.00/30p.
Facilities: T(1 hr)

Woolpit (nr. Bury St. Edmunds)

Woolpit and District Museum Map ref. F7
The Institute
Tel: (01359) 240822
A 17th C. timber-framed building with one permanent display of brickmaking and other displays (changing yearly), depicting the life of a Suffolk village.
Times: Open 10 Apr-26 Sept, Sat, Sun and Bank Hol Mon, 1430-1700.
Fee: Free.
Facilities: T(1 hr)

Machinery & Transport

Barnham (nr. Thetford)

East England Tank Museum Map ref. E4
Tel: (01842) 890010 Web: www.tankmuseum.com
Exhibits of over 70 military vehicles, weapons, uniforms and associated equipment over the last 100 years. Outside and inside exhibits. Military vehicle displays and rides.
Times: Open 1 Feb-28 Nov, Fri, Sat and Bank Hols, 1100-1700; Sun 1100-1600. Mon-Thurs, by appointment only.
Fee: £3.50/£2.50/£2.50/£10.00.
Facilities: P T(1½ hrs)

Carlton Colville (nr. Lowestoft)

East Anglia Transport Museum Map ref. O2
Chapel Road
Tel: (01502) 518459 Web: www.eatm.org.uk
A working museum with one of the widest ranges of street transport vehicles on display and in action. Developing street scene, vehicle rides and a 2ft gauge railway.
Times: Open 9 and 10 Apr, 1400-1700. 11 and 12 Apr, 1100-1700. 3 May-26 Sept, Wed and Sat, 1400-1700; Sun and Bank Hols, 1100-1700. 20 Jul-3 Sept, Tues-Sat, 1400-1700; Sun and Bank Hols, 1100-1700.
Fee: £5.00/£3.50/£3.50 (includes rides).
Facilities: P T(2 hrs)

East Anglia Transport Museum, Carlton Colville

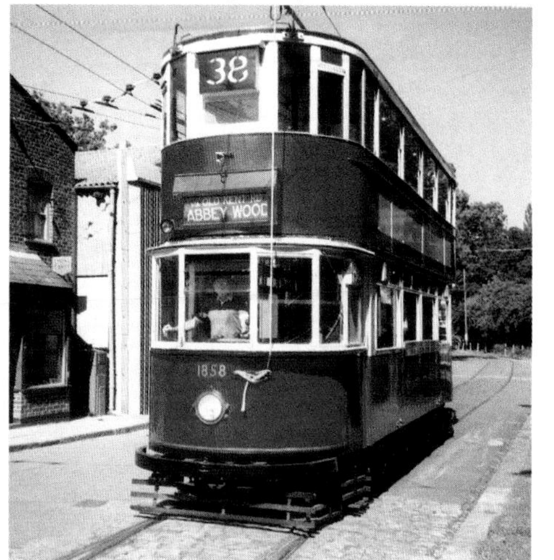

Cotton (nr. Stowmarket)

Mechanical Music Museum and Bygones Trust
Map ref. H6
Blacksmith Road
Tel: (01449) 613876 Web: www.davidivory.co.uk
The Mechanical Music Museum and Bygones at Blacksmith Road, Cotton, nr. Stowmarket, houses a unique collection of music boxes, polyphons, street pianos, barrel organs, fair organs, Wurlitzer Theatre Organ and many unusual items all played.
Times: Open Jun-Sept, Sun, 1430-1730. Fair Organ Enthusiasts Day 3 Oct, 1000-1700. Weekday group tours by arrangement.
Fee: £4.00/£1.00.
Facilities: P T(1½ hrs)

Flixton (nr. Bungay)

Norfolk and Suffolk Aviation Museum Map ref. L3
East Anglia's Aviation Heritage Centre, The Street
Tel: (01986) 896644 Web: www.aviationmuseum.net
A museum with forty aircraft on display, together with a large indoor display of smaller items connected with the history of aviation.
Times: Open 15 Jan-30 Mar, Tues, Wed and Sun, 1000-1600. 1 Apr-30 Oct, Sun-Thurs, 1000-1700. 2 Nov-15 Dec, Tues, Wed and Sun, 1000-1600.
Fee: Free. Donations appreciated.
Facilities: P T(2½ hrs) (on leads)

Ipswich

Ipswich Transport Museum Map ref. J10
Old Trolleybus Depot, Cobham Road
Tel: (01473) 715666
Web: www.ipswichtransportmuseum.co.uk
Over 100 historic vehicles, housed in a former trolleybus depot. All have been built or used in the area. Also history and products of local engineering companies.
Times: Open 21 Mar-28 Nov, Sun and Bank Hol Mon, 1100-1600. School hols, Mon-Fri, 1300-1600.
Fee: £3.00/£1.75/£2.50/£8.50.
Facilities: T(1 hr)

Leiston

Long Shop Museum Map ref. N7
Main Street
Tel: (01728) 832189
Award-winning museum, including Grade II* Listed Long Shop, the first production line for portable steam engines. Discover Leiston's unique history, and the home of the Garrett collection.
Times: Open 1 Apr-31 Oct, Mon-Sat, 1000-1700; Sun, 1100-1700.
Fee: £3.50/£1.00/£3.00.
Facilities: T(1½ hrs)

Lowestoft

Mincarlo Trawler Map ref. P2
Yacht Basin, Lowestoft Harbour
Tel: (01502) 565234
The Mincarlo is a mid-water side-fishing trawler launched in 1962. Contains museum with photographs and displays on the local fishing industries.
Times: Open 17 Apr-1 Nov, daily, 1030-1530.
Fee: Free.
Facilities: T(45 mins)

Wetheringsett (nr. Stowmarket)

Mid-Suffolk Light Railway Museum Map ref. I6
Brockford Station
Tel: (01449) 766899 Web: www.mslr.org.uk
A re-created Mid-Suffolk light railway station. Exhibits relating to the Mid-Suffolk Light Railway, and the restoration of the station and trackwork on part of the original route.
Times: Open 9 Apr-26 Sept, Sun and Bank Hols, 1100-1700. 1-31 Aug, Wed, 1400-1700.
Fee: £1.50/50p/£1.50/£3.50. Special events £5.00/£2.50/£4.50/£12.50.
Facilities: T(2 hrs)

Ipswich Transport Museum

Mills

Herringfleet (nr. Lowestoft)
Herringfleet Marshmill Map ref. N1
Tel: (01473) 583352
The last surviving smock drainage mill (19th C.) in the Broads area, and the last full-size working windmill in the country with four common sails and a tailpole. Access on foot only.
Times: Open National Mills Day, 9 May, Sun, 1300-1700. Open other occasional Suns throughout the year, please contact for details.
Fee: Free.
Facilities: T(1 hr)

Holton St. Peter (nr. Halesworth)
Holton Saint Peter Postmill Map ref. M4/5
Mill House
Tel: (01986) 872367
A restored 18th C. post windmill with four sails and a working fantail.
Times: Open 31 May and 30 Aug, Mon, 1000-1800. By appointment at all other times.
Fee: Free.
Facilities: T(30 mins)

Pakenham (nr. Bury St. Edmunds)
Pakenham Water-Mill Map ref. F6
Mill Road
Tel: (01359) 270570/230275
An 18th C. working water-mill on a Domesday site, with a 1904 Blackstone oil engine, mill pool, short river walk, picnic and barbecue area.
Times: Open 3 Apr-26 Sept, Sat, Sun and Bank Hols, 1400-1730. By appointment at all other times.
Fee: £2.50/£1.50/£2.00.
Facilities: T(1½ hrs)

Saxtead Green (nr. Framlingham)
Saxtead Green Postmill Map ref. K6/7
Tel: (01728) 685789 Web: www.english-heritage.org.uk
An elegant white windmill, dating from 1796. A fine example of a traditional Suffolk postmill. Climb the stairs to the 'buck' to see the machinery, all in working order.
Times: Please contact for details of opening times.
Fee: Please contact for details of admission prices.
Facilities: T(1 hr) (audio tours) **EH**

Stowmarket
Museum of East Anglian Life Map ref. H7/8
See entry in Museums & Galleries section.

Thelnetham (nr. Diss)
Thelnetham Windmill Map ref. G4
Mill Road
Tel: (01473) 727853
A tower windmill, built in 1819, with four very large patent sails driving two pairs of millstones. In full working order.
Times: Open 12 Apr, 30 May, 4 Jul, 8, 29 Aug, 5 Sept, 1100-1700.
Fee: £1.50/25p.
Facilities: T(1 hr)

Thorpeness
Thorpeness Windmill Map ref. N/O7
Tel: (01394) 384948
Web: www.suffolkcoastandheaths.org
A working 19th C. windmill housing displays on the Suffolk Coast and Heaths, Thorpeness village and information on the workings of the mill.
Times: Open 9-12 Apr, 1100-1300 and 1400-1700. 3 Apr-27 Jun, Sat, Sun and Bank Hol Mon, 1100-1300 and 1400-1700. 1 Jul-31 Aug, Mon-Fri, 1400-1700; Sat and Sun, 1100-1300 and 1400-1700. 4-12 Sept, Sat and Sun, 1100-1300 and 1400-1700.
Fee: Free.
Facilities: T(30 mins)

Woodbridge
Buttrums Mill Map ref. K9
Burkitt Road
Tel: (01394) 382045 Web: www.tidemill.org.uk
A fine six storey towermill which is now fully restored with sails and machinery. There is also a display on history and machinery.
Times: Open 11-25 Apr, Sun and Bank Hols, 1400-1730. 1 May-30 Aug, Sat, Sun and Bank Hols, 1400-1730. 5-26 Sept, Sun, 1400-1730.
Fee: £1.50/25p.
Facilities: T(30 mins)

Woodbridge
Woodbridge Tidemill Map ref. K9
Tidemill Quay
Tel: (01473) 626618 Web: www.tidemill.org.uk
A completely restored 18th C. tidalmill. Built in 1793, and used until 1957. The machinery works at varying times, subject to tides.
Times: Open 9-12 Apr, Fri-Mon, 1100-1700. 17, 18 and 24, 25 Apr, Sat and Sun, 1100-1700. 1 May-30 Sept, daily, 1100-1700. 2-31 Oct, Sat and Sun, 1100-1700.
Fee: £2.00/free/£1.50.
Facilities: T(40 mins)

Gardens

Benhall (nr. Saxmundham)
The Walled Garden Map ref. M7
Park Road
Tel: (01728) 602510 Web: www.thewalledgarden.co.uk
A nursery where almost 1,500 varieties of plants are sold and raised. A large garden divided by Yew hedges provides an opportunity to see many of the plants grown to maturity.
Times: Open 2 Jan-7 Feb, Tues-Sat, 0930-dusk. 8 Feb-28 Nov, Tues-Sun, 0930-1700. 29 Nov-18 Dec, Tues-Sat, 0930-dusk.
Fee: Free.
Facilities: P T(1 hr)

Brandon
Brandon Country Park Map ref. C3
See entry in Countryside section.

Coddenham (nr. Ipswich)
Shrubland Gardens Map ref. I9
Shrubland Park
Tel: (01473) 830221 Web: www.shrublandpark.co.uk
Extensive Italianate Victorian garden laid out by Sir Charles Barry in historic parkland. Formal beds, fountains, loggia, wild garden, fine trees and a series of follies.
Times: Open 4 Apr-12 Sept, Sun and Bank Hol Mon, 1400-1700.
Fee: £3.00/£2.00/£2.00.
Facilities: P T(1½ hrs)

East Bergholt
East Bergholt Place Garden Map ref. H11
Tel: (01206) 299224
The garden was laid out at the turn of the century, and covers 15 acres, with fine trees, shrubs, rhododendrons, camellias and magnolias. Specialist plant centre in walled garden.
Times: Open 1 Mar-30 Sept, daily, 1000-1700. Closed 11 Apr.
Fee: £2.50/free.
Facilities: P T(1 hr)

Hadleigh
Guildhall Map ref. G10
See entry in Historic Houses section.

Halesworth
Woottens Plants Map ref. N5
Blackheath, Wenhaston
Tel: (01502) 478258 Web: www.woottensplants.co.uk
Plantmans nursery specialising in auriculas, bearded iris, hemerocallis, pelargoniums, hardy perennials and ornamental grasses. Frequently featured in the press and on television. Display garden.
Times: Nursery open all year, daily, 0930-1700. Closed 24 Dec-1 Jan. Display garden open 1 May-30 Sept, Tues-Thurs, 0930-1630. Iris field open daily, 1-3 and 8, 9 May, then 22 May-6 Jun.
Fee: Free.
Facilities: P T(1½ hrs)

Hartest (nr. Bury St. Edmunds)
Giffords Hall Vineyard and Sweet Pea Centre
Map ref. D9
See entry in Food & Drink section.

Haughley (nr. Stowmarket)
Haughley Park Map ref. G7
See entry in Historic Houses section.

Helmingham
Helmingham Hall Gardens Map ref. J8
Tel: (01473) 890363 Web: www.helmingham.com
A moated and walled garden, with many rare roses, and possibly the best kitchen garden in Britain. New rose garden and herb and knot garden created in the early 1980's.
Times: Open 2 May-12 Sept, Sun, 1400-1800.
Fee: £4.00/£2.00/£3.75.
Facilities: P T(2 hrs) (on leads)

Hengrave (nr. Bury St. Edmunds)
Hengrave Hall Map ref. D6
See entry in Historic Houses section.

Abbey Gardens, Bury St. Edmunds

Horringer (nr. Bury St. Edmunds)
Ickworth House, Park and Gardens Map ref. D7
See entry in Historic Houses section.

Kelsale (nr. Saxmundham)
Laurel Farm Herbs Map ref. M6
Main Road (A12)
Tel: (01728) 668223 Web: www.theherbfarm.co.uk
Well established herb garden to view. Specialist herb grower with a large range of culinary and medicinal pot grown plants. Established since 1985.
Times: Open Jan and Feb, Wed-Fri, 1000-1500. 1 Mar-31 Oct, daily (except Tues), 1000-1700. Nov and Dec, Wed-Fri, 1000-1500. Please telephone to confirm.
Fee: Free.
Facilities: T(1 hr)

Lavenham
Lavenham Guildhall of Corpus Christi Map ref. E/F9
See entry in Historic Houses section.

Lavenham
Little Hall Map ref. E/F9
See entry in Historic Houses section.

Long Melford
Kentwell Hall Map ref. E9
See entry in Historic Houses section.

Long Melford
Melford Hall Map ref. E9/10
See entry in Historic Houses section.

Somerleyton (nr. Lowestoft)
Somerleyton Hall and Gardens Map ref. O1
See entry in Historic Houses section.

Stanton (nr. Bury St. Edmunds)
Wyken Hall Gardens and Wyken Vineyards Map ref. F5/6
Tel: (01359) 250287
Seven acres of vineyard and 4 acres of garden, surrounding an Elizabethan manor house. Woodland walks and 16th C. barn containing a restaurant, cafe and shop.
Times: Open 4 Jan-24 Dec, daily, 1000-1800.
Fee: £2.50/free/£2.00.
Facilities: T(2 hrs) (on leads)

Thornham Magna (nr. Eye)
The Thornham Walled Garden Map ref. H/I5
Tel: (01379) 788700
Web: www.thornhamwalledgarden.com
Restored Victorian glasshouses in the idyllic setting of a 2 acre walled garden, with fruit trees, wide perennial borders and a collection of East Anglian geraniums. Plant sales
Times: Open 2 Jan-31 Mar, daily, 1000-1600. 1 Apr-30 Sept, daily, 0900-1700. 1 Oct-24 Dec, daily, 1000-1600.
Fee: Free.
Facilities: T(1 hr) (on leads)

Helmingham Hall Gardens

Nurseries & Garden Centres

East Bergholt

The Place For Plants Map ref. H11
East Bergholt Place Garden, East Bergholt CO7 6UP
Tel: (01206) 299224
Plant Centre and Garden for specialist and popular plants, voted 7th most recommended nursery in the Country (Gardeners' Favourite Nurseries, by Leslie Geddes-Brown). A plant centre has been set up in the Victorian Walled Garden at East Bergholt Place stocked with an excellent range of plants, shrubs, trees, climbers, herbaceous plants, ferns, grasses, bamboo's, herbs etc. and a selection of terracotta pots. Situated 2 miles east of the A12 on B1070, on the edge of East Bergholt. Plant Centre opens daily, 1000-1700 (closed Easter Sun). Garden open - please see entry in Gardens section on page 280.

Kelsale (nr. Saxmundham)

Laurel Farm Herbs Map ref. M6
Main Road, Kelsale, nr. Saxmundham IP17 2RG
Tel: (01728) 668223
Email: seagontheherbman@aol.com
Web: www.theherbfarm.co.uk
Laurel Farm Herbs, on the main A12 between Saxmundham and Yoxford, is one of Suffolk's longest established herb nurseries. We offer an extensive range of culinary and medicinal plants, including a variety of larger specimens for those who want 'instant' results. In addition to our three sales areas we have a 1,800 sq foot garden, which allows you to see plants as they will be, once they have matured. Hard paths and ramps offer good access to all areas. Open 1000-1700, closed Tues. P T(1 hr)

DID YOU KNOW

The area around Rendlesham Forest is noted as the scene of Britain's most famous UFO incident in 1980, when mysterious strange lights and objects were spotted. There were even rumours of a UFO crashing at an area known as Capel Green.

Weston (nr. Beccles)

Winter Flora

Home and Garden Natural Décor Map ref. N3

Hall Farm, Weston, nr. Beccles NR34 8TT

Tel: (01502) 716810

This family business which began in 1969 is no longer known only for dried flowers. Winter Flora has one of the best selections of silk flowers in East Anglia, a plant centre containing a tempting array of unusual and traditional flowers and shrubs all strengthened by helpful design and plant advice. Numerous treasures reside in the very special plant centre run by Steve Malster, a dedicated plants man who nevertheless maintains the keenest prices, while the large show garden offers many a pleasant spot to sit and gain respite. Coffee Shop. 1 1/2 miles south of Beccles on the A145. Open daily 1000-1700. Closed Easter Day, 24-29 Dec and 1 Jan.

Woodbridge

Notcutts Garden Centres Map ref. K9

Ipswich Road, Woodbridge IP12 4AF

Tel: (01394) 445400 Web: www.notcutts.co.uk

Discover a world of ideas and inspiration around every corner for you, your home and your garden. From fabulous plants to gifts and treats galore, there's so much to see. Gift ideas from around the world, houseplants, books, fresh cut and silk flowers, 3,000 varieties of hardy plants (with a 2 year replacement guarantee), restaurant, expert friendly advice about seasonal and bedding plants, garden furniture and barbecues. Keep an eye open for regular offers on key garden products. Notcutts open 7 days a week, free car-parking plus children's play area.

Flatford Mill

Family Fun

Animal & Bird Collections

Baylham (nr. Ipswich)

Baylham House Rare Breeds Farm Map ref. I9

Mill Lane

Tel: (01473) 830264

Web: www.baylham-house-farm.co.uk

Rare Breeds Farm with cattle, sheep, pygmy goats, poultry and pigs, including Maori pigs called Kune Kunes. The main area of the farm is wheelchair and pushchair friendly. River walk. Picnic area. Disabled toilet. Visitor's Centre with information, gifts, souvenirs and refreshments. Every child gets a free bag of animal food.

Times: Open 14 Feb-31 Oct, daily, from 1100.

Fee: £4.00/£2.00/£3.00.

Facilities: T(1 hr)

New Pleasurewood Hills Leisure Park, Lowestoft

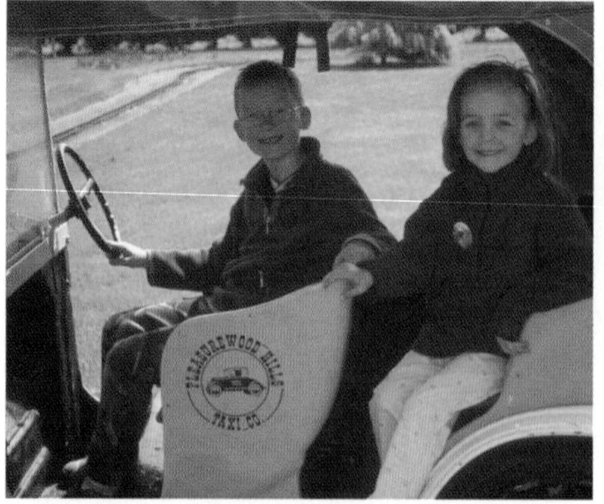

Earsham (nr. Bungay)

Otter Trust Map ref. L3

Tel: (01986) 893470 Web: www.ottertrust.org.uk

A breeding and conservation headquarters, with the largest collection of otters in the world. There are also lakes with a collection of waterfowl and deer.

Times: Open 1 Apr-30 Sept, daily, 1030-1800.

Fee: £6.00/£3.50.

Facilities: T(2 hrs)

Kessingland (nr. Lowestoft)

Suffolk Wildlife Park Map ref. O3

Tel: (01502) 740291 Web: www.suffolkwildlifepark.co.uk

Discover the ultimate African adventure, set in 100 acres of coastal parkland. Experience close encounters with rhino, lions, giraffes, hyenas, zebras and many more.

Times: Open all year, daily, from 1000. Please phone for closing times. Closed 25 Dec and 1 Jan.

Fee: Please contact for details of admission prices.

Facilities: T(4-6 hrs)

Long Melford

Kentwell Hall Map ref. E9

See entry in Historic Houses section.

Newmarket
National Stud Map ref. A7
Tel: (01638) 663464 Web: www.nationalstud.co.uk
A conducted tour which includes top thoroughbred stallions, mares and foals, and gives an insight into the day to day running of a modern stud farm.
Times: Open 1 Mar-30 Sept, Mon-Sat, tours at 1115 and 1430; Sun, tour at 1430. Plus autumn racedays.
Fee: £5.00/£3.50/£4.00/£15.00.
Facilities: Q T(1½ hrs)

Stonham Aspal (nr. Stowmarket)
Redwings Rescue Centre Map ref. I7
Stonham Barns, Pettaugh Road
Tel: 0870 040 0033 Web: www.redwings.co.uk
Home to thirty rescued horses, ponies and donkeys including Harry Potter, a Shetland pony with a club foot. Displays, gifts, refreshments and 'adopt a pony'.
Times: Open 1 Apr-30 Sept, daily, 1000-1600.
Fee: £3.50/£1.50/£2.50. Joint ticket with Suffolk Owl Sanctuary available.
Facilities: T(2 hrs)

Stonham Aspal (nr. Stowmarket)
Suffolk Owl Sanctuary Map ref. I7
Stonham Barns, Pettaugh Road
Tel: (01449) 711425
Web: www.suffolk-owl-sanctuary.org.uk
Outdoor flying arena, featuring frequent demonstrations of birds of prey in flight. Woodland walk, red squirrel enclosure, and aviaries with most species of British owls and raptors. Information centre.
Times: Open all year, daily, summer, 1000-1700; winter, 1000-1630. Closed 23 Dec-2 Jan.
Fee: Free. Donations appreciated.
Facilities: T(2 hrs)

Stowmarket
Museum of East Anglian Life Map ref. H7/8
See entry in Museum & Galleries section.

Wickham Market
Easton Farm Park Map ref. K8
Easton
Tel: (01728) 746475 Web: www.eastonfarmpark.co.uk
Free daily pony rides, pat-a-pet and egg collecting. Lots of farm animals to meet and feed. Play areas, chicks hatching, Suffolk Punch horse talks and woodland/river walks.
Times: Open 14-22 Feb, daily, 1030-1600. 20 Mar-26 Sept, daily, 1030-1800. 23-31 Oct, daily, 1030-1600.
Fee: Please contact for details of admission prices.
Facilities: Q T(4 hrs)

Wickham Market
Valley Farm Camargue Horses Map ref. L8
Valley Farm Riding and Driving Centre
Tel: (01728) 746916 Web: www.valleyfarmonline.co.uk
Britain's only herd of breeding Camargue horses, as featured on television. Animal collection including camel and Suffolk Punches. Horse riding charged separately
Times: Open all year, daily, 1000-1600. Closed 25 and 26 Dec.
Fee: £1.00/£1.00.
Facilities: T(2 hrs)

Amusement/Theme Centres & Parks

Farnham (nr. Saxmundham)
Friday Street Farm Shop - Maize Maze Map ref. M7
Tel: (01728) 602783
Maize maze with quiz. Enjoy hours of fun trying to locate the answers hidden in a few miles of paths. The maze takes a new shape every year and is suitable for all ages.
Times: Open mid Jul-Sept, daily, 0900-1630.
Fee: £3.00/£2.50/£8.00 (family).
Facilities: T(3 hrs)

Felixstowe
Golf FX Map ref. L11
Manning's Amusement Park, Sea Road
Tel: (01394) 282370
Indoor adventure golf with 13 holes of skill, fun and surprises. Suitable for all the family.
Times: Open all year, daily, summer 1000-2200; winter 1000-1800. Closed 25 Dec.
Fee: £2.00/admission under 1m tall £1.50.
Facilities: T(30 mins)

DID YOU KNOW

Holy Trinity Church at Long Melford contains a stained glass window showing Elizabeth Talbot, Duchess of Norfolk. It is said that the artist John Tenniel later used her as the model for the Duchess in 'Alice in Wonderland'.

Felixstowe

Manning's Amusement Park Map ref. L11
Sea Road
Tel: (01394) 282370
Traditional children's amusement park with rides and attractions. Nightclub, sportsbar, amusement arcade and Sunday market.
Times: Open all year, please contact for opening days and times. Children's rides open Easter-30 Sept, Sat, Sun and school hols, 1100-1800. Closed 25 Dec.
Fee: Free. Ride tokens, 50p per token.
Facilities: T(2 hrs)

Ipswich

Ipswich Town Football Club Stadium Tours Map ref. I/J10
Portman Road
Tel: (01473) 400555 Web: www.itfc.co.uk
See behind the scenes at a top football club. From the dressing room to the directors' box - the tour gives you a unique access 'behind the blues'.
Times: By appointment only - contact (01473) 400555 for full details.
Fee: £7.50/£5.00/£5.00/£22.00.
Facilities: T(1½ hrs)

Lowestoft

The East Point Pavilion Visitor Centre Map ref. P2
Royal Plain
Tel: (01502) 533600 Web: www.visit-lowestoft.co.uk
A glass, all-weather Edwardian-style structure with a large indoor play area called Mayhem (for children aged 2-12). Small souvenir shop, restaurant, tearooms and Tourist Information Centre.
Times: Open 2 Jan-31 Mar, Mon-Fri, 1030-1700; Sat and Sun, 1000-1700. 1 Apr-30 Sept, daily, 0930-1730. 1 Oct-31 Dec, Mon-Fri, 1030-1700; Sat and Sun, 1000-1700. Closed 25, 26 Dec and 1 Jan.
Fee: Free. Mayhem Adventure Play £2.95.
Facilities: Q T(1 hr)

Lowestoft

New Pleasurewood Hills Leisure Park Map ref. P2
Leisure Way, Corton
Tel: (01502) 586000 Web: www.pleasurewoodhills.com
Fifty acres of rides, attractions and shows. Tidal wave watercoaster, log flume, chairlift and two railways, pirate ship, parrot/sealion shows, go-karts, rattlesnake coaster and Mega-Drop Tower.
Times: Open 3-18, 24, 25 Apr; 1-3, 8, 9, 15, 16, 22, 23 May; 29 May-5 Sept, daily; 11, 12, 18, 19, 25, 26 Sept; 23-31 Oct. Open from 1000.
Fee: £13.50/£11.50/£46.00 (family).
Facilities: T(6 hrs)

Southwold

Southwold Pier Map ref. O5
North Parade
Tel: (01502) 722105
Web: www.southwoldpier.demon.co.uk
New pier, completed in 2002 - the first built in the UK for over 45 years. Amusements, seaside holiday exhibition, bar/restaurant, gift shop and tea room.
Times: Open 1 Jan-30 Apr, daily, 1000-1600. 1 May-30 Sept, daily, 1000-2200. 1 Oct-31 Dec, daily, 1000-1600. Closed 25 Dec.
Fee: Free.
Facilities: T(3 hrs)

Felixstowe

Children's Indoor Play Centres

Bury St. Edmunds

Activity World Playcentre Map ref. D/E6/7
Station Hill
Tel: (01284) 763799 Web: www.wherekidsplay.co.uk
Indoor children's playground, including giant drop slide, tumble tower, dizzy doughnut and giant ball pit.
Times: Open all year, daily, 0930-1830. Closed 25, 26 Dec and 1 Jan.
Fee: Child £3.95.
Facilities: T(1½ hrs)

Martlesham Heath

Kidz Kingdom Map ref. K10
Gloster Road
Tel: (01473) 611333 Web: www.kingpinbowling.co.uk
Four level structure with slides, ball pools, rope bridge, aerial runways, tots soft play and large bouncy attractions. Also Laser King, a 20 gun laser maze.
Times: Open all year, daily - times vary, please contact for details. Closed 25 and 26 Dec.
Fee: Please contact for details of admission prices.
Facilities: T(2 hrs)

Stowmarket

Playworld/Ocean Adventure Map ref. H7/8
Mid-Suffolk Leisure Centre, Gainsborough Road
Tel: (01449) 674980
A children's indoor play area for the under 10's, with a wide range of inflatables, laser game, grand prix cars, bikes and more.
Times: Playworld - open May-Sept, Mon-Fri, 0930-1900; Sat and Sun, 0900-1800. Ocean Adventure - open all year, Mon-Fri, 0930-1900; Sat and Sun, 0900-1800. Closed 24-26 Dec and 1 Jan.
Fee: Child (under 2) £1.80. Child (over 2) £3.15.
Facilities: T(1½ hrs)

Leisure Pools

Bury St. Edmunds

Bury St. Edmunds Leisure Centre Map ref. D/E6/7
Beetons Way
Tel: (01284) 753496 Web: www.stedmundsbury.gov.uk
Leisure pool with two water flumes, water cannon, pirate galleon and beach area. Also competition pool, sauna-world, sports hall and fitness studio.
Times: Open all year, Mon-Fri, 0630-2230; Sat, 0830-1930; Sun, 0830-2100; Bank Hols, 0900-2200. Contact for specific opening times for each activity.
Fee: Prices vary depending upon activity.
Facilities: T(2-3 hrs)

Felixstowe

Felixstowe Leisure Centre Map ref. L11
Undercliff Road West
Tel: (01394) 670411
Web: www.suffolkcoastal.gov.uk/leisure
Leisure pool with slides. Sauna, steam room, fitness/health suite and indoor bowls rink. Children's indoor soft play area.
Times: Open all year, daily, 0700-2200.
Fee: Prices vary depending upon activity.
Facilities: T(2-3 hrs)

Ipswich

Crown Pools Map ref. I/J10
Crown Street
Tel: (01473) 433655 Web: www.ibcsport.co.uk
Leisure pool with wave machine and fountains, set in a sub tropical atmosphere. Also 25 metre competition pool and health suite.
Times: Open all year. Leisure pool - Mon, 0745-0930 and 1030-2110; Tues-Fri, 0745-2110; Sat and Sun, 0745-1655.
Fee: Prices vary depending upon activity.
Facilities: T(2-3 hrs)

Sudbury

Kingfisher Leisure Centre Map ref. E10
Station Road
Tel: (01787) 375656
Web: http://kingfisher.leisureconnection.co.uk
Leisure complex featuring swimming pool with water flume and beach area. Spa pool, fitness studio, health suite and sauna.
Times: Open all year, Mon-Fri, 0630-2200; Sat, 0700-1900; Sun, 0830-1730.
Fee: Prices vary depending upon activity.
Facilities: T(2-3 hrs)

Easton Farm Park, Wickham Market

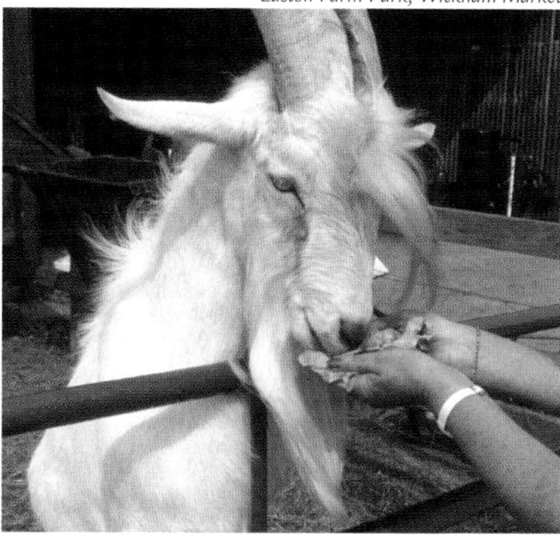

Countryside

The countryside of Suffolk is a unique combination of gently rolling land, woodland, river valleys and estuaries, home to busy market towns and pretty timber-framed/pastel-washed villages. Whilst the forty miles of coastline are designated as 'Heritage Coast', being largely unspoilt, with steep shingle terraces and low-crumbling cliffs - a sign of its constant battle with the sea. A rich agricultural area, the county is noted for its cereal, sugar beet, vegetable and oil-seed rape production, alongside intensive pig rearing units

Special Areas

Suffolk Coastline - an 'Area of Outstanding Natural Beauty', with low crumbling cliffs, sand/shingle beaches, river estuaries, nature reserves, seaside towns and quiet coastal villages. Mini tour - start your journey at England's most easterly point, Lowestoft Ness. From here head south pass Covehithe's severely eroded cliffs to Southwold, where wildlife cruises can be taken along the River Blyth. Take the little ferry to Walberswick (famous for its crabbing contest), for a walk along the beach to Dunwich, where the 12th C. capital of East Anglia was washed away by the sea. Nearby is Dunwich Heath, a unique remnant of the once extensive 'Sandlings' - great between Jun-Sept, when the heather is in bloom. The adjacent RSPB Minsmere Nature Reserve is famous for its rich habitat of reedbeds, artificial lagoons and woodland. Continue south to Aldeburgh to visit the marshes/wetland of North Warren, or take a walk to Snape for a boat trip on the River Alde. On now to Europe's largest vegetated shingle spit, Orford Ness - home to many bird species and seaside flora. Close by is Havergate Island, an important nature reserve. Stop off next at Shingle Street, where you can search for amber. At Bawdsey, take the ferry across the River Deben, which winds downstream past low-wooded hills and sailing hamlets to Woodbridge. Passing Felixstowe, you reach the windswept sand/shingle peninsula of Landguard Point, providing the northern entrance to the Rivers Orwell and Stour. Visit Trimley Marshes, a wetland reserve created from arable farmland in 1990.

The Brecks - see the Countryside section in Norfolk for further information.

The Broads - see the Countryside section in Norfolk for further information.

The Dedham Vale - see the Countryside section in Essex for further information.

The Sandlings - an area of lowland heaths which once stretched right along the Suffolk coastline. Created by prehistoric farmers as they cut back the trees to make clearings for crops - then later the grazing of sheep and rabbits prevented the trees from growing back, allowing heather and gorse to spread. In the 1920s, large areas of forestry were planted. Today the remaining heath-land is fiercely protected and managed - a rich haven for many species of flora and fauna. More information at www.suffolkcoastandheaths.org

Thetford Forest Park - see the Countryside section in Norfolk for further information.

Country Parks & Nature Reserves

Aldeburgh

RSPB North Warren Nature Reserve Map ref. N7/8
Thorpe Road
Tel: (01728) 688481 Web: www.rspb.org.uk
Delightful reserve consists of grazing marshes, reedbeds, heath and woodland. Good for wildfowl in winter, and butterflies and dragonflies in summer. Marsh harriers, nightingales and bitterns.
Times: Open all year, daily, any reasonable time.
Fee: Free.
Facilities: P T(2 hrs) (on leads)

Bradfield St. George (nr. Bury St. Edmunds)

Bradfield Woods Map ref. E7
Tel: (01473) 890089
Web: www.wildlifetrust.org.uk/suffolk
One of Britain's finest ancient woodlands - a haven for wildlife. A working wood, it has been under continuous management since 1252, supplying local needs for firewood and hazel products. SWT.
Times: Open at any reasonable time.
Fee: Free.
Facilities: P T(2 hrs) (on leads)

Kersey

Brandon

Brandon Country Park Map ref. C3
Bury Road
Tel: (01842) 810185
Web: www.suffolkcc.gov.uk/e-ant-t/countryside
30 acres of landscaped parkland, with a lake, walled garden, tree trail and forest walks. Visitor centre open daily. Play area, orienteering course and off-road cycle loops.
Times: Park open all year, daily, dawn-dusk. Visitor centre open 1 Jan-29 Feb, daily, 1000-1600. 1 Mar-31 Oct, Mon-Fri, 1000-1700; Sat and Sun, 1000-1730. 1 Nov-31 Dec, daily, 1000-1600.
Fee: Free.
Facilities: T(1½ hrs)

Brandon

Go Ape! Map ref. D3
High Lodge Forest Centre
Between Brandon and Thetford (off B1107)
Tel: 0870 444 5562 Web: www.goape.cc
Discover the thrill of aerial trekking high above the forest floor. Participants traverse from tree to tree, negotiating rope bridges, scramble nets, tarzan swings and zip slides.
Times: Open all year. 1 Jan-31 Mar, Sat and Sun, 0900-1700 (or 2hrs before the end of daylight). 1 Apr-31 Oct, daily, 0900-1700 (or 2hrs before the end of daylight). 1 Nov-31 Dec, Sat and Sun, 0900-1700 (or 2hrs before the end of daylight). Please phone for Christmas opening.
Fee: £14.50/£9.50.
Facilities: T(2½ hrs)

Brandon

High Lodge Forest Centre Map ref. D3
Between Brandon and Thetford (off B1107)
Tel: (01842) 810271 Web: www.forestry.gov.uk
High Lodge nestles in the heart of the Thetford Forest Park. Centre offers walking, cycling (cycle hire), high ropes course, adventure playground, shop and restaurant.
Times: Open all year, daily, 0900-dusk. Closed 25 Dec.
Fee: £3.50 per car.
Facilities: T(4 hrs)

Bury St. Edmunds

Nowton Park Map ref. E7
Nowton Road
Tel: (01284) 763666 Web: www.stedmundsbury.gov.uk
Previously a country estate, with 170 acres of woodland and pasture. Some formal recreation. All-weather pitch and two football pitches. Children's play area. Visitor centre.
Times: Open all year, daily, 0830-dusk. Visitor centre open weekends, summer, 1100-1700; winter, 1100-1600.
Fee: Free.
Facilities: T(2 hrs) (on leads)

Carlton Colville (nr. Lowestoft)

Carlton Marshes Map ref. O2
Burnt Hill Lane
Tel: (01502) 564250
Web: www.wildlifetrust.org.uk/suffolk
Over 100 acres of grazing marsh, fens and peat pools, set in the Waveney Valley. It is the Broads in miniature. Flower-studded marshes and wintering birds. Visitor Centre. SWT.
Times: Open at any reasonable time.
Fee: Free.
Facilities: T(2 hrs) (on leads)

Clare

Clare Castle Country Park Map ref. C10
Malting Lane
Tel: (01787) 277491
Web: www.suffolkcc.gov.uk/e-ant-t/countryside
A small country park, incorporating the remains of a castle and a Victorian railway station, in a 30-acre site fronting onto the River Stour.
Times: Open all year, daily, dawn-dusk.
Fee: Free.
Facilities: T(2 hrs)

Dunwich Heath Coastal Centre and Beach

West Stow Anglo-Saxon Village

Dunwich

Dunwich Heath Coastal Centre and Beach Map ref. O6
Tel: (01728) 648505 Web: www.nationaltrust.org.uk
Remnant of the once extensive Sandling Heaths, and one of Suffolk's most important nature conservation areas. Many excellent walks and access to beach. Coastguard cottages with observation room, tearoom and shop.
Times: Heath open all year, daily, dawn to dusk. Tearoom and shop open 3 Jan-29 Feb, Sat and Sun. 3 Mar-11 Apr, Wed-Sun. 12-18 Apr, daily. 21 Apr-11 Jul, Wed-Sun. 12 Jul-19 Sept, daily. 22 Sept-19 Dec, Wed-Sun. 27-31 Dec, daily. Daily in half terms. Open from 1000.
Fee: Free. Car park charge £2.00.
Facilities: T(2-3 hrs) NT

Felixstowe

Trimley Marshes Map ref. K11
Tel: (01473) 890089
Web: www.wildlifetrust.org.uk/suffolk
Exciting wetland reserve created entirely from arable land alongside the River Orwell, unbeatable for its sheer number and species of birds. Wonderful estuary views. Visitor Centre. SWT.
Times: Open at any reasonable time.
Fee: Free.
Facilities: T(4 hrs) (on leads)

DID YOU KNOW

The fishermen at Orford once captured a wild man in their nets in 1204. Taken to the castle, he was held there and fed on a diet of fish and meat. Later he escaped, and is depicted on the sign of the oyster restaurant in the town.

Hadleigh

RSPB Wolves Wood Map ref. H10
Tel: (01255) 886043 Web: www.rspb.org.uk
Wolves Wood is one of the few remaining areas of the ancient woodland that used to cover East Anglia. Wide variety of birds, plants and animals.
Times: Open at any reasonable time.
Fee: Free.
Facilities: T(1 hr)

Horringer (nr. Bury St. Edmunds)

Ickworth House, Park and Gardens Map ref. D7
See entry in Historic Houses section.

Knettishall (nr. Thetford)

Knettishall Heath Country Park Map ref. F4
Tel: (01953) 688265
Web: www.suffolkcc.gov.uk/e-ant-t/countryside
Park with 375 acres of Breckland heath and mixed woodlands, with access to the River Ouse along walks. Picnic areas, toilets, and the starting point for The Peddar's Way, Angles Way and Icknield Way long distance footpaths.
Times: Open all year, daily, 0900-dusk. Closed 25 and 26 Dec.
Fee: Free.
Facilities: T(2 hrs)

Lackford (nr. Bury St. Edmunds)

Lackford Lakes Map ref. D6
Tel: (01284) 728706
Web: www.wildlifetrust.org.uk/suffolk
Lackford Lakes lies beside the River Lark, and have been created from former gravel pits. A superb site for wildfowl in both winter and summer. Visitor Centre. SWT.
Times: Reserve open at all times. Centre open all year, Tues-Sun, 1000-1600.
Fee: Free.
Facilities: T(2 hrs)

Needham Market

Needham Lake and Local Nature Reserve Map ref. H8
Tel: (01449) 727150 Web: www.midsuffolkleisure.co.uk
A large man-made lake and nature reserve, with picnic and educational facilities, on the outskirts of Needham Market. Tarmac pathway around the lake.
Times: Open at any reasonable time.
Fee: Free.
Facilities: T(1 hr)

Oulton Broad

Orford

Orford Ness National Nature Reserve Map ref. N9
Tel: (01394) 450900 Web: www.nationaltrust.org.uk
A 10 mile long vegetated shingle spit on the Suffolk coast. It is a national nature reserve and a former top secret military test site. Waymarked trails and displays.
Times: Open 10 Apr-26 Jun, Sat. 29 Jun-2 Oct, Tues-Sat. 9-30 Oct, Sat. Ferries leave Orford Quay from 1000-1400. Last ferry leaves the Ness at 1700.
Fee: National Trust members, £3.80/£1.90. Non-members, £5.80/£2.90.
Facilities: T(2½ hrs) NT

Orford

RSPB Havergate Island Map ref. M/N9
Tel: (01394) 450732 Web: www.rspb.org.uk
Small island set in the River Ore. Mainly a coastal lagoon reserve, important for avocets, terns and other waders. Wildfowl in winter, and a variety of flora in summer.
Times: Open Jan-Mar, 1st Sat of every month. Apr-Aug, 1st and 3rd weekends, and every Thurs. Sept-Dec, 1st Sat of every month. For bookings, please phone RSPB Minsmere on (01728) 648281.
Fee: £5.00/£2.50.
Facilities: T(5 hrs)

Reydon (nr. Southwold)

Hen Reedbed Map ref. N4
Tel: (01473) 890089
Web: www.wildlifetrust.org.uk/suffolk
A blend of reedbeds, fens, dykes and pools created in 1999 to provide new breeding habitat for bittern and other wildlife. A rich mosaic of wetland habitats. SWT.
Times: Open at any reasonable time (daylight hours).
Fee: Free.
Facilities: T(2 hrs) (on leads)

Stutton (nr. Ipswich)

Alton Water Map ref. I11
Holbrook Road
Tel: (01473) 328268 Web: www.anglianwater.co.uk
Largest area of inland water in Suffolk. Visitor centre with cafeteria, panoramic views and cycle hire. Nature reserves, eight mile walk/ten mile cycle track, watersports centre and fishing.
Times: Open all year. Gates open - summer, 0700-2130; winter, 0700-1800. Visitor Centre - daily in summer, 1000-1800; weekends, Bank Hols and school hols only in winter, 1000-dusk.
Fee: Fee.
Facilities: T(3 hrs)

Thornham Magna (nr. Eye)

Thornham Walks Map ref. H/I5
Tel: (01379) 788345 Web: www.midsuffolkleisure.co.uk
12 miles of walks through parkland, woods, meadow and farmland of the Thornham Estate. The walks include a surfaced path suitable for push chairs and wheelchairs.
Times: Open all year, daily, 0900-1800.
Fee: Free. Car park charge, Mon-Sat £2.00; Sun and Bank Hols £2.50.
Facilities: T(2 hrs) (on leads)

Walberswick

Walberswick Visitor Centre Map ref. O5
See entry in Museums & Galleries section.

West Stow (nr. Bury St. Edmunds)

West Stow Country Park Map ref. D5
Icklingham Road
Tel: (01284) 728718
Web: www.stedmundsbury.gov.uk/weststow.htm
Country park with woodland, river, lake, nature trails, walks and bird hides. Large car park with picnic area. Visitor centre with displays, cafeteria and shop.
Times: Open all year, daily, summer 0800-2000; winter 0800-1700.
Fee: Free.
Facilities: T(2 hrs) (on leads)

Westleton (nr. Saxmundham)

RSPB Minsmere Nature Reserve Map ref. N/O6
Tel: (01728) 648281 Web: www.rspb.org.uk
RSPB's flagship reserve on the Suffolk coast, with bird-watching hides and nature trails, year-round events and guided walks. Visitor centre with large shop and tearoom.
Times: Reserve open all year, daily (except Tues), 0900-2100 (or dusk if earlier). Visitor centre open daily (except Tues) - Jan 0900-1600; Feb-Oct 0900-1700; Nov-Dec 0900-1600. Closed 25 and 26 Dec.
Fee: £5.00/£1.50/£3.00/£10.00.
Facilities: T(3 hrs)

Woodbridge

Sandlings Forests Map ref. L/M9, M8, N5/6
Tel: (01394) 450164 Web: www.forestry.gov.uk
The Sandlings covers woods in Rendlesham, Tangham and Dunwich. Diverse mix of conifer plantations, interspersed with broadleaved areas, lowland heath and wetland areas. Forest Centre at Rendlesham with circular walks, cycle trails and adventure playground.
Times: Open all year, daily, any reasonable time.
Fee: Free. Car park charge £1.00.
Facilities: P T(2 1/2 hrs)

Picnic Sites

Barham - beside minor road (off A14) between Claydon and Baylham. 4 miles north west of Ipswich. Map ref. I9
Bramford - on B1067 by River Gipping, 1/2 mile west of Ipswich. Map ref. I10
Bungay - on Outney Road, by River Waveney. Map ref. L3
Cattawade picnic site - on A137/B1070 at Brantham, 3/4 mile north of Manningtree. Map ref. H12
Ferry Road picnic site - beside minor road at Bawdsey Quay, 8 miles south east of Woodbridge. Map ref. L11
Glemsford - by River Stour, 3 miles north west of Sudbury. Map ref. D9
Hadleigh - at start of Riverside Walk, beside minor road to Layham. Access from High Street. Map ref. G10
Haughley - beside A14, 1 1/2 miles north west of Stowmarket. Map ref. G7
Iken Cliff - beside minor road, 2 miles south of Snape. Map ref. M8
Melton Riverside - beside A1152 at Wilford Bridge, 1/2 mile north east of Woodbridge. Map ref. K/L9
Nacton - on minor road, off A1156. 2 miles south east of Ipswich. Map ref. K11
Ramparts Field - off A1101, beside minor road to West Stow. 5 miles north west of Bury St. Edmunds. Map ref. C5
Riverside picnic site - off B1113 at Claydon. 2 miles north west of Ipswich. Map ref. I9
Rodbridge picnic site - beside B1064 between Rodbridge Corner and Cavendish. 3/4 mile north of Sudbury (off A134). Map ref. E10
Sizewell Beach - on minor road off B1122, 1 1/4 miles east of Leiston. Map ref. N7
Stowmarket - picnic sites at Green's Meadow, off Bury Road; Combs Ford, Ipswich Road and Church Meadow, off Poplar Hill. Map ref. H7/8
Sutton Heath picnic sites - beside B1083, 2 miles south east of Woodbridge; and at Hollesley Road, 4 miles south east of Woodbridge. Map ref. L9
Toby's Walks picnic site - beside A12/B1387, 3/4 mile south of Blythburgh. Map ref. N5
Upper Hollesley Common - beside minor road, 5 1/4 miles south east of Woodbridge. Map ref. M10

Forest Enterprise picnic sites in Dunwich, Rendlesham and Tunstall Forests:
Butley Corner picnic site - beside B1084 to Orford, 5 miles north east of Woodbridge. Map ref. M9
Dunwich - on minor road between Blythburgh and Dunwich. Map ref. N6
Rendlesham Forest Centre - access from B1084, Woodbridge to Orford road. Map ref. M9
Sandgall's picnic site - off B1069, on minor road to Iken, 1 mile north east of Tunstall. Map ref. M8

Forest Enterprise picnic sites in Thetford Forest Park:
The Kings Forest - beside B1106, 6 miles north of Bury St. Edmunds. Map ref. D5
Mildenhall - beside A11/A1065, 1/2 mile east of Mildenhall. Map ref. C5
West Stow - on minor road between A1101 and B1106. Access just outside village. 4 miles north west of Bury St. Edmunds. Map ref. D5

Countryside Organisations - Suffolk

English Nature
Regent House, 110 Northgate Street, Bury St. Edmunds, Suffolk IP33 1HP
Tel: (01284) 762218 Web: www.english-nature.gov.uk

Forest Enterprise - East Anglia Forest District
Santon Downham, nr. Brandon, Suffolk IP27 0TJ
Tel: (01842) 810271 Web: www.forestry.gov.uk

The National Trust - Regional Office for East Anglia
Angel Corner, 8 Angel Hill, Bury St. Edmunds, Suffolk IP33 1UZ
Tel: 0870 609 5388 Web: www.nationaltrust.org.uk

The Royal Society for the Protection of Birds (RSPB) - Regional Office for East Anglia
Stalham House, 65 Thorpe Road, Norwich, Norfolk NR1 1UD
Tel: (01603) 661662 Web: www.rspb.org.uk

Suffolk Wildlife Trust (SWT)
Brooke House, The Green, Ashbocking, Suffolk IP6 9JY
Tel: (01473) 890089
Web: www.wildlifetrust.org.uk/suffolk

Activities

Activity Centres

Kennett (nr. Newmarket)

'Wildtracks' Off-road Activity Park Map ref. B6
Chippenham Road
Tel: (01638) 751918 Web: www.wildtracksltd.co.uk
Off-road activity park with military vehicles, 4x4 Range Rovers, quads, karts, clay shooting and motocross bikes.
Times: Open 1st Sun in every month, 1000-1600. Other times by arrangement.
Fee: Various. Entry to park £6.00 per car.
Facilities: T(2-3 hrs) (on leads)

Boat Trips

Beccles

Liana Boat Trip Map ref. N2/3
The Quay, Fen Lane
Tel: (01502) 713196 Web: www.broads-authority.gov.uk
A trip on the Liana offers Edwardian style, travelling along the River Waveney, looking at its scenery and wildlife. Trips go towards Geldeston or Aldeby depending on tides.
Times: Open Apr and May, Sat, Sun and Bank Hols, departing at 1100, 1415 and 1545. Jun-Sept, daily, departing at 1100, 1415 and 1545. Oct, Sat and Sun at 1100, 1415 and 1545.
Fee: £4.50/£3.50/£3.50/£9.00.
Facilities: T(1½ hrs)

Flatford (nr. East Bergholt)

River Stour Trips Map ref. H12
Opposite Bridge Cottage, Flatford Mill
Tel: (01787) 313199 Web: www.riverstourtrust.org
Boat trips on Stour Trusty II, an elegant electric launch designed in Edwardian style. 30 minute round trips to Fen Bridge, or longer charters to Dedham, Stratford or Brantham.
Times: Trips from Easter-end Sept, Sun, Bank Hols and Wed during the school summer holidays. Charters on other days by arrangement. Please contact for further details.
Fee: Please contact for details of admission prices.
Facilities: T(1-3 hrs)

DID YOU KNOW

Borley Rectory (nr. Sudbury) was once the location of the most haunted house in Britain, until it was destroyed by fire in 1939.

Ipswich

Orwell River Cruises Limited Map ref. I/J10
Orwell Quay, Ipswich Wet Dock
Tel: (01473) 836680 Web: www.orwellrivercruises.com
Cruises down the historic and beautiful River Orwell, to Pin Mill, Harwich Harbour and the UK's largest container port at Felixstowe. Themed musical evenings. Private charters.
Times: Regular public cruises 9 Apr-26 Sept - please contact for days and times. Private charters 9 Apr-31 Dec.
Fee: Various different cruise prices, please contact for details. Tickets for public cruises from Ipswich Tourist Information Centre (01473) 258070.
Facilities: T(3½ hrs)

Orford

Lady Florence River Cruises Map ref. N9
Orford Quay
Tel: (07831) 698298 Email: lady-flo@keme.co.uk
Web: www.lady-florence.co.uk
Based at Orford Quay. River cruise for 4 hours with lunch or dinner within the Rivers Alde and Ore. Cruise passes Aldeburgh, The National Trust's Orford Ness and Havergate Island.
Times: Open all year, daily, brunch 0930-1200; lunch 1200-1600; dinner 1600-2000. Champagne high tea, 1 Sept-31 Oct, daily, 1600-1830. Times may vary due to sunset. Please phone for a leaflet, details or prices.
Fee: Prices from £16.95 per person, minimum. Prices depend on the time of year, and food/drinks chosen.
Facilities: T(upto 4 hrs)

Oulton Broad

Waveney River Tours Ltd Map ref. O2
Mutford Lock
Tel: (01502) 574903/(07769) 731389
Daily sailings and private parties. River cruises on the 'Waveney Princess' or 'Enchantress'. Visits to the Berney Arms windmill on Wed, and a day trip to Beccles on Fri.
Times: Open 9 Apr-29 Oct, daily, 0830-1730.
Fee: Please contact for details of admission prices.
Facilities: T(1 hr to whole day)

Southwold

Coastal Voyager Map ref. O5
Southwold Harbour
Tel: (07887) 525082
Web: www.blythweb.co.uk/sail-southwold
Coastal Voyager has it all - offering a variety of sea trips and river cruises departing from Southwold harbour. Including high speed blast trip (1/2hr) and trips along the River Blyth, such as a 31/2hr cruise to Blythburgh.
Times: Open all year, please contact for further details.
Fee: High speed blast trip £15.00/£8.00. 31/2hr river cruise £19.00/£9.00.
Facilities: P T(31/2 hrs)

Sudbury

River Stour Trips Map ref. E10
The Granary, Quay Lane
Tel: (01787) 313199 Web: www.riverstourtrust.org
Boat trips on Rosette, an elegant electric launch designed in Edwardian style. Trips through the picturesque water meadows to Ballingdon, Cornard and Henny. Occasional steam launch trips. Tearoom with home-made cakes.
Times: Trips from Easter-early Oct, Sun, Bank Hols and Wed in Aug. Charters on other days by arrangement. Please contact for further details.
Fee: Please contact for details of admission prices.
Facilities: P T(1-4 hrs)

Waldringfield (nr. Woodbridge)

Deben Cruises Map ref. K10
Waldringfield Boatyard, The Quay
Tel: (01473) 736260
Cruises along the picturesque River Deben, aboard the M.V. Jahan. Trips to Woodbridge or Felixstowe Ferry. Commentary on history of river. Snacks and drinks onboard.
Times: Open May-Sept - please contact for days and times.
Fee: £6.00 (2 hour trip).
Facilities: T(2 hrs)

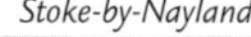

Stoke-by-Nayland

Golf Courses

Ufford Park Hotel, Golf & Leisure Map ref. K/L9
Yarmouth Road, Ufford, nr. Woodbridge IP12 1QW
Tel: (01394) 383555 Fax: (01394) 383582
Web: www.uffordpark.co.uk
Offering a wide range of top quality facilities, Ufford Park is a Best Western Connoisseur hotel, set in 120 acres of historic parkland with 50 en-suite bedrooms, full wedding packages and 7 air-conditioned conference/banqueting rooms. 18 hole, Par 71 golf course, excellent natural drainage for year round play, and purpose built golf academy with expert PGA tuition. Two restaurants, bar meals, light lunches and afternoon teas. Swimming pool, gymnasium, spa, steam/sauna rooms, solarium, beauticians and hairdressers. 11/2 miles from Woodbridge, on the River Deben, and within a few minutes drive from Sutton Hoo Anglo-Saxon burial grounds and our heritage coastline. Access off the A12 past Woodbridge, with 200 parking spaces. Open all year round. OPEN TO NON-RESIDENTS AND NON-MEMBERS.

Cycling

The Miller's Trail is a 23 mile circular route starting at the village of Ixworth (nr. Bury St. Edmunds), and exploring a rich agricultural landscape dotted with historic wind and watermills. The Jockey's Trail starts in the horse-racing capital of the world, Newmarket - with a 28 mile circular route taking in ancient waterways 'lodes' and lavish stud farms. Or head to Carlton Colville (nr. Lowestoft) to try Churches, Copses and Country Lanes, a 24 mile circular route with a plethora of historic churches, crumbling cliffs and old country estates. Saleable maps for all these routes from the East of England Tourist Board on 0870 225 4852. Discover the unique landscapes of The Brecks, with their cycling pack of five routes (small charge) - contact (01842) 765400, or visit www.brecks.org For some off-road routes, try the Rendlesham Forest Centre (nr. Woodbridge), where there are two rides of 6 and 12 miles, or Alton Water (to the south of Ipswich), where an 8 mile (mainly off-road) route encircles the reservoir - there is cycle hire here too. For more information on cycling in the county, visit www.visit-suffolk.org.uk

The Heart of Suffolk Cycle Route - a fully signed circular route of 78 miles through the rural heartland of Suffolk, using a mixture of mainly quiet roads and well-surfaced tracks. This route connects to the National Cycle Network Route 1 (Hull to Harwich). A saleable map/guide to the cycle route (including places to stay) is available from the Mid Suffolk Tourist Information Centre at Stowmarket on (01449) 676800, or visit www.heartofsuffolk.com for further information.

The Suffolk Coastal Cycle Route - explore an area of outstanding natural beauty, with peaceful countryside and unspoilt coastline. This cycle pack details a fully signed circular route of 88 miles (shorter options available), on two fold-out maps, together with information on places to stay and off-road forest rides. This route connects to the National Cycle Network Route 1 (Hull to Harwich). The saleable pack is available from the East of England Tourist Board on 0870 225 4852.

Walking

Long Distance Walks

The Angles Way (78 miles) - linear walk running from Great Yarmouth to Knettishall Heath Country Park (Suffolk). Saleable guide to route available from Sheila Smith, Caldcleugh, Old Buckenham, nr. Attleborough, Norfolk NR17 1RU. Tel: (01953) 861094.

The Icknield Way Path (105 miles) - runs from Ivinghoe Beacon (Buckinghamshire) to Knettishall Heath Country Park (Suffolk), passing through parts of Suffolk. Saleable guide available from the Icknield Way Association, 19 Boundary Road, Bishop's Stortford, Hertfordshire CM23 5LE. Tel: (01279) 504602.

The Sandlings Path (60 miles) - inland route through lowland heaths (Sandlings) between Ipswich and Southwold. Saleable guide available from The Suffolk Coast and Heaths Unit, Dock Lane, Melton, nr. Woodbridge, Suffolk IP12 1PE. Tel: (01394) 384948.

The Stour and Orwell Walk (42 miles) - runs from Felixstowe to Manningtree (Essex). Saleable guide available from The Suffolk Coast and Heaths Unit, Dock Lane, Melton, nr. Woodbridge, Suffolk IP12 1PE. Tel: (01394) 384948.

The Stour Valley Path (60 miles) - linear walk from Newmarket to Manningtree (Essex). Saleable guide available from The Dedham Vale and Stour Valley Countryside Project, c/o Suffolk County Council, Environment and Transport Department, St. Edmund House, Rope Walk, Ipswich, Suffolk IP4 1LZ. Tel: (01473) 583176.

The Suffolk Coast and Heaths Path (50 miles) - linear walk along the coastline from Felixstowe to Lowestoft. Saleable guide available from The Suffolk Coast and Heaths Unit, Dock Lane, Melton, nr. Woodbridge, Suffolk IP12 1PE. Tel: (01394) 384948.

Shorter Walks

Enjoy a walk beside the water - try the 17 mile Gipping Valley Path, which follows the old river towpath between Ipswich and Stowmarket, leaflet from the Gipping Valley Visitor Centre at Barham. The Lark Valley Path (13 miles) runs between Mildenhall and Bury St. Edmunds, or discover the Little Ouse Path between Thetford and Brandon - leaflets and information on these two walks from the Brecks Countryside Project on (01842) 765400, or visit www.brecks.org. Discover nine way-marked circular walks in the Heart of Suffolk, with the help of a guide available from the Mid Suffolk Tourist Information Centre at Stowmarket on (01449) 676800, or visit www.heartofsuffolk.com The Thetford Forest Park is Britain's largest lowland pine forest, and offers a wide range of way-marked trails - more information on (01842) 810271. There's more forest walks at the Rendlesham Forest Centre (nr. Woodbridge). Enjoy a walk through historic estates at Ickworth House (nr. Bury St. Edmunds) and Thornham Walks (nr. Eye). Or discover the landscapes that inspired John Constable with the help of the Constable Country: Keep it Special visitor's guide. Contact the Flatford Tourist Information Centre for a copy on (01206) 299460. For more information on walking in the county, visit www.visit-suffolk.org.uk Of course don't forget the area's country parks, with their various walks and nature trails - see the 'Countryside' section for further information.

Snape Maltings

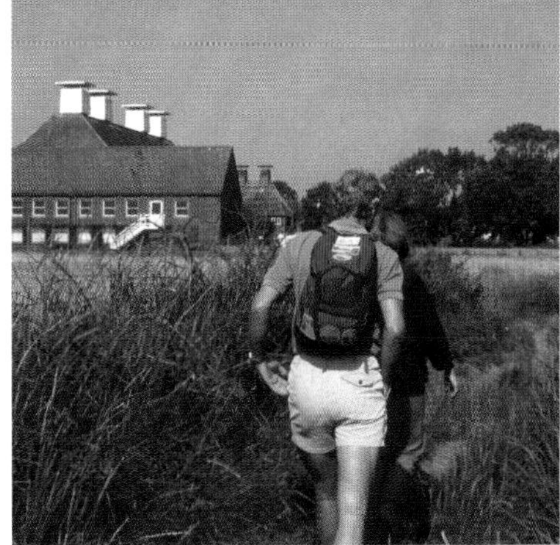

Specialist Holidays & Tours

The National Horseracing Museum Minibus Tours Map ref. A7
99 High Street, Newmarket CB8 8JH
Tel: (01638) 667333 Web: www.nhrm.co.uk
Privileged tours behind the scenes of Newmarket's racing industry. Our regular tour (departs 0920 daily except Suns and Mons) takes you to see horses training on the gallops and in their swimming pool, before going to one of a number of trainers' yards where you will meet staff and their horses. These yards are not normally open to the public. We also have a programme of special tours including our famous all-day Introduction to Racing - our expert will take you racing and explain how it works, including a trip to the start and a visit to the jockey's weighing room. T(2½ hrs)

Suffolk Cycle Breaks
Bradfield Hall Barn, Alder Carr Farm, PO Box 82, Needham Market IP6 8BW
Tel: (01449) 721555 Fax: (01449) 721707
Email: enquiry@cyclebreaks.com
Web: www.cyclebreaks.com www.walkingbreaks.com
Gentle cycling and walking holidays in Suffolk and Norfolk. Luggage transfer and accommodation pre-arranged.

Southwold

Thorpeness Village Map ref. N/O7
Tel: 01728 452176 Web: www.thorpeness.co.uk
This fascinating seaside village on the Suffolk coast was built in the 1920s. Thorpeness Hotel and Golf Club offers comfortable accommodation and a superb 18 hole golf course laid out by James Braid in 1922. The Dolphin Inn offers bed and breakfast and the best of pub food and restaurant facilities, ideal for families visiting the village. In the summer there is outside dining and a BBQ area. The Country Club has seven tennis courts available for hire. The original wings have been sympathetically converted into apartments. There are also function and bar facilities. Guests staying in our village accommodation enjoy a variety of holiday packages all year round. P

Food & Drink

Regional Produce

Suffolk is noted for its delicious meats, such as hams sweet-cured with black treacle, sugar and beer, or dry-cured and oak smoked bacons. Try Newmarket's famous royal-warranted sausages, first made in 1884. Whilst the rich pickings of the sea have brought the coastline great wealth, such as the fishing port of Lowestoft, where herring was once caught by huge fleets of steam drifters. In Dunwich and Aldeburgh you can enjoy some of Britain's best fish and chips, or for the seafood connoisseur try the oysters at Orford. The turning sails and waterwheels of historic mills have been part of Suffolk life for over 800 years, its flour used to make delicious breads and cakes. For a tipple or two, try a glass of Suffolk Cider, or one of the award-winning wines from the area's vineyards. There are also three major brewers, Adnams, Greene King and St. Peter's.

Breweries & Vineyards

Bungay

St. Peter's Brewery and Visitor Centre Map ref. L3
St. Peter's Hall, St. Peter South Elmham
Tel: (01986) 782322 Web: www.stpetersbrewery.co.uk
Opened in 1996, this unique working brewery is housed in 19th C. farm buildings. Restaurant/bar in medieval moated hall dating from 13th C. Brewery shop and visitor centre.
Times: Open all year. Brewery tours - Fri-Sun and Bank Hols, every hour between 1200-1600. Visitor centre and shop - Mon-Fri, 0900-1700; Sat and Sun 1100-1700. Contact for opening times of restaurant/bar.
Fee: Brewery tours/tastings £3.50.
Facilities: Q P T(1 hr)

DID YOU KNOW

Just outside Newmarket is the Gypsy Boy's Grave. In the early 19th C. Joseph was tending his sheep near this spot - but when one of his flock went missing he was accused of stealing. He hanged himself, but as suicides were refused entry to churchyards, he was buried beside the roadside, where fresh flowers are still regularly left today.

Bury St. Edmunds

Greene King Brewery Visitor Centre Map ref. D/E6/7
Westgate Street
Tel: (01284) 714297 Web: www.greeneking.co.uk
Museum providing an insight into the history and art of brewing. Informative and fun tour of the working brewhouse, including a tutored tasting of the beers. Shop and off license.
Times: Open all year, Mon-Sat, 1100-1700; Sun, 1200-1600. Tours, Mon-Sat at 1100 and 1400. Closed 9 Apr, 25 and 26 Dec.
Fee: Museum £2.00/£1.00/£1.50/£5.00. Tours £6.00 (over 12s only).
Facilities: P T(2½ hrs)

Framlingham

Shawsgate Vineyard Map ref. L7
Badingham Road
Tel: (01728) 724060 Web: www.shawsgate.co.uk
An attractive 15-acre vineyard with a modern, well-equipped winery, vineyard walk, guided tours, wine tastings, picnic area, children's play area and shop.
Times: Open all year, daily, 1030-1700. Please contact to confirm times before visiting.
Fee: £4.00/free/£3.50.
Facilities: P T(45 mins)

Hartest (nr. Bury St. Edmunds)

Giffords Hall Vineyard and Sweet Pea Centre
Map ref. D9
Tel: (01284) 830464 Web: www.giffordshall.co.uk
A 33-acre vineyard with vines, a winery, rare breeds of sheep, pigs, free-range chickens, a rose garden, wild flower meadows and a sweet pea centre.
Times: Open 9 Apr-30 Sept, daily, 1100-1800.
Fee: £3.50/free/£3.25.
Facilities: P T(2½ hrs) (on leads)

Hoxne

Horringer (nr. Bury St. Edmunds)

Ickworth House, Park and Gardens Map ref. D7

See entry in Historic Houses section.

Ilketshall St. Lawrence (nr. Halesworth)

The Cider Place Map ref. M4

Cherry Tree Farm

Tel: (01986) 781353

Traditional apple pressing equipment can be seen ready for use. Explanations given on its use, and quality single apple juices and ciders can be sampled and bought.

Times: Open all year, Mon, Tues and Thurs-Sat, 0900-1300 and 1400-1800. Closed 25 and 26 Dec.

Fee: Free.

Facilities: P T(30 mins)

Kirtling (nr. Newmarket)

Sascombe Vineyards Map ref. B8

The Thrift

Tel: (01440) 783100

Organic site with alternative energy, traditional architecture, consultations, talks, mineral water, honey and fine organic dessert-style wines wholesale and retail.

Times: Please contact for details of opening times.

Fee: £3.00.

Facilities: P T(1 hr)

Shotley (nr. Ipswich)

Witenagemot Wines Ltd Map ref. K11

Witenagemot, Below Church

Tel: (01473) 787016 Web: www.witenagemot.co.uk

19 acre vineyard with views over the River Orwell and out to sea. Believed to be ancient vineyard site (5/6th C.) Carp lake, winery and river walks.

Times: Open all year, Fri-Sun, 1100-1800.

Fee: £5.00.

Facilities: P T(2½ hrs)

Stanton (nr. Bury St. Edmunds)

Wyken Hall Gardens and Wyken Vineyards Map ref. F5/6

See entry in Gardens section.

Restaurants

Bury St. Edmunds

Linden Tree Map ref. D/E6/7

7 Out Northgate, Bury St. Edmunds IP33 1JQ

Tel: (01284) 754600

An established Pub/Restaurant, well known for plentiful portions of home-made food and fast service. Reservable non smoking conservatory restaurant, plus table service throughout. Families welcome. Large mature gardens with facilities for children. Average prices: £2-£10 (Lunch). Two courses £10 (evenings). Food served: 1200-1400 (1500 Suns) and 1800-2130. 7 days. P

Bury St. Edmunds

The Priory Hotel and Garden Restaurant

Map ref. D/E6/7

Tollgate, Bury St. Edmunds IP32 6EH

Tel: (01284) 766181 Fax: (01284) 767604

Email: reservations@prioryhotel.co.uk

Web: www.prioryhotel.co.uk

The Priory Hotel and Garden Restaurant is set within extensive gardens, surrounded by historic Priory flint walls. The Grade II listed hotel offers a warm welcome and high levels of individual service, whilst you enjoy the Priory's hospitality, comfort, charm and tranquility. All rooms are en-suite. Free parking for over 70 cars.

Hadleigh

The Marquis of Cornwallis Map ref. G10

Upper Street, Upper Layham, nr. Hadleigh, Ipswich IP7 5JZ

Tel: (01473) 822051

Nestled in Constable countryside, The Marquis of Cornwallis offers a truly traditional welcome. The candle-lit ambience provides the perfect atmosphere for sampling and enjoying its real ales, country wines and traditional English country menu. Perched on the rim of the valley, the Marquis' garden rolls down to the River Brett and provides the perfect location to watch the sun set over the vale. Open daily, we have no petty restrictions, with patrons able to eat in one of the bars, the dining room or the garden. P

Ipswich

The Galley Restaurant Map ref. I/J10

25 St. Nicholas Street, Ipswich IP1 1TW

Tel: (01473) 281131 Web: www.galley.uk.com

This attractive restaurant has an outstanding reputation for the finest food, wines and friendly efficient service. Short walk from town centre and nearby marina development. International cuisine, seafood specialities; daily specials and vegetarian dishes. Alfresco dining. Open for lunch 1200-1400; dinner 1800 until late; Mon-Sat.

Orwell Bridge, Ipswich

Nayland

The White Hart Inn Map ref. F11
11 High Street, Nayland CO6 4JF
Tel: (01206) 263382 (reservations)
Fax: (01206) 263638 Email: Nayhart@aol.com
Web: www.whitehart-nayland.co.uk
A restaurant with guestrooms located in an old coaching house in the heart of Constable Country. Countryside-style cooking with French flair, and the use of seasonal local produce. Wedding Licence. Private function room and terrace available. Light fare lunch menu with á la carte in the evenings. Closed on Mon all day, except Bank Hols. Six bedrooms with en-suite facilities available seven days a week. P

Afternoon Teas

Cavendish

The Sue Ryder Coffee Shop and Museum Map ref. D9
High Street, Cavendish CO10 8AY
Tel: (01787) 282591 Fax: (01787) 282991
Coffee Shop serving lunches and light refreshments, homemade cakes and scones. Gift Shop and beautiful gardens overlooking lake. Museum depicting Sue Ryder's work. Seats up to 90 - parties welcome by arrangement. Admission to museum: £1.00/50p. Open: Daily, 1000-1700. Closed 24-27 Dec. T(1½ hrs)

Walberswick

The Parish Lantern Map ref. O5
On the Village Green, Walberswick IP18 6TT
Tel: (01502) 723173
Visit our celebrated tea room and courtyard garden. Enjoy morning coffee, light lunches, cream teas and home-baked cakes. Original crafts, gifts, clothes and pictures. Set in the unspoilt beauty of the fishing village of Walberswick. Open: 1 Mar-Christmas Eve, daily from 1000. Jan and Feb, Fri, Sat and Sun only, from 1000.

Wingfield (nr. Diss)

Wingfield Arts Tea Room Map ref. J/K4/5
College Yard, Church Road, Wingfield IP21 5RA
Tel: (01379) 384505 Fax: (01379) 384034
Email: info@wingfield-arts.co.uk
Web: www.wingfield-arts.co.uk
Enjoy traditional cakes from local bakeries in the unique atmosphere of our medieval barn or weather permitting, the sun on our terrace overlooking the sculpture garden. Our friendly staff also provide visitors with a choice of hot and cold drinks, and during autumn we have a revised menu to include winter warmer snacks. We are the only tea room in the area and free entry to College Yard means that you can visit as often as you like. Set teas can be arranged when making advance group bookings. Open: Easter-Dec, Wed-Sun from 1400.

Stop & Shop

Aldringham (nr. Leiston)

Aldringham Craft Market Map ref. N7
Aldringham, nr. Leiston IP16 4PY
Tel: (01728) 830397

Family business, established 1958. Three relaxed and friendly galleries offering wide and extensive ranges of British craft products, original paintings, etchings and prints; studio, domestic and garden pottery, wood, leather, glass, jewellery, toys, kites, games, books, maps and many other good things including dolls houses and furniture, ladies' clothes, toiletries and hardy perennial plants. We only stock sensibly-priced, high quality products. Easy car parking; children's play area; coffee shop. Open all year, Mon-Sat, 1000-1730; Sun, 1000-1700.

Beccles

The Parish Lantern Map ref. N2/3
Exchange Square, Beccles NR34 9HH
Tel: (01502) 711700
A rich mix of crafts, gifts, clothes, pictures and jewellery housed in this part 17th C. listed building. Set in the historic market town of Beccles, which features a wealth of period buildings leading down to the River Waveney, 'Gateway to the Broads'. Open Mon-Sat, 0900-1700.

Bungay

Nursey & Son Ltd Map ref. L3
12 Upper Olland St, Bungay NR35 1BQ
Tel: (01986) 892821
Email: tnursey@aol.com
Web: www.nurseyleather.co.uk
Established 1790. Jerkins, gilets, jackets, leather and suede jackets, leather trousers, sheepskin coats, slippers, gloves, hats, rugs etc. The factory shop has a good selection especially for gifts, handbags, wallets, purses, also a wide variety of sub-standard products and oddments. Open Mon-Fri, 1000-1300 and 1400-1700. Closed last week Jul and first week Aug. Nov, Dec and Jan, open 6 days a week. Access, Visa.

Debenham

Carters Teapot Pottery Map ref. J7
Low Road, Debenham IP14 6QU
Tel: (01728) 860475 Fax: (01728) 861110
Email: info@cartersteapots.com
Web: www.cartersteapots.com
It doesn't have to be tea time to visit this Pottery making highly collectable teapots, in the beautiful village of Debenham. Visitors can see from the viewing area how these world renowned teapots are made and painted by hand. Pottery shop selling teapots, mugs and quality seconds. Situated just off the High Street, follow the teapot signs. Parking available. Tea, coffee and light refreshments in the conservatory. Open Mon-Fri, 0900-1730; Sat and Bank Hols, 1030-1630; Sun, 1400-1700.

Monks Eleigh (nr. Lavenham)

Corn Craft and SummerHouse Map ref. G9
Bridge Farm, Monks Eleigh IP7 7AY
Tel: (01449) 740456 Email: rwgage@lineone.net
Web: www.corncraft.co.uk
Situated in converted farm buildings in the heart of Suffolk Countryside between Hadleigh and Lavenham, specialising in the traditional craft of Corn Dolly making, practised on the farm for many years. Also selling a large range of unusual gifts, flowers and crafts.
NEW The SummerHouse selling beautiful and unusual furniture and gifts for the garden and home, offering original design ideas and accessories, with interior design service.
The Tea Room, recently extended to provide seating for 80 people, serving home made refreshments, including light lunches. Easy parking. Open everyday throughout the year, Mon-Sat, 1000-1700; Sun, 1100-1700. T(3 hrs)

Snape (nr. Saxmundham)

Snape Maltings Map ref. M7
Snape, nr. Saxmundham IP17 1SR
Tel: (01728) 688303/5 Web: www.snapemaltings.co.uk
Snape Maltings is a unique collection of 19th C. granaries and malthouses set on the banks of the River Alde. These historic buildings now house a variety of excellent shops and galleries including House and Garden (for furnishings, kitchenware and fine foods), Snape Craft Shop, Books and Cards, Countrywear and Little Rascals. The Granary Tea Shop offers light refreshment, and the award winning Plough and Sail pub specialises in modern British food in a relaxed contemporary setting. Holiday cottages are available to let all year, and painting and craft courses run during the summer months. No admission charge. Free car parking.

Wattisfield

Watson's Potteries Map ref. G5
Wattisfield IP22 1NH
Tel: (01359) 251239 Web: www.henrywatson.com
Henry Watson's Ltd has been manufacturing pottery for over 200 years. Our country gift shop offers a wide choice of excellent quality seconds, including the famous 'Original Suffolk Collection' of terracotta kitchenware and giftware at factory shop prices. See the original kiln and view our craftsmen at work on a guided factory tour by appointment. After browsing, enjoy light refreshments in the relaxed surroundings of our coffee shop. Open Mon-Sat, 0930-1700; Sun, 1100-1700. Find us: On the A143 between Bury St. Edmunds and Diss.

Walberswick

The Parish Lantern Map ref. O5
On the Village Green, Walberswick IP18 6TT
Tel: (01502) 723173
Set in a Grade II listed Georgian building with courtyard garden, The Parish Lantern offers good quality crafts, gifts, clothes and pictures, as well as delicious cream teas and light lunches. The unspoilt sea-side village of Walberswick, with it's picturesque harbour and sandy beach, has long attracted writers and artists, and was once the home of architect and designer Charles Rennie Mackintosh. Close to Minsmere R.S.P.B. Reserve and Dunwich Heath, and just a short ferry ride (in summer) or a pleasant walk from Southwold. Open: 1 Mar-Christmas Eve, daily from 1000. Jan and Feb, Fri, Sat and Sun only, from 1000.

Woolpit (nr. Bury St. Edmunds)

Elm Tree Gallery Map ref. F7
The Old Bakery, Woolpit, nr. Bury St. Edmunds IP30 9QG
Tel: (01359) 240255
An Aladdin's cave of attractive, good quality crafts and gifts, housed in The Old Bakery, a timber-framed building dating from c.1550. The extensive range includes jewellery, textiles, wood, ceramics - including locally crafted Clarecraft figures, Moorcroft pottery and Harmony Kingdom, and one of the best selections of greetings cards in the region. Children's gifts include Ty Beanie Babies. Light refreshments available all day, but limited seating available. Open: All year, Mon-Sat 1000-1800 (closed Bank Hols). Also open on Sun in Dec until Christmas, 1000-1800.

Discovery Tours

Spinning Yarns

Weave your way through the land of the medieval wool industry.

Starting point: Lavenham, Suffolk Map ref. E/F9
Mileage: 10m/16km
Morning - explore Britain's best preserved medieval town, and learn about the wool industry at the Guildhall. Then take the unclassified road to *Long Melford*, now the 'antiques capital of Suffolk'.
Afternoon - visit *Kentwell Hall*, to hear yarns of Tudor times, at one of the annual recreations. End the day by taking the A1092 to the pretty little town of *Clare*. Enjoy the views from the castle mound.

Long Melford

Salty Tales of the Sea

Discover the maritime heritage of the East Coast.

Starting point: Lowestoft, Suffolk Map ref. P2
Mileage: 21m/34km
Morning - visit the harbour, the historic *Mincarlo Trawler*, and the *Lowestoft and East Suffolk Maritime Museum*.
Afternoon - take the A12/B1127 to *Southwold*, and enjoy a pint of ale from the town's own brewery. End the day by taking the A1095 to the A12. Head south, and after 2 miles, turn left to *Dunwich*, a former city lost to the sea. Visit the museum and enjoy some of the best fish and chips in Britain.

Bury St. Edmunds

Under Starter's Orders

Explore the horseracing capital of the world.

Starting point: Newmarket, Suffolk Map ref. A7
Mileage: varied (depending on tour taken)
Morning - go 'behind the scenes' of racing establishments on a unique 'equine tour', including *The National Stud*. Then explore racing history, and ride a horse simulator at *The National Horseracing Museum*.
Afternoon - enjoy an exciting afternoon at the races, where you can cheer your favourite to the winning post!

Bloomin' Beautiful

Discover the spectacular colours and delicate fragrances of some of England's finest gardens.

Starting point: Bury St. Edmunds, Suffolk Map ref. D/E6/7
Mileage: 3m/5km
Morning - explore historic *Bury St. Edmunds*, renowned for its beautiful gardens and parks. The town has twice won the Nations in Bloom 'green oscar'.
Afternoon - take the A143 south west to Horringer, and enjoy the stunning parkland and Italian garden of *Ickworth House*.

An Artist's Inspiration

Visit the places and landscapes which inspired two of Britain's greatest artists.

Starting point: Ipswich, Suffolk Map ref. I/J10
Mileage: 21m/34km
Morning - visit *Christchurch Mansion* to see the Constable and Gainsborough paintings. Then take the A12 south for 6 miles to *East Bergholt*, where John Constable (1776-1837) was born. Continue to nearby *Flatford Mill*, scene of his most famous work "The Haywain".
Afternoon - return to the A12. Head south for 1/2 mile, then take the B1068 (via Stoke-by-Nayland) to the junction with the A134. Turn right to *Sudbury*, and visit the birthplace of Thomas Gainsborough (1727-88).

Strange Tales and Curiosities

Discover the flipside of the east, its customs, stories and local characters.

Starting point: Woodbridge, Suffolk Map ref. K9
Mileage: 26m/42km
Morning - visit the unique *tide mill*, and *Sutton Hoo's* treasure-filled burial site. Then take the A1152/B1084, via UFO country (Rendlesham Forest) to *Orford*. Climb the 12th C. castle and discover the merman story.
Afternoon - take the B1084/B1078 to Tunstall, where you turn right onto the B1069. At Snape, turn right onto the A1094 to the unspoilt seaside town of *Aldeburgh*. Hunt out the little 'Snooks' statue, then follow the coast road north to eccentric *Thorpeness*, and its 'House in the Clouds' and storybook mere.

Milling Mayhem

Discover the turning sails and waterwheels of historic mills. Climb their towers and buy freshly milled flour.

Starting point: Stowmarket, Suffolk Map ref. H7/8
Mileage: 15m/24km
Morning - start at the *Museum of East Anglian Life*, with its reconstructed water mill and wind pump. Then take the A14 west for 5 miles, to join the A1088 north to Ixworth. Just to the south west is *Pakenham*, the last parish in England with a working wind and water mill.
Afternoon - take the A143 to Stanton. End the day at *Wyken Hall* (just to the south along an unclassified road). Explore the gardens and enjoy a cream tea.

DID YOU KNOW

The village of Blaxhall (nr. Wickham Market) is noted for its 'growing stone' - the size of a football a century ago, it has since grown to its present size of about 5 tons.

Fortresses and Fighters

From ancient fortresses to airborne fighters, this is an intriguing insight into the defence of the realm.

Starting point: Bungay, Suffolk Map ref. L3
Mileage: 28m/45km
Morning - explore the remains of the Norman castle at *Bungay*, then take the B1062 to Flixton, and the *Norfolk and Suffolk Aviation Museum*, with its historic aircraft and exhibitions.
Afternoon - take the B1062/A143 to Harleston, where you join the B1116 south to *Framlingham*. Explore the magnificent 12th C. castle. Then continue on the B1116 to visit the *Parham Airfield Museum*, housed in an original wartime control tower.

Animal Magic

Discover British wildlife at its best - owls, horses and avocets.

Starting point: Needham Market, Suffolk Map ref. H8
Mileage: 36m/58km
Morning - leave the town on the B1078. Then take the A140 north for 3 miles to join the A1120 to Stonham Aspal. Enjoy the flying displays at the *Suffolk Owl Sanctuary*. Remain on the A1120 to Earl Soham, then follow the signs to *Easton Farm Park*. You can watch the cows being milked here!
Afternoon - head south east to Wickham Market, and join the A12 north for 12 miles. Just beyond Yoxford, turn right (following signs) to visit the famous *RSPB Minsmere Nature Reserve*.

Woodbridge

Index

A

Abberton Reservoir Visitor Centre, Layer de la Haye . . . 174

Activity World, Hatfield . . . 78

Activity World, Peterborough . . . 115

Activity World and Farmyard Funworld, Bushey . . . 77, 78

Activity World Playcentre, Bury St. Edmunds . . . 287

Ada Cole Rescue Stables, Nazeing . . . 167

Adventure Island, Southend-on-Sea . . . 169

Adventure Island Playbarn, Sawbridgeworth . . . 79

African Violet Centre (The), King's Lynn . . . 228

Alby Crafts, Erpingham . . . 246

Alby Crafts Gardens, Erpingham . . . 224

Aldeburgh Museum (The) . . . 270

Aldenham Country Park, Elstree . . . 78, 82

Aldringham Craft Market . . . 300

Alfred Corry Museum, Southwold . . . 274

Alternative Shopping Guides (The) (advert) . . . 124

Alton Water, Stutton . . . 291

Amber Museum (The), Southwold . . . 275

Ancient House Museum, Clare . . . 271

Ancient House Museum, Thetford . . . 204, 216

Anglesey Abbey, Gardens and Lode Mill, Lode . . . 100, 110, 111

Animal Health Trust Visitor Centre, Kentford . . . 273

Aquasplash, Hemel Hempstead . . . 79

Aqua Park and Jumping Jacks, Norwich . . . 234

Arundel House Hotel, Cambridge . . . 122

Ashridge Estate, Berkhamsted . . . 82

Ashwell Village Museum . . . 65

Audley End House and Park, Saffron Walden . . . 142, 164

Audley End Miniature Railway . . . 157

Awayadays . . . 242

Aylett Nurseries Limited, St. Albans . . . 74

Aythorpe Roding Postmill . . . 159

B

Babylon Gallery, Ely . . . 105

Baconsthorpe Castle . . . 205

Baldock Museum . . . 65

Banham Zoo . . . 230, 231

Bardfield Cage, Great Bardfield . . . 152

Bardfield Vineyard, Great Bardfield . . . 179

Barleylands Craft Village, Billericay . . . 185

Barleylands Farm Centre, Billericay . . . 147, 166

Barn Brasserie (The), Great Tey . . . 182, 183

Barton House Railway, Wroxham . . . 220

Bassingbourn Tower Museum . . . 103

Batchworth Lock Canal Centre, Rickmansworth . . . 67

Battlesbridge Motorcycle Museum and Antiques Centre . . . 147

Baylham House Rare Breeds Farm . . . 284

BBC Essex Garden, Abridge . . . 160

BCA Gallery, Bedford . . . 64

Beans Seal Trips, Morston . . . 240

Beccles and District Museum . . . 270

Bedford (advert) . . . 49

Bedford Butterfly Park, Wilden . . . 77

Bedford Museum . . . 64

Bedford Oasis Beach Pool . . . 79

Bedfords Park Visitor Centre, Romford . . . 175

Beecroft Art Gallery, Westcliff-on-Sea . . . 156

Belfairs Park, Leigh-on-Sea . . . 175

Belhus Woods Country Park, South Ockendon . . . 175

Benington Lordship Gardens . . . 71

Berkhamsted Castle . . . 62

Berney Arms Windmill, Great Yarmouth . . . 222

Beth Chatto Gardens (The), Elmstead Market . . . 161

Big Sky Adventure Play, Peterborough . . . 115

Binham Priory . . . 205

Bircham Contemporary Arts, Holt . . . 211

Bircham Mill, Great Bircham . . . 221

Bishop Bonners Cottage Museum, Dereham . . . 208

Bishops Boats Seal Trips, Blakeney . . . 239

Black Sheep Shop - Black Sheep Jerseys, Aylsham . . . 245
Blacked-Out Britain War Museum, Huntingdon . . . 105
Blackwater Leisure Centre, Maldon . . . 171
Blake Hall Gardens and Museum, Ongar . . . 154, 164
Blake House Craft Centre, Braintree . . . 185
Blakeney Guildhall . . . 202
Blakeney Point National Nature Reserve . . . 236
Blickling Hall, Garden and Park . . . 202, 223, 236
Blooms of Bressingham . . . 226
BMF Events, Peterborough (advert) . . . 17
Bocking Windmill . . . 159
Bomb Group (100th) Memorial Museum, Dickleburgh . . . 209
Bombardment (306th) Group Museum, Thurleigh . . . 65
Bond Street Antiques, Cromer . . . 245
Bourne Mill, Colchester . . . 159
Boxfield Gallery (The), Stevenage . . . 68
Boydells Dairy Farm, Wethersfield . . . 168
Bradfield Woods, Bradfield St. George . . . 288
Braintree District Museum . . . 147
Brampton Wood . . . 116
Brandon Country Park . . . 280, 289
Brandon Heritage Centre . . . 270
Brentwood Museum . . . 147
Bressingham Steam Experience and Gardens . . . 217, 223
Bridewell Museum, Norwich . . . 213
Bridge Cottage, Flatford . . . 263, 271
Bridge End Gardens, Saffron Walden . . . 164
Brightlingsea Museum . . . 148
Britannia Pier, Great Yarmouth . . . 232
British Museum of Miniatures, Wendy . . . 107
Broads Tours Ltd, Wroxham and Potter Heigham . . . 240
Bromham Mill . . . 70
Broom Boats Ltd, Brundall . . . 239
Buckinghamshire Arms (The), Blickling . . . 243
Bungay Castle . . . 268
Bungay Museum . . . 270
Bure Valley Railway, Aylsham . . . 217
Burgh Castle, Great Yarmouth . . . 205
Burghley House, Stamford . . . 100
Burnham-on-Crouch and District Museum . . . 148
Burston Strike School . . . 208
Burwell Museum . . . 103, 108
Bury St. Edmunds Abbey . . . 268
Bury St. Edmunds Art Gallery . . . 270
Bury St. Edmunds Leisure Centre . . . 287
Bushey Museum and Art Gallery . . . 66
Bushmead Priory, Colmworth . . . 62
Butterfly and Wildlife Park, Long Sutton . . . 231
Buttrums Mill, Woodbridge . . . 279

C

Café du Jardin, Ingatestone . . . 184
Cage (The), Parson Drove . . . 106
Caister Roman Site, Great Yarmouth . . . 205
Caistor Roman Town, Caistor St. Edmund . . . 205
Caithness Crystal Visitor Centre, King's Lynn . . . 211, 247
Cambridge American Cemetery, Coton . . . 101
Cambridge and County Folk Museum . . . 103
Cambridge Contemporary Art . . . 103
Cambridge University Botanic Garden . . . 111
Candlemaker and Model Centre, Great Yarmouth . . . 246
Canvey Railway and Model Engineering Club, Canvey Island . . . 157
Capel Manor Gardens, Enfield . . . 71
Carlton Marshes, Carlton Colville . . . 289
Carters Teapot Pottery, Debenham . . . 300
Carter's Vineyards, Boxted . . . 179
Carved Angel, Earls Colne . . . 181
Castle Acre Castle . . . 205
Castle Acre Priory . . . 205
Castle Mound, Bishop's Stortford . . . 62
Castle Point Transport Museum, Canvey Island . . . 157
Castle Rising Castle . . . 205
Cater Museum, Billericay . . . 147

Cathedral and Abbey Church of St. Alban, St. Albans . . . 63

Cathedral Church of St. Mary and St. Helen, Brentwood . . . 143

Cecil Higgins Art Gallery, Bedford . . . 59, 64

Cedars Park, Waltham Cross . . . 72, 83

Central Museum and Planetarium, Southend-on-Sea . . . 155

Charles Burrell Museum, Thetford . . . 216, 219

Chatteris Museum . . . 105

Chelmer and Blackwater Navigation, Chelmsford . . . 173, 177

Chelmsford (advert) . . . 136

Chelmsford Cathedral . . . 143

Chelmsford Museum . . . 149

Chelsworth Open Gardens Day (advert) . . . 20

Chicksands Priory, Shefford . . . 59

Childsplay Adventureland, Colchester . . . 170

Chilford Hall Vineyard, Linton . . . 121

Christchurch Mansion, Ipswich . . . 272

Church Farm Public House, Burgh Castle . . . 243

Cider Place (The), Ilketshall St. Lawrence . . . 298

City of Norwich Aviation Museum, Horsham St. Faith . . . 218

Clacton Pier, Clacton-on-Sea . . . 166, 169

Clare Castle Country Park . . . 289

Cley Mill, Cley-next-the-Sea . . . 221

Clock Tower, St. Albans . . . 63

Coalhouse Fort, East Tilbury . . . 144, 157

Coastal Voyager, Southwold . . . 294

Coggeshall Heritage Centre . . . 149

Colchester (advert) . . . 133

Colchester Castle Museum . . . 144, 149, 150

Colchester Castle Park . . . 162

Colchester Leisure World . . . 171

Colchester Zoo . . . 166

Collectors World of Eric St. John-Foti (The), Downham Market . . . 209, 218

College Lake Wildlife Centre, Tring . . . 68, 83

Colne Valley Railway, Castle Hedingham . . . 157

Congham Hall Herb Garden, Grimston . . . 224

Copt Hall Marshes, Little Wigborough . . . 175

Corn Craft and SummerHouse, Monks Eleigh . . . 300

Cottage Museum, Great Bardfield . . . 152

Creake Abbey, Burnham Market . . . 205

Cressing Temple Barns . . . 144, 160

Crispin's, Messing . . . 183

Cromer Museum . . . 208

Cromer Windmill . . . 70

Cromwell Museum, Huntingdon . . . 106

Crossing House, Shepreth . . . 111

Crown Pools, Ipswich . . . 287

Cudmore Grove Country Park, East Mersea . . . 174

Custom House - Maritime Exhibition, King's Lynn . . . 211

D

Danbury and Lingwood Commons . . . 174

Danbury Country Park . . . 174

De Grey Mausoleum, Flitton . . . 62

de Havilland Aircraft Heritage Centre, London Colney . . . 69

de Vere Arms, Earls Colne . . . 181

Debden Antiques, Saffron Walden . . . 185

Deben Cruises, Waldringfield . . . 294

Dedham Centre Toy Museum . . . 151

Denver Windmill . . . 221

Dinosaur Adventure Park (The), Lenwade . . . 233

Diss Museum . . . 209

Docwra's Manor Garden, Shepreth . . . 111

Dorothy L. Sayers Centre, Witham . . . 156

Dragon Hall, Norwich . . . 203

Dunstable Downs Countryside Centre . . . 81

Dunwich Heath Coastal Centre and Beach . . . 290

Dunwich Museum . . . 271

Dunwich Underwater Exploration Exhibition, Orford . . . 274

Dutch Cottage, Rayleigh . . . 142

Dutch Cottage Museum, Canvey Island . . . 148

Dutch Nursery Garden Centre (The), Coggeshall . . . 165

Duxford Chapel, Whittlesford . . . 102

Duxford Lodge Hotel . . . 123

E

East Anglia Transport Museum, Carlton Colville 277

East Anglian Railway Museum, Colchester 157

East Bergholt Place Garden 280

East England Tank Museum, Barnham 277

East Essex Aviation Society and Museum, St. Osyth 158

East Point Pavilion Visitor Centre (The), Lowestoft 286

East Ruston Old Vicarage Garden 224

Easton Farm Park, Wickham Market 285

Ecotech, Swaffham 216

Eleanor Cross, Waltham Cross 63

Electric Palace Cinema, Harwich (advert) 16

Elephant Playbarn, Knapton 234

Elgood's Brewery and Garden, Wisbech 111, 121

Elizabethan House Museum, Great Yarmouth 202, 209

Elm Tree Gallery, Woolpit 301

Elstow Moot Hall 59, 65

Elton Hall 99, 111

Ely & East Cambridgeshire (advert) 95

Ely Cathedral 101

Ely Museum 105

English Heritage (advert) 2

English School of Falconry - Bird of Prey and Conservation Centre, Biggleswade 76

Epping Forest District Museum, Waltham Abbey 156

Essex Police Museum, Chelmsford 149

Euston Hall, Thetford 266, 267

Eye Castle 268

F

Fakenham Garden Centre 227

Fakenham Museum of Gas and Local History 209

Fairhaven Woodland and Water Garden, South Walsham 225, 228

Fairlands Valley Park, Stevenage 83

Farmland Museum and Denny Abbey (The), Waterbeach 102, 107

Feering and Kelvedon Local History Museum, Kelvedon 153

Feeringbury Manor, Feering 161

Felbrigg Hall 202, 224, 236

Felixstowe Leisure Centre 287

Felixstowe Museum 271

Felsted Vineyard 179

Fenland and West Norfolk Aviation Museum, West Walton 220

Finchingfield (Duck End) Postmill 159

Finchingfield Guildhall and Heritage Centre 151

Fingringhoe Wick Nature Reserve 174

First Garden City Heritage Museum, Letchworth Garden City 66

firstsite @ The Minories Art Gallery, Colchester 149, 160

Fitzwilliam Museum, Cambridge 104

Flag Fen Bronze Age Centre, Peterborough 101, 102, 106

Flitch Way Country Park, Rayne 175

Focal Point Gallery, Southend-on-Sea 155

Ford End Watermill, Ivinghoe 70

Forge Museum and Victorian Cottage Garden (The), Much Hadham 67, 72

Forncett Industrial Steam Museum, Forncett St. Mary 218

Framlingham Castle 268

Freya's Ponyland Rescue Centre and Farm Museum, Braintree 147, 166

Friday Street Farm Shop - Maize Maze, Farnham 285

Fritton Lake Country World 230, 236

Fry Public Art Gallery, Saffron Walden 154

Funstop, Cromer 234

G

Gainsborough's House, Sudbury 267, 275

Galley Restaurant (The), Ipswich 298

Gamlingay Wood 116

Gardens of Easton Lodge (The), Little Easton 163

Gardens of the Rose (The), St. Albans 72

Gibberd Garden (The), Harlow 161

Giffords Hall Vineyard and Sweet Pea Centre, Hartest 280, 297

Glandford Shell Museum . . . 209
Glendale Forge, Thaxted . . . 158
Gnome Magic, Dedham . . . 160, 169
Go Ape, Brandon . . . 289
Go Bananas, Colchester . . . 170
Golf FX, Felixstowe . . . 285
Gooderstone Water Gardens . . . 224
Gorhambury, St. Albans . . . 59, 72
Gosfield Hall . . . 141, 161
Gosfield Lake Resort . . . 174
Grafham Water . . . 116
Grange Barn, Coggeshall . . . 143
Great Dunmow Maltings . . . 145, 152
Great Notley Country Park and Discovery Centre, Braintree . . . 147, 173
Great Walsingham Barns . . . 246
Great Yarmouth Potteries . . . 209
Great Yarmouth Sealife Centre . . . 230
Green Island Garden, Ardleigh . . . 160
Green Quay Environmental Discovery Centre (The), King's Lynn . . . 211, 237
Greene King Brewery Visitor Centre, Bury St. Edmunds . . . 271, 297
Greyfriars Books: the Colchester Bookshop . . . 185
Grimes Graves, Lynford . . . 206
Guildhall, Hadleigh . . . 263, 280
Guildhall of St. George, King's Lynn . . . 202, 212

H

Ha'penny Pier Visitor Centre, Harwich . . . 152
Hadleigh Castle . . . 145
Hadleigh Castle Country Park . . . 174
Hainault Forest Country Park, Chigwell . . . 166, 173
Hales Hall Barn and Gardens, Loddon . . . 206, 224
Halesworth and District Museum . . . 272
Hamerton Zoo Park, Sawtry . . . 113
Hanningfield Reservoir Visitor Centre, Billericay . . . 173
Harbour Lights (Walton-on-the-Naze) Ltd . . . 183
Harleston Museum . . . 211
Harrold-Odell Country Park, Harrold . . . 81
Harwich Lifeboat Museum . . . 152
Harwich Maritime Museum . . . 153
Harwich Redoubt Fort . . . 145
Hatfield Forest, Takeley . . . 166, 176
Hatfield House, Park and Gardens . . . 60, 72, 82
Haughley Park . . . 263, 280
Haverhill and District Local History Centre . . . 272
Hayley Wood, Longstowe . . . 117
Hazle Ceramics Workshop, Great Warley . . . 152, 185
Hedingham Castle, Castle Hedingham . . . 143, 173
Helen of Ranworth Boat Trip . . . 240
Helmingham Hall Gardens . . . 280
Hen Reedbed, Reydon . . . 291
Hengrave Hall . . . 263, 265, 280
Henry Blogg Museum, Cromer . . . 208
Henry Moore Foundation (The), Much Hadham . . 67, 72
Henry Ramey Upcher Lifeboat Museum (The), Sheringham . . . 215
Herb Garden, Wilburton . . . 111
Heritage Centre, Canvey Island . . . 148
Heritage Workshop Centre, Lowestoft . . . 273
Herringfleet Marshmill . . . 279
Hertford Castle . . . 63
Hertford Museum . . . 66
High Lodge Forest Centre, Brandon . . . 289
High Woods Country Park, Colchester . . . 173
Hillside Animal Sanctuary, Frettenham . . . 230
Hilltop Outdoor Centre, Sheringham . . . 242
Hinchingbrooke Country Park, Huntingdon . . . 117
Hitchin British Schools (The) . . . 66
Hitchin Museum and Art Gallery . . . 66, 72
HMS Ganges Association Museum, Shotley Gate . . . 274
Hobbies Museum of Fretwork and Craft Centre, Dereham . . . 208
Hockley Woods, Rayleigh . . . 175
Holkham Hall, Wells-next-the-Sea . . . 204, 216, 238
Holland Haven Country Park, Clacton-on-Sea . . . 173
Hollytrees Museum, Colchester . . . 149
Holme Bird Observatory Reserve (Norfolk Ornithologist's Association), Holme-next-the-Sea . . . 237

Holt Country Park 237

Holton Saint Peter Postmill 279

Hoo Hill Maze, Shefford 71

Horsey Windpump 222

Houghton Hall 202, 211, 224

Houghton House, Ampthill 62

Houghton Mill 110

House on the Hill Toy Museums Adventure, Stansted Mountfitchet 155, 170

Hoveton Hall Gardens, Wroxham 225

HULA Animal Rescue: South Midlands Animal Sanctuary, Aspley Guise 76

Hunstanton Sea Life Sanctuary 231

Hylands House, Widford 142, 164, 176

I

Iceni Brewery, Ickburgh 243

Iceni Village and Museums, Cockley Cley 208, 218

Ickworth House, Park and Gardens, Horringer 263, 281, 290, 298

ILPH Hall Farm, Snetterton 231, 232

Imperial War Museum, Duxford 108

Ingatestone Hall 141, 163

Inspire Discovery Centre, Norwich 213

Into-Food Café, Bressingham 244

Ipswich Museum 272

Ipswich Town Football Club Stadium Tours 286

Ipswich Transport Museum 278

Ipswich Unitarian Meeting House (The) 264

Island Hall, Godmanchester 99

Isleham Priory Church 101

J

John Bunyan Museum and Bunyan Meeting Free Church, Bedford 64

John Dony Field Centre, Luton 81

John Jarrold Printing Museum, Norwich 213

John Russell Gallery (The), Ipswich 272

Joyland, Great Yarmouth 233

Junior Farm at Wroxham Barns 232

K

Kelvedon Hatch Nuclear Bunker, Brentwood 147

Kentwell Hall, Long Melford 264, 265, 281, 284

Kettle's Yard, Cambridge 104

Key Ferry Cruises, Peterborough 119

Kids Kingdom, Southend-on-Sea 171

Kids Klub (advert) 296

Kidz Kingdom, Martlesham Heath 287

Kimbolton Castle 100

Kingfisher Leisure Centre, Sudbury 287

Kingsbury Watermill, St. Albans 70

King's College Chapel, Cambridge 101, 102

Knebworth House, Gardens and Park 61, 72, 82

Knettishall Heath Country Park 290

Kursaal, Southend-on-Sea 170

L

Lackford Lakes 290

Lady Florence River Cruises, Orford 293

Lady of Lee Valley (The), Broxbourne 85

Landguard Fort, Felixstowe 268

Langdon Hills Country Park, Corringham 173

Langdon Visitor Centre and Nature Reserve, Basildon 147, 173

Langham Glass 212, 233, 247

Lanman Museum, Framlingham 272

Laurel Farm Herbs, Kelsale 281, 282

Lavenham Guildhall of Corpus Christi 264, 273, 281

Laxfield and District Museum 273

Layer Marney Tower 142, 163, 166

Lee Valley Leisure Pool, Broxbourne 79

Lee Valley Park Farms, Waltham Abbey 167

Leez Priory, Hartford End 141, 163

Leighton Buzzard Railway 69

Leighton Lady Cruises, Leighton Buzzard 85

Leiston Abbey 269

Letchworth Garden City (advert) 52

Letchworth Museum, Letchworth Garden City 67

Letheringsett Watermill 222

Liana Boat Trip, Beccles . . . 293

Linden Tree, Bury St. Edmunds . . . 298

Lindsell Art Gallery . . . 153

Linton Zoo . . . 113

Litcham Village Museum . . . 212

Little Easton Manor and Barn Theatre . . . 163

Little Gems, Cromer . . . 208

Little Hall, Lavenham . . . 265, 281

Little Legs Playhouse, Bishop's Stortford . . . 78

Long Shop Museum, Leiston . . . 278

Longthorpe Tower . . . 101

Louis Tussauds House of Wax, Great Yarmouth . . . 233

Lowestoft and East Suffolk Maritime Museum . . . 273

Lowestoft Museum . . . 273

Lowestoft Porcelain . . . 273

Lowestoft War Memorial Museum . . . 273

Lowewood Museum, Hoddesdon . . . 66

Luton Museum and Gallery . . . 65

Lynford Arboretum, Mundford . . . 237

Lynn Museum, King's Lynn . . . 212

M

Made in Cley, Cley-next-the-Sea . . . 245

Maeldune Heritage Centre, Maldon . . . 153

Maldon and District Agricultural and Domestic Museum, Goldhanger . . . 151, 157

Maldon District Museum . . . 153

Mangapps Railway Museum, Burnham-on-Crouch . . . 157

Manning's Amusement Park, Felixstowe . . . 286

Mannington Gardens and Countryside . . . 225, 237

Manningtree and District Local History Museum . . . 153

Manor (The), Hemingford Grey . . . 99, 111

Manor House, Bury St. Edmunds . . . 271

March and District Museum . . . 106

Marina Leisure Centre, Great Yarmouth . . . 234

Marks Hall Garden and Arboretum, Coggeshall . . . 160, 173

Marquis of Cornwallis (The), Hadleigh . . . 298

Marsh Farm Country Park, South Woodham Ferrers . . . 167, 176

Marston Vale Millennium Country Park (The), Marston Moretaine . . . 81

Martlesham Heath Control Tower Museum . . . 274

Mead Open Farm, Leighton Buzzard . . . 77

Mechanical Music Museum and Bygones Trust, Cotton . . . 277

Megazone Laser Arena, Rayleigh . . . 169

Melford Hall, Long Melford . . . 266, 281

Melsop Farm Park, Scoulton . . . 231

Merrivale Model Village, Great Yarmouth . . . 233

Mersea Island Museum, West Mersea . . . 156

Mersea Vineyard, East Mersea . . . 179

Mid Norfolk Railway (Dereham to Wymondham Line) . . . 218

Mid Norfolk Railway (County School Station), North Elmham . . . 213, 218

Mid-Suffolk Light Railway Museum, Wetheringsett . . . 278

Midsummer House Restaurant, Cambridge . . . 122

Mildenhall and District Museum . . . 274

Mill Green Museum and Mill, Hatfield . . . 66, 70

Mill Race Nursery Coffee Shop, Aldham . . . 184

Milton Country Park . . . 117

Milton Maize Maze (The) . . . 115

Mincarlo Trawler, Lowestoft . . . 278

Mint (The), Great Yarmouth . . . 233

Mississippi River Boat, Horning . . . 239

Mistley Place Park Animal Rescue Centre . . . 166

Mistley Towers . . . 145

Moggerhanger Park . . . 59, 82

Mole Hall Wildlife Park, Widdington . . . 167, 168

Monster Events Centre, Thurleigh . . . 85

Mossman Collection, Luton . . . 69

Motorboat Museum (The), Pitsea . . . 158

Moulsham Mill, Chelmsford . . . 185

Mountfitchet Castle, Stansted Mountfitchet . . . 146

Mountnessing Windmill . . . 159

Moyse's Hall Museum, Bury St. Edmunds . . . 271

Mr B's Space Chase Quasar, Southend-on-Sea . . . 170

Muckleburgh Collection, Weybourne . . . 218, 220

Mulberry (The), Thetford . . . 244

Mundesley Maritime Museum . . . 213

Museum of East Anglian Life, Stowmarket 275, 279, 285

Museum of Harlow (The) 152, 163

Museum of Power, Langford 158

Museum of St. Albans 68

Museum of Technology, Cambridge 108

Museum of the Broads (The), Stalham 215, 219

Mustard Shop (The), Norwich 213

Myddelton House Gardens, Enfield 72

N

National Horseracing Museum and Tours (The), Newmarket 274, 276, 296

National Stud, Newmarket 285

National Trust (The) (advert) 6

Natural History Museum, Colchester 151

Natural Surroundings, Bayfield 223

Needham Lake and Local Nature Reserve, Needham Market 290

Nene Valley Railway, Stibbington 109

Newbourne Hall 266

New Buckenham Castle 206

New Great Yarmouth Museum 209

New Hall Vineyards, Purleigh 179

New Pleasurewood Hills Leisure Park, Lowestoft 286

New Sun Inn (The), Kimbolton 124

Norfolk and Suffolk Aviation Museum, Flixton 277

Norfolk Broads Yachting Co Ltd, Horning 239

Norfolk Children's Book Centre, Alby 245

Norfolk Herbs, Gressenhall 227

Norfolk Lavender Limited, Heacham 224, 227, 244, 246

Norfolk Motor Cycle Museum, North Walsham 218

Norfolk Nelson Museum, Great Yarmouth 210

Norfolk Shire Horse Centre, West Runton 219, 232

Norfolk Wildlife Centre and Country Park, Great Witchingham 230

Norpar Flowers, Navestock 153, 164

Norris Museum, St. Ives 106

North Elmham Chapel 206

North Herts Leisure Centre, Letchworth Garden City 79

North Norfolk Railway, Sheringham 219

North Weald Airfield Museum 158

Norwich Castle Museum and Art Gallery 207, 214

Norwich Cathedral 206, 207

Norwich Gallery 199, 214

Norwich Puppet Theatre 214

Notcutts (Ansells) Garden Centres, Cambridge 112

Notcutts Garden Centres, Ardleigh 165

Notcutts Garden Centres, Norwich 228

Notcutts Garden Centres, Peterborough 112

Notcutts Garden Centres, St. Albans 75

Notcutts Garden Centres, Woodbridge 283

Nowton Park, Bury St. Edmunds 289

Nursey & Son Ltd, Bungay 300

NWT Broads Wildlife Centre, Ranworth 237

NWT Cley Marshes Nature Reserve, Cley-next-the-Sea 236

NWT Foxley Wood 236

NWT Hickling Broad National Nature Reserve 236, 239

NWT Weeting Heath National Nature Reserve 238

O

Oasis Leisure Centre, Hunstanton 234

Octavia Hill Birthplace Museum, Wisbech 107

Old Bridge Hotel (The), Huntingdon 123

Old Buckenham Mill 222

Old Fire Engine House (The), Ely 123

Old House (The), Rochford 142

Old MacDonalds Educational Farm Park, South Weald 167

Old Merchant's House, Row III House and Greyfriars Cloisters, Great Yarmouth 202, 210

Old Nene Golf and Country Club Ltd, Ramsey 119

Old Swan Teashop (The), Hare Street Village 87

Oliver Cromwell's House, Ely 99, 105

Orford Castle 269

Orford Ness National Nature Reserve 291

Original Great Maze (The), Braintree 168

Origins, Norwich 214

Orton Meadows Golf Course, Peterborough 119

Orton Meadows Pitch & Putt Course, Peterborough . . . 119

Orwell River Cruises Limited, Ipswich . . . 293

Otter Trust, Earsham . . . 284

Oxburgh Hall, Oxborough . . . 203, 225, 237

P

Pakenham Water-Mill . . . 279

Pam Schomberg Gallery, Colchester . . . 151

Panos, Cambridge . . . 123

Paradise Wildlife Park, Broxbourne . . . 77

Parham Airfield Museum . . . 274

Park Farm Snettisham . . . 232

Parkside Pools, Cambridge . . . 115

Parish Lantern (The), Beccles . . . 300

Parish Lantern (The), Walberswick . . . 299, 301

Paxton Pits Nature Reserve, St. Neots . . . 117

Paycockes, Coggeshall . . . 141, 160

PC Arena, Colchester . . . 169

Peckover House and Gardens, Wisbech . . . 100, 111

Pensthorpe Nature Reserve and Gardens . . . 225, 237

Peter Beales Roses, Attleborough . . . 223, 226

Peterborough Cathedral . . . 101

Peterborough Museum and Art Gallery . . . 106

Pettitt's Animal Adventure Park, Reedham . . . 231

Picturecraft of Holt . . . 211

Pitstone Green Museum, Ivinghoe . . . 66, 69

Place for Plants (The), East Bergholt . . . 282

Plantation Garden (The), Norwich . . . 225

Play Rascals, Clacton-on-Sea . . . 170

Playbarn (The), Poringland . . . 231, 234

Playworld/Ocean Adventure, Stowmarket . . . 287

Pleasure Beach, Great Yarmouth . . . 233

Potters Bar Museum . . . 67

Prebendal Manor Medieval Centre (The), Nassington . . . 100, 111

Prickwillow Drainage Engine Museum . . . 109

Priors Hall Barn, Widdington . . . 146

Priory Church of St. Peter, Dunstable . . . 62

Priory Country Park, Bedford . . . 81

Priory Hotel and Garden Restaurant (The), Bury St. Edmunds . . . 298

Priory Maze and Gardens, Beeston Regis . . . 223

Prittlewell Priory, Southend-on-Sea . . . 155

Purfleet Heritage and Military Centre . . . 154

Pykenham Gatehouse, Ipswich . . . 264

Q

Quasar at Rollerworld, Colchester . . . 169, back cover

Queen Elizabeth's Hunting Lodge, Chingford . . . 141

R

RA Boat Trip, Barton Turf . . . 239

Railworld, Peterborough . . . 108

Ramsey Abbey Gatehouse . . . 102

Ramsey Rural Museum . . . 106

Raptor Foundation (The), Woodhurst . . . 115

Raveningham Gardens . . . 225

Rayleigh Mount . . . 145

Rayleigh Windmill and Museum . . . 154, 159

Red House Visitor Centre, Messing . . . 163, 166

Redbourn Village Museum . . . 67

Redbournbury Watermill, St. Albans . . . 70

Redwings Rescue Centre, Stonham Aspal . . . 285

Redwings Visitor Centre, Fritton . . . 230

Reeves Restaurant, Felsted . . . 181

RHS Garden: Hyde Hall, Rettendon . . . 161, 164

Rickmansworth Aquadrome . . . 83

Ridgewell Airfield Commemorative Museum . . . 154

Riverboat Georgina, Cambridge . . . 119

Riverside Ice and Leisure Centre, Chelmsford . . . 171

River Lee Country Park, Waltham Abbey . . . 83, 176

River Stour Trips, Flatford . . . 293

River Stour Trips, Sudbury . . . 294

Rollerworld, Colchester . . . 169, back cover

Roman Catholic Cathedral of St. John the Baptist, Norwich . . . 207

Roman Sandy Story . . . 65

Roman Theatre of Verulamium, St. Albans . . . 62

Roots of Norfolk, Gressenhall . . . 210, 231

Roundwood Garden Centre, Bocking 160
Royal Air Force Air Defence Radar Museum (The), Norwich 214
Royal Gunpowder Mills, Waltham Abbey 156, 176
Royal Naval Patrol Service Association Museum, Lowestoft 273
Royal Norfolk Regimental Museum, Norwich 214
Royal Norfolk Show, Norwich (advert) 20
Royston Cave 63
RSPB Berney Marshes Nature Reserve (and Breydon Water), Great Yarmouth 236
RSPB Fowlmere Nature Reserve 116
RSPB Havergate Island, Orford 291
RSPB Lodge Nature Reserve, Sandy 72, 82
RSPB Minsmere Nature Reserve, Westleton 291
RSPB North Warren Nature Reserve, Aldeburgh 288
RSPB Ouse Washes, March 117
RSPB Rye Meads Nature Reserve, Stanstead Abbots 83
RSPB Snettisham Nature Reserve 237
RSPB Stour Estuary Nature Reserve, Harwich 174
RSPB Strumpshaw Fen Nature Reserve 238
RSPB Titchwell Marsh Nature Reserve 238
RSPB Wolves Wood, Hadleigh 290
Rupert Brooke Museum, Cambridge 104
Rural Discovery Church, Southminster 146
Rye House Gatehouse, Hoddesdon 60

S

Sacrewell Farm and Country Centre, Thornhaugh 107, 110, 115
Saffron Walden Museum 155
Sainsbury Centre for Visual Arts, Norwich 214
St. Albans Organ Museum 68
St. Andrews Church, Greensted 145
St. Andrew's (Minster) Church, Southend-on-Sea 146
St. Benets Abbey, Ludham 206
St. Botolphs Priory, Colchester 144
St. Edmundsbury Cathedral, Bury St. Edmunds 41, 42, 268
St. Ives Bridge Chapel 102
St. James the Less Church, Little Tey 145
St. James's Chapel, Lindsey 269
St. Mary and All Saints Church, Rivenhall 146
St. Mary Magdalene Church, Billericay 143
St. Michael and All Angels Church, Colchester 144
St. Neots Museum 106
St. Neots Picture Gallery, Eynesbury 105
St. Olave's Priory, Herringfleet 269
St. Pauls Walden Bury Garden 72
St. Peter Mancroft Church, Norwich 207
St. Peter's Brewery and Visitor Centre, Bungay 297
St. Peters-on-the-Wall, Bradwell-on-Sea 143
St. Wendreda's Church, March 101
Sandlings Forests, Woodbridge 292
Sandringham 203, 215, 225, 237
Santa Pod Raceway, Podington (advert) 18
Saracen's Head 'With Rooms' (The), Wolterton 244
Sascombe Vineyards, Kirtling 298
Saxtead Green Postmill 279
Scott's Grotto, Ware 63
Searles Golf Resort and Country Club, Hunstanton 241
Searles Sea Tours, Hunstanton 239
Second Air Division Memorial Library, Norwich 215
Sedgwick Museum, Cambridge 104
Seething Airfield Control Tower 215
Shawsgate Vineyard, Framlingham 297
Shaw's Corner, Ayot St. Lawrence 59, 71
Shepreth Wildlife Park (Willersmill) 113, 114
Sheringham Museum 215
Sheringham Park 225, 237
Shirehall Museum and Abbey Gardens, Little Walsingham 206, 212, 224
Shrine of our Lady of Walsingham, Little Walsingham 206
Shrubland Gardens, Coddenham 280
Shuttleworth Collection, Biggleswade 69
Sir Alfred Munnings Art Museum (The), Dedham 151, 161
Skylark Studios, Wisbech 107

Slipper Chapel: Roman Catholic National Shrine, Little Walsingham 206
Snape Maltings 254, 301
Snape Maltings Concert Hall (advert) 17
Somerleyton Hall and Gardens 266, 281
South Creake Maize Maze 233
South Elmham Hall 267, 269
Southchurch Hall Museum, Southend-on-Sea 142, 155
Southend Airshow, Southend-on-Sea (advert) 18
Southend Pier Museum, Southend-on-Sea 155
Southend Planetarium, Southend-on-Sea 155
Southend Sea Life Adventure, Southend-on-Sea 167
Southend-on-Sea Pier 170
Southwold Lifeboat Museum 275
Southwold Museum 275
Southwold Pier 286
Southwold Sailors' Reading Room 275
Splash Leisure Pool (The), Sheringham 234
Stained Glass Museum, Ely 105
Stalham Old Firehouse Museum 215
Stanborough Park, Welwyn Garden City 83
Standalone Farm, Letchworth Garden City 67, 78
Stansted Mountfitchet Windmill 159
Starston Windpump 222
Steeple Bumpstead Pottery and Gallery 275
Steeplegate, Ely 124
Stevenage Museum 68
Stevington Windmill 70
Stock Towermill 159
Stockwood Craft Museum and Gardens, Luton 65, 71
Stondon Museum, Lower Stondon 69
Stracey Arms Drainage Mill, Acle 221
Strangers' Hall Museum, Norwich 203, 215
Straw Museum (The), Hanworth 211
Strumpshaw Old Hall Steam Museum and Farm Machinery Collection 219
Sue Ryder, Walsingham 244
Sue Ryder Coffee Shop and Museum (The), Cavendish 271, 299
Suffolk Cycle Breaks 242, 296
Suffolk Horse Museum, Woodbridge 276
Suffolk Owl Sanctuary, Stonham Aspal 285
Suffolk Wildlife Park, Kessingland 284
Sundon Hills Country Park, Luton 81
Sutton Hoo Burial Site, Woodbridge 269
Sutton Pottery 248
Swaffham Museum 216
Swan at Felsted (The) 180, 181
Sweet Briar Bistro, Attleborough 243
Swiss Garden (The), Old Warden 71

T

Taggart Tile Museum, Great Staughton 105
Tales of the Old Gaol House, King's Lynn 212
Tasburgh Hillfort 207
Tastes of Lincolnshire (advert) 319
Temple Seal Trips, Morston 240
Thaxted Garden for Butterflies (The) 164
Thaxted Guildhall 146, 156
Theatre Royal, Bury St. Edmunds 263, 271
Thelnetham Windmill 279
Thetford Priory 207
Thetford Warren Lodge 204
Thorncroft Clematis Nursery, Reymerston 229
Thorndon Country Park, Brentwood 173
Thorney Abbey Church 102
Thorney Heritage Museum 107
Thornham Walks, Thornham Magna 291
Thornham Walled Garden (The), Thornham Magna 281
Thorpe Wood Golf Course, Peterborough 119
Thorpeness Village 296
Thorpeness Windmill 279
Thorrington Tidemill 159
Thrigby Hall Wildlife Gardens, Filby 230
Thurleigh Farm Centre 77
Thurrock Museum, Grays 152
Thursford Collection 219, 244
Tilbury Fort 146

Tiptree Tearoom, Museum and Shop 156
Toad Hole Cottage Museum, Ludham 213
Toddler World, Dunstable 78
Toddler World, Hatfield 78
Toddler World, Hemel Hempstead 79
Tolhouse Museum, Great Yarmouth 210
Town Hall Centre (The), Braintree 147
Town House Museum of Lynn Life, King's Lynn 212
Trimley Marshes, Felixstowe 290
Tropical Wings Butterfly and Bird Gardens, South Woodham Ferrers 167
Truckfest, Peterborough (advert) 16
True's Yard Fishing Heritage Centre, King's Lynn 212
Tumblewood, Halstead 171
Twinwood Arena and The Glenn Miller Museum, Clapham 64, 69
Tymperleys Clock Museum, Colchester 151

U

Ufford Park Hotel, Golf & Leisure, Woodbridge 294
University Museum of Archaeology and Anthropology, Cambridge 104
University Museum of Zoology, Cambridge 104

V

Valley Farm Camargue Horses, Wickham Market 285
Van Hage Garden Company (The), Bragbury End 73
Van Hage Garden Company (The), Chenies 73
Van Hage Garden Company (The), Great Amwell 74
Verulamium Museum, St. Albans 68
Village Experience (The), Fleggburgh 218, 232

W

Waffle House, St. Albans 87
Walberswick Visitor Centre 275, 291
Walled Garden (The), Benhall 280
Walpole Old Chapel 269
Walpole St. Peter's Church 207
Walpole Water Gardens, Walpole St. Peter 111
Walter Rothschild Zoological Museum (The), Tring 68
Waltham Abbey Church 146
Walton Hall Museum, Linford 153, 158
Walton Maritime Museum, Walton-on-the-Naze 156
Walton Pier, Walton-on-the-Naze 170
Wandlebury Country Park, Babraham 116
Ware Museum 68
Ware Priory 61, 72
Waresley and Gransden Woods 117
Wat Tyler Country Park, Pitsea 175
Waterhall Farm and Craft Centre, Whitwell 78
Waterworld, Thetford 234
Watford Museum 68
Watson's Potteries, Wattisfield 299, 301
Wattisham Airfield Museum, Ipswich 272
Waveney River Tours Ltd, Oulton Broad 293
Weald Country Park, South Weald 176
Weeting Castle 207
Wells Harbour Railway, Wells-next-the-Sea 219
Wells Walsingham Railway, Wells-next-the-Sea 219
Welwyn Roman Baths 63
West Acre Gardens 225
West Stow Anglo-Saxon Village 269
West Stow Country Park 291
Whin Hill Cider, Wells-next-the-Sea 243
Whipple Museum of the History of Science, Cambridge 105
Whipsnade Wild Animal Park, Dunstable 76
White Hart (The), Great Yeldham 183
White Hart Inn (The), Nayland 299
Whittlesey Museum 107
Wicken Corn Windmill 110
Wicken Fen National Nature Reserve 110
Wildfowl and Wetlands Trust, Welney 118
Wildlife Water Trail, Ludham 240
Wildtracks, Kennett 293
William Clowes Museum of Print, Beccles 270
Willingale Churches 146

Willington Dovecote and Stables . . . 62
Willow Farm Flowers, Neatishead . . . 224
Willows Farm Village, London Colney . . . 78
Wimpole Hall and Home Farm, Arrington . . . 99, 111, 113, 116
Windmill (The), Swaffham Prior . . . 110
Wingfield Arts . . . 276, 299
Winter Flora - Home and Garden Natural Décor, Weston . . . 283
Wisbech and Fenland Museum . . . 107
Witenagemot Wines Ltd, Shotley . . . 298
Woburn Abbey . . . 59, 60, 71
Woburn Heritage Centre . . . 65
Woburn Safari Park . . . 76, 77
Wolterton Park, Erpingham . . . 202, 236
Wood Green Animal Shelters, Godmanchester . . . 113
Woodbridge Museum . . . 276
Woodbridge Tidemill . . . 279
Woodforde's Brewery Shop and Visitor Centre, Woodbastwick . . . 243
Woodside Animal Farm, Slip End . . . 77
Woolpit and District Museum . . . 276
Woottens Plants, Halesworth . . . 280
Wrest Park Gardens, Silsoe . . . 71
Wroxham Barns . . . 248
Wroxham Barns Children's Fair . . . 233
Wyken Hall Gardens and Wyken Vineyards, Stanton . . . 281, 298
Wymondham Abbey . . . 207
Wymondham Heritage Museum . . . 216
Wysing Arts, Bourn . . . 103

WANT TO ORDER MORE ???

As a special offer you can purchase additional copies of '**Great Days Out in the East of England**' for only **£3.00 per copy** (that's a 35% saving!!).

Simply complete and return the order form below, ensuring you complete the relevant payment section.
(Unfortunately we can only accept credit/debit card payments - PLEASE DO NOT SEND CASH OR CHEQUES).

Please send me ☐ copies of Great Days Out in the East of England 2004 at the special price of £3.00 per copy (please note this is exclusive of postage and packing which is charged at £1.50 per copy)

Name:

Address:

Country:

Credit/Debit card details: Visa ☐ Mastercard ☐ Switch ☐ (issue no... ....) Delta ☐

Credit card number:

Expiry date: .... Start date (if applicable): ....

Signature: .... Date: ....

Return to: Publications Department, East of England Tourist Board,
Toppesfield Hall, Hadleigh, Suffolk IP7 5DN ENGLAND
Tel: 0870 225 4852 Fax: 0870 225 4890